Beginning COBOL for Programmers

Michael Coughlan

Apress·

Beginning COBOL for Programmers

ISBN-13 (pbk): 978-1-4302-6253-4

ISBN-13 (electronic): 978-1-4302-6254-1

President and Publisher: Paul Manning
Lead Editor: Steve Anglin
Development Editor: Matthew Moodie
Technical Reviewer: Massimo Nardone
Editorial Board: Steve Anglin, Mark Beckner, Ewan Buckingham, Gary Cornell, Louise Corrigan, Jim DeWolf, Jonathan Gennick, Jonathan Hassell, Robert Hutchinson, Michelle Lowman, James Markham, Matthew Moodie, Jeff Olson, Jeffrey Pepper, Douglas Pundick, Ben Renow-Clarke, Dominic Shakeshaft, Gwenan Spearing, Matt Wade, Steve Weiss
Coordinating Editors: Anamika Panchoo and Melissa Maldonado
Copy Editor: Tiffany Taylor
Compositor: SPi Global
Indexer: SPi Global
Artist: SPi Global
Cover Designer: Anna Ishchenko

Distributed to the book trade worldwide by Springer Science+Business Media New York, 233 Spring Street, 6th Floor, New York, NY 10013. Phone 1-800-SPRINGER, fax (201) 348-4505, e-mail orders-ny@springer-sbm.com, or visit www.springeronline.com. Apress Media, LLC is a California LLC and the sole member (owner) is Springer Science + Business Media Finance Inc (SSBM Finance Inc). SSBM Finance Inc is a Delaware corporation.

For information on translations, please e-mail rights@apress.com, or visit www.apress.com.

Apress and friends of ED books may be purchased in bulk for academic, corporate, or promotional use. eBook versions and licenses are also available for most titles. For more information, reference our Special Bulk Sales–eBook Licensing web page at www.apress.com/bulk-sales.

Any source code or other supplementary material referenced by the author in this text is available to readers at www.apress.com. For detailed information about how to locate your book's source code, go to www.apress.com/source-code/.

To my students in grateful thanks for everything you taught me.

Contents at a Glance

Contents

About the Author

Michael Coughlan is a lecturer in the Department of Computer Science and Information Systems at the University of Limerick, Ireland where he teaches e-business, legacy systems, and business oriented programming languages. He has been responsible for teaching COBOL to University of Limerick students since 1980.

Michael wrote the COBOL quick reference for the book *Year 2000 in a Nutshell* by Norman Shakespeare (O'Reilly, 1998), and he created the free online learning resource for COBOL at www.csis.ul.ie/COBOL. This resource is used by students and instructors all over the world, and notes from the website have been translated into a number of languages.

Taught by Cistercian monks in the Knockmealdown mountains of County Waterford, Michael received a B.A. (Mod) in History from Trinity College Dublin, a Graduate Diploma in Computing from the University of Limerick, and an M.Sc. in Information Technology from the University of Ulster.

About the Technical Reviewer

Massimo Nardone holds a Master of Science degree in Computer Science from the University of Salerno, Italy. He worked as a PCI QSA and senior lead IT security/cloud architect for many years, and currently he leads the Security Consulting Team for Hewlett Packard Finland. With more than 19 years of work experience in SCADA, cloud computing, IT infrastructure, mobile, security, and web technology for both national and international projects, Massimo has worked as a project manager, software engineer, research engineer, chief security architect, and software specialist. He worked as visiting lecturer and supervisor for exercises at the Networking Laboratory of the Helsinki University of Technology (Helsinki University of Technology TKK became a part of Aalto University) for the course "Security of Communication Protocols." He holds four international patents (PKI, SIP, SAML, and Proxy areas). This book is dedicated to Pia, Luna, Leo, and Neve, who are my reasons for living.

Acknowledgments

Special thanks go to Steve Anglin, who started the whole process of my writing this book, and to Matthew Moodie, Anamika Panchoo, Melissa Maldonado, and Massimo Nardone, the team of editors at Apress whose work was so invaluable in shaping the text. I would especially like to thank Tiffany Taylor for her excellent suggestions and for all her work in eliminating my errors. Any errors that remain are my responsibility, but without her help, there would be many more of them.

I thank my family for all their support. I thank Redmond O'Brien, who acted as a patient sounding board for ideas, and Dermot Shinners-Kennedy, for our discussions about COBOL. The results of those discussions find many a reflection in this book. Finally, I thank Annette McElligott (HOD) for her support and encouragement in this endeavor.

Thanks also are due to Bill Qualls and Caliber Data Training for granting permission to use their BigDecimal Java example program.

The following acknowledgment is from *American National Standard Programming Language COBOL, X3.23-1985*:

> *Any organization interested in reproducing the COBOL report and specifications in whole or in part, using ideas taken from this report as the basis for an instruction manual or for any other purpose is free to do so. However, all such organizations are requested to reproduce this section as part of the introduction to the document. Those using a short passage, as in a book review, are requested to mention 'COBOL' in acknowledgment of the source, but need not quote this entire section.*
>
> *COBOL is an industry language and is not the property of any company or group of companies, or of any organization or group of organizations.*
>
> *NO warranty, expressed or implied, is made by any contributor or by the COBOL Committee as to the accuracy and functioning of the programming system and language. Moreover, no responsibility is assumed by any contributor, or by the committee, in connection therewith.*
>
> *Procedures have been established for the maintenance of COBOL. Inquiries concerning the procedures for proposing changes should be directed to the Executive Committee of the Conference on Data Systems Languages.*
>
> *The authors and copyright holders of the copyrighted material used herein*
>
> *FLOW-MATIC (Trademark of Sperry Rand Corporation), Programming far the UNIVAC (R) I and II, Data Automation Systems copyrighted 1958, 1959, by Sperry Rand Corporation: IBM Commercial Translator, Form No. F28-80l3, copyrighted 1959 by IBM: FACT, DSI 27A5260-2760, copyrighted 1960 by Min~eapolis- Honeywell*
>
> *have specifically authorized the use of this material in whole or in part, in the COBOL specifications. such authorization extends to the reproduction and use of COBOL specifications in programming manuals or similar publications."*

Preface

It seems strange to be writing a book on COBOL so many years after its death was first predicted. Indeed, COBOL has had such a low profile in recent years that you might be forgiven for thinking that it had all but disappeared. The nature of our industry is such that the new and exciting always gets more airplay than the secure, the accurate, and the reliable. But while Java, C#, Ruby, Python, and Objective C have dominated our consciousness in recent times, in the background billions of lines of COBOL code have quietly gone about supporting the mission-critical applications that make the world work.

Now, after many years, awareness is increasing about COBOL and the huge body of legacy COBOL code. COBOL is mentioned more and more in magazines, in trade journals, and in newspapers. Indeed, you may be reading this book because you have noticed this activity and have become curious about COBOL. You may have wondered why this supposedly dying language is attracting attention recently. The reason is simple. There is a legacy crisis just around the corner, and stakeholders are trying to do something about it.

The problem is, so many attempts to rewrite COBOL legacy systems or replace them with off-the-shelf solutions have ended in failure that custodians of legacy systems are now wary of these approaches to modernization. Migrating the COBOL codebase to take advantage of less-expensive hardware and software is now seen as a more viable, safer, and cheaper alternative to replacement. But keeping, and even growing, the COBOL codebase requires COBOL programmers—and the COBOL workforce is aging and nearing retirement. In an effort to avert the workforce crisis, legacy system stakeholders have implemented initiatives to increase the number of new COBOL programmers entering the marketplace. COBOL implementers such as IBM and Micro Focus have introduced initiatives to encourage colleges and universities around the world to teach COBOL as part of their curriculum, training companies and in-house training groups are once more starting to provide instruction in COBOL, and employers have begun to offer a number of entry-level COBOL positions.

Over the last few years, the demand for programmers has far exceeded the supply. However, as the number of students graduating from computer science courses recovers from the year 2000 downturn, the job market is likely to become more and more competitive. In such a competitive environment, and at a time when the demand for COBOL programmers is increasing, you may find it profitable to have a résumé that includes a knowledge of COBOL.

Who This Book Is For

This book is aimed at programmers familiar with other languages who are curious about COBOL or are working with COBOL legacy systems or who wish to take advantage of COBOL job opportunities. To get the most from this book, you must have some knowledge of programming. It is not an introductory programming text.

How You Should Read This Book

If you are using this book to learn to program in COBOL, rather than just dipping into it to find out how a particular construct or verb works, then you should read the book in the chapter order provided. Many chapters foreshadow or preview material that is dealt with more completely in succeeding chapters. If you read the chapters out of order, you may find the discussion confusing. However, if you wish, you may skip the first chapter, because it deals with such matters as the history of COBOL, the importance for COBOL, and the characteristics of COBOL and COBOL applications. Even if you do skip Chapter 1, you may find it rewarding to read it later. It should provide a ready source of ammunition with which to respond to any expressions of amazement that you are learning COBOL.

CHAPTER 1

■ ■ ■

Introduction to COBOL

When, in 1975, Edsger Dijkstra made his comment that "The use of COBOL cripples the mind; its teaching should, therefore, be regarded as a criminal offence,[1]" he gave voice to, and solidified, the opposition to COBOL in academia. That opposition has resulted in fewer and fewer academic institutions teaching COBOL so that now it has become difficult to find young programmers to replace the aging COBOL workforce.[2-3] This scarcity is leading to an impending COBOL crisis. Despite Dijkstra's comments and the claims regarding COBOL's imminent death, COBOL remains a dominant force in the world of enterprise computing, and attempts to replace legacy COBOL systems have been shown to be difficult, dangerous, and expensive.

In this chapter, I discuss some of the reasons for COBOL's longevity. You're introduced to the notion of an application domain and shown the suitability of COBOL for its target domain. COBOL is one of the oldest computer languages, and the chapter gives a brief history of the language and its four official versions. Later, the chapter presents the evidence for COBOL's dominance in enterprise computing and discusses the enigma of its relatively low profile.

An obvious solution to the scarcity of COBOL programmers is to replace COBOL with a more fashionable programming language. This chapter exposes the problems with this approach and reveals the benefits of retaining, renovating, and migrating the COBOL code.

Finally, I discuss why learning COBOL and having COBOL on your résumé could be useful additions to your armory in an increasingly competitive job market.

What Is COBOL?

COBOL is a high-level programming language like C, C#, Java, Pascal, or BASIC, but it is one with a particular focus and a long history.

COBOL's Target Application Domain

The name COBOL is an acronym that stands for **Co**mmon **B**usiness **O**riented **L**anguage, and this expanded acronym clearly indicates the target domain of the language. Whereas most other high-level programming languages are general-purpose, domain-independent languages, COBOL is focused on business, or enterprise, computing. You would not use COBOL to write a computer game or a compiler or an operating system. With no low-level access, no dynamic memory allocation, and no recursion, COBOL does not have the constructs that facilitate the creation of these kinds of program. This is one of the reasons most universities do not teach COBOL. Because it cannot be used to create data structures such as linked lists, queues, or stacks or to develop algorithms like Quicksort, some other programming language has to be taught to allow instruction in these computer science concepts. The curriculum is so crowded nowadays that there is often no room to introduce two programming languages, especially when one of them seems to offer little educational benefit.

Although COBOL's design may preclude it from being used as a general-purpose programming language, it is well suited for developing long-lived, data-oriented business applications. COBOL's forte is the processing of data transactions, especially those involving money, and this focus puts it at the heart of the mission-critical systems that run the world. COBOL is found in insurance systems, banking systems, finance systems, stock dealing systems, government systems, military systems, telephony systems, hospital systems, airline systems, traffic systems, and many, many others. It may be only a slight exaggeration to say that the world runs on COBOL.

COBOL's Fitness for Its Application Domain

What does it mean to say that a language is well suited for developing business applications? What are the requirements of a language working in the business applications domain? In a series of articles on the topic, Professor Robert Glass[4-7] concludes that such a programming language should exhibit the following characteristics:

- *It should be able to declare and manipulate heterogeneous data.* Unlike other application domains, which mainly manipulate floating-point or integer numbers, business data is a heterogeneous mix of fixed and variable-length character strings as well as integer, cardinal, and decimal numbers.

- *It should be able to declare and manipulate decimal data as a native data type.* In accounting, bank, taxation, and other financial applications, there is a requirement that computed calculations produce *exactly* the same result as those produced by manual calculations. The floating-point calculations commonly used in other application domains often contain minute rounding errors, which, taken over millions of calculations, give rise to serious accounting discrepancies.

■ **Note**   The requirement for decimal data, and the problems caused by using floating-point numbers to represent money values, is explored more fully later in this book.

- *It should have the capability to conveniently generate reports and create a GUI.* Just as calculating money values correctly is important for a business application, so is outputting the results in the format normally used for such business output. GUI screens, with their interactive charts and graphs, although a welcome addition to business applications, have not entirely eliminated the need for traditional reports consisting of column headings, columns of figures, and a hierarchy of subtotals, totals, and final totals.

- *It should be able to access and manipulate record-oriented data masses such as files and databases.* An important characteristic of a business application programming language is that it should have an external, rather than internal, focus. It should concentrate on processing data held externally in files and databases rather than on manipulating data in memory through linked lists, trees, stacks, and other sophisticated data structures.

In an analysis of several programming languages with regard to these characteristics, Professor Glass[6] finds that COBOL is either strong or adequate in all four of these characteristics, whereas the more fashionable domain-independent languages like Visual Basic, Java, and C++ are not. This finding is hardly a great surprise. With the exception of GUIs and databases, these characteristics were designed into COBOL from the outset.

Advocates of domain-independent languages claim that the inadequacies of such a language for a particular application domain can be overcome by the use of function or class libraries. This is partly true. But programs written using bolted-on capabilities are never quite as readable, understandable, or maintainable as programs where these capabilities are an intrinsic part of the base language. As an illustration of this, consider the following two programs: one program is written in COBOL (Listing 1-1), and the other is written in Java (Listing 1-2).

Listing 1-1. COBOL Version

```
IDENTIFICATION DIVISION.
PROGRAM-ID. SalesTax.
WORKING-STORAGE SECTION.
01 beforeTax      PIC 999V99 VALUE 123.45.
01 salesTaxRate  PIC V999   VALUE .065.
01 afterTax      PIC 999.99.
PROCEDURE DIVISION.
Begin.
  COMPUTE afterTax ROUNDED = beforeTax + (beforeTax * salesTaxRate)
  DISPLAY "After tax amount is " afterTax.
```

Listing 1-2. Java Version (from http://caliberdt.com/tips/May03_Java_BigDecimal_Class.htm)

```java
import java.math.BigDecimal;
public class SalesTaxWithBigDecimal
{
  public static void main(java.lang.String[] args)
  {
    BigDecimal beforeTax    = BigDecimal.valueOf(12345, 2);
    BigDecimal salesTaxRate = BigDecimal.valueOf(65, 3);
    BigDecimal ratePlusOne  = salesTaxRate.add(BigDecimal.valueOf(1));
    BigDecimal afterTax     = beforeTax.multiply(ratePlusOne);
    afterTax = afterTax.setScale(2, BigDecimal.ROUND_HALF_UP);
    System.out.println( "After tax amount is " + afterTax);
  }
}
```

The programs do the same job. The COBOL program uses native decimal data, and the Java program creates data-items using the bolted-on BigDecimal class (itself an acknowledgement of the importance of decimal data for this application domain). The programs are presented without explanation (we'll revisit them in Chapter 12; and, if you need it, you can find an explanation there). I hope that, in the course of trying to discover what the programs do, you can agree that the COBOL version is easier to understand—even though you do not, at present, know any COBOL but are probably at least somewhat familiar with syntactic elements of the Java program.

History of COBOL

Detailed histories of COBOL are available elsewhere. The purpose of this section is to give you some understanding of the foundations of COBOL, to introduce some of the major players, and to briefly describe the development of the language through the various COBOL standards.

Beginnings

The history of COBOL starts in April 1959 with a meeting involving computer people, academics, users, and manufacturers to discuss the creation of a common, problem-oriented, machine-independent language specifically designed to address the needs of business[8]. The US Department of Defense was persuaded to sponsor and organize the project. A number of existing languages influenced the design of COBOL. The most significant of these were AIMACO (US Air Force designed), FLOW-MATIC (developed under Rear Admiral Grace Hopper) and COMTRAN (IBM's COMmercial TRANslator).

The first definition of COBOL was produced by the Conference on Data Systems Languages (CODASYL) Committee in 1960. Two of the manufacturer members of the CODASYL Committee, RCA and Remington-Rand-Univac, raced to produce the first COBOL compiler. On December 6 and 7, 1960, the same COBOL program (with minor changes) ran on both the RCA and Remington-Rand-Univac computers.[8]

After the initial definition of the language by the CODASYL Committee, responsibility for developing new COBOL standards was assumed by the American National Standards Institute (ANSI), which produced the next three standards: American National Standard (ANS) 68, ANS 74, and ANS 85. Responsibility for developing new COBOL standards has now been assumed by the International Standards Organization (ISO). ISO 2002, the first COBOL standard produced by this body, defines the object-oriented version of COBOL.

COBOL Standards

Four standards for COBOL have been produced, in 1968, 1974, 1985, and 2002. As just mentioned, the most recent standard (ISO 2002) introduced object orientation to COBOL. This book mainly adheres to the ANS 85 standard; but where this standard departs from previous standards, or where there is an improvement made in the ISO 2002 standard, a note is provided.

The final chapter of the book previews ISO 2002 COBOL. In that chapter, I discuss why object orientation is desirable and what new language elements make it possible to create object-oriented COBOL programs.

COBOL ANS 68

The 1968 standard resolved incompatibilities between the different COBOL versions that had been introduced by various producers of COBOL compilers since the language's creation in 1960. This standard reemphasized the *common* part of the COBOL acronym. The idea, contained in the 1960 language definition, was that the language would be the same across a range of machines.

COBOL ANS 74 (External Subprograms)

The major development of the 1974 standard was the introduction of the CALL verb and external subprograms. Before ANS 74 COBOL, there was no real way to partition a program into separate parts, and this resulted in the huge monolithic programs that have given COBOL such a bad reputation. In these programs, which could be many tens of thousands of lines long, there was no modularization, no functional partitioning, and totally unrestricted access to any variable in the Data Division (more on divisions in Chapter 2).

COBOL ANS 85 (Structured Programming Constructs)

The 1985 standard introduced structured programming to COBOL. The most notable features were the introduction of explicit scope delimiters such as END-IF and END-READ, and contained subprograms. In previous versions of COBOL, the period (full stop) was used to delimit scope. Periods had a visibility problem that, taken along with the fact that they delimited all open scopes, was the cause of many program bugs. Contained subprograms allowed something approaching procedures to be used in COBOL programs for the first time.

COBOL ANS 2002 (OO Constructs)

Object orientation was introduced to COBOL in the ISO 2002 standard. Whereas previous additions had significantly increased the huge COBOL reserved word list, object orientation was introduced with very few additions.

The Argument for COBOL (Why COBOL?)

As you've seen, COBOL is a language with a 50-year history. Many people regard it as a language that has passed its sell-by date—an obsolete language with no relevance to the modern world. In the succeeding pages, I show why, despite its age, programmers should take the time to learn COBOL.

Dominance of COBOL in Enterprise Computing

One reason for learning COBOL is its importance in enterprise computing. Although the death of COBOL has been predicted time and time again, COBOL remains a dominant force at the heart of enterprise computing. In 1997, the Gartner group published a widely reported estimate that of the 300 billion lines of code in the world, 240 billion (80%) were written in COBOL.[9] Around the same time, Capers Jones[10] identified COBOL as the major programming language in the United States, with a software portfolio of 12 million applications and 605 million function points. To put this in perspective, in the same study he estimated that the combined total for C and C++ was 4 million software applications and 261 million points. According to Jones, each function point requires about 107 lines of COBOL; so, in 1996, the software inventory for the United States contained about 64 billion lines of COBOL code. Extrapolating for the world, the Gartner estimate does not seem outside the realms of possibility.

Of course, the 1990s were a long time ago, and in 1996/97, Java had just been created. You might have expected that as Java came to the fore, COBOL would be eclipsed. This did not happen to any significant extent. Much new development has been done in Java, but the existing inventory of COBOL applications has largely remained unaffected. In an OVUM report in 2005,[11] Gary Barnett noted, "Cobol remains the most widely deployed programming language in big business, accounting for 75% of all computer transactions" and "90% of all financial transactions." In that report, Barnett estimated that there "are over 200 billion lines of COBOL in production today, and this number continues to grow by between three and five percent a year."

Even today, COBOL's position in the domain of business computing does not seem to be greatly eroded. In a survey of 357 IT professionals undertaken by *ComputerWorld* in 2012,[2, 12] 54% of respondents said that more than half of all their internal business application code was written in COBOL. When asked to quantify the extent to which languages were used in their organization, 48% said COBOL was used frequently, while only 39% said the same of Java. And as the 2005 OVUM report[11] predicted, new COBOL development is still occurring; 53% of responders said that COBOL was still being used for new development in their organization. Asked to quantify what proportion of new code was written in COBOL 27% said that it was used for more than half of their new development.

Although only tangentially relevant to the issue of COBOL's importance in business computing, one other item of interest came out of the *ComputerWorld* survey.[2, 12] Responders were asked to compare Visual Basic, C#, C++, and Java to COBOL for characteristics such as batch processing, transaction processing, handling of business-oriented features, runtime efficiency, security, reporting, development cost, maintenance cost, availability of programmers, and agility. In every instance except the last two, COBOL scored higher than its more recent counterparts.

Finally, in a May 2013 press release, IBM noted that nearly 15% of all new enterprise application functionality is written in COBOL and that there are more than "200 billion lines of COBOL code being used.[13]"

Danger, Difficulty, and Expense of Replacing Legacy COBOL Applications

The custodians of legacy systems come under a lot of pressure to replace their legacy COBOL code with a more modern alternative. The high cost of maintenance, obsolete hardware, obsolete software, the scarcity of COBOL programmers, the need to integrate with newer software and hardware technologies, the relentless hype surrounding more modern languages—these are all pressures that drive legacy system modernization in general and language replacement in particular. How is it then that the COBOL software inventory seems largely unchanged?

When a legacy system is considered for modernization, a number of alternatives might be considered:

- Replacement with a commercial off-the-shelf (COTS) package

- Complete rewrite

- Automatic language conversion

- Wrapping the legacy system to present a more modern interface

- Code renovation

- Migration to commodity hardware and software

The problem is, experience shows that most modernization attempts that involve replacing the COBOL code fail. Some organizations have spent millions of dollars in repeated attempts to replace their COBOL legacy systems, only to have each attempt fail spectacularly.

Replacement with a COTS Package

Replacement is much harder than it seems. Many legacy COBOL systems implement functionality such as payroll, stock control, and accounting that today would be done by a COTS system. Replacing such a legacy system with a standard COTS package might seem like an attractive option, and in some cases it might be successful; but in many legacy systems, so many proprietary extensions have been added to the standard functionality that replacement is no longer a viable option. Attempting to replace such a legacy system with a COTS package will fail—either completely, causing the replacement attempt to be abandoned; or partially, leading to cost and time overruns and failures in functionality fit.

I know of one instance where a university attempted to replace a COBOL-based Student Record System with a bought-in package as a solution to the Y2K problem. Around September 1999, the school realized that, due to database migration difficulties, the package solution would not be ready in time for the millennium changeover. A successful Y2K remediation of the existing COBOL legacy system was then done, and this bought sufficient time for the new package to be brought on line. Even then, the package only implemented about 80% of the functionality formerly provided by the legacy system.

Complete Rewrite

A complete rewrite in another language is often seen as a viable modernization option. Again, in a restricted set of circumstances, this might be the case. When the documentation created for original legacy system is still available, there is no reason the rewritten replacement should not be as successful as the original. Unfortunately, this happy circumstance is not the case with most legacy systems.

These systems often represent the first parts of the organization to be computerized. They embody the core functionality of the organization; its mission-critical operations; its beating heart. When these systems were created, they replaced the existing manual systems. In the intervening years, the requirements, system architecture, and other documentation have long since been lost. The people who operated the manual system and knew how it worked have either retired or moved on. The rewrite cannot be treated as a greenfield site would be treated, where the requirements could be elicited from stakeholders. For all sorts of legal, customer, and employee reasons, the functionality of the new system must match that of the old. The only source of information about how the system works is embedded in the COBOL code itself. Extracting the business rules from existing legacy code, in order to specify the requirements of the new system, is a very difficult task. The failure rates for most legacy system rewrites are very high.

Automatic Language Conversion

Automatic language conversion is often touted as a solution to the lack of architectural and functional documentation in legacy systems. You don't have to know how the system works, goes the mantra; you can just automatically convert it into a more modern language. But converting legacy COBOL code is a much more difficult task than people realize.[14] Even if the functionality can be reproduced (and this is highly problematic),[3] the resulting code is likely to be an unmaintainable, unreadable mess. It is likely to consist of many more lines of code than the original[15] and to retain the idiom or flavor of COBOL. Although such converted software may be written in the syntax of the target language, it will not look like any kind of a program that a programmer in that language would normally produce. Such automatically produced programs[14] will be so foreign to those who have to maintain them that they are likely to be received with some hostility.

Some organizations advertise their ability to convert legacy COBOL to another language. This is a given; the questions are: how faithful is the conversion and how maintainable is the converted code? Few if any case studies (where they exist at all) mentioned by these organizations address the maintainability problems that may be expected of code produced by automatic language conversion. Although such conversions may alleviate the shortage of COBOL programmers, they probably cause an increase in maintenance costs. It is doubtful if any of these conversions can be deemed a success.

Approaches to legacy system modernization that involve replacing the COBOL code have not been very successful. They either fail completely and have to be abandoned, fail in terms of cost and deadline overruns, or fail in terms of not delivering on maintainability promises.

Wrapping the Legacy System

Most successful modernization efforts retain the COBOL code. Wrapping the legacy code solves interfacing problems but does not address the cost of maintenance, or hardware or software obsolescence problems. On the other hand, it is cheap, it is safe, and it provides an obvious, and immediate, return on investment (ROI).

Code Renovation

Code renovation addresses the cost-of-maintenance problem but none of the others. It is safe and has very good tool support from both COBOL vendors and third parties, but it does not provide an obvious ROI.

Migration to Commodity Hardware and Software

Migration involves moving the legacy COBOL code to modern commodity hardware and software. This approach has some risks, because the COBOL code may have to be changed to accommodate the new hardware and software. However, there is significant tool support to assist migration, and this greatly mitigates the risk of failure. Many case studies point to the success of the migration approach, as borne out by a 2010 report from the Standish Group.[16] This report found that migration and enhancement "stands out as having the highest chance of success and the lowest chance of failure" with the new software development project "six times more likely" and the package replacement project "twice as likely" to fail as migration and enhancement.

Migration solves many of the problems with legacy systems. Obsolescence is addressed by moving to more modern hardware and software. General costs are addressed through the elimination of licensing fees and other costs (in one case study, replacing printed reports with online versions saved $22,000 per year).[17-18] Maintenance costs are often also addressed because code renovation usually precedes a migration. However, interfacing with modern technologies might still be a problem, and there remains the problem of the scarcity of COBOL programmers.

Shortage of COBOL Programmers: Crisis and Opportunity

A major issue that prompts companies to attempt replacement of their legacy COBOL with some other alternative is the perceived scarcity of COBOL programmers. Harry Sneed states this baldly: "The reason for this conversion is that there are no COBOL programmers available. Otherwise the whole system could have been left in COBOL.[3]" He comments that COBOL "is no longer taught in the technical high schools and universities. Therefore, it is very difficult to recruit COBOL programmers. In Austria it is almost impossible to find programmers with knowledge of COBOL. Those few that are left are all close to retirement." Because of their seniority, they are also more expensive than cheap, young Java programmers.

However, the problem is not that there are no COBOL programmers. Capers Jones estimated that there were 550,000 COBOL programmers in the United States to deal with the Y2K problem.[10] Even now, Scott Searle of IBM estimates that the current worldwide population of COBOL programmers is about two million programmers, with about 50,000 of these in India.[19] The real problem is that most of the population of COBOL programmers are nearing retirement age. This is a crisis in the making. As already discussed, it is dangerous and expensive to attempt to replace COBOL legacy systems; but when these COBOL programmers retire, who will maintain the legacy systems?

Legacy system stakeholders are gradually waking up to the problem. Since 2008, there has been a gradual increase in awareness of the need to do something about it. COBOL vendors have encouraged academic training of a new crop of COBOL developers. Micro Focus does this through its Micro Focus Academic Program and Academic Alliance programs, and an IBM initiative in this area has resulted in COBOL being taught in 400 colleges and universities around the world.[19] In addition, the training companies and in-house training groups that traditionally were the main source of COBOL developers are once more starting to take up the strain. For example, the US Postal Service will start its own COBOL training program as its COBOL programmers retire,[20] and the Social Security Administration (SSA)[20] in the United States is going the same route. Manta Technologies is reported to be developing a COBOL training series consisting of nine or ten courses.[21] The company hopes to complete the series by the end of 2013. Some COBOL vendors like Veryant[22] are also providing training courses.

Motivational speakers are often heard to say that the Chinese word for crisis is composed of two characters that represent *danger* and *opportunity*. Although there seems to be some doubt about the veracity of this claim, there is no doubt that in the coming years the crisis caused by the tsunami of retiring programmers represents a golden opportunity for those who can grasp it. The number of students earning computing degrees fell sharply after the year 2000, and this led to a programmer shortfall that has made it a seller's market for computer skills. But student numbers are recovering; and as the job market gets more competitive, having COBOL on your résumé may be a very useful differentiating skill—especially if it is combined with knowledge of Java.

COBOL: The Hidden Asset

The numbers supporting the dominance of COBOL in the business application domain sound incredible. Certainly, a lot of skepticism has been voiced about them on the Internet and elsewhere. But much of the skepticism comes from those who have little or no knowledge of the mainframe arena, an area in which COBOL is strong, if not supreme. You can gain an appreciation for the opposing points of view by reading Jeff Atwood's post "COBOL: Everywhere and nowhere" and the associated comments. His comment that "I have never, in my entire so-called 'professional' programming career, met anyone who was actively writing COBOL code[23]" is indicative of the problem programmers often have when presented statistics regarding the importance of COBOL. Many of the comments that followed Atwood's post reflected that disbelief; but as one commentator remarked, "You want to see COBOL? Go look at a company that processes payroll, or handles trucking, food delivery, or shipping. Look at companies that handle book purchase orders or government disbursements or checking account reconciliation. There's a huge ecosystem of code out there that's truly invisible to those of us who work in and around the Internet.[24]"

Many programmers with a conspiracy-theory bent attempt to prove the impossibility of the COBOL statistics by pointing to the number of lines of code that could be produced by programmers in the given time frame, or by pointing to the impossibility of maintaining the claimed number of lines with the estimated number of COBOL programmers. There are a number of answers to these points.

One answer is that the COBOL code inventory has been hugely bulked out by fourth-generation languages (4GLs) and other COBOL-generating software.[25] 4GLs were all the rage between the 1970s and 1990s, and many produced COBOL code instead of machine code. This was done to give buyers confidence that if the 4GL vendor failed, they would not be left high and dry. In many cases, the vendors did fail, and only the COBOL code was left. In other cases, the programmers took to maintaining the COBOL code directly, and it is now so divorced from the 4GL that there is no point in trying to return to the 4GL code.

Another answer is that programmer productivity seems high because many programs are simply near-copies of existing work. In a legacy system, the enterprise data is often trapped in a variety of storage technologies, from various kinds of database to direct access files and flat files. Nearly every user request to get at that data requires a COBOL program to be written. But these programs are not written from scratch. A programmer creates the program by using the copy, paste, and amend method. The programmer simply copies a similar program, make a few changes, and voilà: a new COBOL program and a big boost to apparent programmer productivity.

If the number of bugs found in legacy systems approached that found in newly minted systems, 2 million programmers might find it very difficult to maintain upwards of 200 billion lines of code. The fact is, though, that unless an environmental change or a user request forces a modification of a legacy system, not much maintenance is required. When a system has been in production for many tens of years, only the blue-moon bugs remain. There is an old joke that goes, "What's the difference between computer hardware and computer software?" The answer is, "If you use hardware long enough, it breaks. But if you use software long enough, it works." A real-world manifestation of David Brin's[26] practice effect, perhaps?

■ **Note** *Blue-moon bugs* are bugs that manifest themselves only as a result of the coincidence of an unusual set of circumstances.

A considerable amount of evidence points to the relatively bug-free status of legacy systems. For instance, when an inventory of software systems was taken in preparation for the Y2K conversion, it was discovered that it had been so long since some of the programs in the inventory had been modified that the source code had been lost. In the opinion of Chris Verhoef, "about 5% of the object code lacks its source code.[27]"

In his paper "Migrating from COBOL to Java,[15]" Harry Sneed mentions that 5 COBOL programmers were responsible for 15,486 function points of legacy COBOL whereas 25 Java developers were responsible for 13,207 function points of Java code. Although it might suit COBOL advocates to believe that COBOL developers are five times more efficient than Java developers, a more realistic explanation is that the legacy system had settled into a largely bug-free equilibrium while the newly minted Java code was still awash with them.

COBOL definitely has a visibility problem. The hype that surrounds some computer languages would have you believe that most of the production business applications in the world are written in Java, C, C++, or Visual Basic and that only a small percentage are written in COBOL. In reality, COBOL is arguably the major programming language for business applications.

One reason for COBOL's low profile lies in the difference between the vertical and horizontal software markets. To use a clothing analogy, an application created for the vertical software market is like a tailored, bespoke suit, whereas an application created for the horizontal software market is like a commodity, off-the-rack suit.

Advantages of Bespoke Software

Why should a company spend millions of dollars to create a bespoke application when it could buy a COTS package? One reason is that because a bespoke application is specifically designed for an organization's particular requirements, it can be tailored to fit in exactly with the way the business or organization operates. Another reason is that it can be customized to interface with other software the company operates, providing a fully integrated IT infrastructure across the whole organization. Yet another reason is that because the company "owns" the software, the company has control over it. But the primary reason for creating a bespoke application is that it can offer an enterprise a competitive advantage over its rivals. Because a bespoke application can incorporate the business processes and business rules that are specific to the company and that do not exist in any packaged solution, it can offer a considerable advantage over competing companies. Owens and Minor[28-29] refer to the specific business rules and processes embedded in their bespoke applications as their "secret sauce."

An example of the effectiveness of bespoke software is the software that first allowed an airline to offer a frequent-flyer program (air miles). That software conferred such an advantage on the airline that competitors were forced to catch up, and frequent-flyer programs are now almost ubiquitous.

Characteristics of COBOL Applications

Software produced for the vertical software market has characteristics that distinguish it from the commodity software you are probably more familiar with. This section examines some characteristics of COBOL applications that you may find surprising.

COBOL Applications Can Be Very Large

Many COBOL applications consist of more than 1 million lines of code, and applications consisting of 6 million lines or more are not considered unusually large in many programming shops:

- In "Revitalizing modifiability of legacy assets,[30]" Niels Veerman mentions a banking company that had "one large system of 2.6 million LOC in almost 1000 programs."

- The Irish Life Group, Ireland's leading life and pensions company, is reported[31] to have completed a legacy system migration project to rehost 3 million lines of COBOL code.

- A Microsoft case study reported that Simon & Schuster had a code inventory of some 5 million lines of COBOL code.[32]

- The Owens and Minor case study mentioned earlier reported that "the company ran its business on 10 million lines of custom COBOL/CICS code.[29]"

- In his paper "A Pilot Project for Migrating COBOL Code to Web Services," Harry Sneed reported a "legacy life insurance system with more than 20 million lines of COBOL code running under IMS on the IBM mainframe.[33]"

- The authors of "Industrial Applications of ASF+SDF" talk about a large suite of mainframe-based COBOL applications that consist of 25,000 programs and 30 million lines of code.[34]

- An audit report by the Office of the Inspector General in 2012 noted that as of June 2010, the US SSA had a COBOL code inventory of "over 60 million lines of COBOL code.[35]"

- The Bank of New York Mellon is quoted as having a software inventory of 112,500 Cobol programs consisting of 343 million lines of code.[2]

- Kwiatkowski and Verhoef report a case study where "a Cobol software portfolio of a large organization operating in the financial sector" consisted of over "18.2 million physical lines of code (LOC).[25]"

COBOL Applications Are Very Long-Lived

The huge investment in creating a software application consisting of millions of lines of COBOL code means the application cannot simply be discarded when a new programming language or technology appears. As a consequence, business applications between 10 and 30 years old are common, and some have been in existence for around 50 years.

A Microsoft case study on the Swedish company Stockholmshem noted that its computer system "was created in 1963 and had been expanded over the years to include roughly 170 online Customer Information Control System (CICS)/COBOL programs and 370 batch COBOL programs.[36]"

Kwiatkowski and Verhoef[25] published a version log (reproduced in Figure 1-1) for a module in the software portfolio of a large financial organization that illustrates the longevity of COBOL programs. Each line of the log is a comment that shows a version number, the name of a programmer, and the date the software was modified. The log shows that maintenance of this module started in 1975. Nor was this the oldest module found. That honor belonged to a program that had been written in 1967. For some readers of this book, the software in this portfolio started life long before they were born.

```
00015 * * * * * * * * VERSION 63 J. NILE MAY 1975 * * * * * * * * *
00016 * * * * * * * * VERSION 64 A.J.SINATRA AUGUST 1976 * * * * * *
00017 * * * * * * * * VERSION 66 BILLY BOLT * NOV 1979 * * * * * *
00018 * * * * * * * * VERSION 67 JOHN DICKSON * OCT 1980 * * * * * * *
00019 * * * * * * * * VERSION 68 M.A. SMITH   * JAN 1985 * * * * * * *
00020 * * * * * * * * VERSION 69 XG500 * NOV 1991 * * * * * *
00021 * * * * * * * * VERSION 70 F. TRIMMER * DEC 1992 * * * * * *
00022 * * * * * * * * VERSION 71 C.COMB    * MRT 1999 * * * * * *
00023 * * * * * * * * VERSION 72 A.B. CREST   * JUL 2000 * * * * * *
```

Figure 1-1. *COBOL module version log. Published in "Recovering Management Information from Source Code," Kwiatkowski and Verhoef*[25]

The longevity of COBOL applications can also be held largely accountable for the predominance of COBOL programs in the Y2K problem (12,000,000 COBOL applications versus 1,400,000 C++ applications in the United States alone).[10] Many years ago, when programmers were writing these applications, they just did not anticipate that the software would last into this millennium.

COBOL Applications Often Run in Critical Areas of Business

COBOL is used for mission-critical applications running in vital areas of the economy. Datamonitor reports that 75% of business data and 90% of financial transactions are processed in COBOL.[37] The serious financial and legal consequences that can result from an application failure is one of the reasons for the near panic over the Y2K problem.

COBOL Applications Often Deal with Enormous Volumes of Data

COBOL's forte is file and record processing. Single files or databases measured in terabytes are not uncommon. The SSA system mentioned earlier, for instance, manages over 1 petabyte (1 petabyte = 1,000 terabytes = 1,000,000 gigabytes) of data,[38] and "Terabytes of new data come in daily.[39]"

Characteristics of COBOL

Although COBOL is a high-level programming language, it is probably quite unlike any language you have ever used. A genealogical tree of programming languages usually places COBOL by itself with no antecedents and no descendants. Occasionally a tree might include FLOW-MATIC and COMTRAN or might show a connection to PL/I (because that language incorporated some COBOL elements). By and large though, COBOL is unique. So even though COBOL supports the familiar elements of a programming language such as variables, arrays, procedures, and selection and iteration control structures, these familiar elements are implemented in an unfamiliar way. It's like going to a foreign country and finding that your rental car uses a stick shift and people drive on the other side of the road: disconcerting.

This section examines some of the general characteristics of COBOL that distinguish it from languages with which you might be more familiar.

COBOL Is Self-Documenting

The most obvious characteristic of COBOL programs is their textual, rather than mathematical, orientation. One of the design goals for COBOL was to make it possible for non-programmers such as supervisors, managers, and users to read and understand COBOL code. As a result, COBOL contains such English-like structural elements as verbs, clauses, sentences, sections, and divisions. As it happens, this design goal was not realized. Managers and users nowadays do not read COBOL programs. Computer programs are just too complex for most nonprofessionals to understand them, however familiar the syntactic elements. But the design goal and its effect on COBOL syntax had one important side effect: it made COBOL the most readable, understandable, and self-documenting programming language in use today. It also made it the most verbose.

It is easy for programmers unused to the business programming paradigm, where programming with a view to ease of maintenance is very important, to dismiss the advantage of COBOL's readability. Not only does this readability generally assist the maintenance process, but the older a program gets, the more valuable readability becomes.

When programs are new, both the in-program comments and the external documentation accurately reflect the program code. But over time, as more and more revisions are applied to the code, it gets out of step with the documentation until the documentation is actually a hindrance to maintenance rather than a help. The self-documenting nature of COBOL means this problem is not as severe with COBOL as it is with other languages.

Readers who are familiar with C, C++, or Java might want to consider how difficult it becomes to maintain programs written in these languages. C programs you wrote yourself are difficult enough to understand when you return to them six months later. Consider how much more difficult it would be to understand a program that was written 15 years previously, by someone else, and which had since been amended and added to by so many others that the documentation no longer accurately reflected the program code. This is a nightmare awaiting maintenance programmers of the future, and it is already peeking over the horizon.

COBOL Is Stable

As a computer language, COBOL evolves with near-glacial slowness. The designers of COBOL do not jump on the bandwagon of every new, popular fad. Changes incorporating new ideas are made to the language only when the new idea has proven itself.

Since its creation in 1960, only four COBOL standards have been produced:

- *ANS 68 COBOL:* Resolved incompatibilities between different COBOL versions

- *ANS 74 COBOL:* Introduced the CALL verb and external subprograms

- *ANS 85 COBOL:* Introduced structured programming and internal subprograms

- *ISO 2002 COBOL:* Introduced object orientation to COBOL

Enterprises running mission-critical applications are unsurprisingly suspicious of change. Many of these organizations stay one version behind the very slow leading edge of COBOL. It is only now that the 2002 version of COBOL has been specified that many will start to move to the 1985 standard. This is one reason this book mainly adheres to the ANS 85 standard.

Conscious of the long life of COBOL applications, backward compatibility has been a major concern of the ANSI COBOL Committee. Very few language elements have been dropped from the language. As a result, programs I wrote in the 1980s for the DEC VAX using VAX COBOL compile, with little or no alteration, on the Micro Focus Visual COBOL compiler. Java, although only created in 1995, is now on its seventh version and already has a very long list of obsolete, deprecated, and removed features. In the years since its creation, Java has removed more language features than COBOL has in the whole of its 50-year history.

COBOL Is Simple

COBOL is a simple language (until the most recent version, it had no pointers, no user-defined functions, and no user-defined types). It encourages a simple, straightforward programming style. Curiously enough, though, despite its limitations, COBOL has proven itself well suited to its target problem domain (business computing). Most COBOL programs operate in a domain where the program complexity lies in the business rules that have to be encoded rather than in the sophistication of the data structures or algorithms required. In cases where sophisticated algorithms are needed, COBOL usually meets the need with an appropriate verb such as SORT or SEARCH.

Earlier in this book, I noted that the limitations of COBOL meant it could not be used to teach computer science concepts. And in the previous paragraph, I noted that COBOL is a simple language with a limited scope of function. These comments pertain to versions of COBOL prior to the ANS 2002 version. With the introduction of OO COBOL, everything has changed. OO COBOL retains all the advantages of previous versions but now includes the following:

- User-defined functions
- Object orientation
- National characters (Unicode)
- Multiple currency symbols
- Cultural adaptability (locales)
- Dynamic memory allocation (pointers)
- Data validation using the new VALIDATE verb
- Binary and floating-point data types
- User-defined data types

COBOL Is Nonproprietary

The COBOL standard does not belong to any particular vendor. It was originally designed to be a "machine independent common language[8]" and to be ported to a wide range of machines. This capability was demonstrated by the first COBOL compilers when the same program was compiled and executed on both the RCA and the Remington-Rand-Univac computers.[8] The ANSI COBOL committee, and now the ISO, define the non-vendor-specific syntax and semantic language standards. COBOL has been ported to virtually every operating system, from every flavor of Windows to every flavor of Unix; from IBM's VM, zOS, and zVSE operating systems, to MPE, MPE-iX, and HP-UX on HP machines; from the Wang VS to GCOS on Bull machines. COBOL runs on computers you have probably never heard of, such as the Data General Nova, SuperNova, and Eclipse MV series; the DEC PDP-11/70 and VAX; the Univac 9000s and the Unisys 2200s; and the Hitachi EX33 and the Bull DPX/20.

COBOL Is Maintainable

COBOL has a 50-year proven track record for application production, maintenance, and enhancement. The indications from the Y2K problem that COBOL applications were cheaper to fix than applications written in more recent languages ($28 per function point versus $35 for C++ and $65 for PL/1) have been supported by the 2012 *ComputerWorld* survey[12] and the 2011/12 CRASH Report.[40] When comparing COBOL maintenance costs to those of Visual Basic, C#, C++, and Java, the *ComputerWorld* survey reported that 72% of respondents found that COBOL was just as good (29%) as these languages or better (43%). Similarly, the CRASH Report found that COBOL had the lowest technical debt (defined in the report as "the effort required to fix problems that remain in the code when an application is released") of any mainstream language, whereas Java-EE, averaging $5.42 per LOC, had the highest.

One reason for the maintainability of COBOL programs was mentioned earlier: the readability of COBOL code. Another reason is COBOL's rigid hierarchical structure. In COBOL programs, all external references, such as references to devices, files, command sequences, collating sequences, the currency symbol, and the decimal point symbol, are defined in the Environment Division.

When a COBOL program is moved to a new machine, has new peripheral devices attached, or is required to work in a different country, COBOL programmers know that the parts of the program that will have to be altered to accommodate these changes will be isolated in the Environment Division. In other programming languages, programmer discipline might ensure that the references liable to change are restricted to one part of the program but they could just as easily be spread throughout the program. In COBOL programs, programmers have no choice. COBOL's rigid hierarchical structure ensures that these items are restricted to the Environment Division.

Summary

Unfortunately, the leaders of the computer science community have taken a very negative view of COBOL from its very inception and therefore have not looked carefully enough to see what good ideas are in there which could be further enlarged, expanded or generalized.

Jean Sammet, "The Early History of COBOL,"
ACM Sigplan Notices 13(8), August 1978

The problem with being such an old language is that COBOL suffers from 50 years of accumulated opprobrium. Criticism of COBOL is often based—if it is based on direct experience at all—on programs written 30 to 50 years ago. The huge monolithic programs, the tangled masses of spaghetti code, and the global data are all hallmarks of COBOL programs written long before programmers knew better. They are not characteristic of programs written using more modern versions of COBOL.

Critics also forget that COBOL is a domain-specific language and criticize it for shortcomings that have little relevance to its target domain. There is little acknowledgement of how well suited COBOL is for that domain. The performance of COBOL compared to other languages in recent surveys underlines its suitability. The 2012 *ComputerWorld* survey[12] compared COBOL with Visual Basic, C#, C++, and Java and reported that, among other things, respondents found it better in terms of batch processing, transaction processing, handling business-oriented features, and maintenance costs. Nor is this a one off: similar results have been reported by other surveys.

There is enormous pressure to replace COBOL legacy systems with systems written in one of the more fashionable languages. The many failures that have attended replacement attempts, however, have given legacy system stakeholders pause for thought. The well-documented dangers of the replacement approach and the relative success of COBOL system migration is leading to a growing reassessment of options. Keeping the COBOL codebase is now seen as a more viable, safer, cheaper alternative to replacement. But this reassessment reveals a problem. Keeping, and even growing, the COBOL codebase requires COBOL programmers, and the COBOL workforce is aging and nearing retirement.

For some years now, programmers have luxuriated in a seller's market. The demand for programmers has been far in advance of the supply. But student numbers in computer science courses around the world are recovering from the Y2K downturn. As these graduates enter the job market, it will become more and more competitive. In a competitive environment, programmers may find that having a résumé that includes COBOL is a useful differentiator.

References

1. Dijkstra EW. How do we tell truths that might hurt? ACM SIGPLAN Notices. 1982; 17(5): 13–15. http://doi.acm.org/10.1145/947923.947924 doi: 10.1145/947923.947924. Originally issued as Memo EWD 498. 1975 Jun.
2. Mitchell RL. Brain drain: where Cobol systems go from here. ComputerWorld. 2012 Mar 14. www.computerworld.com/s/article/9225079/Brain_drain_Where_Cobol_systems_go_from_here_
3. Sneed HM, Erdoes K. Migrating AS400-COBOL to Java: a report from the field. CSMR 2013. Proceedings of the 17th European Conference on Software Maintenance and Reengineering; 2013; Genova, Italy. CSMR; 231–240.
4. Glass R. Cobol—a contradiction and an enigma. Commun ACM. 1997; 40(9): 11–13.
5. Glass R. How best to provide the services IS programmers need. Commun ACM. 1997; 40(12): 17–19.
6. Glass R. COBOL: is it dying—or thriving? Data Base Adv Inf Sy. 1999; 30(1).
7. Glass R. One giant step backward. Commun ACM. 2003; 46(5): 21–23.
8. Sammet J. The early history of COBOL. ACM SIGPLAN Notices. 1978; 13(8) 121–161.
9. Brown GDeW. COBOL: the failure that wasn't. COBOL Report; 1999. CobolReport.com (now defunct)
10. Jones C. The global economic impact of the Year 2000 software problem. Capers Jones. 1996; version 4.
11. Barnett G. The future of the mainframe. Ovum Report. 2005.
12. ComputerWorld. COBOL brain drain: survey results. 2012 Mar 14. www.computerworld.com/s/article/9225099/Cobol_brain_drain_Survey_results
13. Topolski E. IBM unveils new software to enable mainframe applications on cloud, mobile devices. IBM News Room. 2012 May 17. www-03.ibm.com/press/us/en/pressrelease/41095.wss

14. Terekhov AA, Verhoef C. The realities of language conversions. Software, IEEE. 2000; 17(6): 111,124.
15. Sneed HM. Migrating from COBOL to Java. ICSM 2010. Proceedings of International Conference on Software Maintenance; 2010; Timisoara, Romania. IEEE; 1-7.
16. The Standish Group. Modernization: clearing a pathway to success. Report. Boston: The Group; 2010.
17. Organizational tool manufacturer cuts costs by 94 percent with NetCOBOL and NeoTools. Microsoft. 2011. www.gtsoftware.com/resource/organizational-tool-manufacturer-cuts-costs-by-94-percent-with-net-cobol-and-neotools/
18. Productivity tools maker cuts costs 94% with move from mainframe to Windows. Microsoft. 2009 Jul. www.docstoc.com/docs/81151637/Daytimer_MainframeMigration
19. Waters J. Testing mainframe code on your laptop. WatersWorks blog, Application Development Trends (ADT). 2010 Jul 27. http://adtmag.com/blogs/watersworks/2010/07/ibm-mainframes-cobol-recruits.aspx
20. Robinson B. COBOL remains old standby at agencies despite showing its age. Federal Computer Week. 2009 Jul 9. www.fcw.com/Articles/2009/07/13/TECH-COBOL-turns-50.aspx
21. Thomas J. Manta's IBM i COBOL training trifecta. IT Jungle. 2012 Oct 22. www.itjungle.com/tfh/tfh102212-story10.html
22. Veryant announces new COBOL training class. Veryant. 2012 Apr. www.veryant.com/about/news/cobol-training-class.php
23. Atwood J. COBOL everywhere and nowhere. Coding Horror. 2009 Aug 9. www.codinghorror.com/blog/2009/08/cobol-everywhere-and-nowhere.html
24. Campbell G. 2009 Aug 10. Comment on Atwood J. COBOL everywhere and nowhere. Coding Horror. 2009 Aug 9. www.codinghorror.com/blog/2009/08/cobol-everywhere-and-nowhere.html
25. Kwiatkowski ŁM, Verhoef C. Recovering management information from source code. Sci Comput Program. 2013; 78(9): 1368-1406.
26. Brin D. The practice effect. 1984. Reprint, New York: Bantam Spectra; 1995.
27. Verhoef C. The realities of large software portfolios. 2000 Feb 24. www.cs.vu.nl/~x/lsp/lsp.html
28. Case study: Owens & Minor. Robocom. 2011. www.robocom.com/Portals/0/Images/PDF/Owens%20&%20Minor%20Case%20Study.pdf
29. Medical supply distributor avoids costly ERP replacement with migration to Windows Server and SQL Server. Microsoft. 2010 Feb. www.docstoc.com/docs/88231164/Medical-Supply-Distributor-Avoids-Costly-ERP-Replacement-with
30. Veerman N. Revitalizing modifiability of legacy assets. J Softw Maint Evol-R. 2004; 16: 219–254.
31. Holloway N. Micro Focus International plc: Irish Life delivers cost savings and productivity gains through application modernzation program with Micro Focus. 4-Traders.com. 2013 May 30. www.4-traders.com/MICRO-FOCUS-INTERNATIONAL-12467060/news/Micro-Focus-International-plc-Irish-Life-Delivers-Cost-Savings-and-Productivity-Gains-through-Appl-16916097/
32. Mainframe-to-Windows move speeds agility up to 300 percent for global publisher. Microsoft. 2007 Sep. www.platformmodernization.org/microsoft/Lists/SuccessStories/DispForm.aspx?ID=6&RootFolder=%2Fmicrosoft%2FLists%2FSuccessStories
33. Sneed H. A pilot project for migrating COBOL code to web services. Int J Softw Tools Tech Transf. 2009; 11(6): 441–451.
34. Brand M, Deursen A, Klint P, Klusener AS, Meulen E. Industrial applications of ASF+SDF. Amsterdam, The Netherlands: CWI; 1996. Technical report. Also Wirsing M, editor. AMAST'96. Proceedings of the Conference on Algebraic Methodology and Software Technology; 1996; Munich, Germany. Springer-Verlag; 1996.
35. Social Security Administration. The Social Security Administration's software modernization and use of common business oriented language. Audit Report. Office of the Inspector General, Social Security Administration. 2012 May. http://oig.ssa.gov/sites/default/files/audit/full/pdf/A-14-11-11132_0.pdf
36. Property firm migrates from mainframe to Windows, cuts costs 60 percent, ups speed. Microsoft. 2006 Jul. http://cloud.alchemysolutions.com/case-studies/Watch-Stockholmshem-describe-the-modernization-experience Or www.gtsoftware.com/resource/property-management-firm-migrates-from-mainframe-to-windows-cuts-costs-60-percent-ups-speed/ Or http://download.microsoft.com/documents/customerevidence/27759_Stockholmshem_migration_case_study.doc
37. Datamonitor. COBOL—continuing to drive value in the 21st century. Datamonitor; 2008 Nov. Reference code CYBT0006.
38. National Council of Social Security Management Associations Transition White Paper. 2008 Dec. http://otrans.3cdn.net/bfb27060430522c5ae_n0m6iyt3y.pdf
39. Hoover JN. Stimulus funds will go toward new data center for Social Security Administration. InformationWeekUK. 2009 Feb 28. www.informationweek.co.uk/internet/ebusiness/stimulus-funds-will-go-toward-new-data-c/214700005
40. Executive Summary—The CRASH report, 2011/12. CAST. 2012. www.castsoftware.com/research-labs/crash-reports

CHAPTER 2

■ ■ ■

COBOL Foundation

This chapter presents some of the foundational material you require before you can write COBOL programs. It starts by identifying some elements of COBOL that programmers of other languages find idiosyncratic and it explains the reasons for them. You're then introduced to the unusual syntax notation (called *metalanguage*) used to describe COBOL verbs and shown some examples.

COBOL programs have to conform to a fairly rigid hierarchical structure. This chapter introduces the structural elements and explains how each fits into the overall hierarchy. Because the main structural element of a COBOL program is the division, you spend some time learning about the function and purpose of each of the four divisions.

COBOL programs, especially in restrictive coding shops, are required to conform to a number of coding rules. These rules are explained and placed in their historical context.

The chapter discusses the details of name construction; but because name construction is about more than just the mechanics, you also learn about the importance of using descriptive names for both data items and blocks of executable code. The importance of code formatting for visualizing data hierarchy and statement scope is also discussed.

To whet your appetite for what is coming in the succeeding chapters, the chapter includes a number of small example programs and gives brief explanations. The chapter ends by listing the most important COBOL compilers, both free and commercial, available for Windows and UNIX.

COBOL Idiosyncrasies

COBOL is one of the oldest programming languages still in use. As a result, it has some idiosyncrasies, which programmers used to other languages may find irritating. One of the design goals of COBOL was to assist readability by making the language as English-like as possible.[1] As a consequence, the structural concepts normally associated with English prose, such as division, section, paragraph, sentence, verb, and so on, are used in COBOL programs. To further aid readability, the concept of *noise words* was introduced. Noise words are words in a COBOL statement that have no semantic content and are used only to enhance readability by making the statement more English-like.

One consequence of these design decisions is that the COBOL reserved-word list is extensive and contains many hundreds of entries. The reserved words themselves also tend to be long, with words like UNSTRING, EVALUATE, and PERFORM being typical. The English-like structure, the long reserved words, and the noise words makes COBOL programs seem verbose, especially when compared to languages such as C.

When COBOL was designed, today's tools were not available. Programs were written on coding forms (see Figure 2-1), passed to punch-card operators for transfer onto punch cards (see Figure 2-2), and then submitted to the computer operator to be loaded into the computer using a punch-card reader. These media (coding sheets and punch cards) required adherence to a number of formatting restrictions that some COBOL implementations still enforce today, long after the need for them has gone. This book discusses these coding restrictions but doesn't adhere to them. You should be aware, though, that depending on the coding rules in a particular coding shop, you might be obliged to abide by these archaic conventions.

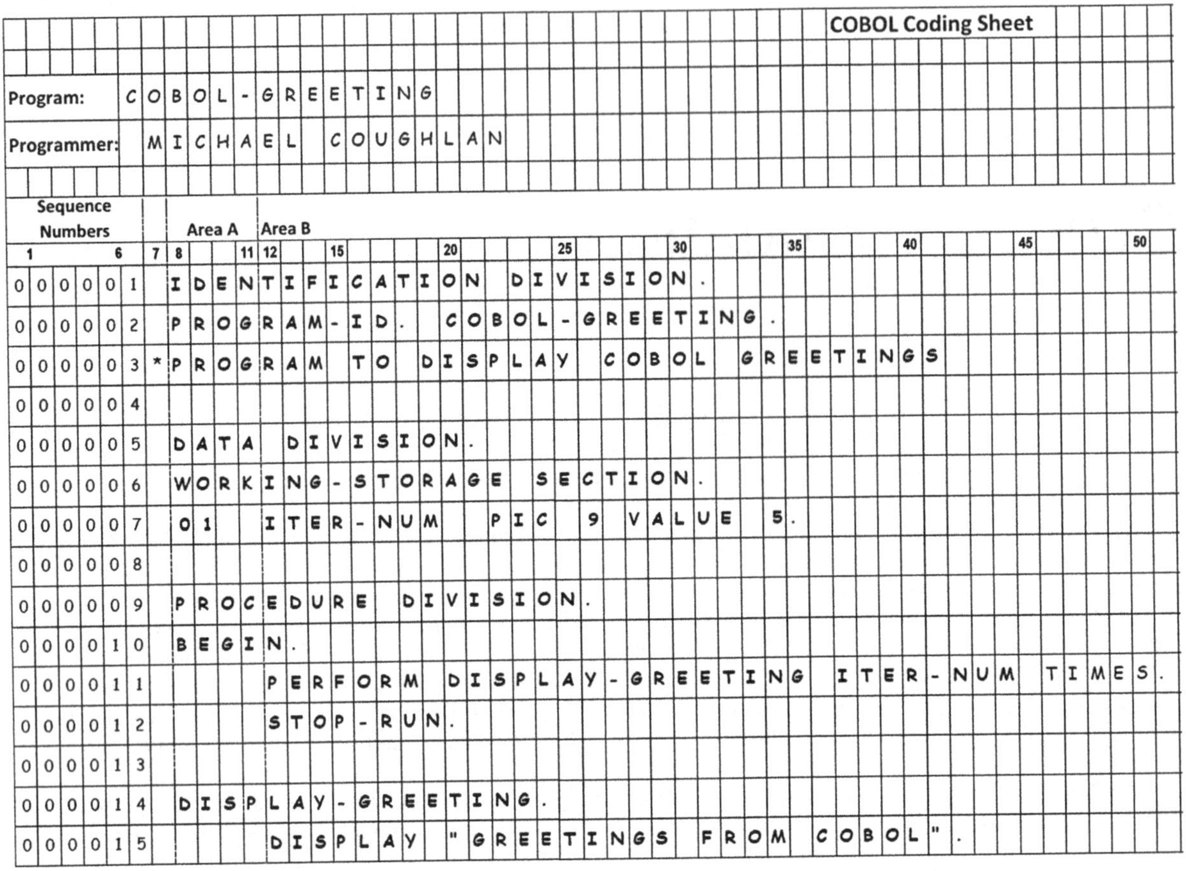

| | | | | | | | | | | | | | | | COBOL Coding Sheet | | | | |

Program: COBOL-GREETING

Programmer: MICHAEL COUGHLAN

Sequence Numbers | Area A | Area B

1	6	7	8	11	12	15	20	25	30	35	40	45	50
0 0 0 0 0 1		IDENTIFICATION DIVISION.
0 0 0 0 0 2		PROGRAM-ID. COBOL-GREETING.
0 0 0 0 0 3	*PROGRAM TO DISPLAY COBOL GREETINGS
0 0 0 0 0 4		
0 0 0 0 0 5		DATA DIVISION.
0 0 0 0 0 6		WORKING-STORAGE SECTION.
0 0 0 0 0 7		01 ITER-NUM PIC 9 VALUE 5.
0 0 0 0 0 8		
0 0 0 0 0 9		PROCEDURE DIVISION.
0 0 0 0 1 0		BEGIN.
0 0 0 0 1 1		PERFORM DISPLAY-GREETING ITER-NUM TIMES.
0 0 0 0 1 2		STOP-RUN.
0 0 0 0 1 3		
0 0 0 0 1 4		DISPLAY-GREETING.
0 0 0 0 1 5		DISPLAY "GREETINGS FROM COBOL".

Figure 2-1. COBOL coding sheet

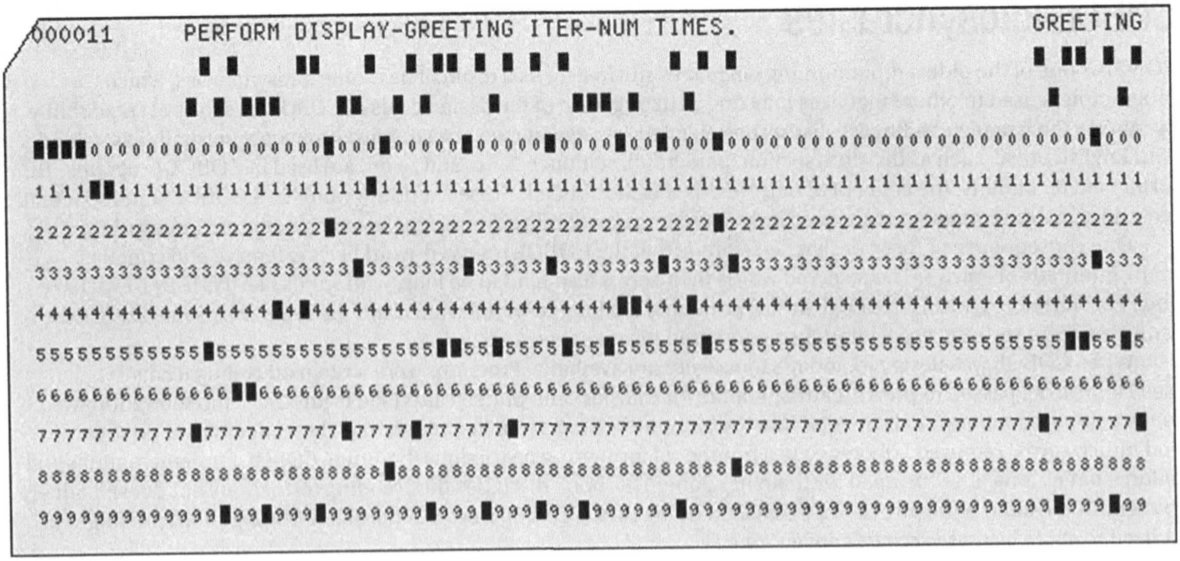

Figure 2-2. COBOL punch card for line 11 of the coding sheet[2]

18

The final COBOL irritant is that although many of the constructs required to write well-structured programs have been introduced into modern COBOL (ANS 85 COBOL and OO-COBOL), the need for backward compatibility means some language elements remain that, if used, make it difficult and in some cases impossible to write good programs. ALTER verb, I'm thinking of you.

COBOL Syntax Metalanguage

COBOL syntax is defined using a notation sometimes called the COBOL *metalanguage.* In this notation

- Words in uppercase are reserved words. When underlined, they are mandatory. When not underlined, they are noise words, used for readability only, and are optional.

- Words in mixed case represent names that must be devised by the programmer (such as the names of data items).

- When material is enclosed in curly braces { }, a choice must be made from the options within the braces. If there is only one option, then that item is mandatory.

- When material is enclosed in square brackets [ ], the material is optional and may be included or omitted as required.

- When the ellipsis symbol ... (three dots) is used, it indicates that the preceding syntactic element may be repeated at your discretion.

- To assist readability, the comma, semicolon, and space characters may be used as separators in a COBOL statement, but they have no semantic effect. For instance, the following statements are semantically identical:

```
ADD Num1 Num2   Num3  TO Result
ADD Num1, Num2, Num3  TO Result
ADD Num1; Num2; Num3  TO Result
```

In addition to the metalanguage diagrams, syntax rules govern the interpretation of metalanguage. For instance, the metalanguage for PERFORM..VARYING (see Figure 2-3) implies that you can have as many AFTER phrases as desired. In fact, as you will discover when I discuss this construct in Chapter 6, only two are allowed.

$$\underline{\text{PERFORM}}\left[\text{1stProc}\left[\left\{\begin{array}{l}\underline{\text{THRU}}\\\underline{\text{THROUGH}}\end{array}\right\}\text{EndProc}\right]\right]\left[\text{WITH}\,\underline{\text{TEST}}\left\{\begin{array}{l}\underline{\text{BEFORE}}\\\underline{\text{AFTER}}\end{array}\right\}\right]$$

$$\underline{\text{VARYING}}\left\{\begin{array}{l}\text{Counter1}\#i\\\text{IndexName1}\end{array}\right\}\underline{\text{FROM}}\left\{\begin{array}{l}\text{StartValue}\#il\\\text{IndexName2}\end{array}\right\}$$

$$\underline{\text{BY}}\,\text{Step Value}\#\,\text{il}\,\underline{\text{UNTIL}}\,\text{Condition1}$$

$$\left[\underline{\text{AFTER}}\left\{\begin{array}{l}\text{Counter2}\#i\\\text{IndexName3}\end{array}\right\}\underline{\text{FROM}}\left\{\begin{array}{l}\text{StartValue2}\#il\\\text{IndexName4}\end{array}\right\}\right]\ldots$$

$$\underline{\text{BY}}\,\text{Step Value2}\#\,\text{il}\,\underline{\text{UNTIL}}\,\text{Condition2}$$

$$\left[\text{StatementBlock}\,\underline{\text{END - PERFORM}}\right]$$

Figure 2-3. PERFORM..VARYING *metalanguage*

Some Notes on Syntax Diagrams

As mentioned in the previous section, the interpretation of the COBOL metalanguage is modified by syntax rules. Because it can be tedious to wade through all the rules for each COBOL construct, this book uses a modified form of the syntax diagram. In this modified diagram, special operand suffixes indicate the type of the operand; these are shown in Table 2-1.

Table 2-1. *Special Metalanguage Operand Suffixes*

Suffix	Meaning
$i	Uses an alphanumeric data item
$il	Uses an alphanumeric data item or a string literal
#i	Uses a numeric data item
#il	Uses a numeric data item or numeric literal
$#i	Uses a numeric or an alphanumeric data item

Example Metalanguage

As an example of how the metalanguage for a COBOL verb is interpreted, the syntax for the COMPUTE verb is shown in Figure 2-4. I'm presenting COMPUTE here because, as the COBOL arithmetic verb (the others are ADD, SUBTRACT, MULTIPLY, DIVIDE) that's closest to the way things are done in many other languages, it will be a point of familiarity. The operation of COMPUTE is discussed in more detail in Chapter 4.

<u>COMPUTE</u> {Result#i [<u>ROUNDED</u>]} ... = Arithmetic Expression

$$\left[\begin{Bmatrix} \text{ON } \underline{\text{SIZE ERROR}} \\ \underline{\text{NOT}} \text{ ON } \underline{\text{SIZE ERROR}} \end{Bmatrix} \text{StatementBlock } \underline{\text{END-COMPUTE}}\right]$$

Figure 2-4. *COMPUTE metalanguage syntax diagram*

The COMPUTE verb assigns the result of an arithmetic expression to a variable or variables. The interpretation of the COMPUTE metalanguage is as follows:

- A COMPUTE statement must start with the keyword COMPUTE.
- The keyword must be followed by the name of a numeric data item that receives the result of the calculation (the suffix #i indicates that the operand must be the name of a numeric data item [variable]).
- The equals sign (=) must be used.
- An arithmetic expression must follow the equals sign.
- The square braces [ ] around the word ROUNDED indicate that rounding is optional. Because the word ROUNDED is underlined, the word must be used if rounding is required.
- The ellipsis symbol (...) indicates that there can more than one Result#i data item.
- The ellipsis occurs outside the curly braces {}, which means each result field can have its own ROUNDED phrase.

In other words, you could have a COMPUTE statement like

```
COMPUTE Result1 ROUNDED, Result2  =  ((9 * 9) + 8) / 5
```

where Result1 would be assigned a value of 18 (rounded 17.8) and Result2 would be assigned a value of 17 (truncated 17.8), assuming both Result1 and Result2 were defined as PIC 99.

Structure of COBOL Programs

COBOL is much more rigidly structured than most other programming languages. COBOL programs are hierarchical in structure. Each element of the hierarchy consists of one or more subordinate elements. The program hierarchy consists of divisions, sections, paragraphs, sentences, and statements (see Figure 2-5).

```
PROGRAM
    DIVISION(s)
        SECTION(s)
            Paragraph(s)
                Sentence(s)
                    Statement(s)
```

Figure 2-5. *Hierarchical COBOL program structure*

A COBOL program is divided into distinct parts called divisions. A division may contain one or more sections. A section may contain one or more paragraphs. A paragraph may contain one or more sentences, and a sentence one or more statements.

■ **Note** Programmers unused to this sort of rigidity may find it irksome or onerous, but this layout offers some practical advantages. Many of the programmatic items that might need to be modified as a result of an environmental change are defined in the ENVIRONMENT DIVISION. External references, such as to devices, files, collating sequences, the currency symbol, and the decimal point symbol are all defined in the ENVIRONMENT DIVISION.

Divisions

The division is the major structural element in COBOL. Later in this chapter, I discuss the purpose of each division. For now, you can note that there are four divisions: the IDENTIFICATION DIVISION, the ENVIRONMENT DIVISION, the DATA DIVISION, and the PROCEDURE DIVISION.

Sections

A section is made up of one or more paragraphs. A section begins with the section name and ends where the next section name is encountered or where the program text ends.

A section name consists of a name devised by the programmer or defined by the language, followed by the word *Section*, followed by a period (full stop). Some examples of section names are given in Example 2-1.

In the first three divisions, sections are an organizational structure defined by the language. But in the PROCEDURE DIVISON, where you write the program's executable statements, sections and paragraphs are used to identify blocks of code that can be executed using the PERFORM or the GO TO.

Example 2-1. Example Section Names

```
SelectTexasRecords SECTION.
FILE SECTION.
CONFIGURATION SECTION.
INPUT-OUTPUT SECTION.
```

Paragraphs

A paragraph consists of one or more sentences. A paragraph begins with a paragraph name and ends where the next section name or paragraph name is encountered or where the program text ends.

In the first three divisions, paragraphs are an organizational structure defined by the language (see Example 2-2). But in the PROCEDURE DIVISON, paragraphs are used to identify blocks of code that can be executed using PERFORM or GO TO (see Example 2-3).

Example 2-2. ENVIRONMENT DIVISION Entries Required for a File Declaration

```
ENVIRONMENT DIVISION.
INPUT-OUTPUT SECTION.
FILE-CONTROL.
    SELECT ExampleFile ASSIGN TO "Example.Dat"
            ORGANIZATION IS SEQUENTIAL.
```

Example 2-3. PROCEDURE DIVISION with Two Paragraphs (Begin and DisplayGreeting)

```
PROCEDURE DIVISION.
Begin.
   PERFORM  DisplayGreeting 10 TIMES.
   STOP RUN.

DisplayGreeting.
   DISPLAY "Greetings from COBOL".
```

Sentences

A sentence consists of one or more statements and is terminated by a period. There must be at least one sentence, and hence one period, in a paragraph. Example 2-4 shows two sentences. The first sentence also happens to be a statement; the second consists of three statements.

Example 2-4. Two Sentences

```
SUBTRACT Tax FROM GrossPay GIVING NetPay.

MOVE .21 TO VatRate
COMPUTE VatAmount = ProductCost * VatRate
DISPLAY "The VAT amount is - " VatAmount.
```

Statements

In COBOL, language statements are referred to as *verbs*. A statement starts with the name of the verb and is followed by the operand or operands on which the verb acts. Example 2-5 shows three statements.

Example 2-5. Three Statements

```
DISPLAY "Enter name " WITH NO ADVANCING
ACCEPT  StudentName
DISPLAY "Name entered was " StudentName
```

In Table 2-2, the major COBOL verbs are categorized by type. The arithmetic verbs are used in computations, the file-handling verbs are used to manipulate files, the flow-of-control verbs are used to alter the normal sequential execution of program statements, the table-handling verbs are used to manipulate tables (arrays), and the string-handling verbs allow such operations as character counting, string splitting, and string concatenation.

Table 2-2. *Major COBOL Verbs, Categorized by Type*

Arithmetic	File Handling	Flow of Control	Assignment & I-O	Table Handling	String Handling
COMPUTE	OPEN	IF	MOVE	SEARCH	INSPECT
ADD	CLOSE	EVALUATE	SET	SEARCH ALL	STRING
SUBTRACT	READ	PERFORM	INITIALIZEACCEPT	SET	UNSTRING
MULTIPLY	WRITE	GO TO	DISPLAY		
DIVIDE	DELETE	CALL			
	REWRITE	STOP RUN			
	START	EXIT PROGRAM			
	SORT				
	RETURN				
	RELEASE				

The Four Divisions

At the top of the COBOL hierarchy are the four divisions. These divide the program into distinct structural elements.

Although some of the divisions may be omitted, the sequence in which they are specified is fixed and must be as follows. Just like section names and paragraph names, division names must be followed by a period:

IDENTIFICATION DIVISION. Contains information about the program

ENVIRONMENT DIVISION. Contains environment information

DATA DIVISION. Contains data descriptions

PROCEDURE DIVISION. Contains the program algorithms

IDENTIFICATION DIVISION

The purpose of the IDENTIFICATION DIVISION is to provide information about the program to you, the compiler, and the linker. The PROGRAM-ID paragraph is the only entry required. In fact, this entry is required in every program. Nowadays all the other entries have the status of comments (which are not processed when the program runs), but you may still find it useful to included paragraphs such as AUTHOR and DATE-WRITTEN.

The PROGRAM-ID is followed by a user-devised name that is used to identify the program internally. This name may be different from the file name given to the program when it was saved to backing storage. The metalanguage for the PROGRAM-ID is

```
PROGRAM-ID. UserAssignedProgramName.
[IS [COMMON] [INITIAL] PROGRAM].
```

The metalanguage items in square braces apply only to subprograms, so I will reserve discussion of these items until later in the book.

When a number of independently compiled programs are combined by the linker into a single executable run-unit, each program is identified by the name given in its PROGRAM-ID. When control is passed to a particular program by means of a CALL verb, the target of the CALL invocation is the name given in the subprogram's PROGRAM-ID for instance:

```
CALL "PrintSummaryReport".
```

Example 2-6 shows an example IDENTIFICATION DIVISION. Pay particular attention to the periods — they are required.

Example 2-6. Sample IDENTIFICATION DIVISION

```
IDENTIFICATION DIVISION.
PROGRAM-ID. PrintSummaryReport.
AUTHOR. Michael Coughlan.
DATE-WRITTEN. 20th June 2013.
```

ENVIRONMENT DIVISION

The ENVIRONMENT DIVISION is used to describe the environment in which the program works. It isolates in one place all aspects of the program that are dependent on items in the environment in which the program runs. The idea is to make it easy to change the program when it has to run on a different computer or one with different peripheral devices or when the program is being used in a different country.

The ENVIRONMENT DIVISION consists of two sections: the CONFIGURATION SECTION and the INPUT-OUTPUT SECTION. In the CONFIGURATION SECTION, the SPECIAL-NAMES paragraph allows you to specify such environmental details as what alphabet to use, what currency symbol to use, and what decimal point symbol to use. In the INPUT-OUTPUT SECTION, the FILE-CONTROL paragraph lets you connect internal file names with external devices and files.

Example 2-7 shows some example CONFIGURATION SECTION entries. A few notes about the listing:

- In some countries the meaning of the decimal point and the comma are reversed. For instance, the number 1,234.56 is sometimes written 1.234,56. The DECIMAL-POINT IS COMMA clause specifies that the program conforms to this scheme.

- The SYMBOLIC CHARACTERS clause lets you assign a name to one of the unprintable characters. In this example, names for the escape, carriage return, and line-feed characters have been defined by specifying their ordinal position (not value) in the character set.

- The SELECT and ASSIGN clauses let you connect the name you use for a file in the program with its actual name and location on disk.

Example 2-7. CONFIGURATION SECTION Examples

```
IDENTIFICATION DIVISION.
PROGRAM-ID. ConfigurationSectionExamples.
AUTHOR. Michael Coughlan.
ENVIRONMENT DIVISION.
CONFIGURATION SECTION.
SPECIAL-NAMES.
    DECIMAL-POINT IS COMMA.
    SYMBOLIC CHARACTERS   ESC  CR  LF
                    ARE   28   14  11.

INPUT-OUTPUT SECTION.
FILE-CONTROL.
    SELECT StockFile ASSIGN TO  "D:\DataFiles\Stock.dat"
            ORGANIZATION IS SEQUENTIAL.
```

DATA DIVISION

The DATA DIVISION is used to describe most of the data that a program processes. The obvious exception to this is literal data, which is defined *in situ* as a string or numeric literal such as "Freddy Ryan" or -345.74.

The DATA DIVISION is divided into four sections:

- The FILE SECTION

- The WORKING-STORAGE SECTION

- The LINKAGE SECTION

- The REPORT SECTION

The first two are the main sections. The LINKAGE SECTION is used only in subprograms, and the REPORT SECTION is used only when generating reports. The LINKAGE and REPORT sections are discussed more fully when you encounter the elements that require them later in the book. For now, only the first two sections need concern you.

File Section

The FILE SECTION describes the data that is sent to, or comes from, the computer's data storage peripherals. These include such devices as card readers, magnetic tape drives, hard disks, CDs, and DVDs.

Working-Storage Section

The WORKING-STORAGE SECTION describes the general variables used in the program. The COBOL metalanguage showing the general structure and syntax of the DATA DIVISION is given in Figure 2-6 and is followed by a fragment of an example COBOL program in Example 2-8.

DATA DIVISION.

$$\left[\begin{array}{l} \text{FILE SECTION.} \\ \textit{file section entries} \end{array}\right]$$

—

$$\left[\begin{array}{l} \text{WORKING – STORAGE SECTION.} \\ \textit{working storages entries} \end{array}\right]$$

$$\left[\begin{array}{l} \text{LINKAGE SECTION.} \\ \textit{linkage section entries} \end{array}\right]$$

$$\left[\begin{array}{l} \text{REPORT SECTION.} \\ \textit{report section entries} \end{array}\right]$$

Figure 2-6. *DATA DIVISION metalanguage*

Example 2-8. Simple Data Declarations

```
IDENTIFICATION DIVISION.
PROGRAM-ID.  SimpleDataDeclarations.
AUTHOR.  Michael Coughlan.
DATA DIVISION.
WORKING-STORAGE SECTION.
01  CardinalNumber       PIC 99     VALUE ZEROS.
01  IntegerNumer         PIC S99    VALUE -14.
01  DecimalNumber        PIC 999V99 VALUE 543.21.
01  ShopName             PIC X(30)  VALUE SPACES.
01  ReportHeading        PIC X(25)  VALUE "=== Employment Report ===".
```

Data Hierarchy

All the data items in Example 2-8 are independent, elementary, items. Although data hierarchy is too complicated a topic to deal with at this point, a preview of hierarchical data declaration is given in BirthDate (see Example 2-9).

Example 2-9. Example of a Hierarchical Data Declaration

```
01  BirthDate.
    02  YearOfBirth.
        03 CenturyOB    PIC 99.
        03 YearOB       PIC 99.
    02  MonthOfBirth    PIC 99.
    02  DayOfBirth      PIC 99.
```

In this declaration, the data hierarchy indicated by the level numbers tells you that the data item BirthDate consists of (is made up of) a number of subordinate data items. The immediate subordinate items (indicated by the 02 level numbers) are YearOfBirth, MonthOfBirth, and DayOfBirth. MonthOfBirth and DayOfBirth are elementary, atomic, items that are not further subdivided. However, YearOfBirth is a data item that *is* further subdivided (indicated by the 03 level numbers) into CenturyOB and YearOB.

In typed languages such as Pascal and Java, understanding what is happening to data in memory is not important. But understanding what is happening to the data moved into a data item is critical in COBOL. For this reason, when discussing data declarations and the assignment of values to data items, I often give a model of the storage. For instance, Figure 2-7 gives the model of the storage for the data items declared in Example 2-9 and shows what happens to the data when you execute the statement - MOVE "19451225" TO BirthDate.

BirthDate							
YearOfBirth				MonthOfBirth		DayOfBirth	
CenturyOB		YearOB					
1	9	4	5	1	2	2	5

Figure 2-7. *Memory model for the data items declared in Example 2-9*

PROCEDURE DIVISION

The PROCEDURE DIVISION is where all the data described in the DATA DIVISION is processed and produced. It is here that you describe your algorithm. The PROCEDURE DIVISION is hierarchical in structure. It consists of sections, paragraphs, sentences, and statements. Only the section is optional; there must be at least one paragraph, one sentence, and one statement in the PROCEDURE DIVISION.

Whereas the paragraph and section names in the other divisions are defined by the language, in the PROCEDURE DIVISION they are chosen by you. The names chosen should reflect the function of the code contained in the paragraph or section.

In many legacy COBOL programs, paragraph and section names were used chiefly as labels to break up the program text and to act as the target of GO TO statements and, occasionally, PERFORM statements. In these programs, GO TOs were used to jump back and forward through the program text in a manner that made the program logic very difficult to follow. This programmatic style was derisively labeled *spaghetti code*.

In this book, I advocate a programming style that eschews the use of GO TOs as much as possible and that uses performs and paragraphs to create single-entry, single-exit, open subroutines. Although the nature of an open subroutine is that control can drop into it, adherence to the single-entry, single-exit philosophy should ensure that this does not happen.

Shortest COBOL Program

COBOL has a very bad reputation for verbosity, but most of the programs on which that reputation was built were written in ANS 68 or ANS 74 COBOL. Those programs are 40 years old. In modern versions of the language, program elements are not required unless explicitly used. For instance, in the ShortestProgram (see Listing 2-1), no entries are required for the ENVIRONMENT and DATA DIVISIONs because they are not used in this program. The IDENTIFICATION DIVISION is required because it holds the mandatory PROGRAM-ID paragraph. The PROCEDURE DIVISION is also required, there must be at least one paragraph in it (DisplayPrompt), and the paragraph must contain at least one sentence (DISPLAY "I did it".). STOP RUN, a COBOL instruction to halt execution of the program, would normally appear in a program but is not required here because the program will stop when it reaches the end of the program text.

Listing 2-1. Shortest COBOL Program

```
IDENTIFICATION DIVISION.
PROGRAM-ID. ShortestProgram.
PROCEDURE DIVISION.
DisplayPrompt.
     DISPLAY "I did it".
```

■ **Note**   Some COBOL compilers require that all the divisions be present in a program. Others only require the
IDENTIFICATION DIVISION and the PROCEDURE DIVISION.

COBOL Coding Rules

Traditionally, COBOL programs were written on coding sheets (see Figure 2-8), punched on to punch cards, and then loaded into the computer via a card reader. Although nowadays most programs are entered directly via screen and keyboard, some COBOL formatting conventions remain that derive from its ancient punch-card history:

- On the coding sheet, the first six character positions are reserved for sequence numbers. Sequence numbers used to be a vital insurance against the disaster of dropping your stack of punch cards.

- The seventh character position is reserved for the continuation character or for an asterisk that denotes a comment line. The continuation character is rarely used nowadays because any COBOL statement can be broken into two lines anywhere (other than in a quoted string) there is a space character.

■ **COBOL Detail**   While other programming languages permit a variety of comment forms (Java for instance supports multiline comments, documentation comments, and end of line comments) COBOL allows only full-line comments. Comment lines are indicated by placing an asterisk in column 7 (if adhering to the strict formatting conventions - see Figure 2-8) or the the first column if using a version of COBOL that does not adhere to archaic formatting conventions. One further note; the Open Source COBOL at Compileonline.com requires comments to begin with *> but like Java you can also place these comments at the end of the line.

Figure 2-8. *Fragment of a coding sheet showing the different program areas*

- The actual program text starts in column 8. The four positions from 8 to 11 are known as Area A, and the positions from 12 to 72 are called Area B.

- The area from position 73 to 80 is the identification area; it was generally used to identify the program. This again was disaster insurance. If two stacks of cards were dropped, the identification allowed the cards belonging to the two programs to be identified.

When a COBOL compiler recognizes the Areas A and B, all division names, section names, paragraph names, file-description (FD) entries, and 01 level numbers must start in Area A. All other sentences must start in Area B.

In some COBOL compilers, it is possible to set a compiler option or include a compiler directive to free you from these archaic formatting conventions. For instance, the Micro Focus Net Express COBOL uses the compiler directive - `$ SET SOURCEFORMAT"FREE"`. Although modern compilers may free you from formatting restrictions, it is probably still a good idea to position items according to the Area A and Area B rule.

Name Construction

COBOL has a number of different user-devised names, such as data names (variable names), paragraph names, section names, and mnemonic names. The rules for name construction are given here along with some advice which all programmers should embrace.

All user-defined names in COBOL must adhere to the following rules:

- They must contain at least 1 character and not more than 30 characters.

- They must contain at least one alphabetic character and must not begin or end with a hyphen.

- They must be constructed from the characters A to Z, the numbers 0 to 9, and the hyphen. Because the hyphen can be mistaken for the minus sign, a word cannot begin or end with a hyphen.

- Names are not case-sensitive. `SalesDate` is the same as `salesDate` or `SALESDATE`.

- None of the many COBOL reserved words may be used as a user-defined name. The huge number of reserved words is one of the annoyances of COBOL. One strategy to avoid tripping over them is to use word doubles such as using `IterCount` instead of `Count`.

Here are some examples of user-defined names:

```
TotalPay
Gross-Pay
PrintReportHeadings
Customer10-Rec
```

Comments about Naming

Data-item names are used to identify variables. In COBOL, all variable data is defined in the DATA DIVISION rather than throughout the program as is done in many other languages. In the PROCEDURE DIVISION, section names and paragraph names are devised by you and are used to identify blocks of executable code.

The proper selection of data-item, section, and paragraph names is probably the most important thing you can do to make your programs understandable. The names you choose should be descriptive. Data-item names should be descriptive of the data they contain; for instance, it is fairly clear what data the data items TotalPay, GrossPay, and NetPay hold. Section and paragraph names should be descriptive of the function of the code contained in the paragraph or section; for instance, these seem fairly descriptive: ApplyValidInsertion, GetPostage, and ValidateCheckDigit. Difficulty in assigning a suitably descriptive name to a block of code should be taken as a sign that the program has been incorrectly partitioned and is likely to offend the Module Strength/Cohesion guidelines[3-6].

Authors writing about other programming languages often make the same point: programmers should choose descriptive names. But in many of these languages, where succinctness appears to be a highly lauded characteristic, the ethos of the language seems to contradict this advice. In COBOL, the language is already so verbose that the added burden of descriptive names is not likely to be a problem.

Comments about Program Formatting

In COBOL, hierarchy is vitally important in the declaration of data. Proper indentation is a very useful aid to understanding data hierarchy (more on this later). Misleading or no indentation is often a source of programming errors. Good programmers seem to understand this instinctively: when student programs are graded, those that correctly implement the specification are often found to have excellent formatting, whereas those with programming errors are often poorly formatted. This is ironic, because the programmers who are most in need of the aid of a well-formatted program seem to be those who pay formatting the least attention. Weak programmers never appear to understand how a poorly formatted program conspires against them and makes it much more difficult to produce code that works.

Proper formatting is also important in the PROCEDURE DIVISION. Even though the scope of COBOL verbs is well-signaled using END delimiters, indentation is still a very useful aid to emphasize scope.

This discussion brings me to an important piece of advice for COBOL programmers. This advice is a restatement of the Golden Rule promulgated by Jesus, Confucius, and others:

> *Write your programs as you would like them written if you were the one who had to maintain them.*

Comments about Programming Style

As noted earlier, data names and reserved words are not case sensitive. The reserved words PROCEDURE DIVISION can be written as uppercase, lowercase, or mixed case. My preference, developed during years of reading program printouts, is to put COBOL reserved words in uppercase and user-defined words in mixed case with capitals at the beginning of each word. Sometimes, for clarity, the words may be separated by a hyphen. This is the style I have chosen for this book because I believe it is the best for a printed format.

I want to stress, though, that this stylistic scheme is a personal preference. Programmers in other languages may be more used to a different scheme, and as long as the scheme is consistently used, it should present no problem. It is worth mentioning that when you start to work in a programming shop, a naming scheme may be forced on you. So perhaps it is not a bad thing to get some practice fitting in with someone else's scheme.

Example Programs

This section provides some example programs to whet your appetite and give you a feel for how a full COBOL program looks. In particular, they give advance warning about how variables (data items) are declared in COBOL. This differs so much from other languages such as C, Java, and Pascal that it is likely to be a matter of some concern, if not consternation. These programs also introduce some of the more interesting and useful features of COBOL.

The COBOL Greeting Program

Let's start with the program you last saw in the COBOL coding sheet (see Figure 2-1). In Listing 2-2 it has been modernized a little by introducing lowercase characters. This basic program demonstrates simple data declaration and simple iteration (looping). The variable IterNum is given a starting value of 5, and the PERFORM executes the paragraph DisplayGreeting five times:

Listing 2-2. The COBOL Greeting Program

```
IDENTIFICATION DIVISION.
PROGRAM-ID. CobolGreeting.
*>Program to display COBOL greetings
DATA DIVISION.
WORKING-STORAGE SECTION.
01  IterNum   PIC 9 VALUE 5.

PROCEDURE DIVISION.
BeginProgram.
   PERFORM DisplayGreeting IterNum TIMES.
   STOP RUN.

DisplayGreeting.
   DISPLAY "Greetings from COBOL".
```

The DoCalc Program

The DoCalc program in Listing 2-3 prompts the user to enter two single-digit numbers. The numbers are added together, and the result is displayed on the computer screen.

Listing 2-3. The DoCalc Example Program

```
IDENTIFICATION DIVISION.
PROGRAM-ID.  DoCalc.
AUTHOR.  Michael Coughlan.
DATA DIVISION.
WORKING-STORAGE SECTION.
01 FirstNum       PIC 9     VALUE ZEROS.
01 SecondNum      PIC 9     VALUE ZEROS.
01 CalcResult     PIC 99    VALUE 0.
01 UserPrompt     PIC X(38) VALUE
                  "Please enter two single digit numbers".
PROCEDURE DIVISION.
CalculateResult.
   DISPLAY UserPrompt
   ACCEPT FirstNum
   ACCEPT SecondNum
   COMPUTE CalcResult = FirstNum + SecondNum
   DISPLAY "Result is = ", CalcResult
   STOP RUN.
```

The program declares three numeric data items (variables): FirstNum for the first number input, SecondNum for the second, and CalcResult to hold the result of the calculation. It also declares a data item to hold the string used to prompt the user to enter two single-digit numbers.

Data declarations in COBOL are very different from the type-based declaration you might be used to in other languages, so some explanation is required. In COBOL, every data-item declaration starts with a level number. Level numbers are used to represent data hierarchy. Because all the items in this example program are independent, elementary data items, they have a level number of 01.

Following the level number is the name of the data item, and this in turn is followed by a storage declaration for the data item. The storage declaration defines the type and size of the storage required. To do this, COBOL uses a kind of "declaration by example" strategy. An example, or picture (hence PIC), is given of the maximum value the data item can hold. The symbols used in the picture declaration indicate the basic type of the item (numeric = 9, alphanumeric = X, alphabetic = A), and the number of symbols used indicates the size.

Consider the following declarations in DoCalc:

```
01 FirstNum      PIC 9  VALUE ZEROS.
01 SecondNum     PIC 9  VALUE ZEROS.
```

These indicate that FirstNum and SecondNum can each hold a cardinal number with a value between 0 and 9. If these data items were required to hold an integer number, the pictures would have to be defined as PIC S9 (signed numeric).

In this program, the picture clauses (which is what they are called) are followed by VALUE clauses specifying that FirstNum and SecondNum start with an initial value of zero. In COBOL, unless a variable is explicitly given an initial value, its value is undefined.

■ **Bug Alert** Numeric data items must be given an explicit numeric starting value by means of the VALUE clause, using the INITIALIZE verb, or by assignment. If a numeric data item with an undefined value is used in a calculation, the program may crash. Of course, a data item with an undefined value may *receive* the result of a calculation because in that case any non-numeric data is overwritten with the calculation result.

The CalcResult data item is defined as follows:

```
01 CalcResult    PIC 99 VALUE 0.
```

This indicates that CalcResult can hold a cardinal number between 0 and 99. It too is initialized to zero, but in this case the value 0 is used rather than the word ZEROS. The word ZEROS is a special COBOL data item called a *figurative constant*. It has the effect of filling the data item with zeros. I have chosen to initialize this variable with the value 0 to make two points. First, numeric values can be used with the VALUE clause. Second, the figurative constant ZEROS should be used in preference to the numeric value because it is clearer than 0, which in some fonts can easily be mistaken for an O.

The UserPrompt data item is defined as follows:

```
01 UserPrompt    PIC X(24) VALUE
                 "Please enter two single digit numbers".
```

This indicates that it can hold an alphanumeric value of up to 24 characters. It has been initialized to a starting string value.

■ **COBOL Detail**   UserPrompt should have been defined as a constant, but COBOL does not allow constants to be created. The nearest you can get to a user-defined constant in COBOL is to assign an initial value to a data item and then not change it. This is a serious deficiency that has finally been addressed in the ISO 2002 version of COBOL by means of the CONSTANT clause.

COBOL PUZZLE

Given the description of BirthDate in Example 2-10, what do you think would be displayed by the COBOL code in Example 2-11?

Example 2-10. BirthDate Data Description

```
01 BirthDate.
   02 YearOfBirth.
      03 CenturyOB    PIC 99.
      03 YearOB       PIC 99.
   02 MonthOfBirth    PIC 99.
   02 DayOfBirth      PIC 99.
```

Example 2-11. Code That Manipulates BirthDate and Its Subordinate Items

```
MOVE 19750215 TO BirthDate
DISPLAY "Month is  = " MonthOfBirth
DISPLAY "Century of birth is = " CenturyOB
DISPLAY "Year of birth is = " YearOfBirth
DISPLAY DayOfBirth "/" MonthOfBirth "/" YearOfBirth
MOVE ZEROS TO YearOfBirth
DISPLAY "Birth date = " BirthDate.
```

The answer is at the end of the chapter.

The Condition Names Program

The final example program for this chapter previews COBOL condition names and the EVALUATE verb. A condition name is a Boolean item that can only take the value true or false. But it is much more than that. A condition name is associated (via level 88) with a particular data item. Rather than setting the condition name to true or false directly, as you might do in other languages, a condition name automatically takes the value true or false depending on the value of its associated data item.

Listing 2-4 accepts a character from the user and displays a message to say whether the character entered was a vowel, a consonant, or a digit. When CharIn receives a character from the user, the associated condition names are all set to true or false depending on the value contained in CharIn.

The EVALUATE verb, which is COBOL's version of switch or case, is shown here at its simplest. It is immensely powerful, complicated to explain, but intuitively easy to use. In this program, the particular WHEN branch executed depends on which condition name is true. See anything familiar, Ruby programmers?

Listing 2-4. Using the EVALUATE Verb

```
IDENTIFICATION DIVISION.
PROGRAM-ID.  ConditionNames.
AUTHOR.  Michael Coughlan.
* Using condition names (level 88's) and the EVALUATE
DATA DIVISION.
WORKING-STORAGE SECTION.
01  CharIn            PIC X.
    88 Vowel          VALUE "a", "e", "i", "o", "u".
    88 Consonant      VALUE "b", "c", "d", "f", "g", "h"
                            "j" THRU "n", "p" THRU "t", "v" THRU "z".
    88 Digit          VALUE "0" THRU "9".
    88 ValidCharacter VALUE "a" THRU "z", "0" THRU "9".
PROCEDURE DIVISION.
Begin.
    DISPLAY "Enter lower case character or digit. Invalid char ends."
    ACCEPT CharIn
    PERFORM UNTIL NOT ValidCharacter
      EVALUATE TRUE
        WHEN Vowel     DISPLAY "The letter " CharIn " is a vowel."
        WHEN Consonant DISPLAY "The letter " CharIn " is a consonant."
        WHEN Digit     DISPLAY CharIn " is a digit."
      END-EVALUATE
      ACCEPT CharIn
    END-PERFORM
    STOP RUN.
```

Chapter Exercise

Write a version of the ConditionNames program in your favorite language. See if you can convince yourself that your version is as clear, concise, readable, and maintainable as the COBOL version.

Where to Get a COBOL Compiler

Now that you've seen the basics of COBOL, it's time to get the software. A couple of years ago, the question of where to get a free COBOL compiler would have been difficult to answer. The policies of COBOL vendors, who were locked into mainframe thought patterns and pricing structures, made it very difficult for interested students to get access to a COBOL compiler. In very recent years, though, and probably in response to the shortage of COBOL programmers, a number of options have become available.

Micro Focus Visual COBOL

Micro Focus COBOL is probably the best-known version of COBOL for Windows PCs. Micro Focus Visual COBOL is the company's most recent version of COBOL. It implements the OO-COBOL standard and integrates either with Microsoft Visual Studio (where it acts as one of the standard .NET languages) or with Eclipse. It is available on Windows, Linux (Red Hat and SuSE) and Unix (Aix, HP-UX, and Solaris).

A personal edition of Visual COBOL is available that is free for non-commercial use. The Visual Studio version can be installed even if Visual Studio is not available, because in that case the Visual Studio Shell edition is installed.

```
www.microfocus.com/product-downloads/vcpe/index.aspx
```

OpenCOBOL

OpenCOBOL is an open source COBOL compiler. The OpenCOBOL web site claims to implement a substantial part of the ANS 85 and ANS 2002 COBOL standards as well as many of the extensions introduced by vendors such as Micro Focus and IBM.

OpenCOBOL translates COBOL into C. The C code can be compiled using the native C compiler on a variety of platforms including Windows, Unix/Linux, and Mac OS X.

The compiler is free and is available from `www.opencobol.org/`.

Raincode COBOL

Raincode is a supplier of programming-language analysis and transformation tools. The company has a version of COBOL available that integrates with Microsoft Visual Studio and generates fully managed .NET code. The COBOL compiler is free from `www.raincode.com/mainframe-rehosting/`.

Compileonline COBOL

An online COBOL compiler is available at `compileonline.com`. Its data input is somewhat problematic, which limits its usefulness, but it can be handy if you just want a quick syntax check. See `www.compileonline.com/compile_cobol_online.php`.

Fujitsu NetCOBOL

Fujitsu NetCOBOL is a very well-known version of COBOL for Windows. NetCOBOL implements a version of the OO-COBOL standard, compiles on the .NET Framework, and can interoperate with other .NET languages such as C# and VB.NET.

A number of other versions of this COBOL are available, including a version for Linux. A trial version is available for download but there is no free version: `www.netcobol.com/product/netcobol-for-net/`.

Summary

This chapter explored part of the foundational material required to write COBOL programs. Some of the material covered was informational, some practical, and some advisory. You saw how COBOL programs are organized structurally and learned the purpose of each of the four divisions. You examined COBOL metalanguage diagrams and the COBOL coding and name construction rules. I offered advice concerning name construction and the proper formatting of program code. Finally, you examined some simple COBOL programs as a preview of the material in coming chapters.

The next chapter examines how data is declared in COBOL. This chapter is only an introduction, though. Data declaration in COBOL is complicated and sophisticated because COBOL is mainly about data manipulation. COBOL data declarations offer many data-manipulation opportunities. Later chapters explore many advanced data-declaration concepts such as condition names, table declarations, the USAGE clause, and data redefinition using the REDEFINES clause.

References

1. Sammet J. The early history of COBOL, 2.6: intended purpose and users. ACM SIGPLAN Notices. 1978; 13(8): 121-161.
2. Kloth RD. Cardpunch emulator. www.kloth.net/services/cardpunch.php
3. Myres G. Composite/structured design. New York: Van Nostrand Reinhold; 1978.
4. Constantine L, with Yourdon E. Structured design. Yourdon Press; 1975.
5. Page-Jones M. Practical guide to structured systems design. 2nd ed. Englewood Cliffs (NJ): Prentice Hall, 1988.
6. Stevens W, Myers G, Constantine L. Structured design. In Yourdon E, editor. Classics in software engineering. Yourdon Press; 1979: 205-232.

COBOL PUZZLE ANSWER

Given the description of BirthDate in Listing 2-5, what do you think would be displayed by the COBOL code in Listing 2-6?

Listing 2-5. BirthDate data description

```
01 BirthDate.
    02 YearOfBirth.
        03 CenturyOB    PIC 99.
        03 YearOB       PIC 99.
    02 MonthOfBirth     PIC 99.
    02 DayOfBirth       PIC 99.
```

Listing 2-6. Code manipulating BirthDate and its subordinate items

```
MOVE 19750215 TO BirthDate
DISPLAY "Month is  = " MonthOfBirth
DISPLAY "Century of birth is = " CenturyOB
DISPLAY "Year of birth is = " YearOfBirth
DISPLAY DayOfBirth "/" MonthOfBirth "/" YearOfBirth
MOVE ZEROS TO YearOfBirth
DISPLAY "Birth date = " BirthDate.
```

COBOL Puzzle Answer

```
Month is  = 02
Century of birth is = 19
Year of birth is =  1952
15/02/1952
Birth date = 00000215
```

CHAPTER 3

■ ■ ■

Data Declaration in COBOL

As you explore the COBOL language, you will notice many differences between it and other programming languages. Iteration, selection, and assignment are all done differently in COBOL than in languages like C, Java, and Pascal. But on the whole, these differences are fairly minor—more a question of nuance than a radical departure. When you are familiar with how iteration and selection work in other languages, COBOL's implementation requires only a small mental adjustment. Assignment might create more of a hiccup, but there is nothing too radical even in that. The real difference between COBOL and these other languages lies in how data is declared.

This chapter explores the different categories of data used in COBOL. It demonstrates how you can create and use items of each category. Because COBOL's approach to data declaration affects assignment in COBOL, that topic is also examined in this chapter.

Categories of Program Data

COBOL programs basically use three categories of data:

- Literals
- Figurative constants
- Data items (variables)

Unlike other programming languages, COBOL does not support user-defined constants.

COBOL Literals

A literal is a data item that consists only of the data item value itself. It cannot be referred to by a name. By definition, literals are constants in that they cannot be assigned a different value.

There are two types of literal:

- Alphanumeric (text/string) literals
- Numeric literals

Alphanumeric Literals

Alphanumeric literals are enclosed in quotes and consist of alphanumeric characters. Here are some examples:

```
"William Murphy",   "1528", "-1528",  "1528.95"
```

> ■ **Note** Enclosing the text in quotes defines the item as an alphanumeric literal even though the literal value may be entirely numeric.

Numeric Literals

Numeric literals may consist of numerals, the decimal point, and the plus or minus sign. Numeric literals are not enclosed in quotes. Here are some examples:

```
1528,    1528.95,   -1528,    +1528
```

Data Items (Variables)

A data item can be defined as a named location in memory in which a program can store a data value and from which it can retrieve the stored value. A **data name**, or identifier, is the name used to identify the area of memory reserved for a data item.

In addition to the data name, a data item must also be described in terms of its basic type (alphabetic, alphanumeric, numeric) and its size. Every data item used in a COBOL program must have a description in the DATA DIVISION.

Data Type Enforcement

Languages such as Pascal, Java, and C# may be described as *strongly typed* languages. In these languages, there are a number of different data types, and the distinction between them is rigorously enforced by the compiler. For instance, if a variable is defined as a float, the compiler will reject a statement that attempts to assign a character value to that variable.

In COBOL, there are only three types of data: numeric, alphanumeric (text/string), and alphabetic. The distinction between these data types is only weakly enforced by the compiler. In COBOL, it is possible to assign a non-numeric value to a data item that has been declared to be numeric.

The problem with this lax approach to data typing is that COBOL programs crash (halt unexpectedly) if they attempt to do computations on numeric data items that contain non-numeric data. In COBOL, therefore, it is the responsibility of the *programmer* to ensure that non-numeric data is never assigned to a numeric data item intended for use in a calculation. Programmers who use strongly typed languages do not need to have this level of discipline because the *compiler ensures* that a variable of a particular type can only be assigned an appropriate value.

> ■ **Bug Alert** Attempting to perform computations on numeric data items that contain non-numeric data is a frequent cause of program crashes for beginning COBOL programmers. This can easily happen if the data item has not been initialized to a valid starting value.

Figurative Constants

Unlike most other programming languages, COBOL does not provide a mechanism for creating user-defined, named constants. This is a serious deficiency. Named constants make a program more readable and more maintainable.

For instance, although a literal value of .06 (representing the current sales tax rate of 6%) could be used throughout a program whenever the sales tax rate was required, the program would be more readable if the value was assigned to the named constant SalesTaxRate. Similarly, using a named constant would make maintenance easier. If the actual sales tax rate changed, only the constant definition would have to be updated instead of all the places in the program where the literal sales tax rate value was used.

In COBOL, a data item can be assigned a value, but there is no way to ensure that, somewhere in the program, some maintenance programmer has not assigned a different value to the data item.

■ **ISO 2002**   Although this book adheres to the ANS 85 standard, you may be interested to know that this deficiency has been addressed in ISO 2002 COBOL standard by means of the CONSTANT clause entry.

Code example:

```
01  SalesTaxRate  CONSTANT AS .06.
```

Although COBOL does not allow user-defined named constants, it does have a set of special constants called *figurative constants*. Figurative constants are special constant values that may be used wherever it is legal to use a literal value. However, unlike a literal, when a figurative constant is assigned to a data item, it fills the entire item, overwriting everything in it. Figurative constants are often used to initialize data items. For instance, MOVE SPACES TO CustomerName fills the whole data item with spaces, and MOVE ZEROS TO FinalTotal fills that data item with zeros. Table 3-1 shows the COBOL figurative constants.

Table 3-1. *Figurative Constants*

Figurative Constant	Behavior
ZERO ZEROS ZEROES	Behaves like one or more instances of the literal value 0. The constants ZERO, ZEROS, and ZEROES are all synonyms. Whichever is used, the effect is exactly the same.
SPACE SPACES	Behaves like one or more instances of the *space* character. SPACE and SPACES are synonyms.
HIGH-VALUE HIGH-VALUES	Behaves like one or more instances of the character in the highest ordinal position in the current collating sequence (usually the ASCII character set). HIGH-VALUE and HIGH-VALUES are synonyms.
LOW-VALUE LOW-VALUES	Behaves like one or more instances of the character in the lowest ordinal position in the current collating sequence (the null character [hex 00] in the ASCII character set). LOW-VALUE and LOW-VALUES are synonyms.
QUOTE QUOTES	Behaves like one or more instances of the quote character. However, it cannot be used to bracket a non-numeric literal instead of the actual quote character. For instance, QUOTE Freddy QUOTE cannot be used in place of "Freddy". QUOTE and QUOTES are synonyms.
ALL literal	Allows an ordinary literal character to behave as if it were a figurative constant.

Elementary Data Items

An *elementary item* is the equivalent of a variable in other languages. It is an atomic data item that is not further subdivided. The type and size of an elementary data item are the type and size specified in its PICTURE clause.

In COBOL, an elementary data item declaration consists of a line of code containing the following mandatory items:

- A level number

- A data-name or identifier

- A PICTURE clause

The declaration may also take a number of optional clauses. The most common optional clause is the VALUE clause, which assigns an initial, or starting, value to a data item.

Elementary data items that are not a subdivision of a group item must use a level number of 01 or 77. This book uses 01 for these items. A discussion of the role of level 77s is reserved for later in this chapter.

■ **Note**   A data item declaration may also take a number of other optional clauses such as USAGE, BLANK WHEN ZERO, and JUSTIFIED.

Declaring Elementary Data Items

In typed languages, the data type specified is important because the type determines the range of values that the item can store and governs the operations that can be applied to it. For instance, a Java int data item can store values between -2,147,483,648 and 2,147,483,647 and can only be used in operations that expect an operand of that, or a compatible, type. From the type of the item, the compiler can establish how much memory to set aside for storing its values.

COBOL is not a *typed* language, so it employs a very different mechanism for describing its data items. COBOL uses what could be described as a "declaration by example" strategy. In effect, you provide the system with an example, or template, or *picture* of the size and type (alphabetic, numeric, alphanumeric) of the item. From this PICTURE clause, the compiler derives the information necessary to allocate the item.

PICTURE Clause Symbols

To create the required picture, you use a set of symbols. The most common symbols used in standard PICTURE clauses are shown in Table 3-2.

Table 3-2. *Common Symbols Used in Standard PICTURE Clauses*

Symbol	Meaning
A	Indicates an occurrence of any alphabetic character (*a* to *z* plus blank) at the corresponding position in the picture: `01 ThreeLetterAcronym    PIC AAA VALUE "DNA".`
X	Indicates an occurrence of any character from the character set at the corresponding position in the picture: `01 Salutation            PIC XXX VALUE "Mr.".`
9	Indicates the occurrence of a digit at the corresponding position in the picture: `01 CardinalValue         PIC 9(4) VALUE 1234.`
V	Indicates the position of the decimal point in a numeric value. It is often referred to as the *assumed decimal point* because it is not part of the value but is rather *information* about the value: `01 TotalSales            PIC 9(5)V99 VALUE ZEROS.`
S	Indicates the presence of a sign, and can only appear at the beginning of a picture: `01 IntegerValue          PIC S9(4) VALUE -1234.`

Note   There are many more picture symbols than those listed in Table 3-2. Most of the remaining symbols will be introduced when you explore edited pictures in Chapter 9.

PICTURE Clause Notes

Although the word `PICTURE` can be used when defining a `PICTURE` clause, it is normal to use the abbreviation `PIC`. The recurring symbols in a `PICTURE` clause can become difficult to count, especially at a glance, so it is normal practice to specify recurring symbols by using a *repeat* factor inside brackets. For instance:

> `PIC 9(8)` is equivalent to `PICTURE 99999999`.
>
> `PIC 9(7)V99` is equivalent to `PIC 9999999V99`.
>
> `PICTURE X(15)` is equivalent to `PIC XXXXXXXXXXXXXXX`.
>
> `PIC S9(5)V9(4)` is equivalent to `PIC S99999V9999`.
>
> `PICTURE 9(18)` is equivalent to `PIC 999999999999999999`.

The repeat factor in brackets is normally used for any picture string with more than three symbols. For instance, a three-digit data item might be described as `PIC 999`, but a four-digit item would be `PIC 9(4)`.

Numeric values can have a maximum of 18 digits, whereas the limit on string values (`PIC X`) is usually system dependent.

ISO 2002   In the 2002 standard, the maximum number of digits in a numeric literal or `PICTURE` clause was increased from 18 digits to 31 digits.

Example Declarations

In typed languages, because the memory required is defined by a variable's data type, a picture of what is happening to the data in the memory is not useful. In COBOL, however, knowing what is happening to the data in memory is very important for a proper understanding of how data declaration and data movement work. For this reason, many of the examples in this book are accompanied by an illustration that attempts to show what is happening to the data.

Consider the examples that follow. A simplified version of what is happening in memory is shown in Example 3-1. Later examples use more granular illustrations that show each character of storage. One thing you can already note from even this simple example is that although TaxRate is given an initial value of .35, what is actually in memory is 35. The V in the PICTURE clause tells COBOL to treat this item as if it had a decimal point in the leftmost character position. Example 3-1 also reveals that the values in alphanumeric data items are left aligned and space filled (the example shows the space character as *), whereas numeric data items seem to be right aligned (they aren't—see the "MOVE Rules" section later in this chapter) and zero filled.

Example 3-1. Data Items and Memory Representation

WORKING-STORAGE SECTION

Num1	Num2	TaxRate	CustomerName
000	015	35	Mike**********

```
DATA DIVISION.
WORKING-STORAGE SECTION.
01 Num1              PIC 999    VALUE ZEROS.
01 Num2              PIC 999    VALUE 15.
01 TaxRate           PIC V99    VALUE .35.
01 CustomerName      PIC X(15) VALUE "Mike".
```

Assignment in COBOL

In typed languages, the assignment operation is simple because assignment is only allowed between items with compatible types. The simplicity of assignment in these languages is achieved at the cost of having a large number of data types.

In COBOL, there are only three basic data types:

- Alphabetic (PIC A)

- Alphanumeric (PIC X)

- Numeric (PIC 9)

But this simplicity is achieved at the cost of having a complex assignment statement.

The MOVE Verb

Assignment in COBOL is achieved using the MOVE verb. The COMPUTE verb, which assigns the result of an arithmetic expression to a data item, should never be used to assign the value of one item to another. Similarly, the SET verb, which can be used to set a condition name to TRUE or to change the value in a table index, should only be used for these specialized purposes. All ordinary assignments should use MOVE.

MOVE Syntax

The MOVE metalanguage makes the verb seem simple but its operation is complicated by a set of governing rules. The metalanguage for MOVE is as follows:

<u>MOVE</u> Source$#il <u>TO</u> Destination$#i...

MOVE copies data from the source identifier (or literal) to one or more destination identifiers. The source and destination identifiers can be group or elementary data items.

In most programming languages, the data movement in an assignment statement is from right to left. That is, data is copied from the source item on the right to the destination item on the left (for example, Dest := Source [Modula-2] or Dest = Source [Java]). COBOL does things differently. In COBOL, the MOVE verb copies data from the source item on the left to the destination item(s) on the right. Almost all the COBOL verbs conform to this pattern of data movement. The COMPUTE verb, which has its destination data item on the left, is the one exception.

MOVE Rules

The major rules for the MOVE verb are given here. As with all the other verbs, you need to consult your COBOL manual for the more esoteric rules:

- The source and destination identifiers can be either elementary or group data items.

- When data is copied into a destination item, the contents of the destination item are completely replaced. The contents of the source item are undisturbed.

- If the number of characters in the source item is *too few* to fill the destination item, the rest of the destination item is filled with zeros or spaces.

- If the number of characters in the source item is *too many* to fit in the destination item, the characters that cannot fit are lost. This is known as *truncation*.

- When the destination item is alphanumeric or alphabetic (PIC X or A), data is copied into the destination area from left to right, with space-filling or truncation on the right.

- When the destination item is numeric or edited numeric, data is *aligned along the decimal point* with zero-filling or truncation as necessary.

- When the decimal point is not explicitly specified in either the source or destination item(s), the item is treated as if it had an assumed decimal point immediately after its rightmost character.

MOVE Combinations

Although COBOL is much less restrictive in this respect than many other languages, certain combinations of sending and receiving data types are not permitted (even by COBOL) and will be rejected by the compiler. The valid and invalid MOVE combinations are shown in Figure 3-1.

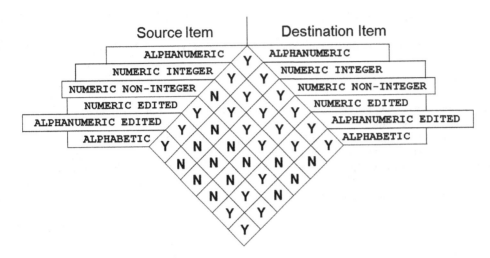

Figure 3-1. *Valid and invalid MOVE combinations*
Source: J.M. Triance, Structured COBOL Reference Summary, National Computing Centre Limited, N.C.C Publications,
1984, page 48.

MOVE Examples

Having a dusty set of rules is all very well, but the operation of the MOVE verb can only be appreciated by examining
some examples. The examples in this section only feature elementary data items. Things get a lot more exciting when
MOVE is used with a group item; you will see some examples of group item moves at the end of the chapter.

Alphanumeric MOVEs

Remember the following rule for alphanumeric MOVEs: when the destination item is alphanumeric or alphabetic
(PIC X or A), data is copied into the destination area from *left* to *right* with space-filling or truncation on the right.

In Example 3-2, the data item Surname is described as having sufficient storage for eight alphanumeric characters.
It has been assigned an initial value of "COUGHLAN".

Example 3-2. Alphanumeric Moves with Truncation and Space Filling

```
01 Surname      PIC X(8)  VALUE "COUGHLAN".
MOVE "SMITH" TO Surname

MOVE "FITZWILLIAM" TO Surname
```

Surname							
C	O	U	G	H	L	A	N
S	M	I	T	H	*	*	*
F	I	T	Z	W	I	L	L

When the first move is executed, "SMITH" is copied into Surname from left to right. Because "SMITH" has too few
characters to fill Surname, the rest of the data item is filled with spaces.

The second move copies "FITZWILLIAM" into Surname from left to right. Because the literal is too large to fit into
Surname, the last three letters (IAM) are truncated.

Numeric MOVEs

Remember the following rule for numeric MOVEs: when the destination item is numeric or edited numeric, data is aligned along the decimal point with zero-filling or truncation as necessary. An edited numeric data item is one that contains symbols such as $ and , and . that format data for output. They are not numeric items, and they can't be used in calculations (except as the receiving field), but they do obey the decimal-point alignment and zero-filling rules. Edited numeric data items are discussed in Chapter 9.

When the decimal point is not explicitly specified in either the source or destination item(s), the item is treated as if it had an assumed decimal point immediately after its rightmost character.

Example Set 1

In Example 3-3, SalePrice is a data item described as PIC 9(4)V99: that is, a decimal number with four digits before the decimal point and two after it. For each MOVE statement, a diagram showing the contents of the SalePrice data item is given. Each diagram shows the actual data moved in black, the filled zeros in grey, and the truncated digits outside the memory area. The position of the assumed decimal point is indicated with an arrow.

When the figurative constant ZEROS (or ZERO or ZEROES) is moved to SalePrice, the data item is filled with zeros.

When the numeric literal 25.5 is moved to SalePrice, there is alignment along the decimal point of the literal and the assumed decimal point in SalePrice, with the result being zero-filling on both the left and right sides.

When 7.553 is moved to SalePrice, there is alignment of the decimal points, with the result being zero-filling on the left and truncation of the digit 3 on the right. In the diagram the truncated digit is shown outside the memory area.

When 93425.158 is moved to SalePrice, there is alignment of the decimal points, with the result that the most significant digit is truncated on the left and the least significant on the right.

The literal value 128 contains no decimal point, so it is treated as if it had a decimal point in the rightmost position. This decimal point is aligned with assumed decimal point in SalePrice, with the result that there is zero filling on the left and right.

Example 3-3. Numeric MOVEs with Alignment Along the Decimal Point, Truncation, and Zero-Filling

```
01 SalePrice        PIC 9(4)V99.

MOVE ZEROS TO SalePrice

MOVE 25.5 TO SalePrice

MOVE 7.553 TO SalePrice

MOVE 93425.158 TO SalePrice

MOVE 128 TO SalePrice
```

SalePrice						
	0	**0**	**0**	**0**	**0**	**0**	
	0	0	**2**	**5**	**5**	0	
	0	0	0	**7**	**5**	**5**	3
9	**3**	**4**	**2**	**5**	**1**	**5**	8
	0	**1**	**2**	**8**	0	0	

⇧
•

Inadvertent truncation is obviously not desirable; but unfortunately, for MOVE operations at least, there is no protection against it. It is up to you to ensure that the data item is large enough to take the data moved into it. Inadvertent truncation is much more likely when calculations are involved. When a number of values are multiplied together, you might not realize that in some cases the result will be too large for the receiving data item. For computations, you can protect against inadvertent truncation by means of the ON SIZE ERROR clause. When this clause is used, it acts like a specialized exception handler. Chapter 4 discusses ON SIZE ERROR when you examine the operation of the COBOL arithmetic verbs.

Example Set 2

In Example 3-4, NumOfEmployees is described as a cardinal number capable of holding a value between 0 and 999. Salary is a decimal number data item with four digits before the decimal point and two after it. CountyName is an alphanumeric data item nine characters long.

The literal value 6745 has no decimal point, so it is treated as if the number has a decimal point in the rightmost position (6745.). NumOfEmployees also contains no explicit decimal point, so it is treated as if the data item has an assumed decimal point specified in the rightmost position:

```
01 NumOfEmployees PIC 999V
```

When the literal 6745 is moved to NumOfEmployees, there is alignment along these decimal points. The result is truncation of the most significant digit.

When NumOfEmployees (treated as if defined as 01 NumOfEmployees PIC 999V) is moved to Salary, which does have an explicit decimal point, there is alignment along the decimal points, with the result being zero-filling on both the left and right.

When the literal value 12.4 is moved to NumOfEmployees (treated as if defined as 01 NumOfEmployees PIC 999V), there is alignment along the decimal points with truncation of the digit 4 on the right and zero-filling on the left.

When the literal "Galway" is moved to CountyName, the data movement starts filling the data item from the left. When the value does not entirely fill the data item, the remaining character positions are space-filled.

When the figurative constant ALL and its associated character literal are moved to a data item, the data item is entirely filled with the character specified. In this example, the character specified after ALL is the hyphen, so CountyName is filled with hyphens.

Example 3-4. Numeric and Alphanumeric MOVEs

```
01 NumOfEmployees       PIC 999.

MOVE 12.4 TO NumOfEmployees

MOVE 6745 TO NumOfEmployees
```

NumOfEmployees				
0	1	2	4	0
7	4	5	0	0

(6 to the left of the second row)

⇑
•

```
01 Salary         PIC 9999V99.

MOVE NumOfEmployees TO Salary
```

Salary					
0	7	4	5	0	0

⇑
•

```
01 CountyName     PIC X(9).

MOVE "GALWAY" TO CountyName

MOVE ALL "@" TO CountyName
```

CountyName								
G	A	L	W	A	Y	*	*	*
@	@	@	@	@	@	@	@	@

Structured Data

In COBOL, the term *elementary item* describes an ordinary data item or variable. An elementary item is a data item that is *atomic*: it has not been further subdivided. Every elementary item must have a PICTURE clause. The PICTURE clause specifies the type and size of the storage required for the data item.

Group Data Items

Sometimes when you are manipulating data it is convenient to treat a collection of elementary items as a single group. For instance, you might want to group the data items Forename, MiddleInitial, and Surname as the group EmployeeName. Alternatively, you might want to group the YearOfBirth, MonthOfBirth, DayOfBirth data items as the group DateOfBirth. In addition, you might want to collect both these group items and some elementary items in an employee record description.

In COBOL, you can easily create groups like these using *group items*. A group item in COBOL is a data item that is a collection of elementary and/or group data items. It is a heterogeneous data structure. In languages like Pascal and Modula-2, group items are referred to as *records*. In C and C++, they are called *structs*. Java has no real equivalent.

The constituent parts of a group item may be elementary items or other group items. But ultimately, every group item must be defined in terms of its subordinate elementary items. Because a group item is ultimately defined in terms of elementary items, it *cannot* have a PICTURE clause, and its size is the sum of the sizes of its subordinate elementary items. A group item is simply a convenient name that you give to a collection of (ultimately) elementary items. Using that name, you can manipulate the collection.

In a group item, the hierarchical relationship between the various subordinate items of the group is expressed using level numbers. The higher the level number, the lower the item is in the hierarchy and the more atomic it is. If a group item is the highest item in a data hierarchy, it is referred to as a *record* and uses the level number 01.

The type of a group item is always assumed to be alphanumeric (PIC X, even if it contains only numeric data items) because a group item may have several different data items and types subordinate to it, and an alphanumeric picture is the only one that can support such collections.

Level Numbers

Level numbers 01 through 49 are the general level numbers used to express data hierarchy. There are also special level numbers such as 66, 77, and 88:

- Level 66 is used with the RENAMES clause. The RENAMES clause allows you to apply a new name to a data-name or group of contiguous data-names. It is similar to the REDEFINES clause; but because of the maintenance problems associated with it, the RENAMES clause has largely fallen into disuse and in some programming shops is banned. You learn more about the operation and shortcomings of the RENAMES clause when the REDEFINES clause is examined later in the book.

- Level 77 is used to identify a noncontiguous, single data item in the WORKING-STORAGE or LINKAGE sections; it cannot be subdivided, and it cannot be part of a group item. In the past, 77s were used for efficiency purposes (77s used less memory than the same items defined as a level 01). Nowadays level 01 is often used instead of 77. Some programming shops take the view that, instead of declaring large numbers of indistinguishable 77s, it is better to collect the individual items into named groups for documentation purposes even if the group, as a group, has no practical purpose. For instance, you might group individual totals such as ShopTotal, CityTotal, StateTotal, and CountryTotal under the group item Totals for documentation purposes. You could not create such a grouping if the items were declared using level 77s.

- Level 88 is used to implement condition names. Whereas level 66 and level 77 are not used in modern COBOL, level 88s and condition names are very important, useful, and unique weapons in COBOL's armory. Chapter 5 provides a detailed examination of the declaration and use of level 88s and condition names.

Data Hierarchy

Level numbers are used to express data hierarchy. The best way to understand the data hierarchy and the data-manipulation opportunities afforded by this organization is by means of an example.

Suppose you want to store information about students. You can create a data item called StudentRec and describe it as follows:

```
01 StudentRec   PIC X(44).
```

You can load some data into StudentRec using this statement:

```
MOVE "1205621William  Fitzpatrick 19751021LM051385" TO StudentRec.
```

Once you have done this, the StudentRec area of storage is instantiated with the data as shown in Example 3-5.

Example 3-5. StudentRec as an Elementary Data Item

```
WORKING-STORAGE SECTION.
01 StudentRec   PIC X(44).
```

StudentRec
1 2 0 5 6 2 1 W I l l i a m   F i t z p a t r i c k   1 9 7 5 1 0 2 1 L M 0 5 1 3 8 5

You can see that the data in StudentRec consists of a number of pieces of information: the student's ID, the student's name, the date of birth, the course ID, and the student's grade point average (GPA). But because you have defined StudentRec as an elementary item (an undifferentiated string of characters), you have no easy way of getting at the individual pieces of data. You can move or display the contents of the entire string, but you cannot easily, for instance, display only the date of birth or the student's name.

What you need to do is to describe StudentRec as a group item that is subdivided into StudentId, StudentName, DateOfBirth, CourseId, and GPA. The revised StudentRec description and the way it appears in storage are shown in Example 3-6.

Example 3-6. StudentRec as a Group Data Item

```
WORKING-STORAGE SECTION.
01 StudentRec.
    02 StudentId        PIC 9(7).
    02 StudentName      PIC X(21).
    02 DateOfBirth      PIC X(8).
    02 CourseId         PIC X(5).
    02 GPA              PIC 9V99.
```

StudentRec				
StudentId	StudentName	DateOfBirth	CourseId	GPA
1 2 0 5 6 2 1	W I l l i a m F i t z p a t r i c k	1 9 7 5 1 0 2 1	L M 0 5 1	3 8 5

StudentRec has been subdivided into a number of individual data items. Because StudentRec is now a group item, it has no PICTURE clause. Its size is the sum of the sizes of the elementary items, and its type is alphanumeric.

Defining StudentRec this way presents you with a number of data-manipulation opportunities. You can still manipulate the whole record. For instance, you can flush the entire 44-character area with spaces using a statement like this:

```
MOVE SPACES TO StudentRec
```

Or you can move the entire contents to another data item with a statement such as

```
MOVE StudentRec to StudentRecCopy
```

But now you can manipulate the individual pieces of data with statements such as these:

```
DISPLAY "Student name = " StudentName
MOVE ZEROS TO StudentId
MOVE "LM067" TO CourseId
DISPLAY "Current GPA = " GPA
MOVE 2.55 TO GPA
MOVE 19751022 TO DateOfBirth
```

It is useful to be able to access the individual pieces of data that constitute StudentRec, but the structure is still not quite granular enough. For instance, you can only access the entire student name. It would be nice to be able to manipulate the forename and the surname individually. Similarly, you would like to be able to access the year, month, and day of birth as separate items.

To make these changes, you need to describe StudentName and DateOfBirth as group items. The revised StudentRec description and the effect of this restructuring on the data storage are shown in Example 3-7.

Example 3-7. StudentRec as a Group Data Item

```
WORKING-STORAGE SECTION.
01 StudentRec.
    02 StudentId        PIC 9(7).
    02 StudentName.
        03 Forename     PIC X(9).
        03 Surname      PIC X(12).
    02 DateOfBirth.
        03 YOB          PIC 9(4).
        03 MOB          PIC 99.
        03 DOB          PIC 99.
    02 CourseId         PIC X(5).
    02 GPA              PIC 9V99.
```

StudentRec																																											
StudentId							StudentName																					DateOfBirth								CourseId					GPA		
							Forename									Surname											YOB				MOB		DOB									
1	2	0	5	6	2	1	W	I	l	l	i	a	m			F	i	t	z	p	a	t	r	i	c	k		1	9	7	5	1	0	2	1	L	M	0	5	1	3	8	5

With this new structure, many more data-manipulation opportunities become available. You can still access StudentRec, StudentId, StudentName, DateOfBirth, CourseId, and GPA as before, but now you can also manipulate the data at a more granular level using statements like these:

```
DISPLAY "Student date of birth is " DOB "/" MOB "/" YOB
DISPLAY "Student name = " Surname "," SPACE Forename
MOVE "Billy" TO Forename
MOVE 22 TO DOB
```

The first statement displays the date of birth on the computer screen:

```
Student date of birth is 21/10/1975
```

The second statement displays the student's name:

```
Student name = Fitzpatrick, William
```

■ **COBOL Detail**   When a figurative constant is used with the DISPLAY verb, it inserts only one character; it does not matter if SPACE or SPACES is used, because they are synonyms. If you wanted to insert two spaces in the previous statement, you would have to write the statement as follows:

```
DISPLAY "Student name = " Surname "," SPACE SPACE Forename
```

Level-Number Relationships Govern Hierarchy

Level numbers express the data hierarchy. A data hierarchy starts with level number 01; the subdivisions then use any number between 02 and 49 to express the hierarchy. The rule to remember is this: a data item with a level number higher than the preceding data item is a subdivision of that data item; a data item with the same level number as the preceding item is at the same level as that item; a data item with a level number lower than the preceding item is at the same level as its first matching preceding level number. For instance, in Example 3-7, Forename has a level number higher than StudentName, so Forename is a subdivision of StudentName. Surname has the same level number as Forename, so it too is a subdivision of StudentName.

In a hierarchical data description, what is important is the *relationship* of the level numbers to one another, not the actual level numbers used. For instance, the record descriptions shown in Example 3-8, Example 3-9, and Example 3-10 are equivalent.

Example 3-8 shows my preferred organization and the one used in this book. This organization seems logical and offers benefits of clarity by making the level numbers coincidental with the levels in the structure.

Example 3-8. Preferred Format

```
01 StudentRec.
    02 StudentId      PIC 9(7).
    02 StudentName.
        03 Forename   PIC X(9).
        03 Surname    PIC X(12).
    02 DateOfBirth.
        03 YOB        PIC 9(4).
        03 MOB        PIC 99.
        03 DOB        PIC 99.
```

```
      02 CourseId      PIC X(5).
      02 GPA           PIC 9V99.
```

Example 3-9 shows that level numbers are used only to show the relationship with the immediately preceding items. For instance, the fact that YOB, MOB, and DOB use level number 14 and Forename and Surname use level 12 is not relevant. What *is* relevant is that the level numbers show that the items are subordinate to their respective preceding items (StudentName in the first case and DateOfBirth in the second).

Example 3-9. Arbitrary Format

```
01 StudentRec.
      07 StudentId      PIC 9(7).
      07 StudentName.
           12 Forename      PIC X(9).
           12 Surname       PIC X(12).
      07 DateOfBirth.
           14 YOB           PIC 9(4).
           14 MOB           PIC 99.
           14 DOB           PIC 99.
      07 CourseId      PIC X(5).
      07 GPA           PIC 9V99.
```

Example 3-10 uses a layout often found in programming shops and COBOL books. This organization lets you create group items by slipping a group item into the description without otherwise disturbing the layout (see the **MOBandDOB** data item in Example 3-11). This seems like a good idea, and it is is part of the coding standards for some programming shops; but over time, this approach causes the structure's clarity to deteriorate. In my view, if the data hierarchy needs to be reorganized, then it should be reorganized properly, so that future maintenance programmers will have no difficulty in comprehending the structure created.

Example 3-10. Common Format

```
01 StudentRec.
      05 StudentId      PIC 9(7).
      05 StudentName.
           10 Forename      PIC X(9).
           10 Surname       PIC X(12).
      05 DateOfBirth.
           10 YOB           PIC 9(4).
           10 MOB           PIC 99.
           10 DOB           PIC 99.
      05 CourseId      PIC X(5).
      05 GPA           PIC 9V99.
```

Example 3-11. Common Format in Use

```
01 StudentRec.
      05 StudentId      PIC 9(7).
      05 StudentName.
           10 Forename      PIC X(9).
           10 Surname       PIC X(12).
      05 DateOfBirth.
           08 YOB           PIC 9(4).
```

```
    08 MOBandDOB.
        10 MOB        PIC 99.
        10 DOB        PIC 99.
    05 CourseId       PIC X(5).
    05 GPA            PIC 9V99.
```

Summary

This chapter provided an introduction to data in COBOL. It introduced the different types of data used, and it showed how you can create and use variable data in the form of elementary data items. The chapter examined the assignment operation and discussed the data-manipulation opportunities afforded by the hierarchical structure of group item data declarations.

But this is just an introduction to data declaration in COBOL. In the rest of this book, you expand your knowledge of data declaration by exploring such topics as the implicit redefinition of data items in the FILE SECTION, the operation of the REDEFINES clause, the preparation of data for output using edited pictures, the USAGE clause, and the declaration of tabular information.

LANGUAGE KNOWLEDGE EXERCISE

Using a 2B pencil, write your answer to each exercise question in the area provided.

1. Create an elementary data item called TaxAmount to hold a value between 0 and 99,999.99.

2. Create an alphanumeric elementary data item called VideoName large enough to hold 35 characters. Define VideoName so that it is initialized with spaces when the program starts.

3. A data item called MinimumWage is defined as PIC 9V99. Show what happens to the data after execution of the statement

   MOVE 123.5 TO MinimumWage

   MinimumWage

   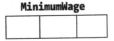

4. A group item called CustomerRec is defined

```
01 CustomerRec.
    02 CustId         PIC 9(5)     VALUE ZEROS.
    02 CustName.
        03 Initials   PIC XX       VALUE SPACES.
        03 Surname    PIC X(4)     VALUE SPACES.
    02 Gender         PIC X.       VALUE SPACES.
    02 Payment        PIC 9(5)V99 VALUE ZEROS.
```

a. A partial diagram representing the CustomerRec is provided. Complete the diagram by showing how the subordinate data items map to the 19 characters of storage reserved for CustomerRec.

b. In the first row of the diagram, show how each VALUE clause initializes the data items in CustomerRec.

c. For each statement in the following program, show what happens to the data in CustomerRec. Use a row for each statement.

```
PROCEDURE DIVISION.
10-BEGIN.
MOVE "45145MCRyanF23445.67" TO CustomerRec
MOVE "Male" TO Gender
MOVE "GSPower" TO CustName
MOVE "Fitzroy" TO Surname
MOVE 34 TO Cust-Payment
STOP RUN.
```

CustomerRec																		
CustId				CustName				Gender				Payment						
				Initials		Surname												

LANGUAGE KNOWLEDGE EXERCISE—ANSWERS

1. Create an elementary data item called TaxAmount to hold a value between 0 and 99,999.99.

```
01 TaxAmount    PIC 9(5)V99.
```

2. Create an alphanumeric elementary data item called VideoName large enough to hold 35 characters. Define VideoName so that it is initialized with spaces when the program starts.

```
01 VideoName    PIC X(35).
```

3. A data item called MinimumWage is defined as PIC 9V99. Show what happens to the data after execution of the statement

MOVE 123.5 TO MinimumWage

MinimumWage

3	5	0

⇧

•

4. A group item called CustomerRec is defined as

```
01 CustomerRec.
   02 CustId          PIC 9(5)     VALUE ZEROS.
   02 CustName.
      03 Initials     PIC XX       VALUE SPACES.
      03 Surname      PIC X(4)     VALUE SPACES.
   02 Gender          PIC X.       VALUE SPACES.
   02 Payment         PIC 9(5)V99  VALUE ZEROS.
```

a. A partial diagram representing the CustomerRec is provided. Complete the diagram by showing how the subordinate data items map to the 19 characters of storage reserved for CustomerRec.

b. In the first row of the diagram, show how each VALUE clause initializes the data items in CustomerRec.

c. For each statement in the following program, show what happens to the data in CustomerRec. Use a row for each statement.

```
PROCEDURE DIVISION.
10-BEGIN.
MOVE "45145MCRyanF23445.67" TO CustomerRec
MOVE "Male" TO Gender
MOVE "GSPower" TO CustName
MOVE "Fitzroy" TO Surname
MOVE 34 TO Cust-Payment
STOP RUN.
```

CustomerRec																		
CustId					CustName						Gender	Payment						
					Initials		Surname											
0	0	0	0	0	*	*	*	*	*	*	*	0	0	0	0	0	0	0
4	5	1	4	5	M	C	R	y	a	n	F	2	3	4	4	5	6	7
4	5	1	4	5	M	C	R	y	a	n	M	2	3	4	4	5	6	7
4	5	1	4	5	G	S	P	o	w	e	M	2	3	4	4	5	6	7
4	5	1	4	5	G	S	F	i	t	z	M	2	3	4	4	5	6	7
4	5	1	4	5	G	S	F	i	t	z	M	0	0	0	3	4	0	0

CHAPTER 4

Procedure Division Basics

The three preceding chapters covered much of the background material you need before you can write useful programs. Chapter 1 was motivational, Chapter 2 dealt with the structure of COBOL programs, and in Chapter 3 you learned how to define the data storage that dynamic programs require to be useful.

The PROCEDURE DIVISION contains the code used to manipulate data described in the DATA DIVISION. This chapter examines some of the basic PROCEDURE DIVISION commands. You learn how to get data from the user, how to use the COBOL arithmetic verbs to do calculations on the data, and how to display the results on the computer screen.

Input and Output with ACCEPT and DISPLAY

In COBOL, the ACCEPT and DISPLAY verbs are used to read from the keyboard and write to the screen. Input and output using these commands is somewhat primitive. The original purpose of these commands was not to communicate with the end user but for use in a batch-programming environment, to allow interaction with the computer operators. Because computer operators are expert users and the level of their interaction with the program was limited to viewing alerts and action prompts or entering the occasional file name, no great sophistication was required in the ACCEPT and DISPLAY commands.

In recent years, however, many implementers have found a need for more powerful versions of ACCEPT and DISPLAY in order to allow online systems to be created. These implementers have augmented the ACCEPT and DISPLAY syntax to allow such things as cursor positioning, character attribute control, and auto-validation of input. In some cases, they have even implemented a special SCREEN SECTION in the DATA DIVISION.

In a real environment, console-based (as opposed to Windows-based) input and output operations would be handled either by implementer-enhanced versions of ACCEPT and DISPLAY or by calls to forms-management or transaction-processing software such as Terminal Data Management System (TDMS), DECforms, and Customer Information Control System (CICS).

This book considers only the standard ACCEPT and DISPLAY syntax. If the vendor of your version of COBOL offers extended ACCEPT and DISPLAY syntax, you should read the manual to discover how these extensions work.

The DISPLAY Verb

The DISPLAY verb is used to send output to the computer screen or to a peripheral device. A single DISPLAY can be used to display several data items or literals or any combination of these. The concatenation required by some other languages is not required for the DISPLAY verb.

Metalanguage diagrams are used to describe the syntax of COBOL verbs and other elements. The metalanguage for the DISPLAY verb is given in Figure 4-1. In case you have forgotten how to interpret these diagrams, see "Metalanguage Reminder" for a brief refresher on the meaning of the symbols.

<u>DISPLAY</u> OutputItem1$#il [OutputItem2$#il]...

[UPONMnemonic-Name][WITH <u>NO</u> <u>ADVANCING</u>]

Figure 4-1. *Metalanguage for the DISPLAY verb*

METALANGUAGE REMINDER

In the COBOL syntax diagrams (the COBOL metalanguage), uppercase words are keywords. If underlined, they are mandatory. In addition

- { } brackets mean one of the options must be selected.

- [ ] brackets mean the item is optional.

- An ellipsis (...) means the item may be repeated at the programmer's discretion.

The symbols used in the syntax diagram identifiers have the following significance:

- $ indicates a string (alphanumeric) item.

- # indicates a numeric item.

- i indicates that the item can be a variable identifier.

- l indicates that the item can be a literal.

Notes

As the ellipsis (...) in the metalanguage shows, a single DISPLAY can be used to display several data items or literals or any combination of these. The items displayed must be USAGE DISPLAY items. USAGE COMP or INDEX will not display correctly. USAGE IS DISPLAY is the default for COBOL data items; it means the data is held in a displayable format. For efficiency purposes, it is also possible to hold data in a binary format that is not displayable. The USAGE clause, which you examine later in the book, is used when you want to hold a data item in one of the more computationally efficient binary formats. For instance:

```
01 SaleValue      PIC 9(5)V99 USAGE IS COMP.
01 TableSubscript  USAGE IS INDEX.
```

The default display device is the computer screen, but you can use other devices for output by specifying a **mnemonic-name** with the UPON clause. Mnemonic-names are used to make programs more readable and more maintainable; they are devised by programmers to represent peripheral devices (such as serial ports). A name is connected to an actual device by an entry in the SPECIAL-NAMES paragraph of the CONFIGURATION SECTION in the ENVIRONMENT DIVISION. The actual device to which the mnemonic-name is connected is defined by the language implementer. Consult your COBOL manual to learn what devices your implementer supports.

Ordinarily, after data is displayed on the computer screen, the onscreen cursor moves to the next row. Sometimes, however, you want the cursor to remain on the same row. In these cases, you can use the WITH NO ADVANCING clause to ensure that the cursor does not move to the next row.

DISPLAY Examples

This section gives some illustrative DISPLAY examples. The DISPLAY in eg1 sends the data in PrinterSetupCodes to the device represented by the mnemonic-name PrinterPort1. The output from the remaining examples is shown in the *Display Results* diagram. Note that in eg4, the separator spaces inserted between the statement operands have no effect on the output. In a COBOL statement, you can insert separator commas, spaces or semicolons wherever you want to make a statement more readable. Also note that in eg5, the figurative constants SPACE and SPACES are synonyms; they both insert only a single space. Note too that no concatenation operator is required to bind the data items and figurative constants into a single string

```
eg1.  DISPLAY PrinterSetupCodes UPON PrinterPort1

eg2.  MOVE 3456 TO FinalTotal
      DISPLAY "The final total is " FinalTotal

eg3.  DISPLAY "One, "    WITH NO ADVANCING
      DISPLAY "two, "    WITH NO ADVANCING
      DISPLAY "three."

eg4.  DISPLAY 1 ","    2     "," 3 "."

eg5.  MOVE 10 TO DayOfBirth
      MOVE 12 TO MonthOfBirth
      MOVE 1975 TO YearOfBirth
      DISPLAY "Date of birth is - "
          DayOfBirth SPACES  MonthOfBirth SPACE YearOfBirth
```

Display Results

```
The final total is 3456
One, two, three.
1,2,3.
Date of birth is - 10 12 1975
```

The ACCEPT Verb

There are two formats for the ACCEPT verb:

- The first gets data from the keyboard or a peripheral device.

- The second lets you access the system date and time (that is, the date and time held in the computer's internal clock) by using certain system variables.

The metalanguage for the two formats of the ACCEPT are shown in Figure 4-2.

Format 1. <u>ACCEPT</u> ReceivingItem$#i [<u>FROM</u> Mnemonic - Name]

Format 2. <u>ACCEPT</u> ReceivingItem$#i <u>FROM</u> $\begin{cases} \underline{\text{DATE}} \text{ [YYYYMMDD]} \\ \underline{\text{DAY}} \text{ [YYYYDDD]} \\ \underline{\text{DAY - OF - WEEK}} \\ \underline{\text{TIME}} \end{cases}$

Figure 4-2. *Metalanguage for the ACCEPT verb*

Rules

When you use the first format, ACCEPT inserts the data typed on the keyboard into the receiving data item. If the FROM option is used, the data inserted into the receiving data item comes from the device indicated by the mnemonic-name. Data is sent to the ReceivingItem according to the rules for alphanumeric moves. If the ReceivingItem is too small to hold the data, the rightmost characters that do not fit are lost. If the ReceivingItem is too large, there is space-filling on the right.

The default input device is the computer keyboard, but you can use other devices by specifying a mnemonic-name with the FROM clause. The mnemonic-name is connected to the actual device by an entry in the SPECIAL-NAMES paragraph, CONFIGURATION SECTION, ENVIRONMENT DIVISION.

When you use the second format, ACCEPT moves the data from one of the system variables (DATE, DAY, DAY-OF-WEEK, TIME) into the receiving data item. Two of the system variables also have optional syntactic elements that allow you to specify that the date be supplied with a four-digit year.

Required Format for System Variables

The declarations and comments that follow show the format required for the data items that ACCEPT values from each of the system variables:

```
01 CurrentDate      PIC 9(6).
* Receiving data item for DATE system variable: Format is YYMMDD


01 DayOfYear        PIC 9(5).
* Receiving data item for DAY system variable: Format is YYDDD


01 DayOfWeek        PIC 9.
* Receiving item for DAY-OF-WEEK: Format is D (1=Monday)


01 CurrentTime      PIC 9(8).
* Receiving item for TIME: Format is HHMMSSss   s = S/100


01 Y2KDate          PIC 9(8).
* Receiving item for DATE YYYYMMDD system variable: Format is YYYYMMDD


01 Y2KDayOfYear       PIC 9(7).
* Receiving item for DAY YYYYDDD system variable: Format is YYYYDDD
```

Example Program: ACCEPT and DISPLAY

Listing 4-1 gives some examples of how to use the ACCEPT and DISPLAY verbs. The examples use both formats of ACCEPT. The first form of ACCEPT is combined with DISPLAY to prompt for and receive a username. The second form gets data from some of the date and time system variables. Finally, all the gathered information is displayed on the computer screen. The results of running the program are shown in the results diagram.

Listing 4-1. ACCEPT and DISPLAY Examples

```
IDENTIFICATION DIVISION.
PROGRAM-ID.  Listing4-1.
AUTHOR.  Michael Coughlan.
DATA DIVISION.
WORKING-STORAGE SECTION.
01  UserName          PIC X(20).

*> Receiving data item for DATE system variable: Format is YYMMDD
01 CurrentDate.
   02  CurrentYear    PIC 99.
   02  CurrentMonth   PIC 99.
   02  CurrentDay     PIC 99.

*> Receiving data item for DAY system variable: Format is YYDDD
01 DayOfYear.
   02  FILLER         PIC 99.
   02  YearDay        PIC 9(3).

*> Receiving item for TIME: Format is HHMMSSss    s = S/100
01 CurrentTime.
   02  CurrentHour    PIC 99.
   02  CurrentMinute  PIC 99.
   02  FILLER         PIC 9(4).

*> Receiving item for DATE YYYYMMDD system variable: Format is YYYYMMDD
01 Y2KDate.
   02 Y2KYear         PIC 9(4).
   02 Y2KMonth        PIC 99.
   02 Y2KDay          PIC 99.

*> Receiving item for DAY YYYYDDD system variable: Format is YYYYDDD
01 Y2KDayOfYear.
   02 Y2KDOY-Year     PIC 9(4).
   02 Y2KDOY-Day      PIC 999.
PROCEDURE DIVISION.
Begin.
    DISPLAY "Please enter your name - " WITH NO ADVANCING
    ACCEPT  UserName
    DISPLAY "********************"
    ACCEPT CurrentDate  FROM DATE
    ACCEPT DayOfYear    FROM DAY
    ACCEPT CurrentTime  FROM TIME
    ACCEPT Y2KDate      FROM DATE YYYYMMDD
```

```
ACCEPT Y2KDayOfYear FROM DAY YYYYDDD
DISPLAY "Name is " UserName
DISPLAY "Date is " CurrentDay "-" CurrentMonth "-" CurrentYear
DISPLAY "Today is day " YearDay " of the year"
DISPLAY "The time is " CurrentHour ":" CurrentMinute
DISPLAY "Y2KDate is " Y2kDay SPACE Y2KMonth SPACE Y2KYear
DISPLAY "Y2K Day of Year is " Y2KDoy-Day " of " Y2KDOY-Year
STOP RUN.
```

```
Please enter your name - Peter Reid
* * * * * * * * * * * * * * * * * * * * * *
Name is Peter Reid
Date is 17-08-13
Today is day 229 of the year
The time is 13:24
Y2KDate is 17 08 2013
Y2K Day of Year is 229 of 2013
```

■ **Note**   The example programs in this book were compiled by using Micro Focus Visual COBOL and capturing the output results. In most cases, the programs were also compiled and run using the web-based open source COBOL compiler at www.compileonline.com/compile_cobol_online.php. If you want to use this compiler, be aware that interactivity is limited and you must enter keyboard input via the site's STDIN Input box. Some tweaking may be required.

Arithmetic in COBOL

Most procedural programming languages perform computations by assigning the result of an arithmetic expression (or function) to a variable. In COBOL, the COMPUTE verb is used to evaluate arithmetic expressions, but there are also specific commands for adding (ADD), subtracting (SUBTRACT), multiplying (MULTIPLY), and dividing (DIVIDE).

Common Arithmetic Template

With the exception of COMPUTE, DIVIDE with REMAINDER, and some exotic formats of ADD and SUBTRACT, most COBOL arithmetic verbs conform to the template metalanguage shown in Figure 4-3. It is useful to review this metalanguage template because it allows me to discuss the clauses and issues that apply to all the arithmetic verbs.

$$\underline{\text{VERB}} \text{ Operand1\#il} \begin{Bmatrix} \underline{\text{TO}} \\ \underline{\text{FROM}} \\ \underline{\text{BY}} \\ \underline{\text{INTO}} \end{Bmatrix} \begin{Bmatrix} \{\text{OperandResult\#i } [\underline{\text{ROUNDED}}]\} \dots \\ \text{Operand\#il } \underline{\text{GIVING}} \{\text{Result\#i } [\underline{\text{ROUNDED}}]\} \dots \end{Bmatrix}$$

$$\left[\begin{Bmatrix} \text{ON } \underline{\text{SIZE ERROR}} \\ \underline{\text{NOT}} \text{ ON } \underline{\text{SIZE ERROR}} \end{Bmatrix} \text{StatementBlock } \underline{\text{END} - \text{VERB}} \right]$$

Figure 4-3. *Metalanguage for a common arithmetic template*

Arithmetic Template Notes

All the arithmetic verbs move the result of a calculation into a receiving data item according to the rules for a numeric move: that is, with alignment along the assumed decimal point and with zero-filling or truncation as necessary. In all the arithmetic verbs except COMPUTE, the result of the calculation is assigned to the rightmost data item(s).

All arithmetic verbs must use numeric literals or numeric data items (PIC 9) that contain numeric data. There is one exception: data items that *receive* the result of the calculation but are not themselves one of the operands (do not contribute to the result) may be numeric or *edited numeric*.

Where the GIVING phrase is used, the item to the right of the word *giving* receives the result of the calculation but does not contribute to it. Where there is more than one item after the word *giving*, each receives the result of the calculation.

Where the GIVING phrase is not used and there is more than one OperandResult#i, Operand#il is applied to each OperandResult#i in turn, and the result of each calculation is placed in each OperandResult#i.

The maximum size of each operand is 18 digits (31 in ISO 2002 COBOL).

Examples of COBOL Arithmetic Statements

Here are a number of examples, each followed by an explanation of the operation:

```
ADD Takings TO CashTotal
* Adds the value in Takings to the value in CashTotal and puts the result in CashTotal

ADD Males TO Females GIVING TotalStudents
* Adds the value in Males to the value in Females and overwrites
* the value in TotalStudents with the result.

ADD Sales TO ShopSales, CountySales, CountrySales
* Adds the value of Sales to ShopSales and puts the result in ShopSales.
* Adds the value of Sales to CountySales and puts the result in CountySales
* Adds the value of Sales to CountrySales and puts the result in CountrySales

SUBTRACT Tax FROM GrossPay
* Subtracts the value in Tax from the value in GrossPay and puts the result in GrossPay.

SUBTRACT Tax FROM GrossPay GIVING NetPay
* Subtracts the value in Tax from the value in GrossPay and puts the result in NetPay.

DIVIDE Total BY Members GIVING MemberAverage ROUNDED
* Divides the value in Total by the value in Members and puts
* the rounded result in MemberAverage.

DIVIDE Members INTO Total GIVING MemberAverage
* Divides the value in Members into the value in Total and puts the result in MemberAverage.

MULTIPLY 10 BY Magnitude
* Multiplies 10 by the value in Magnitude and puts the result in Magnitude.

MULTIPLY Members BY Subs GIVING TotalSubs
* Multiplies the value of Members by the value of Subs and puts the result in TotalSubs.
```

Note that when separating contiguous operands, you may insert commas for clarity. They have no semantic effect, as you will see if you use the following example:

```
DISPLAY "Date of birth = " DayOB, SPACE, MonthOB, SPACE, YearOB
ADD Sales TO ShopSales, CountySales, CountrySales
```

The ROUNDED Phrase

If you use the ROUNDED phrase, then, after decimal point alignment, if the result of the calculation must be truncated on the right side (least significant digits) and the leftmost truncated digit has an absolute value of five or greater, the rightmost digit is increased by one when rounded. That sounds complicated, but it isn't. Let's look at some examples, as shown in Table 4-1.

Table 4-1. *ROUNDED Examples. Digits in the Actual Result column that will be truncated are not in bold*

Actual Result	Receiving Data Item	Truncated Result	Rounded Result
342.736	PIC 999V99	342.73	342.74
342.734	PIC 999V99	342.73	342.73
342.534	PIC 999	342	343
342.464	PIC 999	342	342
5.958	PIC 9V99	5.95	5.96
12.821565	PIC 99V9(5)	12.82156	12.82157

The ON SIZE ERROR

A size error occurs when the computed result is too large or too small to fit into the receiving field. When the ON SIZE ERROR phrase is used, it is followed by a block of COBOL statements that usually alert you that an error condition has occurred. For instance, in the following example, if FinalResult is too small to hold the result of all these multiplications, the ON SIZE ERROR activates and the alert message is displayed:

```
COMPUTE FinalResult = Num1 * Num2 * Num3 * Num4
    ON SIZE ERROR DISPLAY "Alert: FinalResult too small to hold result"
END-COMPUTE
```

The scope of the statement block is delimited by the appropriate END delimiter (END-ADD, END-SUBTRACT, END-MULTIPLY, END-DIVIDE, END-COMPUTE).

The ON SIZE ERROR acts like a specialized exception handler that comes into play if there is division by zero or if unexpected truncation occurs. When a computation is performed and decimal point alignment has occurred between the calculated result and the receiving data item, the result may be truncated on either the left side or the right. If the most significant digits are truncated, the size error activates. If there is truncation of the least significant digits, size error activation depends on whether the ROUNDED phrase is specified. If it is, then truncation of the least significant digits is ignored because using the ROUNDED phrase indicates that you know there will be truncation and have specified rounding to deal with it. Table 4-2 gives some ON SIZE ERROR examples.

Table 4-2. *ON SIZE ERROR Examples. Digits in the Actual Result column that will be truncated are not in bold*

Actual Result	Result Data item	Truncated Result	SIZE ERROR?
761.758	999V99	761.75	**YES** 8 is truncated on the right.
1761.78	999V99	761.78	**YES** 1 is truncated on the left.
374	999	374	**NO**
1761	999	761	**YES** 1 is truncated on the left.
326.475	999V99	326.47	**YES** 5 is truncated on the right.
326.475	999V99 ROUNDED	326.48	**NO** 5 is truncated on the right, but rounding is specified.
1326.475	999V99 ROUNDED	326.48	**YES** 1 is truncated on the left.

Nonconforming Arithmetic Verbs

When the common arithmetic verb template was introduced, I mentioned that there are forms of some verbs that do not conform to the template. This section gives the full metalanguage for COMPUTE, ADD, SUBTRACT, MULTIPLY, and DIVIDE and discusses in more detail the versions of these verbs that do not conform to the template.

The COMPUTE Verb

COMPUTE assigns the result of an arithmetic expression to a data item. The arithmetic expression to the right of the equal sign is evaluated, and the result is assigned to the data item(s) on the left of the equal sign. The arithmetic expression is evaluated according to the normal arithmetic rules. That is, the expression is normally evaluated from left to right, but bracketing and precedence rules (see Table 4-3) can change the order of evaluation.

Table 4-3. *Precedence Rules*

Precedence	Symbol	Meaning
1	**	Power
2	*	Multiply
	/	Divide
3	+	Add
	-	Subtract

■ **Note** Unlike some other programming languages, COBOL provides the ** expression symbol to represent raising to a power.

COMPUTE is the COBOL verb most similar to assignment in other programming languages. For that reason, you may be tempted to use it for plain assignments of data items to data items. COMPUTE should never be used for that purpose; in COBOL, you have the MOVE verb for that.

The familiarity of COMPUTE may also cause you to use it in preference to the other arithmetic verbs. There is no major objection to doing so, but knowledge of the other arithmetic verbs is required if you will be working with legacy systems.

Figure 4-4 shows the metalanguage for the COMPUTE verb.

$$\text{COMPUTE } \{\text{Result\#i} [\, \underline{\text{ROUNDED}} \,]\} \ldots = \text{Arithmetic Expression}$$

$$\left[\left\{ \begin{array}{l} \underline{\text{ON}} \, \underline{\text{SIZE ERROR}} \\ \underline{\text{NOT ON}} \, \underline{\text{SIZE ERROR}} \end{array} \right\} \text{StatementBlock } \underline{\text{END - COMPUTE}} \right]$$

Figure 4-4. COMPUTE metalanguage

COMPUTE Examples

Each example in this section is followed by a diagram that shows the value of the data items before and after COMPUTE executes.

Let's start with some literal values:

```
COMPUTE Result = 90 - 7 * 3 + 50 / 2

01 Result PIC 9(4) VALUE 3333.
```

Before	3333
After	0094

This is equivalent to

```
COMPUTE Result = 90 - (7 * 3) + (50 / 2)

01 Result PIC 9(4) VALUE 3333.
```

Before	3333
After	0094

Here's another example:

```
COMPUTE Euro ROUNDED = Dollar / ExchangeRate
01 Euro         PIC 9(5)V99 VALUE 3425.15.
01 Dollar       PIC 9(5)V99 VALUE 1234.75.
01 ExchangeRate PIC 9V9(4)  VALUE 1.3017.
```

	Euro	Dollar	Exchange Rate
Before	3425.15	1234.75	1.3017
After	0948.57	1234.75	1.3017

The ADD Verb

The ADD verb is used for addition. You might think COMPUTE could be used for that, and of course it can, but sometimes it can be simpler to use ADD. For instance, to increment a counter, you need COMPUTE ItemCount = ItemCount + 1, whereas you could just use ADD 1 TO ItemCount.

The metalanguage for the ADD verb is given in Figure 4-5.

$$\text{ADD Operand\#i1}\dots \begin{cases} \underline{\text{TO}} \quad \{\text{OperandResult\#i} \; [\underline{\text{ROUNDED}}]\}\dots \\ [\underline{\text{TO}}]\text{Operand\#i1} \; \underline{\text{GIVING}} \; \{\text{Result\#i} \; [\underline{\text{ROUNDED}}]\}\dots \end{cases}$$
$$[\text{ON} \; \underline{\text{SIZE ERROR}} \; \text{StatementBlock END - ADD}]$$

Figure 4-5. *ADD verb metalanguage*

Notes

The ADD verb mostly conforms to the common template, but note the ellipsis after the first operand. This means you could have a statement like

```
ADD Num1, Num2, Num3 TO Num4 GIVING Result.
```

What are the semantics of this version of ADD? The items before TO are all added together, and then the result is applied to the operand or operands after TO.

Note also that in the GIVING version of the ADD verb, the word TO is optional (square brackets). This means you could have a statement like

```
ADD Num1, Num2, Num3 GIVING Result.
```

In this version, all the operands before GIVING are added together, and the result is placed in the Result data item.

ADD Examples

Each example in this section is followed by a figure that shows the value of the data items before and after ADD executes:

```
ADD Cash TO Total.
01 Cash  PIC 9(3) VALUE 364.
01 Total PIC 9(4) VALUE 1000.
```

	Cash	Total
Before	364	1000
After	364	**1364**

```
ADD Cash, 20 TO Total.
01 Cash  PIC 9(3) VALUE 364.
01 Total PIC 9(4) VALUE 1000.
```

	Cash	Total
Before	364	1000
After	**364**	**1384**

```
ADD Cash, Checks TO Total.
01 Cash  PIC 9(3) VALUE 364.
01 Total PIC 9(4) VALUE 1000.
01 Checks PIC (4) VALUE 1445.
```

	Cash	Checks	Total
Before	364	1445	1000
After	364	1445	**2809**

The SUBTRACT Verb

The SUBTRACT verb is a specialized verb used for subtraction. It can be more convenient to use SUBTRACT to decrement a counter rather than COMPUTE. For instance, to decrement a counter you need COMPUTE ItemCount = ItemCount − 1, whereas you could just use SUBTRACT 1 FROM ItemCount.

The metalanguage for the SUBTRACT verb is given in Figure 4-6.

$$\text{SUBTRACT Operand\#il}\ldots\{\underline{\text{FROM}}\}\begin{Bmatrix}\{\text{OperandResult\#i } [\underline{\text{ROUNDED}}]\}\ldots \\ \{\text{Operand\#il } \underline{\text{GIVING}} \text{ Result\#i } [\underline{\text{ROUNDED}}]\}\ldots\end{Bmatrix}$$
$$[\text{ON } \underline{\text{SIZE ERROR}} \text{ StatementBlock END-SUBTRACT}]$$

Figure 4-6. *Metalanguage for the SUBTRACT verb*

Notes

The SUBTRACT verb mostly conforms to the common template, but just as with ADD, there is an ellipsis after the first operand. This means you could have statements like these:

```
SUBTRACT Num1, Num2 FROM Num3 GIVING Result.
SUBTRACT Num1, Num2 FROM NumResult1, NumResult2.
```

In the first example, all the items before the word FROM are added together, the combined result is subtracted from num3, and the result is placed in the Result data item.

In the second example, all the items before the word FROM are added together. The combined result is subtracted from NumResult1, and the result is placed in NumResult1. The combined result is also subtracted from NumResult2, and the result of that calculation is placed in NumResult2.

SUBTRACT Examples

Here are some examples of SUBTRACT:

```
SUBTRACT Num1, Num2 FROM Num3 GIVING Result.
01 Num1    PIC 9(4) VALUE 364.
01 Num2    PIC 9(4) VALUE 1000.
01 Num3    PIC 9(4) VALUE 5555.
01 Result  PIC 9(4) VALUE 1445.
```

	Num1	Num2	Num3	Result
Before	364	1000	5555	1445
After	364	1000	5555	**4191**

```
SUBTRACT Num1, Num2 FROM NumResult1, NumResult2.
01 Num1       PIC 9(4) VALUE 364.
01 Num2       PIC 9(4) VALUE 1000.
01 NumResult1 PIC 9(4) VALUE 5555.
01 NumResult2 PIC 9(4) VALUE 1445.
```

	Num1	Num2	NumResult1	NumResult2
Before	364	1000	5555	1445
After	364	1000	**4191**	**0081**

```
SUBTRACT Tax, PRSI, Pension, Levy FROM GrossPay GIVING NetPay.
01 GrossPay PIC 9(4)V99 VALUE 6350.75.
01 Tax      PIC 9(4)V99 VALUE 2333.25.
01 PRSI     PIC 9(4)V99 VALUE 1085.45.
01 Pension  PIC 9(4)V99 VALUE 1135.74.
01 Levy     PIC 9(3)V99 VALUE 170.50.
01 NetPay   PIC 9(4)V99 VALUE ZEROS.
```

	GrossPay	Tax	PRSI	Pension	Levy	NetPay
Before	6350.75	2333.25	1085.45	1135.74	170.50	0000.00
After	6350.75	2333.25	1085.45	1135.74	170.50	**1625.81**

The MULTIPLY Verb

The MULTIPLY verb is one of the arithmetic verbs that fully conforms to the common template given in Figure 4-3. The metalanguage for the MULTIPLY verb is given in Figure 4-7.

$$\text{MULTIPLY Operand\#il } \left\{\underline{\text{BY}}\right\} \begin{cases} \{\text{OperandResult\#i } [\underline{\text{ROUNDED}}]\}\dots \\ \{\text{Operand\#il } \underline{\text{GIVING}} \text{ Result\#i } [\underline{\text{ROUNDED}}]\}\dots \end{cases}$$

$$[\text{ON } \underline{\text{SIZE ERROR}} \text{ StatementBlock END - MULTIPLY}]$$

Figure 4-7. *Metalanguage for the MULTIPLY verb*

MULTIPLY Examples

Here are some examples of MULTIPLY:

```
Multiply Fees BY Members GIVING TotalFees
    DISPLAY "Alert: result to large for TotalFees"
01 Fees       PIC 9(3)V99 VALUE 052.24
01 Members    PIC 9(4)    VALUE 1024.
01 TotalFees  PIC 9(5)V99 VALUE ZEROS.
```

	Fees	Members	TotalFees
Before	052.24	1024	00000.00
After	052.24	1024	**53493.76**

The DIVIDE Verb

The DIVIDE verb has two main formats. The metalanguage for the first format is given in Figure 4-8. This format is unremarkable in that it conforms to the common template. The metalanguage for the second format is given in Figure 4-9. This format does *not* conform to the common template, and it provides operations that cannot be done with COMPUTE. The second format of DIVIDE allows you to get the quotient and the remainder in one operation.

$$\text{DIVIDE Operand\#il } \begin{cases} \underline{\text{BY}} \\ \underline{\text{INTO}} \end{cases} \begin{cases} \{\text{OperandResult\#i } [\underline{\text{ROUNDED}}]\}\dots \\ \{\text{Operand\#il } \underline{\text{GIVING}} \text{ Result\#i } [\underline{\text{ROUNDED}}]\}\dots \end{cases}$$

$$[\text{ON } \underline{\text{SIZE ERROR}} \text{ StatementBlock END - DIVIDE}]$$

Figure 4-8. *Metalanguage for format 1 of the DIVIDE verb*

$$\underline{\text{DIVIDE}} \text{ Operand\#il } \begin{cases} \underline{\text{INTO}} \\ \underline{\text{BY}} \end{cases} \text{Operand\#il } \underline{\text{GIVING}} \{\text{Quotient\#i} [\underline{\text{ROUNDED}}]\} \underline{\text{REMAINDER}} \text{ Remainder\#i}$$

$$\left[\begin{cases} \text{ON } \underline{\text{SIZE ERROR}} \\ \underline{\text{NOT}} \text{ ON } \underline{\text{SIZE ERROR}} \end{cases} \text{StatementBlock } \underline{\text{END - DIVIDE}} \right]$$

Figure 4-9. *Metalanguage for format 2 of the DIVIDE verb*

DIVIDE Examples

Following are some DIVIDE examples; the third example uses the second format.

In this example, 15 is divided into Amount1, and the result is placed in Amount1; 15 is also divided into Amount2, and result is placed in Amount2. The results calculated are not integer values, so there is truncation of the digits to the left of the decimal point:

```
DIVIDE 15 INTO Amount1, Amount2.
01 Amount1    PIC 9(4) VALUE 2444.
01 Amount2    PIC 9(3) VALUE 354.
```

	Amount1	Amount2
Before	2444	354
After	162	023

In this example, the calculated result is not an integer value, so there is truncation of the digits to the left of the decimal point. But because rounding is requested, the result is rounded to 272 (from 271.7826086956522):

```
DIVIDE Qty By Units GIVING Average ROUNDED.
01 Qty      PIC 9(5)  VALUE 31255.
01 Units    PIC 9(3)  VALUE 115.
01 Average  PIC 9(4)  VALUE ZEROS.
```

	Qty	Units	Average
Before	31255	115	0000
After	31255	115	0272

This example uses the second format of DIVIDE. It shows how you can use DIVIDE to get both the quotient and the remainder in one operation:

```
DIVIDE 215 BY 10 GIVING Quotient REMAINDER Rem.
01 Quotient PIC 999  VALUE ZEROS.
01 Rem      PIC 9    VALUE ZEROS.
```

	Quotient	Rem
Before	000	0
After	021	5

Let's Write a Program

Listing 4-2 presents a very simple program that takes two single-digit numbers from the keyboard, multiplies them together, and then displays the result. This program uses only one of the three classic constructs of structured programming. These constructs are

- Sequence
- Selection
- Iteration

In this program, execution starts in the PROCEDURE DIVISION paragraph CalculateResult and then continues through the program statements one by one, in sequence, until STOP RUN is reached.

Obviously, a program like this has limited usefulness. To make it really useful, you need to be able to selectively execute program statements (selection) and specify that others are to be executed over and over again (iteration). You revisit this program in the next two chapters when you are armed with the necessary selection and iteration constructs.

Listing 4-2. Example Program: ACCEPT, DISPLAY, and MULTIPLY

```
IDENTIFICATION DIVISION.
PROGRAM-ID.  Listing4-2.
AUTHOR.  Michael Coughlan.
*> Accepts two numbers from the user, multiplies them together
*> and then displays the result.

DATA DIVISION.
WORKING-STORAGE SECTION.
01  Num1        PIC 9  VALUE 5.
01  Num2        PIC 9  VALUE 4.
01  Result      PIC 99 VALUE ZEROS.

PROCEDURE DIVISION.
CalculateResult.
    DISPLAY "Enter a single digit number - " WITH NO ADVANCING
    ACCEPT Num1
    DISPLAY "Enter a single digit number - " WITH NO ADVANCING
    ACCEPT Num2
    MULTIPLY Num1 BY Num2 GIVING Result
    DISPLAY "Result is = ", Result
    STOP RUN.
```

Summary

In this chapter, you examined the operation of the arithmetic verbs COMPUTE, ADD, SUBTRACT, MULTIPLY, and DIVIDE. The ACCEPT and DISPLAY verbs, which allow you to get input from the keyboard and send output to the screen, were also explored.

The final example program consisted of a sequence of statements that are executed one after another. This kind of program is of limited usefulness. To be truly useful, a program must incorporate iteration and selection. These control structures are explored in the next chapter, along with the jewel in COBOL's crown: condition names.

LANGUAGE KNOWLEDGE EXERCISES

Sharpen up the 2B pencil you used to answer the questions in the last chapter, and fill in the *after* positions for data items that have a *before* entry:

```
01  Num1    PIC 99.
01  Num2    PIC 99.
01  Num3    PIC 99.
01  Num4    PIC 99.
```

Statement	Before Values				After Values			
	Num1	Num2	Num3	Num4	Num1	Num2	Num3	Num4
ADD Num1 TO Num2	25	30						
ADD Num1, Num2 TO Num3, Num4	13	04	05	12				
ADD Num1, Num2, Num3 GIVING Num4	04	03	02	01				
SUBTRACT Num1 FROM Num2 GIVING Num3	04	10	55					
SUBTRACT Num1,Num2 FROM Num3	05	10	55					
SUBTRACT Num1, Num2 FROM Num3 GIVING Num4	05	10	55	20				
MULTIPLY Num1 BY Num2	10	05						
MULTIPLY Num1 BY Num2 GIVING Num3	10	05	33					
DIVIDE Num1 INTO Num2	05	64						
DIVIDE Num2 BY Num1 GIVING Num3 REMAINDER Num4	05	64	24	88				
COMPUTE Num1 = 5 + 10 * 30 / 2	25							

LANGUAGE KNOWLEDGE EXERCISES - ANSWERS

Sharpen up the 2B pencil you used to answer the questions in the last chapter, and fill in the *after* positions for data items that have a *before* entry:

```
01 Num1    PIC 99.
01 Num2    PIC 99.
01 Num3    PIC 99.
01 Num4    PIC 99.
```

Statement	Before Values				After Values			
	Num1	Num2	Num3	Num4	Num1	Num2	Num3	Num4
ADD Num1 TO Num2	25	30			25	**55**		
ADD Num1, Num2 TO Num3, Num4	13	04	05	12	13	04	**22**	**29**
ADD Num1, Num2, Num3 GIVING Num4	04	03	02	01	04	03	02	**09**
SUBTRACT Num1 FROM Num2 GIVING Num3	04	10	55		04	10	**06**	
SUBTRACT Num1,Num2 FROM Num3	05	10	55		05	10	**40**	
SUBTRACT Num1, Num2 FROM Num3 GIVING Num4	05	10	55	20	05	10	55	**40**
MULTIPLY Num1 BY Num2	10	05			10	**50**		
MULTIPLY Num1 BY Num2 GIVING Num3	10	05	33		10	05	**50**	
DIVIDE Num1 INTO Num2	05	64			05	**12**		
DIVIDE Num2 BY Num1 GIVING Num3 REMAINDER Num4	05	64	24	88	05	64	**12**	**04**
COMPUTE Num1 = 5 + 10 * 30 / 2	25				**55**			

CHAPTER 5

∎ ∎ ∎

Control Structures: Selection

The last chapter noted that programs that consist only of a sequence of statements are not very useful. To be useful, a program must use selection constructs to execute some statements rather than others and must use iteration constructs to execute certain statements repeatedly.

In this chapter, you examine the selection constructs available to COBOL. In addition to discussing the IF and EVALUATE statements, this chapter also discusses the condition types recognized by the selection constructs, the creation and use of condition names, the use of the SET verb to manipulate condition names, and the proper naming of condition names.

A number of short example programs are introduced in this chapter. Please keep in mind that these are only used to demonstrate particular language elements. They are not intended as realistic examples.

Selection

In most procedural languages, if and case/switch are the only selection constructs supported. COBOL supports advanced versions of both of these constructs, but it also supports a greater variety of condition types including relation conditions, class conditions, sign conditions, complex conditions, and condition names.

IF Statement

When a program runs, the program statements are executed one after another, in sequence, unless a statement is encountered that alters the order of execution. An IF statement is one of the statement types that can alter the order of execution in a program. It allows you to specify that a block of code is to be executed only if the condition attached to the IF statement is satisfied. The basic metalanguage for the IF statement is given in Figure 5-1.

$$\underline{\text{IF}}\ \text{Condition}\ \text{THEN} \left\{ \begin{array}{l} \text{StatementBlock} \\ \underline{\text{NEXT SENTENCE}} \end{array} \right\}$$

$$\left[\underline{\text{ELSE}} \left\{ \begin{array}{l} \text{StatementBlock} \\ \underline{\text{NEXT SENTENCE}} \end{array} \right\} \right] \left[\underline{\text{END - IF}} \right]$$

Figure 5-1. *Metalanguage for the IF statement/verb*

The StatementBlock following the THEN executes, if the condition is true. The StatementBlock following the ELSE (if used) executes, if the condition is false. The StatementBlock(s) can include any valid COBOL statement including further IF constructs. This allows for nested IF statements.

One difference from many other programming languages is that when a condition is evaluated, it evaluates to either true or false. It does not evaluate to 1 or 0.

The explicit scope delimiter END-IF was introduced in ANS 85 COBOL. In the previous versions of COBOL, scope was delimited by means of the period. Although the scope of the IF statement may still be delimited by a period, the END-IF delimiter should always be used because it makes explicit the scope of the IF statement.

There are two problems with using a period as a scope delimiter:

- Periods are hard to see, and this makes it more difficult to understand the code.

- A period delimits all open scopes, and this is a source of many programming errors.

You explore this topic more fully later in the chapter.

Condition Types

The IF statement is not as simple as the metalanguage in Figure 5-1 seems to suggest. The condition that follows the IF is drawn from one of the condition types shown in Table 5-1. If a condition is not a complex condition, then it is regarded as a simple condition. A simple condition may be negated using the NOT keyword. Bracketing a complex condition causes it to be treated as a simple condition.

Table 5-1. *Condition Types*

Condition Type
Relation
Class
Sign
Complex
Condition names

Relation Conditions

Relation conditions are used to test whether a value is less than, equal to, or greater than another value. These conditions will be familiar to programmers of other languages. The use of words as shown in the relation condition metalanguage in Figure 5-2 may come as bit of a shock, but for most conditions the more familiar symbols (= < > >= <=) may be used. There is one exception to this: unlike in many other languages, in COBOL there is no symbol for NOT. You must use the word NOT if you want to express this condition.

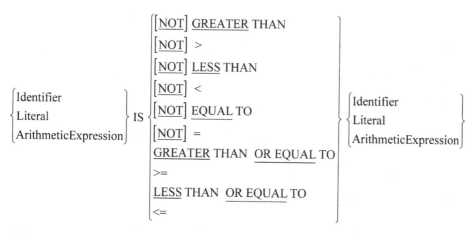

Figure 5-2. Metalanguage for relation conditions

Note that the compared values must be type compatible. For instance, it is not valid to compare a string value to a numeric value. Some examples of relation conditions are shown in Example 5-1. Most of these examples are straight forward, but the final example includes an arithmetic expression. In this case, the arithmetic expression is evaluated and then the result is compared with the value in Num1.

Example 5-1. Some Sample Relation Conditions

```
IF Num1 < 10 THEN
     DISPLAY "Num1  < 10"
END-IF

IF Num1 LESS THAN 10
    DISPLAY "Num1 < 10"
END-IF

IF Num1 GREATER THAN OR EQUAL TO Num2
     MOVE Num1 TO Num2
END-IF

IF Num1 <  (Num2 + ( Num3 / 2))
    MOVE ZEROS TO Num1
END-IF
```

Class Conditions

A class condition does not refer to a class in the OO sense. Instead, it refers to the broad category or class (such as numeric, alphabetic, or alphabetic lower or upper) into which a data item may fall (see the metalanguage for class conditions in Figure 5-3). A class condition is used to discover whether the value of data item is a member of one these classes. For instance, a NUMERIC class condition might be used on an alphanumeric (PIC X) or a numeric (PIC 9) data item to see if it contained numeric data. Or an ALPHABETIC-UPPER class condition might be used to discover if a data item contained only capital letters (see Example 5-2).

$$\text{Identifier IS [\underline{NOT}]} \begin{cases} \underline{\text{NUMERIC}} \\ \underline{\text{ALPHABETIC}} \\ \underline{\text{ALPHABETIC-LOWER}} \\ \underline{\text{ALPHABETIC-UPPER}} \\ \text{UserDefinedClassName} \end{cases}$$

Figure 5-3. *Metalanguage for class conditions*

Example 5-2. Class Condition That Checks Whether the StateName Contains All Capitals

```
IF StateName IS ALPHABETIC-UPPER
    DISPLAY "All the letters in StateName are upper case"
END-IF
```

Notes on Class Conditions

The target of a class test must be a data item with an explicit or implicit usage of DISPLAY. In the case of numeric tests, data items with a usage of PACKED-DECIMAL may also be tested.

The numeric test may not be used with data items described as alphabetic (PIC A) or with group items when any of the elementary items specifies a sign. An alphabetic test may not be used with any data items described as numeric (PIC 9).

The UserDefinedClassName is a name that you can assign to a set of characters. You must use the CLASS clause of the SPECIAL-NAMES paragraph, of the CONFIGURATION SECTION, in the ENVIRONMENT DIVISION, to assign a class name to a set of characters. A data item conforms to the UserDefinedClassName if its contents consist entirely of the characters listed in the definition of the UserDefinedClassName (see Listing 5-1 in the next section).

User-Defined Class Names

Whereas ALPHABETIC and NUMERIC are predefined class names that identify a subset of the character set, the UserDefinedClassName in the metalanguage (see Figure 5-3) is a name that you can assign to a defined subset of characters. To define the subset, you must create a CLASS entry in the SPECIAL-NAMES paragraph, of the CONFIGURATION SECTION, in the ENVIRONMENT DIVISION. The CLASS clause assigns a class name to a defined subset of characters. In a class condition, a data item conforms to the UserDefinedClassName if its contents consist entirely of the characters listed in the definition of the UserDefinedClassName.

Listing 5-1 is an example program that shows how to define and use a user-defined class name. In this listing, two class names are defined: HexNumber and RealName. HexNumber is used to test that NumIn contains only hex digits (0–9 and A–F). RealName is used to test that NameIn contains only valid characters. RealName was created because you can't just use the IS ALPHABETIC class condition to test a name—sometimes names, especially Irish names, contain other characters; such as the apostrophe ('). RealName allows you to test that the name entered contains only characters from the set you have defined.

Listing 5-1. User-Defined Class Names Used with a Class Condition

```
IDENTIFICATION DIVISION.
PROGRAM-ID. Listing5-1.
AUTHOR. Michael Coughlan.
*> Shows how user defined class names are created and used

ENVIRONMENT DIVISION.
CONFIGURATION SECTION.
SPECIAL-NAMES.
    CLASS HexNumber IS "0" THRU "9", "A" THRU "F"
    CLASS RealName  IS "A" THRU "Z", "a" THRU "z", "'", SPACE.

DATA DIVISION.
WORKING-STORAGE SECTION.
01 NumIn      PIC X(4).
01 NameIn     PIC X(15).

PROCEDURE DIVISION.
Begin.
   DISPLAY "Enter a Hex number - " WITH NO ADVANCING
   ACCEPT NumIn.
   IF NumIn IS HexNumber THEN
      DISPLAY NumIn " is a Hex number"
    ELSE
      DISPLAY NumIn " is not a Hex number"
   END-IF

   DISPLAY "--------------------------------"
   DISPLAY "Enter a name - " WITH NO ADVANCING
   ACCEPT NameIn
   IF NameIn IS ALPHABETIC
      DISPLAY NameIn " is alphabetic"
    ELSE
      DISPLAY NameIn " is not alphabetic"
   END-IF

   IF NameIn IS RealName THEN
      DISPLAY NameIn " is a real name"
    ELSE
      DISPLAY NameIn " is not a real name"
   END-IF
   STOP RUN.
```

```
              Listing 5-1 - Run1
Enter a Hex number - 12AF
12AF is a Hex number
-------------------------------------
Enter a name - Liam O'Riordan
Liam O'Riordan  is not alphabetic
Liam O'Riordan  is a real name

              Listing 5-1 - Run2
Enter a Hex number - 12DG
12DG is not a Hex number
-------------------------------------
Enter a name - Li4m O'Riordan
Li4m O'Riordan  is not alphabetic
Li4m O'Riordan  is not a real name

              Listing 5-1 - Run3
Enter a Hex number - 0D0A
0D0A is a Hex number
-------------------------------------
Enter a name - Michael Power
Michael Power  is alphabetic
Michael Power  is a real name
```

How the Program Works

The program accepts a hex number from the user, tests that it contains only valid hex digits, and then displays the appropriate message. The program then accepts a name from the user, uses a class condition to test whether the contents are alphabetic, and displays the appropriate message. The program next tests that NameIn contains only the allowed characters and displays the appropriate message. To give you a feel for how the program works, I ran it a number of times and captured the output (see the output attached to Listing 5-1).

Sign Conditions

The sign condition (see the metalanguage in Figure 5-4) is used to discover whether the value of an arithmetic expression is less than, greater than, or equal to zero. Sign conditions are a shorter way of writing certain relation conditions.

$$\text{ArithmeticExpression IS}\,[\underline{\text{NOT}}]\left\{\begin{array}{l}\underline{\text{POSITIVE}}\\ \underline{\text{NEGATIVE}}\\ \underline{\text{ZERO}}\end{array}\right\}$$

Figure 5-4. *Metalanguage for sign conditions*

In Example 5-3, a sign condition is used to discover whether the result of evaluating an arithmetic expression is a negative value. This example also shows the equivalent relation condition.

Example 5-3. Sign Condition Used to Discover Whether a Result Is Negative

```
IF (Num2 * 10 / 50) - 10 IS NEGATIVE
    DISPLAY "Calculation result is negative"
END-IF

*> the equivalent Relation Condition is

IF (Num2 * 10 / 50) - 10 LESS THAN ZERO
    DISPLAY "Calculation result is negative"
END-IF
```

Complex Conditions

Unlike sign conditions and class conditions, complex conditions (sometimes called compound conditions) should be familiar to programmers of most languages. Even here, however, COBOL has a tweak—in the form of implied subjects—that you may find unusual. The metalanguage for complex conditions is given in Figure 5-5.

$$\text{Condition}\left\{\left\{\begin{array}{l}\underline{\text{AND}}\\ \underline{\text{OR}}\end{array}\right\}\text{Condition}\right\}\ldots$$

Figure 5-5. *Metalanguage for complex conditions*

Complex conditions are formed by combining two or more simple conditions using the conjunction operator OR or AND. Any condition (simple, complex, condition name) may be negated by preceding it with the word NOT. When NOT is applied to a condition, it toggles the true/false evaluation. For instance, if Num1 < 10 is true then NOT Num1 < 10 is false.

Like other conditions in COBOL, a complex condition evaluates to either true or false. A complex condition is an expression. Like arithmetic expressions, a complex condition is evaluated from left to right unless the order of evaluation is changed by precedence rules or by bracketing.

The precedence rules that apply to complex conditions are given in Table 5-2. To assist your understanding, the equivalent arithmetic precedence rules have been given alongside the condition rules.

Table 5-2. *Precedence Rules*

Precedence	Condition Value	Arithmetic Equivalent
1	NOT	**
2	AND	* or /
3	OR	+ or -

Example 5-4. Complex Condition to Detect Whether the Cursor Is Onscreen

```
*> A complex condition example that detects if the cursor position located at
*> ScrnRow, ScrnCol is on screen (the text screen is 24 lines by 80 columns)
   IF (ScrRow > 0 AND ScrRow < 25) AND (ScrCol > 0 AND ScrCol < 81) THEN
      DISPLAY "On Screen"
   END-IF
```

Truth Tables

When a complex condition is being evaluated, it is useful to consider the OR and AND truth tables, shown in Table 5-3.

Table 5-3. OR *and* AND *Truth Tables*

OR Truth Table			AND Truth Table		
Condition	Condition	Result	Condition	Condition	Result
T	T	True	T	T	True
T	F	True	T	F	False
F	T	True	F	T	False
F	F	False	F	F	False

The Effect of Bracketing

Bracketing can make the order of evaluation explicit or can change it. Complex conditions are often difficult to understand, so any aid to clarity is welcome. For that reason, when you have to write a complex condition, you should always use bracketing to make explicit what is intended.

Consider the statement

```
IF NOT Num1 < 25 OR Num2 = 80 AND Num3 > 264 THEN
   DISPLAY "Done"
END-IF
```

The rules of precedence govern how this IF statement is evaluated. You can leave it like this and hope that future readers will understand it, or you can assist their understanding by using bracketing to make explicit the order of evaluation already governed by those rules.

To apply bracketing, you note that NOT takes precedence, so you write (NOT Num1 < 25). AND is next according to the precedence rules, so you bracket the ANDed conditions to give (Num2 = 80 AND Num3 > 264). Finally, the OR is evaluated to give the full condition as

```
IF (NOT Num1 < 25) OR (Num2 = 80 AND Num3 > 264)THEN
    DISPLAY "Done"
END-IF
```

Of course, you can use bracketing to change the order of evaluation. For instance, you can change the previous condition to

```
IF NOT (Num1 < 25 OR Num2 = 80) AND Num3 > 264 THEN
    DISPLAY "Done"
END-IF
```

In the original condition, the order of evaluation was NOT..AND..OR, but the new bracketing changes that order to OR..NOT..AND. This change has a practical effect on the result of the condition.

Suppose all the simple conditions in the original expression are true. The truth table for that expression yields Table 5-4.

Table 5-4. IF Statement Evaluation When All the Simple Conditions Are True

Condition	IF(NOT Num1 < 25)	OR	(Num2 = 80	AND	Num3 > 264)
Expressed as	**(NOT T)**	OR	(T	AND	T)
Evaluates to	(F)	OR	(T	**AND**	**T)**
Evaluates to	(F)	**OR**		(T)	
Evaluates to		**True**			

The re-bracketed expression yields Table 5-5.

Table 5-5. The Rebracketed Truth Table

Condition	IF NOT	(Num1 < 25	OR	Num2 = 80)	AND	Num3 > 264
Expressed as	NOT	(T	**OR**	T)	AND	T
Evaluates to	NOT		(T)		AND	T
Evaluates to		(F)			**AND**	T
			False			

Implied Subjects

Although COBOL is often verbose, it does occasionally provide constructs that enable quite succinct statements to be written. The *implied subject* is one of those constructs.

When, in a complex condition, a number of comparisons have to be made against a single data item, it can be tedious to have to repeat the data item for each comparison. For instance, the example code fragment you saw earlier could be rewritten using implied subjects as

```
IF (ScrRow > 0 AND < 25) AND (ScrCol > 0 AND < 81) THEN
    DISPLAY "On Screen"
END-IF
```

In this case, the implied subjects are ScrRow and ScrCol.

Similarly, using Grade = as the implied subject, you can rewrite

```
IF Grade = "A" OR Grade = "B" OR Grade = "C" THEN DISPLAY "Passed"
```

as

```
IF Grade = "A" OR "B" OR "C" THEN DISPLAY "Passed"
```

Finally, you can use the implied subject Num1 > to rewrite the expression

```
IF Num1 > Num2 AND Num1 > Num3 AND Num1 > Num4 THEN
    DISPLAY "Num1 is the largest"
END-IF
```

as

```
IF Num1 > Num2 AND Num3 AND Num4
    DISPLAY "Num1 is the largest"
END-IF
```

Nested IFs

COBOL allows nested IF statements (see Example 5-5). But be aware that although nested IF statements may be easy to write, they are somewhat difficult to understand when you return to them after an interval of time. Complex, and nested IF, statements are often used as a substitute for clear thinking. When you first attempt to solve a problem, you often don't have a full understanding of it. As a result, your solution may be convoluted and unwieldy. It is often only after you have attempted to solve the problem that you gain sufficient insight to allow you to generate a simpler solution. When you have a better understanding of the problem, you may find that a mere reorganization of your code will greatly reduce both the number and complexity of the IF statements required. Simplicity is difficult to achieve but is a highly desirable objective. It is a principle of good program design that your solution should be only as complex as the problem demands.

Example 5-5. Nested IF..ELSE Statements

```
*> This example uses nested IF statements including IF..THEN..ELSE statements
*> This is quite a straight forward example of nested IFs but nested If & IF.. ELSE statements
*> can get a lot more convoluted and difficult to understand. It is especially difficult if
*> some nested IF statements do not have ELSE branches and others do. It can take some time
*> to untangle which ELSE belongs with which IF
```

```
IF InputVal IS NUMERIC
    MOVE InputVal to Num1
    IF Num1 > 5 AND < 25
        IF Num1 < Num2
            MOVE Num2 TO Num1
          ELSE
            MOVE Num1 TO Num2
        END-IF
        DISPLAY "Num1 & Num2 = " Num1 SPACE Num2
      ELSE
        DISPLAY "Num 1 not in range"
    END-IF
  ELSE
    DISPLAY "Input was not numeric"
END-IF
```

Delimiting Scope: END-IF vs. Period

The scope of an IF statement may be delimited by either an END-IF or a period (full stop). For a variety of reasons, the explicit END-IF delimiter should always be used instead of a period. The period is so problematic that one of the most useful renovations you can perform on legacy COBOL code is to replace the periods with explicit scope delimiters.

There are two main problems with using a period as a scope delimiter. The first is that periods are hard to see, which makes it more difficult to understand the code. The second problem is that a period delimits *all open scopes*. This is a source of many programming errors.

The code fragments in Example 5-6 illustrate the readability problem. Both IF statements are supposed to perform the same task. But the scope of the IF statement on the left is delimited by an END-IF, whereas the statement on the right is delimited by a period.

Example 5-6. Comparing END-IF and Period-Delimited IF Statements

```
Statement1              Statement1
Statement2              Statement2
IF Num1 > Num2 THEN     IF Num1 > Num2 THEN
    Statement3              Statement3
    Statement4              Statement4
END-IF                  Statement5
Statement5              Statement6.
Statement6.
```

Unfortunately, on the right, the programmer has forgotten to follow Statement4 with a delimiting period. This means Statement5 and Statement6 will be included in the scope of the IF. They will be executed only if the condition is true. When periods are used to delimit the scope of an IF statement, this is an easy mistake to make; and, once made, it is difficult to spot. A period is small and unobtrusive compared to an END-IF.

The problem caused by unexpectedly delimiting scope is illustrated by the following code fragment:

```
IF Num1 < 10
    ADD 10 TO Num1
    MULTIPLY Num1 BY 1000 GIVING NUM2
        ON SIZE ERROR  DISPLAY "Error: Num2 too small".
    DISPLAY "When is this shown?".
```

In this fragment, it looks as if the DISPLAY on the final line is executed only when Num1 is less than 10. However, a period has been used to delimit the scope of the ON SIZE ERROR (instead of an END-MULTIPLY delimiter), and that period also delimits the scope of the IF (all open scopes). This means the DISPLAY lies outside the scope of the IF and so is always executed.

If you replace the periods with explicit scope delimiters, you can see more clearly what is happening:

```
IF Num1 < 10
    ADD 10 TO Num1
    MULTIPLY Num1 BY 1000 GIVING NUM2
       ON SIZE ERROR  DISPLAY "Error: Num2 too small"
    END-MULTIPLY
END-IF
    DISPLAY "When is this shown?".
```

Even though the indentation used in this version is just as misleading as the period-based version, you are not misled. The explicit scope delimiters used for the IF and the MULTIPLY make the scope of these statements clear.

The use of delimiting periods in the PROCEDURE DIVISION is such a source of programming errors that a minimum period style of programming has been advocated by Howard Tompkins[1] and Robert Baldwin[2]. In the examples in this book, I use a variation of the style suggested by Tompkins. Tompkins was writing before the 1985 standard was produced and so was not able to incorporate END delimiters into his scheme. Nowadays, you can adopt a style that uses only a single period per paragraph. Although Tompkins has persuasive arguments for placing that period alone on the line in column 12, for aesthetic reasons I use it to terminate the last statement in the paragraph. Whether you prefer the Tompkins lonely period style or my variation, I strongly suggest that you adopt the minimum period style. That way you will save yourself a world of hurt.

Condition Names

Wherever a condition tests a variable for equality to a value, a set of values, or a range of values, that condition can be replaced by a kind of abstract condition called a *condition name*. Wherever it is legal to have a condition, it is legal have a condition name. Just like a condition, a condition name is either true or false.

Condition names allow you to give a meaningful name to a condition while hiding the implementation details of how the condition is detected. For instance,

```
IF CountryCode = 3 OR 7 OR 10 OR 15 THEN
    MOVE 14 TO CurrencyCode
END-IF
```

may be replaced with

```
IF BritishCountry THEN
    SET CurrencyIsPound TO TRUE
END-IF
```

This example illustrates the readability benefits of using condition names. When you encounter code such as

```
IF CountryCode = 3 OR 7 OR 10 OR 15
```

the meaning of what the IF statement is testing is not obvious. You can see that CountryCode is being tested for particular values, but why? What is the significance of the values 3,7,10, and 15? What is the significance of moving 14 to the CurrencyCode? To discover this information, a maintenance programmer has to read external documentation or in-code comments. Now consider the condition name version of the IF statement. It is obvious what you are testing because the test has been given a meaningful name. Similarly, the action taken when BritishCountry is true is also obvious. No documentation and no comments are required.

Ease of maintenance is also improved. If the coding system changed and the countries of the British Isles were now represented by the codes 4, 12, 18, and 25, only the definition of the condition name would have to be changed. In the version that did not use the condition name, you would have to change the code values in all the places in the program where the condition was tested.

Defining Condition Names

Condition names are sometimes called *level 88s* because they are created in the DATA DIVISION using the special level number 88. The metalanguage for defining condition names is given in Figure 5-6.

$$
88\ \text{ConditionName} \left\{ \begin{array}{c} \text{VALUE} \\ \hline \text{VALUES} \end{array} \right\} \left\{ \begin{array}{l} \text{Literal\$\#} \\ \text{LowValuel\$\#} \left\{ \begin{array}{c} \text{THROUGH} \\ \hline \text{THRU} \end{array} \right\} \text{HighValuel \$\#} \end{array} \right\} \cdots
$$

Figure 5-6. *Metalanguage for defining condition names*

Rules

Condition names are always associated with a particular data item and are defined immediately after the definition of that data item. A condition name may be associated with a group data item and elementary data, or even the element of a table. The condition name is automatically set to true or false the moment the value of its associated data item changes.

When the VALUE clause is used with condition names, it does not assign a value. Instead, it identifies the value(s) which, if found in the associated data item, make the condition name true.

When identifying the condition values, a single value, a list of values, a range of values, or any combination of these may be specified. To specify a list of values, the entries are listed after the keyword VALUE. The list entries may be separated by commas or spaces but must terminate with a period.

Single Condition Name, Single Value

In Example 5-7, the condition name CityIsLimerick has been associated with CityCode so that if CityCode contains the value 2 (listed in the CityIsLimerick VALUE clause), the condition name will be automatically set to true.

Example 5-7. Defining and Using a Condition Name

```
DATA DIVISION.
WORKING-STORAGE SECTION.
01  CityCode          PIC 9 VALUE ZERO.
    88 CityIsLimerick VALUE 2.

PROCEDURE DIVISION.
Begin.
    :  :  :  :  :  :  :
    DISPLAY "Enter a city code (1-6) - " WITH NO ADVANCING
    ACCEPT CityCode
```

```
IF CityIsLimerick
   DISPLAY "Hey, we're home."
END-IF
 :   :   :   :   :   :   :
```

In the program fragment, DISPLAY and ACCEPT get a city code from the user. The instant the value in CityCode changes, the CityIsLimerick condition name will be set to true or false, depending on the value in CityCode.

Multiple Condition Names

Several condition names may be associated with a single data item. In Example 5-8, a number of condition names have been associated with CityCode. Each condition name is set to true when CityCode contains the value listed in the condition name VALUE clause. Condition names, like Booleans, can only take the value true or false. If a condition name is not set to true, it is set to false. Table 5-6 shows the Boolean value of each condition name for each value of CityCode.

Example 5-8. Associating Many Condition Names with a Data Item

```
DATA DIVISION.
WORKING-STORAGE SECTION.
01  CityCode PIC 9 VALUE ZERO.
    88 CityIsDublin        VALUE 1.
    88 CityIsLimerick      VALUE 2.
    88 CityIsCork          VALUE 3.
    88 CityIsGalway        VALUE 4.
    88 CityIsSligo         VALUE 5.
    88 CityIsWaterford     VALUE 6.
PROCEDURE DIVISION.
Begin.
    :   :   :   :   :   :   :
    DISPLAY "Enter a city code (1-6) - " WITH NO ADVANCING
    ACCEPT CityCode
    IF CityIsLimerick
       DISPLAY "Hey, we're home."
    END-IF
    IF CityIsDublin
       DISPLAY "Hey, we're in the capital."
    END-IF
    :   :   :   :   :   :   :
```

Table 5-6. *Results for Each Value of CityCode*

Data Item / Condition Name	Data Value / Condition Name Result							
CityCode	**0**	**1**	**2**	**3**	**4**	**5**	**6**	**7-9**
CityIsDublin	False	**TRUE**	False	False	False	False	False	False
CityIsLimerick	False	False	**TRUE**	False	False	False	False	False
CityIsCork	False	False	False	**TRUE**	False	False	False	False
CityIsGalway	False	False	False	False	**TRUE**	False	False	False
CityIsSligo	False	False	False	False	False	**TRUE**	False	False
CityIsWaterford	False	False	False	False	False	False	**TRUE**	False

Overlapping and Multiple-Value Condition Names

When multiple condition names are associated with a single data item, more than one condition name can be true at the same time. In Listing 5-2, UniversityCity is true if CityCode contains any value between 1 and 4. These values overlap the values of the first four condition names, so if UniversityCity is true, then one of those four must also be true.

Listing 5-2. Multiple Condition Names with Overlapping Values

```
IDENTIFICATION DIVISION.
PROGRAM-ID. Listing5-2.
AUTHOR.  Michael Coughlan.
DATA DIVISION.
WORKING-STORAGE SECTION.
01  CityCode PIC 9 VALUE ZERO.
        88 CityIsDublin        VALUE 1.
        88 CityIsLimerick      VALUE 2.
        88 CityIsCork          VALUE 3.
        88 CityIsGalway        VALUE 4.
        88 CityIsSligo         VALUE 5.
        88 CityIsWaterford     VALUE 6.
        88 UniversityCity      VALUE 1 THRU 4.
        88 CityCodeNotValid    VALUE 0, 7, 8, 9.


PROCEDURE DIVISION.
Begin.
    DISPLAY "Enter a city code (1-6) - " WITH NO ADVANCING
    ACCEPT CityCode
    IF CityCodeNotValid
      DISPLAY "Invalid city code entered"
     ELSE
       IF CityIsLimerick
          DISPLAY "Hey, we're home."
       END-IF
       IF CityIsDublin
          DISPLAY "Hey, we're in the capital."
       END-IF
       IF UniversityCity
          DISPLAY "Apply the rent surcharge!"
       END-IF
    END-IF
    STOP RUN.
```

Listing 5-2 Run1

Enter a city code (1-6) - 8
Invalid city code entered
Listing 5-2 Run1

Listing 5-2 Run2

Enter a city code (1-6) - 1
Hey, we're in the capital.
Apply the rent surcharge!

Listing 5-2 Run3

Enter a city code (1-6) - 2
Hey, we're home.
Apply the rent surcharge!

The list of values that follows a condition name may be a single value, a number of values, or a range of values, or any mixture of these. When a range is specified, the word THROUGH or THRU is used to separate the minimum and maximum values in the range. In Listing 5-2, UniversityCity is true if CityCode contains any value between 1 and 4, whereas CityCodeNotValid is true if CityCode contains a value of 0 or 7 or 8 or 9. In Listing 5-2 I have chosen to list the individual values for CityCodeNotValid, but the value list could have been written as:

```
88 CityCodeNotValid    VALUE 0, 7 THRU 9.
```

Table 5-7 shows the Boolean value of the condition names for each value of CityCode.

Table 5-7. *Results for Each Value of CityCode*

Data Item / Condition Name	Data Value / Condition Name Result							
CityCode	0	1	2	3	4	5	6	7 - 9
CityIsDublin	False	**TRUE**	False	False	False	False	False	False
CityIsLimerick	False	False	**TRUE**	False	False	False	False	False
CityIsCork	False	False	False	**TRUE**	False	False	False	False
CityIsGalway	False	False	False	False	**TRUE**	False	False	False
CityIsSligo	False	False	False	False	False	**TRUE**	False	False
CityIsWaterford	False	False	False	False	False	False	**TRUE**	False
UniversityCity	False	**TRUE**	**TRUE**	**TRUE**	**TRUE**	False	False	False
CityCodeNotValid	**TRUE**	False	False	False	False	False	False	**TRUE**

Values Can Be Alphabetic or Numeric

The list of values specified for a condition name can be numeric or alphabetic, as shown in Listing 5-3.

Listing 5-3. Multiple Condition Names with Overlapping Values

```
IDENTIFICATION DIVISION.
PROGRAM-ID. Listing5-3.
AUTHOR.  Michael Coughlan.
DATA DIVISION.
WORKING-STORAGE SECTION.
01 InputChar     PIC X.
   88 Vowel      VALUE   "A","E","I","O","U".
   88 Consonant  VALUE   "B" THRU "D", "F","G","H"
                         "J" THRU "N", "P" THRU "T"
                         "V" THRU "Z".
   88 Digit      VALUE   "0" THRU "9".
   88 ValidChar  VALUE   "A" THRU "Z", "0" THRU "9".

PROCEDURE DIVISION.
Begin.
   DISPLAY "Enter a character :- " WITH NO ADVANCING
   ACCEPT InputChar
   IF ValidChar
      DISPLAY "Input OK"
    ELSE
      DISPLAY "Invalid character entered"
   END-IF
   IF Vowel
      DISPLAY "Vowel entered"
   END-IF
   IF Digit
      DISPLAY "Digit entered"
   END-IF
   STOP RUN.
```

Listing 5-3 Run1

Enter a character :- g
Invalid character entered

Listing 5-3 Run2

Enter a character :- 5
Input OK
Digit entered

Listing 5-3 Run3

Enter a character :- E
Input OK
Vowel entered

List Values Can Be Whole Words

Although I have used single characters in the examples so far, condition names are not restricted to values with only single characters. Whole words can be used if required, as shown in Listing 5-4.

Listing 5-4. Words as Value Items

```
IDENTIFICATION DIVISION.
PROGRAM-ID. Listing5-4.
AUTHOR.  Michael Coughlan.
DATA DIVISION.
WORKING-STORAGE SECTION.
01  MakeOfCar        PIC X(10).
    88 VolksGroup  VALUE "skoda", "seat",
                         "audi", "volkswagen".
    88 GermanMade  VALUE "volkswagen", "audi",
                         "mercedes", "bmw",
                         "porsche".
PROCEDURE DIVISION.
Begin.
    DISPLAY "Enter the make of car - " WITH NO ADVANCING
    ACCEPT MakeOfCar
    IF VolksGroup AND GermanMade
       DISPLAY "Your car is made in Germany by the Volkswagen Group."
     ELSE
       IF VolksGroup
          DISPLAY "Your car is made by the Volkswagen Group."
       END-IF
       IF GermanMade
          DISPLAY "Your car is made in Germany."
       END-IF
    END-IF
    STOP RUN.
```

Using Condition Names Correctly

A condition name should express the true condition being tested. It should not express the test that sets the condition name to true. For instance, in Listing 5-2, a value of 1 in the data item CityCode indicates that the city is Dublin, a value of 2 means the city is Limerick, and so on. These condition names allow you to replace conditions such as

```
IF CityCode = 1
```

and

```
IF CityCode = 2
```

with the more meaningful statements

```
IF CityIsDublin
```

and

```
IF  CityIsLimerick.
```

Many COBOL beginners would use condition names such as CityCodeIs1 or CityCodeIs2 to express these conditions. Those condition names are meaningless because they express the value that makes the condition name true instead of expressing the meaning or significance of CityCode containing a particular value. A value of 1 or 2 in CityCode is how you detect that the city is Dublin or Limerick. It is not the value of CityCode that ultimately interests you; it is the meaning or significance of that value.

Example Program

Listing 5-5 is a small but complete program showing how the BritishCountry and CurrencyIsPound condition names might be defined and used. There is something unusual about this example, however. What do you imagine happens to the associated data item when the CurrencyIsPound condition name is set to true?

Listing 5-5. Detecting BritishCountry and Setting and Using CurrencyIsPound

```
IDENTIFICATION DIVISION.
PROGRAM-ID. Listing5-5.
AUTHOR.  Michael Coughlan.
DATA DIVISION.
WORKING-STORAGE SECTION.
01 CountryCode      PIC 999 VALUE ZEROS.
   88 BritishCountry VALUES 3, 7, 10, 15.

01 CurrencyCode      PIC 99 VALUE ZEROS.
   88 CurrencyIsPound  VALUE 14.
   88 CurrencyIsEuro   VALUE 03.
   88 CurrencyIsDollar VALUE 28.

PROCEDURE DIVISION.
Begin.
    DISPLAY "Enter the country code :- " WITH NO ADVANCING
    ACCEPT CountryCode

    IF BritishCountry THEN
       SET CurrencyIsPound TO TRUE
    END-IF
    IF CurrencyIsPound THEN
       DISPLAY "Pound sterling used in this country"
     ELSE
       DISPLAY "Country does not use sterling"
    END-IF
    STOP RUN.
```

Listing 5-5 Run1

Enter the country code :- 7
Pound sterling used in this country

Listing 5-5 Run2

Enter the country code :- 5
Country does not use sterling

Setting a Condition Name to True

In Listing 5-5, the SET verb is used to set CurrencyIsPound to true. The way condition names normally work is that a value placed into the associated data item automatically sets the condition names that list that value to true. When a condition name is manually set to true using the SET verb, the value listed for that condition name is forced into the associated data item. In Listing 5-5, when the SET verb is used to set CurrencyIsPound to true, the value 14 is forced into CurrencyCode.

When a condition name that lists more than one value is set to true, the first of the values listed is forced into the associated data item. For instance, if BritishCountry were set to true, then the value 3 would be forced into CountryCode.

■ **ISO 2002**   In standard ANS 85 COBOL, the SET verb cannot be used to set a condition name to false. This can be done in ISO 2002 COBOL, but in that case the level 88 entry must be extended to include the phrase

WHEN SET TO <u>FALSE</u> IS LiteralValue$#

To set a condition name to true, you use the SET verb. You might think, therefore, that the SET verb is used only for manipulating condition names. But the SET verb is a strange fish. It is used for a variety of unconnected purposes. For instance, it is used to set a condition name to true. It is used to increment or decrement an index item. It is used to assign the value of an index to an ordinary data item and vice versa. It is used to set On or Off the switches associated with mnemonic names. In ISO 2002 COBOL, it is used to manipulate pointer variables (yes, ISO 2002 COBOL has pointers) and object references. It is often the target of implementer extensions.

Because the SET verb has so many different unrelated uses, instead of dealing with it as a single topic I discuss each format as you examine the construct to which it is most closely related.

SET Verb Metalanguage

Figure 5-7 shows the metalanguage for the version of the SET verb that is used to set a condition name to true. When the SET verb is used to set a condition name, the first condition value specified after the VALUE clause in the definition is moved to the associated data item. So setting the condition name to true changes the value of the associated data item. This can lead to some interesting data-manipulation opportunities.

<u>SET</u> ConditionName ... <u>TO</u> <u>TRUE</u>

Figure 5-7. *Metalanguage for the SET verb condition name version*

In summary, any operation that changes the value of the data item may change the status of the associated condition names, and any operation that changes the status of a condition name will change the value of its associated data item.

SET Verb Examples

In ANS 85 COBOL, you cannot use the SET verb to set a condition name to false. But you can work around this restriction. Consider Example 5-9. This is more a pattern for processing sequential files than real COBOL code, but it serves to illustrate the point.

Example 5-9. Setting the EndOfFile Condition Name

```
01  EndOfFileFlag     PIC 9 VALUE ZERO.
    88 EndOfFile       VALUE 1.
    88 NotEndOfFile    VALUE 0.


    :   :  :  :  :  :  :  :

READ InFile
   AT END SET EndOfFile TO TRUE
END-READ
PERFORM UNTIL EndOfFile
   Process Record
   READ InFile
      AT END SET EndOfFile TO TRUE
   END-READ
END-PERFORM
Set NotEndOfFile TO TRUE.
```

In this example, the condition name EndOfFile has been set up to flag that the end of the file has been reached. You cannot set EndOfFile to false, but you can work around this problem by setting another condition name associated with the same data item to true. When EndOfFile is set to true, 1 is forced into the data item EndOfFileFlag, and this automatically sets NotEndOfFile to false. Similarly, when NotEndOfFile is set to true, 0 is forced into EndOfFileFlag, and this automatically sets EndOfFile to false.

Design Pattern: Reading a Sequential File

Because this is your first look at how COBOL processes sequential (as opposed to direct access) files, it might be useful to preview some of the material in Chapter 7 by providing a brief explanation now. The READ verb copies a record (a discrete package of data) from the file on backing storage and places it into an area of memory set up to store it. When the READ attempts to read a record from the file but discovers that the end of the file has been reached, it activates the AT END clause and executes whatever statements follow that clause.

Example 5-9 shows the pattern you generally use to process a stream of items when you can only discover that you have reached the end of the stream by attempting to read the next item. In this pattern, a loop processes the data in the stream. Outside the loop, you have a read to get the first item in the stream or to discover that the stream is empty. Inside the loop, you have statements to process the stream item and get the next item in the stream.

Why do you have this strange arrangement? The chief reason is that this arrangement allows you to place the read at the end of the loop body so that as soon as the end of the file is detected, the loop can be terminated. If you used a structure such as

```
PERFORM UNTIL EndOfFile
   READ InFile
      AT END SET EndOfFile TO TRUE
   END-READ
   Process Record
END-PERFORM
```

then when the end of file was detected, the program would still attempt to process the nonexistent record. Of course, the last valid record would still be in memory, so that last record would be processed twice. Many COBOL beginners make this programming error.

Many beginners attempt to solve this problem by only processing the record if the end of file has not been detected. They use a structure like this:

```
PERFORM UNTIL EndOfFile
    READ InFile
        AT END SET EndOfFile TO TRUE
    END-READ
    IF NOT EndOfFile
      Process Record
    END-IF
END-PERFORM
```

The problem with this arrangement is that the IF statement will be executed for every record in the file. Because COBOL often deals with very large data sets, this could amount to the execution of millions, maybe even hundreds of millions, of unnecessary statements. It is more elegant and more efficient to use what is called the *read-ahead* technique. The read-ahead has a read outside the loop to get the first record and a read inside the loop to get the remaining records. This approach has the added advantage of allowing the empty file condition to be detected before the loop is entered.

Group Item Condition Names

In Example 5-9, stand-alone condition names were used to flag the end-of-file condition. Because the EndOfFile condition name is closely related to the file, it would be better if the declaration of the condition name were kept with the file declaration. The example program in Listing 5-6 shows how that might be done. It also demonstrates how a condition name can be used with a group (as opposed to elementary) data item.

Listing 5-6. Reading a File and Setting the EndOfStudentFile Condition Name

```
IDENTIFICATION DIVISION.
PROGRAM-ID. Listing5-6.
AUTHOR. Michael Coughlan.
ENVIRONMENT DIVISION.
INPUT-OUTPUT SECTION.
FILE-CONTROL.
    SELECT StudentFile ASSIGN TO "Listing5-6-TData.Dat"
    ORGANIZATION IS LINE SEQUENTIAL.

DATA DIVISION.
FILE SECTION.
FD StudentFile.
01 StudentDetails.
    88  EndOfStudentFile  VALUE HIGH-VALUES.
    02  StudentId       PIC X(8).
    02  StudentName     PIC X(25).
    02  CourseCode      PIC X(5).

PROCEDURE DIVISION.
Begin.
    OPEN INPUT StudentFile
    READ StudentFile
        AT END SET EndOfStudentFile TO TRUE
    END-READ
```

Listing 5-6 Run	
Teresa Casey	08712351 LM042
Padraig Quinlan	08712352 LM051
Kevin Tucker	08712353 LM051
Maria Donovan	08712354 LM042
Liam Lorigan	98712355 LM110
Fiachra Luo	98712356 LM051

```
PERFORM UNTIL EndOfStudentFile
   DISPLAY StudentName SPACE StudentId SPACE CourseCode
   READ StudentFile
      AT END SET EndOfStudentFile TO TRUE
   END-READ
END-PERFORM
CLOSE StudentFile
STOP RUN.
```

In Listing 5-6, the condition name EndOfStudentFile is associated with the group item (which also happens to be a record) StudentDetails. When EndOfStudentFile is set to true, the entire StudentDetails area of storage (38 characters) is flushed with highest possible character value.

This arrangement has two major advantages:

- The EndOfStudentFile condition name is kept with its associated file.

- Flushing the record with HIGH-VALUES at the end of the file eliminates the need for an explicit condition when doing a key-matching update of a sequential file.

Condition Name Tricks

When you become aware that setting a condition name forces a value into the associated data item, it is tempting to see just how far you can take this idea. Listing 5-7 takes advantage of the way condition names work to automatically move an appropriate error message into a message buffer. The program is just a stub to test this error-messaging idea; it doesn't actually validate the date. Instead, the user manually enters one of the codes that would be returned by the date-validation routine.

Listing 5-7. Using Condition Names to Set Up a Date-Validation Error Message

```
IDENTIFICATION DIVISION.
PROGRAM-ID. Listing5-7.
AUTHOR. Michael Coughlan.

DATA DIVISION.
WORKING-STORAGE SECTION.
01 ValidationReturnCode  PIC 9.
   88 DateIsOK              VALUE 0.
   88 DateIsInvalid         VALUE 1 THRU 8.
   88 ValidCodeSupplied     VALUE 0 THRU 8.

01 DateErrorMessage       PIC X(35) VALUE SPACES.
   88 DateNotNumeric        VALUE "Error - The date must be numeric".
   88 YearIsZero            VALUE "Error - The year cannot be zero".
   88 MonthIsZero           VALUE "Error - The month cannot be zero".
   88 DayIsZero             VALUE "Error - The day cannot be zero".
   88 YearPassed            VALUE "Error - Year has already passed".
   88 MonthTooBig           VALUE "Error - Month is greater than 12".
   88 DayTooBig             VALUE "Error - Day greater than 31".
   88 TooBigForMonth        VALUE "Error - Day too big for this month".
```

```
PROCEDURE DIVISION.
Begin.
    PERFORM ValidateDate UNTIL ValidCodeSupplied
    EVALUATE ValidationReturnCode
        WHEN    0    SET DateIsOK       TO TRUE
        WHEN    1    SET DateNotNumeric TO TRUE
        WHEN    2    SET YearIsZero     TO TRUE
        WHEN    3    SET MonthIsZero    TO TRUE
        WHEN    4    SET DayIsZero      TO TRUE
        WHEN    5    SET YearPassed     TO TRUE
        WHEN    6    SET MonthTooBig    TO TRUE
        WHEN    7    SET DayTooBig      TO TRUE
        WHEN    8    SET TooBigForMonth TO TRUE
    END-EVALUATE

    IF DateIsInvalid THEN
        DISPLAY DateErrorMessage
    END-IF
    IF DateIsOK
        DISPLAY "Date is Ok"
    END-IF
    STOP RUN.

ValidateDate.
    DISPLAY "Enter a validation return code (0-8) " WITH NO ADVANCING
    ACCEPT ValidationReturnCode.
```

> Listing 5-7 Run1
>
> Enter a validation return code (0-8) 9
> Enter a validation return code (0-8) 0
> Date is Ok
>
> Listing 5-7 Run2
>
> Enter a validation return code (0-8) 6
> Error - Month is greater than 12
>
> Listing 5-7 Run3
>
> Enter a validation return code (0-8) 8
> Error - Day too big for this month

EVALUATE

In Listing 5-7, the EVALUATE verb is used to SET a particular condition name depending on the value in the ValidationReturnCode data item. You probably did not have much difficulty working out what the EVALUATE statement is doing because it has echoes of how the switch/case statement works in other languages. Ruby programmers, with their when-branched case statement, were probably particularly at home. But the resemblance of EVALUATE to the case/switch used in other languages is superficial. EVALUATE is far more powerful than these constructs. Even when restricted to one subject, EVALUATE is more powerful because it is not limited to ordinal types. When used with multiple subjects, EVALUATE is a significantly more powerful construct. One common use for the multiple-subject EVALUATE is the implementation of decision-table logic.

Decision Tables

A *decision table* is a way to model complicated logic in a tabular form. Decision tables are often used by systems analysts to express business rules that would be too complicated and/or too confusing to express in a textual form.

For instance, suppose an amusement park charges different admission fees depending on the age and height of visitors, according to the following rules:

- If the person is younger than 4 years old, admission is free.

- If the person is between 4 and 7, admission is $10.

- If between 8 and 12, admission is $15.

- If between 13 and 64, admission is $25.

- If 65 or older, admission is $10.

- In addition, in view of the height restrictions on many rides, persons shorter than 48 inches who are between the ages of 8 and 64 receive a discount. Persons between 8 and 12 are charged a $10 admission fee, whereas those between the ages of 13 and 64 are charged $18.

You can represent this textual specification using the decision table in Table 5-8.

Table 5-8. *Amusement Park Decision Table*

Age	Height in inches	Admission
< 4	NA	$0
4 - 7	NA	$10
8 - 12	Height >= 48	$15
8 - 12	Height < 48	$10
13 - 64	Height >= 48 inches	$25
13 - 64	Height < 48	$18
>= 65	NA	$10

EVALUATE Metalanguage

The EVALUATE metalanguage (see Figure 5-8) looks very complex but is actually fairly easy to understand. It is, though, somewhat difficult to explain in words, so I mainly use examples to explain how it works.

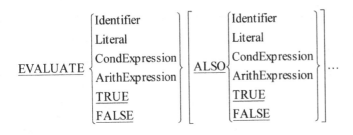

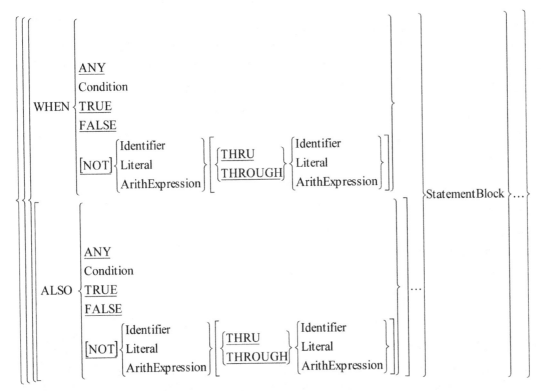

[WHEN OTHER StatementBlock]

END - EVALUATE

Figure 5-8. *Metalanguage for the EVALUATE verb*

Notes

The following are the WHEN branch rules:

- Only one WHEN branch is chosen per execution of EVALUATE.

- The order of the WHEN branches is important because checking of the branches is done from top to bottom.

- If any WHEN branch is chosen, the EVALUATE ends. The break required in other languages to stop execution of the remaining branches is not required in COBOL.

- If none of the WHEN branches can be chosen, the WHEN OTHER branch (if it exists) is executed.

- If none of the WHEN branches can be chosen, and there is no WHEN OTHER phrase, the EVALUATE simply terminates.

The items immediately after the word EVALUATE and before the first WHEN are called *subjects*. The items between the WHEN and its statement block are called *objects*.

The number of subjects must equal the number of objects, and the objects must be compatible with the subjects. For instance, if the subject is a condition, then the object must be either TRUE or FALSE. If the subject is a data item, then the object must be either a literal value or a data item.

Table 5-9 lists the combinations you may have. If there are four subjects, then each WHEN branch must list four objects. If the value of a particular object does not matter, the keyword ANY may be used.

Table 5-9. *EVALUATE Subject/Object Combinations*

	Subject 1		**Subject 2**		**Subject 3**		**Subject 4**	**Action**
EVALUATE	Condition	ALSO	True False	ALSO	Identifier	ALSO	Literal	Statement Block
WHEN	True False	ALSO	Condition	ALSO	Literal	ALSO	Identifier	Statement Block
WHEN	ANY	ALSO	ANY	ALSO	Identifier	ALSO	Literal	Statement Block
WHEN	OTHER							Statement Block
END-EVALUATE	**Object 1**		**Object 2**		**Object 3**		**Object 4**	

EVALUATE Examples

This section looks at three examples of the EVALUATE verb.

Payment Totals Example

Shoppers choose the method of payment as Visa, MasterCard, American Express, Check, or Cash. A program totals the amount paid by each payment method. After a sale, the sale value is added to the appropriate total. Condition names (ByVisa, ByMasterCard, ByAmericanExpress, ByCheck, ByCash) have been set up for each of the payment methods.

You could code this as follows:

```
IF ByVisa ADD SaleValue TO VisaTotal
    ELSE
      IF ByMasterCard ADD SaleValue TO MasterCardTotal
        ELSE
          IF ByAmericanExpress ADD SaleValue TO AmericanExpressTotal
            ELSE
              IF ByCheck ADD SaleValue TO CheckTotal
                ELSE
                  IF ByCash ADD SaleValue TO CashTotal
                  END-IF
              END-IF
          END-IF
      END-IF
END-IF
```

You can replace these nested IF statements with the neater and easier-to-understand EVALUATE statement:

```
EVALUATE TRUE
    WHEN ByVisa            ADD SaleValue TO VisaTotal
    WHEN ByMasterCard      ADD SaleValue TO MasterCardTotal
    WHEN ByAmericanExpress ADD SaleValue TO AmericanExpressTotal
    WHEN ByCheck           ADD SaleValue TO CheckTotal
    WHEN ByCash            ADD SaleValue TO CashTotal
END-EVALUATE
```

In this example, the objects must all be either conditions or condition names, because the subject is TRUE.

Amusement Park Example

EVALUATE can be used to encode a decision table. Listing 5-8 shows how the Amusement Park decision table from Table 5-8 might be encoded.

Listing 5-8. Amusement Park Admission

```
IDENTIFICATION DIVISION.
PROGRAM-ID. Listing5-8.
DATA DIVISION.
WORKING-STORAGE SECTION.
01 Age            PIC 99 VALUE ZERO.
    88 Infant      VALUE 0 THRU 3.
    88 YoungChild  VALUE 4 THRU 7.
    88 Child       VALUE 8 THRU 12.
    88 Visitor     VALUE 13 THRU 64.
    88 Pensioner   VALUE 65 THRU 99.
```

```
01 Height          PIC 999 VALUE ZERO.

01 Admission       PIC $99.99.

PROCEDURE DIVISION.
Begin.
   DISPLAY "Enter age    :- " WITH NO ADVANCING
   ACCEPT Age
   DISPLAY "Enter height :- " WITH NO ADVANCING
   ACCEPT Height

   EVALUATE TRUE        ALSO        TRUE
     WHEN   Infant      ALSO        ANY           MOVE 0  TO Admission
     WHEN   YoungChild  ALSO        ANY           MOVE 10 TO Admission
     WHEN   Child       ALSO    Height >= 48      MOVE 15 TO Admission
     WHEN   Child       ALSO    Height < 48       MOVE 10 TO Admission
     WHEN   Visitor     ALSO    Height >= 48      MOVE 25 TO Admission
     WHEN   Visitor     ALSO    Height < 48       MOVE 18 TO Admission
     WHEN   Pensioner   ALSO        ANY           MOVE 10 TO Admission
   END-EVALUATE

   DISPLAY "Admission charged is " Admission
   STOP RUN.
```

> Listing 5-8 Run1
>
> Enter age   :- 7
> Enter height :- 45
> Admission charged is $10.00
>
> Listing 5-8 Run2
>
> Enter age   :- 9
> Enter height :- 52
> Admission charged is $15.00
>
> Listing 5-8 Run3
>
> Enter age   :- 9
> Enter height :- 45
> Admission charged is $10.00
>
> Listing 5-8 Run4
>
> Enter age   :- 31
> Enter height :- 47

Acme Book Club Example

The Acme Book Club is the largest online book club in the world. The book club sells books to both members and non-members all over the world. For each order, Acme applies a percentage discount based on the quantity of books in the current order, the value of books purchased in the last three months (last quarter), and whether the customer is a member of the Book Club.

Acme uses the decision table in Table 5-10 to decide what discount to apply. Listing 5-9 is a small test program that uses EVALUATE to implement the decision table.

Table 5-10. *Acme Book Club Discount Decision Table*

QtyOfBooks	QuarterlyPurchases (QP)	ClubMember	% Discount
1–5	< 500	ANY	0
1–5	< 2000	Y	7
1–5	< 2000	N	5
1–5	>= 2000	Y	10
1–5	>= 2000	N	8
6–20	< 500	Y	3
6–20	< 500	N	2
6–20	< 2000	Y	12
6–20	< 2000	N	10
6–20	>= 2000	Y	25
6–20	>= 2000	N	15
21–99	< 500	Y	5
21–99	< 500	N	3
21–99	< 2000	Y	16
21–99	< 2000	N	15
21–99	>= 2000	Y	30
21–99	>= 2000	N	20

Listing 5-9. *Acme Book Club Example*

```
IDENTIFICATION DIVISION.
PROGRAM-ID. Listing5-9.
AUTHOR. Michael Coughlan.
DATA DIVISION.
WORKING-STORAGE SECTION.
01 Member          PIC X VALUE SPACE.

01 QP              PIC 9(5) VALUE ZEROS.
*> QuarterlyPurchases

01 Qty             PIC 99 VALUE ZEROS.

01 Discount        PIC 99 VALUE ZEROS.

PROCEDURE DIVISION.
Begin.
    DISPLAY "Enter value of QuarterlyPurchases - " WITH NO ADVANCING
    ACCEPT QP
    DISPLAY "Enter qty of books purchased - " WITH NO ADVANCING
    ACCEPT Qty
```

```
DISPLAY "club member enter Y or N - " WITH NO ADVANCING
ACCEPT Member

EVALUATE Qty        ALSO    TRUE     ALSO Member
  WHEN  1 THRU 5  ALSO QP <   500  ALSO ANY  MOVE 0  TO Discount
  WHEN  1 THRU 5  ALSO QP <  2000  ALSO "Y"  MOVE 7  TO Discount
  WHEN  1 THRU 5  ALSO QP <  2000  ALSO "N"  MOVE 5  TO Discount
  WHEN  1 THRU 5  ALSO QP >= 2000  ALSO "Y"  MOVE 10 TO Discount
  WHEN  1 THRU 5  ALSO QP >= 2000  ALSO "N"  MOVE 8  TO Discount

  WHEN  6 THRU 20 ALSO QP <   500  ALSO "Y"  MOVE 3  TO Discount
  WHEN  6 THRU 20 ALSO QP <   500  ALSO "N"  MOVE 2  TO Discount
  WHEN  6 THRU 20 ALSO QP <  2000  ALSO "Y"  MOVE 12 TO Discount
  WHEN  6 THRU 20 ALSO QP <  2000  ALSO "N"  MOVE 10 TO Discount
  WHEN  6 THRU 20 ALSO QP >= 2000  ALSO "Y"  MOVE 25 TO Discount
  WHEN  6 THRU 20 ALSO QP >= 2000  ALSO "N"  MOVE 15 TO Discount

  WHEN 21 THRU 99 ALSO QP <   500  ALSO "Y"  MOVE 5  TO Discount
  WHEN 21 THRU 99 ALSO QP <   500  ALSO "N"  MOVE 3  TO Discount
  WHEN 21 THRU 99 ALSO QP <  2000  ALSO "Y"  MOVE 16 TO Discount
  WHEN 21 THRU 99 ALSO QP <  2000  ALSO "N"  MOVE 15 TO Discount
  WHEN 21 THRU 99 ALSO QP >= 2000  ALSO "Y"  MOVE 30 TO Discount
  WHEN 21 THRU 99 ALSO QP >= 2000  ALSO "N"  MOVE 20 TO Discount
END-EVALUATE
DISPLAY "Discount = " Discount "%"
STOP RUN.
```

Listing 5-9 Run 1

Enter value of QuarterlyPurchases - 545
Enter qty of books purchased - 14
club member enter Y or N - Y
Discount = 12%

Listing 5-9 Run 2

Enter value of QuarterlyPurchases - 2534
Enter qty of books purchased - 14
club member enter Y or N - Y
Discount = 25%

Listing 5-9 Run 3

Enter value of QuarterlyPurchases - 2534
Enter qty of books purchased - 23
club member enter Y or N - Y
Discount = 30%

Summary

The three classic constructs of structured programming are sequence, selection, and iteration. You have already noted that a COBOL program starts execution with the first statement in the PROCEDURE DIVISION and then continues to execute the statements one after another in sequence until the STOP RUN or the end-of-the-program text is encountered, unless some other statement changes the order of execution. In this chapter, you examined the IF and EVALUATE statements. These statements allow a program to selectively execute program statements. In the next chapter, you discover how iteration, the final classic construct, is implemented in COBOL.

References

1. Tompkins HE. In defense of teaching structured COBOL as computer science (or, notes on being sage struck). ACM SIGPLAN Notices. 1983; 18(4): 86-94.

2. Baldwin RR. A note on H.E. Tompkins's minimum-period COBOL style. ACM SIGPLAN Notices. 1987; 22(5): 27-31. http://doi.acm.org/10.1145/25267.25273

    doi: 10.1145/25267.25273

LANGUAGE KNOWLEDGE EXERCISES

Getting out your 2B pencil once more, write answers to the following questions.

1. For each of the following condition names, which do you consider to be inappropriately named? Suggest more suitable names for these only.

   ```
   01 Country-Code        PIC XX.
      88 Code-Is-US        VALUE "US".
   ```

   _____

   ```
   01 Operating-System    PIC X(15).
      88 Windows-Or-UNIX   VALUE "WINDOWS".
   ```

   _____

   ```
   01 Room-Type           PIC X(20).
      88 Double-Room       VALUE "DOUBLE".
   ```

   _____

   ```
      88 Single-Room       VALUE "SINGLE".
   ```

   _____

2. Write an IF statement that uses the SET verb to manually set the condition name InvalidCode to true if DeptCode contains anything except 1, 6, or 8.

   _____

   _____

   _____

   _____

   _____

   _____

3. Assume the variable DeptCode in question 2 is described as

   ```
   01    DeptCode          PIC 9.
   ```

   _____

   Write a level 88 condition name called InvalidCode that is automatically set to true when the statement ACCEPT DeptCode accepts any value other than 1, 6, or 8.

4. In each of the following five groups of skeleton IF statements, state whether the statements in each group have the same effect (in the sense that they evaluate to true or false). Answer yes or no.

Do these statements have the same effect?   Answer

```
IF Num1 = 1 OR Num1 NOT = 1...
IF NOT (Num1 = 1 AND Num1 = 2) ...

IF TransCode IS NOT = 3 OR Total NOT > 2550  ...
IF NOT (TransCode IS = 3 OR Total > 2550) ...

IF Num1 = 31 OR Num2 = 12 AND Num3 = 23 OR Num4 = 6 ...
IF (Num1 = 31 OR (Num2 = 12 AND Num3 = 23)) OR Num4 = 6 ...

IF Num1 = 15 OR Num1 = 12 OR Num1 = 7 AND City = "Cork" ...
IF (Num1 = 15 OR Num1 = 12 OR Num1 = 7) AND City = "Cork" ...

IF (Num1 = 1 OR Num1 = 2) AND (Num2 = 6 OR Num2 = 8) ...
IF Num1 = 1 OR Num1 = 2 AND Num2 = 6 OR Num2 =  8 ...
```

5. Write an EVALUATE statement to implement the decision part of a game of rock, paper, scissors. Most of the program has been written for you. Just complete the EVALUATE. ADD a WHEN OTHER branch to the EVALUATE to detect when a player enters a code other than 1, 2, or 3.

```
IDENTIFICATION DIVISION.
PROGRAM-ID. Listing5-10.
AUTHOR. Michael Coughlan.
DATA DIVISION.
WORKING-STORAGE SECTION.
01 PlayerGuess-A    PIC 9  VALUE 1.
   88 Rock-A        VALUE 1.
   88 Paper-A       VALUE 2.
   88 Scissors-A    VALUE 3.

01 PlayerGuess-B    PIC 9  VALUE 2.
   88 Rock-B        VALUE 1.
   88 Paper-B       VALUE 2.
   88 Scissors-B    VALUE 3.

PROCEDURE DIVISION.
BEGIN.
    DISPLAY "Guess for player A (1=rock, 2=scissors, 3=paper) : "
            WITH NO ADVANCING
    ACCEPT PlayerGuess-A
    DISPLAY "Guess for player B (1=rock, 2=scissors, 3=paper) : "
            WITH NO ADVANCING
    ACCEPT PlayerGuess-B
```

EVALUATE _____

_____

_____

_____

_____

_____

_____

_____

_____

_____

_____

_____

_____

_____

PROGRAMMING EXERCISE

Listing 4-2 is a program that accepts two numbers from the user, multiplies them together, and then displays the result. Modify the program so that

- It also accepts an operator symbol (+ - / *).

- It uses EVALUATE to discover which operator has been entered and to apply that operator to the two numbers entered.

- It uses the condition name ValidOperator to identify the valid operators and only displays the result if the operator entered is valid.

- The Result data item is changed to accommodate the possibility that subtraction may result in a negative value.

- The Result data item is changed to accommodate the decimal fractions that may result from division. The result data item should be able to accept values with up to two decimal places (for example, 00.43 or 00.74).

LANGUAGE KNOWLEDGE EXERCISES—ANSWERS

1. For each of the following condition names, which do you consider to be inappropriately named? Suggest more suitable names for these only.

```
01 Country-Code        PIC XX.
   88 UnitedStates     VALUE "US".
* Change
* Example of use  - IF UnitedStates DISPLAY "We are in America" END-IF


01 Operating-System    PIC X(15).
   88 Windows          VALUE " WINDOWS".
* Change
* Example of use  - IF Windows DISPLAY "Windows is best" END-IF

01 Room-Type           PIC X(20).
   88 Double-Room      VALUE "DOUBLE".
   88 Single-Room      VALUE "SINGLE".
* No change.
* Example of use -IF Double-Room ADD DoubleRoomSurchage TO RoomRent END-IF
```

2. Write an IF statement that uses the SET verb to manually set the condition name InvalidCode to true if DeptCode contains anything except 1, 6, or 8.

```
IF NOT (DeptCode = 1 OR DeptCode = 6 OR DeptCode = 8) THEN
    SET InvalidCode TO TRUE
END-IF.
```

Or, using implied subjects:

```
IF NOT (DeptCode = 1 OR 6 OR 8) THEN
    SET InvalidCode TO TRUE
END-IF.
```

3. Assume the variable DeptCode in question 2 is described as

```
01 DeptCode        PIC 9.
   88 InvalidCode  VALUE 0, 2 THRU 5,7,9.
```

Write a level 88 condition name called InvalidCode that is automatically set to true when the statement ACCEPT DeptCode accepts any value other than 1, 6, or 8.

4.   In each of the following five groups of skeleton IF statements, state whether the statements in each group have the same effect (in the sense that they evaluate to true or false). Answer yes or no.

Do these statements have the same effect?	Answer
IF Num1 = 1 OR Num1 NOT = 1... IF NOT (Num1 = 1 AND Num1 = 2)...	**YES** In the sense that they are both always true.
IF TransCode IS NOT = 3 OR Total NOT > 2550 ... IF NOT (TransCode IS = 3 OR Total > 2550)...	**NO**
IF Num1 = 31 OR Num2 = 12 AND Num3 = 23 OR Num4 = 6... IF (Num1 = 31 OR (Num2 = 12 AND Num3 = 23)) OR Num4 = 6...	**YES** The brackets only make explicit what is ordained by the precedence rules.
IF Num1 = 15 OR Num1 = 12 OR Num1 = 7 AND City = "Cork"... IF (Num1 = 15 OR Num1 = 12 OR Num1 = 7) AND City = "Cork"...	**NO** In the first Num1=7 AND City=SPACES are ANDed together but in the second City="Cork" is ANDed with the result of the expression in the parentheses
IF (Num1 = 1 OR Num1 = 2) AND (Num2 = 6 OR Num2 = 8) ... IF Num1 = 1 OR Num1 = 2 AND Num2 = 6 OR Num2 = 8 ...	**NO**

5.   Write an EVALUATE statement to implement the decision part of a game of rock, paper, scissors. Most of the program has been written for you. Just complete the EVALUATE. ADD a WHEN OTHER branch to the EVALUATE to detect when a player enters a code other than 1, 2, or 3.

Listing 5-10. Rock, Paper, Scissors Game

```
IDENTIFICATION DIVISION.
PROGRAM-ID. Listing5-10.
AUTHOR. Michael Coughlan.
DATA DIVISION.
WORKING-STORAGE SECTION.
    01 PlayerGuess-A    PIC 9  VALUE 1.
        88 Rock-A         VALUE 1.
        88 Paper-A        VALUE 2.
        88 Scissors-A     VALUE 3.

    01 PlayerGuess-B    PIC 9  VALUE 2.
        88 Rock-B         VALUE 1.
        88 Paper-B        VALUE 2.
        88 Scissors-B     VALUE 3.
```

Listing 5-10 Run1

Guess for player A (1=rock, 2=scissors, 3=paper): 1
Guess for player B (1=rock, 2=scissors, 3=paper): 3
Player A wins

Listing 5-10 Run2

Guess for player A (1=rock, 2=scissors, 3=paper): 1
Guess for player B (1=rock, 2=scissors, 3=paper): 2
Player B wins

Listing 5-10 Run3

Guess for player A (1=rock, 2=scissors, 3=paper): 1
Guess for player B (1=rock, 2=scissors, 3=paper): 1
Draw

```
PROCEDURE DIVISION.
BEGIN.
   DISPLAY "Guess for player A (1=rock, 2=scissors, 3=paper) : "
          WITH NO ADVANCING
   ACCEPT PlayerGuess-A
   DISPLAY "Guess for player B (1=rock, 2=scissors, 3=paper) : "
          WITH NO ADVANCING
   ACCEPT PlayerGuess-B
   EVALUATE  TRUE        ALSO       TRUE
      WHEN Rock-A        ALSO    Rock-B        DISPLAY "Draw"
      WHEN Rock-A        ALSO    Paper-B       DISPLAY "Player B wins"
      WHEN Rock-A        ALSO    Scissors-B    DISPLAY "Player A wins"
      WHEN Paper-A       ALSO    Rock-B        DISPLAY "Player A wins"
      WHEN Paper-A       ALSO    Paper-B       DISPLAY "Draw"
      WHEN Paper-A       ALSO    Scissors-B    DISPLAY "Player B wins"
      WHEN Scissors-A  ALSO      Rock-B        DISPLAY "Player B wins"
      WHEN Scissors-A  ALSO      Paper-B       DISPLAY "Player A wins"
      WHEN Scissors-A  ALSO      Scissors-B  DISPLAY "Draw"
      WHEN OTHER   DISPLAY "Evaluate problem"
   END-EVALUATE
   STOP RUN.
```

PROGRAMMING EXERCISE ANSWER

Listing 5-11. Simple Calculator

```
IDENTIFICATION DIVISION.
PROGRAM-ID.  Listing5-11.
AUTHOR.  Michael Coughlan.
*> Accepts two numbers and an operator from the user.
*> Applies the appropriate operation to the two numbers.

DATA DIVISION.
WORKING-STORAGE SECTION.
01  Num1        PIC 9  VALUE 7.
01  Num2        PIC 9  VALUE 3.
01  Result      PIC --9.99 VALUE ZEROS.
01  Operator    PIC X  VALUE "-".
    88 ValidOperator   VALUES "*", "+", "-", "/".

PROCEDURE DIVISION.
CalculateResult.
    DISPLAY "Enter a single digit number : " WITH NO ADVANCING
    ACCEPT Num1
    DISPLAY "Enter a single digit number : " WITH NO ADVANCING
```

```
ACCEPT Num2
DISPLAY "Enter the operator to be applied : " WITH NO ADVANCING
ACCEPT Operator    EVALUATE Operator
   WHEN "+"    ADD Num2 TO Num1 GIVING Result
   WHEN "-"    SUBTRACT Num2 FROM Num1 GIVING Result
   WHEN "*"    MULTIPLY Num2 BY Num1 GIVING Result
   WHEN "/"    DIVIDE Num1 BY Num2 GIVING Result ROUNDED
   WHEN OTHER DISPLAY "Invalid operator entered"
END-EVALUATE
IF ValidOperator
   DISPLAY "Result is = ", Result
END-IF
STOP RUN.
```

Listing 5-11 Run1

Enter a single digit number : 5
Enter a single digit number : 3
Enter the operator to be applied : /
Result is = 1.67

Listing 5-11 Run2

Enter a single digit number : 5
Enter a single digit number : 3
Enter the operator to be applied : -
Result is = 2.00

Listing 5-11 Run3

Enter a single digit number : 3
Enter a single digit number : 5
Enter the operator to be applied : -
Result is = -2.00

CHAPTER 6

Control Structures: Iteration

The previous chapter dealt with COBOL's selection constructs: IF and EVALUATE. In this chapter, you examine the last of the classic structured programming constructs: iteration.

In almost every programming job, there is some task that needs to be done over and over again. The job of processing a file of records is an iteration of this task: get and process record. The job of getting the sum of a stream of numbers is an iteration of this task: get and add number. The job of searching through an array for a particular value is an iteration of this task: get next element and check element value. These jobs are accomplished using iteration constructs.

Other languages support a variety of iteration constructs, each designed to achieve different things. In Modula-2 and Pascal, While..DO and Repeat..Until implement pre-test and post-test iteration. The for loop is used for counting iteration. The many C-language derivatives use while and do..while for pre-test and post-test iteration, and again the for loop is used for counting iteration.

COBOL supports all these different kinds of iteration, but it has only one iteration construct: the PERFORM verb (see Table 6-1). Pre-test and post-test iteration are supported by PERFORM WITH TEST BEFORE and PERFORM WITH TEST AFTER. Counting iteration is supported by PERFORM..VARYING. COBOL even has variations that are not found in other languages. PERFORM..VARYING, for instance, can take more than one counter, and it has both pre-test and post-test variations. Whereas in most languages the loop target is an inline block of code, in COBOL it can be either an inline block or a named out-of-line block of code.

***Table 6-1.** Iteration Constructs and Their COBOL Equivalents*

	C, C++, Java	Modula-2, Pascal	COBOL
Pre-test	while {}	While..DO	PERFORM WITH TEST BEFORE UNTIL
Post-test	do {} while	Repeat..Until	PERFORM WITH TEST AFTER UNTIL
Counting	for	For..DO	PERFORM..VARYING..UNTIL

Paragraphs Revisited

In the PROCEDURE DIVISION, a paragraph is a block of code to which you have given a name. A paragraph begins with the paragraph name (see Example 6-1) and ends when the next paragraph or section name is encountered or when the end of the program text is reached. The paragraph name must *always* be terminated with a period (full stop).

There may be any number of statements and sentences in a paragraph; but there must be at least one sentence, and the last statement in the paragraph must be terminated with a period. In fact, as I mentioned in the previous chapter, there is a style of COBOL programming called the *minimum-period* style[1,2], which you should adopt. This style suggests that there should be only one period in the paragraph. It is particularly important to adhere to this style when coding inline loops, because a period has the effect of delimiting the scope of an inline PERFORM.

Example 6-1. Two Paragraphs: `ProcessRecord` Ends Where `ProcessOutput` Begins

```
ProcessRecord.
    DISPLAY StudentRecord
    READ StudentFile
        AT END MOVE HIGH-VALUES TO StudentRecord
    END-READ.

ProduceOutput.
    DISPLAY "Here is a message".
```

The PERFORM Verb

Unless it is instructed otherwise, a computer running a COBOL program processes the statements in sequence, starting at the first statement of the PROCEDURE DIVISION and working its way down through the program until the STOP RUN, or the end of the program text, is reached. The PERFORM verb is one way of altering the sequential flow of control in a COBOL program. The PERFORM verb can be used for two major purposes;

- To transfer control to a designated block of code

- To execute a block of code iteratively

Whereas the other formats of the PERFORM verb implement iteration of one sort or another, this first format is used to transfer control to an out-of-line block of code—that is, to execute an open subroutine. You have probably have come across the idea of a subroutine before. A *subroutine* is a block of code that is executed when invoked by name. Methods, procedures, and functions are subroutines. You may not have realized that there are two types of subroutine:

- Open subroutines

- Closed subroutines

If you have learned BASIC, you may be familiar with open subroutines. If you learned C, Modula-2, or Java, you are probably familiar with closed subroutines.

Open Subroutines

An *open* subroutine is a named block of code that control (by which I mean program statement execution) can fall into, or through. An open subroutine has access to all the data items declared in the main program, and it cannot declare any local data items.

Although an open subroutine is normally executed by invoking it by name, it is also possible, unless you are careful, to fall into it from the main program. In BASIC, the GOSUB and RETURN commands allow you to implement open subroutines. Example 6-2 is a short BASIC program that illustrates the fall-through problem. Two outputs are provided: one where the EXIT statement prevents fall-through and the other where control falls through into OpenSub because the EXIT statement has been removed.

Example 6-2. Open Subroutine in Yabasic[3] Showing Output With and Without the EXIT Statement

```
REM Demonstrates Open subroutines in Yabasic
REM When the EXIT is removed, control falls
REM through into OpenSub
REM Author. Michael Coughlan
PRINT "In main"
GOSUB OpenSub
PRINT "Back in main"
EXIT

LABEL OpenSub
  PRINT "In OpenSub"
  RETURN
```

Output - with EXIT removed

Executing the program....
$yabasic main.bas In main
In OpenSub
Back in main
In OpenSub
yabasic: main.bas:9: RETURN without GOSUB

Output - with EXIT in place

Executing the program....
$yabasic main.bas
In main
In OpenSub
Back in main

In some legacy COBOL programs, falling through the program from paragraph to paragraph is a deliberate strategy. In this scheme, which has been called *gravity-driven programming*, control falls through the program until it encounters an IF and GO TO combination that drives it to a paragraph in the code above it; after that, control starts to fall through the program again. Example 6-3 provides an outline of how such a program works (P1, P2, P3, and P4 are paragraph names).

Example 6-3. Model for a Gravity-Driven COBOL Program

```
P1.
  statement
  statement
  statement

P2.
  statement
  statement

P3.
  statement
  IF cond GO TO P2
  statement
  statement
  IF cond GO TO  P3

P4.
  statement
  IF cond GO TO P2
  statement
  statement
  STOP RUN
```

Closed Subroutines

A *closed* subroutine is a named block of code that can *only* be executed by invoking it by name. Control cannot "fall into" a closed subroutine. A closed subroutine can usually declare its own local data, and that data cannot be accessed outside the subroutine. Data in the main program can be passed to the subroutine by means of parameters specified when the subroutine is invoked. In C and Modula-2, procedures and functions implement closed subroutines. In Java, methods are used.

COBOL Subroutines

COBOL supports both open and closed subroutines. Open subroutines are implemented using the first format of the PERFORM verb. Closed subroutines are implemented using the CALL verb and contained or external subprograms. You learn about contained and external subprograms later in the book.

■ **ISO 2002**   ISO 2002 COBOL provides additional support for closed subroutines in the form of methods. Methods in COBOL bear a very strong syntactic resemblance to contained subprograms.

Why Use Open Subroutines?

The open subroutines represented by paragraphs (and sections) are used to make programs more readable and maintainable. Although PERFORMed paragraphs are not as robust as the user-defined procedures or functions found in other languages, they are still useful. They allow you to partition code into a hierarchy of named tasks and subtasks without the formality or overhead involved in coding a procedure or function. COBOL programmers who require the protection of that kind of formal partitioning can use contained or external subprograms.

Partitioning a task into subtasks makes each subtask more manageable; and using meaningful names for the subtasks effectively allows you to document in code what the program is doing. For instance, a block of code that prints report headings can be removed to a paragraph called PrintReportHeadings. The details of *how* the task is being accomplished can be replaced with a name that indicates *what* is being done.

Consider the partitioning and documentation benefits provided by the program skeleton in Example 6-4. The skeleton contains no real code (only PERFORMs and paragraph names), but the hierarchy of named tasks and subtasks allows you to understand that the program reads through a file containing sales records for various shops and for each shop prints a line on the report that summarizes the sales for that shop.

Example 6-4. Program Skeleton

```
PrintSummarySalesReport.
    PERFORM PrintReportHeadings
    PERFORM PrintSummaryBody UNTIL EndOfFile
    PERFORM PrintFinalTotals
    STOP RUN.

PrintSummaryBody.
    PERFORM SummarizeShopSales
            UNTIL ShopId <> PreviousShopId
                OR EndOfFile
    PERFORM PrintShopSummary

SummarizeShopSales.
    Statements
```

```
PrintReportHeadings.
   Statements

PrintShopSummary.
   Statements

PrintFinalTotals.
   Statements
```

Obviously, it is possible to take partitioning to an extreme. You should try to achieve a balance between making the program too fragmented and too monolithic. As a rule of thumb, there should be a good reason for creating a paragraph that contains five statements or fewer.

PERFORM NamedBlock

This first format of the PERFORM (see Figure 6-1) is not an iteration construct. It simply instructs the computer to transfer control to an out-of-line block of code (that is, an open subroutine). The block of code may be a paragraph or a section. When the end of the block is reached, control reverts to the statement (not the sentence) immediately following the PERFORM.

$$\underline{\text{PERFORM}}\left[\text{StartblockName}\left[\left\{\begin{matrix}\underline{\text{THRU}}\\\underline{\text{THROUGH}}\end{matrix}\right\}\text{EndblockName}\right]\right]$$

Figure 6-1. *Metalanguage for PERFORM format 1*

In Figure 6-1, StartblockName and EndblockName are the names of paragraphs or sections. PERFORM..THRU instructs the computer to treat the paragraphs or sections from StartblockName TO EndblockName as a single block of code.

PERFORM s can be nested. A PERFORM may execute a paragraph that contains another PERFORM, but neither direct nor indirect recursion is allowed. Unfortunately, this restriction is not enforced by the compiler, so a syntax error does not result; but your program will not work correctly if you use recursive PERFORMs.

The order of execution of the paragraphs is independent of their physical placement. It does not matter where you put the paragraphs—the PERFORM will find and execute them.

How PERFORM Works

Listing 6-1 shows a short COBOL program that demonstrates how PERFORM works. The program executes as follows:

1. Control starts in paragraph LevelOne, and the message "Starting to run program" is displayed.

2. When PERFORM LevelTwo is executed, control is passed to LevelTwo and the statements in that paragraph start to execute.

3. When PERFORM LevelThree is executed, control passes to LevelThree. When PERFORM LevelFour is executed, the message "Now in LevelFour" is displayed.

4. When the end of LevelFour is reached, *control returns to the statement following the* PERFORM *that invoked it*, and the message "Back in LevelThree" is displayed.

5. When LevelThree ends, control returns to the statement following the PERFORM, and the message "Back in LevelTwo" is displayed. Finally, when LevelTwo ends, control returns to paragraph LevelOne, and the "Back in LevelOne" message is displayed.

6. When STOP RUN is reached, the program stops.

Notice that the order of paragraph execution is independent of physical placement. For instance, although the paragraph LevelTwo comes after LevelThree and LevelFour in the program text, it is executed before them.

As I mentioned earlier, although PERFORMs can be nested, neither direct nor indirect recursion is allowed. So it would not be valid for paragraph LevelThree to contain the statement PERFORM LevelThree. This would be direct recursion. Neither would it be valid for LevelTwo to contain the statement PERFORM LevelOne. This would be indirect recursion because LevelOne contains the instruction PERFORM LevelTwo.

A frequent mistake made by beginning COBOL programmers is to forget to include STOP RUN at the end of the first paragraph. Example 6-5 shows the output that would be produced by Listing 6-1 if you forgot to include STOP RUN. From the output produced, try to follow the order of execution of the paragraphs.

Example 6-5. Output when STOP RUN is missing

```
>  Starting to run program
>  >  Now in LevelTwo
>  >  >  Now in LevelThree
>  >  >  >  Now in LevelFour
>  >  >  Back in LevelThree
>  >  Back in LevelTwo
>  Back in LevelOne
>  >  >  >  Now in LevelFour
>  >  >  Now in LevelThree
>  >  >  >  Now in LevelFour
>  >  >  Back in LevelThree
>  >  Now in LevelTwo
>  >  >  Now in LevelThree
>  >  >  >  Now in LevelFour
>  >  >  Back in LevelThree
>  >  Back in LevelTwo
```

Listing 6-1. Demonstrates How PERFORM Works

```
IDENTIFICATION DIVISION.
PROGRAM-ID. Listing6-1.
AUTHOR. Michael Coughlan.
PROCEDURE DIVISION.
LevelOne.
    DISPLAY "> Starting to run program"
    PERFORM LevelTwo
    DISPLAY "> Back in LevelOne"
    STOP RUN.

LevelFour.
    DISPLAY "> > > > Now in LevelFour".

LevelThree.
```

Program Output

> Starting to run program
> > Now in LevelTwo
> > > Now in LevelThree
> > > > Now in LevelFour
> > > Back in LevelThree
> > Back in LevelTwo
> Back in LevelOne

```
   DISPLAY "> > > Now in LevelThree"
   PERFORM LevelFour
   DISPLAY "> > > Back in LevelThree".

LevelTwo.
   DISPLAY "> > Now in LevelTwo"
   PERFORM LevelThree
   DISPLAY "> > Back in LevelTwo".
```

PERFORM..THRU Dangers

One variation that exists in all the PERFORM formats is PERFORM..THRU. When you use PERFORM..THRU, all the code from StartblockName to EndblockName is treated as a single block of code. Because PERFORM..THRU is generally regarded as a dangerous construct, it should only be used to PERFORM a paragraph and its immediately succeeding paragraph exit.

The problem with using PERFORM..THRU to execute a number of paragraphs as one unit is that, in the maintenance phase of the program's life, another programmer may need to create a new paragraph and may physically place it in the middle of the PERFORM..THRU block. Suddenly the program stops working correctly. Why? Because now PERFORM..THRU is executing an additional, unintentional, paragraph.

Using PERFORM..THRU Correctly

The warning against using PERFORM..THRU is not absolute, because when used correctly, PERFORM..THRU can be very useful. In COBOL there is no way to break out a paragraph that is the target of a PERFORM. All the statements have to be executed until the end of the paragraph is reached. But sometimes, such as when you encounter an error condition, you do not want to execute the remaining statements in the paragraph. This is a circumstance when PERFORM..THRU can be handy.

Consider the program outline in Example 6-6. In this example, control will not return to Begin until SumEarnings has ended, but you do not want to execute the remaining statements if an error is detected. The solution adopted is to hide the remaining statements behind an IF NoErrorFound statement. This might be an adequate solution if there were only one type of error; but if there is more than one type, then nested IF statements must be used. This quickly becomes unsightly and cumbersome.

Example 6-6. Using IFs to Skip Statements When an Error Is Detected

```
PROCEDURE DIVISION.
Begin.
   PERFORM SumEarnings
   STOP RUN.


SumEarnings.
   Statements
   Statements
   IF NoErrorFound
     Statements
     Statements
     IF NoErrorFound
       Statements
       Statements
       Statements
     END-IF
   END-IF.
```

In Example 6-7, PERFORM..THRU is used to deal with the problem in a more elegant manner. The dangers of PERFORM..THRU are ameliorated by having only two paragraphs in the target block and by using a name for the second paragraph that clearly indicates that it is bound to the first.

Example 6-7. Using PERFORM..THRU and GO TO to Skip Statements

```
PROCEDURE DIVISION
Begin.
    PERFORM SumEarnings THRU SumEarningsExit
    STOP RUN.

SumEarnings.
    Statements
    Statements
    IF ErrorFound
        GO TO SumEarningsExit
    END-IF
    Statements
    Statements

    IF ErrorFound
        GO TO SumEarningsExit
    END-IF
    Statements
    Statements
    Statements

SumEarningsExit.
    EXIT.
```

When the statement PERFORM SumEarnings THRU SumEarningsExit is executed, both paragraphs are performed as if they are one paragraph. The GO TO jumps to the exit paragraph, which, because the paragraphs are treated as one, is the end of the block of code. This technique allows you to skip over the code that should not be executed when an error is detected.

The EXIT statement in SumEarningsExit is a dummy statement. It has absolutely no effect on the flow of control. It is in the paragraph merely to conform to the rule that every paragraph must have one sentence. It has the status of a comment.

The PERFORM..THRU and GO TO constructs used in this example are dangerous. GO TO in particular is responsible for the "spaghetti code" that plagues many COBOL legacy systems. For this reason, you should use PERFORM..THRU and GO TO only as demonstrated in Example 6-7.

PERFORM..TIMES

PERFORM..TIMES (see Figure 6-2) is the second format of the PERFORM verb.

$$\underline{PERFORM} \left[StartblockName \left[\begin{Bmatrix} \underline{THRU} \\ \underline{THROUGH} \end{Bmatrix} EndblockName \right] \right]$$

$$RepeatCount\#il \ \underline{TIMES}$$
$$\left[InlineBlock \ \underline{END\text{-}PERFORM} \right]$$

Figure 6-2. Metalanguage for PERFORM format 2

This format has no real equivalent in most programming languages, perhaps because of its limited usefulness. It simply allows a block of code to be executed RepeatCount#il times before returning control to the statement following PERFORM.

Like the other formats of PERFORM, this format allows two types of execution:

- Out-of-line execution of a block of code

- Inline execution of a block of code

Example 6-8 gives some example PERFORM..TIMES statements. These examples specify the RepeatCount using both literals and identifiers and show the inline and out-of-line variants of PERFORM.

Example 6-8. Using PERFORM..TIMES

```
PERFORM PrintBlankLine 10 Times

MOVE 10 TO RepetitionCount
PERFORM DisplayName RepetitionCount TIMES

PERFORM 15 TIMES
  DISPLAY "Am I repeating myself?"
END-PERFORM
```

Inline Execution

Inline execution will be familiar to programmers who have used the iteration constructs (while, do/repeat, for) of most other programming languages. An inline PERFORM iteratively executes a block of code contained within the same paragraph as the PERFORM. That is, the loop body is inline with the rest of the paragraph code. The block of code to be executed starts at the keyword PERFORM and ends at the keyword END-PERFORM (see Listing 6-2).

Listing 6-2. Demonstrates PERFORM..TIMES and Inline vs. Out-of-Line Execution

```
IDENTIFICATION DIVISION.
PROGRAM-ID. Listing6-2.
AUTHOR. Michael Coughlan.
*> in-line and out-of-line PERFORM..TIMES


DATA DIVISION.
WORKING-STORAGE SECTION.
01 NumOfTimes PIC 9 VALUE 5.


PROCEDURE DIVISION.
Begin.
   DISPLAY "About to start in-line Perform"
   PERFORM 4 TIMES
      DISPLAY "> > > > In-line Perform"
   END-PERFORM
   DISPLAY "End of in-line Perform"

   DISPLAY "About to start out-of-line Perform"
   PERFORM OutOfLineCode NumOfTimes TIMES
   DISPLAY "End of out-of-line Perform"
   STOP RUN.


OutOfLineCode.
   DISPLAY "> > > > > Out-of-line Perform".
```

Listing 6-2 Output

About to start in-line Perform
> > > > In-line Perform
> > > > In-line Perform
> > > > In-line Perform
> > > > In-line Perform
End of in-line Perform
About to start out-of-line Perform
> > > > > Out-of-line Perform
> > > > > Out-of-line Perform
> > > > > Out-of-line Perform
> > > > > Out-of-line Perform
> > > > > Out-of-line Perform
End of out-of-line Perform

■ **ANS 85**   In-line PERFORMs were only introduced as part of the ANS 85 COBOL specification. In older legacy systems, the loop body is always out of line.

Out-of-Line Execution

In an out-of-line PERFORM, the loop body is a separate paragraph or section. This is the equivalent, in other languages, of having a procedure, function, or method invocation inside the loop body of a while or for construct.

In an out-of-line PERFORM, the loop body is a separate paragraph or section. This is the equivalent, in other languages,

When a loop is required, but only a few statements are involved, you should use an inline PERFORM. When a loop is required, and the loop body executes some specific task or function, out-of-line code should be used. The paragraph name chosen for the out-of-line code should identify the task or function of the code.

PERFORM..UNTIL

PERFORM..UNTIL (see Figure 6-3) is the third format of the PERFORM verb. This format implements both pre-test and post-test iteration in COBOL. It is the equivalent of Java's while and do..while or Pascal's While and Repeat..Until looping constructs.

$$\underline{\text{PERFORM}}\left[\text{StartBlockName}\left[\left\{\begin{array}{l}\underline{\text{THRU}}\\ \underline{\text{THROUGH}}\end{array}\right\}\text{EndBlockName}\right]\right]\left[\text{WITH}\ \underline{\text{TEST}}\left\{\begin{array}{l}\underline{\text{BEFORE}}\\ \underline{\text{AFTER}}\end{array}\right\}\right]$$

$$\underline{\text{UNTIL}}\,\text{Condition}$$

$$\left[\text{InlineBlock}\ \underline{\text{END - PERFORM}}\right]$$

Figure 6-3. *Metalanguage for PERFORM format 3*

Pre-test and post-test iteration structures seem to be strangely implemented in many languages. Some languages confuse *when* the test is done with *how* the terminating condition is tested (Pascal's While and Repeat structures, for example). In many languages, the test for how the loop terminates emphasizes what makes the loop keep going, rather than what makes it stop. Although this may make formal reasoning about the loop easier, it does not come across as an entirely natural way of framing the question. In your day-to-day life, you do not say, "Heat the water while the water is not boiled" or "Pour water into the cup while the cup is not full."

Pre-test and post-test looping constructs are one area where COBOL seems to have things right. Whether the loop is pre-test or post-test, it is separated from *how* the terminating condition is tested; and the test for termination emphasizes what makes the loop stop, rather than what makes it keep going. In COBOL you might write

```
PERFORM ProcessSalesFile WITH TEST BEFORE
      UNTIL EndOfSalesFile
```

or

```
PERFORM GetNextCharacter WITH TEST AFTER
      UNTIL Letter = "s"
```

Notes on PERFORM..UNTIL

If you use the WITH TEST BEFORE phrase, PERFORM behaves like a while loop and the condition is tested before the loop body is entered. If you use the WITH TEST AFTER phrase, PERFORM behaves like a do..while loop and the condition is tested after the loop body is entered. The WITH TEST BEFORE phrase is the default and so is rarely explicitly stated.

How PERFORM..UNTIL Works

Although flowcharts are generally derided as a program-design tool, they are very useful for showing flow of control. The flowcharts in Figure 6-4 and Figure 6-5 show how the WITH TEST BEFORE and WITH TEST AFTER variations of PERFORM..UNTIL work.

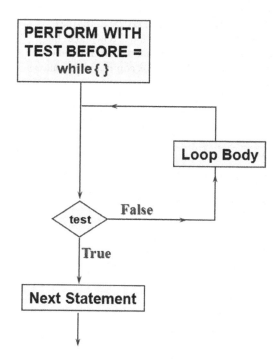

Figure 6-4. *Pre-test loop*

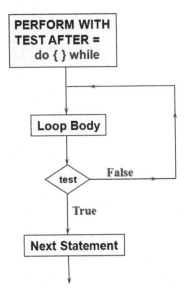

Figure 6-5. *Post-test loop*

Note that the terminating condition is checked only at the beginning of each iteration (PERFORM WITH TEST BEFORE) or at the end of each iteration (PERFORM WITH TEST AFTER). If the terminating condition is reached in the middle of the iteration, the rest of the loop body is still executed. The terminating condition cannot be checked until all the statements in the loop body have been executed. COBOL has no equivalent of the break command that allows control to break out of a loop without satisfying the terminating condition.

PERFORM..VARYING

PERFORM..VARYING (see Figure 6-6) is the final format of the PERFORM verb.

$$\underline{\text{PERFORM}} \left[\text{StartBlockName} \left[\left\{ \begin{matrix} \underline{\text{THRU}} \\ \underline{\text{THROUGH}} \end{matrix} \right\} \text{EndblockName} \right] \right] \left[\text{WITH} \, \underline{\text{TEST}} \left\{ \begin{matrix} \underline{\text{BEFORE}} \\ \underline{\text{AFTER}} \end{matrix} \right\} \right]$$

$$\underline{\text{VARYING}} \left\{ \begin{matrix} \text{Counter1\#i} \\ \text{IndexName1} \end{matrix} \right\} \underline{\text{FROM}} \left\{ \begin{matrix} StartValue\#il \\ IndexName2 \end{matrix} \right\}$$

$$\underline{\text{BY}} \, \text{StepValue\#il} \, \underline{\text{UNTIL}} \, \text{Condition1}$$

$$\left[\underline{\text{AFTER}} \left\{ \begin{matrix} \text{Counter2\#i} \\ \text{IndexName3} \end{matrix} \right\} \underline{\text{FROM}} \left\{ \begin{matrix} StartValue2\#il \\ IndexName4 \end{matrix} \right\} \right. \\ \left. \qquad \underline{\text{BY}} \, \text{StepValue2\#il} \, \underline{\text{UNTIL}} \, \text{Condition2} \right] \dots$$

$$\left[\text{InLineBlock} \, \underline{\text{END - PERFORM}} \right]$$

Figure 6-6. *Metalanguage for PERFORM format 4*

PERFORM..VARYING is used to implement counting iteration. It is similar to the for construct in languages like Pascal, C, and Java. However, there are some differences:

- Most languages permit only one counting variable per loop instruction. COBOL allows up to three. Why only three? Before ANS 85 COBOL, tables were allowed only a maximum of three dimensions, and PERFORM..VARYING was used to process them.

- Both pre-test and post-test variations of counting iteration are supported.

- The terminating condition does not have to involve the counting variable. For instance:

```
PERFORM CountRecordsInFile
        VARYING RecordCount FROM 1 BY 1 UNTIL EndOfFile
```

Notes on PERFORM..VARYING

The inline version of PERFORM..VARYING cannot take the AFTER phrase. This means only one counter may be used with an inline PERFORM.

When you use more than one counter, the counter after the VARYING phrase is the most significant, that after the first AFTER phrase is the next most significant, and the last counter is the least significant. Just like the values in an odometer, the least-significant counter must go through all its values and reach its terminating condition before the next-most-significant counter can be incremented.

The item after the word FROM is the starting value of the counter (initialization). An index item is a special data item. Index items are examined when tables are discussed.

The item after the word BY is the step value of the counter (increment). It can be negative or positive. If you use a negative step value, the counter should be signed (PIC S99, for instance). When the iteration ends, the counters retain their terminating values.

The WITH TEST BEFORE phrase is the default and so is rarely specified.

How PERFORM..VARYING Works

Figure 6-7 shows the flowchart for PERFORM..VARYING..AFTER. Because there is no WITH TEST phrase, WITH TEST BEFORE is assumed. The table shows the number of times the loop body is processed and the value of each counter as displayed in the loop body. The terminating values of the counters are also given.

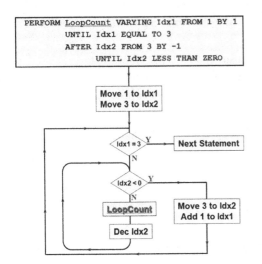

Times	Idx1	Idx2
1	1	3
2	1	2
3	1	1
4	1	0
5	2	3
6	2	2
7	2	1
8	3	0
Terminal	3	3

Figure 6-7. `PERFORM..VARYING..AFTER`

Note how the counter `Idx2` must go through all its values and reach its terminating value before the `Idx1` counter is incremented. An easy way to understand this is to think of it as an odometer. In an odometer, the units counter must go through all its values 0–9 before the tens counter is incremented.

Many of the example programs in this book provide a gentle preview of language elements to come. Listing 6-3 previews edited pictures. Examine the description of `PrnRepCount` provided by its picture, and review the output produced. Can you figure out how the edited picture works? Why do you think it was necessary to move `RepCount` to `PrnRepCount`? Why not just use the edited picture with `RepCount`?

Listing 6-3. Using `PERFORM..VARYING` for Counting

```
IDENTIFICATION DIVISION.
PROGRAM-ID. Listing6-3.
AUTHOR. Michael Coughlan.

DATA DIVISION.
WORKING-STORAGE SECTION.
01 RepCount        PIC 9(4).
01 PrnRepCount     PIC Z,ZZ9.
01 NumberOfTimes   PIC 9(4) VALUE 1000.

PROCEDURE DIVISION.
Begin.
    PERFORM VARYING RepCount FROM 0 BY 50
            UNTIL RepCount = NumberOfTimes
      MOVE RepCount TO PrnRepCount
      DISPLAY "counting " PrnRepCount
    END-PERFORM
    MOVE RepCount TO PrnRepCount
    DISPLAY "If I have told you once, "
    DISPLAY "I've told you " PrnRepCount " times."

    STOP RUN.
```

```
Output from Listing 6-3
counting    0
counting   50
counting  100
counting  150
counting  200
counting  250
counting  300
counting  350
counting  400
counting  450
counting  500
counting  550
counting  600
counting  650
counting  700
counting  750
counting  800
counting  850
counting  900
counting  950
If I have told you once,
I have told you 1,000 times.
```

■ **Answer**   RepCount can't be an edited picture because an edited picture contains non-numeric characters (spaces, in this case), and you can't do computations with non-numeric characters. You have to do the computations with the numeric RepCount and then move it to the edited field PrnRepCount when you want it printed.

The explanation of the operation of PERFORM..VARYING..AFTER compares the construct to an odometer. The program in Listing 6-4 reinforces this idea by using PERFORM..VARYING to emulate an odometer. The program uses both out-of-line and inline versions of PERFORM..VARYING. Notice that when the inline variation is used, you cannot have an AFTER phrase but must instead use nested PERFORMs just as in Java or Pascal. Because the output is voluminous, only the final part is shown here.

Listing 6-4. Odometer Simulation

```
IDENTIFICATION DIVISION.
PROGRAM-ID. Listing6-4.
AUTHOR. Michael Coughlan.

DATA DIVISION.
WORKING-STORAGE SECTION.
01 Counters.
    02 HundredsCount   PIC 99 VALUE ZEROS.
    02 TensCount       PIC 99 VALUE ZEROS.
    02 UnitsCount      PIC 99 VALUE ZEROS.

01 Odometer.
    02 PrnHundreds     PIC 9.
    02 FILLER          PIC X VALUE "-".
    02 PrnTens         PIC 9.
    02 FILLER          PIC X VALUE "-".
    02 PrnUnits        PIC 9.

PROCEDURE DIVISION.
Begin.
    DISPLAY "Using an out-of-line Perform".
    PERFORM CountMileage
            VARYING HundredsCount FROM 0 BY 1 UNTIL HundredsCount > 9
            AFTER TensCount FROM 0 BY 1 UNTIL TensCount > 9
            AFTER UnitsCount FROM 0 BY 1 UNTIL UnitsCount > 9

    DISPLAY "Now using in-line Perform"
    PERFORM VARYING HundredsCount FROM 0 BY 1 UNTIL HundredsCount > 9
        PERFORM VARYING TensCount FROM 0 BY 1 UNTIL TensCount > 9
            PERFORM VARYING UnitsCount FROM 0 BY 1 UNTIL UnitsCount > 9
                MOVE HundredsCount TO PrnHundreds
                MOVE TensCount TO PrnTens
                MOVE UnitsCount TO PrnUnits
                DISPLAY "In - " Odometer
            END-PERFORM
        END-PERFORM
    END-PERFORM
```

Listing 6-4 Partial Output
```
In - 9-8-0
In - 9-8-1
In - 9-8-2
In - 9-8-3
In - 9-8-4
In - 9-8-5
In - 9-8-6
In - 9-8-7
In - 9-8-8
In - 9-8-9
In - 9-9-0
In - 9-9-1
In - 9-9-2
In - 9-9-3
In - 9-9-4
In - 9-9-5
In - 9-9-6
In - 9-9-7
In - 9-9-8
In - 9-9-9
End of odometer simulation.
```

```
    DISPLAY "End of odometer simulation."
    STOP RUN.

CountMileage.
    MOVE HundredsCount TO PrnHundreds
    MOVE TensCount     TO PrnTens
    MOVE UnitsCount    TO PrnUnits
    DISPLAY "Out - " Odometer.
```

You might be wondering why the word FILLER is used in the description of Odometer. In COBOL, instead of having to make up dummy names, you can use FILLER when you need to reserve an area of storage but are never going to refer to it by name. For instance, in the data item Odometer, you want to separate the digits with hyphens, so you declare a character of storage for each hyphen and assign it the value -. But you will never refer to this part of Odometer by name. The hyphens only have significance as part of the group item.

Summary

This chapter examined the iteration constructs supported by COBOL. You learned the differences between COBOL's version of pre-test and post-test iteration and those of other languages. I contrasted counting iteration in its PERFORM..VARYING..AFTER implementation, which has both pre-test and post-test variations, with the offerings of other languages. You also explored the ability to create open subroutines in COBOL, and I provided a rationale for using them.

LANGUAGE KNOWLEDGE EXERCISE

Unleash your 2B pencil. It is exercise time again.

In the columns provided, write out what you would expect to be displayed on the computer screen if you ran the program shown in Listing 6-5. Use the Continue Run column to show what happens after the statement DISPLAY "STOP RUN should be here". has been executed.

Listing 6-5. Program to Test Your Knowledge of the PERFORM Verb

	Start Run	Continue Run
DATA DIVISION. IDENTIFICATION DIVISION. PROGRAM-ID. Listing6-5. AUTHOR. Michael Coughlan. DATA DIVISION. WORKING-STORAGE SECTION. 01 LoopCount PIC 9 VALUE 1. 01 LoopCount2 PIC 9 VALUE 1.		

```
PROCEDURE DIVISION.                          Start Run     Continue Run
P1.
DISPLAY "S-P1"
PERFORM P2
PERFORM P3
MOVE 7 TO LoopCount
PERFORM VARYING LoopCount
FROM 1 BY 1 UNTIL LoopCount = 2
DISPLAY "InLine - " LoopCount
END-PERFORM
DISPLAY "E-P1".
DISPLAY "STOP RUN should be here".

P2.
DISPLAY "S-P2"
PERFORM P5 WITH TEST BEFORE VARYING LoopCount
FROM 1 BY 1 UNTIL LoopCount > 2
DISPLAY "E-P2".

P3.
DISPLAY "S-P3"
PERFORM P5
PERFORM P6 3 TIMES
DISPLAY "E-P3".

P4.
DISPLAY "P4-" LoopCount2
ADD 1 TO LoopCount2.

P5.
DISPLAY "S-P5"
DISPLAY LoopCount "-P5-" LoopCount2
PERFORM P4 WITH TEST AFTER UNTIL LoopCount2 > 2
DISPLAY "E-P5".

P6.
DISPLAY "P6".
```

PROGRAMMING EXERCISE 1

In this programming exercise, you amend the program you wrote for the programming exercise in Chapter 5 (or amend the answer provided in Listing 5-11). That programming exercise required you to create a calculator program, but the program halted after only one calculation.

Amend the program so it runs until the user enters the letter *s* instead of an operator (+ - / *). The result of running the program is shown in the sample output in Example 6-9.

Example 6-9. Sample Run (User Input Shown in Bold)

```
Enter an arithmetic operator (+ - * /) (s to end) : *
Enter a single digit number - 4
Enter a single digit number - 5
Result is = 20.00
Enter an arithmetic operator (+ - * /) (s to end) : +
Enter a single digit number - 3
Enter a single digit number - 3
Result is = 06.00
Enter an arithmetic operator (+ - * /) (s to end) : -
Enter a single digit number - 5
Enter a single digit number - 3
Result is = -02.00
Enter an arithmetic operator (+ - * /) (s to end) : /
Enter a single digit number - 5
Enter a single digit number - 3
Result is = 00.60
Enter an arithmetic operator (+ - * /) (s to end) : s
End of calculations
```

PROGRAMMING EXERCISE 2

Write a program that gets the user's name and a countdown value from the keyboard and then displays a countdown before displaying the name that was entered. Use PERFORM..VARYING to create the countdown.

The program should produce results similar to those shown in Example 6-10. For purposes of illustration, user input is in bold.

Example 6-10. Sample Run

```
Enter your name :- Mike Ryan
Enter the count-down start value :- 05
Getting ready to display your name.
05
04
03
02
01
Your name is Mike Ryan
```

LANGUAGE KNOWLEDGE EXERCISE—ANSWER

```
DATA DIVISION.
IDENTIFICATION DIVISION.
PROGRAM-ID. Listing6-5.
AUTHOR. Michael Coughlan.
DATA DIVISION.
WORKING-STORAGE SECTION.
01 LoopCount  PIC 9 VALUE 1.
01 LoopCount2 PIC 9 VALUE 1.

PROCEDURE DIVISION.
P1.
DISPLAY "S-P1"
PERFORM P2
PERFORM P3
MOVE 7 TO LoopCount
PERFORM VARYING LoopCount
FROM 1 BY 1 UNTIL LoopCount = 2
DISPLAY "InLine - " LoopCount
END-PERFORM
DISPLAY "E-P1".
DISPLAY "STOP RUN should be here".

P2.
DISPLAY "S-P2"
PERFORM P5 WITH TEST BEFORE VARYING LoopCount
FROM 1 BY 1 UNTIL LoopCount > 2
DISPLAY "E-P2".

P3.
DISPLAY "S-P3"
PERFORM P5
PERFORM P6 3 TIMES
DISPLAY "E-P3".

P4.
DISPLAY "P4-" LoopCount2
ADD 1 TO LoopCount2.

P5.
DISPLAY "S-P5"
DISPLAY LoopCount "-P5-" LoopCount2
PERFORM P4 WITH TEST AFTER UNTIL LoopCount2 > 2
DISPLAY "E-P5".

P6.
DISPLAY "P6".
```

Start Run	Continue Run
S-P1	S-P2
S-P2	S-P5
S-P5	1-P5-5
1-P5-1	P4-5
P4-1	E-P5
P4-2	S-P5
E-P5	2-P5-6
S-P5	P4-6
2-P5-3	E-P5
P4-3	E-P2
E-P5	S-P3
E-P2	S-P5
S-P3	3-P5-7
S-P5	P4-7
3-P5-4	E-P5
P4-4	P6
E-P5	P6
P6	P6
P6	E-P3
P6	P4-8
E-P3	S-P5
InLine - 1	3-P5-9
E-P1	P4-9
STOP RUN should be here	E-P5
	P6

PROGRAMMING EXERCISE 1—ANSWER

Listing 6-6. The Full Calculator Program

```
IDENTIFICATION DIVISION.
PROGRAM-ID. Listing6-6.
AUTHOR. Michael Coughlan.
*> Continually calculates using two numbers and an operator
*> Ends when "s" is entered instead of an operator.
DATA DIVISION.
WORKING-STORAGE SECTION.
01 Num1      PIC 9      VALUE ZERO.
01 Num2      PIC 9      VALUE ZERO.
01 Result    PIC --9.99 VALUE ZEROS.
01 Operator  PIC X      VALUE SPACE.
   88 ValidOperator     VALUES "*", "+", "-", "/", "s".
   88 EndOfCalculations VALUE "s".


PROCEDURE DIVISION.
Begin.
   PERFORM GetValidOperator UNTIL ValidOperator
   PERFORM UNTIL EndOfCalculations OR NOT ValidOperator
      PERFORM GetTwoNumbers
      EVALUATE Operator
        WHEN "+" ADD      Num2 TO   Num1 GIVING Result
        WHEN "-" SUBTRACT Num2 FROM Num1 GIVING Result
        WHEN "*" MULTIPLY Num1 BY   Num2 GIVING Result
        WHEN "/" DIVIDE   Num1 BY   Num2 GIVING Result ROUNDED
      END-EVALUATE
      DISPLAY "Result is = ", Result
      MOVE SPACE TO Operator
      PERFORM GetValidOperator UNTIL ValidOperator
   END-PERFORM
   DISPLAY "End of calculations"
   STOP RUN.

GetValidOperator.
   DISPLAY "Enter an arithmetic operator (+ - * /) (s to end) : "
           WITH NO ADVANCING
   ACCEPT Operator.

GetTwoNumbers.
   DISPLAY "Enter a single digit number - " WITH NO ADVANCING
   ACCEPT Num1

   DISPLAY "Enter a single digit number - " WITH NO ADVANCING
   ACCEPT Num2.
```

PROGRAMMING EXERCISE 2—ANSWER

Listing 6-7. Uses PERFORM..VARYING to Display a Countdown from XX to 01

```
IDENTIFICATION DIVISION.
PROGRAM-ID. Listing6-7.
AUTHOR. Michael Coughlan.
DATA DIVISION.
WORKING-STORAGE SECTION.
01 UserName     PIC X(20).
01 StartValue   PIC 99 VALUE ZEROS.
01 Countdown    PIC 99 VALUE ZEROS.

PROCEDURE DIVISION.
DisplayCountdown.
   DISPLAY "Enter your name :- " WITH NO ADVANCING
   ACCEPT UserName

   DISPLAY "Enter the count-down start value :- " WITH NO ADVANCING
   ACCEPT StartValue

   PERFORM VARYING Countdown FROM StartValue BY -1 UNTIL Countdown = ZERO
       DISPLAY Countdown
   END-PERFORM

   DISPLAY "Your name is " UserName
   STOP RUN.
```

References

1. Tompkins HE. In defense of teaching structured COBOL as computer science (or, notes on being sage struck). ACM SIGPLAN Notices. 1983; 18(4): 86-94.

2. Baldwin, RR. A note on H.E. Tompkins's minimum-period COBOL style. ACM SIGPLAN Notices. 1987; 22(5): 27-31. http://doi.acm.org/10.1145/25267.25273

   doi: 10.1145/25267.25273

3. Compiled and run at compileoneline.com—Execute BASIC Program Online (Yabasic 2.9.15). www.compileonline.com/execute_basic_online.php

■ ■ ■

CHAPTER 7

Introduction to Sequential Files

An important characteristic of a programming language designed for enterprise or business computing is that it should have an external, rather than an internal focus. It should concentrate on processing data held externally in files and databases rather than on manipulating data in memory through linked lists, trees, stacks, and other sophisticated data structures. Whereas in most programming languages the focus is internal, in COBOL it is external. A glance at the table of contents of any programming book on Java, C, Pascal, or Ruby emphasizes the point. In most cases, only one chapter, if that, is devoted to files. In this book, over a quarter of the book deals with files: it covers such topics as sequential files, relative files, indexed files, the SORT, the MERGE, the Report Writer, control breaks, and the file-update problem.

COBOL supports three file organizations: sequential files, relative files, and indexed files. Relative and indexed are direct-access file organizations that are discussed later in the book. They may be compared to a music CD on which you select the track you desire. Sequential files are like a music cassette: to listen to a particular song, you must go through all the preceding songs.

This chapter provides a gentle introduction to sequential files. I introduce some of the terminology used when referring to files and explain how sequential files are organized and processed. Every COBOL file organization requires entries in the INPUT-OUTPUT SECTION of the ENVIRONMENT DIVISION and the FILE SECTION of the DATA DIVISION, and these declarations are specified and explained. Because files require more sophisticated data definition than the elementary data items introduced in Chapter 3, this chapter also introduces hierarchically structured data definitions.

What Is a File?

A *file* is a repository for data that resides on backing storage (hard disk, magnetic tape, or CD-ROM). Nowadays, files are used to store a variety of different types of information such as programs, documents, spreadsheets, videos, sounds, pictures, and record-based data. In a record-based file, the data is organized into discrete packages of information. For instance, a customer record holds information about a customer such as their identifying number, name, address, date of birth, and gender. A customer file may contain thousands or even millions of instances of the customer record. In a picture file or music file, by way of contrast, the information is essentially an undifferentiated stream of bytes.

COBOL is often used in systems where the volume of data to be processed is large—not because the data is inherently voluminous, as it is in video or sound files, but because the same items of information have been recorded about a great many instances of the same object. Although COBOL can be used to process other kinds of data files, it is generally used only to process record-based files.

There are essentially two types of record-based file organization—serial files (COBOL calls these sequential files) and direct-access files:

- In a serial file, the records are organized and accessed serially (one after another).

- In a direct-access file, the records are organized in a manner that allows direct access to a particular record based on a key value. Unlike serial files, a record in a direct-access file can be accessed without having to read any of the preceding records.

Terminology

Before I discuss sequential files, I need to introduce some terminology:

- *Field*: An item of information that you are recording about an object (StockNumber, SupplierCode, DateOfBirth, ValueOfSale)

- *Record*: The collection of fields that record information about an object (for example, a CustomerRecord is a collection of fields recording information about a customer)

- *File*: A collection of one or more occurrences (instances) of a record template (structure)

Files, Records, and Fields

It is important to distinguish between the record *occurrence* (the instance or values of a record) and the record *template* (the structure of the record). Every record in a file has a different value but the same structure. For instance, the record template illustrated in Figure 7-1 describes the structure of each record occurrence (instance).

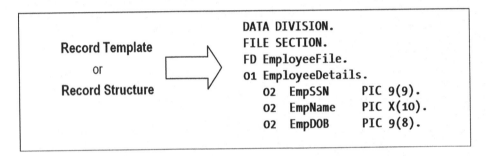

```
                        DATA DIVISION.
  Record Template       FILE SECTION.
        or              FD EmployeeFile.
                        01 EmployeeDetails.
  Record Structure          02  EmpSSN    PIC 9(9).
                            02  EmpName   PIC X(10).
                            02  EmpDOB    PIC 9(8).
```

Figure 7-1. Record template/structure

The occurrences of the employee records (Figure 7-2) are the actual values in the file. There is only one record template, but there are many record instances.

Employee.DAT

EmpSSN	EmpName	EmpDOB
097234562	COUGHLAN	10091961
109724567	RYAN	31121976
329534118	COFFEY	23061964
479423458	O'BRIEN	03111979
587312876	SMITH	12121976

Occurrences (instances)

Figure 7-2. Record occurrences/instances

How Files Are Processed

Before a computer can process a piece of data, the data must be loaded into the computer's main memory (RAM). For instance, if you want to manipulate a picture in Photoshop or edit a file in Word, you have to load the data file into main memory (RAM), make the changes you want, and then save the file on to backing storage (disk).

Programmers in other languages, who may not be used to processing record-based data, often seek to load the entire file into memory as if it were an undifferentiated stream of bytes. For record-based data, this is inefficient and consumes unnecessary computing resources.

A record-based file may consist of millions, tens of millions, or even hundreds of millions of records and may require gigabytes of storage. For instance, suppose you want to keep some basic census information about all the people in the United States. Suppose that each record is about 1,000 characters/bytes (1KB) in size. If you estimate the population of the United States at 314 million, this gives you a size for the file of $1,000 \times 314,000,000 = 314,000,000,000$ bytes = 314GB. Most computers do not have 314GB of RAM available, and those that do are unlikely to be stand-alone machines running only your program. The likelihood is that your program is only one of many running on the machine at the same time. If your program is found to be using a substantial proportion of the available RAM, your manager is going to be less than gruntled.

■ **Note** I once asked an M.Sc. student who was a proficient C++ programmer to write the C++ equivalent of a COBOL file processing program I had written. His first action was to load the entire file into memory. Doing this used an inordinate amount of memory and offered no benefit. He still had to read the file from disk, and the file size so overwhelmed the available RAM that the virtual memory manager had to keep paging to disk.

The data in a record-based file consists of discrete packages of information (records). The correct way to process such a file is to load a record into RAM, process it, and then load the next record. To store the record in memory and allow access to its individual fields, you must declare the record structure (Figure 7-1) in your program. The computer uses your description of the record (the record template) to set aside sufficient memory to store one instance of the record.

The memory allocated for storing a record is usually called a *record buffer*. To process a file, a program reads the records, one at a time, into the record buffer, as shown in Figure 7-3. The record buffer is the only connection between the program and the records in the file.

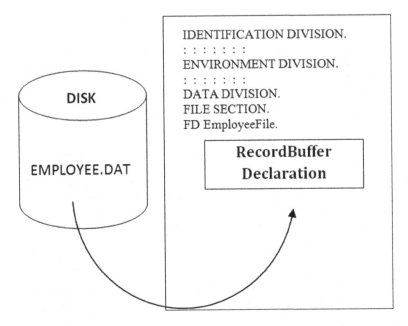

Figure 7-3. *Reading records into the record buffer*

Implications of Buffers

If your program processes more than one file, you have to describe a record buffer for each file. To process all the records in an *input* file, each record instance must be copied (read) from the file into the record buffer when required. To create an *output* file, each record must be placed in the record buffer and then transferred (written) to the file. To transfer a record from an input file to an output file, your program will have to do the following:

- Read the record into the input record buffer.

- Transfer it to the output record buffer.

- Write the data to the output file from the output record buffer.

This type of data transfer between buffers is common in COBOL programs.

File and Record Declarations

Suppose you want to create a file to hold information about your employees. What kind of information do you need to store about each employee?

One thing you need to store is the employee's Name. Each employee is also assigned a unique Social Security Number (SSN), so you need to store that as well. You also need to store the employee's date of birth and gender.

These fields are summarized here:

- Employee SSN

- Employee Name

- Employee DOB

- Employee Gender

■ **Note**   This is for demonstration only. In reality, you would need to include far more items than these.

Creating a Record

To create a record buffer large enough to store one instance of the employee record you must decide on the type and size of each of the fields:

- Employee SSN is nine digits in size, so the data item to hold it is declared as PIC 9(9).

- To store Employee Name, you can assume that you require only 25 characters. So the data item can be declared as PIC X(25).

- Employee Date of Birth requires eight digits, so you can declare it as PIC 9(8).

- Employee Gender is represented by a one-letter character, where *m* is male and *f* is female, so it can be declared as PIC X.

These fields are individual data items, but they are collected together into a record structure as shown in Example 7-1.

Example 7-1. The EmployeeDetails Record Description/Template

```
01 EmployeeDetails.
   02  EmpSSN          PIC 9(9).
   02  EmpName         PIC X(25).
   02  EmpDateOfBirth  PIC 9(8).
   02  EmpGender       PIC X.
```

This record description reserves the correct amount of storage for the record buffer, but it does not allow access to all the individual parts of the record that might be of interest.

For instance, the name is actually made up of the employee's surname and forename. And the date consists of four digits for the year, two digits for the month, and two digits for the day. To be able to access these fields individually, you need to declare the record as shown in Example 7-2.

Example 7-2. A More Granular Version of the EmployeeDetails Record

```
01 EmployeeDetails.
   02  EmpSSN          PIC 9(9).
   02  EmpName.
       03 EmpSurname   PIC X(15).
       03 EmpForename  PIC X(10).
   02  EmpDateOfBirth.
       03 EmpYOB       PIC 9(4).
       03 EmpMOB       PIC 99.
       03 EmpDOB       PIC 99.
   02  EmpGender       PIC X.
```

Declaring the Record Buffer in Your Program

The record description in Example 7-2 sets aside sufficient storage to store one instance of the employee record. This area of storage is the record buffer; it's the only connection between the program and the records in the file. To process the file, you must read the records from the file, one at a time, into the record buffer. The record buffer is connected to the file that resides on backing storage by declarations made in the FILE SECTION of the DATA DIVISION and the SELECT and ASSIGN clause of the ENVIRONMENT DIVISION.

A record template (description/buffer) for every file used in a program must be described in the FILE SECTION by means of an FD (file description) entry. The FD entry consists of the letters FD and an internal name that you assign to the file. The full file description for the employee file might be as shown in Example 7-3.

Example 7-3. The DATA DIVISION Declarations for the Employee File.

```
DATA DIVISION.
FILE SECTION.
FD EmployeeFile.
01 EmployeeDetails.
   02  EmpSSN          PIC 9(9).
   02  EmpName.
       03 EmpSurname   PIC X(15).
       03 EmpForename  PIC X(10).
   02  EmpDateOfBirth.
       03 EmpYOB       PIC 9(4).
       03 EmpMOB       PIC 99.
       03 EmpDOB       PIC 99.
   02  EmpGender       PIC X.
```

In this example, the name EmployeeFile has been assigned as the internal name for the file. This name is then used in the program for file operations such as these:

```
OPEN INPUT EmployeeFile
READ EmployeeFile
CLOSE EmployeeFile
```

The SELECT and ASSIGN Clause

Although you are going to refer to the employee file as EmployeeFile in the program, the actual name of the file on disk is Employee.dat. To connect the name used in the program to the file's actual name on backing storage, you require entries in the SELECT and ASSIGN clause of the FILE-CONTROL paragraph, in the INPUT-OUTPUT SECTION of the ENVIRONMENT DIVISION. As shown in Example 7-4, the SELECT and ASSIGN clause allows you to specify that an internal file name is to be connected to an external data resource. It also lets you specify how the file is organized. In the case of a sequential file, you specify that the file organization is sequential. Sequential files are ordinary text files such as you might create with a text editor.

Example 7-4. Using SELECT and ASSIGN

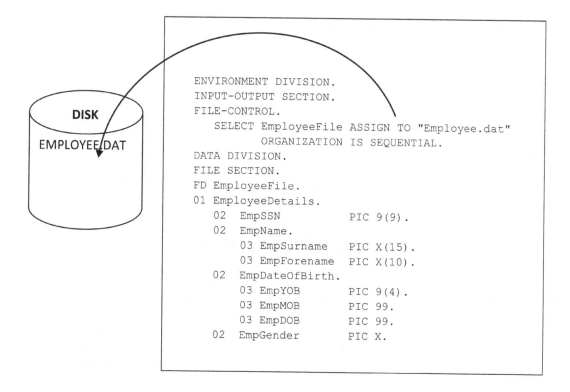

SELECT and ASSIGN Syntax

Here is the SELECT and ASSIGN syntax:

<u>SELECT</u> InternalFileName
    <u>ASSIGN</u> TO ExternalFileSpecification
      [[<u>ORGANIZATION</u> IS] <u>SEQUENTIAL</u>]

■ **Note** The SELECT and ASSIGN clause has far more entries (even for sequential files) than those shown here.
I deal with these entries in this book as you require them.

As illustrated by the examples in Example 7-5, ExternalFileSpecification can be either an identifier or a literal. The identifier or literal can consist of a simple file name or a full or partial file specification. If you use a simple file name, the drive and directory where the program is running are assumed.

When you use a literal, the file specification is hard-coded into the program; but if you want to specify the name of a file when you run the program, you can use an identifier. If an identifier is used, you must move the actual file specification into the identifier before the file is opened.

Example 7-5. Some Example SELECT and ASSIGN Declarations

```
SELECT EmployeeFile
    ASSIGN TO "D:\Cobol\ExampleProgs\Employee.Dat"
    ORGANIZATION IS SEQUENTIAL.

SELECT EmployeeFile
    ASSIGN TO "Employee.Dat"
    ORGANIZATION IS SEQUENTIAL.

SELECT EmployeeFile
    ASSIGN TO EmployeeFileName
    ORGANIZATION IS SEQUENTIAL.
:   :   :   :   :   :   :   :   :   :
MOVE "C:\datafiles\Employee.dat" TO EmployeeFileName
OPEN INPUT EmployeeFile
```

EXTENDED SELECT AND ASSIGN

I mentioned that sequential files are ordinary text files such as might be created with a text editor. This is not entirely true. A text editor appends the Carriage Return (CR) and Line Feed (LF) characters to each line of text. If you specify ORGANIZATION IS SEQUENTIAL and create your test data as lines of text in an ordinary text editor, these extra characters will be counted, and this will throw your records off by two characters each time you read a new record. For this reason, some vendors have extended SELECT and ASSIGN to allow these line-terminating characters to be either ignored or included. For instance, in Micro Focus COBOL, the metalanguage for the SELECT and ASSIGN is

<u>SELECT</u> InternalFileName
    <u>ASSIGN</u> TO ExternalFileSpecification

$$\left[[\underline{\text{ORGANIZATION}} \text{ IS }] \left[\frac{\text{LINE SEQUENTIAL}}{\text{RECORD SEQUENTIAL}} \right] \right]$$

Here LINE SEQUENTIAL means the CR and LF characters are not considered part of the record, and RECORD SEQUENTIAL means they are (same as the standard SEQUENTIAL).

Because it is very convenient to be able to use an ordinary text editor to create test data files, I use the Micro Focus LINE SEQUENTIAL extension in the example programs.

Processing Sequential Files

Unlike direct-access files, sequential files are uncomplicated both in organization and in processing. To write programs that process sequential files, you only need to know four new verbs: OPEN, CLOSE, READ, and WRITE.

The OPEN Statement

Before your program can access the data in an input file or place data in an output file, you must make the file available to the program by OPENing it. When you open a file, you have to indicate how you intend to use it (INPUT, OUTPUT, EXTEND) so the system can manage the file correctly:

$$\text{OPEN} \left\{ \begin{array}{l} \text{INPUT} \\ \text{OUTPUT} \\ \text{EXTEND} \end{array} \right\} \text{InternalFileName} \ldots$$

Opening a file *does not* transfer any data to the record buffer; it simply provides access.

Notes on the OPEN Statement

When a file is opened for INPUT or EXTEND, the file must exist or the OPEN will fail.

When a file is opened for INPUT, the Next Record Pointer is positioned at the beginning of the file. The Next Record Pointer is conceptual; it points to the position in the file where the file system will get or put the next record.

When the file is opened for EXTEND, the Next Record Pointer is positioned after the last record in the file. This allows records to be appended to the file.

When a file is opened for OUTPUT, it is created if it does not exist, and it is overwritten if it already exists.

■ **Bug Alert**   Although the ellipses after InternalFileName in the metalanguage indicate that it is possible to open a number of files with one OPEN statement, it is not advisable to do so. If an error is detected on opening a file and only one OPEN statement has been used to open all the files, the system will not be able to indicate which particular file is causing the problem. If all the files are opened separately, it will.

The CLOSE Statement

The metalanguage for the CLOSE statement is fairly simple:

CLOSE InternalFilename ...

Notes

Before the program terminates, you must make sure the program closes all the open files. Failure to do so may result in some data not being written to the file or users being prevented from accessing the file.

Hard disk access is about a million times slower than RAM access (hard disk access times are measured in milliseconds, whereas RAM access is measured in nanoseconds: 1 millisecond = 1,000 microseconds = 1,000,000 nanoseconds), so data is often cached in memory until a sufficient quantity of records have been accumulated to make the write to disk worthwhile. If the file is not closed, it is possible that these cached records will never be sent to the file.

■ **Bug Alert**   The ellipses in the CLOSE metalanguage indicate that you may specify more than one file name. I advised against this for the OPEN statement; but because very few errors affect the CLOSE statement, the same advice does not hold. For convenience, you can often choose to close multiple files in one CLOSE statement.

The READ Statement

Once the system has opened a file and made it available to the program, it is your responsibility to process it correctly. To process all the records in the file, the program has to transfer them, one record at a time, from the file to the file's record buffer. The READ is provided for this purpose:

READ InternalFilename [NEXT] RECORD

      [INTO Identifier]

       [AT END StatementBlock1]

        [NOT AT END StatementBlock2]

[END-READ]

    The READ statement copies a record occurrence (instance) from the file on backing storage and places it in the record buffer defined for it.

Notes

When the READ attempts to read a record from the file and encounters the end of file marker, the AT END is triggered and StatementBlock1 is executed. If the NOT AT END clause is specified then StatementBlock2 is executed.

    When the INTO clause is used, the data is read into the record buffer and then copied from there, to the Identifier, in one operation. This option creates two copies of the data: one in the record buffer and one in the Identifier. Using the INTO clause is equivalent to reading a record and then moving the contents of the record buffer to the Identifier.

■ **COBOL Detail**　Because AT END is an optional element, you might have wondered how the end-of-file condition can be detected in its absence. COBOL has a special kind of exception handler for files called *declaratives*. When declaratives are specified for a file, any file error—including the end-of-file condition, causes the code in the declaratives to execute. Declaratives are an advanced topic that I address later in the book.

How READ Works

Listing 7-1 is a small program that simply reads the records in the employee file: employee.dat. The test data for the program is given in Figure 7-4. The effect on the data storage of running the program with this data is shown in Figure 7-5.

Listing 7-1. Reading the Employee File

```
IDENTIFICATION DIVISION.
PROGRAM-ID. Listing7-1.
AUTHOR. Michael Coughlan.
ENVIRONMENT DIVISION.
INPUT-OUTPUT SECTION.
FILE-CONTROL.
    SELECT EmployeeFile ASSIGN TO "Employee.dat"
           ORGANIZATION IS LINE SEQUENTIAL.

DATA DIVISION.
FILE SECTION.
FD EmployeeFile.
01 EmployeeDetails.
```

```
88  EndOfEmployeeFile    VALUE HIGH-VALUES.
02  EmpSSN               PIC 9(9).
02  EmpName.
    03 EmpSurname        PIC X(15).
    03 EmpForename       PIC X(10).
02  EmpDateOfBirth.
    03 EmpYOB            PIC 9(4).
    03 EmpMOB            PIC 99.
    03 EmpDOB            PIC 99.
02  EmpGender            PIC X.

PROCEDURE DIVISION.
Begin.
   OPEN INPUT EmployeeFile
   READ EmployeeFile
     AT END SET EndOfEmployeeFile TO TRUE
   END-READ
   PERFORM UNTIL EndOfEmployeeFile
      READ EmployeeFile
        AT END SET EndOfEmployeeFile TO TRUE
      END-READ
   END-PERFORM
   CLOSE EmployeeFile
   STOP RUN.
```

Employee.dat

```
097234562COUGHLAN        MIKE        19610910m
109724567RYAN            MARY        19761231f
329534118COFFEY          MARTIN      19640623m
```

Figure 7-4. Employee.dat test data file

		EmployeeDetails					
	EmpSSN	EmpName		EmpDateOfBirth			EmpGender
		EmpSurname	EmpForename	EmpYOB	EmpMOB	EmpDOB	
Read1	097234562	COUGHLAN	MIKE	1961	09	10	m
Read2	109724567	RYAN	MARY	1976	12	31	f
Read3	329534118	COFFEY	MARTIN	1964	06	23	m
Read4	◆◆◆◆◆◆◆◆◆	◆◆◆◆◆◆◆◆◆◆◆◆◆◆◆	◆◆◆◆◆◆◆◆◆	◆◆◆◆	◆◆	◆◆	◆

Figure 7-5. Effect on data storage of reading each record in the file

The effect on the data storage each time the READ is executed is shown in Figure 7-5:

- Read1 shows the effect of reading the first record. When the record is read from Employee.dat, it is copied into the EmployeeDetails area of storage as shown.

- Read2 and Read3 show the results of reading the second and third records.

- Read4 shows what happens when an attempt to read a fourth record is made. Because there is no fourth record, the AT END activates and the condition name EndOfEmployeeFile is set to TRUE. This condition name is defined on the whole record, and as a result the whole record is filled with HIGH-VALUES (represented here as the ♦ symbol).

■ **Note** Because of space constraints in this book, the various pieces of test data given obviously are not comprehensive enough to test any of the programs adequately. The test data is provided for the purposes of illustration only. You should create your own, more comprehensive test data if you want to test the programs.

Of course, this program does not do anything practical. It reads the file but doesn't do anything with the records it reads. Listing 7-2 tweaks the program a little so that it displays the name and date of birth of each employee in the file. Notice that I have chosen not to display the data items in the same order they are in in the record. The employee name is displayed in forename-surname order, and the date of birth is displayed in the standard U.S. order (month, day, year).

Listing 7-2. Reading the Employee File and Displaying the Records

```
IDENTIFICATION DIVISION.
PROGRAM-ID. Listing7-2.
AUTHOR. Michael Coughlan.
ENVIRONMENT DIVISION.
INPUT-OUTPUT SECTION.
FILE-CONTROL.
    SELECT EmployeeFile ASSIGN TO "Employee.dat"
           ORGANIZATION IS LINE SEQUENTIAL.

DATA DIVISION.
FILE SECTION.
FD EmployeeFile.
01 EmployeeDetails.
   88  EndOfEmployeeFile    VALUE HIGH-VALUES.
   02  EmpSSN               PIC 9(9).
   02  EmpName.
       03 EmpSurname        PIC X(15).
       03 EmpForename        PIC X(10).
   02  EmpDateOfBirth.
       03 EmpYOB            PIC 9(4).
       03 EmpMOB            PIC 99.
       03 EmpDOB            PIC 99.
   02  EmpGender            PIC X.
```

Listing 7-2 Output		
MIKE	COUGHLAN	- 09/10/1961
MARY	RYAN	- 12/31/1976
MARTIN	COFFEY	- 06/23/1964

```
PROCEDURE DIVISION.
Begin.
   OPEN INPUT EmployeeFile
   READ EmployeeFile
     AT END SET EndOfEmployeeFile TO TRUE
   END-READ
   PERFORM UNTIL EndOfEmployeeFile
      DISPLAY EmpForename SPACE EmpSurname " - "
              EmpMOB "/" EmpDOB "/" EmpYOB
      READ EmployeeFile
        AT END SET EndOfEmployeeFile TO TRUE
      END-READ
   END-PERFORM
   CLOSE EmployeeFile
   STOP RUN.
```

The WRITE Statement

The WRITE statement is used to copy data from the record buffer (RAM) to the file on backing storage (tape, disk, or CD-ROM). To write data to a file, the data must be moved to the record buffer (declared in the file's FD entry), and then the WRITE statement is used to send the contents of the record buffer to the file:

$$\underline{\text{WRITE}} \text{ RecordName } \left[\underline{\text{FROM}} \text{ Identifier}\right]$$

$$\left[\left\{ \begin{matrix} \text{BEFORE} \\ \underline{\text{AFTER}} \end{matrix} \right\} \text{ADVANCING} \left\{ \begin{matrix} \text{AdvanceNum} \left[\begin{matrix} \underline{\text{LINE}} \\ \underline{\text{LINES}} \end{matrix} \right] \\ \text{MnemonicName} \\ \underline{\text{PAGE}} \end{matrix} \right\} \right]$$

When WRITE..FROM is used, the data contained in the Identifier is copied into the record buffer and is then written to the file. WRITE..FROM is the equivalent of a MOVE Identifier TO RecordName statement followed by a WRITE RecordName statement.

■ **Note** The full metalanguage for the sequential-file version of WRITE statement is given here, but I postpone discussion of the ADVANCING clause until later in the book. This clause is used when writing print files and is a bit more complicated than it appears on the surface. It is best discussed when considering files with multiple record types.

Write a Record, Read a File

You probably noticed that the metalanguage for the READ and WRITE statements indicates that while you read a file, you write a record. You may have wondered why there is this difference.

So far, you have only seen files that contain one type of record. In the employee file, for example, there is only one type of employee record. But a file may contain a number of different types of record. For instance, if you wanted to update the employee file, you might have a file of transaction records containing both Employee Insertion records and Employee Deletion records. Although an Insertion record would have to contain all the fields in the employee record, a Deletion record would only need the Employee SSN.

The reason you *read a file*, not a record, is that until the record is in the buffer you cannot tell what type of record it is. You have to read the file and then look at the data in the buffer to see what type of record has been supplied. It is your responsibility to discover what type of record has been read into the buffer and then to take the appropriate actions.

The reason you *write a record* instead of a file is that when the output file will contain multiple types of record, you have to specify which record type you want to write to the file.

How WRITE works

Suppose you want to add some records to the end of the employee file. To do so, you use this statement:

```
OPEN EXTEND EmployeeFile
```

This tells the system that you are going to add records to the end of the file. If you opened the file for OUTPUT, then Employee.dat would be replaced (overwritten) with a new version of the employee file.

To write a record to the file, you place the data in the EmployeeDetails record buffer and then use the following statement:

```
WRITE EmployeeDetails
```

The example program fragment in Example 7-6 writes two records to the end of the employee file. Figure 7-6 shows the interaction between the data in memory and the file on backing storage. The first MOVE statement places the record data in the record buffer, and the WRITE statement (Write1) copies it to the file. The second MOVE places the second record in the record buffer, and the WRITE (Write2) copies it to the file.

Example 7-6. Writing Records to the End of a Sequential File

```
PROCEDURE DIVISION.
Begin.
  OPEN EXTEND EmployeeFile

  MOVE "456867564NEWGIRL        MARTHA      19820712f"
        TO EmployeeDetails
  WRITE EmployeeDetails

  MOVE "622842649NEWBOY         MALCOLM     19810925m"
        TO EmployeeDetails
  WRITE EmployeeDetails

  CLOSE EmployeeFile
  STOP RUN.
```

EmployeeDetails						
EmpSSN	EmpName		EmpDateOfBirth			Emp Gender
	EmpSurname	EmpForename	EmpYOB	EmpMOB	EmpDOB	
Write1 456867564	NEWGIRL	MARTHA	1982	07	12	f
Write2 622842649	NEWBOY	MALCOLM	1981	09	25	m

```
                           Employee.dat
       097234562COUGHLAN      MIKE      19610910m
       109724567RYAN         MARY      19761231f
       329534118COFFEY       MARTIN    19640623m
       456867564NEWGIRL      MARTHA    19820712f
       622842649NEWBOY       MALCOLM   19810925m
```

Figure 7-6. *Writing two records to the employee file (see Example 7-6)*

Reading and Writing to the Employee File

The program in Listing 7-3 extends the fragment in Example 7-3 into a full-blown program. However, whereas the data sent to the employee file in Example 7-3 was hard-coded in the form of literal values, in Listing 7-3 the records to be added to the file are obtained from the user. A very simple interface is used to get the records. A template for the record is displayed, and the user then enters the data based on the template. A screen capture shows the data requested from the user and then output when the file is read.

Listing 7-3. Writing and Reading the Employee File

```
IDENTIFICATION DIVISION.
PROGRAM-ID. Listing7-3.
AUTHOR. Michael Coughlan.
ENVIRONMENT DIVISION.
INPUT-OUTPUT SECTION.
FILE-CONTROL.
   SELECT EmployeeFile ASSIGN TO "Employee.dat"
          ORGANIZATION IS LINE SEQUENTIAL.

DATA DIVISION.
FILE SECTION.
FD EmployeeFile.
01 EmployeeDetails.
   88  EndOfEmployeeFile    VALUE HIGH-VALUES.
   02  EmpSSN               PIC 9(9).
   02  EmpName.
       03  EmpSurname       PIC X(15).
       03  EmpForename      PIC X(10).
```

Listing 7-3 Output

```
nnnnnnnnnSSSSSSSSSSSSSSSSSSSFFFFFFFFFFFyyyyMMddG
456867564NEWGIRL      MARTHA  19820712f
nnnnnnnnnSSSSSSSSSSSSSSSSSSSFFFFFFFFFFFyyyyMMddG
622842649NEWBOY       MALCOLM 19810925m
nnnnnnnnnSSSSSSSSSSSSSSSSSSSFFFFFFFFFFFyyyyMMddG

************ End of Input ****************
097234562COUGHLAN      MIKE      19610910m
109724567RYAN          MARY      19761231f
329534118COFFEY        MARTIN    19640623m
456867564NEWGIRL       MARTHA    19820712f
622842649NEWBOY        MALCOLM   19810925m
```

```
    02  EmpDateOfBirth.
        03  EmpYOB          PIC 9(4).
        03  EmpMOB          PIC 99.
        03  EmpDOB          PIC 99.
    02  EmpGender           PIC X.

PROCEDURE DIVISION.
Begin.
    OPEN EXTEND EmployeeFile
    PERFORM GetEmployeeData
    PERFORM UNTIL EmployeeDetails = SPACES
        WRITE EmployeeDetails
        PERFORM GetEmployeeData
    END-PERFORM
    CLOSE EmployeeFile
    DISPLAY "************* End of Input ***************"

    OPEN INPUT EmployeeFile
    READ EmployeeFile
      AT END SET EndOfEmployeeFile TO TRUE
    END-READ
    PERFORM UNTIL EndOfEmployeeFile
        DISPLAY EmployeeDetails
        READ EmployeeFile
          AT END SET EndOfEmployeeFile TO TRUE
        END-READ
    END-PERFORM
    CLOSE EmployeeFile
    STOP RUN.

GetEmployeeData.
    DISPLAY "nnnnnnnnnSSSSSSSSSSSSSSSSFFFFFFFFFFyyyyMMddG"
    ACCEPT EmployeeDetails.
```

Summary

This chapter provided a gentle introduction to sequential files. You learned how to declare the record buffer for a file. You learned how to connect the file's internal file name with its name and location on the backing storage device. You saw how to READ records from a file and how to WRITE them to a file.

Although this chapter is a good start, there is still much more to discover about sequential files. Although I touched on the idea of files that contain multiple record types, I did not explore the full ramifications of this concept; nor did I discuss the true magic of the FILE SECTION. I mentioned print files, but I did not explore the relevant options in the metalanguage; nor did I discuss how to create a print file. I also have not mentioned or discussed the idea of variable-length records. I discussed some of the mechanics of using sequential files in this chapter, but I did not discuss sequential-file processing issues. The chapters that follow explore some of those issues by examining the control-break and file-update problems.

LANGUAGE KNOWLEDGE EXERCISE

Unsheathe your 2B pencil. It is exercise time again.

1. Locate errors in these FILE SECTION entries.

(a)

```
FD SalesFile.
01 SalesRecord          PIC X(13).
    02 SalesmanNumber    PIC 9(7).
    02 SaleValue         PIC 9(5)V99.
```

(b)

```
FD TemperatureFile.
01 DayRecord.
    05 MonthNumber       PIC 99
    05 MaxTemp           PIC 999
    05 MinTemp           PIC 999
    06 AverageTemp       PIC 999
```

(c)

```
FD StudentFile
01 StudentRecord.
02 StudentName.          PIC X(20).
05 StudentInitials       PIC XX.
05 StudnetSurname        PIC X(18).
02 StudentAddress        PIC X(65).
03 AddressLine1.         PIC X(10).
03 AddressLine2          PIC X(10)
03 AddressLine3          PIC X(10).
02 StudentGPA.
05 Year1GPA
10 Sem1GPA               PIC 9V99.
10 Sem2GPA               PIC 9V99.
05 Year2GPA.
10 Sem1GPA               PIC 9V99.
10 Sem2GPA               PIC 9V99.
05 Year3GPA
10 Sem1GPA               PIC 9V99.
10 Sem2GPA               PIC 9V99.
```

2. Complete the SELECT and ASSIGN clause for a sequential file called Stock.dat in the directory C:\COBOL-Data\. The record buffer for the file has this description:

```
FD StockFile.
01 StockRec.
    02 StockNumber     PIC 9(5)
    02 ManfNumber      PIC 9(4)
    02 QtyInStock      PIC 9(6)
    02 ReorderLevel    PIC 9(6)
    02 ReorderQty      PIC 9(6).
```

Write your answer here:

```
IDENTIFICATION DIVISION.
PROGRAM-ID.  Exercise7-2.
ENVIRONMENT DIVISION.
```

PROGRAMMING EXERCISE 1

A StockFile holds details of gadgets sold by the Gadget Shop (GadgetShop.Com). The StockFile is a sequential file sorted in ascending GadgetId order. It is named GadgetStock.dat. Each record has the following description:

Field	Type	Length	Value
GadgetID	N	6	000001–999999
GadgetName	X	30	–
QtyInStock	N	4	0000–9999
Price	N	6	0000.00–9999.99

Write a program to process the data in the StockFile and, for each record, display the item's GadgetName and the total value of the quantity in stock (QtyInStock * Price). When the StockFile has ended, display the total value of all the stock.

Example Test Data

```
123456SoundDisk MP3 Player 4GB        0650003095
234567BioLite Camp Stove              0057029550
345678Collapsible Kettle - Green      0155002590
456789Digital Measuring Jug           0325000895
567890MicroLite LED Torch             0512000745
678901Pocket Sized Fishing Rod        0055001799
```

Note: Place the test data in the data file as one long string.

Example Run

```
SoundDisk MP3 Player 4GB       $20,117.50
BioLite Camp Stove             $16,843.50
Collapsible Kettle - Green      $4,014.50
Digital Measuring Jug           $2,908.75
MicroLite LED Torch             $3,814.40
Pocket Sized Fishing Rod          $989.45
            Stock Total:       $48,688.10
```

PROGRAMMING EXERCISE 2

Amend the program you wrote for exercise 1 so that it adds the following two records to the end of the file. Then display the stock report as before:

```
313245Spy Pen - HD Video Camera     0125003099
593486Scout Cash Capsule - Red      1234000745
```

The records in the StockFile are held in ascending GadgetID order. When you add these two records to the file, the records will be out of order. Without sorting the StockFile after the update, how could you update the file so that the ordering of the records was maintained?

Example Run

```
SoundDisk MP3 Player 4GB       $20,117.50
BioLite Camp Stove             $16,843.50
Collapsible Kettle - Green      $4,014.50
Digital Measuring Jug           $2,908.75
MicroLite LED Torch             $3,814.40
Pocket Sized Fishing Rod          $989.45
Spy Pen - HD Video Camera       $3,873.75
Scout Cash Capsule - Red        $9,193.30
               Stock Total:    $61,755.15
```

LANGUAGE KNOWLEDGE EXERCISES: ANSWERS

Unsheath your 2B pencil. It is exercise time again.

1.   Locate errors in these FILE SECTION entries.

1. Locate errors in these FILE SECTION entries.

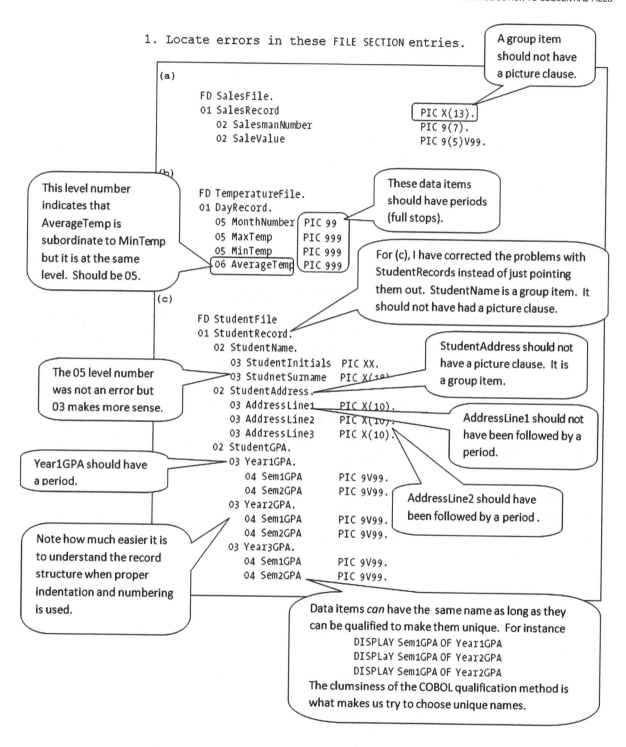

A group item should not have a picture clause.

(a)

```
FD SalesFile.
01 SalesRecord
   02 SalesmanNumber           PIC X(13).
   02 SaleValue                PIC 9(7).
                               PIC 9(5)V99.
```

This level number indicates that AverageTemp is subordinate to MinTemp but it is at the same level. Should be 05.

(b)

```
FD TemperatureFile.
01 DayRecord.
   05 MonthNumber  PIC 99
   05 MaxTemp      PIC 999
   05 MinTemp      PIC 999
   06 AverageTemp  PIC 999
```

These data items should have periods (full stops).

For (c), I have corrected the problems with StudentRecords instead of just pointing them out. StudentName is a group item. It should not have had a picture clause.

(c)

```
FD StudentFile
01 StudentRecord.
   02 StudentName.
      03 StudentInitials  PIC XX.
      03 StudnetSurname    PIC X(19)
   02 StudentAddress.
      03 AddressLine1     PIC X(10).
      03 AddressLine2     PIC X(10).
      03 AddressLine3     PIC X(10).
   02 StudentGPA.
      03 Year1GPA.
         04 Sem1GPA        PIC 9V99.
         04 Sem2GPA        PIC 9V99.
      03 Year2GPA.
         04 Sem1GPA        PIC 9V99.
         04 Sem2GPA        PIC 9V99.
      03 Year3GPA.
         04 Sem1GPA        PIC 9V99.
         04 Sem2GPA        PIC 9V99.
```

The 05 level number was not an error but 03 makes more sense.

StudentAddress should not have a picture clause. It is a group item.

AddressLine1 should not have been followed by a period.

Year1GPA should have a period.

AddressLine2 should have been followed by a period .

Note how much easier it is to understand the record structure when proper indentation and numbering is used.

Data items *can* have the same name as long as they can be qualified to make them unique. For instance

```
DISPLAY Sem1GPA OF Year1GPA
DISPLaY Sem1GPA OF Year2GPA
DISPLAY Sem1GPA OF Year2GPA
```

The clumsiness of the COBOL qualification method is what makes us try to choose unique names.

2. Complete the SELECT and ASSIGN clause for a sequential file called Stock.dat in the directory C:\COBOL-Data\. The record buffer for the file has this description:

```
FD  StockFile.
01  StockRec.
    02  StockNumber    PIC 9(5)
    02  ManfNumber     PIC 9(4)
    02  QtyInStock     PIC 9(6)
    02  ReorderLevel   PIC 9(6)
    02  ReorderQty     PIC 9(6).
```

Write your answer here:

```
IDENTIFICATION DIVISION.
PROGRAM-ID.  Exercise7-2.
ENVIRONMENT DIVISION.
INPUT-OUTPUT SECTION.
FILE-CONTROL.
    SELECT StockFile ASSIGN TO "C:\COBOL-Data\Stock.dat"
        ORGANIZATION IS SEQUENTIAL.
```

PROGRAMMING EXERCISE 1: ANSWER

A StockFile holds details of gadgets sold by the Gadget Shop (GadgetShop.Com). The StockFile is a sequential file sorted in ascending GadgetId order. It is named GadgetStock.dat. Each record has the following description.

Field	Type	Length	Value
GadgetID	N	6	000001-999999
GadgetName	X	30	–
QtyInStock	N	4	0000-9999
Price	N	6	0000.00-9999.99

Write a program to process the data in the StockFile and, for each record, display the item's GadgetName and the total value of the quantity in stock (QtyInStock * Price). When the StockFile has ended, display the total value of all the stock.

Example Test Data

```
123456SoundDisk MP3 Player 4GB        0650003095
234567BioLite Camp Stove              0057029550
345678Collapsible Kettle - Green      0155002590
456789Digital Measuring Jug           0325000895
567890MicroLite LED Torch             0512000745
678901Pocket Sized Fishing Rod        0055001799
```

Note: Place the test data in the data file as one long string.

Example Run

```
SoundDisk MP3 Player 4GB        $20,117.50
BioLite Camp Stove              $16,843.50
Collapsible Kettle - Green       $4,014.50
Digital Measuring Jug            $2,908.75
MicroLite LED Torch              $3,814.40
Pocket Sized Fishing Rod           $989.45
               Stock Total:     $48,688.10
```

Listing 7-4. Displays the Value of the Gadgets in Stock

```
IDENTIFICATION DIVISION.
PROGRAM-ID.  Listing7-4.
AUTHOR. Michael Coughlan

ENVIRONMENT DIVISION.
INPUT-OUTPUT SECTION.
FILE-CONTROL.
    SELECT GadgetStockFile ASSIGN TO "input.txt"
           ORGANIZATION IS LINE SEQUENTIAL.

DATA DIVISION.
FILE SECTION.
FD GadgetStockFile.
01 StockRec.
    88 EndOfStockFile      VALUE HIGH-VALUES.
    02 GadgetID            PIC 9(6).
    02 GadgetName          PIC X(30).
    02 QtyInStock          PIC 9(4).
    02 Price               PIC 9(4)V99.

WORKING-STORAGE SECTION.
01 PrnStockValue.
    02 PrnGadgetName       PIC X(30).
    02 FILLER              PIC XX VALUE SPACES.
    02 PrnValue            PIC $$$,$$9.99.

01 PrnFinalStockTotal.
    02 FILLER              PIC X(16) VALUE SPACES.
    02 FILLER              PIC X(16) VALUE "Stock Total:".
    02 PrnFinalTotal       PIC $$$,$$9.99.

01 FinalStockTotal         PIC 9(6)V99.
01 StockValue              PIC 9(6)V99.
```

```
PROCEDURE DIVISION.
Begin.
    OPEN INPUT GadgetStockFile
    READ GadgetStockFile
        AT END SET EndOfStockFile TO TRUE
    END-READ
    PERFORM DisplayGadgetValues UNTIL EndOfStockFile
    MOVE FinalStockTotal TO PrnFinalTotal
    DISPLAY PrnFinalStockTotal
    CLOSE GadgetStockFile
    STOP RUN.

DisplayGadgetValues.
    COMPUTE StockValue = Price * QtyInStock
    ADD StockValue  TO FinalStockTotal
    MOVE GadgetName TO PrnGadgetName
    MOVE StockValue TO PrnValue
    DISPLAY PrnStockValue
    READ GadgetStockFile
        AT END SET EndOfStockFile TO TRUE
    END-READ.
```

PROGRAMMING EXERCISE 2: ANSWER

Amend the program you wrote for exercise 1 so that it adds the following two records to the end of the file. Then display the stock report as before:

```
313245Spy Pen - HD Video Camera     0125003099
593486Scout Cash Capsule - Red      1234000745
```

The records in the StockFile are held in ascending GadgetID order. When you add these two records to the file, the records will be out of order. Without sorting the StockFile after the update, how could you update the file so that the ordering of the records was maintained?

Example Run

```
SoundDisk MP3 Player 4GB        $20,117.50
BioLite Camp Stove              $16,843.50
Collapsible Kettle - Green       $4,014.50
Digital Measuring Jug            $2,908.75
MicroLite LED Torch              $3,814.40
Pocket Sized Fishing Rod           $989.45
Spy Pen - HD Video Camera        $3,873.75
Scout Cash Capsule - Red         $9,193.30
            Stock Total:        $61,755.15
```

Listing 7-5. Adds Two Records and Then Displays Stock Values Again

```
IDENTIFICATION DIVISION.
PROGRAM-ID.  Listing7-5.
AUTHOR. Michael Coughlan

ENVIRONMENT DIVISION.
INPUT-OUTPUT SECTION.
FILE-CONTROL.
    SELECT GadgetStockFile ASSIGN TO "input.txt"
           ORGANIZATION IS LINE SEQUENTIAL.

DATA DIVISION.
FILE SECTION.
FD GadgetStockFile.
01 StockRec.
    88 EndOfStockFile       VALUE HIGH-VALUES.
    02 GadgetID             PIC 9(6).
    02 GadgetName           PIC X(30).
    02 QtyInStock           PIC 9(4).
    02 Price                PIC 9(4)V99.

WORKING-STORAGE SECTION.
01 PrnStockValue.
    02 PrnGadgetName        PIC X(30).
    02 FILLER               PIC XX VALUE SPACES.
    02 PrnValue             PIC $$$,$$9.99.

01 PrnFinalStockTotal.
    02 FILLER               PIC X(16) VALUE SPACES.
    02 FILLER               PIC X(16) VALUE "Stock Total:".
    02 PrnFinalTotal        PIC $$$,$$9.99.

01 FinalStockTotal         PIC 9(6)V99.
01 StockValue              PIC 9(6)V99.

PROCEDURE DIVISION.
Begin.
    OPEN EXTEND GadgetStockFile
    MOVE "313245Spy Pen - HD Video Camera      0125003099"
        TO StockRec
    WRITE StockRec
    MOVE "593486Scout Cash Capsule - Red       1234000745"
        TO StockRec
    WRITE StockRec
    CLOSE GadgetStockFile

    OPEN INPUT  GadgetStockFile
    READ GadgetStockFile
      AT END SET EndOfStockFile TO TRUE
    END-READ
```

```
        PERFORM DisplayGadgetValues UNTIL EndOfStockFile
        MOVE FinalStockTotal TO PrnFinalTotal
        DISPLAY PrnFinalStockTotal
        CLOSE GadgetStockFile
        STOP RUN.

DisplayGadgetValues.
        COMPUTE StockValue = Price * QtyInStock
        ADD StockValue  TO FinalStockTotal
            MOVE GadgetName TO PrnGadgetName
            MOVE StockValue TO PrnValue
            DISPLAY PrnStockValue
            READ GadgetStockFile
                 AT END SET EndOfStockFile TO TRUE
            END-READ.
```

CHAPTER 8

Advanced Sequential Files

In the previous chapter, you saw how sequential files are declared, written, and read. In this chapter, you continue your exploration of sequential files by examining advanced issues such as multiple-record-type files, print files, and variable-length records.

The previous chapter dealt with sequential files that contained only fixed-length records of a single record type. This chapter shows how a file may have records of different lengths either because the file contains a number of different types of fixed-length records or because it contains variable-length records. The discussion of files that contain multiple record types also considers the implications of these multiple record types for the record buffer.

When the WRITE verb was introduced in the previous chapter, I ignored some of the metalanguage because it dealt with print files. This chapter addresses the issue of print files and shows how they are declared and used. I also discuss the problem caused by the different types of print lines that must be sent to a print file.

Files with Multiple Record Types

Quite often, complex data sets cannot store all their data in just one record type. In such cases, a single file contains more than one type of record. For instance, consider the following problem specification.

Problem Specification

A company has shops all over Ireland. Every night, a sequential file of cash register receipts is sent from each branch to the head office. These files are merged into a single, large, sequential file called the ShopReceiptsFile.

In the ShopReceiptsFile, there are two types of records:

- A ShopDetails record, used to record the ShopId and ShopLocation
- A SaleReceipt record, used to record the ItemId, QtySold, and ItemCost for each item sold

In the file, a single shop record precedes all the SaleReceipt records for a particular shop.

Write a program to process the ShopReceiptsFile and, for each shop in the file, produce a summary line that shows the ShopId of the shop and the total value of sales for that shop.

Implications of Files with Multiple Record Types

As you can see from the previous specification, the ShopReceiptsFile contains two different types of records. When a file contains different record types, the records will have different structures and, possibly, different lengths. In a specification, the different record types are usually represented as shown in Figure 8-1 and Figure 8-2. The ShopDetails record is 35 characters in size, but the SaleReceipt record is only 16 characters. For each shop in the file, there is one ShopDetails record but many SaleReceipt records.

ShopDetails

FieldName	Type	Size	Value
ShopId	X	5	-
ShopLocation	X	30	-

Figure 8-1. ShopDetails description

SaleReceipt

FieldName	Type	Size	Value
ItemId	X	8	-
QtySold	9	3	1–999
ItemCost	9	5	0.00–999.99

Figure 8-2. SaleReceipt description

The different types of records in the ShopReceiptsFile means you need more than one record description in the file's file description (FD) entry. Because record descriptions always begin with level 01, you must provide a 01-level description for each type of record in the file.

Example 8-1 shows the file description for the ShopReceiptsFile. What is not obvious from this description is that even though there are two record descriptions, only one area of memory is reserved for the record buffer, and it is only able to store a single record at a time. Because only one area of memory is reserved, both record descriptions map on to the same record buffer. The size of that record buffer is the size of the largest record.

Example 8-1. File Description for the ShopReceiptsFile

```
FILE SECTION.
FD ShopReceiptsFile.
01 ShopDetails.
    02 ShopId          PIC X(5).
    02 ShopLocation    PIC X(30).

01 SaleReceipt.
    02 ItemId          PIC X(8).
    02 QtySold         PIC 9(3).
    02 ItemCost        PIC 999V99.
```

This is the magic of the FILE SECTION. When, in the FILE SECTION, multiple records are defined in a file's FD entry, all the record descriptions share (map on to) the same area of memory, and all the record descriptions are current (live) at the same time.

Multiple Record Descriptions, One Record Buffer

When multiple records are described for the same FD entry, only a single area of storage (record buffer) is created (the size of the largest record). All the record descriptions map on to this single area of storage, and all the descriptions are current no matter which record is actually in the buffer. Obviously, though, even though both record descriptions are available, only one makes sense for the values in the buffer. For instance, Figure 8-3 is a graphical representation of the shared buffer for the ShopReceiptsFile, and the record currently in the buffer is a SaleReceipt record. If you execute the statement DISPLAY ItemId, the value *ABC12345* is displayed. If you execute DISPLAY QtySold, you get the value *003*. But because both record descriptions are current at the same time, you can also execute DISPLAY ShopLocation, which displays the nonsensical value *34500300399*. It is up to the programmer to know what type of record is in the buffer and to use only the record description that makes sense for those values. The question is, how can you know what type of record has been read into the buffer?

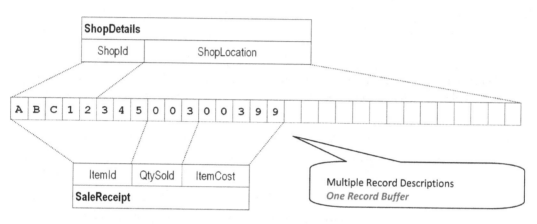

Figure 8-3. *A graphical representation of the shared record buffer*

The Type Code

When a record is read into a shared record buffer, it is your responsibility to discover what type of record has been read in and to refer only to the fields that make sense for that type of record. Looking at the record in Figure 8-3, you might wonder how you can discover what type of record had been read into the buffer. Sometimes you can determine the record type by looking for identifying characteristics that are unique to that type of record, such as a particular value or data type. However, generally it is not possible to establish reliably what type of record is in the buffer simply by examining the buffer values.

A special identifying data item called the *type code* is usually inserted into each record to allow you to distinguish between record types. The type code is usually one character in size and is the first field in each record, but its size and placement are merely conventions. The type code can be placed anywhere in the record and be of any size and any type.

The ShopReceiptsFile uses the character *H* to indicate the ShopDetails record (the header record) and *S* to indicate the SaleReceipt record (the sales record). To detect the type of record read into the buffer, you could use statements such as IF TypeCode = "H" or IF TypeCode = "S". But this is COBOL. It offers a better way. You can define condition names to monitor the type code so that if it contains *H* the condition name ShopHeader is set to true, and if it contains *S* the condition name ShopSale is set to true. The record descriptions required to accommodate these changes for the ShopReceiptsFile are shown in Example 8-2.

Example 8-2. ShopReceiptsFile Record Descriptions with Type Code

```
FILE SECTION.
FD ShopReceiptsFile.
01 ShopDetails.
    02 TypeCode            PIC X.
        88 ShopHeader      VALUE "H".
        88 ShopSale        VALUE "S".
    02 ShopId              PIC X(5).
    02 ShopLocation        PIC X(30).

01 SaleReceipt.
    02 TypeCode            PIC X.
    02 ItemId              PIC X(8).
    02 QtySold             PIC 9(3).
    02 ItemCost            PIC 999V99.
```

A graphical representation of the new record descriptions is shown in Figure 8-4. In this case, there is a ShopDetails record in the buffer. Again, both record descriptions are current (live), but only the ShopDetails record description makes sense for the values in the buffer.

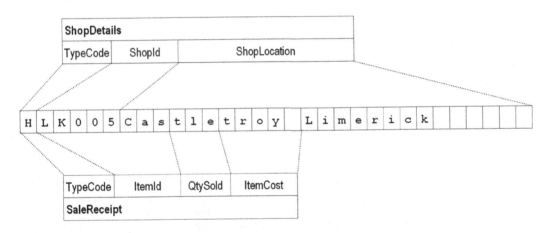

Figure 8-4. *Representation of a record buffer that includes the TypeCode*

When you examined the file description given in Example 8-2, perhaps it occurred to you to ask, why have condition names been defined only for the ShopDetails record and not for the SaleReceipt record? The answer is that TypeCode in both records maps on to the same area of storage; and that because both record descriptions, including the condition names, are current, it does not matter which record is read into the buffer—the condition names can detect it.

Example Program

The program specification given at the beginning of the chapter required you to write a program to process the ShopReceiptsFile. For each shop in the file, you were asked to produce a summary line that shows the ShopId and the total value of sales for that shop. The program to implement the specification is given in Listing 8-1.

Listing 8-1. Summarizes the Header and Sale records of the ShopReceiptsFile

```cobol
IDENTIFICATION DIVISION.
PROGRAM-ID. Listing8-1.
AUTHOR.  Michael Coughlan.
ENVIRONMENT DIVISION.
INPUT-OUTPUT SECTION.
FILE-CONTROL.
    Select ShopReceiptsFile  ASSIGN TO "Listing8-1-ShopSales.Dat"
            ORGANIZATION IS LINE SEQUENTIAL.

DATA DIVISION.
FILE SECTION.
FD ShopReceiptsFile.
01 ShopDetails.
    88 EndOfShopReceiptsFile   VALUE HIGH-VALUES.
    02 RecTypeCode       PIC X.
        88 ShopHeader    VALUE "H".
        88 ShopSale      VALUE "S".
    02 ShopId            PIC X(5).
    02 ShopLocation      PIC X(30).

01 SaleReceipt.
    02 RecTypeCode       PIC X.
    02 ItemId            PIC X(8).
    02 QtySold           PIC 9(3).
    02 ItemCost          PIC 999V99.

WORKING-STORAGE SECTION.
01 PrnShopSalesTotal.
    02 FILLER            PIC X(21) VALUE "Total sales for shop ".
    02 PrnShopId         PIC X(5).
    02 PrnShopTotal      PIC $$$$,$$9.99.

01 ShopTotal            PIC 9(5)V99.

PROCEDURE DIVISION.
ShopSalesSummary.
    OPEN INPUT ShopReceiptsFile
    READ ShopReceiptsFile
        AT END SET EndOfShopReceiptsFile TO TRUE
    END-READ
    PERFORM SummarizeCountrySales
        UNTIL EndOfShopReceiptsFile
    CLOSE ShopReceiptsFile
    STOP RUN.

SummarizeCountrySales.
    MOVE ShopId  TO PrnShopId
    MOVE ZEROS TO ShopTotal
    READ ShopReceiptsFile
        AT END SET EndOfShopReceiptsFile TO TRUE
    END-READ
```

```
    PERFORM SummarizeShopSales
            UNTIL ShopHeader OR EndOFShopReceiptsFile
    MOVE ShopTotal TO PrnShopTotal
    DISPLAY PrnShopSalesTotal.

SummarizeShopSales.
    COMPUTE  ShopTotal = ShopTotal + (QtySold * ItemCost)
    READ ShopReceiptsFile
        AT END SET EndOfShopReceiptsFile TO TRUE
    END-READ.
```

Some basic test data and the results produced by running the program against this test data are shown in Figure 8-5.

```
HID006This is location of shop ID006
SItemId2500500595
SItemId2201500395
SItemId1000100195
SItemId0300100350
SItemId2500100195
SItemId2100100350
HID001This is location of shop ID001
SItemId0500500595
SItemId0201500395
SItemId1000100195
SItemId0300100350
HID002This is location of shop ID002
SItemId1500500595
SItemId0100100350
HID003This is location of shop ID003
SItemId0500500595
SItemId0201500395
SItemId1211501395
SItemId0500100195
SItemId1500100195
SItemId2100100350
SItemId0500100195
```

```
                    Run of Listing 8-1
Total sales for shop ID006      $99.90
Total sales for shop ID001      $94.45
Total sales for shop ID002      $33.25
Total sales for shop ID003    $1,702.60
```

Figure 8-5. *Basic test data for Listing 8-1*

When you consider the solution produced in Listing 8-1, you may be a little puzzled. Where is the IF statement that checks whether the record is a ShopHeader or a ShopSale record? The answer to this question lies in the approach to the problem solution. Many programmers would solve the problem by having a loop to read the records in the file and an IF statement to check what kind type of record has been read. If a ShopSale record was read, then the required computations would be done; and if a ShopDetails record was read, the summary line would be produced and displayed. This is not a terrible solution for a problem of this size; but when you get to control breaks—a type of problem of which this is a near relation—this type of solution quickly becomes complicated.

The solution adopted in Listing 8-1 involves examining the structure of the records in the ShopReceiptsFile and producing a solution that reflects that structure. What do I mean by the *structure* of the file? The records in the file are not thrown randomly into the file: they are grouped by shop, and each grouping starts with a ShopDetails header record followed by many SaleReceipt records. The solution in Listing 8-1 reflects the structure of the file. It has a loop to process the SaleReceipt records and an outer loop to process the whole file. You know you have come to the end of the sales records for a particular shop when you encounter the ShopDetails record for the next shop. At that point, you display the summary information you have accumulated for the previous shop. A graphical representation of this solution as applied to the test data is given in Figure 8-6.

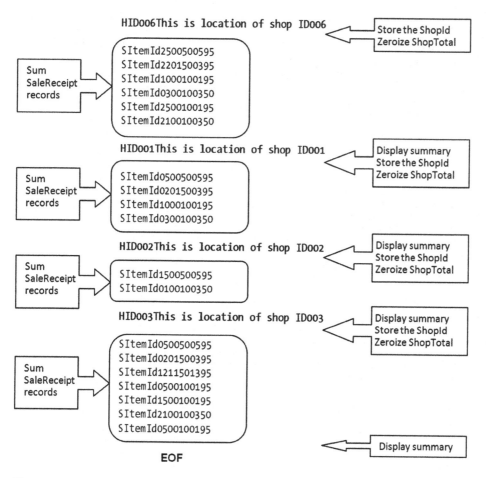

Figure 8-6. *Representation of the solution as applied to the test data*

■ **Note** This solution uses the Micro Focus LINE SEQUENTIAL extension. The reason is that when a file contains records of different lengths, the system has to use a record terminator to detect when one record ends and the next begins. The record terminator is specified by the language implementer. Where the terminator is not a fixed implementer default, it can be specified by using the RECORD DELIMITER IS clause in the file's SELECT and ASSIGN clause.

Because there is no generic, standard way of specifying the terminator, I chose to use the Micro Focus LINE SEQUENTIAL extension. When LINE SEQUENTIAL is used, each record is terminated by the carriage return and line feed ASCII characters. Adopting this extension has the added benefit that the test data can be written using a standard text editor such as Microsoft Notepad.

Specification Amendment

In a file such as ShopReceiptsFile, which consists of groups that contain a header record followed by many body records, there is often a third type of record. A footer record is frequently used to ensure that the group is complete and that none of the records in the group body has been lost. The footer record might simply contain a count of the records in the group body, or it might do some calculations to produce a checksum.

Let's amend the ShopReceiptsFile to include the footer record; and let's amend the specification to say that if the record count in the footer record is not the same as the actual record count, then an error message should be displayed instead of the sales total. The footer record is indicated by the *F* character.

A program to implement the specification is given in Listing 8-2.

Listing 8-2. Summarizes the Header, Sale, and Footer records of the ShopReceiptsFile

```
IDENTIFICATION DIVISION.
PROGRAM-ID. Listing8-2.
AUTHOR.  Michael Coughlan.
ENVIRONMENT DIVISION.
INPUT-OUTPUT SECTION.
FILE-CONTROL.
    Select ShopReceiptsFile  ASSIGN TO "Listing8-2-ShopSales.dat"
            ORGANIZATION IS LINE SEQUENTIAL.

DATA DIVISION.
FILE SECTION.
FD ShopReceiptsFile.
01 ShopDetails.
    88 EndOfShopReceiptsFile   VALUE HIGH-VALUES.
    02 TypeCode          PIC X.
        88 ShopHeader    VALUE "H".
        88 ShopSale      VALUE "S".
        88 ShopFooter    VALUE "F".
    02 ShopId            PIC X(5).
    02 ShopLocation      PIC X(30).

01 SaleReceipt.
    02 TypeCode          PIC X.
    02 ItemId            PIC X(8).
    02 QtySold           PIC 9(3).
    02 ItemCost          PIC 999V99.

01 ShopSalesCount.
    02 TypeCode          PIC X.
    02 RecCount          PIC 9(5).

WORKING-STORAGE SECTION.
01 PrnShopSalesTotal.
    02 FILLER            PIC X(21) VALUE "Total sales for shop ".
    02 PrnShopId         PIC X(5).
    02 PrnShopTotal      PIC $$$$,$$9.99.
```

```
01 PrnErrorMessage.
   02 FILLER              PIC X(15) VALUE "Error on Shop: ".
   02 PrnErrorShopId      PIC X(5).
   02 FILLER              PIC X(10) VALUE " RCount = ".
   02 PrnRecCount         PIC 9(5).
   02 FILLER              PIC X(10) VALUE " ACount = ".
   02 PrnActualCount      PIC 9(5).

01 ShopTotal             PIC 9(5)V99.
01 ActualCount           PIC 9(5).

PROCEDURE DIVISION.
ShopSalesSummary.
    OPEN INPUT ShopReceiptsFile
    PERFORM GetHeaderRec
    PERFORM SummarizeCountrySales
        UNTIL EndOfShopReceiptsFile
    CLOSE ShopReceiptsFile
    STOP RUN.


SummarizeCountrySales.
    MOVE ShopId  TO PrnShopId, PrnErrorShopId
    MOVE ZEROS TO ShopTotal

    READ ShopReceiptsFile
        AT END SET EndOfShopReceiptsFile TO TRUE
    END-READ
    PERFORM SummarizeShopSales
            VARYING ActualCount FROM 0 BY 1 UNTIL ShopFooter
    IF RecCount = ActualCount
       MOVE ShopTotal TO PrnShopTotal
       DISPLAY PrnShopSalesTotal
     ELSE
       MOVE RecCount TO PrnRecCount
       MOVE ActualCount TO PrnActualCount
       DISPLAY PrnErrorMessage
    END-IF
    PERFORM GetHeaderRec.

SummarizeShopSales.
    COMPUTE  ShopTotal = ShopTotal + (QtySold * ItemCost)
    READ ShopReceiptsFile
        AT END SET EndOfShopReceiptsFile TO TRUE
    END-READ.


GetHeaderRec.
    READ ShopReceiptsFile
        AT END SET EndOfShopReceiptsFile TO TRUE
    END-READ.
```

The new test data and the result of running the program against that test data are shown in Figure 8-7.

```
HID006This is location of shop ID006
SItemId2500500595
SItemId2201500395
SItemId1000100195
SItemId0300100350
SItemId2500100195
SItemId2100100350
F00006
HID001This is location of shop ID001
SItemId0500500595
SItemId0201500395
SItemId1000100195
SItemId0300100350
F00006
HID002This is location of shop ID002
SItemId1500500595
SItemId0100100350
F00002
HID003This is location of shop ID003
SItemId0500500595
SItemId0201500395
SItemId1211501395
SItemId0500100195
SItemId1500100195
SItemId2100100350
SItemId0500100195
F00007
```

```
                   Run of Listing 8-2
Total sales for shop ID006      $99.90
Error on Shop: ID001 RCount = 00006 ACount = 00004
Total sales for shop ID002      $33.25
Total sales for shop ID003   $1,702.60
```

Figure 8-7. *Test data and results for Listing 8-2*

Some Comments about the Program

The GetHeaderRec paragraph has only one statement. Ordinarily this would be bad practice, but in this instance, I wanted to use the paragraph name to indicate the purpose of this particular READ statement. In a real program, the PERFORM GetHeaderRec statements would be replaced with the READ in the GetHeaderRec paragraph.

The logic of the program has been changed, because now the end of the shop group is indicated by the presence of a footer record. The sale records for each shop group are counted by means of the PERFORM..VARYING. For a variety of reasons, including book space constraints, the only error the program checks for is missing sale receipt records. It is assumed that in all other respects, the file is correct.

Printer Sequential Files

In a business or enterprise environment, the ability to print reports is an important property for a programming language. COBOL allows programmers to write to the printer, either directly or through an intermediate print file. COBOL treats the printer as a serial file but uses a special variant of the WRITE verb to control the placement of lines on the page. Printing is regarded as so important that not only does COBOL have the printer sequential files discussed in this section, but it also supports a special set of declarations and verbs that together constitute the COBOL Report Writer. The Report Writer introduces elements of declarative programming to COBOL. It is discussed in detail in a later chapter.

SELECT and ASSIGN

As with ordinary sequential files, the internal name used for the print file is associated with an external device, which could be an actual printer or a print file. A *print file* is a file that contains embedded printer control codes such as form feed. Generally, you write to a print file; but in a COBOL programming shop, your program may well have direct control of the printer. The metalanguage for print files is given in Figure 8-8. Since ORGANIZATION IS SEQUENTIAL is the default it may be omitted.

SELECT InternalFileName

    ASSIGN TO { Implementer Name / ExternalFileSpecification }

    [[ORGANIZATION IS] SEQUENTIAL]

Figure 8-8. Print file SELECT and ASSIGN metalanguage

Notes

Where direct control of the printer is assumed, the internal print name is assigned to an `ImplementerName`, which depends on the vendor. For instance, in HP COBOL (really VAX COBOL), the `ImplementerName` is `LINE-PRINTER` (see Example 8-3) and the name is attached to an actual printer by a `LINE-PRINTER IS DeviceName` entry in the `SPECIAL-NAMES` paragraph (`CONFIGURATION SECTION`, `ENVIRONMENT DIVISION`).

Example 8-3. SELECT and ASSIGN clauses for a Print File and a Print Device

```
SELECT MembershipReport ASSIGN TO "MembershipRpt.rpt".
SELECT MembershipReport ASSIGN TO LINE-PRINTER.
```

What Is in a Report

Even when the Report Writer is not directly used, a report created with a printer sequential file consists of groups of printed lines of different types. For instance, suppose you want to print a report that lists the membership of your local golf club. This report might consist of the following types of print lines:

- **Page Heading**
  Rolling Greens Golf Club - Membership Report

- **Page Footing**
  Page: *PageNum*

- **Column Headings**
  MemberID Member Name Type Gender

- **Membership detail line**
  MemberID MemberName MembershipType Gender

- **Report Footing**
  **** End of Membership Report ****

To set up the printer sequential file, you must create an FD for the file and a print record for each type of print line that will appear on the report. For instance, for the golf club membership report, you have to have the records shown in Example 8-4.

Example 8-4. Print Lines Required for the Golf Club Membership Report

```
01  PageHeading.
    02 FILLER          PIC X(44)
       VALUE "Rolling Greens Golf Club - Membership Report".

01  PageFooting.
    02 FILLER          PIC X(15) VALUE SPACES.
    02 FILLER          PIC X(7)  VALUE "Page : ".
    02 PrnPageNum      PIC Z9.

01  ColumnHeadings     PIC X(41)
                       VALUE "MemberID  Member Name        Type Gender".

01  MemberDetailLine.
    02 FILLER          PIC X  VALUE SPACES.
    02 PrnMemberId     PIC 9(5).
    02 FILLER          PIC X(4) VALUE SPACES.
    02 PrnMemberName   PIC X(20).
    02 FILLER          PIC XX VALUE SPACES.
    02 PrnMemberType   PIC X.
    02 FILLER          PIC X(4) VALUE SPACES.
    02 PrnGender       PIC X.

01  ReportFooting      PIC X(38)
       VALUE "**** End of Membership Report ****".
```

Problem of Multiple Print Records

When you reviewed the different types of print lines in Example 8-4, you may have realized that there is a problem. As you saw in the previous section, if a file is declared as having multiple record types, all the records map on to the same physical area of storage. This does not cause difficulties if the file is an input file, because only one type of record at a time can be in the buffer. But as you can see from the print line declarations in Example 8-4, the information in many print lines is static. It is assigned using the VALUE clause and instantiated as soon as the program starts. This means all the record values have to be in the record buffer at the same time, which is obviously impossible. In fact, to prevent the creation of print records in the FILE SECTION, there is a COBOL rule stating that, in the FILE SECTION, the VALUE clause can only be used with condition names (that is, it cannot be used to give an item an initial value).

Solution to the Multiple Print Record Problem

The solution to the problem of declaring print records is to declare the print line records in the WORKING-STORAGE SECTION and to declare a record in the file's FD entry in the FILE SECTION, which is the size of the largest print line record. You print a print line by moving it from the WORKING-STORAGE SECTION, to the record in the FILE SECTION; then that record is written to the print file. This is shown graphically in Example 8-5.

Example 8-5. Writing to a Print File

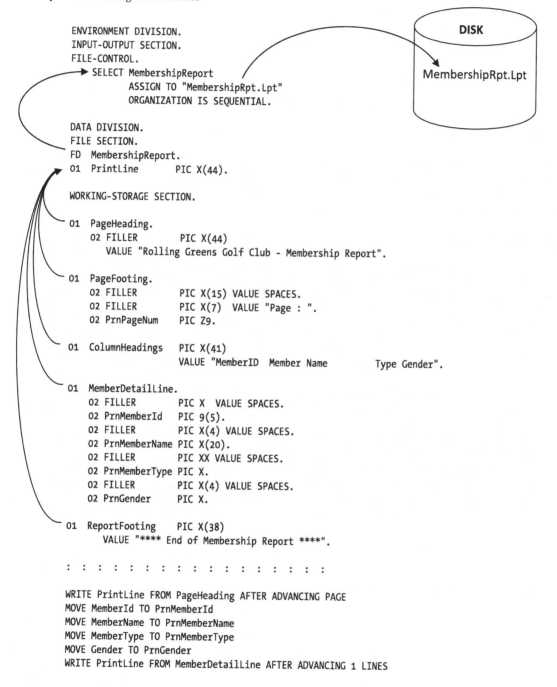

```
ENVIRONMENT DIVISION.
INPUT-OUTPUT SECTION.
FILE-CONTROL.
    SELECT MembershipReport
           ASSIGN TO "MembershipRpt.Lpt"
           ORGANIZATION IS SEQUENTIAL.

DATA DIVISION.
FILE SECTION.
FD  MembershipReport.
01  PrintLine        PIC X(44).

WORKING-STORAGE SECTION.

01  PageHeading.
    02 FILLER        PIC X(44)
       VALUE "Rolling Greens Golf Club - Membership Report".

01  PageFooting.
    02 FILLER        PIC X(15) VALUE SPACES.
    02 FILLER        PIC X(7)  VALUE "Page : ".
    02 PrnPageNum    PIC Z9.

01  ColumnHeadings   PIC X(41)
                     VALUE "MemberID  Member Name         Type Gender".

01  MemberDetailLine.
    02 FILLER        PIC X  VALUE SPACES.
    02 PrnMemberId   PIC 9(5).
    02 FILLER        PIC X(4) VALUE SPACES.
    02 PrnMemberName PIC X(20).
    02 FILLER        PIC XX VALUE SPACES.
    02 PrnMemberType PIC X.
    02 FILLER        PIC X(4) VALUE SPACES.
    02 PrnGender     PIC X.

01  ReportFooting    PIC X(38)
       VALUE "**** End of Membership Report ****".

 :  :  :  :  :  :  :  :  :  :  :  :  :  :  :  :  :

WRITE PrintLine FROM PageHeading AFTER ADVANCING PAGE
MOVE MemberId TO PrnMemberId
MOVE MemberName TO PrnMemberName
MOVE MemberType TO PrnMemberType
MOVE Gender TO PrnGender
WRITE PrintLine FROM MemberDetailLine AFTER ADVANCING 1 LINES
```

DISK

MembershipRpt.Lpt

WRITE Syntax Revisited

When I discussed the WRITE statement in the previous chapter, I noted that I was postponing discussion of the ADVANCING CLAUSE until I dealt with print files. To refresh your memory, the metalanguage for the WRITE statement is given in Figure 8-9.

WRITE RecordName[FROM Identifier]

$$\left[\begin{array}{l} \begin{Bmatrix} \underline{BEFORE} \\ \underline{AFTER} \end{Bmatrix} \text{ADVANCING} \begin{Bmatrix} \text{AdvanceNum} \begin{bmatrix} \underline{LINE} \\ \underline{LINES} \end{bmatrix} \\ \text{MnemonicName} \\ \underline{PAGE} \end{Bmatrix} \end{array}\right]$$

Figure 8-9. *Metalanguage for the* WRITE *verb*

The syntax for writing to print files is more complicated than that used for writing in ordinary sequential files because it must contain entries to allow you to control the vertical placement of the print lines. For instance, the statement WRITE PrintLine BEFORE ADVANCING 2 LINES sends the data in PrintLine to the printer, after which the printer advances two lines.

Notes on WRITE

The ADVANCING clause is used to position the lines on the page when writing to a print file or a printer. The ADVANCING clause uses the BEFORE or AFTER phrase to specify whether advancing is to occur before the line is printed or after.

The PAGE option writes a form feed (goes to a new page) to the print file or printer. MnemonicName refers to a vendor-specific page control command. It is defined in the SPECIAL-NAMES paragraph.

When you write to a print file, you generally use the WRITE..FROM option because the print records are described in the WORKING-STORAGE SECTION. When the WRITE..FROM option is used, the data in the source area is moved into the record buffer and then the contents of the buffer are written to the print file. WRITE..FROM is the equivalent of a MOVE SourceItem TO RecordBuffer statement followed by a WRITE RecordBuffer statement.

SOME IGNORED WRITE VERB ENTRIES

I have ignored some print-related formats of the WRITE verb on the basis that if you need this level of print sophistication, you should be using the Report Writer. The full WRITE syntax includes the END-OF-PAGE clause, as shown in the following illustration; this is connected to the LINAGE clause specified in the file's FD entry. The LINAGE clause specifies the number of lines that can fit on a page, and this in turn allows the end of the page to be automatically detected. If you want to explore this further, you should read your implementer manual.

WRITE RecordName [FROM Identifier]

$$\left[\begin{array}{l} \begin{Bmatrix} \underline{BEFORE} \\ \underline{AFTER} \end{Bmatrix} \text{ADVANCING} \begin{Bmatrix} \text{AdvanceNum} \begin{bmatrix} \underline{LINE} \\ \underline{LINES} \end{bmatrix} \\ \text{MnemonicName} \\ \underline{PAGE} \end{Bmatrix} \end{array}\right]$$

$$\left[\text{AT} \begin{Bmatrix} \underline{END\text{-}OF\text{-}PAGE} \\ \underline{EOP} \end{Bmatrix} StatementBlock \right]$$

$$\left[\underline{NOT} \text{ AT} \begin{Bmatrix} \underline{END\text{-}OF\text{-}PAGE} \\ \underline{EOP} \end{Bmatrix} StatementBlock \right]$$

[END-WRITE]

Example Program

Listing 8-3 contains a program that produces a simple report to show a golf club's membership list. The program keeps a count of the number of lines printed; it changes the page and prints the headings again when the line count is greater than 49. A page count is also kept, and this is printed at the bottom of each page. The report produced by running the program is shown in Figure 8-10.

Listing 8-3. Program to Print the Golf Club Membership Report

```
IDENTIFICATION DIVISION.
PROGRAM-ID. Listing8-3.
AUTHOR. Michael Coughlan.
ENVIRONMENT DIVISION.
INPUT-OUTPUT SECTION.
FILE-CONTROL.
    SELECT MembershipReport
          ASSIGN TO " Listing8-3-Members.rpt"
          ORGANIZATION IS SEQUENTIAL.

    SELECT MemberFile  ASSIGN TO "Listing8-3Members.dat"
          ORGANIZATION IS LINE SEQUENTIAL.

DATA DIVISION.
FILE SECTION.
FD  MembershipReport.
01  PrintLine        PIC X(44).

FD  MemberFile.
01  MemberRec.
    88 EndOfMemberFile   VALUE HIGH-VALUES.
    02 MemberId       PIC X(5).
    02 MemberName     PIC X(20).
    02 MemberType     PIC 9.
    02 Gender         PIC X.


WORKING-STORAGE SECTION.
01  PageHeading.
    02 FILLER         PIC X(44)
       VALUE "Rolling Greens Golf Club - Membership Report".

01  PageFooting.
    02 FILLER         PIC X(15) VALUE SPACES.
    02 FILLER         PIC X(7)  VALUE "Page : ".
    02 PrnPageNum     PIC Z9.

01  ColumnHeadings   PIC X(41)
                     VALUE "MemberID  Member Name          Type Gender".

01  MemberDetailLine.
    02 FILLER         PIC X  VALUE SPACES.
    02 PrnMemberId    PIC 9(5).
```

```
        02 FILLER       PIC X(4) VALUE SPACES.
        02 PrnMemberName PIC X(20).
        02 FILLER       PIC XX VALUE SPACES.
        02 PrnMemberType PIC X.
        02 FILLER       PIC X(4) VALUE SPACES.
        02 PrnGender    PIC X.

   01  ReportFooting    PIC X(38)
           VALUE "**** End of Membership Report ****".

   01  LineCount        PIC 99 VALUE ZEROS.
        88 NewPageRequired  VALUE 40 THRU 99.

   01  PageCount        PIC 99 VALUE ZEROS.

PROCEDURE DIVISION.
PrintMembershipReport.
    OPEN INPUT MemberFile
    OPEN OUTPUT MembershipReport
    PERFORM PrintPageHeadings
    READ MemberFile
        AT END SET EndOfMemberFile TO TRUE
    END-READ
    PERFORM PrintReportBody UNTIL EndOfMemberFile
    WRITE PrintLine FROM ReportFooting AFTER ADVANCING 5 LINES
    CLOSE MemberFile, MembershipReport
    STOP RUN.

PrintPageHeadings.
    WRITE PrintLine FROM PageHeading AFTER ADVANCING PAGE
    WRITE PrintLine FROM ColumnHeadings AFTER ADVANCING 2 LINES
    MOVE 3 TO LineCount
    ADD 1 TO PageCount.

PrintReportBody.
    IF NewPageRequired
       MOVE PageCount TO PrnPageNum
       WRITE PrintLine FROM PageFooting AFTER ADVANCING 5 LINES
       PERFORM PrintPageHeadings
    END-IF.
    MOVE MemberId    TO PrnMemberId
    MOVE MemberName  TO PrnMemberName
    MOVE MemberType  TO PrnMemberType
    MOVE Gender      TO PrnGender
    WRITE PrintLine FROM MemberDetailLine AFTER ADVANCING 1 LINE
    ADD 1 TO LineCount
    READ MemberFile
        AT END SET EndOfMemberFile TO TRUE
    END-READ.
```

```
Rolling Greens Golf Club - Membership Report

Meml  Rolling Greens Golf Club - Membership Report
 A1:
 A1:  MemberID   Member Name           Type Gender
 A1:   F0003    Niamh Lynch              1    F
 A1:   F0104    Michael Roddy            1    M
 A1:   F0105    Rolling Greens Golf Club - Membership Report
 A1:   F0106
 A1:   F0107     MemberID   Member Name          Type Gender
 B0:   F0128      L0022    Michael O'Brien        1    M
 B0:   F0129      L0023    Donal O'Donoghue       1    M
 B0:   F0130      M0024    Mark Deasy             1    M
 B0:   F0131      M0025    Joseph  Kiely          2    M
 B0:   F0132      M0026    Martin Goodwin         1    M
 B0:   F0133      M0027    Mary Maher             1    F
 B0:   G0212      M0028    David Hayes            1    M
 C2:   G0311      M0029    Kevin Kirwan           1    M
 C2:   G0410      M0030    Arthur McCormack       1    M
 C2:   G0509
 C2:   G0608
 C2:   G0707
 C2:   G0806
 C2:   H1234     **** End of Membership Report ****
 C2:   H1235    Eoghan O'Toole        2     M
 D6:   H1236    Hao Ming O'Connor     1     M
 D7:   H1237    Donald Hogan          2     M
 D7:   H1238    Ciara Ryan            1     F
 D8:   H1239    Shu Carroll           3     F
 D9:   H1240    Shane Reen            1     M
 D9:   H1241    Matthew Ryan          1     M
 E1:   H1242    William Carty         2     M
 E1:   K0012    Shane Cronin          1     M
 E1:   K0013    Kristofer Geraghty    2     M
 E1:   K0014    Padraig Webster       1     M
 E1:   K0015    David McWeeney        1     M
 E1:   K0016    Sharon Doyle          1     F
 E1:   K0017    Aaron Brady           1     M
 E1:   K0018    Jay Mc Carthy         1     M
 F0(   L0019    Barry Murphy          1     M
 F0(   L0020    Triona  Keyes         1     F
       L0021    Patrick Gillen        3     M



                 Page :   2
```

Figure 8-10. *Report produced by Listing 8-3*

Report Writer Version

The Report Writer has been mentioned a number of times in this chapter, so it might be useful to compare the PROCEDURE DIVISION of the program in Listing 8-3 with the PROCEDURE DIVISION of the Report Writer version of the report shown in Example 8-6. How is it able to do so much work with so little PROCEDURE DIVISION code? A short answer is that that is the magic of the Report Writer and declarative programming. A detailed answer will have to wait until I examine the Report Writer in a later chapter.

Example 8-6. PROCEDURE DIVISION for Report Writer Version of the Golf Club Membership Report

```
PROCEDURE DIVISION.
PrintMembershipReport.
    OPEN INPUT MemberFile
    OPEN OUTPUT MembershipReport
    INITIATE ClubMemebershipReport
    READ MemberFile
        AT END SET EndOfMemberFile TO TRUE
    END-READ
    PERFORM UNTIL EndOfMemberFile
       GENERATE MemberLine
       READ MemberFile
         AT END SET EndOfMemberFile TO TRUE
       END-READ
    END-PERFORM
    TERMINATE ClubMemebershipReport
    CLOSE MemberFile, MembershipReport
    STOP RUN.
```

Variable-Length Records

COBOL programs normally process fixed-length records, but sometimes files contain records of different lengths. In the first section of this chapter, you saw that a file might consist of a number of different record types. But even though, taken as a whole, the records in the file vary in size, each record type is a fixed-length record. You can, however, have true variable-length records, meaning you do not know the structure or size of the records (although you have to know the maximum size and may know the minimum size). For instance, in an ordinary text file such as might be produced by MS Notepad, the lines of text have no structure and vary in size from line to line. This section demonstrates how files containing true variable-length records may be declared and processed.

FD Entries for Variable-Length Records

When the FD entry for sequential files was introduced, you only saw a simplified version that consisted of the letters *FD* followed by the file name. Actually, the FD entry can be more complex than you have seen so far, and it can have a large number of subordinate clauses (see your implementer manual or help files). Some of these clauses are not required for all computers. For instance, the BLOCK CONTAINS clause is only required for computers where the number of characters read or written in one I/O operation is under programmatic control. If the block size is fixed, it is not required. Other clauses are syntax retained from previous versions of COBOL and are now treated as comments. I ignore these. Some clauses are important for direct-access file organizations; I deal with these when I examine these file organizations. The RECORD IS VARYING IN SIZE clause allows you to specify that a file contains variable-length records. The metalanguage for the expanded FD entry is given in Figure 8-11 and Example 8-7 demonstrates how to use these new FD entries.

FD *FileName*

    <u>RECORD</u> IS <u>VARYING</u> IN SIZE

    [[FROM *SmallestSize#l*][TO *LargestSize#l*]CHARACTERS]

    [<u>DEPENDING</u> ON *RecordSize#i*]

Figure 8-11. RECORD IS VARYING *clause for variable-length records*

Notes on Varying-Length Records

The RECORD IS VARYING IN SIZE clause without the DEPENDING ON phrase is not strictly required, because the compiler can work out this information from the record sizes. That is why it was not included in the multiple record-type declarations in the first section of this chapter.

The RecordSize#i in the DEPENDING ON phase must be an elementary unsigned integer data-item declared in the WORKING-STORAGE SECTION. When a record defined with the RECORD IS VARYING IN SIZE..DEPENDING ON phrase is read from a file, the length of the record read in to the buffer is moved into the RecordSize#i data item. When a record defined with RECORD IS VARYING IN SIZE..DEPENDING ON is written to a file, the length of the record to be written must first be moved to RecordSize#i data-item, and then the WRITE statement must be executed.

Example 8-7. FD Entries with the RECORD IS VARYING Phrase

```
FD Textfile
   RECORD IS VARYING IN SIZE
   FROM 1 TO 80 CHARACTERS
   DEPENDING ON TextLineLength.
```

Or we may define the file as -

```
FD Textfile
   RECORD IS VARYING IN SIZE
   DEPENDING ON TextLineLength.
```

Example Program

Listing 8-4 is an example program that demonstrates how to read a file that contains variable-length records. One problem with variable-length records is that although the records are variable length, the buffer into which they are read is fixed in size. So if only the characters that have been read from the file are required, they must be extracted from the record buffer. In this program, reference modification and NameLength are used to slice NameLength number of characters from the buffer. *Reference modification* is a COBOL string-handling facility that you explore in a later chapter. To demonstrate that you have extracted only the required characters, asterisks are used to bracket the names. Figure 8-12 is a diagrammatic representation of how reference modification is used to extract the name from the record buffer.

Listing 8-4. Processing Variable-Length Records

```
IDENTIFICATION DIVISION.
PROGRAM-ID.  Listing8-4.
AUTHOR.  Michael Coughlan.
* This program demonstrates how to read variable length records.
* It also demonstrates how a file may be assigned its actual name
* at run time rather than compile time (dynamic vs static).
* The record buffer is a fixed 40 characters in size but the
* lengths or names vary so Reference Modification is used to extract
* only the  number of characters from the record buffer.

ENVIRONMENT DIVISION.
INPUT-OUTPUT SECTION.
FILE-CONTROL.
   SELECT LongNameFile
         ASSIGN TO NameOfFile
         ORGANIZATION IS LINE SEQUENTIAL.
```

```
DATA DIVISION.
FILE SECTION.
FD LongNameFile
   RECORD IS VARYING IN SIZE
   DEPENDING ON NameLength.
01 LongNameRec        PIC X(40).
   88 EndOfNames      VALUE HIGH-VALUES.

WORKING-STORAGE SECTION.
01 NameLength         PIC 99.
01 NameOfFile         PIC X(20).

PROCEDURE DIVISION.
Begin.
   DISPLAY "Enter the name of the file :- "
      WITH NO ADVANCING
   ACCEPT NameOfFile.
   OPEN INPUT LongNameFile.
   READ LongNameFile
     AT END SET EndOfNames TO TRUE
   END-READ
   PERFORM UNTIL EndOfNames
      DISPLAY "***" LongNameRec(1:NameLength) "***"
      READ LongNameFile
        AT END SET EndOfNames TO TRUE
      END-READ
   END-PERFORM
   CLOSE LongNameFile
   STOP RUN.
```

Run of Listing8-4

```
Enter the name of the file :-
longnames.dat
***Oscar Fingal O'Flahertie Wills Wilde***
***Colm Padraig Brendan Ryan***
***Kevin Tucker Barry***
***Maria  Roseanna Catherine Donovan***
***Liam  Sean Lorigan***
***Maeve Fitzgibbon Mencke***
***Shane Philip Adrian Cross***
***Stephen Rory Mulhall***
***Niamh Karen Ciara   Lynch***
***Darren Peter  Hastings***
***Aoife Triona Ryan***
***Hao Ming Barry O'Connor***
```

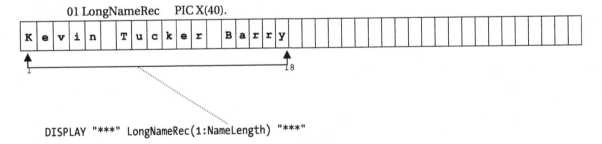

DISPLAY "***" LongNameRec(1:NameLength) "***"

Figure 8-12. *Using reference modification to extract the name from the record*

Summary

This chapter examined how files that contain records of different lengths may be defined and used. The first section of the chapter dealt with files in which the record lengths are different because the file contains fixed-length records of different types. The last section dealt with files that contain real variable-length records. The middle section of the chapter discussed the problem of print files. It explained why the different types of print lines required when printing a report cannot be declared as different records in the file's FD entry but must instead be declared in the WORKING-STORAGE SECTION.

In the next chapter, you continue your exploration of printed output by examining edited pictures. Edited pictures allow you to format data for output. In some of the example programs in this and previous chapters, I have used edited pictures without explanation because the context made obvious what was happening. But seeing edited pictures in action and knowing how to use them are different things. The next chapter examines edited pictures in detail and discusses how to format data so that leading zeros are suppressed; so that the currency symbol floats against the non-zero digits of the number; and so that blanks, commas, zeros, and slashes are inserted where they are required. Table 8-1 gives a preview of some of the formatting that can be applied to data.

Table 8-1. *Preview of Some of the Edited Picture Formatting Effects*

Effect	Value
Original value	00014584.95
With commas inserted	00,014,584.95
With zero-suppression added	14,584.95
With check security and currency symbol added	$***14,584.95
With floating + sign	+14,584.95
With floating currency symbol	$14,584.95
With zeros inserted after the decimal point	$14,584.00
With slashes inserted in the middle of the number	00/014/584.95
With three zeros inserted in the number	00014000584.95
With three blanks inserted in the number	00014 584.95

PROGRAMMING EXERCISE 1

It is exercise time again. Now, where did you put that 2B pencil? Write a program to satisfy the following specification.

University Entrants Summary Report

A program is required that will process the first-year-student entrants file (Entrants.dat) to produce a summary that shows the number of first-year students in each course. The summary should be displayed on the screen ordered by ascending CourseCode. An output template is given next.

Output Template

```
    First Year Entrants Summary
    Course Code     NumOfStudents
       LM999           9,999
       LM999           9,999
    :               :
    :               :
       LM999           9,999
       LM999           9,999

 Total Students:  99,999
```

Entrants File

The entrants file (Entrants.dat) is a sequential file sequenced on ascending CourseCode. The records in the file have the following description:

Field	Type	Length	Value
StudentId	9	8	0-99999999
CourseCode	X	5	-
Gender	X	1	M/F

Some Statements You Need for Your Program

To make this programming exercise easier, some of the statements and data declarations required for your program are given next.

Executable Statements

```
DISPLAY Headingline1
DISPLAY Headingline2
DISPLAY CourseLine
DISPLAY SPACES
DISPLAY FinalTotalLine
MOVE CourseCode TO PrnCourseCode
MOVE CourseTotal TO PrnCourseTotal
MOVE FinalTotal TO PrnFinalTotal
READ EntrantsFile
    AT END SET EndOfFile TO TRUE
END-READ
OPEN INPUT EntrantsFile
CLOSE EntrantsFile
ADD 1 TO CourseTotal, FinalTotal
MOVE ZEROS TO CourseTotal
MOVE ZEROS TO FinalTotal
MOVE CourseCode TO PrevCourseCode
```

Some Data Descriptions

```
01 HeadingLine1      PIC X(31) VALUE "    First Year Entrants Summary".
01 HeadingLine2      PIC X(31) VALUE "   Course Code    NumOfStudents".
01 CourseLine.
   02 FILLER         PIC X(5) VALUE SPACES.
   02 PrnCourseCode  PIC X(5).
   02 FILLER         PIC X(10) VALUE SPACES.
   02 PrnCourseTotal PIC Z,ZZ9.
01 FinalTotalLine.
   02 FILLER         PIC X(19) VALUE "  Total Students:".
   02 PrnFinalTotal  PIC ZZ,ZZ9.
01 CourseTotal       PIC 9(4).
01 FinalTotal        PIC 9(5).
01 PrevCourseCode    PIC X(5).
```

PROGRAMMING EXERCISE 2

Change the program you wrote for Programming Exercise 1 so that it now writes the report to a print file.

The answer to this exercise is given below. Because exercise 1 is substantially the same as exercise 2, the same answer should serve both.

PROGRAMMING EXERCISES 1 AND 2: ANSWER

```
IDENTIFICATION DIVISION.
PROGRAM-ID.  Listing8-5.
AUTHOR.  Michael Coughlan.
* This program processes the first year students entrants file to produce
* a summary report sequenced on ascending Course Code that shows the number
* of first year students* in each course.
* The Entrants File is a sequential file sequenced on ascending CourseCode.

ENVIRONMENT DIVISION.
INPUT-OUTPUT SECTION.
FILE-CONTROL.
   SELECT EntrantsFile ASSIGN TO "Listing8-5-Entrants.Dat"
          ORGANIZATION IS LINE SEQUENTIAL.

   SELECT SummaryReport ASSIGN TO "Listing8-5-Summary.Rpt"
          ORGANIZATION IS SEQUENTIAL.

DATA DIVISION.
FILE SECTION.
FD EntrantsFile.
01 StudentRecord.
   88 EndOfEntrantsFile      VALUE HIGH-VALUES.
   02 StudentId              PIC 9(8).
   02 CourseCode             PIC X(5).
   02 Gender                 PIC X.
```

```
FD SummaryReport.
01 PrintLine                   PIC X(35).

WORKING-STORAGE SECTION.
01 HeadingLine1      PIC X(31) VALUE "    First Year Entrants Summary".

01 HeadingLine2      PIC X(31) VALUE "   Course Code      NumOfStudents".

01 CourseLine.
   02 FILLER         PIC X(5) VALUE SPACES.
   02 PrnCourseCode  PIC X(5).
   02 FILLER         PIC X(10) VALUE SPACES.
   02 PrnCourseTotal PIC BBZZ9.

01 FinalTotalLine.
   02 FILLER         PIC X(19) VALUE " Total Students:".
   02 PrnFinalTotal  PIC BZ,ZZ9.

01 CourseTotal       PIC 9(4) VALUE ZEROS.
01 FinalTotal        PIC 9(5) VALUE ZEROS.
01 PrevCourseCode    PIC X(5) VALUE ZEROS.

PROCEDURE DIVISION.
ProduceSummaryReport.
   OPEN INPUT EntrantsFile
   OPEN OUTPUT SummaryReport
   WRITE PrintLine FROM HeadingLine1 AFTER ADVANCING PAGE
   WRITE PrintLine FROM HeadingLine2 AFTER ADVANCING 2 LINES
   READ EntrantsFile
     AT END SET EndOfEntrantsFile TO TRUE
   END-READ
   PERFORM UNTIL EndOfEntrantsFile
     MOVE CourseCode TO PrnCourseCode, PrevCourseCode
     MOVE ZEROS TO CourseTotal
     PERFORM UNTIL CourseCode NOT = PrevCourseCode
        ADD 1 TO CourseTotal, FinalTotal
        READ EntrantsFile
          AT END SET EndOfEntrantsFile TO TRUE
        END-READ
     END-PERFORM
     MOVE CourseTotal TO PrnCourseTotal
     WRITE PrintLine FROM CourseLine AFTER ADVANCING 1 LINE
   END-PERFORM
   MOVE FinalTotal TO PrnFinalTotal
   WRITE PrintLine FROM FinalTotalLine AFTER ADVANCING 2 LINES
   CLOSE EntrantsFile, SummaryReport

   STOP RUN.
```

CHAPTER 9

Edited Pictures

In the previous chapter, you saw how a printed report may be created by sending data directly to the printer or to a print file. In this chapter, you continue your exploration of printed output by examining how data may be formatted for output.

Most users of the data produced by a COBOL report program are not content with the simple raw, unformatted data. Unformatted data is difficult to read, so users want it presented in a way that makes it easier to understand. This is especially true of numeric data. Users may want numeric values separated into thousands, and they may want leading zeros to be suppressed. If the report contains currency values, then users may want the currency symbol to be printed, and they may want the symbol floated up against the first non-zero digit. In COBOL, all these effects and more can be achieved using edited pictures.

Edited Pictures

Edited pictures are picture clauses that format data intended for output to a screen or a printer. To enable the data items to be formatted, special symbols are embedded in the picture clause. These symbols supplement the basic 9, X, A, V, and S picture clause symbols. The additional symbols are referred to as *edit symbols*, and picture clauses that include edit symbols are called *edited Pictures*. The term *edit* is used because the edit symbols cause the data in the edited item to be changed or "edited."

When numeric data is moved into an edited numeric data item, it obeys the rules for numeric moves, with decimal-point alignment and zero-filling or truncation as necessary. Although an edited numeric data item cannot be used as an active operand in a computation, it may be used as the receiving field of a computation. That is, it may be used to the right of the word GIVING.

Formatting Output

The last chapter ended with an example that showed a number of the formatting effects that may be applied to a data value. The example did not show how those effects were achieved. You start this chapter by revisiting that example and examining a program that shows how edited pictures were used to achieve those effects. After you have seen how edited pictures are used in a program, this chapter explores the topic of edited pictures in detail. You examine the different kinds of editing that may be applied to data, and you expand your knowledge of the special symbols used to create edited pictures.

Table 9-1 restates the example given in Table 8-1 in the previous chapter. This example shows some of the different kinds of formatting that may be applied to a data value. Among the effects are numeric values divided into thousands by commas, suppression of leading zeros, and the plus sign and the currency symbol floating up against the first non-zero value.

Table 9-1. *Edited Picture Formatting Effects*

Effect	Value
Original value	00014584.95
With commas inserted	00,014,584.95
With zero-suppression added	14,584.95
With check security and currency symbol added	$***14,584.95
With floating + sign	+14,584.95
With floating currency symbol	$14,584.95
With zeros inserted after the decimal point	$14,584.00
With slashes inserted in the middle of the number	00/014/584.95
With three zeros inserted in the number	00014000584.95
With three blanks inserted in the number	00014 584.95

Immediate Editing

The most important thing to know about an edited picture is that the data formatting is not done when the edited data is output to a printer or a computer screen; it is immediate. The moment data is moved into an edited item, the data itself is modified according to the formatting instructions specified by the edited picture.

It can be very useful to know that when a data value is moved into an edited item, it is immediately formatted; once you know that, you can think of a number of manipulations that you can do to the edited data to achieve interesting effects. For instance, you could use COBOL string-handling to replace the floating dollar sign with the Euro, Yen, or other currency symbol; or you might replace the slash symbol in a date with the hyphen or some other separator. Later, this chapter returns to this idea and looks at some examples.

Example Program

Listing 9-1 is a simple program that shows how the formatting effects of Table 9-1 were achieved. This program has been pared down to its essential elements so that you can concentrate on the editing effects. The program uses the DISPLAY statement to output the edited data to the screen.

Listing 9-1. Using Edited Pictures to Format Data for Output

```
IDENTIFICATION DIVISION.
PROGRAM-ID. Listing9-1.
AUTHOR. Michael Coughlan.
DATA DIVISION.
WORKING-STORAGE SECTION.
01 NumericValue    PIC 9(8)V99  VALUE 00014584.95.
01 Edit1    PIC  99,999,999.99.
01 Edit2    PIC  ZZ,ZZZ,ZZ9.99.
01 Edit3    PIC  $*,***,**9.99.
01 Edit4    PIC  ++,+++,++9.99.
01 Edit5    PIC  $$,$$$,$$9.99.
01 Edit6    PIC  $$,$$$,$$9.00.
```

```
01 Edit7     PIC   99/999/999.99.
01 Edit8     PIC   99999000999.99.
01 Edit9     PIC   99999BBB999.99.


PROCEDURE DIVISION.
Begin.
MOVE NumericValue TO Edit1
DISPLAY "Edit1 = " Edit1

MOVE NumericValue TO Edit2
DISPLAY "Edit2 = " Edit2

MOVE NumericValue TO Edit3
DISPLAY "Edit3 = " Edit3

MOVE NumericValue TO Edit4
DISPLAY "Edit4 = " Edit4

MOVE NumericValue TO Edit5
DISPLAY "Edit5 = " Edit5

MOVE NumericValue TO Edit6
DISPLAY "Edit6 = " Edit6

MOVE NumericValue TO Edit7
DISPLAY "Edit7 = " Edit7

MOVE NumericValue TO Edit8
DISPLAY "Edit8 = " Edit8

MOVE NumericValue TO Edit9
DISPLAY "Edit9 = " Edit9


STOP RUN.
```

Listing 9-1 Output

```
Edit1 = 00,014,584.95
Edit2 =    14,584.95
Edit3 = $***14,584.95
Edit4 =    +14,584.95
Edit5 =    $14,584.95
Edit6 =    $14,584.00
Edit7 = 00/014/584.95
Edit8 = 00014000584.95
Edit9 = 00014   584.95
```

The data item NumericValue is a decimal number. The V in the picture clause indicates the position of the assumed decimal point; but the actual decimal point, which is a text character, is not held in the data item. To display or print an actual decimal point, you must use an edited picture containing the decimal-point editing symbol. If you examine the Edit1 data item in Listing 9-1, you see that the V, which normally indicates the position of the decimal point, has been replaced by the actual decimal-point character.

When the value in NumericValue is moved into the edited item, the data is immediately modified according to the formatting specified by the edit symbols. A brief explanation of the effect of moving data from NumericValue to each of the edited items is given next:

- When NumericValue is moved to Edit1, the assumed decimal point in NumericValue aligns with the actual decimal point in Edit1, and the actual decimal-point character is inserted. In addition, commas are inserted where they are specified in the edited picture.

- The zero-suppression symbol **Z** in Edit2 modifies the data so that leading zeros are replaced with spaces.

- In Edit3, the edit symbols cause the dollar sign to be inserted and the leading zeros to be replaced with asterisks.

- The plus-sign symbols in Edit4 cause the sign to float up against the first non-zero digit.

- The data in Edit5 is similarly modified, but using the dollar sign.

- The editing specified for Edit6 inserts two zeros after the decimal point. This means when the data is moved into Edit6 and there is alignment along the decimal point, there is no room for the digits 9 and 5, which are truncated.

- Edit7 shows how the slash character can be inserted into a number. The slash is used to good effect when formatting dates, but it is used here to show that it is not restricted to date values.

- In Edit8, the zero edit symbol is used to insert zeros into the middle of the number.

- In Edit9, the blank symbol B is used to insert spaces or blanks into the middle of the number. This can be useful for formatting dates or for aligning report headings or values.

Types of Editing

There are two basic types of editing in COBOL: insertion editing, and suppression and replacement editing. Insertion editing modifies the data value by inserting additional characters into the data. This type of editing has the following subcategories:

- Simple insertion

- Special insertion

- Fixed insertion

- Floating insertion

Suppression and replacement editing modifies the data value by suppressing leading zeros and replacing them with a replacement character. This type of editing has the following subcategories:

- Zero-suppression and replacement with spaces

- Zero-suppression and replacement with asterisks (*)

■ **COBOL Detail**   Zero-suppression and replacement with spaces can also be achieved by using the BLANK WHEN ZERO clause. This clause can sometimes be useful because it may be used with a picture clause that contains editing symbols (except the asterisk [*] replacement symbol). For instance, 01 BlankedNumber PIC +$$$,$$9 BLANK WHEN ZERO.

Editing Symbols

Special picture symbols are used in an edited-picture clause to specify the formatting required. Table 9-2 shows the special picture clause symbols used in edited pictures and categorizes them by the type of editing they are used for.

Table 9-2. *Editing Symbols*

Edit Symbol	Editing Type
, B O /	Simple insertion
.	Special insertion
+ - CR DB $	Fixed insertion
+ - $	Floating insertion
Z *	Suppression and replacement

Insertion Editing

Insertion editing is so named because the edit symbol is inserted into the data value at the same position it occupies in the picture clause. As mentioned earlier, there are four types of insertion editing: simple insertion, special insertion, fixed insertion, and floating insertion. The following sections explore these types of editing in more detail.

Simple-Insertion Editing

A simple-insertion edited picture consists of a PICTURE string that specifies the relevant insertion character(s) in the required character position. When a data value is moved into the edited item, the insertion characters are inserted into the item at the position specified in the PICTURE. Simple insertion may be used with both numeric-edited and alphanumeric-edited data items.

As shown in Table 9-2, the comma, the blank or space, the zero, and the slash are the simple-insertion editing symbols. In simple insertion, all the inserted characters count toward the number of characters printed or displayed. For instance, an item described as PIC 9999/99/99 occupies ten character positions when printed. You need to be aware of this when designing report layouts.

How the Symbols Work

The comma symbol (,) instructs the computer to insert a comma at the character position where the symbol occurs. The comma counts toward the size of the printed item. When used with zero-suppression and replacement or floating insertion, the comma operates in a special way: if all characters to the left of the comma are zeros, the comma is replaced with the appropriate character (currency symbol, asterisk, or space).

The space or blank (B), slash (/), and zero (0) symbols instruct the computer to insert the appropriate character at the position where the symbol occurs in the PICTURE string.

Simple-Insertion Examples

Table 9-3 gives some simple-insertion example PICTURE strings, shows the formatting that these edited pictures apply to data values, and provides a comment that explains what is done.

Table 9-3. *Simple-Insertion Examples*

Sending		Receiving		Comments
Picture	Data	Picture	Result	
PIC X(8)	MikeRyan	PIC X(4)BBX(4)	Mike□□Ryan	Spaces are inserted. Size = 10 characters.
PIC X(9)	10Jan2013	PIC XX/XXX/(4)	10/Jan/2013	Slashes are inserted. Size = 11 characters.
PIC 9(6)	123456	PIC 999,999	123,456	Comma is inserted. Size = 7 characters.
PIC 9(6)	000045	PIC 9(3),9(3)	000,045	Comma is inserted. Note the leading zeros. Size = 7 characters.
PIC 9(6)	000045	PIC ZZZ,ZZZ	□□□□□45	Leading zeros are replaced with spaces (represented by □). Because there is a zero to the left of the comma, it is replaced by a space. Size = 7 characters.
PIC 9(6)	000345	PIC ***,***	****345	Zero-suppression and the zero to the left of the comma cause the comma to be replaced by an asterisk. Size = 7 characters.
PIC 9(6)	002345	PIC ***,***	**2,345	Zero-suppression is used, but there is a non-zero to the left of the comma, so the comma is inserted. Size = 7 characters.
PIC 9(8)	12252013	PIC 99B99B9999	12□25□2013	Spaces are inserted. Size = 10 characters.
PIC 9(8)	12252013	PIC 99/99/9999	12/25/2013	Slashes are inserted. Size = 10 characters.
PIC 9(6)	7654329	PIC 990099	430029	No explicit decimal point in either the sending or receiving field means each is treated as if it had a decimal point in the rightmost position. The zero characters are inserted, so there is only room in the data for four of the sending field's digits. After decimal-point alignment, digits 765 are truncated. Size = 6 characters.
PIC 9(4)V999	7654329	PIC 999.009	654.003	The assumed decimal point aligns with the actual decimal point in the receiving field, causing the most significant digit (7) to be truncated. The zero characters are inserted after the decimal point, which only leaves room for one digit; so the digits 29 are truncated on the left. Size= 7 characters.

Special-Insertion Editing

The only special-insertion symbol is the decimal point. The decimal-point insertion symbol has the effect of inserting an actual decimal point into the edited item. This type of editing is called *special insertion* because of the effect on data moved into the edited item. Data sent to the edited field is aligned along the decimal point, with zero-filling or truncation as required. The decimal point is inserted in the character position where the symbol occurs, and there may be only one decimal point. The decimal-point symbol cannot be mixed with either the V (assumed decimal point) or the P (scaling position) symbol. The purpose and operation of the P symbol is explored later in this chapter.

Special-Insertion Examples

Table 9-4 gives some special-insertion example picture strings and shows the formatting that these edited pictures apply to data values. You probably noticed that the last example in Table 9-3 was an example of special insertion as well as simple insertion.

Table 9-4. *Special-Insertion Editing Examples*

Sending		Receiving		Comments
Picture	Data	Picture	Result	
PIC 9(3)V99	63485	PIC 9999.99	0634.85	The decimal point is inserted; and after alignment, the digits of the sending item are inserted to the left and right of the decimal point, with the result that there is zero-filling on the left. Size = 7 characters.
PIC 9(4)V99	063485	PIC 9999.9	0634.8	The decimal point is inserted; and after alignment, the digits of the sending item are inserted to the left and right of the decimal point, with the result that there is truncation on the right (5). Size = 6 characters.
PIC 9(4)V99	363485	PIC 999.99	634.85	The decimal point is inserted; and after alignment, the digits of the sending item are inserted to the left and right of the decimal point with the result that there is truncation on the left (3). Size = 6 characters.
PIC 9(4)	3485	PIC 999.99	485.00	The decimal point is inserted. The sending field is treated as if it had a decimal point in the rightmost position. After alignment, there is truncation of the leftmost digit (3) and zero-filling on the left. Size = 6 characters.

Fixed-Insertion Editing

Fixed-insertion editing is so named because it inserts the edit symbol in a fixed position at the beginning or end of the edited item. The fixed insertion editing symbols are as follows:

- The plus (+) and minus (-) signs

- The letters CR and DB, representing credit and debit

- The currency symbol (usually the $ sign)

Like the other insertion edit symbols, the fixed-insertion symbols count toward the size of the printed item.

Plus and Minus Symbols

The plus (+) and minus (-) symbols must be placed in the first or last character position of the PICTURE string. The operation of the plus and minus edit symbols is not as straightforward as it may appear. The rules governing their operation are as follows:

- If the plus symbol is specified, then a minus sign is inserted if the value is negative and a plus sign is inserted if the value is positive.

- If the minus symbol is specified, then a minus sign is inserted if the value is negative but a *space* is inserted if the value is positive. So the minus symbol is only used to highlight negative values. If you always want the appropriate sign to be inserted, use the plus symbol.

CR and DB

CR and DB stand for credit and debit, respectively. But what a credit is and what a debit is depends on which side of the balance sheet you are on. Therefore, the rule with the CR and DB symbols is that both are inserted only if the value is negative. CR and DB count toward the data-item size, occupy two character positions, and may only appear in the last character position of the edit PICTURE string.

The Currency Symbol

The currency symbol (usually $) must be one of the leading characters of the edit PICTURE string. It may be preceded by a plus or a minus sign.

The default currency symbol is the dollar sign ($); but as shown in Listing 9-2, it may be changed to a different symbol by the CURRENCY SIGN IS clause, in the SPECIAL-NAMES paragraph, CONFIGURATION SECTION, ENVIRONMENT DIVISION.

Listing 9-2. Using the CURRENCY SIGN Clause to Change the Currency Symbol

```
IDENTIFICATION DIVISION.
PROGRAM-ID. Listing9-2.
AUTHOR. Michael Coughlan.

ENVIRONMENT DIVISION.
CONFIGURATION SECTION.
SPECIAL-NAMES.
```

```
     CURRENCY SIGN IS "£".
DATA DIVISION.
WORKING-STORAGE SECTION.
01 Edit1     PIC  £££,££9.99.


PROCEDURE DIVISION.
Begin.
   MOVE 12345.95 TO Edit1
   DISPLAY "Edit1 = " Edit1
   STOP RUN.
```

Listing 9-2 Output

```
Edit1 = £12,345.95
```

In Listing 9-3, multiple currency sign declarations are used to create a currency converter program. Several CURRENCY SIGN declarations are made (note that while there are several clauses there is only one sentence and hence one period) and then each edited picture uses the appropriate currency symbol.

Listing 9-3. Using Multiple CURRENCY SIZE clauses

```
IDENTIFICATION DIVISION.
PROGRAM-ID. Listing9-3.
AUTHOR. Michael Coughlan.
ENVIRONMENT DIVISION.
CONFIGURATION SECTION.
SPECIAL-NAMES.
    CURRENCY SIGN IS "£"
    CURRENCY SIGN IS "$"
    CURRENCY SIGN IS "¥".
DATA DIVISION.
WORKING-STORAGE SECTION.
01  DollarValue      PIC 9999V99.

01  PrnDollarValue   PIC $$$,$$9.99.
01  PrnYenValue      PIC ¥¥¥,¥¥9.99.
01  PrnPoundValue    PIC £££,££9.99.

01  Dollar2PoundRate PIC 99V9(6) VALUE 0.640138.
01  Dollar2YenRate   PIC 99V9(6) VALUE 98.6600.

PROCEDURE DIVISION.
Begin.
   DISPLAY "Enter a dollar value to convert :- " WITH NO ADVANCING
   ACCEPT DollarValue
   MOVE DollarValue TO PrnDollarValue

   COMPUTE PrnYenValue ROUNDED = DollarValue * Dollar2YenRate

   COMPUTE PrnPoundValue ROUNDED = DollarValue * Dollar2PoundRate
```

```
DISPLAY "Dollar value    = " PrnDollarValue
DISPLAY "Yen value       = " PrnYenValue
DISPLAY "Pound value     = " PrnPoundValue
```

```
                      Listing 9-3 Output
Enter a dollar value to convert :- 123.45
Dollar value    =      $123.45
Yen value       = ¥12,179.58
Pound value     =       £79.03
```

Fixed-Insertion Examples

Table 9-5 gives examples of fixed insertion using the plus and minus edit symbols. Table 9-6 does the same for the CR and DB edit symbols.

Table 9-5. *Fixed-Insertion Editing with the Plus and Minus Symbols*

Sending		Receiving		Comments
Picture	Data	Picture	Result	
PIC S9(4)	-4174	PIC -9999	-4174	A negative value moved into an item edited with a minus sign inserts the minus sign. Size = 5 characters.
PIC S9(4)	-4174	PIC 9999-	4174-	When the minus sign is in the last character position, the minus is inserted into the last character position. Size = 5 characters.
PIC S9(4)	+4174	PIC -9999	□4174	A positive value moved into an item edited with a minus sign inserts a space character in the position of the minus symbol. Size = 5 characters.
PIC S9(4)	+4174	PIC +9999	+4174	A positive value moved into an item edited with a plus sign inserts a plus sign. Size = 5 characters.
PIC S9(4)	-174	PIC +9999	-0174	A negative value moved into an item edited with a plus sign inserts a minus sign. Size = 5 characters.
PIC S9(4)	-174	PIC 9999+	0174-	A negative value moved into an item edited with a plus sign inserts a minus sign in the character position of the plus symbol. Size = 5 characters.

Table 9-6. *Fixed-Insertion Editing with CR, DB, and the Currency Symbol*

Sending		Receiving		Comments
Picture	Data	Picture	Result	
PIC 999	174	PIC $9999	$0174	The $ sign is inserted. Size = 5 characters.
PIC S999	-174	PIC -$9999	-$0174	The minus symbol is used before the $ and the value is negative, so both are inserted. Size = 6 characters.
PIC S999	-174	PIC -$9999CR	-$0174CR	The minus symbol is used at the start of the edit string and CR at the end. The value is negative, so the minus and CR are both inserted. Size = 8 characters.
PIC S999	+174	PIC +$9999CR	+$0174□□	A plus sign is used before the $ and the value is positive, so a plus sign is inserted. The CR symbol is used; but because the value is positive, spaces are inserted. Size = 8 characters.
PIC S9(4)	-4174	PIC 9999CR	4174CR	The value is negative, so CR is inserted. Size = 6 characters.
PIC S9(4)	+4174	PIC 9999CR	4174□□	The value is positive, so spaces are inserted. Size = 6 characters.
PIC S9(4)	-4174	PIC 9999DB	4174DB	The value is negative, so DB is inserted. Size = 6 characters.
PIC S9(4)	+4174	PIC 9999DB	4174□□	The value is positive, so spaces are inserted. Size = 6 characters.
PIC S9(4)	-174	PIC 9999+	0174-	A negative value moved into an item edited with a plus sign inserts a minus sign in the character position of the plus symbol. Size = 5 characters.

Floating Insertion

The problem with fixed-insertion editing is that data formatted using it can be somewhat unsightly. Values like $00019,825.75 and -0000135 are more acceptably presented as $19,825.75 and -135. What makes these formats more presentable is that the leading zeros have been suppressed and the editing symbol has been "floated" up against the first non-zero digit. In COBOL, this effect can be achieved using floating insertion. Floating insertion can only be applied to numeric-edited data items.

The floating-insertion symbols are the plus and minus signs and the currency symbol. Floating insertion suppresses leading zeros and floats the insertion symbol up against the first non-zero digit. Every floating symbol counts toward the size of the printed item. Each floating-insertion symbol—with the exception of the leftmost symbol, which is always inserted—is a placeholder that may be replaced by a space or a digit. This means at least one symbol is always inserted, even though this may be at the cost of truncating the number.

Floating-Insertion Examples

The examples in Table 9-7 show how you can use floating-insertion editing. You should pay particular attention to how floating insertion deals with the comma when this symbol is combined with the floating-insertion symbols (see the second example).

Table 9-7. *Floating-Insertion Editing with Plus, Minus, and the Currency Symbol*

Sending		Receiving		Comments
Picture	Data	Picture	Result	
PIC 9(4)V99	000000	PIC $$,$$9.99	****$0.00	The currency symbol floats against the digit in the leftmost numeric position. The zeros to the left of the currency symbol are replaced by spaces. Size = 9 characters.
PIC 9(4)V99	174.75	PIC $$,$$9.99	**$174.75	The currency symbol replaces the comma because there are no digits to the left of the comma (rule prevents $,174.75). Size = 9 characters.
PIC 9(4)V99	4174.75	PIC $$,$$9.99	$4,174.75	A comma is inserted. Size = 9 characters.
PIC 9(4)V99	4174.75	PIC $$,$$9.00	$4,174.00	The zeros are inserted to the right of the decimal point. After decimal-point alignment, the least significant digits (75) of the value are lost. Size = 9 characters.
PIC 9(5)V99	34174.75	PIC $$,$$9.99	$4,174.75	The leftmost currency symbol cannot be replaced by a digit, which means after alignment the most significant digit (3) is lost. Size = 9 characters.
PIC S9(3)	-26	PIC +++9	*-26	The character positions to the left of the currency symbol are occupied by spaces. Size = 4 characters.
PIC S9(3)	+426	PIC +++9	+426	Size = 4 characters.
PIC S9(3)	-426	PIC ---9	-426	Size = 4 characters.
PIC S9(3)	+426	PIC ---9	□426	A positive value and the minus symbol mean the symbol is replaced by space. Size = 4 characters.
PIC S9(4)	+6426	PIC +++9	+426	The leftmost plus symbol cannot be replaced by a digit, which means after alignment the most significant digit (6) is lost. Size = 4 characters.

Suppression-and-Replacement Editing

Suppression-and-replacement editing is used to replace leading zeroes from the value to be edited with the replacement symbol. Like floating insertion, suppression and replacement can only be applied to numeric-edited data items. There are two varieties of suppression-and-replacement editing:

- Suppression of leading zeros and replacement with spaces
- Suppression of leading zeros and replacement with asterisks

The suppression and replacement symbols are the letter Z and the asterisk (*). Using Z in an edited picture instructs the computer to suppress a leading zero in that character position and replace it with a space. Using * in an edited picture instructs the computer to replace a leading zero with an asterisk. The picture clause symbol 9 cannot appear to the left of the replacement symbols (Z or *). If all the character positions in a data item are Z editing symbols and the sending item is 0, then only spaces will be printed. Replacement with spaces is done for aesthetic reasons, but replacement with asterisks is often done as a security measure on checks.

Suppression-and-Replacement Examples

Table 9-8 shows how you can use suppression and replacement. As with the examples in Table 9-7, you should pay particular attention to how suppression-and-replacement editing deals with the comma when this symbol is combined with the replacement symbols.

Table 9-8. Suppression-and-Replacement Editing Examples

Sending		Receiving		Comments
Picture	Data	Picture	Result	
PIC 9(4)	0000	PIC Z,ZZZ	☐☐☐☐☐	The value is zero, and the edit string instructs the computer to replace the leading zeros with spaces. Size= 5 characters.
PIC 9(4)	8317	PIC Z,Z99	8,317	If there are no leading zeros, there is no replacement. Size= 5 characters.
PIC 9(4)	0317	PIC Z,Z99	☐☐317	When there are only zeros to the left of the comma, the comma is replaced with the replacement symbol. Size= 5 characters.
PIC 9(4)	0007	PIC Z,Z99	☐☐☐07	The edited value is 07 because the edit picture does not require replacement for the last two digits. Size= 5 characters.
PIC 9(4)	0000	PIC ****	****	The value is zero, and the edit string instructs the computer to replace the leading zeros with asterisks. Size= 4 characters.
PIC 9(4)	0083	PIC ****	**83	Leading zeros are replaced with asterisks. Size= 4 characters.

(continued)

Table 9-8. (*continued*)

Sending		Receiving		Comments
Picture	**Data**	**Picture**	**Result**	
PIC 9(4)	8317	PIC $*,**9.00	$8,317.00	No replacement occurs, but the currency symbol, comma, and zeros are inserted.
				Size = 9 characters.
PIC 9(4)	0317	PIC $*,**9.00	$**317.00	The comma is replaced with an asterisk.
				Size = 9 characters.
PIC 9(4)	0017	PIC $*,999.00	$**017.00	The comma is replaced with an asterisk.
				Size = 9 characters.

Example Print Lines

Example 9-1 shows some print lines. Note how the edit symbol B is used for spacing. If this were not done, additional data items filled with spaces, as shown in Example 9-2, would have to be used.

Example 9-1. Example Print Lines Containing Edited Pictures

```
01  Cust-Sales-Line.
    02  Prn-Cust-Name        PIC X(20).
    02  Prn-Cust-Id          PIC BBB9(5).
    02  Prn-Cust-Sales       PIC B(5)ZZ9.
    02  Prn-Qty-Sold         PIC B(5)ZZ,ZZ9.
    02  Prn-Sales-Value      PIC BBBB$$$,$$9.99.

01  Total-Sales-Line.
    02  FILLER               PIC X(33) VALUE SPACES.
    02  FILLER               PIC X(19) VALUE "TOTAL SALES      :".
    02  Prn-Total-Sales      PIC B(6)ZZ,ZZ9.
```

Example 9-2. Spacing with Space-Filled Data Items

```
01  Cust-Sales-Line.
    02  Prn-Cust-Name        PIC X(20).
    02  FILLER               PIC XXX VALUE SPACES.
    02  Prn-Cust-Id          PIC 9(5).
    02  FILLER               PIC X(5) VALUE SPACES.
    02  Prn-Cust-Sales       PIC ZZ9.
    02  FILLER               PIC X(5) VALUE SPACES.
    02  Prn-Qty-Sold         PIC ZZ,ZZ9.
    02  FILLER               PIC X(4) VALUE SPACES.
    02  Prn-Sales-Value      PIC $$$,$$9.99.
```

Immediate Editing

I noted earlier that the moment a value is placed into an edited data item, the value is modified according the formatting specified by the edit string. This section examines examples that show some of the interesting effects you can achieve by taking advantage of the way editing works.

In Figure 9-1, the data item SouthAfricanPay uses the dollar sign as the floating-insertion symbol. Obviously, this is a problem. The currency of South Africa is the Rand, which is represented by the character R. What you want is a floating R character rather than a floating dollar sign. Unfortunately, you cannot change the currency symbol to R using the CURRENCY SIGN clause: restrictions are placed on the characters that can be used with that clause, and R is one of the restricted characters. So what can you do? Immediate editing gives you the answer. You replace the dollar sign that has floated against the number, with an R.

```
01 SouthAfricanPay  PIC $$$,$$9.99.

::  ::  ::  ::  ::  ::  ::  ::  ::

MOVE 12345.67 TO SouthAfricanPay.
INSPECT SouthAfricanPay REPLACING ALL "$" BY  "R".
DISPLAY SouthAfricanPay
```

	01 SouthAfricanPay PIC $$$,$$9.99.
After MOVE	$12,345.67
After INSPECT	R12,345.67

Figure 9-1. *The floating Rand symbol*

Example Program

Listing 9-4 uses zero suppression and replacement by asterisks to create a starred rating system. In this system, a rating of 5 is shown as 5 asterisks, 4 is shown as 4 asterisks, and so on. The COMPUTE statement produces the values 10000, *1000, **100, ***10, ****1, and *****. The INSPECT replaces each 1 and each 0 in Stars with a space. INSPECT Stars CONVERTING "10" TO SPACES is a shorthand way of writing - INSPECT Stars REPLACING ALL "1" BY SPACE, ALL "0" BY SPACE. You'll examine INSPECT in detail in Chapter 15.

Listing 9-4. Starred Rating System

```
IDENTIFICATION DIVISION.
PROGRAM-ID. Listing9-4.
AUTHOR. Michael Coughlan.

DATA DIVISION.
WORKING-STORAGE SECTION.
01 Stars        PIC *****.
01 NumOfStars   PIC 9.
```

```
PROCEDURE DIVISION.
Begin.
    PERFORM VARYING NumOfStars FROM 0 BY 1 UNTIL NumOfStars > 5
        COMPUTE Stars = 10 ** (4 - NumOfStars)
        INSPECT Stars CONVERTING "10" TO SPACES
        DISPLAY NumOfStars " = " Stars
    END-PERFORM
    STOP RUN.
```

Listing 9-4 Output

```
0 =

1 = *

2 = **

3 = ***

4 = ****

5 = *****
```

PICTURE String Restrictions

Some combinations of picture symbols are not permitted. Table 9-9 shows the combinations of symbols that are allowed. You should now be familiar with all these PICTURE symbols except P: the P symbol is a scaling symbol.

Table 9-9. *PICTURE String Restrictions*

Character	May Be Followed By
P	P B 0 / , + - CR DB 9 V
B	P B 0 / , . + - CR DB 9 V
0	P B 0 / , . + - CR DB 9 V
/	P B 0 / , . + - CR DB 9 V
,	P B 0 / , . + - CR DB 9 V
.	B 0 / , . + - CR DB 9
+	P B 0 / , . + $ 9 V
-	P B 0 / , . - $ 9 V
CR or DB	Nothing at all
$	P B 0 / , . + - CR DB $ 9 V
9	P B 0 / , . + - CR DB 9 V
V	B 0 / , + - CR DB 9

The PICTURE Clause Scaling Symbol

The P symbol in a PICTURE clause specifies a decimal-point scaling position. It is used to save storage when the magnitude of a number is significantly larger than the required precision. For instance, suppose you are required to store numbers that contain whole billions. You could use a declaration such as PIC 9(12), which requires 12 characters, or you could use the scaling symbol P to define the item as PIC 999P(9). This definition requires only three characters and can store a value between 001,000,000,000 and 999,000,000,000.

The P symbol is not often used, but a description of how it operates is included here for completeness. By default, when no assumed decimal point is explicitly defined, the data item is treated as if it had a decimal point in the rightmost position. The P symbol allows you to change that by defining the assumed decimal point to be to the left or right of the digits, depending on where the P symbol is placed. Each P symbol represents one decimal scaling position.

In Example 9-3, LargeScaledNumber occupies only three characters of storage but can hold a value as high as 99,900,000. Similarly, ScaledBillions occupies only three characters of storage but can hold a number as large as 999,000,000,000, while SmallScaledNumber can hold a number as small as 0.00000001.

Example 9-3. Scaling, Which Allows Numbers to Be Defined Using Less Storage

```
01 SmallScaledNumber  PIC P(5)999 VALUE .00000423.
01 LargeScaledNumber  PIC 999P(5) VALUE 45600000.00.
01 ScaledBillions     PIC 999P(9)    VALUE ZEROS.
```

Rules

If the symbol P is used more than once, it can only occur as a contiguous string of Ps at the leftmost or rightmost end of the PICTURE string. The assumed decimal point symbol (V) can be used for clarity, but it has no semantic effect, and when used it must appear to the left of the leftmost P or to the right of the rightmost P. For instance, to clarify where the decimal point is, you could define the Example 9-3 data items as follows:

```
01 SmallScaledNumber  PIC VPPPPP999 VALUE .00000423.
01 LargeScaledNumber  PIC 999PPPPPV VALUE 45600000.00.
01 ScaledBillions     PIC 999PPPPPPPPPV    VALUE ZEROS.
```

The P symbols do not count toward the size of the item. However, each P counts toward the maximum number of digit positions (18) in a numeric item.

The P symbol cannot be used if the explicit decimal-point edit symbol is used in the PICTURE string.

All computations and other operations performed against scaled data items behave as if the decimal point were in the scaled position. For instance, as shown in Listing 9-5, the result of adding LargeScaledNumber to the data item containing the value 11,111,111.00 is 56,711,111.00.

Listing 9-5. Using the Scaling Symbol P

```
IDENTIFICATION DIVISION.
PROGRAM-ID. Listing9-5.
AUTHOR. Michael Coughlan.
DATA DIVISION.
WORKING-STORAGE SECTION.
01 SmallScaledNumber  PIC VP(5)999    VALUE .00000423.
01 LargeScaledNumber  PIC 999P(5)V    VALUE 45600000.00.
01 ScaledBillions     PIC 999P(9)     VALUE ZEROS.

01 SmallNumber        PIC 9V9(8)      VALUE 1.11111111.
01 LargeNumber        PIC 9(8)V9      VALUE 11111111.

01 PrnSmall           PIC 99.9(8).
01 PrnLarge           PIC ZZ,ZZZ,ZZ9.99.
01 PrnBillions        PIC ZZZ,ZZZ,ZZZ,ZZ9.

PROCEDURE DIVISION.
Begin.
    MOVE SmallScaledNumber TO PrnSmall
    MOVE LargeScaledNumber TO PrnLarge
    DISPLAY "Small scaled = " PrnSmall
    DISPLAY "Large scaled = " PrnLarge

    ADD SmallScaledNumber TO SmallNumber
    ADD LargeScaledNumber TO LargeNumber
    MOVE SmallNumber TO PrnSmall
    MOVE LargeNumber TO PrnLarge
    DISPLAY "Small  = " PrnSmall
    DISPLAY "Large  = " PrnLarge

    MOVE 123456789012  TO ScaledBillions
    MOVE ScaledBillions  TO PrnBillions
    DISPLAY "Billions = " PrnBillions
    STOP RUN.
```

Listing 9-5 Output

```
Small scaled = 00.00000423
Large scaled = 45,600,000.00
Small  = 01.11111534
Large  = 56,711,111.00
Billions = 123,000,000,000
```

Summary

This chapter continued the exploration of printed output that began in the last chapter. You discovered how data can be formatted for output using edited pictures. You explored the different kinds of editing supported by COBOL, from simple insertion of the comma, the currency symbol, and the plus and minus signs; to the more sophisticated floating insertion, which floats these last symbols against the number being displayed or printed; to zero-suppression and replacement with asterisks or spaces. You learned that the editing effect is immediate, and you saw some of the interesting post-edit manipulations you can do on the edited data item. Finally, you examined how the PICTURE symbol P may be used to store a very large or very small value in only a few characters of storage.

The next chapter examines some of the problems of processing sequential files. In particular, you look at some of the difficulties of the file-update problem and learn how to write control-break programs.

LANGUAGE KNOWLEDGE EXERCISE

The time has come once more to unlimber those 2B pencils and answer some exercise questions.

1. For each part, examine the formatted results produced for the various data values. Deduce what the edited picture would have to be to produce the formatted results shown from the data values given.

a.

Sending	Data	Result	Edited Picture
PIC 9(5)	12345	12345	
	01234	*1234	
	00123	**123	
	00012	**012	

b.

Sending	Data	Result	Edited Picture
PIC 9(6)	412345	$12345	
	000123	**$123	
	000001	****$1	
	000000	******	

c.

Sending	Data	Result	Edited Picture
PIC 9(6)V99	012345	$123.00	
	000123	$**1.00	
	000025	$**0.00	
	000000	$**0.00	

d.

Sending	Data	Result	Edited Picture
PIC S9(4)	1234	+1234	
	-0012	**-12	
	0004	***+4	
	0000	*****	

2. Show the formatted result that will be produced when the data value is moved to the edited picture.

Sending	Data	Result	Edited Picture
9(6)	000321		PIC ZZZ,999
9(6)	004321		PIC ZZZ,999
9(6)	000004		PIC ZZZ,999
9(6)	654321		PIC ZZZ,ZZZ.00
9999V99	654321		PIC ZZZ,ZZZ.ZZ
9999V99	004321		PIC $$,$$9.99
9999V99	000078		PIC $$,$$9.99
9999V99	000078		PIC $Z,ZZ9.99
S9999V99	000078		PIC $Z,ZZ9.99CR
S9999V99	-045678		PIC $Z,ZZ9.99CR
S9(6)	-123456		PIC -999,999
S9(6)	123456		PIC -999,999
S9(6)	123456		PIC +999,999
S9(6)	-123456		PIC +999,999
S9(6)	001234		PIC ++++,++9
9(6)	123456		PIC 99B99B99
9(6)	001234		PIC Z(6).00
9(6)	000092		PIC ZZZZZZ00
X(5)	123GO		PIC XBXBXBBXX
9999V99	000123		PIC $***,**9.99
99999V99	24123.45		PIC $$,$$9.99

PROGRAMMING EXERCISE 1

The Genealogists Society of Ireland wishes to discover the most popular surname used in each of the 26 counties in the Irish Republic. In order to obtain this information, the society has acquired a file containing a subset of data from the most recent census.

Write a program that will process the census file and produce a report that shows, for each county, the most popular surname and the number of times it occurs.

The census file is a standard sequential file with fixed-length fields. Each record contains a census number, a surname, and a county name. The file has been sorted and is now ordered on ascending `Surname` within ascending `CountyName`. Each record in the file has the following description:

Field	Type	Length	Value
CensusNumber	N	8	00000001-99999999
Surname	X	20	-
CountyName	X	9	-

The report should take the format shown in the following report template. The `Count` field is a count of the number of times the surname occurs in the county. In the `Count` field, thousands should be separated using a comma; and the field should be zero-suppressed up to, but not including, the last digit:

```
          Popular Surname Report
CountyName Surname             Count
Carlow    XXXXXXXXXXXXXXXXXXXX XXX,XXX
Cavan     XXXXXXXXXXXXXXXXXXXX XXX,XXX
Clare     XXXXXXXXXXXXXXXXXXXX XXX,XXX
::  ::  :: ::  ::  ::  ::  ::  ::  ::  ::
Westmeath XXXXXXXXXXXXXXXXXXXX XXX,XXX
Wicklow   XXXXXXXXXXXXXXXXXXXX XXX,XXX
Wexford   XXXXXXXXXXXXXXXXXXXX XXX,XXX
************ end of report ***************
```

LANGUAGE KNOWLEDGE EXERCISES: ANSWERS

The time has come once more to unlimber those 2B pencils and answer the following exercise questions.

1. For each part, examine for formatted results produced for the various data values.
    Deduce what the edited picture would have to be to produce the formatted results from
    the data values given.

a.

Sending	Data	Result	Edited Picture
PIC 9(5)	12345	12345	PIC ZZ999
	01234	*1234	
	00123	**123	
	00012	**012	

b.

Sending	Data	Result	Edited Picture
PIC 9(6)	412345	$12345	PIC $(6) or $$$$$$
	000123	**$123	
	000001	****$1	
	000000	******	

c.

Sending	Data	Result	Edited Picture
PIC 9(6)V99	012345	$123.00	PIC $ZZ9.00
	000123	$**1.00	
	000025	$**0.00	
	000000	$**0.00	

d.

Sending	Data	Result	Edited Picture
PIC S9(4)	1234	+1234	PIC +(5) or +++++
	-0012	**-12	
	0004	***+4	
	0000	*****	

2. Show the formatted result that will be produced when the data value is moved to the edited picture.

Sending	Data	Result	Edited Picture
9(6)	000321	***321	PIC ZZZ,999
9(6)	004321	**4,321	PIC ZZZ,999
9(6)	000004	****004	PIC ZZZ,999
9(6)	654321	654,321.00	PIC ZZZ,ZZZ.00
9999V99	654321	**6,543.21	PIC ZZZ,ZZZ.ZZ
9999V99	004321	***$43.21	PIC $$,$$9.99
9999V99	000078	****$0.78	PIC $$,$$9.99
9999V99	000078	$****0.78	PIC $Z,ZZ9.99
S9999V99	000078	$****0.78	PIC $Z,ZZ9.99CR
S9999V99	-045678	$**456.78CR	PIC $Z,ZZ9.99CR
S9(6)	-123456	-123,456	PIC -999,999
S9(6)	123456	*123,456	PIC -999,999
S9(6)	123456	+123,456	PIC +999,999
S9(6)	-123456	-123,456	PIC +999,999
S9(6)	001234	**+1,234	PIC ++++,++9
9(6)	123456	12*34*56	PIC 99B99B99
9(6)	001234	**1234.00	PIC Z(6).00
9(6)	000092	****9200	PIC ZZZZZZ00
X(5)	123GO	1*2*3**GO	PIC XBXBXBBXX
9999V99	000123	$******1.23	PIC $***,**9.99
99999V99	24123.45	$4,123.45	PIC $$,$$9.99

PROGRAMMING EXERCISE 1: ANSWER

The answer to this exercise is found in the next chapter, where it appears an an example.

CHAPTER 10

⬛ ⬛ ⬛

Processing Sequential Files

Previous chapters introduced the mechanics of creating and reading sequential files. This chapter introduces the two most important sequential-file processing problems: control breaks and the file update problem.

Both control breaks and the file update problem involve manipulating ordered sequential files so the chapter begins with a discussion of how sequential files are organized and the difference between ordered and unordered sequential files.

The next section discusses control-break problems. These normally occur when a hierarchically structured printed report has to be produced. But control breaks are not limited to printed reports. Any problem that processes a stream of ordered data and requires action to be taken when one of the items on which the stream is ordered changes, is a control-break problem.

The final section introduces the file-update problem. This involves the thorny difficulty of how to apply a sequential file of ordered transaction records to an ordered sequential master file. This section starts gently by showing how transaction files containing updates of only a single type may be applied to a master file. I then discuss the record buffer implications of transaction files that contain different types of records and introduce a simplified version of the file-update problem. Finally, I discuss and demonstrate an algorithm, based on academic research, which addresses the full complexity of the file-update problem.

File Organization vs. Method of Access

Two important characteristics of files are data organization and method of access. *Data organization* refers to the way the file's records are organized on the backing storage device. COBOL recognizes three main types of file organization:

- *Sequential:* Records are organized serially.

- *Relative:* A direct-access file is used and is organized on relative record number.

- *Indexed:* A direct-access file is used and has an index-based organization.

Method of access refers to the way in which records are accessed. Some approaches to organization are more versatile than others. A file with indexed or relative organization may still have its records accessed sequentially; but the records in a sequential file can only be accessed sequentially.

To understand the difference between file organization and method of access, consider them in the context of a library with a large book collection. Most of the books in the library are organized by Dewey Decimal number; but some, awaiting shelving, are organized in the order in which they were purchased. A reader looking for a book in the main part of the library might find it by looking up its Dewey Decimal number in the library index or might just go the particular section and browse through the books on the shelves. Because the books are organized by Dewey Decimal number, the reader has a choice regarding the method of access. But if the desired book is in the newly acquired section, the reader has no choice. They have to browse through all the titles to find the one they want. This is the difference between direct-access files and sequential files. Direct-access files offer a choice of access methods. Sequential files can only be processed sequentially.

Sequential Organization

Sequential organization is the simplest type of file organization. In a sequential file, the records are arranged serially, one after another, like cards in a dealing shoe. The only way to access a particular record is to start at the first record and read all the succeeding records until the required record is found or until the end of the file is reached.

Ordered and Unordered Files

Sequential files may be ordered or unordered (they should really be called *serial* files). In an ordered file, the records are sequenced (see Table 10-1) on a particular field in the record, such as CustomerId or CustomerName. In an unordered file, the records are not in any particular order.

Table 10-1. *Ordered and Unordered Files*

Ordered File	Unordered File
Record-KeyA	Record-KeyM
Record-KeyB	Record-KeyH
Record-KeyD	Record-KeyO
Record-KeyG	Record-KeyB
Record-KeyH	Record-KeyN
Record-KeyK	Record-KeyA
Record-KeyM	Record-KeyT
Record-KeyO	Record-KeyK
Record-KeyT	Record-KeyG

The ordering of the records in a file has a significant impact on the way in which it is processed and the processing that can be applied to it.

Control-Break Processing

Control-break processing is a technique generally applied to an ordered sequential file in order to create a printed report. But it can also be used for other purposes such as creating a summary file. For control-break processing to work, the input file must be sorted in the same order as the output to be produced.

A control-break program works by monitoring one or more *control items* (fields in the record) and taking action when the value in one of the control items changes (the *control break*). In a control-break program with multiple control-break items, the control breaks are usually hierarchical, such that a break in a major control item automatically causes a break in the minor controls even if the actual value of the minor item does not change. For instance, Figure 10-1 partially models a file that holds details of magazine sales. When the major control item changes from England to Ireland, this also causes the minor control item to break even though its value is unchanged. You can see the logic behind this: it is unlikely that the same individual (Maxwell) lives in both countries.

MagazineSales file

CountryName	CustomerName
England	Abbot
England	Abbot
England	Lowe
England	Lyon
England	Lyon
England	Maxwell
England	Maxwell
Ireland	Maxwell
Ireland	Maxwell
Ireland	Maxwell
Ireland	Molloy
Ireland	Molloy
Ireland	Power
Scotland	Campbell
Scotland	Campbell
Scotland	MacDonald
Scotland	MacKenzie
Scotland	MacKenzie
Scotland	Stewart

Figure 10-1. *Partial model of a file containing details of magazine sales. A major control break also causes a break of the minor control item*

Specifications that Require Control Breaks

To get a feel for the kinds of problems that require a control-break solution, consider the following specifications.

Specification Requiring a Single Control Break

Write a program to process the UnemploymentPayments file to produce a report showing the annual Social Welfare unemployment payments made in each county in Ireland. The report must be printed and sequenced on ascending CountyName. The UnemploymentPayments file is a sequential file ordered on ascending CountyName.

In this specification, the control-break item is the CountyName. The processing required is to sum the payments for a particular county and then, when the county names changes, to print the county name and the total unemployment payments for that county.

Specification Requiring Two Control Breaks

A program is required to process the MagazineSales file to produce a report showing the total spent by customers in each country on magazines. The report must be printed on ascending CustomerName within ascending CountryName. The MagazineSales file is a sequential file ordered on ascending CustomerName within ascending CountryName.

Figure 10-1 models the MagazineSales file and shows what is meant by "ordered on ascending CustomerName within ascending CountryName." Notice how the records are in order of ascending country name, but all the records for a particular country are in order of ascending customer name.

In this specification, the control-break items are the CountryName (major) and the CustomerName (minor).

Specification Requiring Three Control Breaks

Electronics2Go has branches in a number of American states. A program is required to produce a report showing the total sales made by each salesperson, the total sales for each branch, the total sales for each state, and a final total of sales for the entire United States. The report must be printed on ascending SalespersonId within ascending BranchId within ascending StateName.

The report is based on the CompanySales file. This file holds details of sales made in all the branches of the company. It is a sequential file, ordered on ascending SalespersonId, within ascending BranchId, within ascending StateName.

In this specification, the control-break items are the StateName (major), the BranchId (minor), and the SalespersonId (most minor).

Detecting the Control Break

A major consideration in a control-break program is how to detect the control break. If you examine the data in Figure 10-1, you can see the control breaks quite clearly. When the country name changes from England to Ireland, a major control break has occurred. When the customer surname changes from Molloy to Power, a minor control break has occurred. It is easy for *you* to see the control breaks in the data file, but how can you detect these control breaks programmatically?

The way you do this is to compare the value of the control field in the record against the previous value of the control field. How do you know the previous value of the control field? You must store it in a data item specifically set up for the purpose. For instance, if you were writing a control-break program for the data in Figure 10-1, you might create the data items PrevCountryName and PrevCustomerName to store the control-break values. Detecting the control break then simply becomes a matter of comparing the values in these fields with the values in the fields of the current record.

Writing a Control-Break Program

The first instinct programmers seem to have when writing a control-break program is to code the solution as a single loop and to use IF statements (often nested IF statements) to handle the control breaks. This approach results in a cumbersome solution. A better technique is to recognize the structure of the data in the data file and in the report and to create a program that echoes that structure. This echoed structure uses a hierarchy of loops to process the control breaks. This idea is not original; it is essentially that advocated by Michael Jackson in Jackson Structured Programming (JSP).[1]

When you use this approach, the code for processing each control item becomes

```
Initialize control items  (Totals and PrevControlItems)
Loop Until control break
Finalize control items (Print Totals)
```

---

[1]Michael Jackson. Principles of Program Design. Academic Press, 1975.

Control-Break Program Template

Example 10-1 gives a template for writing a control-break program. The program structure echoes the structure of the input and output data. The control breaks are processed by a hierarchy of loops, where the inner loop processes the most minor control break.

Example 10-1. Template for Control-Break Programs

```
OPEN File
Read next record from file
PERFORM UNTIL EndOfFile
    MOVE ZEROS TO totals of ControlItem1
    MOVE ControlItem1 TO PrevControlItem1
    PERFORM UNTIL ControlItem1 NOT EQUAL TO PrevControlItem1
                OR EndOfFile
      MOVE ZEROS TO totals of ControlItem2
      MOVE ControlItem2 TO PrevControlItem2
      PERFORM UNTIL ControlItem2 NOT EQUAL TO PrevControlItem2
            OR   ControlItem1 NOT EQUAL TO PrevControlItem1
            OR   EndOfFile
        Process record
        Read next record from file
      END-PERFORM
      Process totals of ControlItem2
    END-PERFORM
    Process totals of ControlItem1
END-PERFORM
Process final totals
CLOSE file
```

Three-Level Control Break

Let's see how all this works in an actual example. As the basis for the example, let's use a modified version of the three-control-break specification given earlier.

Electronics2Go has branches in a number of American states. A program is required to produce a summary report showing the total sales made by each salesperson, the total sales for each branch, the total sales for each state, and a final total of sales for the entire United States. The report must be printed on ascending SalespersonId in ascending BranchId in ascending StateName.

The report is based on the Electronics2Go sales file. This file holds details of sales made in all the branches of the company. It is a sequential file, ordered on ascending SalespersonId, within ascending BranchId, within ascending StateName. Each record in the sales file has the following description:

Field	Type	Length	Value
StateName	X	14	-
BranchId	X	5	-
SalespersonId	X	6	99999X (M/F)
ValueOfSale	9	6	0000.00–9999.99

The report format should follow the template in Figure 10-2. In the report template, the SalesTotal field is the sum of the sales made by this salesperson. The Branch Total is the sum of the sales made by each branch. The State Total is the sum of the sales made by all the branches in the state. The Final Total is the sum of the sales made in the United States.

```
        Electronics2Go Sales Report
State Name      Branch  SalesId  SalesTotal

XXXXXXXXXXXXXX  XXXXX    XXXXX   XXXXXXXXX
                         XXXXX   XXXXXXXXX
                         XXXXX   XXXXXXXXX
                         Branch Total:    XXXXXXXXXX

                XXXXX    XXXXX   XXXXXXXXX
                         XXXXX   XXXXXXXXX
                         XXXXX   XXXXXXXXX
                         XXXXX   XXXXXXXXX
                         Branch Total:    XXXXXXXXXX
                          State Total:   XXXXXXXXXXX

XXXXXXXXXXXXXX  XXXXX    XXXXX   XXXXXXXXX
                         XXXXX   XXXXXXXXX
                         XXXXX   XXXXXXXXX
                         Branch Total:    XXXXXXXXXX

XXXXXXXXXXXXXX  XXXXX    XXXXX   XXXXXXXXX
                         XXXXX   XXXXXXXXX
                         XXXXX   XXXXXXXXX
                          Branch Total:    XXXXXXXXXX
                          State Total:   XXXXXXXXXXX
                          Final Total: XXXXXXXXXXXXX
```

Figure 10-2. *Template for the Electronics2Go sales report*

In all sales value fields, leading zeros should be suppressed and the dollar symbol should float against the value. The State Name and the Branch should be suppressed after their first occurrence. For simplicity, the headings are only printed once, so no page count or line numbers need be tracked.

■ **Note** The full state name is used in every record of the sales file. This is a waste of space. Normally a code representing the state would be used, and the program would convert this code into a state name by means of a lookup table. Because you have not yet encountered lookup tables, I have decided to use the full state name in the file.

Three-Level Control-Break Program

Listing 10-1 shows a program that implements the Electronics2Go Sales Report specification.

Listing 10-1. Three-Control-Break Electronics2Go Sales Report

```
IDENTIFICATION DIVISION.
PROGRAM-ID. Listing10-1.
AUTHOR. Michael Coughlan.
* A three level Control Break program to process the Electronics2Go
* Sales file and produce a report that shows the value of sales for
* each Salesperson, each Branch, each State, and for the Country.
* The SalesFile is sorted on ascending SalespersonId within BranchId
* within Statename.
* The report must be printed in the same order


ENVIRONMENT DIVISION.
INPUT-OUTPUT SECTION.
FILE-CONTROL.
SELECT SalesFile ASSIGN TO "Listing10-1TestData.Dat"
                 ORGANIZATION IS LINE SEQUENTIAL.

SELECT SalesReport ASSIGN TO "Listing10-1.RPT"
                   ORGANIZATION IS LINE SEQUENTIAL.


DATA DIVISION.
FILE SECTION.
FD  SalesFile.
01  SalesRecord.
       88 EndOfSalesFile VALUE HIGH-VALUES.
       02 StateName        PIC X(14).
       02 BranchId         PIC X(5).
       02 SalesPersonId    PIC X(6).
       02 ValueOfSale      PIC 9(4)V99.

FD SalesReport.
01 PrintLine              PIC X(55).


WORKING-STORAGE SECTION.
01  ReportHeading.
       02 FILLER            PIC X(35)
          VALUE "        Electronics2Go Sales Report".

01  SubjectHeading.
       02 FILLER            PIC X(43)
          VALUE "State Name      Branch  SalesId  SalesTotal".

01  DetailLine.
       02 PrnStateName       PIC X(14).
          88 SuppressStateName VALUE SPACES.
       02 PrnBranchId        PIC BBX(5).
          88 SuppressBranchId  VALUE SPACES.
       02 PrnSalespersonId   PIC BBBBX(6).
       02 PrnSalespersonTotal PIC BB$$,$$9.99.
```

```cobol
01  BranchTotalLine.
    02 FILLER            PIC X(43)
       VALUE "                      Branch Total:     ".
    02 PrnBranchTotal    PIC $$$,$$9.99.

01  StateTotalLine.
    02 FILLER            PIC X(40)
       VALUE "                    State Total :   ".
    02 PrnStateTotal     PIC $$,$$$,$$9.99.

01  FinalTotalLine.
    02 FILLER            PIC X(39)
       VALUE "                   Final Total :".
    02 PrnFinalTotal     PIC $$$,$$$,$$9.99.

01  SalespersonTotal     PIC 9(4)V99.
01  BranchTotal          PIC 9(6)V99.
01  StateTotal           PIC 9(7)V99.
01  FinalTotal           PIC 9(9)V99.

01  PrevStateName        PIC X(14).
01  PrevBranchId         PIC X(5).
01  PrevSalespersonId    PIC X(6).

PROCEDURE DIVISION.
Begin.
    OPEN INPUT SalesFile
    OPEN OUTPUT SalesReport
    WRITE PrintLine FROM ReportHeading  AFTER ADVANCING 1 LINE
    WRITE PrintLine FROM SubjectHeading AFTER ADVANCING 1 LINE

    READ SalesFile
       AT END SET EndOfSalesFile TO TRUE
    END-READ
    PERFORM UNTIL EndOfSalesFile
       MOVE StateName TO PrevStateName, PrnStateName
       MOVE ZEROS TO StateTotal
       PERFORM SumSalesForState
             UNTIL StateName NOT = PrevStateName
                 OR EndOfSalesFile
       MOVE StateTotal TO PrnStateTotal
       WRITE PrintLine FROM StateTotalLine AFTER ADVANCING 1 LINE
    END-PERFORM

    MOVE FinalTotal TO PrnFinalTotal
    WRITE PrintLine FROM FinalTotalLine AFTER ADVANCING 1 LINE

    CLOSE SalesFile, SalesReport
    STOP RUN.
```

```
SumSalesForState.
    WRITE PrintLine FROM SPACES AFTER ADVANCING 1 LINE
    MOVE BranchId TO PrevBranchId, PrnBranchId
    MOVE ZEROS TO BranchTotal
    PERFORM SumSalesForBranch
            UNTIL BranchId NOT = PrevBranchId
                OR StateName NOT = PrevStateName
                OR EndOfSalesFile
      MOVE BranchTotal TO PrnBranchTotal
      WRITE PrintLine FROM BranchTotalLine AFTER ADVANCING 1 LINE.

SumSalesForBranch.
    MOVE SalespersonId TO PrevSalespersonId, PrnSalespersonId
    MOVE ZEROS TO SalespersonTotal
    PERFORM SumSalespersonSales
            UNTIL SalespersonId NOT = PrevSalespersonId
                OR BranchId    NOT = PrevBranchId
                OR StateName   NOT = PrevStateName
                OR EndOfSalesFile
    MOVE SalespersonTotal TO PrnSalespersonTotal
    WRITE PrintLine FROM DetailLine AFTER ADVANCING 1 LINE
    SET SuppressBranchId TO TRUE
    SET SuppressStateName TO TRUE.

SumSalespersonSales.
    ADD ValueOfSale TO SalespersonTotal, BranchTotal, StateTotal, FinalTotal
    READ SalesFile
      AT END SET EndOfSalesFile TO TRUE
    END-READ.
```

Program Notes

The program in Listing 10-1 is fairly straightforward, once you understand that its structure mirrors the structure of the data and the report. It is interesting to contrast this program with a similar program given on the web site The American Programmer[2]. That program uses the single loop and IF statement approach mentioned earlier. One objection to this approach is that the three control items are tested for every record in the file.

I draw your attention to the way in which the StateName and BranchId are suppressed after their first occurrence in Listing 10-1. This is done to make the report look less cluttered. To implement the suppression, the condition-name technique that you have seen in a number of other example programs is used. I could have implemented the suppression using a statement such as MOVE SPACES TO PrnStateName, but it would not have been obvious why the data item was being filled with spaces. The purpose of the statement SET SuppressStateName TO TRUE is easier to understand.

Test Data and Results

Due to space constraints, Figure 10-3 shows only a portion of the test data file and the report produced from that data is shown.

---

[2]The Three Level Subtotal (Control Break) COBOL Program, TheAmericanProgrammer.Com, http://theamericanprogrammer.com/programming/08-brklv3.shtml.

```
           Electronics2Go Sales Report              Test Data
   State Name      Branch  SalesId  SalesTotal   Arkansas    KA12312344M011111
                                                 Arkansas    KA12312345F011111
   Arkansas        KA123   12344M    $111.11      Arkansas    KA12312345F011111
                           12345F    $222.22      Arkansas    KA12312347M033333
                           12347M    $333.33      Arkansas    KA12312348F022222
                           12348F    $444.44      Arkansas    KA12312348F022222
                           12349M    $555.55      Arkansas    KA12312349M055555
                           Branch Total:   $1,666.65   Arkansas    KA12423456F022222
                                                 Arkansas    KA12423456F022222
                   KA124   23456F    $666.66      Arkansas    KA12423456F022222
                           23457F    $777.77      Arkansas    KA12423457F077777
                           23456F    $888.88      Arkansas    KA12423456F044444
                           Branch Total:   $2,333.31   Arkansas    KA12423456F044444
                                                 Arkansas    KA12811345F001117
                   KA128   11345F     $33.54      Arkansas    KA12811345F001118
                           44444M  $1,711.16      Arkansas    KA12811345F001119
                           55555M    $166.75      Arkansas    KA12844444M055555
                           Branch Total:   $1,911.45   Arkansas    KA12844444M055555
                                                 Arkansas    KA12844444M055555
                   KA411   00123F  $4,133.32      Arkansas    KA12844444M002225
                           11111F  $6,177.90      Arkansas    KA12844444M002226
                           22222M  $3,157.05      Arkansas    KA12855555M003333
                           Branch Total:  $13,468.27   Arkansas    KA12855555M003334
                           State Total :  $19,379.68   Arkansas    KA12855555M003335
                                                 Arkansas    KA12855555M003336
   Florida         LF111   00123F    $188.15      Arkansas    KA12855555M003337
                           33123F     $39.45      Arkansas    KA41100123F104443
                           55123F     $66.55      Arkansas    KA41100123F204444
                           Branch Total:    $294.15   Arkansas    KA41100123F104445
                                                 Arkansas    KA41111111F304446
                                                 Arkansas    KA41111111F104447
                                                 Arkansas    KA41111111F104448
                                                 Arkansas    KA41111111F104449
                                                 Arkansas    KA41122222M100234
                                                 Arkansas    KA41122222M110235
                                                 Arkansas    KA41122222M105236
```

Figure 10-3. Fragment of the report produced and part of the test data file

An Atypical Control Break

The program in Listing 10-1 is a typical control-break program, but control-break problems come in a variety of shapes and sizes. For instance, you have probably realized by now that Exercise 1 at the end of the last chapter is a control-break problem but not a typical one. I didn't provide a solution at the time because I wanted you discover for yourself some of the difficulties with this kind of problem and how easy it is to get dragged into a convoluted solution. Before I present my solution, let's look at the specification again.

Specification

The Genealogists Society of Ireland wishes to discover the most popular surname used in each of the 26 counties in the Irish Republic. In order to obtain this information, the society has acquired a file containing a subset of data from the most recent census.

A program is required that will process the census file and produce a report that shows, for each county, the most popular surname and the number of times it occurs.

The census file is a standard sequential file with fixed-length fields. Each record contains a census number, a surname, and a county name. The file has been sorted and is now ordered on ascending Surname in ascending CountyName. Each record in the file has the following description:

Field	Type	Length	Value
CensusNumber	9	8	00000001–99999999
Surname	X	20	-
CountyName	X	9	-

The report should take the format shown in the following report template. The Count field is a count of the number of times the Surname occurs in the county. In the Count field, thousands should be separated using a comma, and the field should be zero-suppressed up to, but not including, the last digit:

```
                Popular Surname Report
CountyName      Surname                 Count
Carlow          XXXXXXXXXXXXXXXXXXXX   XXX,XXX
Cavan           XXXXXXXXXXXXXXXXXXXX   XXX,XXX
Clare           XXXXXXXXXXXXXXXXXXXX   XXX,XXX
::   ::   ::    ::   ::   ::   ::   ::   ::   ::
Westmeath       XXXXXXXXXXXXXXXXXXXX   XXX,XXX
Wicklow         XXXXXXXXXXXXXXXXXXXX   XXX,XXX
Wexford         XXXXXXXXXXXXXXXXXXXX   XXX,XXX


************* end of report **************
```

Atypical Control-Break Program

This is not a typical control-break program (see Listing 10-2). Instead of printing the total number of occurrences of the surname when there is a change of surname (as a classic control-break program would do), there is a check to see if this surname is the most popular. A line is printed only when the major control item (the county name) changes. When that happens, the county name and the most popular surname are printed. There is a trap here for the unwary: when the control break occurs, it is too late to move the county name to the print line, because at this point the county name in the buffer is the next county. The solution is to move PrevCountyName to the print line or to, as is done in this program, prime the print line with the correct county name before entering the loop that processes all the surnames in that county.

Listing 10-2. Two-Level Control-Break Program Showing the Most Popular Surnames in the Counties of Ireland

```
IDENTIFICATION DIVISION.
PROGRAM-ID. Listing10-2.
AUTHOR. Michael Coughlan.
* Control Break program to process the Census file and produce
* a report that shows, for each county, the most popular surname
* and the number of times it occurs.
* The Records in the sequential Census file are ordered on
* ascending Surname within ascending CountyName.
* The report must be printed in ascending CountyName order
```

```
ENVIRONMENT DIVISION.
INPUT-OUTPUT SECTION.
FILE-CONTROL.
SELECT CensusFile ASSIGN TO "Listing10-2TestData.Dat"
                ORGANIZATION IS LINE SEQUENTIAL.

SELECT SurnameReport  ASSIGN TO "Listing10-2.RPT"
                ORGANIZATION IS LINE SEQUENTIAL.


DATA DIVISION.
FILE SECTION.
FD  CensusFile.
01  CensusRec.
      88 EndOfCensusFile VALUE HIGH-VALUES.
      02 CensusNum          PIC 9(8).
      02 Surname            PIC X(20).
      02 CountyName         PIC X(9).


FD SurnameReport.
01 PrintLine               PIC X(45).


WORKING-STORAGE SECTION.
01  ReportHeading.
      02 FILLER             PIC X(13) VALUE SPACES.
      02 FILLER             PIC X(22)
         VALUE "Popular Surname Report".


01  SubjectHeading.
      02 FILLER             PIC X(42)
         VALUE "CountyName  Surname                    Count".


01  CountySurnameLine.
      02 PrnCountyName      PIC X(9).
      02 FILLER             PIC X(3) VALUE SPACES.
      02 PrnSurname         PIC X(20).
      02 PrnCount           PIC BBBZZZ,ZZ9.


01  ReportFooter           PIC X(43)
      VALUE "************ end of report **************".


01  PrevCountyName         PIC X(9).
01  PrevSurname            PIC X(20).
01  MostPopularSurname     PIC X(20).
01  MostPopularCount       PIC 9(6).
01  SurnameCount           PIC 9(6).


PROCEDURE DIVISION.
Begin.
   OPEN INPUT CensusFile
   OPEN OUTPUT SurnameReport
   WRITE PrintLine FROM ReportHeading  AFTER ADVANCING 1 LINE
   WRITE PrintLine FROM SubjectHeading AFTER ADVANCING 1 LINE
```

```
        READ CensusFile
            AT END SET EndOfCensusFile TO TRUE
        END-READ
        PERFORM UNTIL EndOfCensusFile
            MOVE CountyName TO PrevCountyName, PrnCountyName
            MOVE ZEROS  TO MostPopularCount
            MOVE SPACES TO MostPopularSurname
            PERFORM FindMostPopularSurname
                    UNTIL CountyName NOT EQUAL TO PrevCountyName
                        OR EndOfCensusFile
            MOVE MostPopularCount   TO PrnCount
            MOVE MostPopularSurname TO PrnSurname
            WRITE PrintLine FROM CountySurnameLine AFTER ADVANCING 1 LINE
        END-PERFORM

        WRITE PrintLine FROM ReportFooter AFTER ADVANCING 2 LINES
        CLOSE CensusFile, SurnameReport
        STOP RUN.

    FindMostPopularSurname.
        MOVE Surname TO PrevSurname
        PERFORM CountSurnameOccurs VARYING SurnameCount FROM 0 BY 1
                UNTIL Surname NOT EQUAL TO PrevSurname
                    OR CountyName NOT EQUAL TO PrevCountyName
                    OR EndOfCensusFile

        IF SurnameCount > MostPopularCount
            MOVE SurnameCount TO MostPopularCount
            MOVE PrevSurname  TO MostPopularSurname
        END-IF.

    CountSurnameOccurs.
        READ CensusFile
            AT END SET EndOfCensusFile TO TRUE
        END-READ.
```

Program Notes

The census file is ordered on ascending Surname in ascending CountyName, and that is the same order required for the printed report. The control items are CountyName and Surname. The data items PrevSurname and PrevCountyName are used to detect the control breaks. Similar to Listing 10-1, the structure of this program echoes the structure of the input file and the output report.

Test Data and Results

Figure 10-4 shows the report produced by the program and a small portion of the test data file used.

Popular Surname Report			Test Data	
CountyName	Surname	Count	00660861AGNEW	CARLOW
CARLOW	BOURKE	32	04358072AGNEW	CARLOW
CAVAN	DOHERTY	1,296	04418761AHERN	CARLOW
CLARE	O'NEILL	36	08311181AHERN	CARLOW
CORK	COLLINS	10	07778114AHERN	CARLOW
DONEGAL	BROWN	5	06863734AHERN	CARLOW
DUBLIN	SAVAGE	5	04402884AMBROSE	CARLOW
GALWAY	LYONS	36	08685554AMBROSE	CARLOW
KERRY	COLLINS	6	07792108ANDREWS	CARLOW
KILDARE	BUCKELY	5	00444018APPLEBY	CARLOW
KILKENNY	COLLINS	6	01057045APPLEBY	CARLOW
LAOIS	COAKLEY	7	05662481ASHE	CARLOW
LIMERICK	MACDONAGH	40	01031598ASHE	CARLOW
LONGFORD	FINE	5	00655862ASHE	CARLOW
LOUTH	COLLINS	5	02988155ASHTON	CARLOW
MAYO	BERRY	4	07726846BAKER	CARLOW
MEATH	BERRY	5	07112469BAKER	CARLOW
MONAGHAN	WHEALAN	5	07148094BAKER	CARLOW
ROSCOMMON	COLLINS	7	03879251BARKER	CARLOW
SLIGO	ASHTON	4	09206688BARKER	CARLOW
TIPPERARY	COLLINS	6	09590803BARKER	CARLOW
WATERFORD	COUGHLAN	10	01843122BARKER	CARLOW
WESTMEATH	AGNEW	5	07123677BARON	CARLOW
WEXFORD	BOLGER	6	00495541BARR	CARLOW
WICKLOW	RUTLAND	6	06897641BARRY	CARLOW
			03609815BEGLEY	CARLOW
************ end of report **************			04659971BERMINGHAM	CARLOW
			02865489BERMINGHAM	CARLOW

Figure 10-4. *The report produced by the program, and part of the test data file*

Updating Sequential Files

It is easy to add records to an unordered sequential file because you can simply add them to the end of the file by opening the file for EXTEND. For instance:

```
OPEN EXTEND UnorderedFile
WRITE UnorderedRec
```

When a file is OPENed for EXTEND, the Next Record Pointer is positioned at the end of the file. When records are written to the file, they are appended to the end.

Although you can add records to an unordered sequential file, the records in a sequential file cannot be deleted or updated *in situ*. The only way to delete records from a sequential file is to create a *new file*, which does not contain them; and the only way to update records is to create a *new file* that contains the updated records. A record update involves changing the value of one or more of its fields. For instance, you might change the value of the CustomerAddress or CustomerPhoneNumber field of a customer record, or you might change the value of the QtyInStock or ReorderLevel field of a stock record.

■ **COBOL Detail** Although, in standard COBOL, sequential files cannot be deleted or updated *in situ* many vendors, including Micro Focus, allow this for disk-based files.

Because updating or deleting records in a sequential file requires you to read all the records in the file and to create a new file that has the changes applied to it, it is computationally too expensive to apply these operations to the file one at a time. Updates to sequential files are normally done in batch mode. That is, all the updates are gathered together into what is often referred to as the *transaction file* and then applied to the target file in one go or *batch*. The target file is often referred to as the *master file*.

As you have seen, you can add records to an unordered sequential file by opening the file for EXTEND and writing the records to the end of it. But if you want to update or delete records, you must have a way of identifying the record you want to update or delete. A *key field* is normally used to achieve this. A key field is a field in the record whose value can be used to identify that record. For instance, in a stock record, the StockNumber might be used as the key field. When you apply transaction records to a master file, you compare the key field in the transaction record with that in the master file record. If there is a match, you can apply the delete or update to that master file record. This key-comparison operation is called *record matching*.

For record matching to work correctly, the transaction file and the master file must be ordered on the same key value. Record matching does not work if either file is unordered or if the files are ordered on different key fields. If you need convincing of this, PERFORM (that is, go there, do the exercise, and then come back) the Language Knowledge Exercise at the end of the chapter. That exercise will help you understand the problems of trying to apply batched transactions to an unordered master file.

Applying Transactions to an Ordered Sequential File

You start this section by looking at programming templates that show how to apply each type of transaction (insertion, deletion, and update) to an ordered sequential file. To complicate matters, most transaction files consist of a mixture of transaction types. Therefore, this section considers the data-declaration implications of mixed transaction types, and you examine an example program that applies a variety of transaction types to an ordered sequential file.

Inserting Records in an Ordered Sequential File

When you want to add records to an unordered sequential file, you just OPEN the file for EXTEND and then write the records to the file. You can't do that with an ordered sequential file because if you do, the records will no longer be in order.

When you insert records into an ordered sequential file, a major consideration must be to preserve the ordering. To insert records, you must create a new file that consists of all the records of the old file with the new records inserted into their correct key-value positions. When you are inserting records into an ordered file, you also have to be aware of the possibility that the record you are trying to insert will have the same key value as one already in the file. This is an error condition. For instance, you can't have two customer records with the same CustomerId value.

Figure 10-5 is a template that outlines the algorithm required to insert records from an ordered transaction file into their correct positions in an ordered master file. There are three files. The *transaction file* (TF) contains the three records you want to insert. The *master file* (MF) is the file into which you wish to insert these records. Because the MF is a sequential file, the only way to insert the records is to create a new file that contains the inserted records. This is the *new master file* (NMF).

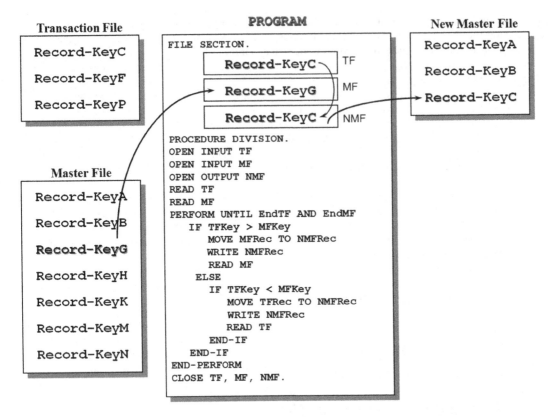

Figure 10-5. *Inserting records into an ordered sequential file*

The program starts by opening the files and reading a record from each of the two input files. This is the equivalent of the read-ahead technique that you saw in Chapter 5. Before you enter the loop that processes the files, you start with a record in each file buffer. The loop is executed until the end of both files, because regardless of which file ends first, the remaining records of the other must be written to the NMF.

With Record-KeyC in one buffer (TF) and Record-KeyA in the other (MF), the key field values are compared. When the transaction is greater than the master (as is the case here), the condition indicates that the position where the transaction record must be inserted has not yet been reached, so the MF record is written to the NMF. Because the MF record in the buffer has been dealt with (consumed), you read the MF to get a new record. This is the record: Record-KeyB.

When the key values are compared, the transaction key is still greater the master, so this record too is written to the NMF and another is read from the MF. This is the record: Record-KeyG.

Now you have reached the point in the program captured by Figure 10-5. This time, the key value in the TF is less than that of the MF, so the transaction record is written to the NMF. Because the record in the TF buffer has been consumed, a new record is read into the buffer, and the process continues until both files end.

To simplify the template, the condition where the key values are equal has been omitted. If this condition occurs, then a transaction error has occurred, because for record-matching purposes, the key values must be unique.

If you examine the algorithm provided, you might be puzzled that there appears to be no code to write out the remaining records to the NMF when one file ends before the other. The explanation for this lies in the end-of-file condition name associated with each file. These might be described as in Example 10-2.

Example 10-2. Partial Record Descriptions for the Transaction and Master Files

```
FD TransactionFile
01 TFRec.
   88 EndTF  VALUE HIGH-VALUES.
   02 TFKey     PIC X(?).
        etc

FD MasterFile
01 MFRec.
   88 EndMF  VALUE HIGH-VALUES.
   02 MFKey     PIC X(?).
        etc
```

When the end of either file is encountered, its associated condition name is set to true; this has the side effect of filling its record area (including its key field) with HIGH-VALUES (the highest possible character value). Subsequent key comparisons cause the remaining records to be written to the NMF. For instance, from the test data in Figure 10-1, it is clear that the TF will end first. When the EndTF condition name is set to true, TFkey contains HIGH-VALUES. In the key comparison, TFKey is greater than MFKey, and this results in the master record being written to the NMF. If the MF ends first, MFKey is filled with HIGH-VALUES, and the key comparisons then causes the remaining transaction records to be written to the NMF.

Updating Records in an Ordered Sequential File

The template for updating records in an ordered sequential file is shown in Figure 10-6. The diagram captures the program action at the point where Record-KeyH has been read into the TF record buffer and the MF record buffer. Both records are combined to produce the updated record Record-KeyH+, which is then sent to the NMF.

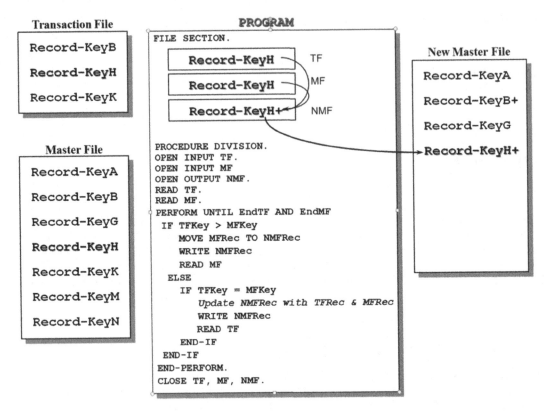

Figure 10-6. *Updating records in an ordered sequential file*

When you apply an update to the MF, you combine the records from the TF and the MF because the transaction record only consist of the key field and the field(s) to be updated. For instance, in a stock-file update, the update record in the TF might contain the fields shown in Example 10-3, whereas the MF might contain those shown in Example 10-4.

Example 10-3. Fields in the Update Record of a Transaction File

```
FD TransactionFile.
01 TFRec.
   02 StockId-TF        PIC X(?).
   02 QtyInStock-TF      PIC 9(?).
```

Example 10-4. Fields in the Record of a Stock Master File

```
FD StockMasterFile.
01 StockMFRec.
   02 StockId-MF         PIC X(?).
   02 Description-MF      PIC X(?).
   02 ManfId-MF          PIC X(?).
   02 ReorderLevel-MF    PIC 9(?).
   02 ReorderQty-MF      PIC 9(?).
   02 QtyInStock-MF      PIC 9(?).
```

The template in Figure 10-6 does not check for the error condition where the record to be updated does not exist in the MF. This condition is detected when the value in TFKey is less than that in MFKey. You can test this yourself by including the record Record-KeyD in the transaction file and then applying the transactions manually.

Deleting Records from an Ordered Sequential File

Figure 10-7 shows the template for deleting records from an ordered sequential file. The diagram captures the action just after Record-KeyK has been read into the MF record buffer. When the keys are equal, you have found the MF record to be deleted. So what action do you take to delete it? No action! You just don't send it to the NMF. Because both the transaction record and the master record have been consumed, you need to get the next record from each file.

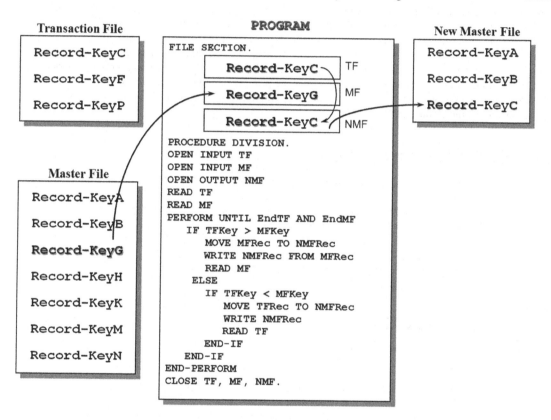

Figure 10-7. Deleting records from an ordered sequential file

When I discussed how to update an ordered sequential file, I noted that the transaction record contained fewer fields than the MF record. The delete operation takes this even further. To delete a record, the transaction record only needs the key field.

As before, the template does not check for the error condition where the record to be deleted does not exist in the MF. Just like the update operation, this condition is detected when the value in TFKey is less than that in MFKey. You can test this yourself by adding the record Record-KeyC to the records in the TF and then applying the transactions manually.

The File-Update Problem: Simplified

The previous section showed how various types of updates can be applied to an ordered sequential file. But you considered each of these types of updates in isolation. The TF consisted of records of only one type; it contained a batch of deletions, or a batch of insertions, or a batch of updates. In reality, all these different kinds of transaction records would be gathered together into one transaction file. Having multiple record types in the transaction file is good for processing efficiency, but it considerably complicates the update logic.

The problem of how to update an ordered sequential file is known as the *file-update problem*. The file-update problem is much more difficult than it appears on the surface and has been the subject of some research. Of particular interest is Barry Dwyer's paper "One More Time—How to Update a Master File.[3]" The algorithm described in his paper is implemented in Listing 10-2.

This section considers a simplified version of updating a file containing multiple record types. In this version, multiple updates for a particular master record are allowed, but an insertion record cannot be followed by any other operation for the same record. That restriction reveals the further levels of complexity of the file-update problem. Obviously, in a stock file, there might be a number of stock movements (additions and subtractions from stock) for a particular stock item. But in some cases, there might be an insertion for a particular stock item followed by stock movements and other updates for that item. In such a situation, the order in which the transactions are applied is important, because obviously you want to insert the record before you apply updates to it. These and other issues considerably complicate the file-update problem.

Updating a Stock File: Problem Specification

To explore some of the complexities of applying transactions of different types to a master file, consider the following problem specification.

A stock file holds details of gadgets sold by Gadget Shop (GadgetShop.Com). It is a sequential file sorted on ascending GadgetId. Each record in the file has the following description:

Field	Type	Length	Value
GadgetId	9	6	000001–999999
GadgetName	X	30	-
QtyInStock	9	4	0000–9999
Price	9	6	0000.00–9999.99

To update the stock file, a number of different kinds of update records have been gathered together into a sequential transaction file.

The records in transaction file have seen sorted into ascending GadgetId order. Within GadgetId, the transactions are sorted by the order in which they were submitted. There are three different types of transaction records: insertion records to add a new line of stock, deletion records to delete a line of stock, and price-change records change the Price of a line of stock. Obviously, you could also have stock-movement records to add and subtract inventory from the QtyInStock field, but that would needlessly complicate this example.

Because there are three different types of records in the transaction file, you need to have three different record descriptions. But as you discovered in Chapter 8, when a file contains multiple types of records, you must have some way of identifying which record type has been read into the record buffer. To distinguish one type of record from

---

[3]Barry Dwyer. 1981. One more time—how to update a master file. *Commun. ACM* 24, 1 (January 1981), 3-8. DOI=10.1145/358527.358534 http://doi.acm.org/10.1145/358527.358534.

another, a special field called a *type code* is inserted into each transaction record. In the transaction file used to update Gadget Shop's stock file, a type code value of 1 is used to represent insertions, 2 represents deletions, and 3 represents a price change. The records in the transaction file have the following descriptions:

Insertion Record

Field	Type	Length	Value
TypeCode	9	1	1
GadgetId	9	6	000001–999999
GadgetName	X	30	-
QtyInStock	9	4	0000–9999
Price	9	6	0000.00–9999.99

Deletion Record

Field	Type	Length	Value
TypeCode	9	1	2
GadgetId	9	6	000001–999999

Price Change Record

Field	Type	Length	Value
TypeCode	9	1	3
GadgetId	9	6	000001–999999
Price	9	6	0000.00–9999.99

Because there are three different types of records in the file, you must have three record descriptions in the FD entry for the transaction file (see Example 10-5).

Example 10-5. Record Descriptions for the Transaction File

```
FD TransactionFile.
01 InsertionRec.
   02 TypeCode       PIC 9.
   02 GadgetId       PIC 9(6).
   02 GadgetName     PIC X(30).
   02 QtyInStock     PIC 9(4).
   02 Price          PIC 9(4)V99.

01 DeletionRec.
   02 TypeCode       PIC 9.
   02 GadgetID       PIC 9(6).

01 PriceChangeRec.
   02 TypeCode       PIC 9.
   02 GadgetID       PIC 9(6).
   02 Price          PIC 9(4)V99.
```

Buffer Implications of Multiple Record Types

You discovered in Chapter 8 that when a file contains multiple record types, a record declaration (starting with a 01 level number) must be created for each type of record. But even though there are different types of records in the file, and there are separate record declarations for each record type, only a *single record buffer* is created for the file. All the record descriptions map on to this area of storage, which is the size of the largest record. Figure 10-8 shows the mapping of the transaction records on to the record buffer. All the identifiers in all the mapped records are current/active at the same time, but only one set of identifiers makes sense for the particular record in the buffer. In Figure 10-8, the record in the buffer is an insertion record (TypeCode = 1), so even though you *could* execute the statement MOVE Price TO PrnPrice, it wouldn't make sense to do so. Because there is an insertion record in the buffer, Price has the value "Ice Cr."

Figure 10-8. *Schematic showing the mapping of records on to the record buffer*

When you examine the record descriptions in Example 10-5 and the record schematic in Figure 10-8, you may notice that both TypeCode and GadgetId occur in all three record descriptions. You may wonder if is it permitted to use the same data name in different records. And if it is permitted, how can the data name be referenced uniquely?

Although it is legal to use the same data name in different records (but not in the same group item), in order to uniquely identify the record you want, you must qualify it with the record or group name. For instance, you can refer to the GadgetId in PriceChangeRec by using the form GadgetId OF PriceChangeRec.

But even though it is *legal* to declare GadgetId in all the records, and even though you must declare the storage for GadgetId in all the records, you don't actually *need* to use the name GadgetId in all the records. Because all the records map on to the same area of storage, it does not matter which GadgetId you refer to—they all access the same value in the record. So no matter which record is in the buffer, a statement that refers to GadgetId OF InsertRec will still access the correct value.

The same logic applies to the TypeCode. The TypeCode is in the same place in all three record types, so it doesn't matter which one you use—they all access the same area of memory. When an area of storage must be declared, but you don't care what name you give it, you don't have to make up a dummy name. You use the special name FILLER.

Example 10-6 shows a revised version of the three record descriptions. In this version, only the items that have to be named are given data names. The record schematic for this revised version is shown in Figure 10-9.

Example 10-6. Revised Record Descriptions

```
FD TransactionFile.
01 InsertionRec.
   02 TypeCode      PIC 9.
   02 GadgetId      PIC 9(6).
   02 GadgetName    PIC X(30).
   02 QtyInStock          PIC 9(4).
   02 Price         PIC 9(4)V99.

01 DeletionRec.
   02 FILLER        PIC 9(7).

01 PriceChangeRec.
   02 FILLER        PIC 9(7).
   02 Price         PIC 9(4)V99.
```

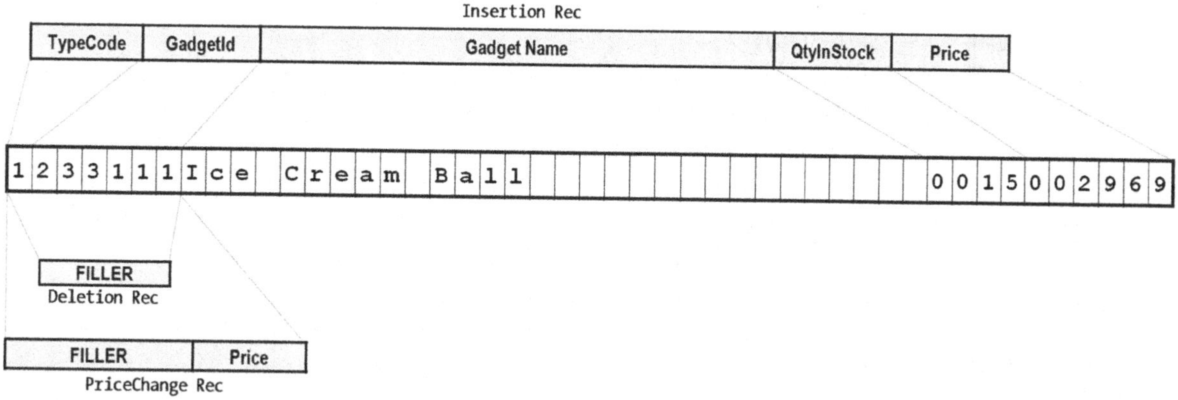

Figure 10-9. *Mapping of transaction records on to the record buffer*

File Update Program

The program required to apply the transaction file to the gadget stock file is shown in Listing 10-3.

Listing 10-3. File Update—Insert not followed by updates to inserted record

```
IDENTIFICATION DIVISION.
PROGRAM-ID.  Listing10-3.
AUTHOR. Michael Coughlan
* Applies the transactions ordered on ascending GadgetId-TF to the
* MasterStockFile ordered on ascending GadgetId-MF.
* Assumption: Insert not followed by updates to inserted record
*             Multiple updates per master record permitted
```

```
ENVIRONMENT DIVISION.
INPUT-OUTPUT SECTION.
FILE-CONTROL.
    SELECT MasterStockFile ASSIGN TO "Listing10-3Master.dat"
            ORGANIZATION IS LINE SEQUENTIAL.

    SELECT NewStockFile ASSIGN TO "Listing10-3NewMast.dat"
            ORGANIZATION IS LINE SEQUENTIAL.

    SELECT TransactionFile ASSIGN TO "Listing10-3Trans.dat"
            ORGANIZATION IS LINE SEQUENTIAL.

DATA DIVISION.
FILE SECTION.
FD MasterStockFile.
01 MasterStockRec.
    88 EndOfMasterFile        VALUE HIGH-VALUES.
    02 GadgetId-MF            PIC 9(6).
    02 GadgetName-MF          PIC X(30).
    02 QtyInStock-MF          PIC 9(4).
    02 Price-MF               PIC 9(4)V99.

FD NewStockFile.
01 NewStockRec.
    02 GadgetId-NSF           PIC 9(6).
    02 GadgetName-NSF         PIC X(30).
    02 QtyInStock-NSF         PIC 9(4).
    02 Price-NSF              PIC 9(4)V99.

FD TransactionFile.
01 InsertionRec.
    88 EndOfTransFile         VALUE HIGH-VALUES.
    02 TypeCode-TF            PIC 9.
        88 Insertion          VALUE 1.
        88 Deletion           VALUE 2.
        88 UpdatePrice        VALUE 3.
    02 GadgetId-TF            PIC 9(6).
    02 GadgetName-IR          PIC X(30).
    02 QtyInStock-IR          PIC 9(4).
    02 Price-IR               PIC 9(4)V99.

01 DeletionRec.
    02 FILLER                 PIC 9(7).

01 PriceChangeRec.
    02 FILLER                 PIC 9(7).
    02 Price-PCR              PIC 9(4)V99.

WORKING-STORAGE SECTION.
01  ErrorMessage.
    02 PrnGadgetId            PIC 9(6).
    02 FILLER                 PIC XXX VALUE " - ".
```

```
    02 FILLER              PIC X(45).
        88 InsertError        VALUE "Insert Error - Record already exists".
        88 DeleteError        VALUE "Delete Error - No such record in Master".
        88 PriceUpdateError VALUE "Price Update Error - No such record in Master".


PROCEDURE DIVISION.
Begin.
    OPEN INPUT  MasterStockFile
    OPEN INPUT  TransactionFile
    OPEN OUTPUT NewStockFile
    PERFORM ReadMasterFile
    PERFORM ReadTransFile
    PERFORM UNTIL EndOfMasterFile AND EndOfTransFile
        EVALUATE TRUE
          WHEN GadgetId-TF > GadgetId-MF  PERFORM CopyToNewMaster
          WHEN GadgetId-TF = GadgetId-MF  PERFORM TryToApplyToMaster
          WHEN GadgetId-TF < GadgetId-MF  PERFORM TryToInsert
        END-EVALUATE
    END-PERFORM


    CLOSE MasterStockFile, TransactionFile, NewStockFile
    STOP RUN.


CopyToNewMaster.
    WRITE NewStockRec FROM MasterStockRec
    PERFORM ReadMasterFile.


TryToApplyToMaster.
    EVALUATE TRUE
        WHEN UpdatePrice MOVE Price-PCR TO Price-MF
        WHEN Deletion    PERFORM ReadMasterFile
        WHEN Insertion   SET InsertError TO TRUE
                         DISPLAY ErrorMessage
    END-EVALUATE
    PERFORM ReadTransFile.


TryToInsert.
    IF Insertion     MOVE GadgetId-TF TO GadgetId-NSF
                     MOVE GadgetName-IR TO GadgetName-NSF
                     MOVE QtyInStock-IR TO QtyInStock-NSF
                     MOVE Price-Ir TO Price-NSF
                     WRITE NewStockRec
        ELSE
          IF UpdatePrice
             SET PriceUpdateError TO TRUE
          END-IF
          IF Deletion
             SET DeleteError TO TRUE
          END-IF
          DISPLAY ErrorMessage
    END-IF
    PERFORM ReadTransFile.
```

```
ReadTransFile.
    READ TransactionFile
        AT END SET EndOfTransFile TO TRUE
    END-READ
    MOVE GadgetId-TF TO PrnGadgetId.

ReadMasterFile.
    READ MasterStockFile
        AT END SET EndOfMasterFile TO TRUE
    END-READ.
```

Program Notes

Three files are used in the program. The master file, the transaction file and the new master file. The gadget stock file is known as the MasterStockFile, the transaction file is called the TransactionFile, and the new master file, produced by applying the transactions to the master file is known as the NewStockFile.

Applying the updates requires a considerable amount of data movement from fields in one stock record to another. To avoid the tedium of having to qualify each field reference, a suffix has been applied to the relevant fields to distinguish them from one another. The suffix MF (master File) is applied to records of the MasterStockFile, NSF is applied to records of the NewStockFile, and TF is applied to the common fields (TypeCode and GadgetId) of the TransactionFile.

Reading the TransactionFile and the MasterStockFile are operations that occur in a number of places. To avoid having to write out the READ statement in full each time, I have placed them in a paragraph which I then invoke by means of a PERFORM. While this makes the program textually shorter, you should be aware that performance will be impacted. Similarly, I have placed the statement MOVE GadgetId-TF TO PrnGadgetId in the ReadTransFile paragraph where it sets the GadgetId into the ErrorMessage every time a record is read. This placement means only one instance of this statement is required but again this saving is achieved at the cost of a slight impact on performance (because you really only need to do this if there is an error).

The GadgetId is moved into the ErrorMessage area every time a transaction record is read but you may be wondering how the actual error message gets into the ErrorMessage area. I won't go into a full explanation here but I will remind you that when a condition name is set to TRUE it pushes its value item into the associated data item. If that isn't a sufficient hint, then you may need to review Chapter 5 where condition names were discussed.

The paragraph CopyToNewMaster copies the MasterStockFile record to the NewStockFile when there are no transactions to be applied to the MasterStockFile record (GadgetId-TF > GadgetId-MF) but it is also the paragraph that writes the MasterStockRec after updates have been applied to it. How does this happen? Consider this sequence of events happening in the program:

GadgetId-TF = GadgetId-MF and an update is applied to the MasterStockRec

The next transaction record is read

GadgetId-TF = GadgetId-MF and another update is applied to the MasterStockRec

The next transaction record is read (because the transaction records are in ascending sequence this transaction must be equal to or greater than the master)

GadgetId-TF > GadgetId-MF and the updated MasterStockRec is written to the NewStockFile

When the keys are equal, the update is applied to the MasterStockRec, when eventually the transaction key is greater than the master file key (the only possible condition because the files are ordered), the updated record is written to the new master file.

Test Data and Results

The test data files for the program are given Figure 10-10. As usual, I've kept them short because of space constraints and to make them easy to understand. For the transaction file, I have taken advantage of the fact the record buffer is the size of the largest record, to add text that identifies the purpose of each test. For instance, a delete record in a real transaction file would only consist of the type code and the key.

TransactionFile	MasterStockFile (record to be deleted in bold)	
1113111Valid Insert @ start of file 1111004149	113434Mini Retro Popcorn Maker	1111004149
3234567033333 Valid Price Update	123456SoundDisk MP3 Player 4GB	0650003095
1266111Valid Insert @ middle of file 1111002379	234567BioLite Camp Stove	0057029550
2334222 Invalid Delete	266999The Original Bacon Kit	1111002379
1345678 Invalid Insert 0155002590	345678Collapsible Kettle - Green	0155002590
3345678003333 Valid Update	456789Digital Measuring Jug	0325000895
2567890 Valid Delete MicroLiteLEDTorch	**567890MicroLite LED Torch**	**0512000745**
3578901001799 Invalid Update	678901Pocket Sized Fishing Rod	0055001799
3789111003333 First update to 789111	789111Ice Cream Ball	1111002969
3789111009393 Second update to 789111		
1888111Valid Insert @ end of file 1111002969		

Figure 10-10. *Test data and results*

The results from running the program are shown in Figure 10-11.

NewStockFile (inserts & updates in bold)		Listing 10-3 Output
113111Valid Insert @ start of file	**1111004149**	334222 - Delete Error - No such record in Master
113434Mini Retro Popcorn Maker	1111004149	345678 - Insert Error - Record already exists
123456SoundDisk MP3 Player 4GB	0650003095	578901 - Price Update Error - No such record in Master
234567BioLite Camp Stove	0057**033333**	
266111Valid Insert @ middle of file	**1111002379**	
266999The Original Bacon Kit	1111002379	
345678Collapsible Kettle - Green	0155**003333**	
456789Digital Measuring Jug	0325000895	
678901Pocket Sized Fishing Rod	0055001799	
789111Ice Cream Ball	1111**009393**	
888111Valid Insert @ end of file	**1111002969**	

Figure 10-11. *Listing 10-3 results*

The Full File Update Problem

Listing 10-3 provides a gentle introduction to the file update problem but the algorithm used in that program only works for a limited form of the problem. The algorithm does not work when an insert can be followed by updates to the record to be inserted. The reason the algorithm does not work for the extended version of problem is that now the updates can be applied to either the master file or the transaction file. In the Listing 10-3 algorithm, the updates are applied only to the master file. This seemingly small change makes the task a very slippery fish indeed. The moment you think you have solved the problem by placing a read here or a write there some other difficulty rears its ugly head. The best way to get a feel for the complications that this simple specification change causes, is to try it yourself. Using Listing 10-3 as the basis for your program, attempt to change the program so that it also allows an insertion to be followed by updates to the inserted record.

Fortunately, you don't have to rely on your own resources to come up with a solution. People have gone before you, and you can stand on their shoulders. Listing 10-4 demonstrates a solution to the problem based on the algorithm described by Barry Dwyer in "One More Time - How to Update a Master File."[3]

The main elements of the algorithm are the ChooseNextKey and SetInitialStatus paragraphs, the RecordInMaster and RecordNotInMaster condition names, and the loop PERFORM ProcessOneTransaction UNTIL GadgetID-TF NOT = CurrentKey.

ChooseNextKey allows the program to decide if the transaction file or the master file will be the focus of updates. The key of whichever file is the focus is recorded in CurrentKey.

SetInitialStatus uses the condition names RecordInMaster and RecordNotInMaster to record whether or not the record is currently included in the master file. Later the RecordInMaster condition name is used to decide whether the record is to be included in the new master file.

The ProcessOneTransaction loop applies all the transactions that apply to the record of focus while the keys are equal. When the loop exits, the RecordInMaster condition name is tested to see if the record of focus should be included in the new master file.

Full File Update Program

Listing 10-4 is the final program.

Listing 10-4. Caption

```
IDENTIFICATION DIVISION.
PROGRAM-ID.  Listing10-4.
AUTHOR. Michael Coughlan
* File Update program based on the algorithm described by Barry Dwyer in
* "One more time - How to update a Master File"
* Applies the transactions ordered on ascending GadgetId-TF to the
* MasterStockFile ordered on ascending GadgetId-MF.
* Within each key value records are ordered on the sequence in which
* events occurred in the outside world.
* All valid, real world, transaction sequences are accommodated

ENVIRONMENT DIVISION.
INPUT-OUTPUT SECTION.
FILE-CONTROL.
    SELECT MasterStockFile ASSIGN TO "Listing10-4Master.dat"
           ORGANIZATION IS LINE SEQUENTIAL.
```

```
        SELECT NewStockFile ASSIGN TO "Listing10-4NewMast.dat"
            ORGANIZATION IS LINE SEQUENTIAL.

        SELECT TransactionFile ASSIGN TO "Listing10-4Trans.dat"
            ORGANIZATION IS LINE SEQUENTIAL.

    DATA DIVISION.
    FILE SECTION.
    FD MasterStockFile.
    01 MasterStockRec.
        88 EndOfMasterFile      VALUE HIGH-VALUES.
        02 GadgetID-MF          PIC 9(6).
        02 GadgetName-MF        PIC X(30).
        02 QtyInStock-MF        PIC 9(4).
        02 Price-MF             PIC 9(4)V99.

    FD NewStockFile.
    01 NewStockRec.
        02 GadgetID-NSF         PIC 9(6).
        02 GadgetName-NSF       PIC X(30).
        02 QtyInStock-NSF       PIC 9(4).
        02 Price-NSF            PIC 9(4)V99.

    FD TransactionFile.
    01 InsertionRec.
        88 EndOfTransFile       VALUE HIGH-VALUES.
        02 TypeCode-TF          PIC 9.
            88 Insertion        VALUE 1.
            88 Deletion         VALUE 2.
            88 UpdatePrice      VALUE 3.
        02 RecordBody-IR.
            03 GadgetID-TF      PIC 9(6).
            03 GadgetName-IR    PIC X(30).
            03 QtyInStock-IR    PIC 9(4).
            03 Price-IR         PIC 9(4)V99.

    01 DeletionRec.
        02 FILLER               PIC 9(7).

    01 PriceChangeRec.
        02 FILLER               PIC 9(7).
        02 Price-PCR            PIC 9(4)V99.

    WORKING-STORAGE SECTION.
    01 ErrorMessage.
        02 PrnGadgetId          PIC 9(6).
        02 FILLER               PIC XXX VALUE " - ".
        02 FILLER               PIC X(45).
            88 InsertError        VALUE "Insert Error - Record already exists".
            88 DeleteError        VALUE "Delete Error - No such record in Master".
            88 PriceUpdateError  VALUE "Price Update Error - No such record in Master".
```

```
01 FILLER                    PIC X VALUE "n".
   88 RecordInMaster         VALUE "y".
   88 RecordNotInMaster      VALUE "n".

01 CurrentKey                PIC 9(6).

PROCEDURE DIVISION.
Begin.
   OPEN INPUT  MasterStockFile
   OPEN INPUT  TransactionFile
   OPEN OUTPUT NewStockFile
   PERFORM ReadMasterFile
   PERFORM ReadTransFile
   PERFORM ChooseNextKey
   PERFORM UNTIL EndOfMasterFile AND EndOfTransFile
      PERFORM SetInitialStatus
      PERFORM ProcessOneTransaction
            UNTIL GadgetID-TF NOT = CurrentKey
*     CheckFinalStatus
      IF RecordInMaster
         WRITE NewStockRec
      END-IF
      PERFORM ChooseNextKey
    END-PERFORM

    CLOSE MasterStockFile, TransactionFile, NewStockFile
    STOP RUN.

ChooseNextKey.
   IF GadgetID-TF < GadgetID-MF
      MOVE GadgetID-TF TO CurrentKey
    ELSE
      MOVE GadgetID-MF TO CurrentKey
   END-IF.

SetInitialStatus.
   IF GadgetID-MF =  CurrentKey
      MOVE MasterStockRec TO NewStockRec
      SET RecordInMaster TO TRUE
      PERFORM ReadMasterFile
    ELSE SET RecordNotInMaster TO TRUE
   END-IF.

ProcessOneTransaction.
*  ApplyTransToMaster
   EVALUATE TRUE
       WHEN Insertion   PERFORM ApplyInsertion
       WHEN UpdatePrice PERFORM ApplyPriceChange
       WHEN Deletion    PERFORM ApplyDeletion
     END-EVALUATE.
     PERFORM ReadTransFile.
```

```
ApplyInsertion.
    IF RecordInMaster
       SET InsertError TO TRUE
       DISPLAY ErrorMessage
     ELSE
       SET RecordInMaster TO TRUE
       MOVE RecordBody-IR TO NewStockRec
    END-IF.

ApplyDeletion.
    IF RecordNotInMaster
       SET DeleteError TO TRUE
       DISPLAY ErrorMessage
     ELSE SET RecordNotInMaster TO TRUE
    END-IF.

ApplyPriceChange.
    IF RecordNotInMaster
       SET PriceUpdateError TO TRUE
       DISPLAY ErrorMessage
     ELSE
       MOVE Price-PCR TO Price-NSF
    END-IF.

ReadTransFile.
    READ TransactionFile
        AT END SET EndOfTransFile TO TRUE
    END-READ
    MOVE GadgetID-TF TO PrnGadgetId.

ReadMasterFile.
    READ MasterStockFile
        AT END SET EndOfMasterFile TO TRUE
    END-READ.
```

Program Notes

I have incorporated an optimization in Listing 10-4 that might welcome some explanation. Before you write an insert record to the master file in Listing 10-3, the fields in the record are transferred one by one to the NewStockRec. You couldn't just move the InsertionRec to the NewStockRec because the InsertionRec also includes the TypeCode field. In Listing 10-4, this problem has been solved by restructuring the Insertion records so that the fields you have to move to the NewStockRec are subordinate to a group item called RecordBody-IR. This means in Listing 10-4, instead of moving the contents of the insertion record to the new master record field by field, you just MOVE RecordBody-IR TO NewStockRec. The record schematic for this restructured record is shown in Figure 10-12. The record remains the same size. But now you have an additional data name with which to manipulate the data in the record.

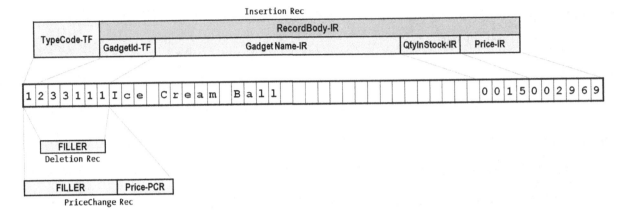

Figure 10-12. *Revised record schematic showing the restructured Insertion record*

Test Data and Results

The test data for the program is shown in Figure 10-13.

TransactionFile	MasterStockFile (record to be deleted shown in bold)	
1113111Valid Insert @ start of file 1111004149	113434Mini Retro Popcorn Maker	1111004149
3234567033333 Valid Price Update	123456SoundDisk MP3 Player 4GB	0650003095
1266111Valid Insert @ middle of file 1111002379	234567BioLite Camp Stove	0057029550
2334222 Invalid Delete	266999The Original Bacon Kit	1111002379
1333333Valid Insert & updates 1111003333	345678Collapsible Kettle - Green	0155002590
3333333006666 First update to 333333	456789Digital Measuring Jug	0325000895
3333333009999 Second update to 333333	**567890MicroLite LED Torch**	**0512000745**
1345678 Invalid Insert 0155002590	678901Pocket Sized Fishing Rod	0055001799
3345678003333 Valid Update	789111Ice Cream Ball	1111002969
2567890 Valid Delete MicroLiteLEDTorch		
3578901001799 Invalid Update		
3789111003333 First update to 789111		
3789111009393 Second update to 789111		
1888111Valid Insert @ end of file 1111002969		

Figure 10-13. *Test data for Listing 10-4*

The result of running the program against that test data is shown in Figure 10-14.

```
NewStockFile  (inserts & updates in bold)

113111Valid Insert @ start of file  1111004149
113434Mini Retro Popcorn Maker       1111004149
123456SoundDisk MP3 Player 4GB       0650003095
234567BioLite Camp Stove             0057033333
266111Valid Insert @ middle of file 1111002379
266999The Original Bacon Kit         1111002379
333333Valid Insert & updates         1111009999
345678Collapsible Kettle - Green     0155003333
456789Digital Measuring Jug          0325000895
678901Pocket Sized Fishing Rod       0055001799
789111Ice Cream Ball                 1111009393
888111Valid Insert @ end of file     1111002969
```

Figure 10-14. *Results of running Listing 10-4*

Summary

This chapter introduced two of the most important sequential file processing problems. The chapter began by examining how sequential files are organized and discussing the difference between ordered and unordered sequential files. The next section introduced the class of problems known as control-break problems. The final section introduced the thorny problem of the sequential File Update.

The section that discussed control-break problems included an example program to produce a printed report involving a three level control break. A second example program implemented an atypical control break problem and was intended to show that a control break solution may be applied to a number of different types of problem.

In the final section, I discussed how to apply updates to an ordered sequential file and included two examples programs. The first example implemented a solution to a simplified version of the file update problem while the second applied the algorithm described by Dwyer[3] and Dijkstra.[4]

In the specification for Listing 10-1, I mentioned that using the full state name in every record was very wasteful and that a more realistic scenario would use a state code instead of the full name. I noted that in that case you would have to convert the state code to a state name by means of a lookup table. In the next chapter, which will discuss how tabular data is implemented in COBOL, you revisit the Listing 10-1 specification to create a more realistic scenario that will require you to incorporate a state lookup table into the program.

LANGUAGE KNOWLEDGE EXERCISE

Unleash your 2B pencil once more. It is time for some exercises. These exercises are designed to allow you to prove to yourself that it is not possible to update an unordered sequential file.

No answers are provided for these questions.

1. The transaction file and the master file in Figure 10-15 are unordered sequential files. Using the algorithm outlined in Figure 10-15 manually attempt to update the master file records to produce a new master file that contains the updated records.

---

[4]Dijkstra, E.W. A Discipline of Programming. Prentice-Hall, Englewood Cliffs, N.J.,1976.

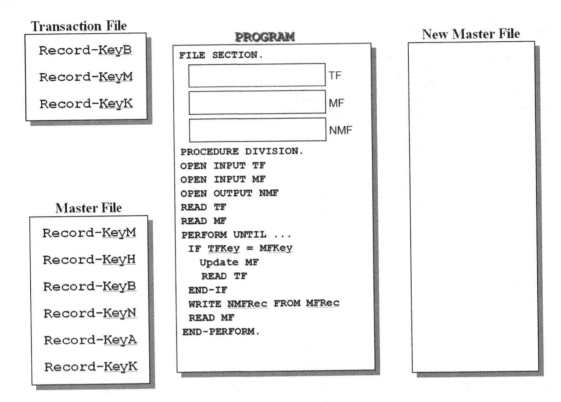

Figure 10-15. *Attempting to update an unordered sequential file*

2. The transaction file and the master file in Figure 10-15 are unordered sequential files. Using the algorithm outlined in Figure 10-16 manually attempt to delete the master file records to produce a new master file that does not contain the deleted records.

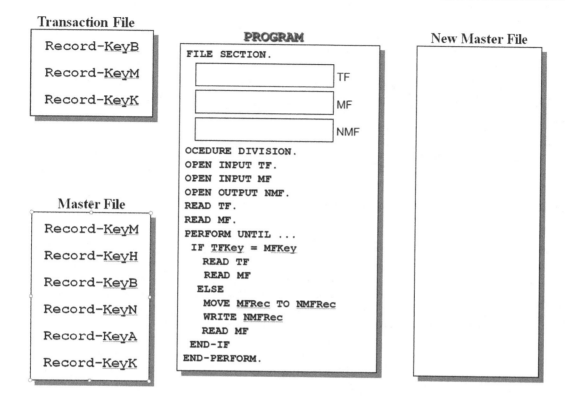

Figure 10-16. *Attempting to delete from an unordered sequential file*

PROGRAMMING EXERCISE

Listing 10-4 applies the File Update algorithm described by Dwyer[3] to implement an update of the Gadget Shop's Stock MF. However, in that implementation only the Price field is updated. Now you need to modify that program so that it can also update the QtyInStock field.

Change the program in Listing 10-4 so that it handle stock movement updates as well as price change updates. To accommodate this change in the specification two new record types will have to be added to the transaction file. These new transaction records are the AddToStock record indicated by a type code of 4 and the SubtractFromStock record indicated by a type code of 5.

The record descriptions for the MF and the new version of the TF are given here.

The Stock MF is a sequential file ordered on ascending GadgetId. Each record has the following description.

StockMaster Record

Field	Type	Length	Value
GadgetId	9	6	000001–999999
GadgetName	X	30	-
QtyInStock	9	4	0000–9999

Field	Type	Length	Value
Price	9	6	0000.00-9999.99

The TF is a sequential file ordered on ascending GadgetId. In each set of records with the same GadgetId the records are ordered in sequence in which the transactions occurred in the real world. Records in the TF have the following descriptions:

Insertion record

Field	Type	Length	Value
TypeCode	9	1	1
GadgetId	9	6	000001-999999
GadgetName	X	30	-
QtyInStock	9	4	0000-9999
Price	9	6	0000.00-9999.99

Deletion record

Field	Type	Length	Value
TypeCode	9	1	2
GadgetId	9	6	000001-999999

PriceChange record

Field	Type	Length	Value
TypeCode	9	1	3
GadgetId	9	6	000001-999999
Price	9	6	0000.00-9999.99

AddToStock record

Field	Type	Length	Value
TypeCode	9	1	4
GadgetId	9	6	000001-999999
QtyToAdd	9	4	0000-9999

SubtractFromStock record

Field	Type	Length	Value
TypeCode	9	1	5
GadgetId	9	6	000001-999999
QtyToSubtract	9	4	0000-9999

TestData

To test your program you can use the test data shown below in Figure 10-17.

TransactionFile		MasterStockFile (record to be deleted shown in bold)	
1113111Valid Insert @ start of file	1111004149	113434Mini Retro Popcorn Maker	1111004149
3234567033333 Valid Price Update		123456SoundDisk MP3 Player 4GB	0650003095
1266111Valid Insert @ middle of file	1111002379	234567BioLite Camp Stove	0057029550
52669991111 Valid Subtract from stock		266999The Original Bacon Kit	1111002379
52669990003 Invalid subtract - not enough		345678Collapsible Kettle - Green	0155002590
42669994444 Valid Add to stock		456789Digital Measuring Jug	0325000895
52669990404 Valid Subtract from stock		**567890MicroLite LED Torch**	**0512000745**
2334222 Invalid Delete		678901Pocket Sized Fishing Rod	0055001799
1333333Valid Insert & updates	1111003333	789111Ice Cream Ball	1111002969
3333333006666 First update to 333333			
3333333009999 Second update to 333333			
1345678 Invalid Insert	0155002590		
3345678003333 Valid Update			
2567890 Valid Delete MicroLiteLEDTorch			
3578901001799 Invalid Update			
3789111003333 First update to 789111			
3789111009393 Second update to 789111			
1888111Valid Insert @ end of file	1111002969		

***Figure 10-17.** Test data including add and subtract from stock transactions*

Notes

There is an additional error conditions to be noted. If the GadgetId-TF < GadgetId-MF and the type code is 4 or 5 then an error has occurred (no matching master file record) but it is also an error if the transaction is a SubtractFromStock record but the QtyInStock in the MF is less than the QtyToSubtract in the SubtractFromStock record

PROGRAMMING EXERCISE - ANSWER

***Listing 10-5.** Update with added AddToStock and SubtractFromStock transactions*

```
IDENTIFICATION DIVISION.
PROGRAM-ID.  Listing10-5.
AUTHOR. Michael Coughlan
* File Update program based on the algorithm described by Barry Dwyer in
* "One more time - How to update a Master File"
* Applies the transactions ordered on ascending GadgetId-TF to the
* MasterStockFile ordered on ascending GadgetId-MF.
* Within each key value records are ordered on the sequence in which
```

```
* events occurred in the outside world.
* All valid, real world, transaction sequences are accommodated
* This version includes additions and subtractions from QtyInStock

ENVIRONMENT DIVISION.
INPUT-OUTPUT SECTION.
FILE-CONTROL.
    SELECT MasterStockFile ASSIGN TO "Listing10-5Master.dat"
            ORGANIZATION IS LINE SEQUENTIAL.

    SELECT NewStockFile ASSIGN TO "Listing10-5NewMast.dat"
            ORGANIZATION IS LINE SEQUENTIAL.

    SELECT TransactionFile ASSIGN TO "Listing10-5Trans.dat"
            ORGANIZATION IS LINE SEQUENTIAL.

DATA DIVISION.
FILE SECTION.
FD MasterStockFile.
01 MasterStockRec.
    88 EndOfMasterFile      VALUE HIGH-VALUES.
    02 GadgetID-MF          PIC 9(6).
    02 GadgetName-MF        PIC X(30).
    02 QtyInStock-MF        PIC 9(4).
    02 Price-MF             PIC 9(4)V99.

FD NewStockFile.
01 NewStockRec.
    02 GadgetID-NSF         PIC 9(6).
    02 GadgetName-NSF       PIC X(30).
    02 QtyInStock-NSF       PIC 9(4).
    02 Price-NSF            PIC 9(4)V99.

FD TransactionFile.
01 InsertionRec.
    88 EndOfTransFile       VALUE HIGH-VALUES.
    02 TypeCode-TF          PIC 9.
        88 Insertion        VALUE 1.
        88 Deletion         VALUE 2.
        88 UpdatePrice      VALUE 3.
        88 StockAddition    VALUE 4.
        88 StockSubtraction VALUE 5.
    02 RecordBody-IR.
        03 GadgetID-TF      PIC 9(6).
        03 GadgetName-IR    PIC X(30).
        03 QtyInStock-IR    PIC 9(4).
        03 Price-IR         PIC 9(4)V99.

01 DeletionRec.
    02 FILLER               PIC 9(7).
```

```
01 PriceChangeRec.
   02 FILLER              PIC 9(7).
   02 Price-PCR           PIC 9(4)V99.

01 AddToStock.
   02 FILLER              PIC 9(7).
   02 QtyToAdd            PIC 9(4).

01 SubtractFromStock.
   02 FILLER              PIC 9(7).
   02 QtyToSubtract       PIC 9(4).

WORKING-STORAGE SECTION.
01 ErrorMessage.
   02 PrnGadgetId         PIC 9(6).
   02 FILLER              PIC XXX VALUE " - ".
   02 FILLER              PIC X(46).
      88 InsertError         VALUE "Insert Error - Record already exists".
      88 DeleteError         VALUE "Delete Error - No such record in Master".
      88 PriceUpdateError    VALUE "Price Update Error - No such record in Master".
      88 QtyAddError         VALUE "Stock Add Error - No such record in Master".
      88 QtySubtractError    VALUE "Stock Subtract Error - No such record in Master".
      88 InsufficientStock   VALUE "Stock Subtract Error - Not enough stock".

01 FILLER                 PIC X VALUE "n".
   88 RecordInMaster         VALUE "y".
   88 RecordNotInMaster      VALUE "n".

01 CurrentKey             PIC 9(6).

PROCEDURE DIVISION.
Begin.
   OPEN INPUT  MasterStockFile
   OPEN INPUT  TransactionFile
   OPEN OUTPUT NewStockFile
   PERFORM ReadMasterFile
   PERFORM ReadTransFile
   PERFORM ChooseNextKey
   PERFORM UNTIL EndOfMasterFile AND EndOfTransFile
      PERFORM SetInitialStatus
      PERFORM ProcessOneTransaction
            UNTIL GadgetID-TF NOT = CurrentKey
*     CheckFinalStatus
      IF RecordInMaster
         WRITE NewStockRec
      END-IF
      PERFORM ChooseNextKey
   END-PERFORM

   CLOSE MasterStockFile, TransactionFile, NewStockFile
   STOP RUN.
```

```
ChooseNextKey.
   IF GadgetID-TF < GadgetID-MF
      MOVE GadgetID-TF TO CurrentKey
    ELSE
      MOVE GadgetID-MF TO CurrentKey
   END-IF.


SetInitialStatus.
   IF GadgetID-MF =  CurrentKey
      MOVE MasterStockRec TO NewStockRec
      SET RecordInMaster TO TRUE
      PERFORM ReadMasterFile
    ELSE SET RecordNotInMaster TO TRUE
   END-IF.


ProcessOneTransaction.
*  ApplyTransToMaster
   EVALUATE TRUE
       WHEN Insertion        PERFORM ApplyInsertion
       WHEN UpdatePrice      PERFORM ApplyPriceChange
       WHEN Deletion         PERFORM ApplyDeletion
       WHEN StockAddition     PERFORM ApplyAddToStock
       WHEN StockSubtraction PERFORM ApplySubtractFromStock
    END-EVALUATE.
    PERFORM ReadTransFile.


ApplyInsertion.
   IF RecordInMaster
      SET InsertError TO TRUE
      DISPLAY ErrorMessage
    ELSE
      SET RecordInMaster TO TRUE
      MOVE RecordBody-IR TO NewStockRec
   END-IF.


ApplyDeletion.
   IF RecordNotInMaster
      SET DeleteError TO TRUE
      DISPLAY ErrorMessage
    ELSE SET RecordNotInMaster TO TRUE
   END-IF.


ApplyPriceChange.
   IF RecordNotInMaster
      SET PriceUpdateError TO TRUE
      DISPLAY ErrorMessage
    ELSE
      MOVE Price-PCR TO Price-NSF
   END-IF.
```

```
ApplyAddToStock.
    IF RecordNotInMaster
       SET QtyAddError TO TRUE
       DISPLAY ErrorMessage
     ELSE
       ADD QtyToAdd TO QtyInStock-NSF
    END-IF.


ApplySubtractFromStock.
    IF RecordNotInMaster
       SET QtySubtractError TO TRUE
       DISPLAY ErrorMessage
     ELSE
       IF QtyInStock-NSF < QtyToSubtract
          SET InsufficientStock TO TRUE
          DISPLAY ErrorMessage
        ELSE
          SUBTRACT QtyToSubtract FROM QtyInStock-NSF
       END-IF
    END-IF.


ReadTransFile.
    READ TransactionFile
        AT END SET EndOfTransFile TO TRUE
    END-READ
    MOVE GadgetID-TF TO PrnGadgetId.


ReadMasterFile.
    READ MasterStockFile
        AT END SET EndOfMasterFile TO TRUE
    END-READ.
```

CHAPTER 11

■ ■ ■

Creating Tabular Data

This chapter and the next return to the DATA DIVISION to explore more data-declaration concepts. In this chapter, I discuss how to create and manipulate tabular data. I compare and contrast COBOL tables with the arrays used in many other programming languages. Chapter 12 covers more advanced data declaration using the USAGE, REDEFINES, and RENAMES clauses.

The chapter starts with a discussion of the similarities and differences between arrays and tables. You then see how COBOL tables are declared using the OCCURS clause and manipulated using subscripts. I introduce a scenario to explain why tabular data is required and end the scenario with an example program that uses a simple one-dimensional table as part of the solution.

The middle section of the chapter introduces the concept of group items as table elements and demonstrates this in an example program. Multidimensional tables are then introduced. You learn the best way to depict a multidimensional COBOL table graphically; and I again address the contrast between arrays and tables, which is more pronounced with multidimensional tables. I present an example program using a two-dimensional table as part of its solution and introduce a scenario requiring a three-dimensional table.

In the chapter's final section, I show how to create prefilled tables using the REDEFINES clause. You see this demonstrated in an example program that uses a table prefilled with the names of the American states. I also discuss some of the table declaration changes introduced with the ANS 85 standard.

Tables vs. Arrays

Most programming languages have a facility to create tabular information. Tabular information consists of multiple occurrences of a homogeneous data item.

Most programming languages use the term *array* to describe these multiple-occurrence data items, but COBOL uses the term *table*. This is not just a difference of nomenclature. In most languages (including Basic, Pascal, Java, FORTRAN, and Ada), arrays look and work similarly; but COBOL tables, although they have some similarities to arrays, have a number of minor and major differences.

Table/Array Definition

Tables and arrays are so similar that you can use the same definition for them. A table/array may be defined as a contiguous sequence of memory locations that all have the same name and that are uniquely identified by that name and by their position in the sequence. The position index is called a *subscript*, and the individual components of the table/array are referred to as *elements*.

Table/Array Differences

If the same definition can be used for tables and arrays, what is the difference between them? The first difference affects the C language derivatives (C++, Java, and C#). In these languages, arrays start at element 0 and go to the maximum size of the array minus one. This arrangement is a rich source of programming errors for beginner programmers who have difficulty coming to grips with this displaced referencing: for instance, element[9] is the *tenth* element in the array. In COBOL, tables start at element 1 (not 0) and go to the maximum size of the table. In a COBOL table, element(9) is the *ninth* element of the table.

A major difference between COBOL tables and arrays is that COBOL tables are declared using record descriptions. The nature of a record description is that there is a hierarchical relationship between the items in the record. Consequently, one item in a multidimensional table must always be subordinate to another. Arrays have no such hierarchical relationship. An array is simply a matrix of cells that are referenced using row and column subscripts. The hierarchical structuring of COBOL tables allows data-manipulation opportunities that are not available to languages that use arrays.

Declaring Tables

Tables are declared using an extension to the PICTURE clause, called the OCCURS clause. The metalanguage for the basic OCCURS clause is as follows:

```
OCCURS TableSize#1 TIMES
```

To declare a table, you define the type and size of the table element, and then you use the OCCURS clause to specify how many times the element occurs. In the following NFL-Stadium example, the type and size of the element are defined by its subordinate data items. Each element is alphanumeric and 35 characters (30 + 5) in size:

```
01 SoccerStadiumName    PIC X(25) OCCURS 20 TIMES.


01 NFL-Stadium  OCCURS 31 TIMES.
   02 NFL-StadiumName      PIC X(30).
   02 NFL-StadiumCapacity  PIC 9(5).
```

OCCURS Clause Rules

Here are the rules for the OCCURS clause:

- Any data item whose description includes an OCCURS clause must be subscripted when referred to. For example:

```
DISPLAY SoccerStadiumName(15)
MOVE NFL-Stadium(12) TO NFL-Stadium(7)
```

- Any data item that is subordinate to a group item whose description contains an OCCURS clause must be subscripted when referred to. For example:

```
DISPLAY NFL-StadiumName(7)
DISPLAY NFL-StadiumCapacity(7)
```

Subscript Rules

Now let's look at the subscript rules:

- A subscript is a bracketed numeric index (or something that evaluates to one) that points to a particular element (or part of an element) of the table. The subscript immediately follows the element name.

- The numeric index must be a positive integer, a data name that represents one, or a simple expression that evaluates to one.

- The numeric index is a value between one and the number of elements in the table, inclusive.

- When more than one subscript is used, they must be separated from one another by commas.

- One subscript must be specified for each dimension of the table. There must be one subscript for a one-dimensional table, two subscripts for a two-dimensional table, and three for a three-dimensional table.

- The first subscript applies to the first OCCURS clause, the second applies to the second OCCURS clause, and so on.

- Subscripts must be enclosed in rounded brackets: ( ).

Here are some examples:

```
MOVE ZEROS TO StateSalesTotal(35)
ADD BranchSales TO StateSalesTotal(StateNum)
ADD BranchSales TO StateSalesTotal(StateNum + 1)
ADD BranchSales TO StateSalesTotal(StateNum - 2)
ADD MonthlyBranchSales TO StateSalesTotal(StateNum, MonthNum)
DISPLAY "Stadium Name is " StadiumName(24)
DISPLAY "Stadium Capacity is " StadiumCapacity(24)
```

Why Use Tabular Data?

Let's start this introduction to tabular data by setting up a hypothetical problem. In the course of exploring the problem and a number of variations, I will show how tables are defined and used in COBOL.

First Specification

YoreCandyShoppe is a franchise that sells old-time candy at branches all over the United States. A program is required that will sum the candy sales for all the YoreCandyShoppe branches in the country. The sales data is obtained from a sales file containing the candy sales for each branch. The sales file is a sequential file sequenced on ascending BranchId. Each record of the file may be described using the following record description:

```
01 BranchSalesRec.
   88 EndOfSalesFile  VALUE HIGH-VALUES.
   02 BranchId    PIC 9(7).
   02 StateNum    PIC 99.
   02 CandySales  PIC 9(7)V99.
```

To save file space, a two-digit numeric value is used to represent the state instead of a state name.

The program to perform this task is very simple. All you have to do is set up a variable to hold the total candy sales and then add CandySales from each record to TotalCandySales. A fragment of the program required to do this is given in Example 11-1.

Example 11-1. PROCEDURE DIVISION of a Program to Sum Total Candy Sales

```
PROCEDURE DIVISION.
Begin.
    OPEN INPUT SalesFile
    READ SalesFile
        AT END SET EndOfSalesFile TO TRUE
    END-READ
    PERFORM UNTIL EndOfSalesFile
        ADD CandySales TO TotalCandySales
        READ SalesFile
            AT END SET EndOfSalesFile TO TRUE
        END-READ
    END-PERFORM.
    DISPLAY "Total candy sales for the US : ", TotalCandySales
    CLOSE SalesFile
    STOP RUN.
```

Second Specification

The program to solve the problem set in the first specification is simple. But suppose the specification is changed so that instead of being asked for the country's total candy sales, you are asked to calculate the total sales for each state.

One approach to this new problem would be to sort the file on StateNum. This would turn the requirement into a simple control-break problem (that is, process all the records for one state, output the result, and then go on to the next). But the issue with this solution is that sorting is a comparatively slow, disk-intensive procedure. You want to avoid having to adopt this solution if possible. Is there any other way to solve the problem?

You could create 50 variables (one for each state) to hold the sales totals. Then, in the program, you could use an EVALUATE statement to add CandySales to the appropriate total. For example:

```
EVALUATE StateNum
    WHEN    1       ADD CandySales TO State1SalesTotal
    WHEN    2       ADD CandySales TO State2SalesTotal
    WHEN    3       ADD CandySales TO State3SalesTotal
            ..... 47 more WHEN branches
END-EVALUATE
```

This solution is not very satisfactory. You need a specific WHEN branch to process each state, and you have to declare 50 data items to hold the sales totals. And when you want to display the results, you must use 50 DISPLAY statements:

```
DISPLAY "State 1 total is ", State1SalesTotal
DISPLAY "State 2 total is ", State2SalesTotal
DISPLAY "State 3 total is ", State3SalesTotal
            ..... 47 more DISPLAY statements
```

But this poor attempt at a solution does contain the germ of an idea of how to solve the problem. It is interesting to note that the processing of each WHEN branch is the same: CandySales is added to the sales total for a particular state. You could replace all 50 WHEN branches with one statement if you could generalize to something like this:

```
ADD the CandySales to the StateSalesTotal location indicated by the StateNum.
```

There is also something interesting about the 50 data items. They all have exactly the same PICTURE, and they all have, more or less, the same name: StateSalesTotal. The only way you can distinguish between one StateSalesTotal and another is by attaching a number to the name: State1SalesTotal, State2SalesTotal, State3SalesTotal, and so on.

When you see a group of data items that all have the same name and the same description and are only distinguished from one another by a number attached to the name, you know that you have a problem crying out for a table-based solution.

Using a Table for the State Sales Totals

In COBOL, you declare a table by specifying the type (or structure) of a single item (element) of the table and then specifying that the data item is to be repeated a given number of times. For instance, StateSalesTable may be defined as follows:

```
01 StateSalesTable.
   02 StateSalesTotal      PIC 9(8)V99  OCCURS 50 TIMES.
```

StateSalesTable can be represented diagrammatically as shown in Figure 11-1. All the elements of the table have the name StateSalesTotal; you can refer to a specific one by using that name followed by an integer value in brackets. So, StateSalesTotal(3) refers to the third element of the table, and StateSalesTotal(13) refers to the thirteenth element.

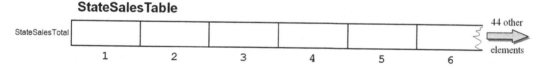

Figure 11-1. *Diagrammatic representation of StateSalesTable*

But when you refer to an element, you don't have to use a numeric literal. You can use anything that evaluates to a numeric value between 1 and the size of the table—even a simple arithmetic expression.

So the solution to the problem of summing the candy sales for each state is to use a table to hold a StateSalesTotal for each state and to use StateNum to access the correct element in the table.

Once you realize that you can use a table to hold the sales totals and StateNum as an index into the table, the solution to the problem becomes very simple. A program to read the sales file, sum the sales, and display the results is given in Listing 11-1. In this example, to keep the program simple and focus on table creation and handling, I chose to display the results rather than write them to a print file.

Listing 11-1. Summing Candy Sales for Each State

```cobol
IDENTIFICATION DIVISION.
PROGRAM-ID.  Listing11-1.
AUTHOR. Michael Coughlan
* Program to sum the CandySales for each branch of YoreCandyShoppe
* and display the results in StateNum order
* Using as input the Sequential BranchSalesFile ordered on ascending BranchId

ENVIRONMENT DIVISION.
INPUT-OUTPUT SECTION.
FILE-CONTROL.
    SELECT BranchSalesFile ASSIGN TO "Listing11-1BranchSales.dat"
           ORGANIZATION IS LINE SEQUENTIAL.

DATA DIVISION.
FILE SECTION.
FD BranchSalesFile.
01 BranchSalesRec.
    88 EndOfSalesFile  VALUE HIGH-VALUES.
    02 BranchId        PIC 9(7).
    02 StateNum        PIC 99.
    02 CandySales      PIC 9(7)V99.

WORKING-STORAGE SECTION.
01 StateSalesTable.
    02 StateSalesTotal  PIC 9(8)V99  OCCURS 50 TIMES.

01 StateIdx          PIC 99.
01 PrnStateSales     PIC $$$,$$$,$$9.99.

PROCEDURE DIVISION.
Begin.
    MOVE ZEROS TO StateSalesTable
    OPEN INPUT BranchSalesFile
    READ BranchSalesFile
       AT END SET EndOfSalesFile TO TRUE
    END-READ
    PERFORM UNTIL EndOfSalesFile
       ADD CandySales TO StateSalesTotal(StateNum)
       READ BranchSalesFile
          AT END SET EndOfSalesFile TO TRUE
       END-READ
    END-PERFORM
    DISPLAY "   YoreCandyShoppe Sales by State"
    DISPLAY "   ----------------------------"
    PERFORM VARYING StateIdx FROM 1 BY 1
            UNTIL StateIdx GREATER THAN 50
       MOVE StateSalesTotal(StateIdx) TO PrnStateSales
```

```
        DISPLAY "State ", StateIdx
                " sales total is " PrnStateSales
    END-PERFORM
    CLOSE BranchSalesFile
    STOP RUN.
```

Third Specification: Group Items as Table Elements

The elements of a table do not have to be elementary items. An element can be a group item. In other words, each element can be subdivided into two or more subordinate items.

Suppose the specification of the YoreCandyShoppe sales-report program changes so that in addition to summing the candy sales for each state, the program should count the number of branches and compute the average sales for the state. Final country totals should also be produced, showing Total-US-Sales, US-BranchCount, and Average-US-Sales.

One solution to this problem would be to set up two separate tables: one to hold state sales and another to hold the count of the number of branches in the state (see Example 11-2).

Example 11-2. The Two-Table Solution

```
01 StateSalesTable.
   02 StateSalesTotal      PIC 9(8)V99  OCCURS 50 TIMES.

01 StateBranchesTable.
   02 StateBranchCount      PIC 9(5)  OCCURS 50 TIMES.
```

Then all that would be required to calculate the average sales for the state would be a statement such as

```
COMPUTE AverageStateSales = StateSalesTotal(StateNum) / StateBranchCount(StateNum)
```

This is probably the way you would solve the problem in most languages. But in COBOL you can also set up a single table in which each element is defined as a group item that consists of the StateSalesTotal and the StateBranchCount (see Example 11-3).

Example 11-3. Solution Using the Group Item as a Table Element

```
01 StateSalesTable.
   02 StateTotals OCCURS 50 TIMES.
      03 StateSalesTotal    PIC 9(8)V99.
      03 StateBranchCount   PIC 9(5).
```

To calculate the average sales, you can use the same COMPUTE statement as before:

```
COMPUTE AverageStateSales = StateSalesTotal(StateNum) / StateBranchCount(StateNum)
```

A diagrammatic representation of this table description is shown in Figure 11-2. Each element of the table now consists of two parts: StateSalesTotal and StateBranchCount. These are subordinate to the StateTotals element. Data-manipulation opportunities abound. All these data names allow you to manipulate the data in the table at different levels of granularity. You can use the following commands:

- MOVE ZEROS TO StateSalesTable: See Figure 11-2. Fills the whole table with zeros.

- MOVE StateTotals(2) TO StateTotals(5): See Figure 11-2. Copies the contents of one element, including both subordinate items, to another element.

- DISPLAY StateBranchCount(3): Displays the contents of the StateBranchCount part of element 3.

- ADD CandySales TO StateSalesTotal(3): Adds CandySales to the contents of the StateSalesTotal part of element 3.

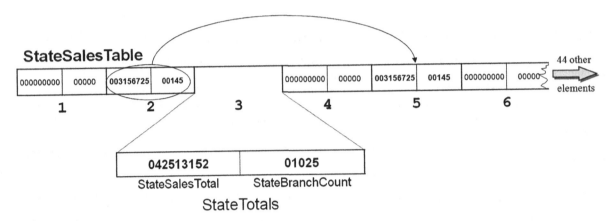

Figure 11-2. Table elements as group items. Element 3 is exploded to show details

Tabular Data Program

Listing 11-2 is a solution to the problem posed by the changed specification. It uses the table defined in Example 11-3.

Listing 11-2. Table Elements as Group Items

```
IDENTIFICATION DIVISION.
PROGRAM-ID.  Listing11-2.
AUTHOR. Michael Coughlan
* Program that for each state and for the whole US
* sums the CandySales for each branch of YoreCandyShoppe
* counts the number of branches
* calculates the average sales per state and displays the results in StateNum order
* Uses as input the Sequential BranchSalesFile ordered on ascending BranchId

ENVIRONMENT DIVISION.
INPUT-OUTPUT SECTION.
FILE-CONTROL.
    SELECT BranchSalesFile ASSIGN TO "Listing11-2BranchSales.dat"
           ORGANIZATION IS LINE SEQUENTIAL.

DATA DIVISION.
FILE SECTION.
FD BranchSalesFile.
01 BranchSalesRec.
    88 EndOfSalesFile  VALUE HIGH-VALUES.
    02 BranchId               PIC 9(7).
    02 StateNum               PIC 99.
    02 CandySales             PIC 9(7)V99.
```

```
       WORKING-STORAGE SECTION.
       01 StateSalesTable.
          02 StateTotals OCCURS 50 TIMES.
             03 StateSalesTotal    PIC 9(8)V99.
             03 StateBranchCount   PIC 9(5).


       01 StateIdx              PIC 99.


       01 ReportHeading1        PIC X(35)
                                VALUE "     YoreCandyShoppe Sales by State".
       01 ReportHeading2        PIC X(35)
                                VALUE "     -------------------------------".
       01 ReportHeading3        PIC X(47)
                                VALUE "State  Branches      StateSales    AverageSales".

       01 DetailLine.
          02 PrnStateNum         PIC BZ9.
          02 PrnBranchCount      PIC B(3)ZZ,ZZ9.
          02 PrnStateSales       PIC B(5)$$$,$$$,$$9.99.
          02 PrnAveageSales      PIC BB$$$,$$$,$$9.99.

       01 US-Totals.
          02 US-TotalSales       PIC 9(9)V99.
          02 US-BranchCount      PIC 9(6).
          02 PrnUS-TotalSales    PIC $,$$$,$$$,$$9.99.
          02 PrnUS-BranchCount   PIC B(9)ZZZ,ZZ9.
          02 PrnUS-AverageSales  PIC BBBB$$$,$$$,$$9.99.


       PROCEDURE DIVISION.
       Begin.
          MOVE ZEROS TO StateSalesTable
          OPEN INPUT BranchSalesFile
          READ BranchSalesFile
             AT END SET EndOfSalesFile TO TRUE
          END-READ
          PERFORM UNTIL EndOfSalesFile
             ADD CandySales TO StateSalesTotal(StateNum), US-TotalSales
             ADD 1 TO StateBranchCount(StateNum), US-BranchCount
             READ BranchSalesFile
               AT END SET EndOfSalesFile TO TRUE
             END-READ
          END-PERFORM
          PERFORM PrintResults

          CLOSE BranchSalesFile
          STOP RUN.

       PrintResults.
          DISPLAY ReportHeading1
          DISPLAY ReportHeading2
```

```
DISPLAY ReportHeading3
PERFORM VARYING StateIdx FROM 1 BY 1
        UNTIL StateIdx GREATER THAN 50
   MOVE StateIdx TO PrnStateNum
   MOVE StateSalesTotal(StateIdx) TO PrnStateSales
   MOVE StateBranchCount(StateIdx) TO PrnBranchCount
   COMPUTE PrnAveageSales = StateSalesTotal(StateIdx) / StateBranchCount(StateIdx)
   DISPLAY DetailLine
END-PERFORM
MOVE US-TotalSales TO PrnUS-TotalSales
MOVE US-BranchCount TO PrnUS-BranchCount
COMPUTE PrnUS-AverageSales = US-TotalSales / US-BranchCount
DISPLAY "YoreCandyShoppe branches in the US = " PrnUS-BranchCount
DISPLAY "YoreCandyShoppe sales in the US    = " PrnUS-TotalSales
DISPLAY "YoreCandyShoppe average US sales   = " PrnAveageSales.
```

Multidimensional Tables

Listing 11-2 uses a table in which each element is a group item that consists of the StateSalesTotal and the StateBranchCount. But the table is still a single-dimensional table. Sometimes the solution to a problem demands a multidimensional table approach. A multidimensional table is one in which each element of the table is itself a table. This section considers multidimensional tables in the context of a specification change for the YoreCandyShoppe sales report.

Suppose each YoreCandyShoppe branch is asked to provide more granular sales data. Instead of reporting sales for the entire year, each branch must now report sales for each month. To do this, the sales record for each branch must be changed to accommodate a 12-element table of sales data. The new record description is given in Example 11-4.

Example 11-4. New Record Description That Records Candy Sales for Each Month

```
01 BranchSalesRec.
   88 EndOfSalesFile  VALUE HIGH-VALUES.
   02 BranchId                PIC 9(7).
   02 StateNum                PIC 99.
   02 SalesForMonth           PIC 9(5)V99 OCCURS 12 TIMES.
```

The report produced from the sales file must reflect this more granular data and is now required to show the following:

- Total sales for each state

- The count of the number of branches in the state

- Average sales per branch for each state

- Sales per month for each state

- Final country totals showing Total-US-Sales, US-BranchCount, and Average-US-Sales

In the program that implemented the previous specification, the sales for each state and the number of branches in each state were recorded in a 50-element table. In this version, instead of the total sales for the year, you have to record the sales per month. To do that, you need a two-dimensional table as described in Example 11-5.

Example 11-5. Two-dimensional Table to Record Sales per Month and the Number of Branches in the State

```
01 StateSalesTable.
   02 State OCCURS 50 TIMES.
      03 StateBranchCount   PIC 9(5).
      03 StateMonthSales    PIC 9(5)V99 OCCURS 12 TIMES.
```

COBOL DETAIL

If you wanted to manipulate the table at a further level of granularity, you could describe the table as

```
01 StateSalesTable.
   02 State OCCURS 50 TIMES.
      03 StateBranchCount   PIC 9(5).
      03 StateSales.
         04 StateMonthSales PIC 9(5)V99 OCCURS 12 TIMES.
```

The table description in Example 11-5 highlights a difference between COBOL tables and arrays. In other languages, two arrays would be required to record this information: a two-dimensional table to record the state sales per month and a one-dimensional table to record the number of branches per state. You can also record the data using two tables in COBOL, as shown in Example 11-6; but COBOL's hierarchical structuring allows you to combine both tables so that each element of the first dimension consists of the BranchCount and a 12-element table containing the sales for each month.

Example 11-6. A Two-Table Solution

```
01 StateSalesTable.
   02 State OCCURS 50 TIMES.
      03 StateMonthSales    PIC 9(5)V99 OCCURS 12 TIMES.

01 StateBranchesTable.
   02 State OCCURS 50 TIMES.
      03 StateBranchCount   PIC 9(5).
```

Multidimensional Program

Listing 11-3 is a solution to the changed specification that uses the two-dimensional table described in Example 11-5.

Listing 11-3. Using a Two-dimensional Table to Solve the Problem Posed by the Changed Specification

```
IDENTIFICATION DIVISION.
PROGRAM-ID.  Listing11-3.
AUTHOR. Michael Coughlan
* Program that for each state and for the whole US
* sums the Monthly Sales for each branch of YoreCandyShoppe, counts the number of
* branches and displays the State Sales per month in StateNum order
* Calculates the US sales, the number of branches in the US and the average US sales
* Uses as input the Sequential BranchSalesFile ordered on ascending BranchId
```

```
ENVIRONMENT DIVISION.
INPUT-OUTPUT SECTION.
FILE-CONTROL.
    SELECT BranchSalesFile ASSIGN TO "Listing11-3BranchSales.dat"
           ORGANIZATION IS LINE SEQUENTIAL.

DATA DIVISION.
FILE SECTION.
FD BranchSalesFile.
01 BranchSalesRec.
    88 EndOfSalesFile  VALUE HIGH-VALUES.
    02 BranchId             PIC 9(7).
    02 StateNum             PIC 99.
    02 SalesForMonth        PIC 9(5)V99 OCCURS 12 TIMES.

WORKING-STORAGE SECTION.
01 StateSalesTable.
    02 State OCCURS 50 TIMES.
       03 StateBranchCount  PIC 9(5).
       03 StateMonthSales   PIC 9(5)V99 OCCURS 12 TIMES.

01 ReportHeading.
    02  FILLER              PIC X(20)  VALUE SPACES.
    02  FILLER              PIC X(38) VALUE "YoreCandyShoppe Monthly Sales by State".

01 ReportUnderline.
    02  FILLER              PIC X(20)  VALUE SPACES.
    02  FILLER              PIC X(38) VALUE ALL "-".

01 ReportSubjectHeadings1.
    02 FILLER               PIC X(12)  VALUE "State    NOBs".
    02 FILLER               PIC X(63)
       VALUE  "     Jan        Feb        Mar        Apr        May        Jun".

01 ReportSubjectHeadings2.
    02 FILLER               PIC X(12) VALUE SPACES.
    02 FILLER               PIC X(63)
       VALUE  "     Jul        Aug        Sep        Oct        Nov        Dec".

01 DetailLine1.
    02 PrnStateNum          PIC BZ9.
    02 PrnBranchCount       PIC BBZZ,ZZ9.
    02 PrnMonthSales1       PIC B$$$,$$9.99 OCCURS 6 TIMES.

01 DetailLine2.
    02 FILLER               PIC X(11) VALUE SPACES.
    02 PrnMonthSales2       PIC B$$$,$$9.99 OCCURS 6 TIMES.
```

```
01 US-Totals.
   02 US-TotalSales        PIC 9(9)V99.
   02 US-BranchCount       PIC 9(6).
   02 PrnUS-TotalSales     PIC $,$$$,$$$,$$9.99.
   02 PrnUS-BranchCount    PIC B(9)ZZZ,ZZ9.
   02 PrnUS-AverageSales   PIC BB$$$,$$$,$$9.99.

01 StateIdx                PIC 99.
01 MonthIdx                PIC 99.


PROCEDURE DIVISION.
Begin.
   MOVE ZEROS TO StateSalesTable
   OPEN INPUT BranchSalesFile
   READ BranchSalesFile
      AT END SET EndOfSalesFile TO TRUE
   END-READ
   PERFORM UNTIL EndOfSalesFile
      ADD 1 TO StateBranchCount(StateNum), US-BranchCount
      PERFORM VARYING MonthIdx FROM 1 BY 1 UNTIL MonthIdx > 12
         ADD SalesForMonth(MonthIdx) TO
            StateMonthSales(StateNum, MonthIdx), US-TotalSales
      END-PERFORM
      READ BranchSalesFile
         AT END SET EndOfSalesFile TO TRUE
      END-READ
   END-PERFORM
   PERFORM DisplayResults
   CLOSE BranchSalesFile
   STOP RUN.


DisplayResults.
   DISPLAY ReportHeading
   DISPLAY ReportUnderline
   DISPLAY ReportSubjectHeadings1
   DISPLAY ReportSubjectHeadings2
   PERFORM VARYING StateIdx FROM 1 BY 1
         UNTIL StateIdx GREATER THAN 50
      MOVE StateIdx TO PrnStateNum
      MOVE StateBranchCount(StateIdx) TO PrnBranchCount
      PERFORM VARYING MonthIdx FROM 1 BY 1 UNTIL MonthIdx > 6
         MOVE StateMonthSales(StateIdx, MonthIdx) TO PrnMonthSales1(MonthIdx)
      END-PERFORM
      PERFORM VARYING MonthIdx FROM 7 BY 1 UNTIL MonthIdx > 12
         MOVE StateMonthSales(StateIdx, MonthIdx) TO PrnMonthSales2(MonthIdx - 6)
      END-PERFORM
      DISPLAY DetailLine1
      DISPLAY DetailLine2
      DISPLAY SPACES
   END-PERFORM
```

```
MOVE US-TotalSales TO PrnUS-TotalSales
MOVE US-BranchCount TO PrnUS-BranchCount
COMPUTE PrnUS-AverageSales = US-TotalSales / US-BranchCount
DISPLAY "YoreCandyShoppe branches in the US = " PrnUS-BranchCount
DISPLAY "YoreCandyShoppe sales in the US    = " PrnUS-TotalSales
DISPLAY "YoreCandyShoppe average US sales   = " PrnUS-AverageSales.
```

Correct Depiction of COBOL Tables

Two-dimensional tables are often depicted using a grid of rows and columns. This is an accurate representation for arrays, but for COBOL tables it has the flaw that it does not accurately reflect the data hierarchy.[1]

The table described in Example 11-5 allows you to manipulate the table using statements such as MOVE ZEROS TO State(1) and MOVE 123 TO BranchCount(2). In a row-and-column grid depiction, it is not clear how such manipulations are possible.

The diagram in Figure 11-3 uses the correct representation for StateSalesTable. This diagram expresses the data hierarchy inherent in the table description where one OCCURS clause is subordinate to another. With this representation, you can see how statements such as MOVE ZEROS TO State(1) and MOVE 123 TO StateBranchCount(2) affect the values in the table.

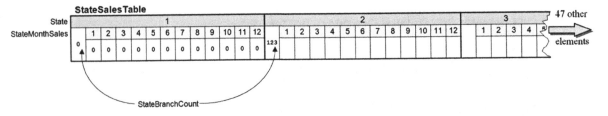

Figure 11-3. *Diagram showing the hierarchy in a COBOL table description*

Three-Dimensional Tables

In COBOL, multidimensional tables rarely have more than three dimensions. Prior to the ANS 85 version of COBOL, a maximum of three dimensions were permitted; the restriction on PERFORM..VARYING that allows only three counting variables harks back to those days. In the ANS 85 and ISO 2002 COBOL standards, the maximum number of dimensions is seven.

A discussion of how three-dimensional tables are created and processed should help to solidify your understanding of multidimensional tables. This time, however, I present the problem specification and show the declarations necessary to create the three-dimensional table, but I don't write a full program. I leave that as an exercise for you at the end of the chapter.

Keep in mind that this specification is designed with an eye toward what is easy to present diagrammatically rather than toward realism.

Problem Specification

The U.S. Census Bureau has provided you with a subset of census data in a file containing the age category, gender, state number, and car-ownership information of every person in the country. The CensusFile is an unordered sequential file, and its records have the following description:

Field	Type	Length	Value
StateNum	9	2	1–50
AgeCategory	9	1	1 = Child 2 = Teen 3 = Adult
GenderCategory	9	1	1 = Female 2 = Male
CarOwner	X	1	Y or N

You are required to write a program to process the CensusFile and display the number of males and females in each AgeCategory (Child, Teen, and Adult) in each state, as shown in Figure 11-4.

```
Population Details Report
State   Male       Female     Male       Female     Male       Female
Num     Adults     Adults     Teens      Teens      Children   Children
XX      XXXXXXXXXX XXXXXXXXXX XXXXXXXXXX XXXXXXXXXX XXXXXXXXXX XXXXXXXXXX
XX      XXXXXXXXXX XXXXXXXXXX XXXXXXXXXX XXXXXXXXXX XXXXXXXXXX XXXXXXXXXX
XX      XXXXXXXXXX XXXXXXXXXX XXXXXXXXXX XXXXXXXXXX XXXXXXXXXX XXXXXXXXXX
                              etc.
```

Figure 11-4. *Report template*

To accumulate the population totals for each state, you use the three-dimensional table defined in Example 11-7.

Example 11-7. Three-dimensional Table to Hold Population Totals

```
01 US-PopulationTable.
   02 State OCCURS 50 TIMES.
      03 AgeCategory OCCURS 3 TIMES.
         04 GenderCategory OCCURS 2 TIMES.
            05 PopTotal   PIC 9(8).
```

For each record that you read from the CensusFile, you execute the following statement:

```
ADD 1 TO PopTotal(StateNum, Age, Gender)
```

Depicting a Three-dimensional Table

Figure 11-5 is a depiction of the three-dimensional table defined in the Example 11-7.

US-PopulationTable

State	1						2						1	48 other elements
AgeCategory	1		2		3		1		2		3		1	
GenderCategory	1	2	1	2	1	2	1	2	1	2	1	2	1	2
PopTotal	00000000	00000000	00000000	00000000	00000000	00000000		00000000		156	00000000	00000000		

Figure 11-5. *Structure of a three-dimensional table*

The data in the table has been changed by executing the following statements:

```
MOVE ZEROS TO State(1)
MOVE ZEROS TO AgeCategory(2,3)
MOVE ZEROS TO GenderCategory (3,1,1)
MOVE ZEROS TO PopTotal(2,1,2)
MOVE 156 TO PopTotal(2,2,2)
```

As you can see from these statements, the data names defined in the table allow you to manipulate the table at various levels of granularity. When you refer to the State data item, you must use one subscript because it is a data item whose description contains an OCCURS clause. When you refer to AgeCategory, you must use two subscripts because AgeCategory is subordinate to an item that contains an OCCURS clause, and it itself contains an OCCURS clause. Finally, when you refer to GenderCategory and PopTotal, you must use three subscripts: GenderCategory is subordinate to two items that contain an OCCURS clause, and it contains an OCCURS clause itself; and PopTotal is subordinate to three items that contain an OCCURS clause. PopTotal and GenderCategory are data names that refer to the same area of storage. The US-PopulationTable could have been defined as

```
01 US-PopulationTable.
    02 State OCCURS 50 TIMES.
        03 AgeCategory OCCURS 3 TIMES.
            04 GenderCategory PIC 9(8) OCCURS 2 TIMES.
```

However, the PopTotal data item was added for clarity, as documentation.

Prefilled Tables

In all the examples in this chapter, the table used has been filled with data in the course of running the program. Sometimes, however, the table needs to be prefilled with data values. When the program starts, the table must already have been instantiated with the data values.

For instance, in Listing 11-3, when you display the results, you display a state number instead of the name of the state. Obviously it would be better to display the actual state name. A simple way to do this is to set up a prefilled table containing the names of the states and then display the appropriate name using a statement such as DISPLAY StateName(StateIdx).

REDEFINES Clause

To set up a prefilled table in COBOL, you have to use a special data-description clause called the REDEFINES clause. The REDEFINES clause is not limited to creating prefilled tables. It is a powerful data-manipulation language element that is used for a number of purposes. I discuss the REDEFINES clause in detail in Chapter 12, including its full syntax, the semantic rules that apply to it, and the many ways it may be used. In this chapter, I discuss the REDEFINES clause only in the context of creating prefilled tables.

When a file contains different types of records, a record description is created for each record type in the FILE SECTION. However, all these record descriptions map on to the same area of storage. They are, in effect, redefinitions of the area of storage. The REDEFINES clause allows you to achieve the same effect for units smaller than a record and in the other parts of the DATA DIVISION—not just the FILE SECTION.

Creating Prefilled Tables of Values

You can use the REDEFINES clause to create a prefilled table by applying the following procedure:

1. Reserve an area of storage, and use the VALUE clause to fill it with the values required in the table.

2. Use the REDEFINES clause to redefine the area of memory as a table.

For instance, to create a table prefilled with the names of the months, the first step is to reserve an area of storage and fill it with the names of the months (see Example 11-8). The diagram in Example 11-8 depicts the undifferentiated area of storage filled with the month names.

Example 11-8. Setting Up an Area of Storage Containing the Month Names

```
01 MonthTable.
   02 MonthValues.
      03 FILLER      PIC X(18) VALUE "January  February".
      03 FILLER      PIC X(18) VALUE "March    April".
      03 FILLER      PIC X(18) VALUE "May      June".
      03 FILLER      PIC X(18) VALUE "July     August".
      03 FILLER      PIC X(18) VALUE "SeptemberOctober".
      03 FILLER      PIC X(18) VALUE "November December".
```

The next step is to redefine the area of storage to impose a table definition on it, as shown in Example 11-9. Now MonthName(3) contains the value "March", and MonthName(6) contains "June".

Example 11-9. Redefining the Area of Storage as a Table

```
01 MonthTable.
   02 MonthValues.
      03 FILLER      PIC X(18) VALUE "January  February".
      03 FILLER      PIC X(18) VALUE "March    April".
      03 FILLER      PIC X(18) VALUE "May      June".
      03 FILLER      PIC X(18) VALUE "July     August".
      03 FILLER      PIC X(18) VALUE "SeptemberOctober".
```

```
    03 FILLER      PIC X(18) VALUE "November December".
 02 FILLER REDEFINES MonthValues.
    03 MonthName OCCURS 12 TIMES PIC X(9).
```

1	2	3	4	5	6	6 other
January	February	March	April	May	June	elements

Creating a Prefilled Two-dimensional Table

To set up a two-dimensional table prefilled with data values, you use the same procedure as for a one-dimensional table. First you create an area of storage that contains the values you want in the table, and then you redefine the area as a table.

Suppose a company pays a bonus depending on ServiceCategory and MaritalStatus, as shown in Table 11-1. You can set up a prefilled table as shown in Example 11-10. In this table, Bonus(4,1) = 135 and Bonus(2,2) = 085. The data items MaritalStatus and Bonus refer to the same area of storage. The Bonus data item has been added for purposes of clarity.

Table 11-1. *Bonus Table*

	Service Category			
	5–10 years	11–20 years	21–30 years	30–50 years
Single	050	085	100	135
Married	075	120	150	175

Example 11-10. Two-dimensional Bonus Table

```
01 BonusTable.
   02 BonusValues   PIC X(24) VALUE "050075085120100150135175".
   02 FILLER REDEFINES BonusValues.
      03 ServiceCategory OCCURS 4 TIMES.
         04 MaritalStatus OCCURS 2 TIMES.
            05 Bonus   PIC 9(3).
```

BonusTable

ServiceCategory	1		2		3		4	
MaritalStatus	1	2	1	2	1	2	1	2
Bonus	050	075	085	120	100	150	135	175

Prefilled Table Program

The program in Listing 10-1 in Chapter 10 implemented a three-level control break. In the discussion of that program, I noted that in order to reduce the amount of storage occupied by the data file, the normal practice would be to use a state number instead of a state name. I mentioned that in such a program, when it is necessary to print out the state name, the state number is converted to a name by means of a lookup table.

So let's write a program to the same specification as Listing 10-1, except that now the records in the Sales file should use a state number rather than the full state name. The revised program specification follows.

Revised Specification

Electronics2Go has branches in a number of American states. A program is required to produce a report showing the total sales made by each salesperson, the total sales for each branch, the total sales for each state, and a final total showing the total sales for the entire United States. The report must be printed by ascending SalespersonId within ascending BranchId within ascending StateName.

The report is based on the Electronics2Go sales file. This file holds details of sales made in all the branches of the company. It is a sequential file, ordered on ascending SalespersonId within ascending BranchId within ascending StateNum. Each record in the sales file has the following description:

Field	Type	Length	Value
StateNum	9	2	01–50
BranchId	X	5	-
SalespersonId	X	6	99999X (M/F)
ValueOfSale	9	6	0000.00–9999.99

The report format should follow the template shown in Figure 11-6.

```
        Electronics2Go Sales Report
State Name      Branch  SalesId  SalesTotal

XXXXXXXXXXXXXX  XXXXX     XXXXXX  XXXXXXXXX
                          XXXXXX  XXXXXXXXX
                          XXXXXX  XXXXXXXXX
                          Branch Total:    XXXXXXXXXX

                XXXXX     XXXXXX  XXXXXXXXX
                          XXXXXX  XXXXXXXXX
                          XXXXXX  XXXXXXXXX
                          XXXXXX  XXXXXXXXX
                          Branch Total:    XXXXXXXXXX
                           State Total:    XXXXXXXXXXXX

XXXXXXXXXXXXXX  XXXXX     XXXXXX  XXXXXXXXX
                          XXXXXX  XXXXXXXXX
                          XXXXXX  XXXXXXXXX
                          Branch Total:    XXXXXXXXXX

XXXXXXXXXXXXXX  XXXXXX    XXXXXX  XXXXXXXXX
                          XXXXXX  XXXXXXXXX
                          XXXXXX  XXXXXXXXX
                          Branch Total:    XXXXXXXXXX
                           State Total:    XXXXXXXXXXXX
                           Final Total: XXXXXXXXXXXXXX
```

Figure 11-6. *Template for the Electronics2Go sales report*

Final Prefilled Table Program

The program in Listing 11-4 implements the final specification.

Listing 11-4. Report with Three Control Breaks, Using a State Name Table (Changes from Listing 10-1 Shown in Bold)

```
IDENTIFICATION DIVISION.
PROGRAM-ID. Listing11-4.
AUTHOR. Michael Coughlan.
* A three level Control Break program to process the Electronics2Go
* Sales file and produce a report that shows the value of sales for
* each Salesperson, each Branch, each State, and for the Country.
* The SalesFile is sorted on ascending SalespersonId within BranchId
* within StateNum.
* The report must be printed in SalespersonId within BranchId
* within StateName.  There is a correspondence between StateNum order
* and StateName order such that the order of records in
* the file is the same if the file is ordered on ascending StateNum
* as it is when the file is ordered on ascending StateName

ENVIRONMENT DIVISION.
INPUT-OUTPUT SECTION.
FILE-CONTROL.
SELECT SalesFile ASSIGN TO "Listing11-4TestData.Dat"
                 ORGANIZATION IS LINE SEQUENTIAL.

SELECT SalesReport ASSIGN TO "Listing11-4.RPT"
                 ORGANIZATION IS LINE SEQUENTIAL.

DATA DIVISION.
FILE SECTION.
FD  SalesFile.
01  SalesRecord.
        88 EndOfSalesFile VALUE HIGH-VALUES.
        02 StateNum        PIC 99.
        02 BranchId        PIC X(5).
        02 SalesPersonId   PIC X(6).
        02 ValueOfSale     PIC 9(4)V99.

FD SalesReport.
01 PrintLine               PIC X(55).

WORKING-STORAGE SECTION.
01  StateNameTable.
    02 StateNameValues.
        03 FILLER  PIC X(14) VALUE "Alabama".
        03 FILLER  PIC X(14) VALUE "Alaska".
        03 FILLER  PIC X(14) VALUE "Arizona".
        03 FILLER  PIC X(14) VALUE "Arkansas".
        03 FILLER  PIC X(14) VALUE "California".
        03 FILLER  PIC X(14) VALUE "Colorado".
        03 FILLER  PIC X(14) VALUE "Connecticut".
```

```
        03 FILLER  PIC X(14) VALUE "Delaware".
        03 FILLER  PIC X(14) VALUE "Florida".
        03 FILLER  PIC X(14) VALUE "Georgia".
        03 FILLER  PIC X(14) VALUE "Hawaii".
        03 FILLER  PIC X(14) VALUE "Idaho".
        03 FILLER  PIC X(14) VALUE "Illinois".
        03 FILLER  PIC X(14) VALUE "Indiana".
        03 FILLER  PIC X(14) VALUE "Iowa".
        03 FILLER  PIC X(14) VALUE "Kansas".
        03 FILLER  PIC X(14) VALUE "Kentucky".
        03 FILLER  PIC X(14) VALUE "Louisiana".
        03 FILLER  PIC X(14) VALUE "Maine".
        03 FILLER  PIC X(14) VALUE "Maryland".
        03 FILLER  PIC X(14) VALUE "Massachusetts".
        03 FILLER  PIC X(14) VALUE "Michigan".
        03 FILLER  PIC X(14) VALUE "Minnesota".
        03 FILLER  PIC X(14) VALUE "Mississippi".
        03 FILLER  PIC X(14) VALUE "Missouri".
        03 FILLER  PIC X(14) VALUE "Montana".
        03 FILLER  PIC X(14) VALUE "Nebraska".
        03 FILLER  PIC X(14) VALUE "Nevada".
        03 FILLER  PIC X(14) VALUE "New Hampshire".
        03 FILLER  PIC X(14) VALUE "New Jersey".
        03 FILLER  PIC X(14) VALUE "New Mexico".
        03 FILLER  PIC X(14) VALUE "New York".
        03 FILLER  PIC X(14) VALUE "North Carolina".
        03 FILLER  PIC X(14) VALUE "North Dakota".
        03 FILLER  PIC X(14) VALUE "Ohio".
        03 FILLER  PIC X(14) VALUE "Oklahoma".
        03 FILLER  PIC X(14) VALUE "Oregon".
        03 FILLER  PIC X(14) VALUE "Pennsylvania".
        03 FILLER  PIC X(14) VALUE "Rhode Island".
        03 FILLER  PIC X(14) VALUE "South Carolina".
        03 FILLER  PIC X(14) VALUE "South Dakota".
        03 FILLER  PIC X(14) VALUE "Tennessee".
        03 FILLER  PIC X(14) VALUE "Texas".
        03 FILLER  PIC X(14) VALUE "Utah".
        03 FILLER  PIC X(14) VALUE "Vermont".
        03 FILLER  PIC X(14) VALUE "Virginia".
        03 FILLER  PIC X(14) VALUE "Washington".
        03 FILLER  PIC X(14) VALUE "West Virginia".
        03 FILLER  PIC X(14) VALUE "Wisconsin".
        03 FILLER  PIC X(14) VALUE "Wyoming".
    02 FILLER REDEFINES StateNameValues.
       03 StateName PIC X(14) OCCURS 50 TIMES.
```

```
01  ReportHeading.
    02 FILLER              PIC X(35)
       VALUE "         Electronics2Go Sales Report".

01  SubjectHeading.
    02 FILLER              PIC X(43)
       VALUE "State Name     Branch  SalesId  SalesTotal".

01  DetailLine.
    02 PrnStateName        PIC X(14).
       88 SuppressStateName VALUE SPACES.
    02 PrnBranchId         PIC BBX(5).
       88 SuppressBranchId  VALUE SPACES.
    02 PrnSalespersonId    PIC BBBBX(6).
    02 PrnSalespersonTotal PIC BB$$,$$9.99.

01  BranchTotalLine.
    02 FILLER              PIC X(43)
       VALUE "                        Branch Total:     ".
    02 PrnBranchTotal      PIC $$$,$$9.99.

01  StateTotalLine.
    02 FILLER              PIC X(40)
       VALUE "                    State Total :  ".
    02 PrnStateTotal       PIC $$,$$$,$$9.99.

01  FinalTotalLine.
    02 FILLER              PIC X(39)
       VALUE "                      Final Total :".
    02 PrnFinalTotal       PIC $$$,$$$,$$9.99.

01  SalespersonTotal      PIC 9(4)V99.
01  BranchTotal           PIC 9(6)V99.
01  StateTotal            PIC 9(7)V99.
01  FinalTotal            PIC 9(9)V99.

01  PrevStateNum          PIC 99.
01  PrevBranchId          PIC X(5).
01  PrevSalespersonId     PIC X(6).

PROCEDURE DIVISION.
Begin.
   OPEN INPUT SalesFile
   OPEN OUTPUT SalesReport
   WRITE PrintLine FROM ReportHeading  AFTER ADVANCING 1 LINE
   WRITE PrintLine FROM SubjectHeading AFTER ADVANCING 1 LINE

   READ SalesFile
      AT END SET EndOfSalesFile TO TRUE
   END-READ
   PERFORM UNTIL EndOfSalesFile
```

```
            MOVE StateNum TO PrevStateNum,
            MOVE StateName(StateNum) TO PrnStateName
          MOVE ZEROS TO StateTotal
          PERFORM SumSalesForState
                  UNTIL StateNum NOT = PrevStateNum
                      OR EndOfSalesFile
          MOVE StateTotal TO PrnStateTotal
          WRITE PrintLine FROM StateTotalLine AFTER ADVANCING 1 LINE
        END-PERFORM


        MOVE FinalTotal TO PrnFinalTotal
        WRITE PrintLine FROM FinalTotalLine AFTER ADVANCING 1 LINE


        CLOSE SalesFile, SalesReport
        STOP RUN.


  SumSalesForState.
        WRITE PrintLine FROM SPACES AFTER ADVANCING 1 LINE
        MOVE BranchId TO PrevBranchId, PrnBranchId
        MOVE ZEROS TO BranchTotal
        PERFORM SumSalesForBranch
                UNTIL BranchId NOT = PrevBranchId
                    OR StateNum NOT = PrevStateNum
                    OR EndOfSalesFile
          MOVE BranchTotal TO PrnBranchTotal
          WRITE PrintLine FROM BranchTotalLine AFTER ADVANCING 1 LINE.


  SumSalesForBranch.
        MOVE SalespersonId TO PrevSalespersonId, PrnSalespersonId
        MOVE ZEROS TO SalespersonTotal
        PERFORM SumSalespersonSales
                UNTIL SalespersonId NOT = PrevSalespersonId
                    OR BranchId    NOT = PrevBranchId
                    OR StateNum   NOT = PrevStateNum
                    OR EndOfSalesFile
        MOVE SalespersonTotal TO PrnSalespersonTotal
        WRITE PrintLine FROM DetailLine AFTER ADVANCING 1 LINE
        SET SuppressBranchId TO TRUE
        SET SuppressStateName TO TRUE.


  SumSalespersonSales.
        ADD ValueOfSale TO SalespersonTotal, BranchTotal, StateTotal, FinalTotal
        READ SalesFile
          AT END SET EndOfSalesFile TO TRUE
        END-READ.
```

ANS 85 Table Changes

The ANS 85 COBOL standard introduced a number of changes to tables. Among these changes is a method that lets you create prefilled tables without using the REDEFINES clause, as long as the number of values is small. For large amounts of data, the REDEFINES clause is still required.

The new method works by assigning the values to a group name defined over a subordinate table. For instance, in Example 11-11, the data item Day actually declares the table, but I have given the table the overall group name DayTable. Assigning the values to this group name fills the area of the table with the values.

Example 11-11. Creating a Prefilled Table Without the REDEFINES Clause

```
01 DayTable VALUE "MonTueWedThrFriSatSun".
   02 Day OCCURS 7 TIMES PIC X(3).
```

Mon	Tue	Wed	Thr	Fri	Sat	Sun
Day(1)	Day(2)	Day(3)	Day(4)	Day(5)	Day(6)	Day(7)

The ANS 85 COBOL standard also introduced some changes to the way tables are initialized. In the previous versions of COBOL, initializing a table was never a problem if the elements of the table were elementary items. All that was required was to move the initializing value to the table's group name. For instance, the statement MOVE ZEROS TO DriverTable initializes the following table to zeros:

```
01 DriverTable.
   02 StateDrivers  PIC 9(7) OCCURS 50 TIMES.
```

But initializing a table was much more difficult if each element was a group item that contained different types of data. For instance, in the following table, the StateDrivers part of the element had to be initialized to zeros, and the StateName part had to be initialized to spaces. The only way do this was to initialize the items, element by element, using iteration:

```
01 DriverTable.
   02 State OCCURS 50 TIMES.
      03 StateDrivers  PIC 9(7).
      03 StateName     PIC X(14).
```

The ANS 85 standard introduced a new way to initialize table elements that solves this problem. A table cannot be initialized by assigning an initial value to each part of an element using the VALUE clause. The following description initializes the StateDrivers part of the element to zeros and the StateName part to spaces:

```
01 DriverTable.
   02 State OCCURS 50 TIMES.
      03 StateDrivers  PIC 9(7)  VALUE ZEROS.
      03 StateName     PIC X(14) VALUE SPACES.
```

This example shows the ANS 85 changes that allow table elements to be initialized when a program starts; but sometimes data items need to be reinitialized while a program is running. The ANS 85 standard added the INITIALIZE verb for this purpose. The INITIALIZE verb sets data items, including table elements, either to their MOVE fill value (zero for numeric items, spaces for alphabetic or alphanumeric items) or to a specified compatible replacement value. The metalanguage for the INITIALIZE verb is given in Figure 11-7.

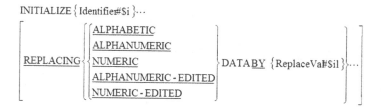

Figure 11-7. *Metalanguage for the* INITIALIZE *verb*

A large number of rules govern the operation of the INITIALIZE verb. For full details, please consult your COBOL manual. To get a feel for how INITIALIZE operates, examine output produced by the code in Example 11-12.

Example 11-12. *Example Uses of the* INITIALIZE *Verb*

```
01 GroupItem.
    02 Data1    PIC X(7).
    02 Data2    PIC 9(5).
    02 Data3    PIC 99/99/99.
    02 Data4    PIC +99.99.
    02 Data5    PIC $$,$$9.99.
:   :   :   :   :   :   :   :   :   :   :
PROCEDURE DIVISION.
Begin.
    MOVE ALL "-" TO GroupItem
    INITIALIZE GroupItem
    DISPLAY "Init1__" Data1 "__" Data2 "__" Data3 "__" Data4 "__" Data5.

    INITIALIZE GroupItem REPLACING ALPHANUMERIC BY "Michael"
                          NUMERIC BY 54321.

    DISPLAY "Init2__" Data1 "__" Data2 "__" Data3 "__" Data4 "__" Data5.

    STOP RUN.
```

Example 11-12 Output
Init1__   __00000__00/00/00__+00.00__ $0.00
Init2__Michael__54321__00/00/00__+00.00__ $0.00

Summary

This chapter introduced the concept of tabular data. You learned how to create tables using the OCCURS clause and were introduced to the notion of group items as table elements. I discussed multidimensional tables and showed how to create, use, and graphically depict them. In the final section, you saw how to use the REDEFINES clause to create a table prefilled with table values, and I discussed the table declaration changes that were introduced with the ANS 85 standard.

The next chapter discusses the other uses of the REDEFINES clause and introduces the similar but ill-favored RENAMES clause. You learn about the importance of decimal arithmetic for the business and enterprise programming domains and discover the use and purpose of the USAGE clause.

PROGRAMMING EXERCISE

Earlier in this chapter, I presented a problem specification and suggested an approach to solving the problem that involved using a three-dimensional table. Although the table was defined in Example 11-7, no solution was given. Because you have a problem and no solution, this is an excellent opportunity for you to get some practice using three-dimensional tables.

A subset of the U.S. census data has been made available to you by the U.S. Census Bureau (not really—this is just the specification scenario) in an unordered sequential file called the CensusFile. The CensusFile contains the age category (adult, teen, child), gender, state number, and car-ownership information of every person in the country. Each record in the file has the following description:

Field	Type	Length	Value
StateNum	9	2	1–50
Age	9	1	1 = Child 2 = Teen 3 = Adult
Gender	9	1	1 = Female 2 = Male
CarOwner	X	1	Y or N

Write a program to process the CensusFile and produce a Population Details Report that displays the number of males and females in each AgeCategory (Child, Teen, and Adult) in each state. The report format should be as shown in Figure 11-8.

```
                    Population Details Report
State    Male      Female      Male      Female    Male       Female
Num     Adults     Adults     Teens      Teens    Children   Children
XX    XXXXXXXXXX XXXXXXXXXX XXXXXXXXXX XXXXXXXXXX XXXXXXXXXX XXXXXXXXXX
XX    XXXXXXXXXX XXXXXXXXXX XXXXXXXXXX XXXXXXXXXX XXXXXXXXXX XXXXXXXXXX
XX    XXXXXXXXXX XXXXXXXXXX XXXXXXXXXX XXXXXXXXXX XXXXXXXXXX XXXXXXXXXX
                            etc.
```

Figure 11-8. *Template for the Population Details Report*

Specification Extension

Change the three-dimensional table so that it can be used to accumulate the number of car owners in each state. Change the program so that the format of the report now conforms to the template in Figure 11-9.

```
                    Population Details Report
State    Car      Male      Female     Male      Female     Male       Female
Name    Owners   Adults     Adults    Teens      Teens    Children   Children
XX    XXXXXXXXXX XXXXXXXXXX XXXXXXXXXX XXXXXXXXXX XXXXXXXXXX XXXXXXXXXX XXXXXXXXXX
XX    XXXXXXXXXX XXXXXXXXXX XXXXXXXXXX XXXXXXXXXX XXXXXXXXXX XXXXXXXXXX XXXXXXXXXX
XX    XXXXXXXXXX XXXXXXXXXX XXXXXXXXXX XXXXXXXXXX XXXXXXXXXX XXXXXXXXXX XXXXXXXXXX
                            etc.
```

Figure 11-9. *Template for the Population Details Report that includes car ownership details*

References

1. Fowler GC, Glorfeld LW. COBOL tables: A proposed standard of presentation. SIGCSE Bull. 1983; 15(1): 200-203. http://doi.acm.org/10.1145/952978.801046

   doi=10.1145/952978.801046

CHAPTER 12

■ ■ ■

Advanced Data Declaration

In the last chapter, you learned how to create and use a one-dimensional prefilled table. In this chapter, I continue the discussion of the REDEFINES clause and demonstrate how you can use it to create a two-dimensional prefilled table.

When I introduced the REDEFINES clause in the previous chapter, I did so informally. This chapter formally introduces the REDEFINES clause, including the metalanguage syntax and the semantic rules that apply. It also includes several examples of the other ways in which REDEFINES may be applied.

Because the RENAMES clause is similar to REDEFINES, I introduce RENAMES in this chapter. You learn about the metalanguage syntax for the clause, explore the semantic rules, and see some examples of how to use RENAMES.

The sections discussing the REDEFINES and RENAMES clauses are followed by an introduction to the USAGE clause. I discuss the advantages and disadvantages of USAGE IS DISPLAY (the default). I cover the metalanguage syntax and the semantic rules and examine USAGE IS COMP, USAGE IS PACKED-DECIMAL, and USAGE IS INDEX in more detail. Finally, you learn about the purpose and operation of the SYNCHRONIZED clause.

The final section discusses the importance of fixed-point decimal arithmetic to COBOL's claim of fitness for creating business or enterprise applications. You learn about the problems with doing financial and commercial calculations using floating-point arithmetic. I discuss the Java BigDecimal class and highlight some of the problems with using it, and I contrast COBOL's native support for decimal arithmetic with the bolted-on capability provided by BigDecimal.

The Redefines Clause

In the previous chapter, you used the REDEFINES clause to create a prefilled table of values. I noted at the time that the REDEFINES clause has a number of other uses; this chapter discusses how you can use REDEFINES to achieve powerful data-manipulation effects. However, before I discuss the other uses of REDEFINES, let's revisit its use in creating prefilled tables. Listing 11-4 used the REDEFINES clause to create a table prefilled with the names of the American states. Although it was interesting to see how to create a prefilled table by laying down the values in memory and then using REDEFINES to redefine the area of memory as a table, the mapping between the actual values in memory and the table definition was straightforward because only a one-dimensional table was required. In Listing 12-1, later in this section, you see how to create a prefilled two-dimensional table of values.

Specification: Aromamora Base Oil Sales Report

The following specification defines a program that demonstrates how to create and use a prefilled two-dimensional table of values.

Aromamora PLC is a company that sells essential and base (carrier) oils to aromatherapists, health shops, and other mass users of essential oils. Every month, details of the sales of base oils to these customers are gathered together into a sales file (Listing 12-1.Dat in the code download). A program is required that produces a summary report from this file. The report should show the value of the base oils purchased by each customer and should be printed sequenced on ascending CustomerId.

The Sales File

The sales file contains details of sales to all Aromamora customers. It is a sequential file ordered on ascending CustomerId. The records in the sales file have the following description:

Field	Type	Length	Value
CustomerId	9	5	0–99999
CustomerName	X	20	-
OilId	X	3	B01–B14
UnitSize	9	1	1/2/3
UnitsSold	9	3	1–999

Report Template

The report format is given in the template shown in Figure 12-1.

```
Aromamora Base Oils Summary Sales Report

Cust Id  Customer Name          ValueOfSales

 XXXXX   XXXXXXXXXXXXXXXXXXXX    XXXXXXXXXXX

 XXXXX   XXXXXXXXXXXXXXXXXXXX    XXXXXXXXXXX

 XXXXX   XXXXXXXXXXXXXXXXXXXX    XXXXXXXXXXX

 XXXXX   XXXXXXXXXXXXXXXXXXXX    XXXXXXXXXXX


************** End of Report **************
```

Figure 12-1. *Report template for Aromamora Summary Sales Report*

Notes

Here are some things to consider:

- The *B* in the OilId indicates that this is a base oil.
- UnitSize represents the size of the oil container purchased. There are only three sizes for base oils: 1 (50ml), 2 (100ml), and 3 (200ml).
- ValueOfSales is the sum of the ValueOfSale calculated for each record.

- • ValueOfSale is UnitsSold * UnitCost(OilNum,Unitsize).

- • The OilName and UnitCost are obtained from a prefilled table of values (see the program outline for details). The two-dimensional table required to hold these values is shown in Figure 12-2.

		1	2	3
1	Almond	$02.00	$03.50	$06.50
2	Aloe vera	$04.75	$08.50	$16.25
3	Apricot kernel	$02.50	$04.25	$07.75
4	Avocado	$02.75	$04.75	$08.75
5	Coconut	$02.75	$04.75	$08.95
6	Evening primrose	$03.75	$06.55	$12.25
7	Grape seed	$01.85	$03.25	$06.00
8	Peanut	$02.75	$04.25	$07.95
9	Jojoba	$07.25	$13.25	$25.00
10	Macadamia	$03.25	$05.75	$10.95
11	Rosehip	$05.25	$09.95	$18.50
12	Sesame	$02.95	$04.25	$07.50
13	Walnut	$02.75	$04.55	$08.25
14	Wheatgerm	$04.50	$07.75	$14.25

Figure 12-2. *Table of oil names and unit costs*

Oil Costs Table

Aromamora sells 14 kinds of base oil. The cost of each type of base oil in each of the three container sizes (50ml, 100ml, and 200ml) is given by the table in Figure 12-2. For instance, almond oil costs $02.00 for the 50ml size, $03.50 for 100ml size, and $06.50 for 200ml size.

Example 12-1 demonstrates how you can translate the information given in Figure 12-1 into a prefilled COBOL table. You start by laying down in memory the information you want in the table. Obviously you have to omit the dollar sign and decimal point because those are text and you need to do calculations on the data in the table. At this point, you have a block of undifferentiated data in memory as follows:

```
Almond           020003500650
Aloe vera        047508501625
Apricot kernel   025004250775
Avocado          027504750875
Coconut          027504750895
Evening primrose037506551225
Grape seed       018503250600
Peanut           027504250795
```

```
Jojoba          072513252500
Macadamia       032505751095
Rosehip         052509951850
Sesame          029504250750
Walnut          027504550825
Wheatgerm       045007751425
```

The final step in creating the table is to use the REDEFINES clause to impose a table definition on the area of memory, as shown in Example 12-1. Once the data is redefined, you can access it using the table. For instance, OilName(9) = Jojoba, and UnitCost(9,2) = 1325.

Example 12-1. Table Definition of the Two-Dimensional Table Shown in Figure 12-1

```
01  OilsTable.
    02  OilTableValues.
        03 FILLER  PIC X(28) VALUE "Almond          020003500650".
        03 FILLER  PIC X(28) VALUE "Aloe vera       047508501625".
        03 FILLER  PIC X(28) VALUE "Apricot kernel  025004250775".
        03 FILLER  PIC X(28) VALUE "Avocado         027504750875".
        03 FILLER  PIC X(28) VALUE "Coconut         027504750895".
        03 FILLER  PIC X(28) VALUE "Evening primrose037506551225".
        03 FILLER  PIC X(28) VALUE "Grape seed      018503250600".
        03 FILLER  PIC X(28) VALUE "Peanut          027504250795".
        03 FILLER  PIC X(28) VALUE "Jojoba          072513252500".
        03 FILLER  PIC X(28) VALUE "Macadamia       032505751095".
        03 FILLER  PIC X(28) VALUE "Rosehip         052509951850".
        03 FILLER  PIC X(28) VALUE "Sesame          029504250750".
        03 FILLER  PIC X(28) VALUE "Walnut          027504550825".
        03 FILLER  PIC X(28) VALUE "Wheatgerm       045007751425".
    02  FILLER REDEFINES OilTableValues.
        03 BaseOil OCCURS 14 TIMES.
           04 OilName    PIC X(16).
           04 UnitCost   PIC 99V99 OCCURS 3 TIMES.
```

Program

This is a typical one-level control-break program. I have kept the program simple (see Listing 12-1) to allow you to focus on the declaration and use of the two-dimensional table. Note that in a real situation, the oil-cost table would not be static as it is in this program. The cost data is likely to change, so for maintenance reasons the table would probably be instantiated from a file. A portion of the sales file used to the test the program and the summary report produced from that file are shown in Figure 12-3 in the next section.

Listing 12-1. Aromamora Base Oils Summary Sales Report

```
IDENTIFICATION DIVISION.
PROGRAM-ID. Listing12-1.
AUTHOR.  Michael Coughlan.
* This program produces a summary report showing the sales of base oils
* to Aromamora customers by processing the OilSalesFile.  The OilSalesFile is a
* sequential file ordered on ascending CustomerId.  The report is required to be
* printed in ascending CustomerId order.
```

```
ENVIRONMENT DIVISION.
INPUT-OUTPUT SECTION.
FILE-CONTROL.
        SELECT BaseOilsSalesFile ASSIGN TO "Listing12-1.Dat"
                ORGANIZATION IS LINE SEQUENTIAL.

        SELECT SummaryReport ASSIGN TO "Listing12-1.Rpt"
                ORGANIZATION IS LINE SEQUENTIAL.

DATA DIVISION.
FILE SECTION.
FD  BaseOilsSalesFile.
01  SalesRec.
        88  EndOfSalesFile         VALUE HIGH-VALUES.
        02  CustomerId             PIC X(5).
        02  CustomerName           PIC X(20).
        02  OilId.
            03  FILLER             PIC X.
            03  OilNum             PIC 99.
        02  UnitSize               PIC 9.
        02  UnitsSold              PIC 999.


FD SummaryReport.
01 PrintLine                       PIC X(45).


WORKING-STORAGE SECTION.
01  OilsTable.
        02  OilTableValues.
            03 FILLER  PIC X(28) VALUE "Almond          020003500650".
            03 FILLER  PIC X(28) VALUE "Aloe vera       047508501625".
            03 FILLER  PIC X(28) VALUE "Apricot kernel  025004250775".
            03 FILLER  PIC X(28) VALUE "Avocado         027504750875".
            03 FILLER  PIC X(28) VALUE "Coconut         027504750895".
            03 FILLER  PIC X(28) VALUE "Evening primrose037506551225".
            03 FILLER  PIC X(28) VALUE "Grape seed      018503250600".
            03 FILLER  PIC X(28) VALUE "Peanut          027504250795".
            03 FILLER  PIC X(28) VALUE "Jojoba          072513252500".
            03 FILLER  PIC X(28) VALUE "Macadamia       032505751095".
            03 FILLER  PIC X(28) VALUE "Rosehip         052509951850".
            03 FILLER  PIC X(28) VALUE "Sesame          029504250750".
            03 FILLER  PIC X(28) VALUE "Walnut          027504550825".
            03 FILLER  PIC X(28) VALUE "Wheatgerm       045007751425".
        02  FILLER REDEFINES OilTableValues.
            03 BaseOil OCCURS 14 TIMES.
               04 OilName   PIC X(16).
               04 UnitCost  PIC 99V99 OCCURS 3 TIMES.

01  ReportHeadingLine      PIC X(41)
            VALUE " Aromamora Base Oils Summary Sales Report".
```

```
01  TopicHeadingLine.
    02  FILLER              PIC X(9)  VALUE "Cust Id".
    02  FILLER              PIC X(15) VALUE "Customer Name".
    02  FILLER              PIC X(7)  VALUE SPACES.
    02  FILLER              PIC X(12) VALUE "ValueOfSales".


01  ReportFooterLine      PIC X(43)
          VALUE "************* End of Report **************".


01  CustSalesLine.
    02  PrnCustId          PIC B9(5).
    02  PrnCustName        PIC BBBX(20).
    02  PrnCustTotalSales  PIC BBB$$$$,$$9.99.

01  CustTotalSales        PIC 9(6)V99.
01  PrevCustId            PIC X(5).
01  ValueOfSale           PIC 9(5)V99.

PROCEDURE DIVISION.
Print-Summary-Report.
    OPEN OUTPUT SummaryReport
    OPEN INPUT BaseOilsSalesFile

    WRITE PrintLine FROM ReportHeadingLine AFTER ADVANCING 1 LINE
    WRITE PrintLine FROM TopicHeadingLine  AFTER ADVANCING 2 LINES

    READ BaseOilsSalesFile
        AT END SET EndOfSalesFile TO TRUE
    END-Read

    PERFORM PrintCustomerLines UNTIL EndOfSalesFile

    WRITE PrintLine FROM ReportFooterLine AFTER ADVANCING 3 LINES

    CLOSE SummaryReport, BaseOilsSalesFile
    STOP RUN.

PrintCustomerLines.
    MOVE ZEROS TO CustTotalSales
    MOVE CustomerId TO PrnCustId, PrevCustId
    MOVE CustomerName TO PrnCustName

    PERFORM UNTIL CustomerId NOT = PrevCustId
        COMPUTE ValueOfSale = UnitsSold * UnitCost(OilNum, UnitSize)
        ADD ValueOfSale TO CustTotalSales
        READ BaseOilsSalesFile
            AT END SET EndOfSalesFile TO TRUE
        END-Read
    END-PERFORM

    MOVE CustTotalSales TO PrnCustTotalSales
    WRITE PrintLine FROM CustSalesLine AFTER ADVANCING 2 LINES.
```

Test Data and Results

Due to space constraints, only a portion of the test data file is shown (see Figure 12-3).

Sales File (Listing12-1.Dat)

```
12332SCENTIMENTS        B122100
12332SCENTIMENTS        B112150
12332SCENTIMENTS        B143050
12332SCENTIMENTS        B121150
12332SCENTIMENTS        B123250
12344AROMANTICS         B112115
12344AROMANTICS         B132325
12344AROMANTICS         B082005
12344AROMANTICS         B092105
12350EATS OF EDEN       B081025
12350EATS OF EDEN       B081050
12350EATS OF EDEN       B031100
12350EATS OF EDEN       B021022
12350EATS OF EDEN       B011100
123520ILS FOR ALL       B031045
123520ILS FOR ALL       B032055
123520ILS FOR ALL       B051035
123520ILS FOR ALL       B112025
123520ILS FOR ALL       B121015
123520ILS FOR ALL       B121065
123520ILS FOR ALL       B141005
123520ILS FOR ALL       B133005
123520ILS FOR ALL       B132005
123520ILS FOR ALL       B121105
123520ILS FOR ALL       B121115
123520ILS FOR ALL       B112145
123520ILS FOR ALL       B092005
123520ILS FOR ALL       B062005
123520ILS FOR ALL       B042005
123520ILS FOR ALL       B043005
22342SCENTS OF SMELL    B032050
22342SCENTS OF SMELL    B061050
22342SCENTS OF SMELL    B092050
22342SCENTS OF SMELL    B082050
22342SCENTS OF SMELL    B092050
etc.
```

Summary Report (Listing12-1.Rpt)

```
      Aromamora Base Oils Summary Sales Report

 Cust Id   Customer Name              ValueOfSales

  12332    SCENTIMENTS                  $4,947.50

  12344    AROMANTICS                   $4,035.50

  12350    EATS OF EDEN                   $760.75

  12352    OILS FOR ALL                 $3,272.00

  22342    SCENTS OF SMELL              $1,937.50

  22346    AROMANIACS                     $500.25

  22354    COMMON SCENTS                $3,400.00

  32348    HEAVEN SCENT                 $3,552.50

  32350    OILS WELL THAT ENDS             $25.00

  32358    SCENTS OF DECORUM            $5,282.50

  42346    OIL IN GOOD TIME               $105.00

  42348    SCENTS OF FOREBODING           $122.00

  52332    MAKING SCENTS OF IT             $77.25

  52336    SCENTSUALITY                   $161.00

  52338    ODOURS OF SANCTITY              $44.75

  52346    OILS FAYRE IN LOVE               $1.85

  52348    PERFECT SCENTS               $3,362.50

************* End of Report *************
```

Figure 12-3. Partial test data and results produced

The REDEFINES Clause

So far, I have dealt informally with the REDEFINES clause. You have seen how to use it to create a prefilled table of values, but I have not formally defined what REDEFINES does or explored its other uses.

When a file contains different types of records, you must create a separate record description for each record type in the file's FD entry. You have seen that all these record descriptions map on to the same area of storage. They are, in effect, redefinitions of the area of storage. What the REDEFINES clause allows you to do is to achieve the same effect for units smaller than a record and in parts of the DATA DIVISION other than the FILE SECTION. The REDEFINES clause lets you give different data descriptions to the same area of storage.

REDEFINES Syntax

The syntax metalanguage for the REDEFINES clause is given in Figure 12-4. Identifier1 is the data item that originally defines the area of storage, and Identifier2 is the data item that redefines it.

$$\text{Level} - \text{No} \begin{Bmatrix} \text{Identifier2} \\ \text{FILLER} \end{Bmatrix} \underline{\text{REDEFINES}}\,\text{Identifier1}$$

Figure 12-4. Syntax metalanguage for the REDEFINES clause

REDEFINES Notes

The metalanguage defines the syntax of the REDEFINES clause, but there are also a number of semantic rules that must be obeyed when you use REDEFINES:

- The REDEFINES clause must immediately follow Identifier2 (that is, REDEFINES must come before PIC [see Example 12-2]).

- The level numbers of Identifier1 and Identifier2 must be the same and cannot be 66 or 88.

- The data description of Identifier1 cannot contain an OCCURS clause (that is, you can't redefine a table element).

- If there are multiple redefinitions of the same area of storage, then they must all redefine the data item that originally defined the area (see Example 12-5).

- The redefining entries (Identifier2) cannot contain VALUE clauses except in condition name entries.

- No entry with a level number lower (that is, higher in the hierarchy) than the level number of Identifier1 and Identifier2 can occur between Identifier1 and Identifier2.

- Entries redefining the area must immediately follow those that originally defined it.

- Only entries subordinate to Identifier1 are allowed between Identifier1 and Identifier2.

- The REDEFINES clause must not be used for records (01 level) described in the FILE SECTION because multiple 01 entries for the same file are implicit redefinitions of the first 01 level record.

REDEFINES Examples

The best way to understand how the REDEFINES clause works is to explore some of the ways it may be used through a number of examples.

REDEFINES Example 1

Some COBOL statements, such as UNSTRING, require their receiving fields to be alphanumeric (PIC X) data items. This is inconvenient if the value of the data item is actually numeric, because then a MOVE is required to place the value into a numeric item. If the value contains a decimal point, this creates even more difficulties.

For example, suppose an UNSTRING statement has just extracted the text value "5432195" from a string, and you want to move this value to a numeric item described as PIC 9(5)V99. An ordinary MOVE is not going to work because the computer will not know that you want the item treated as if it were the value 654321.95.

The REDEFINES clause allows you to solve this problem neatly because you can UNSTRING the number into TextValue and then treat TextValue as if it were described as PIC 9(5)V99 (see Example 12-2). If TextValue contains the alphanumeric value "65432195", then NumericValue, which REDEFINES it, sees the value as 654321.95 (see Figure 12-5).

Example 12-2. Redefining an Alphanumeric Item as a Decimal Data Item

```
01 RedefinesExample1.
   02 TextValue     PIC X(8).
   02 NumericValue REDEFINES TextValue PIC 9(6)V99.
```

Figure 12-5. *Memory model showing the result of redefinition*

REDEFINES Example 2

The first example showed how you can use the REDEFINES clause to treat a set of alphanumeric digits as a decimal number. This example explores a similar problem. When a program ACCEPTs a decimal number from a user, the decimal point is included. This is a problem because this decimal point is a text character. If you move a numeric literal (such as 1234.55) that contains a decimal point into a numeric data item that contains an assumed decimal point (such as PIC 9(5)V99), the actual and assumed decimal points align. This does not happen when you move an item containing the decimal point text character. In fact, if you move an item containing an actual decimal point into a numeric data item and then try to perform an arithmetic calculation on that data item, the program will crash (halt unexpectedly).

A solution to this problem is given in Example 12-3. When a number containing an actual decimal point is accepted from the user, the UNSTRING verb is used to split the input string into the digits before the decimal point and those after the decimal point. Although WorkArea contains only numeric digits, because it is a group item, its type is alphanumeric, and so it can't be used in a calculation. The solution is to redefine WorkArea as WorkNum, which is a numeric data item that can be used in calculations. A model of the redefined data items is given in Figure 12-6.

Example 12-3. Redefining Two Data Items as a Single Numeric Item

```
WORKING-STORAGE SECTION.
01  InputString    PIC X(8).


01  WorkArea.
    02 Fnum     PIC 9(5) VALUE ZEROS.
    02 Snum     PIC 99   VALUE ZEROS.
01  WorkNum REDEFINES WorkArea PIC 99999V99.


01 EditedNum    PIC ZZ,ZZ9.99.


PROCEDURE DIVISION.
Begin.
    DISPLAY "Enter a decimal number - " WITH NO ADVANCING
    ACCEPT InputString
    UNSTRING InputString DELIMITED BY ".", ALL SPACES
        INTO Fnum, Snum
    MOVE WorkNum TO EditedNum
    DISPLAY "Decimal Number = " EditedNum
    ADD 10 TO WorkNum
    MOVE WorkNum TO EditedNum
    DISPLAY "Decimal Number = " EditedNum
```

<u>Example 12-3 Output</u>
```
Enter a decimal number - 1234.55
Decimal Number =   1,234.55
Decimal Number =   1,244.55
```

Figure 12-6. *Model showing WorkArea, Fnum, and Snum redefined as WorkNum*

REDEFINES Example 3

Working with percentages often presents a problem. If the percentage is held as an integer, then calculations are complicated by having to divide by 100. For instance, COMPUTE PercentOfBase = BaseAmount * PercentToApply /100.

On the other hand, if the percentage is held as a decimal fraction, then calculations are made simpler but communication with users is complicated because now they have to input or print the percentage as a decimal fraction rather than a whole number.

The solution is to take in the percentage as an integer value and then use REDEFINES to treat it as a decimal fraction. Example 12-4 is a program fragment that shows how this works.

Example 12-4. Using REDEFINES to Allow Different Views of a Percentage Value

```
DATA DIVISION.
WORKING-STORAGE SECTION.
01  PercentToApply    PIC 9(3).
01  Percentage REDEFINES PercentToApply PIC 9V99.

01  BaseAmount        PIC 9(5) VALUE 10555.
01  PercentOfBase     PIC ZZ,ZZ9.99.
01  PrnPercent        PIC ZZ9.

PROCEDURE DIVISION.
Begin.
    MOVE 23 TO PercentToApply
    COMPUTE PercentOfBase = BaseAmount * Percentage
    DISPLAY "23% of 10555 is = " PercentOfBase
    MOVE PercentToApply to PrnPercent
    DISPLAY "Percentage applied was " PrnPercent "%"
    STOP RUN.
```

<u>Example 12-4 Output</u>
```
23% of 10555 is =   2,427.65
Percentage applied was   23%
```

REDEFINES Example 4

The REDEFINES clause is also useful when you need to treat a numeric item as if it had its decimal point in a different place. For instance, Example 12-5 shows how you can use the REDEFINES clause to provide time conversions between seconds, milliseconds, microseconds, and nanoseconds.

The main purpose of Example 12-5 is to illustrate the rule that if there are multiple redefinitions of an area of storage, they must all refer to the data item that originally defined the area of storage.

Example 12-5. Time Conversion by Multiple Redefinition

```
WORKING-STORAGE SECTION.
01 NanoSecs     PIC 9(10).
01 MicroSecs    REDEFINES NanoSecs PIC 9999999V999.
01 MilliSecs    REDEFINES NanoSecs PIC 9999V999999.
01 Seconds      REDEFINES NanoSecs PIC 9V999999999.

01 EditedNum    PIC Z,ZZZ,ZZZ,ZZ9.99.

PROCEDURE DIVISION.
Begin.
    MOVE 1234567895 TO NanoSecs
    MOVE NanoSecs TO EditedNum
    DISPLAY EditedNum " NanoSecs"
```

```
MOVE MicroSecs TO EditedNum
DISPLAY EditedNum " MicroSecs"

MOVE MilliSecs TO EditedNum
DISPLAY EditedNum " MilliSecs"

MOVE Seconds TO EditedNum
DISPLAY EditedNum " Seconds"
STOP RUN.
```

Example 12-5 Output

```
1,234,567,895.00 NanoSecs
    1,234,567.89 MicroSecs
        1,234.56 MilliSecs
            1.23 Seconds
```

The RENAMES Clause

As you have seen, the REDEFINES clause allows you to give a new data definition and name to an area of storage. The RENAMES clause lets you give a new name (or alias) to a data item or a collection of data items. This can be useful when you want to regroup a number of elementary data items in a record so that they can belong to the original as well as to the new group.

The RENAMES clause is used with the special level number 66. In the same way that condition names are sometimes called level eighty-eights, RENAMES data items are sometimes called *level sixty-sixes*.

Because of the maintenance problems associated with RENAMES , it has largely fallen into disuse; and in some programming shops, it is banned. I include it here only for completeness.

RENAMES Syntax

The syntax metalanguage for the RENAMES clause is given in Figure 12-7. Identifier2 [THRU Identifier3] is the original area of storage, and Identifier1 is the new name that you can use to manipulate it.

66 Identifier1 <u>RENAMES</u> Identifer2 $\left[\left\{ {{\text{THRU} \atop \text{THROUGH}}} \right\} \text{Identifer3} \right]$

Figure 12-7. *RENAMES metalanguage*

RENAMES Notes

The syntax diagram in Figure 12-7 is modified by the following semantic rules:

- The level number of Identifier2 and Identifier3 cannot be 77, 88, 01, or 66.

- Identifier2 and Identifier3 must not contain an OCCURS clause or be subordinate to a data item that contains an OCCURS clause.

- No data item between Identifier2 and Identifier3 can contain an OCCURS clause.

- RENAMES entries must follow the last data-description entry of a record (can't be in the middle of a record description).

RENAMES Examples

Listing 12-2 contains a number of examples that show how to use the RENAMES clause.

Listing 12-2. RENAMES Examples

```
IDENTIFICATION DIVISION.
PROGRAM-ID. Listing12-2
AUTHOR. Michael Coughlan.
* RENAMES clause examples
DATA DIVISION.
WORKING-STORAGE SECTION.
01 StudentRec.
   02 StudentId      PIC 9(8)  VALUE 12345678.
   02 GPA            PIC 9V99  VALUE 3.25.
   02 ForeName       PIC X(6)  VALUE "Matt".
   02 SurName        PIC X(8)  VALUE "Cullen".
   02 Gender         PIC X     VALUE "M".
   02 PhoneNumber    PIC X(14) VALUE "3536120228233".

66 PersonalInfo RENAMES ForeName  THRU PhoneNumber.
66 CollegeInfo   RENAMES StudentId THRU SurName.
66 StudentName   RENAMES ForeName  THRU SurName.

01 ContactInfo.
   02 StudName.
      03 StudForename  PIC X(6).
      03 StudSurname   PIC X(8).
   02 StudGender       PIC X.
   02 StudPhone        PIC X(14).

66 MyPhone RENAMES StudPhone.

PROCEDURE DIVISION.
Begin.
    DISPLAY "Example 1"
    DISPLAY "All information = " StudentRec
    DISPLAY "College info    = " CollegeInfo
    DISPLAY "Personal Info   = " PersonalInfo

    DISPLAY "Example 2"
    DISPLAY "Combined names  = " StudentName

    MOVE PersonalInfo TO ContactInfo

    DISPLAY "Example 3"
    DISPLAY "Name    is " StudName
    DISPLAY "Gender  is " StudGender
    DISPLAY "Phone   is " StudPhone

    DISPLAY "Example 4"
    DISPLAY "MyPhone is " MyPhone
    STOP RUN.
```

```
                    Listing 12-2 Output
Example 1
All information = 12345678325Matt  Cullen  M3536120228233
College info    = 12345678325Matt  Cullen
Personal Info   = Matt  Cullen  M3536120228233

Example 2
Combined names  = Matt  Cullen

Example 3
Name    is Matt  Cullen
Gender  is M
Phone   is 3536120228233

Example 4
MyPhone is 3536120228233
```

Listing Notes

Listing 12-2 contains a number of RENAMES clause examples. The first example uses the RENAMES clause to rename sections of the StudentRec to allow the college and personal information parts of the record to be accessed separately. No new data storage is created when this is done, but the existing storage is given new names. This example also shows that multiple, overlapping, RENAMES may be used.

The second example renames the elementary data items ForeName and SurName as StudentName so they can be treated as a single item (that is, members of a group item). For the purpose of contrast, in the record ContactInfo I made these items subordinate to a group item.

The third example shows that the renamed data can be manipulated using the new name. I moved PersonalInfo to ContactInfo and then displayed the individual fields in ContactInfo.

The final example shows that you can also use RENAMES to rename a single item.

The USAGE Clause

Computers store their data in the form of binary digits. Apart from cardinal numbers (positive integers), all other data stored in the computer's memory uses some sort of formatting convention.

For instance, text data is stored using an encoding sequence like ASCII or EBCDIC. An encoding system is simply a convention that specifies that a particular set of bits represents a particular character. For instance, Figure 12-8 shows the bit configuration used to represent an uppercase *A* in the ASCII and EBCDIC encoding sequences.

SYSTEM	CHAR	HEX	DEC	8	4	2	1	8	4	2	1
ASCII	"A"	41	65	0	1	0	0	0	0	0	1
EBCDIC	"A"	C1	193	1	1	0	0	0	0	0	1

Figure 12-8. *Uppercase A in the ASCII and EBCDIC encoding sequences*

Representation of Numeric Data

COBOL gives you a lot of control over how numeric data is held in memory. In COBOL, numeric data can be held as text digits (ASCII digits), as twos-complement binary numbers, or as decimal numbers (using binary-coded decimal [BCD]).

You use the USAGE clause to specify how a data item is to be stored in the computer's memory. Every data item declared in a COBOL program has a USAGE clause—even when no explicit clause is specified. When there is no explicit USAGE clause, the default USAGE IS DISPLAY is applied. USAGE IS DISPLAY has been used in all the examples so far.

Disadvantage of USAGE DISPLAY

For text items, or for numeric items that will not be used in a computation (phone numbers, account numbers, and so son), the default of USAGE IS DISPLAY presents no problems. But the default usage is not the most efficient way to store data that will be used in a calculation.

When numeric items (PIC 9 items) have a usage of DISPLAY, they are stored as ASCII digits (see the ASCII digits 0–9 in the ASCII table in Figure 12-9).

Char	Dec	Hex	Binary
0	48	30	00110000
1	49	31	00110001
2	50	32	00110010
3	51	33	00110011
4	52	34	00110100
5	53	35	00110101
6	54	36	00110110
7	55	37	00110111
8	56	38	00111000
9	57	39	00111001

Figure 12-9. *Table of ASCII digits*

Consider the program fragment in Example 12-6. Figure 12-10 shows what would happen if computations were done directly on numbers stored in this format. Because none of the data items have an explicit USAGE clause, they default to USAGE IS DISPLAY. This means the values in the variables Num1, Num2, and Num3 are stored as ASCII digits. This in turn means the digit 4 in Num1 is encoded as 00110100 and the digit 1 in Num2 is encoded as 00110001. When these binary numbers are added together, the result, as shown in Figure 12-10, is the binary value 01100101, which is the ASCII code for the lowercase letter *e*.

Example 12-6. Arithmetic on Items Held as USAGE IS DISPLAY

```
Num1    PIC 9 VALUE 4.
Num2    PIC 9 VALUE 1.
Num3    PIC 9 VALUE ZERO.
:   :   :   :   :   :   :   :
ADD Num1, Num2 GIVING Num3.
```

Figure 12-10. *Adding two ASCII digits gives the wrong result*

When calculations are done with numeric data items using USAGE IS DISPLAY, the computer has to convert the numeric values to their binary equivalents before the calculation can be done. When the result has been computed, the computer must reconvert it to ASCII digits. Conversion to and from ASCII digits slows down computations.

For this reason, data that is heavily involved in computation is often declared using one of the usages optimized for computation, such as USAGE IS COMPUTATIONAL.

Advantage of USAGE IS DISPLAY

Although it is computationally inefficient, there are a number of advantages to holding numeric data as text digits. One obvious advantage is that USAGE DISPLAY items can be output to the computer screen by the DISPLAY verb without the need for conversion. Another advantage is portability. Files whose data is encoded as text can be processed without difficulty on different makes of computers or using other programming languages. In contrast, the chosen binary formats of some computers and the Big Endian/Little Endian byte order preference of others means that non-text files produced on one make of computer are often difficult to read on another make of computer or even using another programming language or utility program on the same computer.

STORAGE OF MULTIBYTE NUMBERS

Some computers store numeric binary values using a byte order where the low-order byte of a number is stored at the lowest memory address, and the high-order byte at the highest address. This is known as the *Little Endian* byte order. For instance, a four-byte-long integer value would be stored as

```
Byte0 at BaseAddress+0
Byte1 at BaseAddress+1
Byte2 at BaseAddress+2
Byte3 at BaseAddress+3
```

In contrast, in *Big Endian* computers, the high-order byte of the number is stored at the lowest memory address, and the low-order byte at the highest address. For instance:

```
Byte3 at BaseAddress +0
Byte2 at BaseAddress +1
Byte1 at BaseAddress +2
Byte0 at BaseAddress +3
```

The advantages of the USAGE IS DISPLAY format and the speed of modern computers means that the USAGE clause is an optimization that is only worth doing if the data item will be used in thousands of computations.

USAGE Clause Syntax

As you have seen, the default representation (USAGE IS DISPLAY) used by COBOL for numeric data items can negatively impact the speed of computations. USAGE is used for purposes of optimization of both speed and storage. It allows you to control the way data items (normally numeric data items) are stored in memory. One important point to note is that because computers can be quite different under the skin (for instance, register size and Endian order), the COBOL standard leaves the actual implementation of the binary data items to the compiler implementer. This means a COMP item on one computer may not be exactly the same as a COMP item on another computer.

The metalanguage syntax diagram for the USAGE clause is given in Figure 12-11, and some example declarations are shown in Example 12-7.

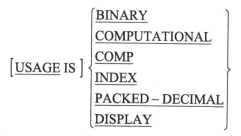

Figure 12-11. *The USAGE clause metalanguage*

Example 12-7. Example USAGE Clause Declarations

```
01 Num1            PIC 9(5)V99  USAGE IS COMP.
01 Num2            PIC 99       USAGE IS PACKED-DECIMAL.
01 IdxItem    USAGE IS INDEX.

01 FirstGroup    COMP.
    02 Item1    PIC 999.
    02 Item2    PIC 9(4)V99.
    02 Item3    PIC S9(5) COMP SYNC.
```

Notes

Here are some things to note:

- The USAGE clause may be used with any data description entry except those with level numbers of 66 or 88.

- When the USAGE clause is declared for a group item, the usage specified is applied to every item in the group. The group item itself is still treated as an alphanumeric data item (see FirstGroup in Example 12-7).

- The USAGE clause of an elementary item cannot override the USAGE clause of the group to which it is subordinate (for instance, in Example 12-7, the USAGE of Item3 is COMP because that is the USAGE of FirstGroup).

- USAGE IS COMPUTATIONAL and COMP or BINARY are synonyms of one another.

- The USAGE IS INDEX clause is used to provide an optimized table subscript.

- Any item declared with USAGE IS INDEX can only appear in

  - A SEARCH or SET statement

  - A relation condition

  - The USING phrase of the PROCEDURE DIVISION

  - The USING phrase of the CALL statement

- The picture string of a COMP or PACKED-DECIMAL item can contain only the symbols 9, S, V, and/or P.

- The picture clause used for COMP and PACKED-DECIMAL items must be numeric.

■ **Bug Alert**   Group items are always treated as alphanumeric, and this can cause problems when there are subordinate COMP items. For instance, suppose you defined a group of data items as follows:

```
01 SecondGroup.
  02 NumItem1   PIC 9(3)V99 USAGE IS COMP.
  02 NumItem2   PIC 99V99   USAGE IS COMP.
```

and then applied a statement such as MOVE ZEROS TO SecondGroup to it.

On the surface, it appears that the statement is moving the numeric value 0 to NumItem1 and NumItem2; but because SecondGroup is an alphanumeric item, what is actually moved into NumItem1 and NumItem2 is the ASCII digit "0". When an attempt is made to use NumItem1 or NumItem2 in a calculation, the program will crash because these data items contain non-numeric data.

COMP Explanation

COMP items are held in memory as pure binary twos-complement numbers. You don't have to understand how twos-complement numbers work or how they are stored, but you must understand the storage requirements for fields described as COMP. The storage requirements are shown in Table 12-1. For instance, the declaration

```
01 TotalCount   PIC 9(7) USAGE IS COMP
```

requires a LongWord (4 bytes) of storage.

Table 12-1. *Storage Requirements of COMP Data Items*

Number of Digits	Storage Required
PIC 9(1 to 4)	1 Word (2 bytes)
PIC 9(5 to 9)	1 LongWord (4 bytes)
PIC 9(10 to 18)	1 QuadWord (8 bytes)

PACKED-DECIMAL Explanation

Data items declared as PACKED-DECIMAL are held in binary-coded decimal (BCD) form. Instead of representing the value as a single binary number, the binary value of each digit is held in a nibble (half a byte). The sign is held in a separate nibble in the least significant position of the item (see Figure 12-12).

```
01 Num1    PIC S9    VALUE +5    USAGE PACKED-DECIMAL.
```

5	✦

```
01 Num2    PIC S9(2) VALUE -32   USAGE PACKED-DECIMAL.
```

0	3	2	-

```
01 Num3    PIC S9(3) VALUE +262 USAGE PACKED-DECIMAL.
```

2	6	2	✦

Figure 12-12. *Memory representation of BCD numbers*

The SYNCHRONIZED Clause

The SYNCHRONIZED clause is sometimes used with USAGE IS COMP or USAGE IS INDEX items. It is used to optimize speed of processing, but it does so at the expense of increased storage requirements.

Many computer memories are organized in such a way that there are natural addressing boundaries, such as word boundaries. If no special action is taken, some data items in memory may straddle these boundaries. This may cause processing overhead because the CPU may need two fetch cycles to retrieve the data from memory. The SYNCHRONIZED clause is used to explicitly align COMP and INDEX items along their natural word boundaries. Without SYNCHRONIZED, data items are aligned on byte boundaries. The metalanguage for SYNCHRONIZED is given in Figure 12-13.

$$\begin{Bmatrix} \text{SYNCHRONIZED} \\ \text{SYNC} \end{Bmatrix} \begin{bmatrix} \text{LEFT} \\ \text{RIGHT} \end{bmatrix}$$

Figure 12-13. *Metalanguage for the SYNCHRONIZED clause*

The effect of the SYNCHRONIZED clause is implementation dependent. You need to read your implementer manual to see how it works on your computer (in some cases it may have no effect). To illustrate how SYNCHRONIZED works in general, assume that a COBOL program is running on a word-oriented computer where the CPU fetches data from memory a word at a time. Suppose the program performs a calculation on the number stored in the variable TwoBytes (as shown in Figure 12-14). Because of the way the data items have been declared, the number stored in TwoBytes straddles a word boundary. In order to use the number, the CPU has to execute two fetch cycles: one to get the first part of the number in Word2 and the second to get the second part of the number in Word3. This double fetch slows down calculations.

```
01 ThreeBytes   PIC XXX    VALUE "CAT".
01 TwoBytes     PIC 9(4)   COMP.
```

C	A	T	number

Word1 Word2 Word3

Figure 12-14. *With no SYNCHRONIZED clause, numbers may straddle word boundaries*

When the SYNCHRONIZED clause is used, as shown in Figure 12-15, TwoBytes is aligned along the word boundary, so the CPU only has to do one fetch cycle to retrieve the number from memory. This speeds up processing, but at the expense of wasting some storage (the second byte of Word2 is no longer used).

```
01 ThreeBytes  PIC XXX    VALUE "CAT".
01 TwoBytes    PIC 9(4)   COMP SYNC.
```

Figure 12-15. With the SYNCHRONIZED, clause numbers are aligned along word boundaries

Nonstandard USAGE Extensions

The USAGE clause is one of the areas where many implementers have introduced extensions to the COBOL standard. It is not uncommon to see COMP-1, COMP-2, COMP-3, COMP-4, COMP-5, and POINTER usage items in programs written using these extensions.

Even though COMP-1 and COMP-2 are extensions to the COBOL standard, many implementers seem to use identical representations for these usages. Comp-1 is usually defined as a single-precision, floating-point number, adhering to the IEEE specification for such numbers (Real or float in typed languages). Comp-2 is usually defined as an IEEE double-precision, floating-point number (LongReal or double in typed languages). COMP-3 items are usually defined as BCD numbers. The official introduction of PACKED-DECIMAL in the ANS 85 version of COBOL has made this extension unnecessary.

Decimal Arithmetic

One of COBOL's strengths, and one of its main claims to fitness for writing business and enterprise applications, is its native support for fixed-point decimal arithmetic. Until the problems associated with floating-point arithmetic are pointed out to them, most programmers are not even aware that there is a problem. In the Java community, this is such a problem that even now articles and forum posts are still produced warning of the dangers of using float or double for currency calculations.

The problem with floating-point arithmetic is this: binary floating-point numbers (such as those with a type of real, float, or double) cannot represent common decimal fractions exactly. For instance, common decimal fractions like 0.1 do not have a terminating binary representation. Just as 1/3 is a repeating fraction in decimal, 1/10 is a repeating fraction in binary. As a result, floating-point numbers can't be used safely for financial calculations. In fact, they cannot be used for any calculations where the result produced is required to match those that might be calculated by hand.

In an article on the Java Performance Tuning Guide[1], Mikhail Vorontsov emphasizes this point when he notes that double calculations are not precise even for simple operations such as addition and subtraction. For instance, he notes that the Java statement

```
System.out.println( "362.2 - 362.6 = " + ( 362.2 - 362.6 ) );
```

produces the output

```
362.2 - 362.6 = -0.4000000000000341
```

The advantage of doing computations using fixed-point decimal arithmetic, as COBOL does, is that everyday numbers such as 0.1 can be represented exactly and the results of COBOL calculations do exactly match those that might be produced by hand.

Doing computations using floating-point arithmetic causes tiny inaccuracies that lead to unacceptable errors when taken over millions of computations. For instance, suppose you are required to calculate a tax of 15% on a 70-cent telephone call that is then rounded to the nearest cent[2]. Using the Java compiler at compileonline.com, the calculation 0.70 * 1.15 produces a result of 0.8049999999999999, which rounds down to 0.80 cents. The correct result should have been 0.805, which would round up to 0.81 cents. This difference of a cent per calculation, when taken over a million calculations of this kind, would result in an undercharge of ten thousand dollars.

If floating-point arithmetic is so problematic, how do languages that do not have native support for fixed-point decimal arithmetic deal with the problem? Nowadays, they implement a class to support decimal arithmetic operations. However, implementing such a class is not a trivial undertaking. Java's original implementation of the BigDecimal class was so flawed that IBM raised a Java Specification Request (JSR)[2] detailing the problems and requesting changes. These changes were implemented and shipped with Java 1.5 in 2004.

So does the revised BigDecimal class solve the problems with decimal arithmetic in Java? Only partly; decimal arithmetic in Java is implemented as a class instead of as a native type, and computations using the class are cumbersome, unnatural, and slow. For instance, Vorontsov[1] found that 100 million BigDecimal calculations took 8.975 seconds, while the same number of double calculations took only 0.047 seconds. BigDecimal operations can be called unnatural in the sense that Java floating-point numbers and integers can use the standard assignment operator (=) and the standard arithmetic operators (+ - / *), whereas the BigDecimal class has to use its class methods. For instance, to multiply two BigDecimal numbers, you might use a statement like

```
calcResult = num1.multiply(num2);
```

instead of

```
calcResult = num1 * num2;
```

Early in Chapter 1, I showed you a Java program that used the BigDecimal class and asked you to compare it to the COBOL version for readability. I was confident then that you would be able to appreciate the readability of the COBOL version even though at the time you had not yet been introduced to the elements of the language. However, now that we have a more level playing field, let's look at those programs again (reprinted Listings 1-1 and 1-2).

Listing 1-1. COBOL Version

```
IDENTIFICATION DIVISION.
PROGRAM-ID. SalesTax.
DATA DIVISION.
WORKING-STORAGE SECTION.
01 beforeTax        PIC 999V99   VALUE 123.45.
01 salesTaxRate     PIC V999     VALUE .065.
01 afterTax         PIC 999.99.
PROCEDURE DIVISION.
Begin.
    COMPUTE afterTax ROUNDED = beforeTax + (beforeTax * salesTaxRate)
    DISPLAY "After tax amount is " afterTax.
```

Listing 1-2. Java Version (from http://caliberdt.com/tips/May03_Java_BigDecimal_Class.htm)

```
import java.math.BigDecimal;
public class SalesTaxWithBigDecimal
{
  public static void main(java.lang.String[] args)
  {
    BigDecimal beforeTax = BigDecimal.valueOf(12345, 2);
    BigDecimal salesTaxRate = BigDecimal.valueOf(65, 3);
    BigDecimal ratePlusOne = salesTaxRate.add(BigDecimal.valueOf(1));
```

```
    BigDecimal afterTax = beforeTax.multiply(ratePlusOne);
    afterTax = afterTax.setScale(2, BigDecimal.ROUND_HALF_UP);
    System.out.println( "After tax amount is " + afterTax);
  }
}
```

The COBOL version uses native fixed-point decimal arithmetic and is able to use all the standard arithmetic operators. The Java version has to use the BigDecimal methods to do even simple calculations. The COBOL program is 10 lines and 335 characters long, whereas the Java program is 13 lines and 484 characters long. Reminded me again. Which one is the verbose language?

Summary

This chapter explored the operation of advanced data-declaration clauses such as the REDEFINES clause, the RENAMES clause, and the USAGE clause. It showed how you can use REDEFINES clauses to redefine an area of storage with a new name and new data description. You saw how to use RENAMES to group a set of data items under a new name. You also learned how to use the USAGE clause to change the default DISPLAY data format to one of the binary formats such as COMPUTATIONAL or PACKED-DECIMAL. The operation of these binary formats was explored in more depth, and the computational efficiency of the binary formats was weighed against the portability of the DISPLAY format. You investigated the operation-modifying SYNCHRONIZED clause and learned about the USAGE clause extensions provided by many COBOL implementers. The chapter ended with a discussion of the problems inherent in using floating-point arithmetic for financial and commercial calculations and the contrast between COBOL's native support for decimal arithmetic and the bolted-on capability provided by Java's BigDecimal class.

The next chapter returns to the topic of tabular data to introduce the SEARCH and SEARCH ALL verbs. Searching tabular data for a particular value is a common operation, but it can be tricky to get the search algorithms right. For this reason, COBOL provides SEARCH and SEARCH ALL. The SEARCH ALL verb allows you to apply a binary search to a table, and SEARCH applies a linear search.

LANGUAGE KNOWLEDGE EXERCISES

Sometimes the most instructive lessons arise from the mistakes you make. The debugging exercises that follow are based on some programming errors I made when I was learning to program in COBOL.

Locate your 2B pencil, and provide answers to the problems.

The Problems

The first two programs go into an infinite loop (never halt) and have to be stopped by the user. The third program sometimes crashes with the error message shown in the accompanying runs. The fourth program sometimes goes into an infinite loop.

Examine each program, and use the accompanying runs to discover the bug or bugs responsible for the problem. Identify the problem, and show how you would correct the program to make it work correctly.

Program 1

This program goes into an infinite loop. Examine the program in Listing 12-3 and the program output and try to figure out what is going wrong. Identify the problem, and suggest a solution.

Listing 12-3. Program Does Not Halt

```
IDENTIFICATION DIVISION.
PROGRAM-ID. Listing12-3.
AUTHOR.  Michael Coughlan.

DATA DIVISION.
WORKING-STORAGE SECTION.
01 Counters.
    02 Counter1        PIC 99.
    02 Counter2        PIC 99.
    02 Counter3        PIC 9.

PROCEDURE DIVISION.
Begin.
    DISPLAY "Debug 1.  Discover why I can't stop."
    PERFORM EternalLooping VARYING Counter1
        FROM 13 BY -5 UNTIL Counter1 LESS THAN 2
        AFTER Counter2 FROM 15 BY -4
            UNTIL Counter2 LESS THAN 1
        AFTER Counter3 FROM 1 BY 1
            UNTIL Counter3 GREATER THAN 5

    STOP RUN.

EternalLooping.
    DISPLAY "Counters 1, 2 and 3 are -> "
            Counter1 SPACE  Counter2 SPACE Counter3.
```

Answer:

_____
_____
_____
_____
_____
_____
_____
_____
_____
_____

```
         Listing 12-3 Output

Debug 1.  Discover why I can't stop.
Counters 1, 2 and 3 are -> 13 15 1
Counters 1, 2 and 3 are -> 13 15 2
Counters 1, 2 and 3 are -> 13 15 3
Counters 1, 2 and 3 are -> 13 15 4
Counters 1, 2 and 3 are -> 13 15 5
Counters 1, 2 and 3 are -> 13 11 1
Counters 1, 2 and 3 are -> 13 11 2
Counters 1, 2 and 3 are -> 13 11 3
Counters 1, 2 and 3 are -> 13 11 4
Counters 1, 2 and 3 are -> 13 11 5
Counters 1, 2 and 3 are -> 13 07 1
Counters 1, 2 and 3 are -> 13 07 2
Counters 1, 2 and 3 are -> 13 07 3
Counters 1, 2 and 3 are -> 13 07 4
Counters 1, 2 and 3 are -> 13 07 5
Counters 1, 2 and 3 are -> 13 03 1
Counters 1, 2 and 3 are -> 13 03 2
Counters 1, 2 and 3 are -> 13 03 3
Counters 1, 2 and 3 are -> 13 03 4
Counters 1, 2 and 3 are -> 13 03 5
Counters 1, 2 and 3 are -> 13 01 1
Counters 1, 2 and 3 are -> 13 01 2
Counters 1, 2 and 3 are -> 13 01 3
Counters 1, 2 and 3 are -> 13 01 4
Counters 1, 2 and 3 are -> 13 01 5
Counters 1, 2 and 3 are -> 13 03 1
Counters 1, 2 and 3 are -> 13 03 2
Counters 1, 2 and 3 are -> 13 03 3
Counters 1, 2 and 3 are -> 13 03 4
Counters 1, 2 and 3 are -> 13 03 5
Counters 1, 2 and 3 are -> 13 01 1
Counters 1, 2 and 3 are -> 13 01 2
Counters 1, 2 and 3 are -> 13 01 3
Counters 1, 2 and 3 are -> 13 01 4
Counters 1, 2 and 3 are -> 13 01 5
Counters 1, 2 and 3 are -> 13 03 1
Counters 1, 2 and 3 are -> 13 03 2
Counters 1, 2 and 3 are -> 13 03 3
Counters 1, 2 and 3 are -> 13 03 4
Counters 1, 2 and 3 are -> 13 03 5
Counters 1, 2 and 3 are -> 13 01 1
Counters 1, 2 and 3 are -> 13 01 2
         < Interrupted by user>
```

Program 2

This program also goes into an infinite loop. Examine the program in Listing 12-4 and the program output, and try to figure out what is going wrong. Identify the problem, and suggest a solution.

Listing 12-4. What Is Wrong with This Program?

```
IDENTIFICATION DIVISION.
PROGRAM-ID.  Listing12-4.
AUTHOR.  Michael Coughlan.

DATA DIVISION.
WORKING-STORAGE SECTION.
01    Counters.
      02    Counter1     PIC 99.
      02    Counter2     PIC 9.
      02    Counter3     PIC 9.

PROCEDURE DIVISION.
Begin.
    DISPLAY "Debug2.  Why can't I stop?"
    PERFORM EternalLooping VARYING Counter1
         FROM 1 BY 1 UNTIL Counter1 GREATER THAN 25
         AFTER Counter2 FROM 1 BY 1
                   UNTIL Counter2 GREATER THAN 9
         AFTER Counter3 FROM 1 BY 1
                   UNTIL Counter3 EQUAL TO 5
    STOP RUN.

EternalLooping.
    DISPLAY "Counters 1, 2 and 3 are "
            Counter1 SPACE Counter2 SPACE Counter3.
```

Answer: _____

_____

_____

_____

_____

_____

```
       Listing 12-4 Output

Debug2.  Why can't I stop?
Counters 1, 2 and 3 are 01 1 1
Counters 1, 2 and 3 are 01 1 2
Counters 1, 2 and 3 are 01 1 3
Counters 1, 2 and 3 are 01 1 4
Counters 1, 2 and 3 are 01 2 1
Counters 1, 2 and 3 are 01 2 2
Counters 1, 2 and 3 are 01 2 3
Counters 1, 2 and 3 are 01 2 4
Counters 1, 2 and 3 are 01 3 1
Counters 1, 2 and 3 are 01 3 2
Counters 1, 2 and 3 are 01 3 3
Counters 1, 2 and 3 are 01 3 4
Counters 1, 2 and 3 are 01 4 1
Counters 1, 2 and 3 are 01 4 2
Counters 1, 2 and 3 are 01 4 3
Counters 1, 2 and 3 are 01 4 4
Counters 1, 2 and 3 are 01 5 1
Counters 1, 2 and 3 are 01 5 2
Counters 1, 2 and 3 are 01 5 3
Counters 1, 2 and 3 are 01 5 4
Counters 1, 2 and 3 are 01 6 1
Counters 1, 2 and 3 are 01 6 2
Counters 1, 2 and 3 are 01 6 3
Counters 1, 2 and 3 are 01 6 4
Counters 1, 2 and 3 are 01 7 1
Counters 1, 2 and 3 are 01 7 2
Counters 1, 2 and 3 are 01 7 3
Counters 1, 2 and 3 are 01 7 4
Counters 1, 2 and 3 are 01 8 1
Counters 1, 2 and 3 are 01 8 2
Counters 1, 2 and 3 are 01 8 3
Counters 1, 2 and 3 are 01 8 4
Counters 1, 2 and 3 are 01 9 1
Counters 1, 2 and 3 are 01 9 2
Counters 1, 2 and 3 are 01 9 3
Counters 1, 2 and 3 are 01 9 4
Counters 1, 2 and 3 are 01 0 1
Counters 1, 2 and 3 are 01 0 2
Counters 1, 2 and 3 are 01 0 3
Counters 1, 2 and 3 are 01 0 4
Counters 1, 2 and 3 are 01 1 1
Counters 1, 2 and 3 are 01 1 2
Counters 1, 2 and 3 are 01 1 3
Counters 1, 2 and 3 are 01 1 4
< Interrupted by user>
```

Program 3

This program sometimes crashes. When it crashes, it produces the error message shown. From the two program outputs shown (one successful and one where the program crashes to produce the error message) and an examination of the program, try to work out why the program crashes. Identify the problem, and suggest a solution.

Listing 12-5. Program Crashes When Numbers Are Even; OK When Odd.

```
IDENTIFICATION DIVISION.
PROGRAM-ID. Debug3.
AUTHOR.  Michael Coughlan.
ENVIRONMENT DIVISION.
INPUT-OUTPUT SECTION.
FILE-CONTROL.
     SELECT PersonFile ASSIGN TO "PERSON.DAT"
          ORGANIZATION IS LINE SEQUENTIAL.

DATA DIVISION.
FILE SECTION.
FD PersonFile.
01 PersonRec          PIC X(10).
     88 EndOfFile     VALUE HIGH-VALUES.

WORKING-STORAGE SECTION.
01 Surname            PIC X(10).
     88 EndOfData     VALUE SPACES.
01 Quotient           PIC 9(3).
01 Rem                PIC 9(3).
01 NumberOfPeople     PIC 9(3) VALUE ZERO.

PROCEDURE DIVISION.
Begin.
     OPEN OUTPUT PersonFile
     DISPLAY "Debug3"
     DISPLAY "Enter list of Surnames."
     DISPLAY "Press RETURN after each name."
     DISPLAY "To finish press return
with no value."
     DISPLAY "This will fill Surname
with spaces"
     DISPLAY "Name -> " WITH NO ADVANCING
     ACCEPT Surname
     PERFORM GetPersons UNTIL EndOfData
     CLOSE PersonFile
```

Listing12-5 Output

```
Debug3
Enter list of Surnames.
Press RETURN after each name.
To finish press return with no value.
This will fill Surname with spaces
Name -> Power
Name -> Ryan
Name -> Smith
Name ->
Power
Ryan
Smith
Odd number of people
```

Listing12-5 Output

```
Debug3
Enter list of Surnames.
Press RETURN after each name.
To finish press return with no value.
This will fill Surname with spaces
Name -> Power
Name -> Ryan
Name -> Smith
Name -> Roddy
Name ->
Power
Ryan
Smith
Roddy
Even number of people
```

Error Message after program crash

```
148     Wrong open mode or access mode
        for write: PERSON.DAT
```

```
OPEN INPUT PersonFile
READ PersonFile
    AT END SET EndOfFile TO TRUE
END-READ
PERFORM CountPersons UNTIL EndOfFile.
CLOSE PersonFile

DIVIDE NumberOfPeople BY 2
    GIVING Quotient REMAINDER Rem

IF Rem = 0
    DISPLAY "Even number of people"
ELSE
    DISPLAY "Odd number of people"

STOP RUN.

GetPersons.
    WRITE PersonRec FROM Surname
    DISPLAY "Name -> " WITH NO ADVANCING
    ACCEPT Surname.

CountPersons.
    DISPLAY PersonRec
    ADD 1 TO NumberOfPeople
    READ PersonFile
        AT END SET EndOfFile TO TRUE
    END-READ.
```

Program 4

Sometimes this program goes into an infinite loop (does not halt). From the two program outputs shown (one where the program halts naturally and one where it has to be halted by the user) and an examination of the program, try to work out why the program sometimes does not halt. Identify the problem, and suggest a solution.

Listing 12-6. Program Sometimes Goes into an Infinite Loop

```
IDENTIFICATION DIVISION.
PROGRAM-ID. Debug4.
AUTHOR.  Michael Coughlan.

DATA DIVISION.
WORKING-STORAGE SECTION.
01 Counter1       PIC 99.
01 InNumber       PIC 9.
01 Result         PIC 999.
```

```
          Listing12-6 Output

DEBUG4.   Sometimes I just don't stop
Enter number 0-9 :--> 4
Counter1 = 01   Result = 004
Counter1 = 02   Result = 008
Counter1 = 03   Result = 012
Counter1 = 04   Result = 016
Counter1 = 05   Result = 020
Counter1 = 06   Result = 024
Counter1 = 07   Result = 028
Counter1 = 08   Result = 032
Counter1 = 09   Result = 036
Counter1 = 10   Result = 040
Back in main paragraph now
```

```
PROCEDURE DIVISION.
Begin.
    DISPLAY "DEBUG4.  Sometimes I just don't stop"
    DISPLAY "Enter number 0-9 :--> " WITH NO ADVANCING
    ACCEPT InNumber
    PERFORM EternalLooping
        VARYING Counter1 FROM 1 BY 1
        UNTIL Counter1 GREATER THAN 10

    DISPLAY "Back in main paragraph now"
    STOP RUN.

EternalLooping.
    COMPUTE Result = InNumber * Counter1
    IF Result > 60
        MOVE 99 TO Counter1
    END-IF
    DISPLAY "Counter1 = " Counter1 "  Result = " Result.
```

```
Listing12-6 Output

DEBUG4.   Sometimes I just don't stop
Enter number 0-9 :--> 7
Counter1 = 01   Result = 007
Counter1 = 02   Result = 014
Counter1 = 03   Result = 021
Counter1 = 04   Result = 028
Counter1 = 05   Result = 035
Counter1 = 06   Result = 042
Counter1 = 07   Result = 049
Counter1 = 08   Result = 056
Counter1 = 99   Result = 063
Counter1 = 00   Result = 000
Counter1 = 01   Result = 007
Counter1 = 02   Result = 014
Counter1 = 03   Result = 021
Counter1 = 04   Result = 028
Counter1 = 05   Result = 035
Counter1 = 06   Result = 042
Counter1 = 07   Result = 049
Counter1 = 08   Result = 056
Counter1 = 99   Result = 063
Counter1 = 00   Result = 000
Counter1 = 01   Result = 007
Counter1 = 02   Result = 014
Counter1 = 03   Result = 021
Counter1 = 04   Result = 028
         < Interrupted by user>
```

LANGUAGE KNOWLEDGE EXERCISES—ANSWERS

Program 1
Problem Cause

The problem here is that Counter1 and Counter2 go negative but are described as PIC 99—a description that only allows positive values. The problem with Counter1 is masked by the problem with Counter2. You can see the effect of the problem with Counter2 in the program output fragment shown in Figure 12-16. When Counter2 has a value of 03, the next value it should take is -1; but because Counter2 is described as PIC 99, it cannot hold a negative value. This means the sign is lost, and instead of -1, the value of Counter2 is 1. Therefore, Counter2 never reaches its terminating value, and the loop never terminates.

```
PERFORM EternalLooping VARYING Counter1
        FROM 13 BY -5 UNTIL Counter1 LESS THAN 2
        AFTER Counter2 FROM 15 BY -4
            UNTIL Counter2 LESS THAN 1
        AFTER Counter3 FROM 1 BY 1
            UNTIL Counter3 GREATER THAN 5
```

```
Counters 1, 2 and 3 are -> 13 03 4
Counters 1, 2 and 3 are -> 13 03 5
Counters 1, 2 and 3 are -> 13 01 1
Counters 1, 2 and 3 are -> 13 01 2
Counters 1, 2 and 3 are -> 13 01 3
Counters 1, 2 and 3 are -> 13 01 4
Counters 1, 2 and 3 are -> 13 01 5
Counters 1, 2 and 3 are -> 13 03 1
Counters 1, 2 and 3 are -> 13 03 2
Counters 1, 2 and 3 are -> 13 03 3
```

Figure 12-16. Fragment of output from Listing 12-3 highlighting the problem area

Problem Solution

The solution to the problem is to describe Counter1 and Counter2 as PIC S99.

Program 2
Problem Cause

The problem here is that Counter2 is described as PIC 9. You can see the problem by examining the flowchart in Figure 12-17.

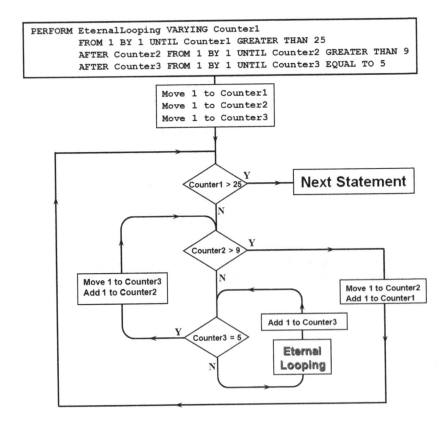

Figure 12-17. Flowchart showing how the three-counter PERFORM..VARYING works

Suppose the program is at the point where Counter2 has a value of 9 and Counter3 has a value of 5. At this point the condition Counter3 = 5 is satisfied, and Counter3 is reset to 1 while Counter2 is incremented, making it equal to 10. Because Counter2 is described as PIC 9, there is only room for one digit, so the 1 is truncated, leaving Counter2 with a value of 0. When the Counter2 > 9 condition is tested, it is not satisfied, and the loop never ends.

Problem Solution

The solution to the problem is to describe Counter2 as PIC 99.

Program 3
Problem Cause

The problem here is that the IF before the STOP RUN does not have an explicit terminator. This means the scope of the IF is terminated by the period that follows the STOP RUN; and this means the scope of the ELSE branch of the IF includes the STOP RUN:

```
DIVIDE NumberOfPeople BY 2
    GIVING Quotient REMAINDER Rem

IF Rem = 0
    DISPLAY "Even number of people"
ELSE
    DISPLAY "Odd number of people"

STOP RUN.

GetPersons.
   WRITE PersonRec FROM Surname
   DISPLAY "Name -> " WITH NO ADVANCING
   ACCEPT Surname.
```

Failing to specify the scope of the IF with an explicit terminator has the following effect. When there is an odd number of people, the ELSE branch is taken, the STOP RUN is executed, and the program stops normally; but when there is an even number of people, the ELSE branch is not taken, the STOP RUN is not executed, and control falls into the GetPersons paragraph where it tries to write to the closed PersonFile. This write attempt crashes the program and produces the error message.

Problem Solution

Add an explicit scope delimiter to the IF statement:

```
IF Rem = 0
    DISPLAY "Even number of people"
ELSE
    DISPLAY "Odd number of people"
END-IF

STOP RUN.
```

Program 4
Problem Cause

The problem with this program is that the programmer tries to modify the PERFORM..VARYING counter variable Counter1 in order to force the loop to terminate prematurely. Unfortunately, the programmer has not consulted the flowchart shown in Figure 12-18. That flowchart shows that as control exits, the paragraph Counter1 is incremented. Because Counter1 has been given a value of 99 in the paragraph, the increment brings it to 100. But Counter1 is described as PIC 99 and only has room for two digits. This means the 1 is truncated, leaving Counter1 with a value of 00. Because the terminating condition Counter1 > 10 has not been satisfied, the loop will not terminate.

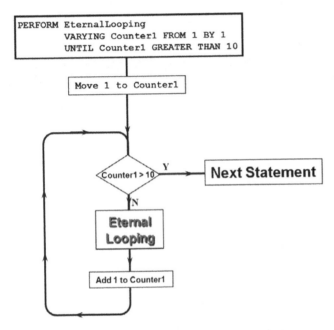

Figure 12-18. *Flowchart showing how the single-counter PERFORM..VARYING works*

Problem Solution

A simple solution is to change the description of Counter1 to PIC 999. A more complex solution would require you rewrite the program so that it does not require the counting variable to be changed in the loop. When you use a construct such as the PERFORM..VARYING, you make a contract with the reader that construct will operate in the normal way and that the counting variable will take the values specified in the PERFORM. If you break that contract, you create uncertainty in the mind of the reader not only for this loop but also for all the loops in the program. Now the reader has to scrutinize each one to make sure they work as expected.

References

1. Vorontsov M. Using double/long vs. BigDecimal for monetary calculations. 2013 Feb. http://java-performance.info/bigdecimal-vs-double-in-financial-calculations/
2. IBM. Decimal arithmetic FAQ. 2008. http://speleotrove.com/decimal/decifaq.html

CHAPTER 13

Searching Tabular Data

In previous chapters, you saw how to create and use tabular data. This chapter returns to the issue of processing tabular data to examine the operation of the SEARCH and SEARCH ALL verbs. SEARCH is used for linear searches, and SEARCH ALL is used for binary searches.

The chapter begins by noting that when you use SEARCH or SEARCH ALL, the table they are searching must have an associated table index. You learn the metalanguage for the INDEXED BY clause used to specify the table index and explore the nature of the index data item. Because index data items can't be manipulated by ordinary COBOL verbs, the chapter introduces the versions of the SET verb that are used to assign, increment, and decrement table index values.

With the background material covered, you see how the SEARCH verb operates on single-dimension tables and work through an example. The chapter highlights the limitations of the SEARCH with regard to searching multidimensional tables and suggests, and demonstrates, a solution.

The SEARCH verb searches a table serially. To search a table using a binary search, you must use SEARCH ALL. You learn that the SEARCH ALL can only work correctly if the table is ordered, and the chapter discusses the extension to the OCCURS clause that allows you to identify the data item on which the table is ordered. You see how a binary search works along with an example of the operation of SEARCH ALL.

Finally, the chapter introduces the notion of variable-length tables. Although variable-length tables are not truly dynamic, they are still useful, because the variable size limitations are obeyed by COBOL verbs such as the SEARCH and SEARCH ALL. You see this with an example program.

SEARCHING Tabular Data

The task of searching a table to determine whether it contains a particular value is a common operation. The method used to search a table depends heavily on the way the values are organized in the table. If the values are not ordered, then the only strategy available is a linear search. A linear search starts at the first element and then examines each succeeding element until the item is found or until the end of the table is reached (item not found). If the values are ordered, then you have the option of using either a linear search or a binary search. A binary search works by dividing the table in half and determining whether the item sought is in the top half of the table or the bottom half. This process continues until the item is found or it is determined that the item is not in the table.

COBOL has special verbs that let you search tables using either strategy. The SEARCH verb is used for linear searches, and the SEARCH ALL verb is used for binary searches.

Searching Using SEARCH and SEARCH ALL

One advantage of using SEARCH or SEARCH ALL rather than a handcrafted search is that because these are specialized instructions, their operation can be optimized. Part of that optimization involves creating a special subscript to be used when searching the table. You create this special subscript using an extension to the OCCURS clause called the INDEXED BY clause.

INDEXED BY Clause

Before you can use SEARCH or SEARCH ALL to search a table, you must define the table as having an index item associated with it. Using an index makes the searching more efficient. Because the index is linked to a particular table, the compiler—taking into account the size of the table—can choose the most efficient representation possible for the index. This speeds up the search.

The index is specified by the IndexName given in an INDEXED BY clause attached to the OCCURS clause. The extended OCCURS clause metalanguage is shown in Figure 13-1.

<u>OCCURS</u> TableSize# 1 TIMES
[<u>INDEXED</u> BY IndexName ...]

Figure 13-1. *OCCURS metalanguage, including the INDEXED BY clause*

The following are some things to consider about Figure 13-1:

- The index defined in a table declaration is associated with that table and is the subscript that SEARCH or SEARCH ALL uses to access the table.

- The only entry that needs to be made for an IndexName is to use it in an INDEXED BY phrase. It does not require a PICTURE clause, because the compiler handles its declaration automatically.

- Because of its special binary representation, the table index cannot be displayed, and its value cannot be manipulated using ordinary COBOL verbs such as MOVE, ADD, and SUBTRACT. Only four COBOL verbs can change the value of a table index: SEARCH, SEARCH ALL, PERFORM..VARYING, and SET.

- Index names must be unique.

- An index is only valid for the table to which it is bound. An index bound to one table cannot be used with another table.

Using SET to Manipulate the Table Index

A table index is a special data item. It has no PICTURE clause, it is associated with a particular table, and the compiler defines the index using the most computationally efficient representation possible. Because of its special binary representation, the table index cannot be displayed and can only be assigned a value, or have its value assigned, by the SET verb. Similarly, the SET verb must be used to increment or decrement the value of an index item.

The metalanguage for the formats of the SET verb that are used to manipulate the value of an index item are given in Figure 13-2.

$$\underline{SET}\ \left\{\begin{matrix} \text{IndexName} \\ \text{Identifier\#\$} \end{matrix}\right\}\ ...\ \underline{TO}\ \left\{\begin{matrix} \text{IndexName} \\ \text{DataItem\#\$il} \end{matrix}\right\}$$

$$\underline{SET}\ \{\text{IndexName}\}...\left\{\begin{matrix} \underline{UP} \\ \underline{DOWN} \end{matrix}\right\}\ \underline{BY}\ \left\{\begin{matrix} \text{IncrementVal\# il} \\ \text{DecrementVal\# il} \end{matrix}\right\}$$

Figure 13-2. *Metalanguage for SET formats used to manipulate index values*

The SEARCH Verb

When the values in a table are not ordered, the only searching strategy available is a linear search. You start at the first element and then search through the table serially, element by element, until either you find the item you seek or you reach the end of the table. You use the SEARCH verb when you want to search a table serially. The metalanguage for the SEARCH verb is given in Figure 13-3.

$$\underline{\text{SEARCH}} \quad \text{TableName} \left[\underline{\text{VARYING}} \left\{ \begin{array}{l} \text{Indentifier\#}\,i \\ \text{IndexItem} \end{array} \right\} \right]$$

$$\left[\text{AT}\ \underline{\text{END}}\ \text{StatementBlock} \right]$$

$$\left\{ \underline{\text{WHEN}}\ \text{Condition} \left\{ \begin{array}{l} \text{StatementBlock} \\ \underline{\text{NEXT SENTENCE}} \end{array} \right\} \right\} \cdots$$

$$\underline{\text{END} - \text{SEARCH}}$$

Figure 13-3. *Metalanguage for the SEARCH verb*

Note the following about Figure 13-3:

- Before you can use SEARCH to search TableName, you must define a table index for the table in an INDEXED BY clause attached to the OCCURS clause that defines the table. The index specified in the INDEXED BY clause of TableName is the controlling index (subscript) of SEARCH. The controlling index controls the submission of the elements, or element items, for examination by the WHEN phrase of SEARCH. A SEARCH can have only one controlling index.

- TableName must identify a data item in the table hierarchy with both OCCURS and INDEXED BY clauses.

- SEARCH searches a table serially, starting at the element pointed to by the table index. This means the table index is under your control.

- Because the table index is under your control, before SEARCH executes you must SET the table index to point to one of the elements in the table (usually the first element).

- When SEARCH executes, the table index cannot have a value less than one or greater than the size of the table, or SEARCH will immediately terminate.

- The VARYING phrase is used for a number of purposes:

    - When more than one index is attached to the table (note the ellipsis after IndexName in Figure 13-1), IndexItem identifies the IndexName that SEARCH uses as the table index.

    - When IndexItem is an index attached to another table or is a data item defined as USAGE IS INDEX, SEARCH increments the IndexItem at the same time and by the same amount as the table index.

    - When a non-index data item is used, SEARCH increments the data item by one each time it increments the table index.

- If AT END is specified and the index is incremented beyond the highest legal occurrence for the table (that is, the item has not been found), then the statement following AT END is executed and SEARCH terminates.

- The WHEN conditions attached to SEARCH are evaluated in turn. As soon as one is true, the statements following the WHEN phrase are executed, SEARCH ends, and the table index remains set at the value it had when the condition was satisfied.

SEARCH Examples

This section contains a number of examples that show how SEARCH is used. The section starts with a simple example by way of introduction and then ratchets up the complexity.

Letter Position Example

The example shown in Listing 13-1 uses SEARCH to discover the alphabet position of a letter entered by the user.

Listing 13-1. Finding the Position of a Letter in the Alphabet

```
IDENTIFICATION DIVISION.
PROGRAM-ID.  Listing13-1.
AUTHOR.  Michael Coughlan.
DATA DIVISION.
WORKING-STORAGE SECTION.
01 LetterTable.
   02 TableValues.
      03 FILLER PIC X(13)
         VALUE "ABCDEFGHIJKLM".
      03 FILLER PIC X(13)
         VALUE "NOPQRSTUVWXYZ".
   02 FILLER REDEFINES TableValues.
      03 Letter PIC X OCCURS 26 TIMES
                     INDEXED BY LetterIdx.

01 IdxValue  PIC 99 VALUE ZEROS.

01 LetterIn  PIC X.
   88 ValidLetter VALUE "A" THRU "Z".

PROCEDURE DIVISION.
FindAlphabetLetterPosition.
   PERFORM WITH TEST AFTER UNTIL ValidLetter
      DISPLAY "Enter an uppercase letter please - " WITH NO ADVANCING
      ACCEPT LetterIn
   END-PERFORM
   SET LetterIdx TO 1
   SEARCH Letter
      WHEN Letter(LetterIdx) = LetterIn
         SET IdxValue TO LetterIdx
         DISPLAY LetterIn, " is in position ", IdxValue
   END-SEARCH
   STOP RUN.
```

```
                  Listing13-1 Output
Enter an uppercase letter please - Q
Q is in position 17
```

I use a loop to get a valid uppercase letter from the user. Because the loop will exit only when a valid letter has been entered, the AT END clause is not used in SEARCH because the letter is always found in the table.

LetterIdx is the table index. It is automatically incremented by SEARCH. Note how it is associated with the table by means of the INDEXED BY clause.

Before SEARCH executes, the SET verb is used to set the table index (LetterIdx) to the position in the table where I want SEARCH to start.

Finally, because LetterIdx is a special binary index item, you can't display its value directly. So IdxValue, a numeric data item whose value can be displayed, is set to value of LetterIdx, and then IdxValue is displayed.

American States Example

The program in Listing 13-2 uses SEARCH to interrogate a table of American states, their ISO two-letter codes, and their capitals. The user is asked to choose the state code, state name, or state capital as their search term. Whichever is chosen, the program displays the other two. For instance, if the user chooses to search on the state code, then the program displays the state name and the state capital. If the state name is chosen, then the program displays the state code and state capital.

Listing 13-2. Given One of StateCode, StateName, or StateCapital, Display the Other Two

```
IDENTIFICATION DIVISION.
PROGRAM-ID.  Listing13-2.
AUTHOR.  Michael Coughlan.
DATA DIVISION.
WORKING-STORAGE SECTION.
01 StatesTable.
    02 StateValues.
        03 FILLER PIC X(60)
           VALUE "ALAlabama       Montgomery   AKAlaska       Juneau".
        03 FILLER PIC X(60)
           VALUE "AZArizona       Phoenix      ARArkansas     Little Rock".
        03 FILLER PIC X(60)
           VALUE "CACalifornia    Sacramento   COColorado     Denver".
        03 FILLER PIC X(60)
           VALUE "CTConnecticut   Hartford     DEDelaware     Dover".
        03 FILLER PIC X(60)
           VALUE "FLFlorida       Tallahassee  GAGeorgia      Atlanta".
        03 FILLER PIC X(60)
           VALUE "HIHawaii        Honolulu     IDIdaho        Boise".
        03 FILLER PIC X(60)
           VALUE "ILIllinois      Springfield  INIndiana      Indianapolis".
        03 FILLER PIC X(60)
           VALUE "IAIowa          Des Moines   KSKansas       Topeka".
        03 FILLER PIC X(60)
           VALUE "KYKentucky      Frankfort    LALouisiana    Baton Rouge".
        03 FILLER PIC X(60)
           VALUE "MEMaine         Augusta      MDMaryland     Annapolis".
        03 FILLER PIC X(60)
           VALUE "MAMassachusetts Boston       MIMichigan     Lansing".
        03 FILLER PIC X(60)
           VALUE "MNMinnesota     Saint Paul   MSMississippi  Jackson".
        03 FILLER PIC X(60)
           VALUE "MOMissouri      Jefferson CityMTMontana      Helena".
```

```
        03 FILLER PIC X(60)
            VALUE "NENebraska      Lincoln      NVNevada        Carson City".
        03 FILLER PIC X(60)
            VALUE "NHNew Hampshire Concord      NJNew Jersey    Trenton".
        03 FILLER PIC X(60)
            VALUE "NMNew Mexico    Santa Fe     NYNew York      Albany".
        03 FILLER PIC X(60)
            VALUE "NCNorth CarolinaRaleigh      NDNorth Dakota  Bismarck".
        03 FILLER PIC X(60)
            VALUE "OHOhio          Columbus     OKOklahoma      Oklahoma City".
        03 FILLER PIC X(60)
            VALUE "OROregon        Salem        PAPennsylvania  Harrisburg".
        03 FILLER PIC X(60)
            VALUE "RIRhode Island  Providence   SCSouth CarolinaColumbia".
        03 FILLER PIC X(60)
            VALUE "SDSouth Dakota  Pierre       TNTennessee     Nashville".
        03 FILLER PIC X(60)
            VALUE "TXTexas         Austin       UTUtah          Salt Lake City".
        03 FILLER PIC X(60)
            VALUE "VTVermont       Montpelier   VAVirginia      Richmond".
        03 FILLER PIC X(60)
            VALUE "WAWashington    Olympia      WVWest Virginia Charleston".
        03 FILLER PIC X(60)
            VALUE "WIWisconsin     Madison      WYWyoming       Cheyenne".
    02 FILLER REDEFINES StateValues.
        03 State OCCURS 50 TIMES
                INDEXED BY StateIdx.
            04 StateCode    PIC XX.
            04 StateName    PIC X(14).
            04 StateCapital PIC X(14).

01 StateNameIn          PIC X(14).

01 StateCapitalIn       PIC X(14).

01 StateCodeIn          PIC XX.

01 SearchChoice         PIC 9 VALUE ZERO.
    88 ValidSearchChoice VALUES 1, 2, 3, 4.
    88 EndOfInput        VALUE 4.

PROCEDURE DIVISION.
Begin.
    PERFORM WITH TEST AFTER UNTIL EndOfInput
        PERFORM WITH TEST AFTER UNTIL ValidSearchChoice
            DISPLAY SPACES
            DISPLAY "Search by StateCode (1), StateName (2), StateCapital (3), STOP (4) - "
                    WITH NO ADVANCING
            ACCEPT SearchChoice
        END-PERFORM
```

```
        SET StateIdx TO 1
        EVALUATE SearchChoice
            WHEN 1 PERFORM GetNameAndCapital
            WHEN 2 PERFORM GetCodeAndCapital
            WHEN 3 PERFORM GetCodeAndName
        END-EVALUATE
    END-PERFORM
    STOP RUN.


GetNameAndCapital.
    DISPLAY "Enter the two letter State Code - " WITH NO ADVANCING
    ACCEPT StateCodeIn
    MOVE FUNCTION UPPER-CASE(StateCodeIn) TO StateCodeIn
    SEARCH State
        AT END DISPLAY "State code " StateCodeIn " does not exist"
        WHEN StateCode(StateIdx) = StateCodeIn
            DISPLAY "State Name    = " StateName(StateIdx)
            DISPLAY "State Capital = " StateCapital(StateIdx)
    END-SEARCH.


GetCodeAndCapital.
    DISPLAY "Enter the State Name - " WITH NO ADVANCING
    ACCEPT StateNameIn
    SEARCH State
        AT END DISPLAY "State Name " StateNameIn " does not exist"
        WHEN FUNCTION UPPER-CASE(StateName(StateIdx)) = FUNCTION UPPER-CASE(StateNameIn)
            DISPLAY "State Code    = " StateCode(StateIdx)
            DISPLAY "State Capital = " StateCapital(StateIdx)
    END-SEARCH.


GetCodeAndName.
    DISPLAY "Enter the State Capital - " WITH NO ADVANCING
    ACCEPT StateCapitalIn
    SEARCH State
        AT END DISPLAY "State capital " StateCapitalIn " does not exist"
        WHEN FUNCTION UPPER-CASE(StateCapital(StateIdx)) = FUNCTION UPPER-CASE(StateCapitalIn)
            DISPLAY "State Code = " StateCode(StateIdx)
            DISPLAY "State Name = " StateName(StateIdx)
    END-SEARCH.
```

Listing13-2 Output

```
Search by StateCode (1), StateName (2), StateCapital (3), STOP (4) - 3
Enter the State Capital - deS mOines
State Code = IA
State Name = Iowa


Search by StateCode (1), StateName (2), StateCapital (3), STOP (4) - 2
Enter the State Name - iowA
State Code   = IA
State Capital = Des Moines


Search by StateCode (1), StateName (2), StateCapital (3), STOP (4) - 1
Enter the two letter State Code - ia
State Name   = Iowa
State Capital = Des Moines


Search by StateCode (1), StateName (2), StateCapital (3), STOP (4) - 3
Enter the State Capital - saint paul
State Code = MN
State Name = Minnesota


Search by StateCode (1), StateName (2), StateCapital (3), STOP (4) - 4
```

The program contains a table prefilled with the state codes, state names, and state capitals of the American states. The user provides any one of the three (state code, state name, or state capital), and SEARCH returns the other two from the table.

Most of the program is straightforward and doesn't require any explanation. However, each of the three paragraphs GetNameAndCapital, GetCodeAndCapital, and GetCodeAndName makes use of *intrinsic functions*. You have not encountered intrinsic functions yet. You won't examine them formally until chapter 15, but I have introduced them here by way of a preview.

A *function* is a closed subroutine (block of code) that substitutes a returned value for its invocation. In Java, a method with a non-void return value type is a function. COBOL does not have user-defined functions, but it does have a number of built-in system functions called intrinsic functions.

The problem with using user input for comparison purposes is that you have to compare like with like. *Alaska* is not the same as *alaska* or *ALASKA* or *aLaska*. In GetCodeAndCapital and GetCodeAndName, the intrinsic function UPPER-CASE is used to convert the table data item and the data entered by the user to uppercase to ensure that the program is comparing like with like. In the comparison, the intrinsic function invocation is replaced by the returned function result, and then the comparison is done. For instance, an IF statement such as

```
IF FUNCTION UPPER-CASE("rEdMond") = FUNCTION UPPER-CASE("REDmond")
```

becomes

```
IF "REDMOND" = "REDMOND"
```

In GetNameAndCapital, I could have used the intrinsic function the same way as in GetCodeAndCapital and GetCodeAndName; but because the state code is already in uppercase, I took the opportunity to show another way of using intrinsic functions. In this paragraph, I use the intrinsic function to convert the user input to uppercase by moving the converted input data back into the input data item StateCodeIn.

Searching Multidimensional Tables

In the notes on SEARCH, I observed that SEARCH can have only one controlling index (the IndexName specified in the INDEXED BY phrase attached to the table being searched). Because SEARCH can have only one controlling index, SEARCH can only be used to search a single dimension of a table at a time. If the table to be searched is multidimensional, then *you* must control the indexes of the other dimensions.

Listing 13-3 is a small program that demonstrates how to use SEARCH to search a two-dimensional table. The program sets Appointment(3, 2) and Location(3, 2) to "Peter's Wedding" and "Saint John's Church". SEARCH is then used to search the appointments timetable for the appointment details of "Peter's Wedding". When found, these details are displayed.

Listing 13-3. Program Demonstrating How to Search a Two-Dimensional Table

```
IDENTIFICATION DIVISION.
PROGRAM-ID. Listing13-3.
AUTHOR. Michael Coughlan.
DATA DIVISION.
WORKING-STORAGE SECTION.
01 MyTimeTable.
    02 DayOfApp OCCURS 5 TIMES INDEXED BY DayIdx.
        03 HourOfApp OCCURS 9 TIMES INDEXED BY HourIdx.
            04 Appointment     PIC X(15).
            04 Location        PIC X(20).

01 AppointmentType         PIC X(15).

01 DaySub                  PIC 9.
01 HourSub                 PIC 9.

01 FILLER                  PIC 9 VALUE ZERO.
    88 AppointmentNotFound     VALUE ZERO.
    88 AppointmentFound        VALUE 1.

01 DayValues VALUE "MonTueWedThuFri".
    02 DayName    PIC XXX OCCURS 5 TIMES.

01 TimeValues   VALUE " 9:0010:0011:0012:0013:0014:0015:0016:0017:00".
    02 TimeValue    PIC X(5) OCCURS 9 TIMES.

PROCEDURE DIVISION.
Begin.
    MOVE "Peter's Wedding" TO AppointmentType, Appointment(2, 3)
    MOVE "Saint John's Church" TO Location(2, 3)
    SET DayIdx TO 1.
    PERFORM UNTIL AppointmentFound OR DayIdx > 5
      SET HourIdx TO 1
      SEARCH HourOfApp
        AT END SET DayIdx UP BY 1
        WHEN AppointmentType = Appointment(DayIdx, HourIdx)
            SET AppointmentFound TO TRUE
            SET HourSub TO HourIdx
            SET DaySub TO DayIdx
```

```
Listing13-3 Output

Peter's Wedding is on Tue
at 11:00 in Saint John's Church
```

```
            DISPLAY AppointmentType " is on " DayName(DaySub)
            DISPLAY "at " TimeValue(HourSub) " in " Location(DayIdx, HourIdx)
    END-SEARCH
  END-PERFORM
  IF AppointmentNotFound
     DISPLAY "Appointment " AppointmentType " was not in the timetable"
  END-IF
  STOP RUN.
```

The table used to hold the appointment timetable is described in Example 13-1 and is graphically depicted in Figure 13-4.

Example 13-1. Declarations for the Table Used to Record Appointments

```
01 MyTimeTable.
   02 DayOfApp OCCURS 5 TIMES INDEXED BY DayIdx.
      03 HourOfApp OCCURS 9 TIMES INDEXED BY HourIdx.
         04 Appointment    PIC X(15) VALUE SPACES.
         04 Location        PIC X(20) VALUE SPACES.
```

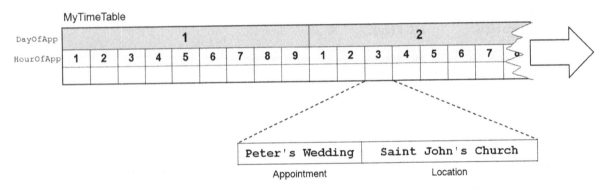

Figure 13-4. *Graphical depiction of the two-dimensional table* MyTimeTable

As you can see by examining Figure 13-4, in this two-dimensional table each day element consists of a table of hour elements. The table of hour elements is the SEARCH target. In most searches of a multidimensional table, the SEARCH target is the lowest data item in the hierarchy that contains both a OCCURS and an INDEXED BY clause. In this case, HourOfApp is the SEARCH target. In SEARCH, the controlling index is the item attached to the target table by an INDEXED BY clause. In this case, it is HourIdx.

Because SEARCH can have only one controlling index, you have to control the other. In this program, the SET verb is used to control the value in DayIdx, and HourIdx is under the control of SEARCH.

When SEARCH executes, it searches whichever of the HourOfApp tables is pointed to by DayIdx. If the appointment is not found, AT END activates, DayIdx is incremented, and SEARCH is executed again, this time examining the HourOfApp table in the next DayOfApp element. If the appointment is found, WHEN activates, and the HourIdx and DayIdx values are used to display the time (24-hour format) and day of the appointment. DayName and TimeValue are set up using the facility introduced in the ANS 85 version of COBOL that allows you to create prefilled tables without using the REDEFINES clause.

Searching the First Dimension of a Two-Dimensional Table

Listing 13-3 uses SEARCH to search the second dimension of the two-dimensional table. It does not normally make sense to search the first dimension of a two-dimensional table, because as you can see from Figure 13-4, each element at that level contains a table, not a discrete value. Sometimes, though, you need to perform such a search.

Suppose you have a two-dimensional table that records the number of jeans sold in three different colors in 150 shops. Suppose for each group of jeans sales totals, you also record the shop name. The table to record this information is described in Example 13-2 and is graphically depicted in Figure 13-5.

Example 13-2. Description of JeansSalesTable

```
01 JeansSalesTable.
   02 Shop OCCURS 150 TIMES INDEXED BY ShopIdx.
      03 ShopName        PIC X(15).
      03 JeansColor OCCURS 3 TIMES INDEXED BY ColorIdx.
         04 TotalSold       PIC 9(5).
```

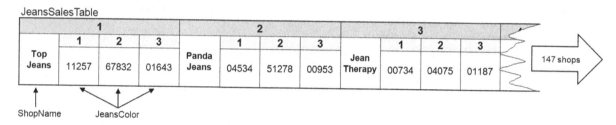

Figure 13-5. Graphical depiction of JeansSalesTable

Listing 13-4 is a simple program that shows how to use SEARCH to search the first dimension of a two-dimensional table. To keep the program simple, I haven't filled the table with all the values shown in Figure 13-5; only the element Shop(3) is filled with data values.

Listing 13-4. Searching the First Dimension of a Two-Dimensional Table

```
IDENTIFICATION DIVISION.
PROGRAM-ID. Listing13-4.
AUTHOR. Michael Coughlan.
DATA DIVISION.
WORKING-STORAGE SECTION.
01 JeansSalesTable.
   02 Shop OCCURS 150 TIMES INDEXED BY ShopIdx.
      03 ShopName        PIC X(15) VALUE SPACES.
      03 JeansColor OCCURS 3 TIMES.
         04 TotalSold     PIC 9(5)  VALUE ZEROS.

01 ShopQuery            PIC X(15).

01 PrnWhiteJeans.
   02 PrnWhiteTotal     PIC ZZ,ZZ9.
   02 FILLER            PIC X(12) VALUE " white jeans".
```

```
01 PrnBlueJeans.
    02 PrnBlueTotal      PIC ZZ,ZZ9.
    02 FILLER            PIC X(12) VALUE " blue  jeans".

01 PrnBlackJeans.
    02 PrnBlackTotal     PIC ZZ,ZZ9.
    02 FILLER            PIC X(12) VALUE " black jeans".

PROCEDURE DIVISION.
Begin.
    MOVE "Jean Therapy" TO ShopName(3), ShopQuery
    MOVE 00734 TO TotalSold(3, 1)
    MOVE 04075 TO TotalSold(3, 2)
    MOVE 01187 TO TotalSold(3, 3)

    SET ShopIdx TO 1
    SEARCH Shop
       AT END Display "Shop not found"
       WHEN ShopName(ShopIdx) = ShopQuery
           MOVE TotalSold(ShopIdx, 1) TO PrnWhiteTotal
           MOVE TotalSold(ShopIdx, 2) TO PrnBlueTotal
           MOVE TotalSold(ShopIdx, 3) TO PrnBlackTotal
           DISPLAY "Sold by " ShopQuery
           DISPLAY PrnWhiteJeans
           DISPLAY PrnBlueJeans
           DISPLAY PrnBlackJeans
    END-SEARCH
    STOP RUN.
```

Listing13-4 Output
Sold by Jean Therapy
734 white jeans
4,075 blue jeans
1,187 black jeans

The SEARCH ALL Verb

As I noted earlier in this chapter, the method used to search a table depends heavily on the way the values are organized in the table. If the values are not ordered, then the only strategy available is a linear search. If the values are ordered, then you have the option of using either a linear search or a binary search. This section introduces SEARCH All, the COBOL verb used for binary searches.

Because SEARCH ALL implements a binary search, it only works on an ordered table. The table must be ordered on the values in the element or, where the element is a group item, on a data item within the element. The item on which the table is ordered is known as the *key field* and is identified using the KEY IS phrase in the table declaration.

KEY IS Clause

The KEY IS clause is used to identify the data item on which the table to be searched is ordered. If you want to search a table using SEARCH ALL, the table declaration must contain a KEY IS phrase. The OCCURS metalanguage that includes the KEY IS clause is given in Figure 13-6.

OCURS TableSize#1 TIMES

$$\begin{bmatrix} \begin{cases} \underline{\text{ASCENDING}} \\ \underline{\text{DESCENDING}} \end{cases} \text{KEY IS TableItem\$\#i} \dots \end{bmatrix} \dots$$

$\begin{bmatrix} \underline{\text{INDEXED}} \text{ BY IndexName} \dots \end{bmatrix}$

Figure 13-6. *OCCURS metalanguage including the KEY IS clause*

How a Binary Search Works

I have mentioned that SEARCH ALL implements a binary search. Before discussing SEARCH ALL itself, let's take the time to refresh your memory about how a binary search works.

A binary search works by repeatedly dividing the search area into a top half and a bottom half, deciding which half contains the required item, and making that half the new search area. The search continues halving the search area like this until the required item is found or the search discovers that the item is not in the table.

The algorithm for a binary search is given in Example 13-3.

Example 13-3. Binary Search Algorithm

```
PERFORM UNTIL ItemFound OR ItemNotInTable
   COMPUTE Middle = (Lower + Upper) / 2
   EVALUATE TRUE
      WHEN Lower > Upper THEN SET ItemNotInTable TO TRUE
      WHEN KeyField(Middle) < SearchItem THEN Lower = Middle + 1
      WHEN KeyField(Middle) > SearchItem THEN Upper = Middle -1
      WHEN KeyField(Middle) = SearchItem THEN SET ItemFound TO TRUE
   END-EVALUATE
END-PERFORM
```

To illustrate how this algorithm works, let's consider it in the context of a table containing the letters of the alphabet. The table holding the letters is described in Example 13-4, and its representation in memory is illustrated pictorially in Figure 13-7.

Example 13-4. Table Prefilled with the Letters of the Alphabet

```
01  LetterTable.
    02 LetterValues.
       03 FILLER PIC X(13)
          VALUE "ABCDEFGHIJKLM".
       03 FILLER PIC X(13)
          VALUE "NOPQRSTUVWXYZ".
    02 FILLER REDEFINES LetterValues.
       03 Letter PIC X OCCURS 26 TIMES
                     ASCENDING KEY IS Letter
                     INDEXED BY LetterIdx.
```

LetterTable

Figure 13-7. *Table containing the letters of the alphabet*

Suppose you want to search LetterTable to find the position of the letter *R*. The general binary search algorithm introduced in Example 13-3 can be made more specific to the problem, as shown in Example 13-5. Figure 13-8 shows a succession of diagrams illustrating the application of this algorithm.

Example 13-5. Binary Search to Find the Letter R

```
PERFORM UNTIL ItemFound OR ItemNotInTable
    COMPUTE Middle = (Lower + Upper) / 2
    EVALUATE TRUE
        WHEN Lower > Upper THEN SET ItemNotInTable TO TRUE
        WHEN Letter(Middle) < "R" THEN Lower = Middle + 1
        WHEN Letter(Middle) > "R"  THEN Upper = Middle -1
        WHEN Letter(Middle) = "R"  THEN SET ItemFound TO TRUE
    END-EVALUATE
END-PERFORM
```

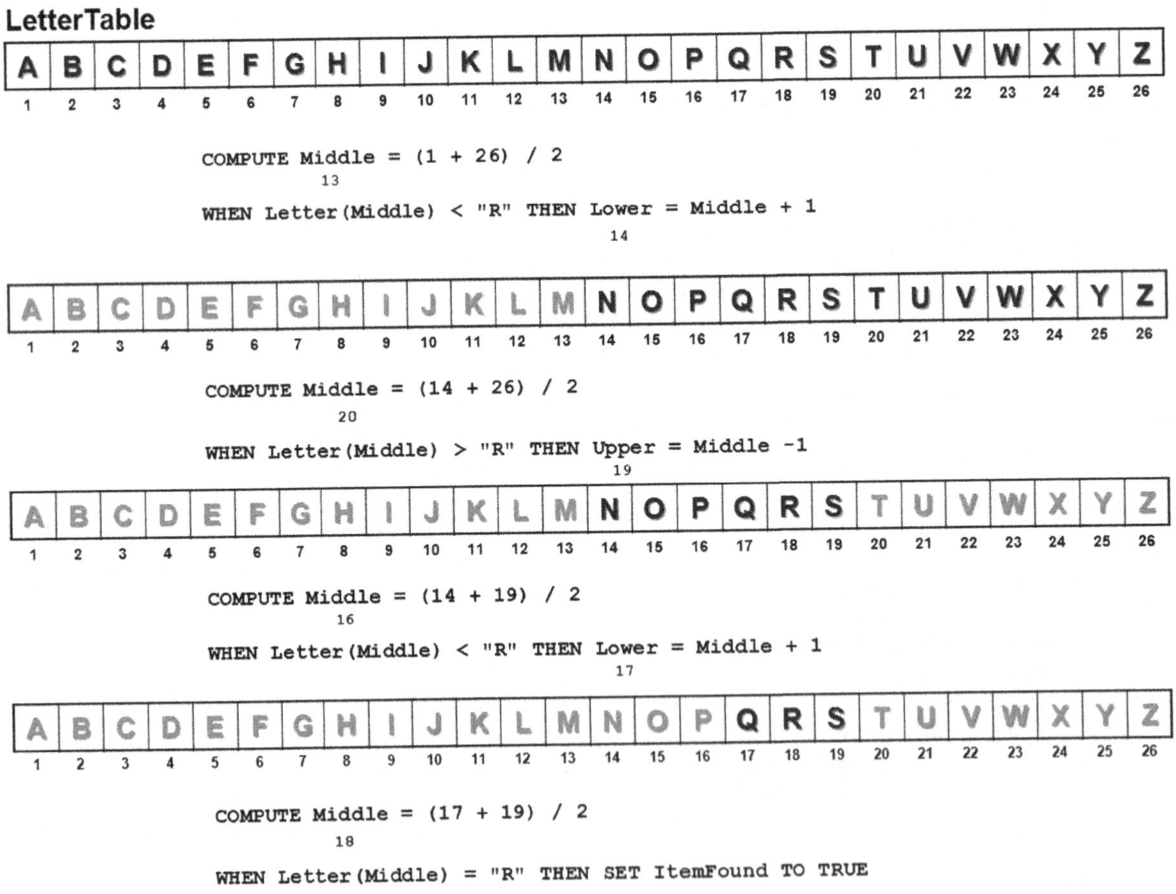

LetterTable

Figure 13-8. *Finding the letter R using a binary search*

SEARCH ALL

The metalanguage for SEARCH ALL is given in Figure 13-9.

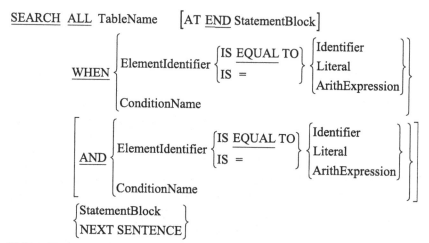

END – SEARCH

Figure 13-9. *Metalanguage for SEARCH ALL*

Consider the following:

- The OCCURS clause of the table to be searched must have a KEY IS clause in addition to an INDEXED BY clause. The KEY IS clause identifies the data item on which the table is ordered.

- When you use SEARCH ALL, you do not need to set the table index to a starting value because SEARCH ALL controls it automatically.

- ElementIdentifier must be the item referenced by the table's KEY IS clause.

- ConditionName may have only one value, and it must be associated with a data item referenced by the table's KEY IS clause.

■ **Bug Alert** SEARCH ALL presents no problems when the table is fully loaded (all the elements have been assigned data values); but if the table is not fully loaded, then SEARCH ALL may not function correctly because the values in the unloaded part of the table will not be in key order. To rectify this problem, before you load the table you should fill it with HIGH-VALUES if the key is ascending or LOW-VALUES if the key is descending. See Listing 13-5 for an example.

Listing 13-5 is a simple program that displays the country name when the user enters a two-letter Internet code. Unlike the other example programs in this chapter, the table data in Listing 13-5 is obtained from a file that is loaded into the table at runtime. This is a much more realistic scenario for any sort of volatile data. Countries come and go and change their names with sufficient frequency that loading the table from a file makes good sense from a maintenance perspective. The table can hold up to 250 countries, but the country-code file contains only 243 entries at present.

Listing 13-5. Displaying the Corresponding Country Name When the User Enters a Country Code

```
IDENTIFICATION DIVISION.
PROGRAM-ID. Listing13-5.
AUTHOR. Michael Coughlan.

ENVIRONMENT DIVISION.
INPUT-OUTPUT SECTION.
FILE-CONTROL.
       SELECT CountryCodeFile ASSIGN TO "Listing13-5.dat"
                 ORGANIZATION IS LINE SEQUENTIAL.

DATA DIVISION.
FILE SECTION.
FD CountryCodeFile.
01 CountryCodeRec.
    88 EndOfCountryCodeFile VALUE HIGH-VALUES.
    02 CountryCodeCF    PIC XX.
    02 CountryNameCF    PIC X(25).

WORKING-STORAGE SECTION.
01 CountryCodeTable.
    02 Country OCCURS 300 TIMES
               ASCENDING KEY IS CountryCode
               INDEXED BY Cidx.
       03 CountryCode   PIC XX.
       03 CountryName   PIC X(25).

01 CountryCodeIn        PIC XX.
    88 EndOfInput       VALUE SPACES.

01 FILLER               PIC 9 VALUE ZERO.
    88 ValidCountryCode VALUE 1.
```

```
Listing 13-5 Output

Enter a country code (space to stop) :- ie
ie is Ireland

Enter a country code (space to stop) :- AZ
AZ is Azerbaijan

Enter a country code (space to stop) :- za
za is South Africa

Enter a country code (space to stop) :- us
us is United States

Enter a country code (space to stop) :- tt
tt is Trinidad and Tobago

Enter a country code (space to stop) :- qq
Country code qq is not valid

Enter a country code (space to stop) :- zw
zw is Zimbabwe

Enter a country code (space to stop) :-
```

```
PROCEDURE DIVISION.
Begin.
    PERFORM LoadCountryCodeTable
    PERFORM WITH TEST AFTER UNTIL EndOfInput
       PERFORM WITH TEST AFTER UNTIL ValidCountryCode OR EndOfInput
          DISPLAY "Enter a country code (space to stop) :- "
                    WITH NO ADVANCING
          ACCEPT CountryCodeIn
          SEARCH ALL Country
             AT END IF NOT EndOfInput
                       DISPLAY "Country code " CountryCodeIn " is not valid"
                    END-IF
             WHEN CountryCode(Cidx) = FUNCTION UPPER-CASE(CountryCodeIn)
             DISPLAY CountryCodeIn " is " CountryName(Cidx)
          END-SEARCH
          DISPLAY SPACES
       END-PERFORM
    END-PERFORM
    STOP RUN.
```

```
LoadCountryCodeTable.
* Loads table with HIGH-VALUES so the SEARCH ALL works when the table is partially loaded
    MOVE HIGH-VALUES TO CountryCodeTable
    OPEN INPUT CountryCodeFile
    READ CountryCodeFile
       AT END SET EndOfCountryCodeFile TO TRUE
    END-READ

    PERFORM VARYING Cidx FROM 1 BY 1 UNTIL EndOfCountryCodeFile
        MOVE CountryCodeRec TO Country(Cidx)
        READ CountryCodeFile
            AT END SET EndOfCountryCodeFile TO TRUE
        END-READ
    END-PERFORM
    CLOSE CountryCodeFile.
```

Variable-Length Tables

All the examples you have seen so far have used fixed-length tables. You may have wondered if COBOL supports variable-length tables. The answer is that it does support variable-length tables—of a sort.

You can declare variable-length tables using extensions to the OCCURS clause, as shown in Figure 13-10. Although you can dynamically alter the number of *element occurrences* in a variable-length table, the amount of storage allocated is fixed. It is defined by the value of LargestSize#i and is assigned at compile time. Standard COBOL has no mechanism for dynamically changing the amount of storage allocated to a table.

$$\underline{OCCURS} \, SmallestSize\#1 \, \underline{TO} \, LargestSize\#1 \, \underline{TIMES} \, \underline{DEPENDING} \, \underline{ON} \, TableSize\#i$$

$$\left[\begin{Bmatrix} \underline{ASCENDING} \\ \underline{DESCENDING} \end{Bmatrix} KEY \, IS \, TableItem\$\#i \ldots \right] \ldots$$

$$\left[\underline{INDEXED} \, BY \, IndexName \ldots \right]$$

Figure 13-10. *Full OCCURS metalanguage, including the entries required for variable-length tables and the SEARCH and SEARCH ALL verbs*

Note that this format of the OCCURS clause may only be used to vary the number of elements in the first dimension of a table.

An example declaration is shown in Example 13-6.

Example 13-6. Example Variable-Length Table Declaration

```
01 BooksReservedTable.
   02 BookId    PIC 9(7) OCCURS 1 TO 10
                DEPENDING ON NumOfReservations.
```

The program in Listing 13-5 fills the table with HIGH-VALUES in order to get SEARCH ALL to work correctly, because the table was only partially populated (250 elements in size but only 243 countries). You could achieve the same effect by declaring the table as a variable-length table.

Although variable-length tables are not dynamic (the storage allocated is defined by the table's maximum size), they are treated by COBOL verbs as if they were dynamic. For instance, when you use SEARCH or SEARCH ALL with the table, only the elements between SmallestSize#i and TableSize#i are interrogated.

Listing 13-6 revisits the program from Listing 13-5 to emphasize these points.

Listing 13-6. SEARCH ALL Used with a Variable-Length Table

```
IDENTIFICATION DIVISION.
PROGRAM-ID. Listing13-6.
AUTHOR. Michael Coughlan.


ENVIRONMENT DIVISION.
INPUT-OUTPUT SECTION.
FILE-CONTROL.
        SELECT CountryCodeFile ASSIGN TO "Listing13-6.dat"
                ORGANIZATION IS LINE SEQUENTIAL.


DATA DIVISION.
FILE SECTION.
FD CountryCodeFile.
01 CountryCodeRec.
    88 EndOfCountryCodeFile VALUE HIGH-VALUES.
    02 CountryCodeCF    PIC XX.
    02 CountryNameCF    PIC X(25).

WORKING-STORAGE SECTION.
01 CountryCodeTable.
    02 Country OCCURS 1 TO 300 TIMES
                DEPENDING ON NumberOfCountries
                ASCENDING KEY IS CountryCode
                INDEXED BY Cidx.
        03 CountryCode  PIC XX.
        03 CountryName  PIC X(25).

01 CountryCodeIn        PIC XX.
    88 EndOfInput       VALUE SPACES.

01 FILLER               PIC 9 VALUE ZERO.
    88 ValidCountryCode VALUE 1.

01 NumberOfCountries    PIC 999.

PROCEDURE DIVISION.
Begin.
    PERFORM LoadCountryCodeTable
    PERFORM WITH TEST AFTER UNTIL EndOfInput
        PERFORM WITH TEST AFTER UNTIL ValidCountryCode OR EndOfInput
            DISPLAY "Enter a country code (space to stop) :- "
                    WITH NO ADVANCING
            ACCEPT CountryCodeIn
            PERFORM SearchCountryCodeTable
            DISPLAY SPACES
        END-PERFORM
    END-PERFORM
```

```
                        Listing 13-6 Output

    Enter a country code (space to stop) :- us
    us is United States

    Enter a country code (space to stop) :- az
    az is Azerbaijan

    Enter a country code (space to stop) :- za
    za is South Africa

    Enter a country code (space to stop) :- zz
    Country code zz is not valid

    Enter a country code (space to stop) :- ie
    ie is Ireland

    Enter a country code (space to stop) :-

    ZZ is  **** FOUND ****
```

```
        MOVE 244 TO NumberOfCountries
        MOVE "ZZ" TO CountryCodeIn
        PERFORM SearchCountryCodeTable
        STOP RUN.

SearchCountryCodeTable.
    SEARCH ALL Country
        AT END IF NOT EndOfInput
                    DISPLAY "Country code " CountryCodeIn " is not valid"
                END-IF
        WHEN CountryCode(Cidx) =  FUNCTION UPPER-CASE(CountryCodeIn)
            DISPLAY CountryCodeIn " is " CountryName(Cidx)
    END-SEARCH.

LoadCountryCodeTable.
    OPEN INPUT CountryCodeFile
    READ CountryCodeFile
    AT END SET EndOfCountryCodeFile TO TRUE
    END-READ

    PERFORM VARYING NumberOfCountries FROM 1 BY 1 UNTIL EndOfCountryCodeFile
        MOVE CountryCodeRec TO Country(NumberOfCountries)
        READ CountryCodeFile
            AT END SET EndOfCountryCodeFile TO TRUE
        END-READ
    END-PERFORM
    MOVE "ZZ **** FOUND ****" TO Country(244)
    CLOSE CountryCodeFile.
```

The program in Listing 13-6 is the same as Listing 13-5, with the following changes:

- Variable-length tables are used. When the country data is loaded into the table from the file, the table increases in size as each record is read (see VARYING NumberOfCountries).

- Once the table has been loaded from the file, the value "ZZ **** FOUND ****" is loaded into element 244. The purpose of this is to prove that SEARCH ALL recognizes the table size specified in NumberOfCountries.

- In this program, I moved SEARCH ALL to its own paragraph because I need to use it in two different parts of the program and I don't want to repeat the code.

- When the program runs, the user enters a number of country codes, and the country names are returned. Note that this all works correctly even though the table has not had HIGH-VALUES moved to it.

- Then user enters ZZ. This is the country code of the entry I placed beyond the end of the table (as identified by NumberOfCountries). SEARCH ALL reports that it can't find this country code.

- When the loop exits, the program increases NumberOfCountries to 244, and the search is attempted again. This time SEARCH ALL does find the ZZ country code, because this time the code is the table.

Summary

This chapter examined SEARCH and SEARCH ALL, the COBOL verbs that allow you to search tabular data. The chapter introduced the INDEXED BY and KEY IS extensions to the OCCURS clause. These extensions are required when you want to use SEARCH and SEARCH ALL to search a table. You saw how to use SEARCH for linear searches of single-dimension tables and how, by controlling one of the indexes yourself, you can even use SEARCH to search a multidimensional table. The chapter showed how a binary search works and demonstrated how to use SEARCH ALL to search a table. Finally, you were introduced to the topic of variable-length tables and learned to declare and use them.

The next chapter introduces the SORT and MERGE verbs. SORT is generally used to sort files, but it may also be used to sort a table. As I noted when discussing sequential files in Chapter 7, many operations on sequential files are not possible unless the files are ordered. For this reason, many programs begin by sorting the file into the required order.

PROGRAMMING EXERCISE 1

Prepare your 2B pencil; it's exercise time again. In this program, you will use your knowledge of variable-length tables and the SEARCH verb.

A program is required that will report the frequency of all the words in a document. To make the problem easier, the document has been split into individual words, one word per record. The program should be able to report on a maximum of 1,000 words.

The document words are held in an unordered sequential file called DocWords.dat. Each record has the following description:

Field	Type	Length	Value
Word	X	20	-

Write a program to read a file of document words and produce a report that shows the top ten words in descending order of frequency. The report template is as follows:

```
Top Ten Words In Document
 Pos   Occurs   Document Word
  1.    XXX     XXXXXXXXXXXXXXXXXXXX
  2.    XXX     XXXXXXXXXXXXXXXXXXXX
  3.    XXX     XXXXXXXXXXXXXXXXXXXX
  4.    XXX     XXXXXXXXXXXXXXXXXXXX
  5.    XXX     XXXXXXXXXXXXXXXXXXXX
  6.    XXX     XXXXXXXXXXXXXXXXXXXX
  7.    XXX     XXXXXXXXXXXXXXXXXXXX
  8.    XXX     XXXXXXXXXXXXXXXXXXXX
  9.    XXX     XXXXXXXXXXXXXXXXXXXX
 10.    XXX     XXXXXXXXXXXXXXXXXXXX
```

PROGRAMMING EXERCISE 2

The task in this exercise is to write a program that accepts ten numbers from the user, places them in a table, and then detects and reports on the following states:

- No zeros found in the table

- Only one zero found in the table

- Two zeros found, but no numbers between the two zeros

- Two zeros, and between them an even number of non-zeros

- Two zeros, and between them an odd number of non-zeros

PROGRAMMING EXERCISE 1: ANSWER

Listing 13-7. Program to Find the Top Ten Words in a Document

```
IDENTIFICATION DIVISION.
PROGRAM-ID. Listing13-7.
AUTHOR. Michael Coughlan.

ENVIRONMENT DIVISION.
INPUT-OUTPUT SECTION.
FILE-CONTROL.
      SELECT DocWordsFile ASSIGN TO "Listing13-7.DAT"
                  ORGANIZATION IS LINE SEQUENTIAL.

DATA DIVISION.
FILE SECTION.
FD DocWordsFile.
01 WordIn               PIC X(20).
   88 EndOfDocWordsFile VALUE HIGH-VALUES.

WORKING-STORAGE SECTION.
01 WordFreqTable.
   02 Word OCCURS 0 TO 2000 TIMES
            DEPENDING ON NumberOfWords
            INDEXED BY Widx.
      03 WordFound   PIC X(20).
      03 WordFreq    PIC 9(3).

01 TopTenTable.
   02 WordTT   OCCURS 11 TIMES
            INDEXED BY TTidx.
      03 WordFoundTT  PIC X(20) VALUE SPACES.
      03 WordFreqTT   PIC 9(3)  VALUE ZEROS.

01 NumberOfWords        PIC 9(4) VALUE ZERO.
```

```
01 ReportHeader          PIC X(27) VALUE " Top Ten Words In Document".

01 SubjectHeader         PIC X(29) VALUE "Pos   Occurs    Document Word".

01 DetailLine.
   02 PrnPos             PIC Z9.
   02 FILLER             PIC X VALUE ".".
   02 PrnFreq            PIC BBBBBZZ9.
   02 PrnWord            PIC BBBBBX(20).


01 Pos                   PIC 99.


PROCEDURE DIVISION.
Begin.
    OPEN INPUT DocWordsFile
    READ DocWordsFile
      AT END SET EndOfDocWordsFile TO TRUE
    END-READ
    PERFORM LoadWordFreqTable UNTIL EndOfDocWordsFile
    PERFORM FindTopTenWords
          VARYING Widx FROM 1 BY 1 UNTIL Widx > NumberOfWords
    PERFORM DisplayTopTenWords
    CLOSE DocWordsFile
    STOP RUN.


LoadWordFreqTable.
* The AT END triggers when Widx is one greater than the current size of the
* table so all we have to do is extend the table and write into the new table
* element
    SET Widx TO 1
    SEARCH Word
      AT END ADD 1 TO NumberOfWords
             MOVE 1 TO WordFreq(Widx)
             MOVE FUNCTION LOWER-CASE(WordIn) TO WordFound(Widx)
      WHEN   FUNCTION LOWER-CASE(WordIn) = WordFound(Widx)
             ADD 1 TO WordFreq(Widx)
    END-SEARCH
    READ DocWordsFile
      AT END SET EndOfDocWordsFile TO TRUE
    END-READ.


FindTopTenWords.
    PERFORM VARYING TTidx FROM 10 BY -1 UNTIL TTidx < 1
      IF WordFreq(Widx) > WordFreqTT(TTidx)
        MOVE WordTT(TTidx) TO WordTT(TTidx + 1)
        MOVE Word(Widx) TO WordTT(TTidx)
      END-IF
    END-PERFORM.


DisplayTopTenWords.
```

Listing13-7 Output		
Top Ten Words In Document		
Pos	Occurs	Document Word
1.	69	and
2.	42	will
3.	30	remote
4.	29	web
5.	24	procedures
6.	21	services
7.	20	other
8.	18	with
9.	17	them
10.	16	from

```
    DISPLAY ReportHeader
    DISPLAY SubjectHeader
    PERFORM  VARYING TTidx FROM 1 BY 1 UNTIL TTIdx > 10
       SET Pos TO TTidx
       MOVE Pos TO PrnPos
       MOVE WordFoundTT(TTidx) TO PrnWord
       MOVE WordFreqTT(TTidx) TO PrnFreq
       DISPLAY DetailLine
    END-PERFORM
```

PROGRAMMING EXERCISE 2: ANSWER

Listing 13-8. Program to Find the Number of Zeros in a List of Ten Numbers

```
IDENTIFICATION DIVISION.
PROGRAM-ID. Listing13-8.
AUTHOR. Michael Coughlan.
DATA DIVISION.
WORKING-STORAGE SECTION.
01 NumberArray.
   02 Num PIC 99 OCCURS 10 TIMES
                INDEXED BY Nidx.

01 FirstZeroPos          PIC 99 VALUE ZERO.
   88 NoZeros            VALUE 0.

01 SecondZeroPos         PIC 99 VALUE ZERO.
   88 OneZero            VALUE 0.

01 ValuesBetweenZeros    PIC 9 VALUE ZERO.
   88 NoneBetweenZeros   VALUE 0.

PROCEDURE DIVISION.
Begin.
  DISPLAY "Enter 10 two digit numbers "
  PERFORM VARYING Nidx FROM 1 BY 1 UNTIL Nidx > 10
    DISPLAY "Enter number - "  SPACE WITH NO ADVANCING
    ACCEPT Num(Nidx)
  END-PERFORM

  SET Nidx TO 1
  SEARCH Num
    AT END SET NoZeros TO TRUE
    WHEN Num(Nidx) = ZERO
     SET FirstZeroPos TO Nidx
     SET Nidx UP BY 1
     SEARCH Num
       AT END SET OneZero TO TRUE
       WHEN Num(Nidx) = ZERO
```

```
                SET SecondZeroPos TO Nidx
                COMPUTE ValuesBetweenZeros = (SecondZeroPos - 1) - FirstZeroPos
        END-SEARCH
END-SEARCH

EVALUATE TRUE
    WHEN NoZeros      DISPLAY "No zeros found"
    WHEN OneZero      DISPLAY "Only one zero found"
    WHEN NoneBetweenZeros DISPLAY "No numbers between the two zeros"
    WHEN FUNCTION REM(ValuesBetweenZeros, 2)= ZERO
                      DISPLAY "Even number of non-zeros between zeros"
    WHEN OTHER        DISPLAY "Odd number of non-zeros between zeros"
END-EVALUATE
STOP RUN.
```

▪ ▪ ▪

CHAPTER 14

Sorting and Merging

If there is one thing you should have learned from the chapters on sequential files, it is that your processing options are very limited if a sequential file is not ordered. Solutions based on control breaks, and the file-update problem, are impossible unless the file is ordered on some key field. In previous chapters, I mentioned the very useful program design technique called *beneficial wishful thinking* in which, when you are confronted by a difficult programming problem, you imagine a set of circumstances under which the difficulty would be greatly reduced and then try to bring about that set of circumstances. In the context of sequential files, you will often find yourself confronted with problems that would be much easier to solve if the file was ordered. A solution based on the beneficial wishful thinking approach first puts the file into the required order.

In this chapter, you discover how to use the SORT verb to sort a sequential file in ascending or descending order. You learn how to use an INPUT PROCEDURE to filter or modify the records presented for sorting and how to use an OUTPUT PROCEDURE to process the sorted records instead of sending them directly to an output file. In addition, you see how to use the MERGE verb to merge the records in two or more ordered files to create a combined file with the records in the correct order.

SORTING

I noted in previous chapters that it is possible to apply processing to an ordered sequential file that is difficult, or impossible, when the file is unordered. In cases where you need to apply ordered processing to an unordered sequential file, part of the solution must be to sort the file. COBOL provides the SORT verb for this purpose.

The SORT verb is usually used to sort sequential files. Some programmers claim that the SORT verb is unnecessary, preferring to use an implementer-provided or "off-the-shelf" sort. However, one major advantage of using the SORT verb is that it enhances the portability of COBOL programs. Because the SORT verb is available in every COBOL compiler, when a program that uses SORT has to be moved to a different computer system, it can make the transition without requiring any changes to the SORT. This is rarely the case when programs rely on an implementer-supplied or bought-in sort.

Simple Sorting

The syntax for the simple SORT is given in Figure 14-1. This version of SORT takes the records in the InFileName file, sorts them on the WorkSortKey#$i key or keys, and writes the sorted records to the OutFileName file.

$$\underline{SORT} \text{ SDWorkFileName} \left\{ ON \begin{Bmatrix} \underline{ASCENDING} \\ \underline{DESCENDING} \end{Bmatrix} KEY \{ WorkSortKey\#\$i \} ... \right\} ...$$

$$[WITH \underline{DUPLICATES} IN ORDER]$$
$$[\underline{COLLATING} \underline{SEQUENCE} IS AlphabetName]$$
$$\{ \underline{USING} \{ InFileName \} ... \}$$
$$\{ \underline{GIVING} \{ OutFileName \} ... \}$$

Figure 14-1. *Metalanguage for the simple version of SORT*

Some example SORT statements are given in Example 14-1.

Example 14-1. Example SORT Statements

```
SORT WorkFile
    ON ASCENDING BookId-WF
                 AuthorName-WF
    USING BookSalesFileUS, BookSalesFileEU
    GIVING SortedBookSales

SORT WorkFile
    ON DESCENDING NCAP-Result-WF
       ASCENDING  ManfName-WF, VehicleName-WF
    USING NCAP-TestResultsFile
    GIVING Sorted-NCAP-TestResultsFile
```

Simple Sorting Notes

Consider the following:

- SDWorkFileName identifies a temporary work file that the sort process uses as a kind of scratch pad for sorting. The file is defined in the FILE SECTION using a sort description (SD) rather than a file description (FD) entry. Even though the work file is a temporary file, it must still have associated SELECT and ASSIGN clauses in the ENVIRONMENT DIVISION. You can give this file any name you like; I usually call it WorkFile as I did in Example 14-1.

- SDWorkFileName file is a sequential file with an organization of RECORD SEQUENTIAL. Because this is the default organization, it is usually omitted (see Listing 14-1).

- Each WorkSortKey#$i identifies a field in the record of the work file. The sorted file will be ordered on this key field(s).

- When more than one WorkSortKey#$i is specified, the keys decrease in significance from left to right (the leftmost key is the most significant, and the rightmost is the least significant).

- InFileName and OutFileName are the names of the input and output files, respectively.

- If more than one InFileName is specified, the files are combined (OutFileSize = InFile1Size + InFile2Size) and then sorted.

- If more than one OutFileName is specified, then each file receives a copy of the sorted records.

- If the DUPLICATES clause is used, then when the file has been sorted, the final order of records with duplicate keys (keys with the same value) is the same as that in the unsorted file. If no DUPLICATES clause is used, the order of records with duplicate keys is undefined.

- AlphabetName is an alphabet name defined in the SPECIAL-NAMES paragraph of the ENVIRONMENT DIVISION. This clause is used to select the character set the SORT verb uses for collating the records in the file. The character set may be STANDARD-1 (ASCII), STANDARD-2 (ISO 646), NATIVE (may be defined by the system to be ASCII or EBCDIC; see your implementer manual), or user defined.

- SORT can be used anywhere in the PROCEDURE DIVISION except in an INPUT PROCEDURE (SORT) or OUTPUT PROCEDURE (SORT or MERGE) or in the DECLARATIVES SECTION. The purpose of the INPUT PROCEDURE and OUTPUT PROCEDURE is explained later in this chapter, but an explanation of the DECLARATIVES SECTION has to wait until Chapter 18.

- The records described for the input file (USING) must be able to fit into the records described for SDWorkFileName.

- The records described for SDWorkFileName must be able to fit into the records described for the output file (GIVING).

- The description of WorkSortKey#$i cannot contain an OCCURS clause (it cannot be a table), nor can it be subordinate to an entry that contains one.

- The InFileName and OutFileName files are automatically opened by the SORT. When the SORT executes, they *must not already be open*.

How the Simple SORT Works

Figure 14-2 shows how the simple version of SORT works. In this case, the diagram uses the example in Listing 14-1 to illustrate the point. The sort process takes records from the unsorted BillableServicesFile, sorts them using WorkFile (the temporary work area), and, when the records have been sorted, sends them to SortedBillablesFile. After sorting, the records in the SortedBillablesFile will be ordered on ascending SubscriberId.

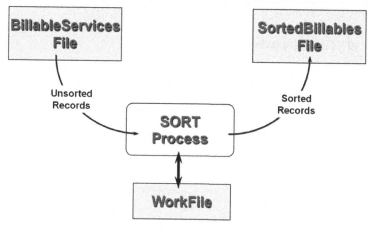

```
SORT WorkFile ON ASCENDING KEY SubscriberId-WF
     USING   BillableServicesFile
     GIVING SortedBillablesFile.
```

Figure 14-2. *Diagram showing how the simple SORT works*

Simple Sorting Program

Universal Telecoms has subscribers all over the United States. Each month, the billable activities of these subscribers are gathered into a file. BillableServicesFile is an unordered sequential file. Each record has the following description:

Field	Type	Length	Value
SubscriberId	9	10	–
ServiceType	9	1	1(text)/2(voice)
ServiceCost	9	6	0.10–9999.99

A program is required to produce a report that shows the value of the billable services for each subscriber (see Listing 14-1). In the report, BillableValue is the sum of the ServiceCost fields for each subscriber. The report must be printed on ascending SubscriberId and have the following format:

```
Universal Telecoms Monthly Report
SubscriberId      BillableValue
XXXXXXXXXX        XXXXXXXXXXX
XXXXXXXXXX        XXXXXXXXXXX
XXXXXXXXXX        XXXXXXXXXXX
```

Listing 14-1. A simple SORT applied to the BillableServicesFile

```
IDENTIFICATION DIVISION.
PROGRAM-ID. Listing14-1.
AUTHOR. Michael Coughlan.
ENVIRONMENT DIVISION.
INPUT-OUTPUT SECTION.
FILE-CONTROL.
    SELECT WorkFile ASSIGN TO "WORK.TMP".

    SELECT BillableServicesFile  ASSIGN TO "Listing14-1.dat"
            ORGANIZATION LINE SEQUENTIAL.

    SELECT SortedBillablesFile   ASSIGN TO "Listing14-1.Srt"
            ORGANIZATION LINE SEQUENTIAL.

DATA DIVISION.
FILE SECTION.

FD  BillableServicesFile.
01  SubscriberRec-BSF      PIC X(17).

SD  WorkFile.
01  WorkRec.
    02 SubscriberId-WF    PIC 9(10).
    02 FILLER             PIC X(7).

FD  SortedBillablesFile.
01  SubscriberRec.
    88 EndOfBillablesFile    VALUE HIGH-VALUES.
    02 SubscriberId       PIC 9(10).
```

```
    02 ServiceType        PIC 9.
    02 ServiceCost        PIC 9(4)V99.


WORKING-STORAGE SECTION.
01 SubscriberTotal        PIC 9(5)V99.

01 ReportHeader           PIC X(33) VALUE "Universal Telecoms Monthly Report".

01 SubjectHeader          PIC X(31) VALUE "SubscriberId      BillableValue".

01 SubscriberLine.
    02 PrnSubscriberId    PIC 9(10).
    02 FILLER             PIC X(8) VALUE SPACES.
    02 PrnSubscriberTotal PIC $$$,$$9.99.

01 PrevSubscriberId       PIC 9(10).


PROCEDURE DIVISION.
Begin.
    SORT WorkFile ON ASCENDING KEY SubscriberId-WF
           USING BillableServicesFile
           GIVING SortedBillablesFile
    DISPLAY ReportHeader
    DISPLAY SubjectHeader
    OPEN INPUT SortedBillablesFile
    READ SortedBillablesFile
      AT END SET EndOfBillablesFile TO TRUE
    END-READ
    PERFORM UNTIL EndOfBillablesFile
       MOVE SubscriberId TO PrevSubscriberId, PrnSubscriberId
       MOVE ZEROS TO SubscriberTotal
       PERFORM UNTIL SubscriberId NOT EQUAL TO PrevSubscriberId
          ADD ServiceCost TO SubscriberTotal
          READ SortedBillablesFile
               AT END SET EndOfBillablesFile TO TRUE
          END-READ
       END-PERFORM
       MOVE SubscriberTotal TO PrnSubscriberTotal
       DISPLAY SubscriberLine
    END-PERFORM
    CLOSE SortedBillablesFile
    STOP RUN.
```

Program Notes

I have kept this program simple for reasons of clarity and space, and because you will meet a more fully worked version of the program when I explore advanced versions of the SORT. Because the SORT uses a disk-based WorkFile, it is slower than purely RAM-bound operations. You should be aware of this whenever you are considering using SORT. You should probably use SORT only when no practical RAM-based solution is available; and even then, you should ensure that only the data items required in the sorted file are sorted. This may involve leaving out some of the records or changing the record size.

In this instance, sorting the file does seem to be the only viable option. There are millions of telephone subscribers, and, in the course of a month, they make many calls and send hundreds of texts. So `BillableServicesFile` contains tens of millions, or hundreds of millions, of records. In COBOL, the only possible RAM-based solution (you can't create dynamic structures like trees or linked lists pre–ISO 2002) would be to use a table (one element per subscriber) to sum the subscribers' `ServiceCost` fields. That solution has many problems. The array would have to contain millions of elements, you would have to ensure that the elements were in `SubscriberId` order, and, because new subscribers are constantly joining, the table would have to be redimensioned every time the program ran.

You may wonder why the example uses different record descriptions for the three files when the records are identical. The reason is that although the records are identical, they are used in different ways in the program, and the granular data descriptions reflect way the records are used.

The input file is used only by the SORT, so while you have to define how much storage a record will occupy you never need to refer to the individual fields. You could fully define the record as follows:

```
01  UnsortedSubcriberRec.
    02 SubscriberId      PIC 9(10).
    02 ServiceType       PIC 9.
    02 ServiceCost       PIC 9(4)V99
```

But then you would either have to use slightly different field names for the sorted file or qualify them using references such as `SubscriberId OF SubscriberRec`.

In `WorkFile`, only the data items on which the file is to be sorted (mentioned in the KEY phrase) need to be explicitly defined. In this case, the only item that must be explicitly identified is `SubscriberId-WF`.

The sorted file is normally the file that the program uses to do whatever work is required. This generally means that all, or nearly all, of the data items are mentioned by name in the program; and, hence, they have to be declared. Normally, the record description for this file fully defines the record.

Using Multiple Keys

If you examine the SORT metalanguage in Figure 14-1, you will realize not only that can a file be sorted on a number of keys but also that one key can be ascending while another is descending. This is illustrated in Table 14-1 and Example 14-2. The table contains student results that have been sorted into descending `StudentId` order within ascending GPA order. Notice that GPA is the major key and that `StudentId` is only in descending sequence within GPA. This is because the first key named in a SORT statement is the major key, and keys become less significant with each successive declaration.

Example 14-2. SORT with One Key Descending and Another Ascending

```
SORT WorkFile ON DESCENDING GPA
              ASCENDING  StudentId
              USING   StudentResultsFile
              GIVING  SortedStudentsResultsFile
```

Table 14-1. *Ascending StudentId within Descending GPA*

SortedStudentsResultsFile

GPA	StudentId	Record remainder
4	11234598	Et cetera
4	22334567	Et cetera
4	33435678	Et cetera
4	44245666	Et cetera
3.50	11103456	Et cetera
3.50	22234567	Et cetera
3.50	33315432	Et cetera
3.25	11114321	Et cetera
3.25	22228676	Et cetera
3.25	33339758	Et cetera
3.25	44449878	Et cetera
3.25	55559990	Et cetera
3.25	66669990	Et cetera
3.15	11111345	Et cetera
3.15	22222567	Et cetera
3.00	11111123	Et cetera
3.00	22222254	Et cetera
3.00	33333356	Et cetera
3.00	44444487	Et cetera
2.75	11111117	Et cetera
2.75	33333336	Et cetera
etc.	etc.	etc.

SORT with Procedures

The simple version of SORT takes the records from InFileName, sorts them, and then outputs them to OutFileName. Sometimes, however, not all the records in the unsorted file are required in the sorted file, or not all the data items in the unsorted file record are required in the record of the sorted file. For instance, suppose the specification for the Universal Telecoms Monthly Report changes so that you are only required to show the value of the *voice calls* made by subscribers. In that situation, the text records (ServiceType = 1) are not required in the sorted file. Similarly, if the specification changes so that the *number* of texts and phone calls is required rather than their *value,* you do not need the ServiceCost data item in sorted file records. In both cases, processing must be applied, to eliminate unwanted records or alter their format, before the records are submitted to the sort process. This processing is achieved by specifying INPUT PROCEDURE with SORT.

Sometimes, to reduce the number of files that have to be declared, you may find it useful to process the records directly from the sort process instead of creating a sorted file and then processing that. For instance, you could create the Universal Telecoms Monthly Report directly instead of creating a sorted file and then processing the sorted file to create the report. Such processing is accomplished by using OUTPUT PROCEDURE with SORT.

An INPUT PROCEDURE is a block of code that consists of one or more sections or paragraphs that execute, having been passed control by SORT. When the block of code has finished, control reverts to SORT. An OUTPUT PROCEDURE works in a similar way.

Figure 14-3 gives the metalanguage for the full SORT including the INPUT PROCEDURE and the OUTPUT PROCEDURE.

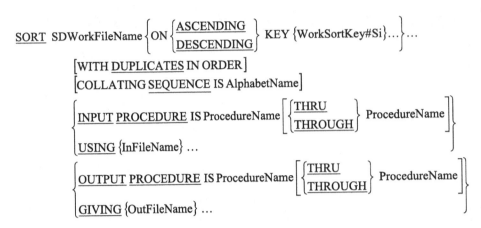

Figure 14-3. *Metalanguage for the full version of the SORT verb*

INPUT PROCEDURE Notes

You should consider the following when using an INPUT PROCEDURE:

- The block of code specified by the INPUT PROCEDURE allows you to select which records, and what format of records, are submitted to the sort process. Because an INPUT PROCEDURE executes before the SORT sorts the records, only the data that is actually required in the sorted file is sorted.

- When you use an INPUT PROCEDURE, it replaces the USING phrase. The ProcedureName in the INPUT PROCEDURE phrase identifies a block of code that uses the RELEASE verb to supply records to the sort process. The INPUT PROCEDURE must contain at least one RELEASE statement to transfer the records to the work file (identified by SDWorkFileName).

- The INPUT PROCEDURE finishes before the sort process sorts the records supplied to it by the procedure. That's why the records are RELEASEd to the work file. They are stored there until the INPUT PROCEDURE finishes, and then they are sorted.

- Neither an INPUT PROCEDURE nor an OUTPUT PROCEDURE can contain a SORT or MERGE statement.

- The pre–ANS 85 COBOL rules for the SORT verb stated that the INPUT PROCEDURE and OUTPUT PROCEDURE had to be self-contained sections of code and could not be entered from elsewhere in the program.

- In the ANS 85 version of COBOL, the INPUT PROCEDURE and OUTPUT PROCEDURE can be any contiguous group of paragraphs or sections. The only restriction is that the range of paragraphs or sections used must not overlap.

OUTPUT PROCEDURE Notes

You should consider the following when using an OUTPUT PROCEDURE:

- An OUTPUT PROCEDURE retrieves sorted records from the work file using the RETURN verb. An OUTPUT PROCEDURE must contain at least one RETURN statement to get the records from the work file.

- An OUTPUT PROCEDURE only executes after the file has been sorted.

- If you use an OUTPUT PROCEDURE, the SORT..GIVING phrase cannot be used.

How an INPUT PROCEDURE Works

A simple SORT works by taking records from the USING file, sorting them, and then writing them to the GIVING file. When an INPUT PROCEDURE is used, there is no USING file, so the sort process has to get its records from the INPUT PROCEDURE. The INPUT PROCEDURE uses the RELEASE verb to supply the records to the work file of the SORT, one at a time.

Although an INPUT PROCEDURE usually gets the records it supplies to the sort process from an input file, the records can originate from anywhere. For instance, if you wanted to sort the elements of a table, you could use INPUT PROCEDURE to send the elements, one at a time, to the sort process (see Listing 14-7, in the section "Sorting Tables Program"). Or, if you wanted to sort the records as they were entered by the user, you could use INPUT PROCEDURE to get the records from the user and supply them to the sort process (see Listing 14-3, later in this section). When an INPUT PROCEDURE gets its records from an input file, it can select which records to send to the sort process and can even alter the structure of the records before they are sent.

Creating an INPUT PROCEDURE

When you use an INPUT PROCEDURE, a RELEASE verb must be used to send records to the work file associated with SORT. The work file is declared in an SD entry in the FILE SECTION. RELEASE is a special verb used only in INPUT PROCEDUREs to send records to the work file. It is the equivalent of a WRITE command and works in a similar way. The metalanguage for the RELEASE verb is given in Figure 14-4.

RELEASE SDWorkRecordName [FROM Identifier]

Figure 14-4. *Metalanguage for the RELEASE verb*

A template for an INPUT PROCEDURE that gets records from an input file and releases them to the SORT work file is given in Example 14-3. Notice that the work file is not opened in the OUTPUT PROCEDURE. The work file is automatically opened by the SORT.

Example 14-3. INPUT PROCEDURE File-Processing Template

```
OPEN INPUT InFileName
READ InFileName RECORD
PERFORM UNTIL TerminatingCondition
    RELEASE SDWorkRec
    READ InFileName RECORD
END-PERFORM
CLOSE InFileName
```

Using an INPUT PROCEDURE to Select Records

Suppose that the specification for the Universal Telecoms Monthly Report is changed so that only the value of the *voice calls* made by subscribers is required. Figure 14-5 shows how you can use an INPUT PROCEDURE between the input file and the sort process to filter out the unwanted text (ServiceType = 1) records. Listing 14-2 implements the specification change and also produces a more fully worked version. In this program, the report is written to a print file rather than just displayed on the computer screen.

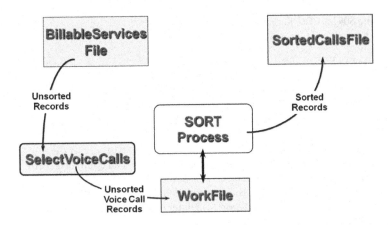

```
SORT WorkFile ON ASCENDING KEY SubscriberId-WF
     INPUT PROCEDURE IS SelectVoiceCalls
     GIVING SortedCallsFile
```

Figure 14-5. INPUT PROCEDURE *used to select the voice call records*

Listing 14-2. Using an INPUT PROCEDURE to Select Only Voice Calls Records

```
IDENTIFICATION DIVISION.
PROGRAM-ID. Listing14-2.
AUTHOR. Michael Coughlan.
ENVIRONMENT DIVISION.
INPUT-OUTPUT SECTION.
FILE-CONTROL.
    SELECT WorkFile ASSIGN TO "WORK.TMP".

    SELECT BillableServicesFile  ASSIGN TO "Listing14-2.dat"
           ORGANIZATION LINE SEQUENTIAL.

    SELECT SortedCallsFile   ASSIGN TO "Listing14-2.Srt"
             ORGANIZATION LINE SEQUENTIAL.

    SELECT PrintFile  ASSIGN TO "Listing14-2.prn"
             ORGANIZATION LINE SEQUENTIAL.

DATA DIVISION.
FILE SECTION.
FD  BillableServicesFile.
01  SubscriberRec-BSF.
```

```
    88 EndOfBillableServicesFile VALUE HIGH-VALUES.
    02 FILLER              PIC X(10).
    02 FILLER              PIC 9.
       88 VoiceCall        VALUE 2.
    02 FILLER              PIC X(6).


SD  WorkFile.
01  WorkRec.
    02 SubscriberId-WF     PIC 9(10).
    02 FILLER              PIC X(7).


FD  SortedCallsFile.
01  SubscriberRec.
    88 EndOfCallsFile      VALUE HIGH-VALUES.
    02 SubscriberId        PIC 9(10).
    02 ServiceType         PIC 9.
    02 ServiceCost         PIC 9(4)V99.


FD PrintFile.
01 PrintRec               PIC X(40).


WORKING-STORAGE SECTION.
01 SubscriberTotal        PIC 9(5)V99.

01 ReportHeader           PIC X(33) VALUE "Universal Telecoms Monthly Report".

01 SubjectHeader          PIC X(31) VALUE "SubscriberId        BillableValue".

01 SubscriberLine.
   02 PrnSubscriberId      PIC 9(10).
   02 FILLER               PIC X(8) VALUE SPACES.
   02 PrnSubscriberTotal   PIC $$$,$$9.99.

01 PrevSubscriberId       PIC 9(10).

PROCEDURE DIVISION.
Begin.
    SORT WorkFile ON ASCENDING KEY SubscriberId-WF
          INPUT PROCEDURE IS SelectVoiceCalls
          GIVING SortedCallsFile
    OPEN OUTPUT PrintFile
    OPEN INPUT SortedCallsFile
    WRITE PrintRec FROM ReportHeader AFTER ADVANCING PAGE
    WRITE PrintRec FROM SubjectHeader AFTER ADVANCING 1 LINE

    READ SortedCallsFile
      AT END SET EndOfCallsFile TO TRUE
    END-READ
    PERFORM UNTIL EndOfCallsFile
      MOVE SubscriberId TO PrevSubscriberId, PrnSubscriberId
      MOVE ZEROS TO SubscriberTotal
      PERFORM UNTIL SubscriberId NOT EQUAL TO PrevSubscriberId
```

```
            ADD ServiceCost TO SubscriberTotal
            READ SortedCallsFile
                AT END SET EndOfCallsFile TO TRUE
            END-READ
        END-PERFORM
        MOVE SubscriberTotal TO PrnSubscriberTotal
        WRITE PrintRec FROM SubscriberLine AFTER ADVANCING 1 LINE
    END-PERFORM
    CLOSE SortedCallsFile, PrintFile
    STOP RUN.


SelectVoiceCalls.
    OPEN INPUT BillableServicesFile
    READ BillableServicesFile
        AT END SET EndOfBillableServicesFile TO TRUE
    END-READ
    PERFORM UNTIL EndOfBillableServicesFile
        IF VoiceCall
            RELEASE WorkRec FROM SubscriberRec-BSF
        END-IF
        READ BillableServicesFile
            AT END SET EndOfBillableServicesFile TO TRUE
        END-READ
    END-PERFORM
    CLOSE BillableServicesFile.
```

The file declarations are once more of interest. Because only the voice call records are released to the work file, you need to be able to detect which records are voice call records. To do this, you cannot declare SubscriberRec-BSF as an undifferentiated group of 17 characters, as in Listing 14-1. Instead, you isolate the ServiceType character position so that you can monitor it with the condition name VoiceCall. Because you never refer to ServiceType in the PROCEDURE DIVISION, you do not explicitly name it but instead give it the generic name FILLER.

Using an INPUT PROCEDURE to Modify Records

In addition to selecting which records to send to be sorted, you can also use an INPUT PROCEDURE to modify the records before releasing them to the sort process. Suppose the specification for the Universal Telecoms Monthly Report is changed again. Now you are now required to count the *number of calls made* and the *number of texts sent* by each subscriber. Because sorting is a slow, disk-based process, every effort should be made to reduce the amount of data that has to be sorted. The ServiceCost data item is not required to produce the report, so you do not need to include it in the records sent to the work file. You can use an INPUT PROCEDURE to modify the input record so that only the required data items are submitted to the SORT.

Listing 14-3 implements the specification change, and Figure 14-6 shows how the INPUT PROCEDURE sits between the input file and the sort process to modify the records before they are released to the work file.

Listing 14-3. Using an INPUT PROCEDURE to Modify the Record Structure

```
IDENTIFICATION DIVISION.
PROGRAM-ID. Listing14-3.
AUTHOR. Michael Coughlan.
ENVIRONMENT DIVISION.
INPUT-OUTPUT SECTION.
FILE-CONTROL.
```

```cobol
        SELECT WorkFile ASSIGN TO "WORK.TMP".

        SELECT BillableServicesFile  ASSIGN TO "Listing14-3.dat"
               ORGANIZATION LINE SEQUENTIAL.

        SELECT SortedSubscriberFile   ASSIGN TO "Listing14-3.Srt"
               ORGANIZATION LINE SEQUENTIAL.

        SELECT PrintFile  ASSIGN TO "Listing14-3.prn"
               ORGANIZATION LINE SEQUENTIAL.

DATA DIVISION.
FILE SECTION.
FD  BillableServicesFile.
01  SubscriberRec-BSF.
    88 EndOfBillableServicesFile VALUE HIGH-VALUES.
    02 SubscriberId-BSF   PIC 9(10).
    02 ServiceType-BSF    PIC 9.
    02 FILLER             PIC X(6).

SD  WorkFile.
01  WorkRec.
    02 SubscriberId-WF    PIC 9(10).
    02 ServiceType-WF     PIC 9.

FD  SortedSubscriberFile.
01  SubscriberRec.
    88 EndOfCallsFile    VALUE HIGH-VALUES.
    02 SubscriberId       PIC 9(10).
    02 ServiceType        PIC 9.
       88 VoiceCall       VALUE 2.

FD PrintFile.
01 PrintRec              PIC X(40).

WORKING-STORAGE SECTION.
01 CallsTotal            PIC 9(4).

01 TextsTotal            PIC 9(5).

01 ReportHeader          PIC X(33) VALUE "Universal Telecoms Monthly Report".

01 SubjectHeader         PIC X(31) VALUE "SubscriberId    Calls     Texts".

01 SubscriberLine.
   02 PrnSubscriberId    PIC 9(10).
   02 FILLER             PIC X(6) VALUE SPACES.
   02 PrnCallsTotal      PIC Z,ZZ9.
   02 FILLER             PIC X(4) VALUE SPACES.
   02 PrnTextsTotal      PIC ZZ,ZZ9.
```

```cobol
01 PrevSubscriberId        PIC 9(10).

PROCEDURE DIVISION.
Begin.
    SORT WorkFile ON ASCENDING KEY SubscriberId-WF
            INPUT PROCEDURE IS ModifySubscriberRecords
            GIVING SortedSubscriberFile
    OPEN OUTPUT PrintFile
    OPEN INPUT SortedSubscriberFile
    WRITE PrintRec FROM ReportHeader AFTER ADVANCING PAGE
    WRITE PrintRec FROM SubjectHeader AFTER ADVANCING 1 LINE

    READ SortedSubscriberFile
      AT END SET EndOfCallsFile TO TRUE
    END-READ
    PERFORM UNTIL EndOfCallsFile
       MOVE SubscriberId TO PrevSubscriberId, PrnSubscriberId
       MOVE ZEROS TO CallsTotal, TextsTotal
       PERFORM UNTIL SubscriberId NOT EQUAL TO PrevSubscriberId
          IF VoiceCall ADD 1 TO CallsTotal
             ELSE ADD 1 TO TextsTotal
          END-IF
          READ SortedSubscriberFile
               AT END SET EndOfCallsFile TO TRUE
          END-READ
       END-PERFORM
       MOVE CallsTotal TO PrnCallsTotal
       MOVE TextsTotal TO PrnTextsTotal
       WRITE PrintRec FROM SubscriberLine AFTER ADVANCING 1 LINE
    END-PERFORM
    CLOSE SortedSubscriberFile, PrintFile
    STOP RUN.

ModifySubscriberRecords.
    OPEN INPUT BillableServicesFile
    READ BillableServicesFile
         AT END SET EndOfBillableServicesFile TO TRUE
    END-READ
    PERFORM UNTIL EndOfBillableServicesFile
       MOVE SubscriberId-BSF TO SubscriberId-WF
       MOVE ServiceType-BSF  TO ServiceType-WF
       RELEASE WorkRec
       READ BillableServicesFile
            AT END SET EndOfBillableServicesFile TO TRUE
       END-READ
    END-PERFORM
    CLOSE BillableServicesFile.
```

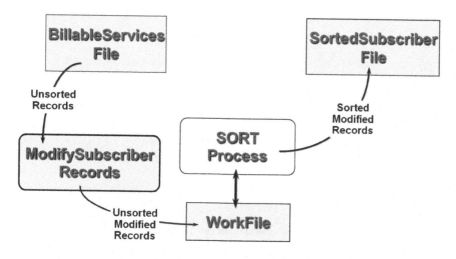

```
SORT WorkFile ON ASCENDING KEY SubscriberId-WF
     INPUT PROCEDURE IS ModifySubscriberRecords
     GIVING SortedSubscriberFile
```

Figure 14-6. *Using an INPUT PROCEDURE to modify the subscriber records*

As before, the record declarations are of some interest. For reasons of clarity, I chose to explicitly identify the data items in SubscriberRec-BSF that are being preserved in WorkRec. You may, on consideration of the character positions, wonder if you could simply move SubscriberRec-BSF to WorkRec and let MOVE truncation eliminate the unwanted data. If those are your thoughts, then you are correct. You could save yourself some typing by doing that.

Feeding SORT from the Keyboard

As I mentioned earlier, and as you can see from Figure 14-5 and Figure 14-6, when an INPUT PROCEDURE is used, it is responsible for supplying records to the sort process. The records supplied can come from anywhere. They can come from a file, a table, or (as in this example) directly from the user.

The program in Listing 14-4 gets records directly from the user, sorts them on ascending StudentId, and then outputs them to SortedStudentFile. The diagram in Figure 14-7 represents the process. Note that the sort process only sorts the file when the INPUT PROCEDURE has finished.

Listing 14-4. Feeding SORT from the Keyboard

```
IDENTIFICATION DIVISION.
PROGRAM-ID.  Lsiting14-4.
AUTHOR.  Michael Coughlan.
ENVIRONMENT DIVISION.
INPUT-OUTPUT SECTION.
FILE-CONTROL.
    SELECT StudentFile ASSIGN TO "Listing14-4.DAT"
           ORGANIZATION IS LINE SEQUENTIAL.

    SELECT WorkFile ASSIGN TO "WORK.TMP".
```

```
DATA DIVISION.
FILE SECTION.
FD StudentFile.
01 StudentDetails      PIC X(32).
* The StudentDetails record has the description shown below.
* But in this program I don't actually need to refer to any
* of the items in the record and so have described it as PIC X(32)
* 01 StudentDetails
*    02   StudentId       PIC 9(8).
*    02   StudentName.
*         03 Surname      PIC X(8).
*         03 Initials     PIC XX.
*    02   DateOfBirth.
*         03 YOBirth      PIC 9(4).
*         03 MOBirth      PIC 9(2).
*         03 DOBirth      PIC 9(2).
*    02   CourseCode      PIC X(5).
*    02   Gender          PIC X.

SD WorkFile.
01 WorkRec.
   88 EndOfInput         VALUE SPACES.
   02 FILLER             PIC X(8).
   02 SurnameWF          PIC X(8).
   02 FILLER             PIC X(16).

PROCEDURE DIVISION.
Begin.
    SORT WorkFile ON ASCENDING KEY SurnameWF
         INPUT PROCEDURE IS GetStudentDetails
         GIVING StudentFile
    STOP RUN.

GetStudentDetails.
    DISPLAY "Use the template below"
    DISPLAY "to enter your details."
    DISPLAY "Enter spaces to end.".
    DISPLAY "NNNNNNNNSSSSSSSSIIYYYYMMDDCCCCCG".
    ACCEPT  WorkRec.
    PERFORM UNTIL EndOfInput
       RELEASE WorkRec
       ACCEPT WorkRec
    END-PERFORM.
```

Listing 14-4 Input

```
Use the template below
to enter your details.
Enter spaces to end.
NNNNNNNNSSSSSSSSIIYYYYMMDDCCCCCG
12345678Molloy  DJ19940107LM051M
13456789Ryan    TT19951213LM051F
12986378Smith   AJ19910221LM069M
12764523Luskin  WA19951111LM051M
11349872O'Brien RR19941010LM110F
13246454Sheridan
13456723Andrews
12987786Williams
12111234Cullen
```

SortedStudentFile

```
13456723Andrews DD19941212LM110M
12111234Cullen  MM19920314LM114M
12764523Luskin  WA19951111LM051M
12345678Molloy  DJ19940107LM051M
11349872O'Brien RR19941010LM110F
13456789Ryan    TT19951213LM051F
13246454SheridanVV19920918LM069F
12986378Smith   AJ19910221LM069M
12987786WilliamsRR19920817LM051M
```

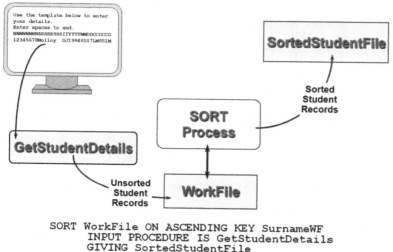

```
SORT WorkFile ON ASCENDING KEY SurnameWF
     INPUT PROCEDURE IS GetStudentDetails
     GIVING SortedStudentFile
```

Figure 14-7. Supplying SORT records directly from the user

OUTPUT PROCEDURE

An INPUT PROCEDURE allows you to filter, or alter, records before they are supplied to the sort process. This can substantially reduce the amount of data that has to be sorted. An OUTPUT PROCEDURE has no such advantage. An OUTPUT PROCEDURE only executes when the sort process has already sorted the file.

Nevertheless, an OUTPUT PROCEDURE is useful when you don't need to preserve the sorted file. For instance, if you are sorting records to produce a one-off report, you can use an OUTPUT PROCEDURE to create the report directly, without first having to create a file containing the sorted records. This saves you the effort of having to define an unnecessary file. An OUTPUT PROCEDURE is also useful when you want to alter the structure of the records written to the sorted file. For instance, if you were required to produce a summary file from the sorted records, you could use an OUTPUT PROCEDURE to summarize the sorted records and then write each of the summary records to summary file. The resulting file would contain summary records, rather than the detail records contained in the unsorted file.

How the OUTPUT PROCEDURE Works

A simple SORT takes the records from the unsorted input file, sorts them, and then outputs them to the sorted output file. As Figure 14-8 shows, the OUTPUT PROCEDURE breaks the connection between the SORT and the output file. The OUTPUT PROCEDURE uses the RETURN verb to retrieve sorted records from the work file. It may then send the retrieved records to the output file, but it doesn't have to. Once the OUTPUT PROCEDURE has retrieved the sorted records from the work file, it can do whatever it likes with them. For instance, it can summarize them, alter them, put them into a table, display them on the screen, or send them to the output file. When the OUTPUT PROCEDURE does send the sorted records to an output file, it can control which records, and what type of records, appear in the file.

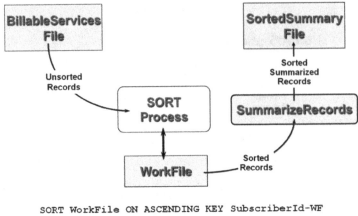

```
SORT WorkFile ON ASCENDING KEY SubscriberId-WF
     INPUT PROCEDURE IS SummarizeRecords
     GIVING SortedSummaryFile
```

Figure 14-8. *Using an OUTPUT PROCEDURE TO summarize records*

Creating an OUTPUT PROCEDURE

When you use an OUTPUT PROCEDURE, you must use the RETURN verb to retrieve records from the work file associated with the SORT. RETURN is a special verb used only in OUTPUT PROCEDUREs. It is the equivalent of the READ verb and works in a similar way. The metalanguage for the RETURN verb is given in Figure 14-9.

RETURN SDFileName RECORD [INTO Identifier]

        AT END StatementBlock

END - RETURN

Figure 14-9. *Metalanguage for the RETURN verb*

Example 4-4 shows an operational template for an OUTPUT PROCEDURE that gets records from the work file and writes them to an output file. Notice that the work file is not opened in the OUTPUT PROCEDURE; the work file is automatically opened by the SORT.

Example 14-4. OUTPUT PROCEDURE File-Processing Template

```
OPEN OUTPUT OutFile
RETURN SDWorkFile RECORD
PERFORM UNTIL TerminatingCondition
    Setup OutRec
    WRITE OutRec
    RETURN SDWorkFile RECORD
END-PERFORM
CLOSE OutFile
```

Using an OUTPUT PROCEDURE to Produce a Summary File

The example in Listing 14-5 returns to the specification for the Universal Telecoms Monthly Report. However, the specification has been changed again. This time, instead of producing a report, you are required to produce a summary file. The summary file is a sequential file, ordered on ascending `SubscriberId`. Each subscriber record in the summary file summarizes all the records in `BillableServicesFile` for that subscriber. Each record in the file has the following description:

Field	Type	Length	Value
SubscriberId	9	10	–
CostOfTexts	9	6	0.10–9999.99
CostOfCalls	9	8	0.10–999999.99

Listing 14-5. Using an OUTPUT PROCEDURE to Create a Summary File

```
IDENTIFICATION DIVISION.
PROGRAM-ID. Listing14-5.
AUTHOR. Michael Coughlan.
ENVIRONMENT DIVISION.
INPUT-OUTPUT SECTION.
FILE-CONTROL.
    SELECT WorkFile ASSIGN TO "WORK.TMP".

    SELECT BillableServicesFile  ASSIGN TO "Listing14-5.dat"
            ORGANIZATION LINE SEQUENTIAL.

    SELECT SortedSummaryFile  ASSIGN TO "Listing14-5.Srt"
                ORGANIZATION LINE SEQUENTIAL.

DATA DIVISION.
FILE SECTION.
FD  BillableServicesFile.
01  SubscriberRec-BSF     PIC X(17).

SD  WorkFile.
01  WorkRec.
    88 EndOfWorkFile      VALUE HIGH-VALUES.
    02 SubscriberId-WF    PIC 9(10).
    02 FILLER             PIC 9.
       88 TextCall        VALUE 1.
       88 VoiceCall       VALUE 2.
    02 ServiceCost-WF     PIC 9(4)V99.

FD  SortedSummaryFile.
01  SummaryRec.
    02 SubscriberId       PIC 9(10).
    02 CostOfTexts        PIC 9(4)V99.
    02 CostOfCalls        PIC 9(6)V99.
```

```
PROCEDURE DIVISION.
Begin.
    SORT WorkFile ON ASCENDING KEY SubscriberId-WF
          USING BillableServicesFile
          OUTPUT PROCEDURE IS CreateSummaryFile
    STOP RUN.

CreateSummaryFile.
    OPEN OUTPUT SortedSummaryFile
    RETURN WorkFile
      AT END SET EndOfWorkFile TO TRUE
    END-RETURN
    PERFORM UNTIL EndOfWorkFile
       MOVE ZEROS TO CostOfTexts, CostOfCalls
       MOVE SubscriberId-WF TO SubscriberId
       PERFORM UNTIL SubscriberId-WF NOT EQUAL TO SubscriberId
          IF VoiceCall
             ADD ServiceCost-WF TO CostOfCalls
           ELSE
             ADD ServiceCost-WF TO CostOfTexts
          END-IF
          RETURN WorkFile
             AT END SET EndOfWorkFile TO TRUE
          END-RETURN
       END-PERFORM
       WRITE SummaryRec
    END-PERFORM
    CLOSE SortedSummaryFile.
```

Figure 14-8 illustrates the process of producing the summary file. The SORT takes records from BillableServicesFile and sorts them, and then the OUTPUT PROCEDURE summarizes them and writes the summary records to SortedSummaryFile.

The data items in BillableServicesFile are not referred to in the program and so are not explicitly defined, although the storage they require is reserved (PIC X(17)). For reasons of brevity, and because it would obscure the core logic, the program does not check the data for validity.

Some Interesting Programs

You have seen how you can use an INPUT PROCEDURE to process records before they are sent to a SORT and how you can use an OUTPUT PROCEDURE to process the sorted records. But each was used in isolation. You can achieve some interesting results by using them in concert.

Sorting Student Records into Date-of-Entry Order

Suppose there exists an unordered sequential file of student records, and each record in the file has the following description:

Field	Type	Length	Value
StudentId	9	7	YYxxxxx
CourseCode	9	5	LMxxx

StudentId is a number that consists of two digits representing the year of entry followed by six other digits. Write a program to sort StudentFile on the "real" ascending StudentId.

This specification presents an interesting issue. It says that the file should be ordered on the "real" ascending StudentId. This means the IDs of students who entered the university after the year 2000 should appear after those of students who entered the university before 2000. This is a problem because you can't just sort the records in ascending StudentId order, as is demonstrated in Figure 14-10.

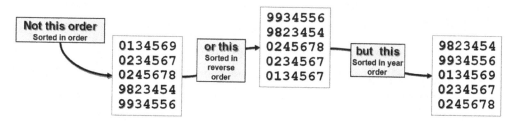

Figure 14-10. Showing the real StudentId sort order

How can this be done? Listing 14-6 solves the problem by using an INPUT PROCEDURE to alter StudentId to add the millennium to the date-of-entry part. Then the altered records are sorted, and the OUTPUT PROCEDURE strips off the millennium digits.

Listing 14-6. Using INPUT PROCEDURE and OUTPUT PROCEDURE in Concert

```
IDENTIFICATION DIVISION.
PROGRAM-ID.  Listing14-6.
AUTHOR.  Michael Coughlan.
ENVIRONMENT DIVISION.
INPUT-OUTPUT SECTION.
FILE-CONTROL.
    SELECT UnsortedStudentsFile ASSIGN TO "Listing14-6.DAT"
        ORGANIZATION IS LINE SEQUENTIAL.

    SELECT WorkFile ASSIGN TO "Workfile.tmp".

    SELECT SortedStudentsFile  ASSIGN TO "Listing14-6.srt"
            ORGANIZATION IS LINE SEQUENTIAL.

DATA DIVISION.
FILE SECTION.
FD UnsortedStudentsFile.
```

```cobol
01 StudentRecUF.
    88  EndOfUnsortedFile  VALUE HIGH-VALUES.
    02  StudentIdUF.
        03 MillenniumUF    PIC 99.
        03 FILLER          PIC 9(5).
    02  RecBodyUF          PIC X(14).

SD WorkFile.
01 StudentRecWF.
    88  EndOfWorkFile  VALUE HIGH-VALUES.
    02  FullStudentIdWF.
        03 MillenniumWF    PIC 99.
        03 StudentIdWF     PIC 9(7).
    02  RecBodyWF          PIC X(14).

FD SortedStudentsFile.
01 StudentRecSF.
    02  StudentIdSF        PIC 9(7).
    02  RecBodySF          PIC X(14).

PROCEDURE DIVISION.
Begin.
    SORT WorkFile ON ASCENDING KEY FullStudentIdWF
        INPUT PROCEDURE  IS AddInMillennium
        OUTPUT PROCEDURE IS RemoveMillennium
    STOP RUN.

AddInMillennium.
    OPEN INPUT UnsortedStudentsFile
    READ UnsortedStudentsFile
        AT END SET EndOfUnsortedFile TO TRUE
    END-READ
    PERFORM UNTIL EndOfUnsortedFile
        MOVE RecBodyUF TO RecBodyWF
        MOVE StudentIDUF    TO StudentIdWF
        IF MillenniumUF < 70
            MOVE 20 TO MillenniumWF
        ELSE
            MOVE 19 TO MillenniumWF
        END-IF
        RELEASE StudentRecWF
        READ UnsortedStudentsFile
            AT END SET EndOfUnsortedFile TO TRUE
        END-READ
    END-PERFORM
    CLOSE UnsortedStudentsFile.

RemoveMillennium.
    OPEN OUTPUT SortedStudentsFile
    RETURN WorkFile
        AT END SET EndOfWorkFile TO TRUE
```

```
END-RETURN
PERFORM UNTIL EndOfWorkFile
    MOVE RecBodyWF    TO RecBodySF
    MOVE StudentIdWF TO StudentIdSF
    WRITE StudentRecSF
    RETURN WorkFile
      AT END SET EndOfWorkFile TO TRUE
    END-RETURN
END-PERFORM
CLOSE SortedStudentsFile.
```

Sorting Tables

Versions of COBOL before ISO 2002 did not allow you to apply a SORT to a table. But it was possible to work around this restriction by using an INPUT PROCEDURE to release table elements to the work file and an OUTPUT PROCEDURE to get the sorted element-records from the work file and put them back into the table. The process is illustrated in Figure 14-11; see Listing 14-7.

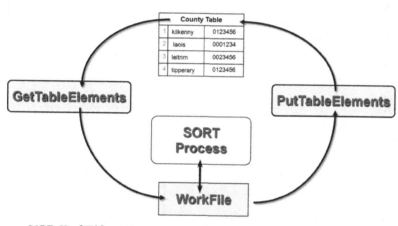

```
SORT WorkFile ON ASCENDING KEY CountyName-WF
       INPUT PROCEDURE IS GetTableElements
       OUTPUT PROCEDURE IS PutTableElements
```

Figure 14-11. *Using INPUT PROCEDURE and OUTPUT PROCEDURE to sort a table*

Listing 14-7. Sorting a Table Using INPUT PROCEDURE and OUTPUT PROCEDURE

```
IDENTIFICATION DIVISION.
PROGRAM-ID. Listing14-7.
DATA DIVISION.
WORKING-STORAGE SECTION.
01 CountyTable.
    02 TableValues.
        03 FILLER  PIC X(16)  VALUE "kilkenny 0080421".
        03 FILLER  PIC X(16)  VALUE "laois    0058732".
        03 FILLER  PIC X(16)  VALUE "leitrim  0025815".
        03 FILLER  PIC X(16)  VALUE "tipperary0140281".
        03 FILLER  PIC X(16)  VALUE "waterford0101518".
```

```
        03 FILLER   PIC X(16)   VALUE "westmeath0072027".
        03 FILLER   PIC X(16)   VALUE "carlow   0045845".
        03 FILLER   PIC X(16)   VALUE "wicklow  0114719".
        03 FILLER   PIC X(16)   VALUE "cavan    0056416".
        03 FILLER   PIC X(16)   VALUE "clare    0103333".
        03 FILLER   PIC X(16)   VALUE "meath    0133936".
        03 FILLER   PIC X(16)   VALUE "monaghan 0052772".
        03 FILLER   PIC X(16)   VALUE "offaly   0063702".
        03 FILLER   PIC X(16)   VALUE "roscommon0053803".
        03 FILLER   PIC X(16)   VALUE "sligo    0058178".
        03 FILLER   PIC X(16)   VALUE "cork     0448181".
        03 FILLER   PIC X(16)   VALUE "donegal  0137383".
        03 FILLER   PIC X(16)   VALUE "dublin   1122600".
        03 FILLER   PIC X(16)   VALUE "galway   0208826".
        03 FILLER   PIC X(16)   VALUE "wexford  0116543".
        03 FILLER   PIC X(16)   VALUE "kerry    0132424".
        03 FILLER   PIC X(16)   VALUE "kildare  0163995".
        03 FILLER   PIC X(16)   VALUE "limerick 0175529".
        03 FILLER   PIC X(16)   VALUE "longford 0031127".
        03 FILLER   PIC X(16)   VALUE "louth    0101802".
        03 FILLER   PIC X(16)   VALUE "mayo     0117428".
     02 FILLER REDEFINES TableValues.
        03    CountyDetails OCCURS 26 TIMES
              INDEXED BY Cidx.
           04 CountyName   PIC X(9).
           04 CountyPop    PIC 9(7).


01 PrnCountyPop           PIC Z,ZZZ,ZZ9.


PROCEDURE DIVISION.
Begin.
    DISPLAY "County name order"
    SORT CountyDetails ON ASCENDING KEY CountyName
    PERFORM DisplayCountyTotals
            VARYING Cidx FROM 1 BY 1 UNTIL Cidx GREATER
THAN 26.

    DISPLAY SPACES
    DISPLAY "County population order"
    SORT CountyDetails ON DESCENDING KEY CountyPop
    PERFORM DisplayCountyTotals
            VARYING Cidx FROM 1 BY 1 UNTIL Cidx GREATER
THAN 26.

    STOP RUN.

DisplayCountyTotals.
    MOVE CountyPop(Cidx) TO PrnCountyPop
    DISPLAY CountyName(Cidx) " is " PrnCountyPop
```

LISTING 14-7 Output

```
County name order
carlow      is       45,845
cavan       is       56,416
clare       is      103,333
cork        is      448,181
donegal     is      137,383
dublin      is    1,122,600
galway      is      208,826
kerry       is      132,424
kildare     is      163,995
kilkenny    is       80,421
laois       is       58,732
leitrim     is       25,815
limerick    is      175,529
longford    is       31,127
louth       is      101,802
mayo        is      117,428
meath       is      133,936
monaghan    is       52,772
offaly      is       63,702
roscommon   is       53,803
sligo       is       58,178
tipperary   is      140,281
waterford   is      101,518
westmeath   is       72,027
wexford     is      116,543
wicklow     is      114,719
```

```
County population order
dublin      is    1,122,600
cork        is      448,181
galway      is      208,826
limerick    is      175,529
kildare     is      163,995
tipperary   is      140,281
donegal     is      137,383
meath       is      133,936
kerry       is      132,424
mayo        is      117,428
wexford     is      116,543
wicklow     is      114,719
clare       is      103,333
louth       is      101,802
waterford   is      101,518
kilkenny    is       80,421
westmeath   is       72,027
offaly      is       63,702
laois       is       58,732
sligo       is       58,178
cavan       is       56,416
roscommon   is       53,803
monaghan    is       52,772
carlow      is       45,845
longford    is       31,127
leitrim     is       25,815
```

Sorting Tables: ISO 2002 Changes

Listing 14-7 shows how to sort a table using an INPUT PROCEDURE and an OUTPUT PROCEDURE. The problem with this solution is the work file. The sort operation, being bound to a file on backing storage, is comparatively slow. Sorting the table would be faster if it could be done wholly in memory.

Sorting a table directly in memory is exactly what the ISO 2002 version of COBOL now allows. The metalanguage for this SORT format is given in Figure 14-12, and Listing 14-8 shows how you can use this format to sort the County table from Listing 14-7.

$$\underline{\text{SORT}}\ \text{TableName}\ \left\{\text{ON} \left\{\begin{array}{l}\underline{\text{ASCENDING}}\\ \underline{\text{DESCENDING}}\end{array}\right\} \text{KEY} \{\text{TableElement}\}\dots\right\}\dots$$

$$\left[\text{WITH} \underline{\text{DUPLICATES}} \text{IN ORDER}\right]$$

$$\left[\text{COLLATING} \underline{\text{SEQUENCE}} \left\{\begin{array}{l}\text{IS AlphabetName1}\ [\text{AlphabetName2}]\\ \left\{\begin{array}{l}\text{FOR} \underline{\text{ALPHANUMERIC}} \text{IS AlphabetName1}\\ \text{FOR} \underline{\text{NATIONAL}} \text{IS AlphabetName2}\end{array}\right\}\end{array}\right\}\right]$$

Figure 14-12. *Metalanguage for the ISO 2002 version of SORT*

Listing 14-8. Applying SORT Directly to a Table

```
IDENTIFICATION DIVISION.
PROGRAM-ID. Listing14-8.
*> ISO 2002 Applying the SORT to a table
DATA DIVISION.
WORKING-STORAGE SECTION.
01 CountyTable.
   02 TableValues.
      03 FILLER  PIC X(16)  VALUE "kilkenny 0080421".
      03 FILLER  PIC X(16)  VALUE "laois    0058732".
      03 FILLER  PIC X(16)  VALUE "leitrim  0025815".
      03 FILLER  PIC X(16)  VALUE "tipperary0140281".
      03 FILLER  PIC X(16)  VALUE "waterford0101518".
      03 FILLER  PIC X(16)  VALUE "westmeath0072027".
      03 FILLER  PIC X(16)  VALUE "carlow   0045845".
      03 FILLER  PIC X(16)  VALUE "wicklow  0114719".
      03 FILLER  PIC X(16)  VALUE "cavan    0056416".
      03 FILLER  PIC X(16)  VALUE "clare    0103333".
      03 FILLER  PIC X(16)  VALUE "meath    0133936".
      03 FILLER  PIC X(16)  VALUE "monaghan 0052772".
      03 FILLER  PIC X(16)  VALUE "offaly   0063702".
      03 FILLER  PIC X(16)  VALUE "roscommon0053803".
      03 FILLER  PIC X(16)  VALUE "sligo    0058178".
      03 FILLER  PIC X(16)  VALUE "cork     0448181".
      03 FILLER  PIC X(16)  VALUE "donegal  0137383".
      03 FILLER  PIC X(16)  VALUE "dublin   1122600".
      03 FILLER  PIC X(16)  VALUE "galway   0208826".
      03 FILLER  PIC X(16)  VALUE "wexford  0116543".
      03 FILLER  PIC X(16)  VALUE "kerry    0132424".
      03 FILLER  PIC X(16)  VALUE "kildare  0163995".
      03 FILLER  PIC X(16)  VALUE "limerick 0175529".
```

```
        03 FILLER  PIC X(16)  VALUE "longford 0031127".
        03 FILLER  PIC X(16)  VALUE "louth    0101802".
        03 FILLER  PIC X(16)  VALUE "mayo     0117428".
    02 FILLER REDEFINES TableValues.
        03   CountyDetails OCCURS 26 TIMES
             INDEXED BY Cidx.
             04 CountyName  PIC X(9).
             04 CountyPop   PIC 9(7).

01 PrnCountyPop            PIC Z,ZZZ,ZZ9.

PROCEDURE DIVISION.
Begin.
    DISPLAY "County name order"
    SORT CountyDetails ON ASCENDING KEY CountyName
    PERFORM DisplayCountyTotals
          VARYING Cidx FROM 1 BY 1 UNTIL Cidx GREATER THAN 26.

    DISPLAY SPACES
    DISPLAY "County population order"
    SORT CountyDetails ON ASCENDING KEY CountyPop
    PERFORM DisplayCountyTotals
          VARYING Cidx FROM 1 BY 1 UNTIL Cidx GREATER THAN 26.

    STOP RUN.

DisplayCountyTotals.
    MOVE CountyPop(Cidx) TO PrnCountyPop
    DISPLAY CountyName(Cidx) " is " PrnCountyPop.
```

■ **Note**   For full details, read your implementer manual.

Merging Files

It is often useful to combine two or more files into a single large file. If the files are unordered, this is easy to accomplish because you can simply append the records in one file to the end of the other. But if the files are ordered, the task is somewhat more complicated—especially if there are more than two files—because you must preserve the ordering in the combined file.

In COBOL, instead of having to write special code every time you want to merge files, you can use the MERGE verb. MERGE takes a number of files, all ordered on the same key values, and combines them based on those key values. The combined file is then sent to an output file or an OUTPUT PROCEDURE.

MERGE Verb

The metalanguage for the MERGE verb is given in Figure 14-13. It should be obvious from the metalanguage that MERGE shares many of same declarations required for SORT. Just like SORT, MERGE uses a temporary work file that must be defined using an SD entry in the FILE SECTION. Also just as with SORT, the KEY field (on which the files are merged) must be a data item declared in the work file. And just as with SORT, you can use an OUTPUT PROCEDURE to get records from the work file before sending them to their ultimate destination. Unlike with SORT, however, no INPUT PROCEDURE is permitted.

$$\underline{\text{MERGE}}\ \text{SDWorkFileName} \left\{ \underline{\text{ON}} \left\{ \begin{matrix} \underline{\text{ASCENDING}} \\ \underline{\text{DESCENDING}} \end{matrix} \right\} \underline{\text{KEY}} \left\{ \text{MergeKeyIdentifier} \right\} \dots \right\} \dots$$

$$\left[\underline{\text{COLLATING}} \underline{\text{SEQUENCE}} \underline{\text{IS}} \text{AlphabetName} \right]$$

$$\underline{\text{USING}} \text{InFileName1} \left\{ \text{InFileName2} \right\} \dots$$

$$\left\{ \begin{matrix} \underline{\text{OUTPUT}} \underline{\text{PROCEDURE}} \underline{\text{IS}} \text{ProcedureName} \left[\left\{ \begin{matrix} \underline{\text{THRU}} \\ \underline{\text{THROUGH}} \end{matrix} \right\} \text{ProcedureName} \right] \\ \underline{\text{GIVING}} \left\{ \text{MergedFileName} \right\} \dots \end{matrix} \right\}$$

Figure 14-13. *Metalanguage for the MERGE verb*

MERGE Notes

You should consider the following when using MERGE:

- The results of the MERGE verb are predictable only when the records in the USING files are ordered as described in the KEY clause associated with the MERGE. For instance, if the MERGE statement has an ON DESCENDING KEY StudentId clause, then all the USING files must be ordered on descending StudentId.

- As with SORT, SDWorkFileName is the name of a temporary file, with an SD entry in the FILE SECTION, SELECT and ASSIGN entries in the INPUT-OUTPUT SECTION, and an organization of RECORD SEQUENTIAL.

- Each MergeKeyIdentifier identifies a field in the record of the work file. The merged files are ordered on this key field(s).

- When more than one MergeKeyIdentifier is specified, the keys decrease in significance from left to right (the leftmost key is most significant, and the rightmost is least significant).

- InFileName and MergedFileName are the names of the input file to be merged and the resulting combined file produced by the MERGE, respectively. These files are automatically opened by the MERGE. When the MERGE executes, they must not be already open.

- AlphabetName is an alphabet name defined in the SPECIAL-NAMES paragraph of the ENVIRONMENT DIVISION. This clause is used to select the character set the SORT verb uses for collating the records in the file. The character set may be STANDARD-1 (ASCII), STANDARD-2 (ISO 646), NATIVE (may be defined by the system to be ASCII or EBCDIC; see your implementer manual), or user defined.

- MERGE can use an OUTPUT PROCEDURE and the RETURN verb to get merged records from SDWorkFileName.

- The OUTPUT PROCEDURE executes only after the files have been merged and must contain at least one RETURN statement to get the records from SortFile.

Merging Province Sales Files

Listing 14-9 is an example program that uses MERGE to combine four sequential files, each ordered on ascending ProductCode. The program is based on the following specification.

Listing 14-9. Merging ProvinceSales Files and Producing a Sales Summary File

```
IDENTIFICATION DIVISION.
PROGRAM-ID. Listing14-9.
AUTHOR. Michael Coughlan.
ENVIRONMENT DIVISION.
INPUT-OUTPUT SECTION.
FILE-CONTROL.
    SELECT UlsterSales    ASSIGN TO "Listing14-9ulster.dat"
            ORGANIZATION IS LINE SEQUENTIAL.

    SELECT ConnachtSales  ASSIGN TO "Listing14-9connacht.dat"
            ORGANIZATION IS LINE SEQUENTIAL.

    SELECT MunsterSales   ASSIGN TO "Listing14-9munster.dat"
            ORGANIZATION IS LINE SEQUENTIAL.

    SELECT LeinsterSales  ASSIGN TO "Listing14-9leinster.dat"
            ORGANIZATION IS LINE SEQUENTIAL.

    SELECT SummaryFile    ASSIGN TO "Listing14-9.sum"
                ORGANIZATION IS LINE SEQUENTIAL.

    SELECT WorkFile       ASSIGN TO "WORK.TMP".

DATA DIVISION.
FILE SECTION.
FD  UlsterSales.
01  FILLER              PIC X(12).

FD  ConnachtSales.
01  FILLER              PIC X(12).

FD  MunsterSales.
01  FILLER              PIC X(12).

FD  LeinsterSales.
01  FILLER              PIC X(12).

FD  SummaryFile.
01  SummaryRec.
    02 ProductCode-SF    PIC X(6).
    02 TotalSalesValue   PIC 9(6)V99.
```

```
SD   WorkFile.
01   WorkRec.
        88 EndOfWorkfile        VALUE HIGH-VALUES.
        02 ProductCode-WF       PIC X(6).
        02 ValueOfSale-WF       PIC 9999V99.


PROCEDURE DIVISION.
Begin.
     MERGE WorkFile ON ASCENDING KEY ProductCode-WF
         USING UlsterSales, ConnachtSales, MunsterSales, LeinsterSales
         OUTPUT PROCEDURE IS SummarizeProductSales

     STOP RUN.

SummarizeProductSales.
     OPEN OUTPUT SummaryFile
     RETURN WorkFile
        AT END SET EndOfWorkfile TO TRUE
     END-RETURN

     PERFORM UNTIL EndOfWorkFile
        MOVE ZEROS TO TotalSalesValue
        MOVE ProductCode-WF TO ProductCode-SF
        PERFORM UNTIL ProductCode-WF NOT EQUAL TO ProductCode-SF
           ADD ValueOfSale-WF TO TotalSalesValue
           RETURN WorkFile
              AT END SET EndOfWorkfile TO TRUE
           END-RETURN
        END-PERFORM
        WRITE SummaryRec
     END-PERFORM
     CLOSE SummaryFile.
```

Every month, the TrueValue head office receives a file from its branch in each of the four provinces of Ireland. Each file records the sales made in that province. A program is required that will combine these four files and, from them, produce a summary file that records the total value of the sales of each product sold by the company. The summary file must be ordered on ascending ProductCode. The record description for each of the four files is as follows:

Field	Type	Length	Value
ProductCode	X	6	–
ValueOfSale	9	6	0–9999.99

The record description for the summary file is shown next:

Field	Type	Length	Value
ProductCode	X	6	–
TotalValueOfSale	9	8	0–999999.99

Summary

This chapter explored the SORT and MERGE verbs. You discovered how to define the work file that SORT uses as a temporary scratch pad when sorting. You saw how to create an INPUT PROCEDURE to filter or alter the records sent to the work file and how to create an OUTPUT PROCEDURE to get and process the sorted records from the work file. You also learned that you can use the INPUT PROCEDURE and OUTPUT PROCEDURE in concert to achieve interesting results: you can sort a table by using an INPUT PROCEDURE to get the elements from the table and release them to the work file and an OUTPUT PROCEDURE to retrieve the sorted element-records from the work file and place them back in the table. In addition, the ISO 2002 version of COBOL allows you to sort a table directly. Finally, you saw how to use the MERGE verb to combine identically ordered files into one file that preserves the ordering.

The next chapter introduces COBOL string handling. In many other languages, string manipulation is achieved by using a library of string functions. In COBOL, string manipulation uses intrinsic functions, reference modification, and the STRING, UNSTRING, and INSPECT verbs.

PROGRAMMING EXERCISE 1

Visitors to an Irish web site are asked to fill in a guestbook form. The form requests the name of the visitor, their country of origin, and a comment. These fields are stored as a fixed length record in GuestBookFile. GuestBookFile is an unordered sequential file, each record of which has the following description:

Field	Type	Length	Value
GuestName	X	20	–
CountryName	X	20	–
GuestComment	X	40	–

You are required to write a program to print a report that shows the number of visitors from each foreign (non-Irish) country. The report must be printed in ascending CountryName sequence. Because the records in GuestBookFile are not in any particular order, before the report can be printed, the file must be sorted by CountryName. The report template is as follows:

```
    Foreign Guests Report
Country                 Visitors
XXXXXXXXXXXXXXXXXXXX    XXXXX
XXXXXXXXXXXXXXXXXXXX    XXXXX
XXXXXXXXXXXXXXXXXXXX    XXXXX
XXXXXXXXXXXXXXXXXXXX    XXXXX
XXXXXXXXXXXXXXXXXXXX    XXXXX
XXXXXXXXXXXXXXXXXXXX    XXXXX
XXXXXXXXXXXXXXXXXXXX    XXXXX
XXXXXXXXXXXXXXXXXXXX    XXXXX
XXXXXXXXXXXXXXXXXXXX    XXXXX
XXXXXXXXXXXXXXXXXXXX    XXXXX
XXXXXXXXXXXXXXXXXXXX    XXXXX
XXXXXXXXXXXXXXXXXXXX    XXXXX

    ***** End of report *****
```

PROGRAMMING EXERCISE 1: ANSWER

Because only foreign visitors are of interest, there is no point in sorting the entire file. An INPUT PROCEDURE is used to select only the records of visitors from foreign (non-Irish) countries. An OUTPUT PROCEDURE is used to create the report.

When you examine the fields of a GuestBookFile record, notice that, for the purposes of this report, GuestName and GuestComment are irrelevant. The only field you need for the report is the CountryName field. So in addition to selecting only foreign guests, the INPUT PROCEDURE alters the structure of the records supplied to the sort process. Because the new records are only 20 characters in size, rather than 80 characters, the amount of data that has to be sorted is substantially reduced.

Listing 14-10. Using an INPUT PROCEDURE to Modify and Filter the Records in the Input File

```
IDENTIFICATION DIVISION.
PROGRAM-ID.  Listing14-10.
AUTHOR.  Michael Coughlan.
ENVIRONMENT DIVISION.
INPUT-OUTPUT SECTION.
FILE-CONTROL.
   SELECT GuestBookFile
         ASSIGN TO "Listing14-10.Dat"
         ORGANIZATION IS LINE SEQUENTIAL.

   SELECT WorkFile
         ASSIGN TO "Work.Tmp".

   SELECT ForeignGuestReport
         ASSIGN TO "Listing14-10.rpt"
         ORGANIZATION IS LINE SEQUENTIAL.

DATA DIVISION.
FILE SECTION.
FD GuestBookFile.
01 GuestRec.
   88  EndOfFile  VALUE HIGH-VALUES.
   02  GuestNameGF       PIC X(20).
   02  CountryNameGF      PIC X(20).
       88 CountryIsIreland VALUE "IRELAND".
   02  GuestCommentGF     PIC X(40).

SD WorkFile.
01 WorkRec.
   88 EndOfWorkFile       VALUE HIGH-VALUES.
   02 CountryNameWF       PIC X(20).

FD ForeignGuestReport.
01 PrintLine              PIC X(38).
```

```
WORKING-STORAGE SECTION.
01 Heading1                 PIC X(25)
        VALUE "   Foreign Guests Report".


01 Heading2.
   02 FILLER                PIC X(22) VALUE "Country".
   02 FILLER                PIC X(8)  VALUE "Visitors".


01 CountryLine.
   02 PrnCountryName        PIC X(20).
   02 PrnVisitorCount       PIC BBBZZ,ZZ9.


01 ReportFooting           PIC X(27)
        VALUE "  ***** End of report *****".


01 VisitorCount            PIC 9(5).


PROCEDURE DIVISION.
Begin.
    SORT WorkFile ON ASCENDING CountryNameWF
        INPUT PROCEDURE IS SelectForeignGuests
        OUTPUT PROCEDURE IS PrintGuestsReport.


    STOP RUN.


PrintGuestsReport.
    OPEN OUTPUT ForeignGuestReport
    WRITE PrintLine FROM Heading1
        AFTER ADVANCING PAGE
    WRITE PrintLine FROM Heading2
        AFTER ADVANCING 1 LINES


    RETURN WorkFile
        AT END SET EndOfWorkfile TO TRUE
    END-RETURN
    PERFORM PrintReportBody UNTIL EndOfWorkfile


    WRITE PrintLine FROM ReportFooting
        AFTER ADVANCING 2 LINES
    CLOSE ForeignGuestReport.


 PrintReportBody.
    MOVE CountryNameWF TO PrnCountryName
    MOVE ZEROS TO VisitorCount
    PERFORM UNTIL CountryNameWF NOT EQUAL TO PrnCountryName
       ADD 1 TO VisitorCount
       RETURN WorkFile
          AT END SET EndOfWorkfile TO TRUE
       END-RETURN
    END-PERFORM
```

```
        MOVE VisitorCount TO PrnVisitorCount
        WRITE PrintLine FROM CountryLine
              AFTER ADVANCING 1 LINE.

    SelectForeignGuests.
        OPEN INPUT GuestBookFile.
        READ GuestBookFile
           AT END SET EndOfFile TO TRUE
        END-READ
        PERFORM UNTIL EndOfFile
           IF NOT CountryIsIreland
              MOVE CountryNameGF TO CountryNameWF
              RELEASE WorkRec
           END-IF
           READ GuestBookFile
              AT END SET EndOfFile TO TRUE
           END-READ
        END-PERFORM
        CLOSE GuestBookFile.
```

CHAPTER 15

String Manipulation

In many languages, string manipulation is achieved by using a library of string functions or, as in Java, the methods of a String class. COBOL also uses a library of string-manipulation functions, but most string manipulation is done using reference modification and the three string-handling verbs: STRING, UNSTRING, and INSPECT.

This chapter starts by examining the string-handling verbs. These verbs allow you to count and replace characters, and concatenate and split strings. You are then introduced to reference modification, which lets you treat any string as an array of characters. Finally, you learn about the intrinsic functions used for string and date manipulation.

The INSPECT Verb

The INSPECT verb has four formats;

- The first format is used for counting characters in a string.

- The second replaces a group of characters in a string with another group of characters.

- The third combines both operations in one statement.

- The fourth format converts each character in a set of characters to its corresponding character in another set of characters.

Before starting a formal examination of the INSPECT formats, let's get a feel for how the verb operates by looking at a short program (see Listing 15-1). The program accepts a line of text from the user and then counts and displays how many times each letter of the alphabet occurs in the text.

Listing 15-1. Finding the Number of Times Each Letter Occurs in a Line of Text

```
IDENTIFICATION DIVISION.
PROGRAM-ID. Listing15-1.
AUTHOR. Michael Coughlan.
DATA DIVISION.
WORKING-STORAGE SECTION.
01 TextLine       PIC X(80).

01 LowerCase      PIC X(26) VALUE "abcdefghijklmnopqrstuvwxyz".

01 UpperCase      VALUE "ABCDEFGHIJKLMNOPQRSTUVWXYZ".
   02 Letter      PIC X OCCURS 26 TIMES.
```

```
01 idx                PIC 99.

01 LetterCount        PIC 99.

01 PrnLetterCount     PIC Z9.

PROCEDURE DIVISION.
Begin.
    DISPLAY "Enter text : " WITH NO ADVANCING
    ACCEPT TextLine
    INSPECT TextLine
            CONVERTING LowerCase TO UpperCase

    PERFORM VARYING idx FROM 1 BY 1 UNTIL idx > 26
       MOVE ZEROS TO LetterCount
       INSPECT TextLine TALLYING LetterCount FOR ALL Letter(idx)
       IF LetterCount > ZERO
          MOVE LetterCount TO PrnLetterCount
          DISPLAY "Letter " Letter(idx) " occurs " PrnLetterCount " times"
       END-IF
    END-PERFORM
    STOP RUN.
```

```
                    Listing 15-1 output
Enter text : That time of year thou mayst in me behold
Letter A occurs  3 times
Letter B occurs  1 times
Letter D occurs  1 times
Letter E occurs  4 times
Letter F occurs  1 times
Letter H occurs  3 times
Letter I occurs  2 times
Letter L occurs  1 times
Letter M occurs  3 times
Letter N occurs  1 times
Letter O occurs  3 times
Letter R occurs  1 times
Letter S occurs  1 times
Letter T occurs  5 times
Letter U occurs  1 times
Letter Y occurs  2 times
```

The program gets a line of text from the user. It then uses INSPECT..CONVERTING to convert all the characters to their uppercase equivalents.

The UpperCase data item in this program does double duty. It is used in INSPECT CONVERTING as an ordinary alphanumeric data item, but it is also defined as a 26-element prefilled table of letters. Using this table, the PERFORM loop supplies the letters one at a time to INSPECT..TALLYING, which counts the number of times each letter occurs in TextLine. It stores the count in LetterCount. If the letter occurred in TextLine, then the count is displayed.

There are some interesting things to note about this program. First, since intrinsic functions were introduced in the ANS 85 version of COBOL, is it no longer necessary to use INSPECT.. CONVERTING to convert characters to uppercase. Nowadays you can use the UPPER-CASE function. This function has the added benefit that it can do the conversion without changing the original text. Second, you don't actually need to hold the letters of the alphabet as a table. Reference modification allows you to treat any alphanumeric data item as a table of characters. Listing 15-2 shows a version of the program that incorporates these modernizations.

Listing 15-2. Modernized Version of the Program in Listing 15-1

```
IDENTIFICATION DIVISION.
PROGRAM-ID. Listing15-2.
AUTHOR. Michael Coughlan.
DATA DIVISION.
WORKING-STORAGE SECTION.
01 TextLine         PIC X(80).

01 Letters          PIC X(26) VALUE "ABCDEFGHIJKLMNOPQRSTUVWXYZ".

01 LetterPos        PIC 99.

01 LetterCount      PIC 99.

01 PrnLetterCount   PIC Z9.
```

```
PROCEDURE DIVISION.
Begin.
   DISPLAY "Enter text : " WITH NO ADVANCING
   ACCEPT TextLine
   PERFORM VARYING LetterPos  FROM 1 BY 1 UNTIL LetterPos  > 26
     MOVE ZEROS TO LetterCount
     INSPECT FUNCTION UPPER-CASE(TextLine)
             TALLYING LetterCount FOR ALL Letters(LetterPos:1)
     IF LetterCount > ZERO
        MOVE LetterCount TO PrnLetterCount
        DISPLAY "Letter " Letters(LetterPos:1) " occurs " PrnLetterCount " times"
     END-IF
   END-PERFORM
   STOP RUN.
```

INSPECT..TALLYING: Format 1

INSPECT..TALLYING counts the number of occurrences of a character in a string. The metalanguage for this version of INSPECT is given in Figure 15-1.

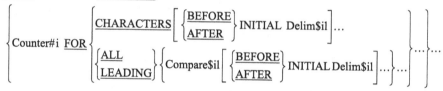

INSPECT SourceStr$i TALLYING

Figure 15-1. *Metalanguage for* INSPECT..TALLYING

This version of INSPECT works by scanning the source string SourceStr$i from left to right, counting the occurrences of all characters or just a specified character:

- The behavior of INSPECT is modified by the LEADING, ALL, BEFORE, and AFTER phrases. An ALL, LEADING, or CHARACTERS phrase may only be followed by one BEFORE and one AFTER phrase.

- As indicated by the ellipsis after the final bracket, you can use a number of counters—each with its own modifying phrases—with an INSPECT..TALLYING statement.

- If Compare$il or Delim$il is a figurative constant, it is one character in size.

Modifying Phrases

The operation of INSPECT is governed by the modifying phrases used. The meaning of these phrases is as follows:

BEFORE: Designates the characters to the left of the associated delimiter (Delim$il) as valid. If the delimiter is not present in SourceStr$i, then using the BEFORE phrase implies that all the characters are valid.

AFTER: Designates the characters to the right of the associated delimiter (Delim$il) as valid. If the delimiter is not present in the SourceStr$i, then using the AFTER phrase implies that there are no valid characters in the string.

ALL: Counts all Compare$il characters from the first matching valid character to the first invalid one.

LEADING: Counts leading Compare$il characters from the first matching valid character encountered to the first nonmatching or invalid character.

INSPECT..TALLYING Examples

Example 15-1 shows some example INSPECT statements, and Listing 15-3 presents a small program. The program's task is to count the number of vowels and the number of consonants in a line of text entered by the user.

Example 15-1. Some INSPECT..TALLYING Example Statements

```
INSPECT TextLine TALLYING UnstrPtr FOR LEADING SPACES.

INSPECT TextLine TALLYING
        eCount FOR ALL "e" AFTER  INITIAL "start"
                           BEFORE INITIAL "end".

INSPECT TextLine TALLYING
        aCount FOR ALL "a"
        eCount FOR ALL "e"
        oCount FOR ALL "o"

INSPECT FUNCTION REVERSE(TextLine) TALLYING
        TrailingSpaces FOR LEADING SPACES
COMPUTE StrLength = FUNCTION LENGTH(TextLine) - TrailingSpaces
```

Listing 15-3. Counting Vowels and Consonants

```
IDENTIFICATION DIVISION.
PROGRAM-ID. Listing15-3.
AUTHOR. Michael Coughlan.
DATA DIVISION.
WORKING-STORAGE SECTION.
01 TextLine        PIC X(80).

01 VowelCount      PIC 99 VALUE ZERO.

01 ConsonantCount  PIC 99 VALUE ZERO.

PROCEDURE DIVISION.
Begin.
    DISPLAY "Enter text : " WITH NO ADVANCING
    ACCEPT TextLine
    INSPECT FUNCTION UPPER-CASE(TextLine) TALLYING
            VowelCount FOR ALL "A" "E" "I" "O" "U"
            ConsonantCount FOR ALL
            "B" "C" "D" "F" "G" "H" "J" "K" "L" "M" "N" "P"
            "Q" "R" "S" "T" "V" "W" "X" "Y" "Z"

    DISPLAY "The line contains " VowelCount " vowels and "
            ConsonantCount " consonants."
    STOP RUN.
```

Listing 15-3 output
Enter text : When to the Sessions of Sweet Silent thought
The line contains 13 vowels and 24 consonants.

Programmatic Detour

There are a number of ways to solve the problem of finding the number of vowels and consonants in a line of text. Although it is not strictly string manipulation, I'd like to explore an alternative solution to Listing 15-3 here, because it allows me to introduce an aspect of condition names that you have not seen before. In the solution in Listing 15-4, TextLine is defined as an array of characters. A PERFORM is used to step through the array and, at each character, test whether it is a vowel or a consonant; whichever it is, the PERFORM then increments the appropriate total. The interesting part is the way you discover whether the character is a vowel or a consonant.

You may not have realized that a condition name can be set to monitor a table element. That is what the program in Listing 15-4 does. Once the condition names for vowels and consonants are set up, all the program needs to do is test which condition name is set to TRUE for the character under consideration and then increment the appropriate count.

Listing 15-4. Using a Table Element Condition to Count Vowels and Consonants

```
IDENTIFICATION DIVISION.
PROGRAM-ID. Listing15-4.
AUTHOR. Michael Coughlan.
DATA DIVISION.
WORKING-STORAGE SECTION.
01 TextLine.
    02 Letter          PIC X OCCURS 80 TIMES.
        88 Vowel       VALUE  "A" "E" "I" "O" "U".
        88 Consonant   VALUE  "B" "C" "D" "F" "G" "H" "J" "K" "L" "M" "N" "P"
                              "Q" "R" "S" "T" "V" "W" "X" "Y" "Z".
01 VowelCount          PIC 99 VALUE ZERO.
01 ConsonantCount      PIC 99 VALUE ZERO.
01 idx                 PIC 99.
PROCEDURE DIVISION.
Begin.
    DISPLAY "Enter text : " WITH NO ADVANCING
    ACCEPT TextLine
    MOVE FUNCTION UPPER-CASE(TextLine) TO TextLine
    PERFORM VARYING idx FROM 1 BY 1 UNTIL idx > 80
        IF Vowel(idx) ADD 1 TO VowelCount
          ELSE IF Consonant(idx) ADD 1 TO ConsonantCount
        END-IF
    END-PERFORM
    DISPLAY "The line contains " VowelCount " vowels and " ConsonantCount " consonants."
    STOP RUN.
```

```
                          Listing 15-4 output
Enter text : When in disgrace with fortune and men's eyes
The line contains 13 vowels and 23 consonants.
```

INSPECT .. REPLACING: Format 2

INSPECT..REPLACING replaces characters in the string with a replacement character. The metalanguage for this version of INSPECT is given in Figure 15-2.

INSPECT SourceStr$i <u>REPLACING</u>

Figure 15-2. *Metalanguage for* `INSPECT..REPLACING`

This version of INSPECT works by scanning the source string SourceStr$i from left to right and replacing occurrences of all characters with a replacement character, or replacing specified characters with replacement characters:

- The behavior of the INSPECT is modified by the LEADING, ALL, FIRST, BEFORE, and AFTER phrases. An ALL, LEADING, FIRST, or CHARACTERS phrase may only be followed by one BEFORE phrase and one AFTER phrase.

- If Compare$il or Delim$il is a figurative constant, it is one character in size. But when Replace$il is a figurative constant, its size equals that of Compare$il.

- The sizes of Compare$il and Replace$il must be equal.

- When there is a CHARACTERS phrase, the size of ReplaceChar$il and the delimiter that may follow it (Delim$il) must be one character.

Modifying Phrases

Like INSPECT..TALLYING, the operation of INSPECT..REPLACING is governed by the modifying phrases used. The meaning of these phrases is as follows:

> BEFORE: Designates the characters to the left of its associated delimiter (Delim$il) as valid. If the delimiter is not present in SourceStr$i, then using the BEFORE phrase implies that all the characters are valid.

> AFTER: Designates the characters to the right of its associated delimiter (Delim$il) as valid. If the delimiter is not present in the SourceStr$i, then using the AFTER phrase implies that there are no valid characters in the string.

> ALL: Replaces all Compare$il characters with the Replace$il characters from the first matching valid character to the first invalid one.

> FIRST: Causes only the first valid character(s) to be replaced.

INSPECT..REPLACING Examples

The INSPECT..REPLACING statements in Example 15-2 work on the data in StringData to produce the results shown in the storage schematics. Assume that before each INSPECT executes, the value "FFFAFFFFFFQFFFZ" (shown in the Before row) is moved to StringData.

Example 15-2. Example INSPECT..REPLACING Statements with Results

1.   INSPECT StringData REPLACING ALL "F" BY "G"
        AFTER INITIAL "A" BEFORE INITIAL "Q"

2.   INSPECT StringData REPLACING ALL "F" BY "G"
        AFTER INITIAL "A" BEFORE INITIAL "Z"

3.   INSPECT StringData REPLACING FIRST "F" BY "G"
        AFTER INITIAL "A" BEFORE INITIAL "Q"

4.   INSPECT StringData REPLACING
        ALL "FFFF" BY "DOGS"
        AFTER INITIAL "A" BEFORE INITIAL "Z"

5.   INSPECT StringData REPLACING
        CHARACTERS BY "z" BEFORE INITIAL "Q"

01 StringData PIC X(15).														
Before	F	F	F	A	F	F	F	F	F	F	Q	F	F	F	Z
After 1	F	F	F	A	G	G	G	G	G	G	Q	F	F	F	Z
After 2	F	F	F	A	G	G	G	G	G	G	Q	G	G	G	Z
After 3	F	F	F	A	G	F	F	F	F	F	Q	G	G	G	Z
After 4	F	F	F	A	D	O	G	S	F	F	Q	F	F	F	Z
After 5	z	z	z	z	z	z	z	z	z	z	Q	F	F	F	Z

INSPECT: Format 3

The third format of INSPECT simply allows you to combine the operation of the two previous formats in one statement. Please see those formats for explanations and examples. The metalanguage for the third INSPECT format is shown in Figure 15-3. This format is executed as though two successive INSPECT statements are applied to SourceStr$i, the first being an INSPECT..TALLYING and the second an INSPECT.. REPLACING.

INSPECT SourceStr$i <u>TALLYING</u>

$$
\left\{ \text{Counter\#i} \ \underline{\text{FOR}} \left\{ \begin{array}{l} \underline{\text{CHARACTERS}} \left[\left\{ \begin{array}{l} \underline{\text{BEFORE}} \\ \underline{\text{AFTER}} \end{array} \right\} \text{INITIAL Delim\$il} \right] \ldots \\[2em] \left\{ \begin{array}{l} \underline{\text{ALL}} \\ \underline{\text{LEADING}} \end{array} \right\} \left\{ \text{Compare\$il} \left[\left\{ \begin{array}{l} \underline{\text{BEFORE}} \\ \underline{\text{AFTER}} \end{array} \right\} \text{INITIAL Delim\$il} \right] \ldots \right\} \ldots \end{array} \right\} \ldots \right\} \ldots
$$

<u>REPLACING</u>

$$
\left\{ \begin{array}{l} \underline{\text{CHARACTERS}} \ \text{BY ReplaceChar\$il} \left[\left\{ \begin{array}{l} \underline{\text{BEFORE}} \\ \underline{\text{AFTER}} \end{array} \right\} \text{INITIAL Delim\$il} \right] \ldots \\[3em] \left\{ \begin{array}{l} \underline{\text{ALL}} \\ \underline{\text{LEADING}} \\ \underline{\text{FIRST}} \end{array} \right\} \left\{ \text{Compare\$il BY Replace\$il} \left[\left\{ \begin{array}{l} \underline{\text{BEFORE}} \\ \underline{\text{AFTER}} \end{array} \right\} \text{INITIAL Delim\$il} \right] \ldots \right\} \ldots \end{array} \right\} \ldots
$$

Figure 15-3. *Metalanguage for format 3 of* INSPECT

INSPECT .. CONVERTING: Format 4

INSPECT..CONVERTING seems very similar to INSPECT..REPLACING but actually works quite differently. It is used to convert one list of characters to another list of characters on a character-per-character basis. The metalanguage for this version of INSPECT is given in Figure 15-4.

INSPECT SourceStr$i <u>CONVERTING</u>

Compare$il <u>TO</u> Convert$il

$$
\left[\left\{ \begin{array}{l} \underline{\text{BEFORE}} \\ \underline{\text{AFTER}} \end{array} \right\} \text{INITIAL Delim\$il} \right] \ldots
$$

Figure 15-4. *Metalanguage for* INSPECT..CONVERTING

Using INSPECT .. CONVERTING

INSPECT..CONVERTING works on individual characters. If any of the Compare$il list of characters are found in SourceStr$i, they are replaced by the characters in Convert$il on a one-for-one basis. For instance, in Figure 15-5, an *F* found in StringData is converted to *z*, *X* is converted to *y*, *T* is converted to *a*, and *D* is converted to *b*.

Figure 15-5. INSPECT..CONVERTING *showing the conversion strategy*

The INSPECT..CONVERTING in Figure 15-5 is the equivalent of the following:

```
INSPECT StringData REPLACING
ALL "F" BY "z",
    "X" BY "y",
    "T" BY "a",
    "D" BY "b"
```

These are some rules for INSPECT..CONVERTING:

- Compare$il and Convert$il must be equal in size.

- When Convert$il is a figurative constant, its size equals that of Compare$il.

- The same character cannot appear more than once in Compare$il, because each character in the Compare$il string is associated with a replacement character. For instance, INSPECT StringData CONVERTING "XTX" TO "abc" is not allowed because the system won't know if X should be converted to *a* or *c*.

INSPECT..CONVERTING Examples

You saw an example of INSPECT..CONVERTING in Listing 15-1, where it was used to convert text to uppercase. That example is repeated in Listing 15-3, but here it demonstrates that Compare$il and Convert$il can be either strings or data items containing string values.

Example 15-3. Using INSPECT..CONVERTING to Convert Text to Uppercase or Lowercase

```
DATA DIVISION.
WORKING-STORAGE SECTION.
01 TextLine        PIC X(60).
01 LowerCase       PIC X(26) VALUE "abcdefghijklmnopqrstuvwxyz".
01 UpperCase       PIC X(26) VALUE "ABCDEFGHIJKLMNOPQRSTUVWXYZ".

PROCEDURE DIVISION.
Begin.
    DISPLAY "Enter text : " WITH NO ADVANCING
    ACCEPT TextLine

    INSPECT TextLine CONVERTING
            "abcdefghijklmnopqrstuvwxyz" TO
            "ABCDEFGHIJKLMNOPQRSTUVWXYZ"
    DISPLAY "Entered text in upper case = " TextLine

    INSPECT TextLine CONVERTING UpperCase TO LowerCase
    DISPLAY "Entered text in lower case = " TextLine.
```

Sometimes when you want to process the words in a line of text, especially if you want to recognize the words, you may need to get rid of the punctuation marks. Example 15-4 uses INSPECT..CONVERTING to convert punctuation marks in the text to spaces. UNSTRING is then used to unpack the words from the text.

Example 15-4. Using INSPECT..CONVERTING to Convert Punctuation Marks to Spaces

```cobol
ACCEPT TextLine
INSPECT TextLine CONVERTING ",.;:?!-_" TO SPACES
MOVE 1 TO UnstrPtr
PERFORM UNTIL EndOfText
    UNSTRING TextLine DELIMITED BY ALL SPACES
            INTO UnpackedWord
            WITH POINTER UnstrPtr
    DISPLAY UnpackedWord
END-PERFORM
```

The final example (Example 15-5) shows how you can use INSPECT..CONVERTING to implement a simple encoding mechanism. It converts the character *0* to character *5, 1* to *2, 2* to *9, 3* to *8*, and so on. Conversion starts when the characters *@>* are encountered in the string and stops when *<@* appears.

Example 15-5. Using INSPECT..CONVERTING to Implement an Encoding Mechanism

```cobol
WORKING-STORAGE SECTION.
01 TextLine         PIC X(70).

01 UnEncodedText    PIC X(10) VALUE "0123456789".

01 EncodedText      PIC X(10) VALUE "5298317046".

PROCEDURE DIVISION.
Begin.
    DISPLAY "Text : "
            WITH NO ADVANCING
    ACCEPT TextLine
    INSPECT TextLine CONVERTING
        UnEncodedText  TO  EncodedText
        AFTER  INITIAL "@>"
        BEFORE INITIAL "<@"

    DISPLAY "Encoded   = " TextLine

    INSPECT TextLine CONVERTING
        EncodedText  TO  UnEncodedText
        AFTER  INITIAL "@>"
        BEFORE INITIAL "<@"

    DISPLAY "UnEncoded = " TextLine

    STOP RUN.
```

```
                      Example 15-5 output
Text : My home number is @> 353-61-43975689373 <@. Call me!
Encoded   = My home number is @> 818-72-38601746808 <@. Call me!
UnEncoded = My home number is @> 353-61-43975689373 <@. Call me!
```

String Concatenation

String concatenation involves joining the contents of two or more source strings or partial source strings to create a single destination string. In COBOL, string concatenation is done using the STRING verb. Before I discuss the STRING verb formally, let's look at some examples to get a feel for what it can do.

The first example concatenates the entire contents of the identifiers String1 and String2 with the literal "LMO51" and puts the resulting sting into DestString:

```
STRING String1, String2, "LMO51" DELIMITED BY SIZE
    INTO DestString
END-STRING
```

The second example concatenates the entire contents of String1, the partial contents of String2 (all the characters up to the first space), and the partial contents of String3 (all the characters up to the word *unique*) and puts the concatenated string in DestString.

```
STRING
    String1 DELIMITED BY SIZE
    String2 DELIMITED BY SPACES
    String3 DELIMITED BY "unique"
INTO DestString
END-STRING
```

The STRING Verb

The metalanguage for the STRING verb is given in Figure 15-6.

$$
\text{STRING} \left\{ \text{SourceString\$il} \ldots \underline{\text{DELIMITED}} \text{ BY} \left\{ \begin{matrix} \text{Delim\$il} \\ \underline{\text{SIZE}} \end{matrix} \right\} \right\} \ldots
$$

$$
\underline{\text{INTO}} \text{ DestString\$i}
$$
$$
\left[\text{WITH } \underline{\text{POINTER}} \text{ Pointer\#i} \right]
$$
$$
\left[\text{ON } \underline{\text{OVERFLOW}} \text{ StatementBlock} \right]
$$
$$
\left[\underline{\text{NOT}} \text{ ON } \underline{\text{OVERFLOW}} \text{ StatementBlock} \right]
$$
$$
\left[\underline{\text{END - STRING}} \right]
$$

Figure 15-6. Metalanguage for the STRING verb

The STRING verb moves characters from the source string (SourceString$il) to the destination string (DestString$il). Data movement is from left to right. The leftmost character of the source string is moved to the leftmost position of the destination string, then the next-leftmost character of the source string is moved to the next-leftmost position of the destination string, and so on. Note that no space filling occurs; and unless characters in the destination string are explicitly overwritten, they remain undisturbed.

When a number of source strings are concatenated, characters are moved from the leftmost source string first until either that string is exhausted or the delimiter (Delim$il) is encountered in that string. When transfer from that source string finishes, characters are moved from the next-leftmost source string. This proceeds until either the strings are exhausted or the destination string is full. At that point, the STRING operation finishes.

The following rules apply to the operation of the STRING verb:

- The ON OVERFLOW clause executes if valid characters remain to be transferred in the source string but the destination string is full.

- When a WITH POINTER phrase is used, its value determines the starting character position for insertion into the destination string. As each character is inserted into the destination string, the pointer is incremented. When the pointer points beyond the end of the destination string, the STRING statement stops.

- When the WITH POINTER phrase is used, then before the STRING statement executes, the program must set Pointer#i to an initial value greater than zero and less than the length of the destination string.

- If the WITH POINTER phrase is not used, operation on the destination field starts from the leftmost position.

- Pointer#i must be an integer item, and its description must allow it to contain a value one greater than the size of the destination string. For instance, a pointer declared as PIC 9 is too small if the destination string is ten characters long.

- The DELIMITED BY SIZE clause causes the whole of the sending field to be added to the destination string.

- Where a literal can be used, you can use a figurative constant (such as SPACES) except for the ALL *literal* figurative constant.

- When a figurative constant is used, it is one character in size.

- The destination item DestString$i must be either an elementary data item without editing symbols or the JUSTIFIED clause.

- Data movement from a particular source string ends when one of the following occurs:

  - The end of the source string is reached.

  - The end of the destination string is reached.

  - The delimiter is detected.

- The STRING statement ends when one of the following is true:

  - All the source strings have been processed.

  - The destination string is full.

  - The pointer points outside the string.

String Concatenation Example

Example 15-6 shows how you can build a destination string a piece at a time by executing several separate STRING statements. Each time a STRING statement executes, the current value of StrPtr governs where the characters from the source string are inserted into the destination string.

Example 15-6. STRING Examples Showing How to Use the WITH POINTER Phrase

```
DATA DIVISION.
WORKING-STORAGE SECTION.
01 DayStr     PIC XX VALUE "5".
01 MonthStr   PIC X(9) VALUE "September".
01 YearStr    PIC X(4) VALUE "2013".
01 DateStr    PIC X(16) VALUE ALL "@".
01 StrPtr     PIC 99.

PROCEDURE DIVISION.
Begin.
DISPLAY DateStr
MOVE 1 TO StrPtr
```

```
┌──────────────────────────────┐
│      Example 15-6 output      │
│                              │
│  @@@@@@@@@@@@@@@@             │
│  5,@@@@@@@@@@@@@@             │
│  5,September,@@@@             │
│  5,September,2013             │
└──────────────────────────────┘
```

```
STRING DayStr  DELIMITED BY SPACES
       ","      DELIMITED BY SIZE
       INTO DateStr WITH POINTER StrPtr
END-STRING
DISPLAY DateStr

STRING MonthStr DELIMITED BY SPACES
       ","      DELIMITED BY SIZE
       INTO DateStr WITH POINTER StrPtr
END-STRING
DISPLAY DateStr

STRING YearStr  DELIMITED BY SIZE
       INTO DateStr WITH POINTER StrPtr
END-STRING
DISPLAY DateStr.
```

String Splitting

String splitting involves chopping a string into a number of smaller strings. In COBOL, string splitting is done using the UNSTRING verb. Before I discuss the UNSTRING verb formally, let's look at some examples to see what UNSTRING can do.

The first example uses UNSTRING to break a customer name into its three constituent parts: first name, middle name, and surname. For instance, the string "John Joseph Ryan" is broken into the three strings "John", "Joseph", and "Ryan":

```
UNSTRING CustomerName DELIMITED BY ALL SPACES
    INTO FirstName, SecondName, Surname
END-UNSTRING
```

The second example breaks an address string (where the parts of the address are separated from one another by commas) into separate address lines. The address lines are stored in a six-element table. Not all addresses have six parts exactly, but you can use the TALLYING clause to discover how many parts there are:

```
UNSTRING CustAddress DELIMITED BY ","
    INTO AdrLine(1), AdrLine(2), AdrLine(3),
        AdrLine(4), AdrLine(5), AdrLine(6)
    TALLYING IN AdrLinesUsed
END-UNSTRING
```

The final example breaks a simple comma-delimited record into its constituent parts. Because the fields are not fixed length, they need to be validated for length—and that requires finding out how long each field is. The COUNT IN clause, which counts the number of characters transferred to a particular destination field, is used to determine the actual length of the field:

```
UNSTRING SupplierRec DELIMITED BY ","
    INTO Supplier-Code    COUNT IN SuppCodeCount
         Supplier-Name    COUNT IN SuppNameCount
         Supplier-Address COUNT IN SuppAdrCount
END-UNSTRING
```

The UNSTRING Verb

The metalanguage for the UNSTRING verb is given in Figure 15-7.

UNSTRING SourceStr$i
      [DELIMITED BY [ALL] Delim$il [OR [ALL] Delim$il]...]
      INTO {DestStr$i [DELIMITER IN HoldDelim$i]
                      [COUNT IN CharCounter#i]}...
      [WITH POINTER Pointer#i]
      [TALLYING IN DestCounter#i]
      [ON OVERFLOW StatementBlock]
      [NOT ON OVERFLOW StatementBlock]
      [END - UNSTRING]

Figure 15-7. *Metalanguage for the UNSTRING verb*

UNSTRING copies characters from the source string to the destination string until a condition is encountered that terminates data movement. When data movement ends for a particular destination string, the next destination string becomes the receiving area, and characters are copied into it until once again a terminating condition is encountered. Characters are copied from the source string to the destination strings according to the rules for MOVE, with space filling or truncation as necessary.

Strictly speaking, END-UNSTRING is only required to delimit the scope of the OVERFLOW statement block. You will notice, however, that I have a tendency to use it to indicate the end of every UNSTRING statement. This is just a personal preference.

Data-Movement Termination

When you use the DELIMITED BY clause, data movement from the source string to the current destination string ends when either of the following occurs:

- A delimiter is encountered in the source string

- The end of the source string is reached

When the DELIMITED BY clause is not used, data movement from the source string to the current destination string ends when either of these is true:

- The destination string is full.

- The end of the source string is reached.

UNSTRING Termination

The UNSTRING statement terminates in the following cases:

- All the characters in the source string have been examined.

- All the destination strings have been processed.

- Some error condition is encountered (such as the pointer pointing outside the source string).

UNSTRING Clauses

As you can see by examining the metalanguage, the operation of UNSTRING is modified by a number of clauses. These clauses affect the operation of UNSTRING as follows:

DELIMITED BY: When the DELIMITED BY clause is used, characters are examined in the source string and copied to the current destination string until one of the specified delimiters is encountered in the source string or the end the source string is reached. If there is not enough room in the destination string to take all the characters sent to it from the source string, the remaining characters are truncated/lost. When the delimiter is encountered in the source string, the next destination string becomes current, and characters are transferred into it from the source string. Delimiters are not transferred or counted in CharCounter#i.

ON OVERFLOW: When ON OVERFLOW activates, the statement block following it is executed. ON OVERFLOW activates if

- The unstring pointer (Pointer#i) is not pointing to a character position within the source string when UNSTRING executes (that is, Pointer#i is 0 or is greater than the size of the string).

- All the destination strings have been processed, but there are still valid unexamined characters in the source string.

The statements following NOT ON OVERFLOW are executed if UNSTRING is about to terminate successfully.

COUNT IN: The COUNT IN clause is associated with a particular destination string and holds a count of the number of characters passed to the destination string, regardless of whether they were truncated.

DELIMITER IN: A DELIMITER IN clause is associated with a particular destination string. HoldDelim$i holds the delimiter that was encountered in the source string. If the DELIMITER IN phrase is used with the ALL phrase, then only one occurrence of the delimiter is moved to HoldDelim$i.

TALLYING IN: Only one TALLYING clause can be used with each UNSTRING. It holds a count of the number of destination strings affected by the UNSTRING operation.

WITH POINTER: When the WITH POINTER clause is used, the Pointer#i data item holds the position of the next *non-delimiter* character to be examined in the source string. Pointer#i must be large enough to hold a value one greater than the size of the source string, because when UNSTRING ends, it will be pointing to one character position beyond the end of the string.

ALL: When the ALL phrase is used, contiguous delimiters are treated as if only one delimiter had been encountered. If ALL is not used, contiguous delimiters result in spaces being sent to some of the destination strings.

Notes on UNSTRING

Bear the following in mind when you use UNSTRING:

- Where a literal can be used, any figurative constant can be used except the ALL *literal* figurative constant.

- When a figurative constant is used, it is one character long.

- The delimiter is moved into HoldDelim$i according to the rules for MOVE.

- The DELIMITER IN and COUNT IN phrases may be specified only if the DELIMITED BY phrase is used.

Language Knowledge Examples

This section presents a number of UNSTRING examples. These are not real-world examples but are rather intended to show how UNSTRING and its clauses operate.

UNSTRING: Demonstrating the COUNT IN Clause

Listing 15-5 demonstrates how to chop a string into separate strings based on a delimiter and how to keep a count of the number of characters transferred to each destination string. Note that DestStr2 is larger than the data copied to it and so is space filled. DestStr3 is too small to hold the characters transferred to it, so they are truncated; but the count still notes how many characters were transferred (08). The count for DestStr4 seems incorrect, but the literal assigned to xString is not long enough to fill it and so it is space filled. When UNSTRING copies "of sweet silent" to DestStr4, it copies these trailing spaces; they can't all fit into DestStr4 and so are truncated but counted.

Listing 15-5. UNSTRING Example 1

```
IDENTIFICATION DIVISION.
PROGRAM-ID.  Listing15-5.
AUTHOR.  Michael Coughlan.

DATA DIVISION.
WORKING-STORAGE SECTION.
01 xString        PIC X(45) VALUE "When,to the,sessions,of sweet silent".
01 DestinationStrings.
   02 DestStr1   PIC X(4).
   02 DestStr2   PIC X(10).
   02 DestStr3   PIC X(3).
   02 DestStr4   PIC X(18).

01 CharCounts.
   02 CCount      PIC 99  OCCURS 4 TIMES.

PROCEDURE DIVISION.
Begin.
    UNSTRING xString delimited by ","
        INTO DestStr1 COUNT IN CCount(1)
             DestStr2 COUNT IN CCount(2)
             DestStr3 COUNT IN CCount(3)
             DestStr4 COUNT IN CCount(4)
    END-UNSTRING

    DISPLAY DestStr1 " = " CCount(1)
    DISPLAY DestStr2 " = " CCount(2)
    DISPLAY DestStr3 " = " CCount(3)
    DISPLAY DestStr4 " = " CCount(4)
    STOP RUN.
```

```
            Listing 15-5 Output

When = 04
to the     = 06
ses = 08
of sweet silent    = 24
```

UNSTRING: Demonstrating ON OVERFLOW and the Effect of Delimiters

Listing 15-6 contains three UNSTRING examples. Example 2 demonstrates the activation of the ON OVERFLOW clause. Because no delimiter is specified, all the text in DateStr is eligible for transfer; and as each destination item is filled, the next one becomes the current target. There are not enough destination items to take all the data: the remaining characters ("19" and the trailing spaces) are eligible for transfer, but there are no destination strings left to take them. So, ON OVERFLOW activates, and the message "Characters unexamined" is displayed.

Listing 15-6. The ON OVERFLOW Clause and the Effect of Delimiters

```
IDENTIFICATION DIVISION.
PROGRAM-ID.  Listing15-6.
AUTHOR.  Michael Coughlan.

DATA DIVISION.
WORKING-STORAGE SECTION.
01 DateStr       PIC X(15).

01 DateRec.
    02 DayStr     PIC XX.
    02 MonthStr   PIC XX.
    02 YearStr    PIC X(4).

PROCEDURE DIVISION.
Begin.
*>Unstring example 2
    MOVE "19-08-2012" TO DateStr
    UNSTRING DateStr INTO DayStr, MonthStr, YearStr
        ON OVERFLOW DISPLAY "Characters unexamined"
    END-UNSTRING
    DISPLAY DayStr SPACE MonthStr SPACE YearStr
    DISPLAY "_____"
    DISPLAY SPACES

*>Unstring example 3
    MOVE "25-07-2013lost" TO DateStr.
    UNSTRING DateStr DELIMITED BY "-"
        INTO DayStr, MonthStr, YearStr
        ON OVERFLOW DISPLAY "Characters unexamined"
    END-UNSTRING.
    DISPLAY DayStr SPACE MonthStr SPACE YearStr
    DISPLAY "_____"
    DISPLAY SPACES

*>Unstring example 4
    MOVE "30end06end2014" TO DateStr
    UNSTRING DateStr DELIMITED BY "end"
        INTO DayStr, MonthStr, YearStr
        ON OVERFLOW DISPLAY "Characters unexamined"
    END-UNSTRING
    DISPLAY DayStr SPACE MonthStr SPACE YearStr

    STOP RUN.
```

Listing 15-6 Output
Characters unexamined 19 -0 8-20
25 07 2013
30 06 2014

Example 3 demonstrates the difference when a delimiter is specified. ON OVERFLOW does not activate in this case because all the characters have been copied to the destination strings. UNSTRING tries to copy "2013lost" into YearStr, but because there is not sufficient room, some of the transferred characters are truncated.

Example 4 demonstrates that the delimiter does not have to be a single character. It can be a word or any other group of characters.

UNSTRING: The Effect of the ALL Delimiter

Listing 15-7 also contains three UNSTRING examples. Example 5 demonstrates the use of the ALL delimiter, which treats successive occurrences of a delimiter as one occurrence. This is contrasted with Example 6, where the same delimiter configuration is used but the ALL phrase is omitted. In this example, each occurrence of the delimiter is treated as separate instance; the result is shown in the following storage schematic.

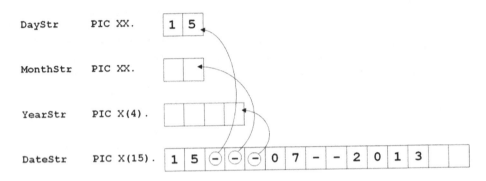

Listing 15-7. The ALL Delimiter and the DELIMITER IN Phrase

```
IDENTIFICATION DIVISION.
PROGRAM-ID.  Listing15-7.
AUTHOR.  Michael Coughlan.

DATA DIVISION.
WORKING-STORAGE SECTION.
01 DateStr       PIC X(15).

01 DateRec.
    02 DayStr     PIC XX.
    02 MonthStr   PIC XX.
    02 YearStr    PIC X(4).

01 Delims.
    02 HoldDelim OCCURS 3 TIMES PIC X.

PROCEDURE DIVISION.
Begin.
*>Unstring example 5
    MOVE "15---07--2013" TO DateStr.
    UNSTRING DateStr DELIMITED BY ALL "-"
        INTO DayStr, MonthStr, YearStr
        ON OVERFLOW DISPLAY "Characters unexamined"
```

```
               Listing 15-7 Output

    15  07  2013
    _____

    Characters  unexamined
    15
    _____

    /  delimits  15
    -  delimits  07
    @  delimits  2013
```

```
          END-UNSTRING
          DISPLAY DayStr SPACE MonthStr SPACE YearStr
          DISPLAY "_____"
          DISPLAY SPACES

 *>Unstring example 6
          MOVE "15---07--2013" TO DateStr.
          UNSTRING DateStr DELIMITED BY "-"
              INTO DayStr
                   MonthStr
                   YearStr
              ON OVERFLOW DISPLAY "Characters unexamined"
          END-UNSTRING
          DISPLAY DayStr SPACE MonthStr SPACE YearStr
          DISPLAY "_____"
          DISPLAY SPACES

 *>Unstring example 7
          MOVE "15/07-----2013@" TO DateStr
          UNSTRING DateStr DELIMITED BY "/" OR "@" OR ALL "-"
              INTO DayStr   DELIMITER in HoldDelim(1)
                   MonthStr DELIMITER in HoldDelim(2)
                   YearStr  DELIMITER in HoldDelim(3)
              ON OVERFLOW DISPLAY "Characters unexamined"
          END-UNSTRING
          DISPLAY HoldDelim(1) " delimits " DayStr
          DISPLAY HoldDelim(2) " delimits " MonthStr
DISPLAY HoldDelim(3) " delimits " YearStr

          STOP RUN.
```

Example 7 shows how you can use the DELIMITER IN clause to store a delimiter that causes character transfer to cease for a particular destination field.

String-Splitting Program

The examples so far have shown you aspects of the UNSTRING verb's operation. Listing 15-8 is a more real-world example. The problem specification is as follows: Write a program that accepts a person's full name from the user and reduces it to the initials of the first and middle names followed by the surname. For instance, William Henry Ford Power becomes W. H. F. Power.

Listing 15-8. UNSTRING and STRING Used in Combination

```
IDENTIFICATION DIVISION.
PROGRAM-ID.  Listing15-8.
AUTHOR.  Michael Coughlan.

DATA DIVISION.
WORKING-STORAGE SECTION.
01 OldName      PIC X(80).
```

```
01 TempName.
   02 NameInitial  PIC X.
   02 FILLER       PIC X(19).

01 NewName         PIC X(30).

01 UnstrPtr        PIC 99.
   88 NameProcessed VALUE 81.

01 StrPtr          PIC 99.

PROCEDURE DIVISION.
ProcessName.
   DISPLAY "Enter a name - " WITH NO ADVANCING
   ACCEPT OldName
   MOVE 1 TO UnstrPtr, StrPtr
   UNSTRING OldName DELIMITED BY ALL SPACES
      INTO TempName WITH POINTER UnstrPtr
   END-UNSTRING
   PERFORM UNTIL NameProcessed
      STRING NameInitial "." SPACE DELIMITED BY SIZE
         INTO NewName WITH POINTER StrPtr
      END-STRING
      UNSTRING OldName DELIMITED BY ALL SPACES
         INTO TempName WITH POINTER UnstrPtr
      END-UNSTRING
   END-PERFORM
   STRING TempName DELIMITED BY SIZE
         INTO NewName WITH POINTER StrPtr
   END-STRING
   DISPLAY "Processed name = " NewName
   STOP RUN.
```

Reference Modification

Reference modification is a special COBOL facility that allows you to treat any USAGE IS DISPLAY item as if it were an array of characters but it defines access to the characters in a special way. To access substrings using reference modification, as shown in the metalanguage in Figure 15-8, you must specify the following:

- The name of the data item (DataItemName) to be referenced
- The start-character position of the substring (StartPos)
- The number of characters in the substring (SubStrLength)

DataItemName (StartPos[: SubStrLength])

Figure 15-8. *Metalanguage syntax for reference modification*

The metalanguage syntax is modified by the following sematic rules:

- StartPos is the character position of the first character in the substring, and SubStrLength is the number of characters in the substring. StartPos and SubStrLength must each be a positive integer or an expression that evaluates to one.

- DataItemName can be subscripted and/or qualified.

- DataItemName can be the alphanumeric value returned by a function.

- As indicated by the square brackets, SubStrLength may be omitted, in which case the substring from StartPos to the end of the string is assumed.

- You can use reference modification almost anywhere an alphanumeric data item is permitted.

To get a feel for the way reference modification works, let's look at some examples. You start with some abstract examples and then see how you can use reference modification in a more practical situation.

The three DISPLAYs in Example 15-7 use reference modification to display substrings of xString. The storage schematic shows how each example extracts the substring from xString:

- DISPLAY xString(11:5) displays a substring of five characters starting at the position of the eleventh character.

- DISPLAY xString(17:SubStrSize) demonstrates that you can use a numeric data item in place of the literal and displays eight characters starting with the seventeenth.

- DISPLAY xString(StartPos:) shows that when you omit SubStrLength, the substring consists of the characters from the start character to the end of the string.

Example 15-7. Extracting a Substring Using Reference Modification

```
01 SubStrSize   PIC 99 VALUE 8.

01 StartPos     PIC 99 VALUE 28.

01 xString      PIC X(40) VALUE "One day I wrote her name upon the strand".
```

DISPLAY xString(11:5)

DISPLAY xString(17:SubStrSize)

DISPLAY xString(StartPos:)

Example 15-7 Output

wrote

her name

on the strand

The two DISPLAY statements in Example 15-8 demonstrate the other ways of defining the substring. The MOVE statement shows how you can use reference modification to insert characters into a string:

- DISPLAY xString(12:SubstrSize - 5) shows that you can use an arithmetic expression as SubStrLength.

- DISPLAY FUNCTION UPPER-CASE(xString)(Startpos - 7 : 4) demonstrates that you can apply reference modification to a function result. It also shows that StartPos may be an arithmetic expression.

- MOVE " text insert " TO XString(31:6) demonstrates how to use reference modification to insert text into a string. Note that the SubStrLength given specifies the number of characters in the string that will be overwritten. For instance, in this example only 6 characters are overwritten, even though there are 13 characters in the moved text.

Example 15-8. Applying Reference Modification to an Alphanumeric String

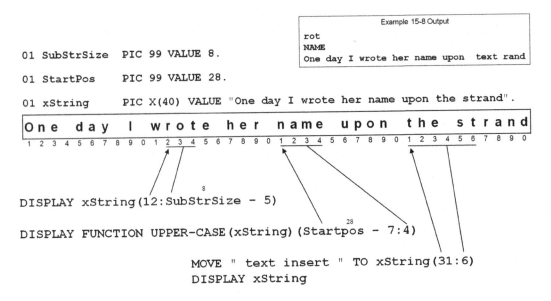

Example 15-9 shows how to apply reference modification to the numeric data item nString and the edited numeric data item enString:

- In nString, reference modification is used to display the dollars and cents parts of a numeric value.

- In enString, reference modification is used to overwrite the check-security asterisks with the @ symbol. Note that ALL "@" is a figurative constant that is used to fill the four character positions specified by the reference modifier.

Example 15-9. Applying Reference Modification to Numeric Data Items

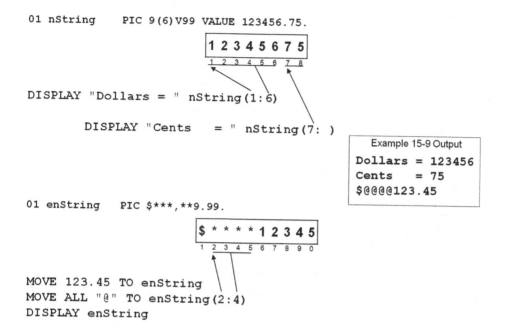

```
01 nString     PIC 9(6)V99 VALUE 123456.75.
```

```
DISPLAY "Dollars = " nString(1:6)
```

```
        DISPLAY "Cents   = " nString(7: )
```

```
01 enString    PIC $***,**9.99.
```

```
MOVE 123.45 TO enString
MOVE ALL "@" TO enString(2:4)
DISPLAY enString
```

```
Example 15-9 Output
Dollars = 123456
Cents   = 75
$@@@@123.45
```

Intrinsic Functions

User-defined functions of one sort or another are a standard part of many programming languages. The ANS 85 version of COBOL does not support user-defined functions, but it has introduced a library of standard functions called *intrinsic functions.*

Intrinsic functions fall into three broad categories: date functions, numeric functions, and string functions. Because this chapter is about string manipulation, I discuss the string functions in some detail. I also look at the date functions and some of the numeric functions that I have found particularly useful. For the remaining functions you should consult your implementer manual.

Using Intrinsic Functions

Like a function in another language, an intrinsic function is replaced by the function result in the position where the function occurs. Wherever you can use a literal, you can use an intrinsic function that returns a result of the same type.

An intrinsic function consists of three parts:

- The start of the function is signalled by the FUNCTION keyword.

- The FUNCTION keyword is followed by the name of the function.

- The name of the function is immediately followed by a bracketed list of parameters or arguments.

- The intrinsic function template is

  FUNCTION FunctionName(Parameter)

  where FunctionName is the name of the function and Parameter is one or
  more parameters/arguments supplied to the function.

For instance, the following examples show how to use intrinsic functions in a number of different contexts. In some cases, the result of the function is assigned to a data item; in others (as in the first example), it is used directly in the place of a literal or data item. Sometimes the parameters/arguments are numeric, and other times they are alphabetic. Some functions use only one parameter, others take multiple parameters, and still others do not require a parameter:

```
DISPLAY FUNCTION UPPER-CASE("this will be in upper case").
MOVE FUNCTION ORD("A") TO OrdPos
MOVE FUNCTION RANDOM(SeedValue) TO RandomNumber
MOVE FUNCTION RANDOM TO NextRndNumber
COMPUTE Result = FUNCTION MOD(25, 10)
MOVE FUNCTION ORD-MAX(12 23 03 78 65) TO MaxOrdPos
```

When you use intrinsic functions, you must bear in mind a number of things:

- Intrinsic functions return a result of Alphanumeric, Numeric (includes integer), or Integer (does not allow the decimal point).

- The result returned by an alphanumeric function has an implicit usage of DISPLAY. This is why the result returned by FUNCTION UPPER-CASE may be used directly with the DISPLAY verb.

- Intrinsic functions that return a numeric value are always considered to be signed and can only be used in an arithmetic expression or a MOVE statement.

- Intrinsic functions that return a non-integer numeric value can't be used where an integer value is required.

String Functions

Table 15-1 lists the intrinsic functions that allow manipulation of strings. The table uses the parameter name to indicate the type of the parameter required, as follows:

Alpha indicates Alphanumeric.

Num indicates any Numeric.

PosNum indicates a positive Numeric.

Int indicates any Integer.

PosInt indicates a positive Integer.

Any indicates that the parameter may be of any type.

Table 15-1. *String Functions, Grouped by Type of Operation*

Function Name	Result Type	Comment
CHAR(PosInt)	Alphanumeric	Returns the character in the collating sequence at ordinal position PosInt.
ORD(Alpha)	Integer	Returns the ordinal position of character Alpha.
ORD-MAX({Any}...)	Integer	Returns the ordinal position of whichever parameter in the list has the highest value. All parameters must be of the same type. The parameter list may be replaced by an array. If an array is used, the reserved word ALL may be used as the array subscript to indicate all the elements of the array.
ORD-MIN({Any}...)	Integer	Returns the ordinal position of whichever parameter in the list has the lowest value. All parameters must be of the same type. The parameter list may be replaced by an array.
LENGTH(Any)	Integer	Returns the number of characters in the data item Any. Not as useful as it sounds. It returns the value given in the item's picture clause. For instance, Length(StrItem) returns 18 if the picture clause is PIC X(18).
REVERSE(Alpha)	Alphanumeric	Returns a character string with the characters in Alpha reversed.
LOWER-CASE(Alpha)	Alphanumeric	Returns a character string with the characters in Alpha changed to their lowercase equivalents.
UPPER-CASE(Alpha)	Alphanumeric	Returns a character string with the characters in Alpha changed to their uppercase equivalents.

If a function takes a parameter list (indicated by {Any}... in the function definition), the parameter list may be replaced by an array. The reserved word ALL is used as the array subscript to indicate all the elements of the array.

For instance, the ORD-MAX function may take a parameter list, or you can use an array as the parameter, as shown in the following example:

```
MOVE FUNCTION ORD-MAX(12 23 03 78 65) TO OrdPos
```

or

```
MOVE FUNCTION ORD-MAX(IntElement(ALL)) TO OrdPos
```

String Intrinsic Function Examples

Listing 15-9 solves no specific problem. It merely consists of a number of intrinsic function examples.

Listing 15-9. String Manipulation with Intrinsic Functions

```
IDENTIFICATION DIVISION.
PROGRAM-ID.  Listing15-9.
AUTHOR.  Michael Coughlan.
*> Intrinsic Function examples
```

```
DATA DIVISION.
WORKING-STORAGE SECTION.
01 OrdPos          PIC 99.

01 TableValues     VALUE "123411457429130938637306851419883522700467".
   02 Num          PIC 99 OCCURS 21 TIMES.

01 idx             PIC 9.

01 xString         PIC X(45)
                   VALUE "This string is 33 characters long".

01 xWord           PIC X(10).

01 CharCount       PIC 99.

01 TextLength      PIC 99.

PROCEDURE DIVISION.
Begin.
*> eg1. In the ASCII collating sequence W has a code of 87 but an ordinal
*> position of 88.
   DISPLAY "eg1. The character in position 88 is = " FUNCTION CHAR(88)

*> eg2. Using ordinal positions to spell out my name
   DISPLAY SPACES
   DISPLAY "eg2. My name is " FUNCTION CHAR(78)   FUNCTION CHAR(106)
                             FUNCTION CHAR(108) FUNCTION CHAR(102)

*> eg3. Finding the ordinal position of a particular character
   DISPLAY SPACES
   MOVE FUNCTION ORD("A") TO OrdPos
   DISPLAY "eg3. The ordinal position of A is = " OrdPos

*> eg4. Using CHAR and ORD in combination to display the sixth letter of the alphabet
   DISPLAY SPACES
   DISPLAY "eg4. The sixth letter of the alphabet is "
           FUNCTION CHAR(FUNCTION ORD("A") + 5)

*> eg5. Finding the position of the highest value in a list of parameters
   DISPLAY SPACES
   MOVE FUNCTION ORD-MAX("t" "b" "x" "B" "4" "s" "b") TO OrdPos
   DISPLAY "eg5. Highest character in the list is at pos " OrdPos

*> eg6. Finding the position of the lowest value in a list of parameters
   DISPLAY SPACES
   MOVE FUNCTION ORD-MIN("t" "b" "x" "B" "4" "s" "b") TO OrdPos
   DISPLAY "eg6. Lowest character in the list is at pos " OrdPos
```

Listing 15-9 Output
eg1. The character in position 88 is = W
eg2. My name is Mike
eg3. The ordinal postion of A is = 66
eg4. The sixth letter of the alphabet is F

```
*> eg7.Finding the position of the highest value
in a table
   DISPLAY SPACES
   MOVE FUNCTION ORD-MAX(Num(ALL)) TO OrdPos
   DISPLAY "eg7. Highest value in the table is at pos "
        OrdPos

*> eg8. Finding the highest value in a table
   DISPLAY SPACES
   DISPLAY "eg8. Highest value in the table = "
Num(FUNCTION ORD-MAX(Num(ALL)))
```

```
                        Listing 15-9 Output
  eg5. Highest character in the list is at pos 03

  eg6. Lowest character in the list is at pos 05

  eg7. Highest value in the table is at pos 16

  eg8. Highest value in the table = 88

  eg9.
  TopPos 1 = 88
  TopPos 2 = 85
  TopPos 3 = 74
```

```
*> eg9. Finds the top three values in a table by finding the top
*> overwrites it with zeros to remove it from consideration
*> then finds the next top and so on
   DISPLAY SPACES
   DISPLAY "eg9."
   PERFORM VARYING idx FROM 1 BY 1 UNTIL idx > 3
      DISPLAY "TopPos " idx " = " Num(FUNCTION ORD-MAX(Num(ALL)))
      MOVE ZEROS TO Num(FUNCTION ORD-MAX(Num(ALL)))
   END-PERFORM

*> eg10. Finding the length of a string
   DISPLAY SPACES
   DISPLAY "eg10. The length of xString is " FUNCTION LENGTH(xString) " characters"

*> eg11. Finding the length of the text in a string
   DISPLAY SPACES
   INSPECT FUNCTION REVERSE(xString) TALLYING CharCount
        FOR LEADING SPACES
   COMPUTE TextLength = FUNCTION LENGTH(xString) - CharCount
   DISPLAY "eg11. The length of text in xString is " TextLength " characters"

*> eg12. Discover if a word is a palindrome
   DISPLAY SPACES
   DISPLAY "eg12."
   MOVE ZEROS TO CharCount
   DISPLAY "Enter a word - " WITH NO ADVANCING
   ACCEPT xWord
   INSPECT FUNCTION REVERSE(xWord)
        TALLYING CharCount FOR LEADING SPACES
   IF FUNCTION UPPER-CASE(xWord(1:FUNCTION LENGTH(xWord) - CharCount)) EQUAL TO
      FUNCTION UPPER-CASE(FUNCTION REVERSE(xWord(1:FUNCTION LENGTH(xWord)- CharCount)))
      DISPLAY xWord " is a palindrome"
    ELSE
      DISPLAY xWord " is not a palindrome"
   END-IF
   STOP RUN.
```

```
                        Listing 15-9 Output
  eg10. The length of xString is 45 characters

  eg11. The length of text in xString is 33 characters

  eg12.
  Enter a word - RoTatOr
  RoTatOr     is a palindrome
```

Program Explanation

These examples build on one another so that although the early ones are straightforward, the later ones are somewhat more complex and require explanation. One thing you will realize from these examples is that COBOL's intrinsic functions are not as effective as functions in other languages. For one thing, the requirement to precede every intrinsic function with the word FUNCTION makes nesting functions cumbersome. For another, the function library is incomplete. You often have to use INSPECT, UNSTRING, and STRING to compensate for omissions. On the other hand, not being able to nest functions deeply may be a good thing. For instance, eg12 would require more typing but would be easier to understand and debug if coded as follows:

```
*>eg12. Discover if a word is a palindrome
   DISPLAY SPACES
   DISPLAY "eg12."
   MOVE ZEROS TO CharCount
   DISPLAY "Enter a word - " WITH NO ADVANCING
   ACCEPT xWord

   INSPECT FUNCTION REVERSE(xWord) TALLYING CharCount
         FOR LEADING SPACES

   MOVE FUNCTION UPPER-CASE(xWord) TO xWord

   COMPUTE TextLength = FUNCTION LENGTH(xWord) - CharCount

   IF xWord(1:TextLength) EQUAL TO FUNCTION REVERSE(xWord(1:TextLength))
      DISPLAY xWord " is a palindrome"
    ELSE
      DISPLAY xWord " is not a palindrome"
   END-IF
```

Let's look at how these examples work:

- eg1 uses the CHAR function to return the eighty-eighth character (*W*) of the ASCII collating sequence. In most languages, you would be required to supply the ASCII value, whereas in COBOL you supply the ordinal position. If you are used to dealing with ASCII values, the ordinal position will seem to be off by one: for example, the ASCII value of *W* is 87.

- eg2 uses the CHAR function to display the name *Mike*.

- eg3 demonstrates that the ORD function is the opposite of CHAR. Whereas CHAR returns the character at the ordinal position supplied, ORD returns the ordinal position of the character supplied. As you no doubt know, *A* is ASCII value 65, but its ordinal position is returned as 66.

- eg4 is the first use of nested functions. CHAR and ORD are used in combination. ORD("A") returns the position of the first letter in the alphabet, and the sixth is five letters on from that.

- eg5 and eg6 demonstrate using the ORD-MAX function to find the position of the highest value in the supplied list.

- eg7 demonstrates how to use ORD-MAX to find the position of the highest value in a table.

- eg8 uses nesting and ORD-MAX to find the highest *value in a table.*

- Eg9 uses the techniques demonstrated in eg7 and eg8 to find the top three values in a table. Each time through the loop, the highest value is found, displayed, and then overwritten with zeros to remove it from consideration the next time around. This solution does have the drawback of destroying some of the values in the table.

- eg10 and eg11: one problem COBOL has is that alphanumeric data items are fixed in length, so if the text does not fill the data item, the data item is space-filled to the right. For certain kinds of processing, this is a problem. eg10 shows how to get the length of a data item, and eg11 shows how to use the length of the data item to get the *length of the text* in that data item.

- eg12 brings together much of the material covered in this chapter. The task is to discover whether a word entered by the user is a palindrome (reads the same backward as forward). As I noted earlier, the nesting of functions makes the program much more difficult to understand.

  This is the algorithm: using the technique of eg11, find the actual length of the word. Use reference modification to select only the word from the data item xWord, change it to uppercase, and compare it to a reversed, uppercased, version of the word. If they are equal, then the word is a palindrome.

DATE Functions

Date functions are a homogeneous group of functions that are often very useful. Table 15-2 lists the functions. The table uses the same parameter type indicators as Table 15-1 (Alpha, Num, PosNum, Int, PosInt, Any).

Table 15-2. *Date Functions*

Function Name	Result Type	Comment
CURRENT-DATE	Alphanumeric	Returns a 21-character string representing the current date and time, and the difference between the local time and Greenwich Mean Time. The format of the string is YYYYMMDDHHMMsshhxhhmm, where YYYY is the year, MM is the month, DD is the day of the month, HH is the hour (24-hour time), MM is the minutes, ss is the seconds, and hh is the hundredths of a second. In addition, xhhmm is the number of hours and minutes the local time is ahead of or behind GMT (x = + or - or 0). If x = 0, the hardware cannot provide this information.
DATE-OF-INTEGER(PosInt)	Integer of the form YYYYMMDDD	Converts the integer date PosInt (representing the number of days that have passed since Dec 31, 1600 in the Gregorian calendar) to a standard date. Returns the standard date in the form YYYYMMDD. This function can be useful when you are calculating the number of days between two dates.
DAY-OF-INTEGER(PosInt)	Integer of the form YYYYDDD	Converts the integer date PosInt (representing the number of days that have passed since Dec 31, 1600 in the Gregorian calendar) to a standard date of the form YYYYDDD (sometimes called a Julian date).
INTEGER-OF-DATE(PosInt)	Integer	Converts the standard date PosInt (in the form YYYYMMDD) into the equivalent integer date. If PosInt is not a valid date, then zeros are returned.
INTEGER-OF-DAY(PosInt)	Integer	Converts the standard date PosInt (in the form YYYYDDD—a Julian date) into the equivalent integer date.
WHEN-COMPILED	Integer	Returns the date and time the program was compiled. Uses the same format as CURRENT-DATE.

DATE Examples

Like the previous listing, Listing 15-10 solves no specific problem but is instead a collection of examples that show how to use intrinsic functions to manipulate dates.

Listing 15-10. Using Intrinsic Functions to Manipulate Dates

```
IDENTIFICATION DIVISION.
PROGRAM-ID.  Listing15-10.
AUTHOR.  Michael Coughlan.
*> Date Functions

DATA DIVISION.
WORKING-STORAGE SECTION.
01 DateAndTimeNow.
    02 DateNow.
        03 YearNow              PIC 9(4).
        03 MonthNow             PIC 99.
        03 DayNow               PIC 99.
    02 TimeC.
        03 HourNow              PIC 99.
        03 MinNow               PIC 99.
        03 SecNow               PIC 99.
        03 FILLER               PIC 99.
    02 GMT.
        03 GMTDiff              PIC X.
            88 GMTNotSupported  VALUE "0".
        03 GMTHours             PIC 99.
        03 GMTMins              PIC 99.

01  BillDate                    PIC 9(8).
01  DateNowInt                  PIC 9(8).
01  DaysOverdue                 PIC S999.
01  NumOfDays                   PIC 999.

01  IntFutureDate               PIC 9(8).
01  FutureDate                  PIC 9(8).
01  DisplayDate REDEFINES FutureDate.
    02 YearD                    PIC 9999.
    02 MonthD                   PIC 99.
    02 DayD                     PIC 99.

01 DateCheck                    PIC 9(8) VALUE ZEROS.
    88 DateIsNotValid           VALUE ZEROS.
    88 DateIsValid              VALUE 1 THRU 99999999.

PROCEDURE DIVISION.
Begin.
*> eg1 This example gets the current date and displays
*> the constituent parts.
    DISPLAY "eg1 - get the current date"
    MOVE FUNCTION CURRENT-DATE TO DateAndTimeNow
```

```
        DISPLAY "Current Date is "
                MonthNow "/" DayNow "/" YearNow
        DISPLAY "Current Time is "
                HourNow ":" MinNow ":" SecNow
    IF GMTNotSupported
        DISPLAY "This computer cannot supply the time"
        DISPLAY "difference between local and GMT."
      ELSE
        DISPLAY "The local time is - GMT "
                    GMTDiff GMTHours ":" GMTMins
    END-IF.


*> eg2. In this example bills fall due 30 days
*> from the billing date.
    DISPLAY SPACES
    DISPLAY "eg2 - find the difference between two dates"
    DISPLAY "Enter the date of the bill (yyyymmdd) - " WITH NO ADVANCING
    ACCEPT BillDate
    MOVE DateNow TO DateNowInt
    COMPUTE DaysOverDue =
            (FUNCTION INTEGER-OF-DATE(DateNowInt))
          - (FUNCTION INTEGER-OF-DATE(BillDate) + 30)

    EVALUATE TRUE
        WHEN DaysOverDue > ZERO
            DISPLAY "This bill is overdue."
        WHEN DaysOverDue = ZERO
            DISPLAY "This bill is due today."
        WHEN DaysOverDue < ZERO
            DISPLAY "This bill is not yet due."
    END-EVALUATE

*> eg3. This example displays the date NumOfDays days
*> from the current date
    DISPLAY SPACES
    DISPLAY "eg3 - find the date x days from now"
    DISPLAY "Enter the number of days - " WITH NO ADVANCING
    ACCEPT NumOfDays
    COMPUTE IntFutureDate = FUNCTION INTEGER-OF-DATE(DateNowInt) + NumOfDays + 1
    MOVE FUNCTION DATE-OF-INTEGER(IntFutureDate) TO FutureDate
    DISPLAY "The date in " NumOfDays " days time will be "
            MonthD "/" DayD "/" YearD

*> eg4. This takes advantage of the fact that DATE-OF-INTEGER
*> requires a valid date to do some easy date validation

    DISPLAY SPACES
    DISPLAY "eg4 - validate the date"
    PERFORM WITH TEST AFTER UNTIL DateIsValid
        DISPLAY "Enter a valid date (yyyymmdd) - " WITH NO ADVANCING
        ACCEPT DateNowInt
```

```
      COMPUTE DateCheck = FUNCTION INTEGER-OF-DATE(DateNowInt)
      IF DateIsNotValid
         DISPLAY DateNowInt " is not a valid date"
         DISPLAY SPACES
      END-IF
   END-PERFORM
   DISPLAY "Thank you! " DateNowInt " is a valid date."

   STOP RUN.
```

Listing 15-10 Output

```
eg1 - get the current date
Current Date is 12/18/2013
Current Time is 11:51:10
The local time is - GMT +00:00


eg2 - find the difference between two dates
Enter the date of the bill (yyyymmdd) - 20131117
This bill is overdue.


eg3 - find the date x days from now
Enter the number of days - 13
The date in 013 days time will be 01/01/2014


eg4 - validate the date
Enter a valid date (yyyymmdd) - 20131305
20131305 is not a valid date


Enter a valid date (yyyymmdd) - 20130931
20130931 is not a valid date


Enter a valid date (yyyymmdd) - 20130930
Thank you! 20130930 is a valid date.
```

DATE Program Explanation

Most of these examples are straightforward and require little explanation. Only eg2 and eg4 should present any difficulty:

- eg2 calculates the difference between the due date (bill date + 30) and today's date and, by subtracting one from the other, determines whether the bill is overdue (more than 30 days old).

- eg4 invokes the INTEGER-OF-DATE function for the sole purpose of checking whether the date is valid. If an invalid date is supplied to INTEGER-OF-DATE, the function returns zeros.

Summary

This chapter introduced COBOL string manipulation. You discovered how to use INSPECT to count, convert, and replace characters in a string. You saw how to use the STRING verb to concatenate strings and UNSTRING to split a string into substrings. In addition to learning the basics of the string-handling verbs, you saw how to augment their capabilities by using reference modification and intrinsic functions.

All the examples you have examined so far have been small, stand-alone programs. But in a large COBOL system, the executables usually consist of a number of programs, separately compiled and linked together to produce a single run unit. In the next chapter, you learn how to use contained and external subprograms to create a single run unit from a number of COBOL programs. COBOL subprograms introduce a number of data-declaration issues, so Chapter 16 also examines the COPY verb and the IS GLOBAL and IS EXTERNAL clauses.

LANGUAGE KNOWLEDGE EXERCISES

Ah! Exercise time again. Now, where did you put your 2B pencil?

Q1 Assume that for each INSPECT statement, StringVar1 has the value shown in the **Ref** row of the following table. Show what value StringVar1 holds after each INSPECT statement is executed:

1. INSPECT StringVar1 REPLACING LEADING "W" BY "6"

2. INSPECT StringVar1 REPLACING ALL "W" BY "7"   AFTER INITIAL "Z"
   BEFORE INITIAL "Q"

3. INSPECT StringVar1 REPLACING ALL "WW" BY "me" BEFORE INITIAL "ZZ"

4. INSPECT StringVar1 CONVERTING "WZQ" TO "abc"

01 StringVar1 PIC X(16) VALUE "WWWWZWWWWWZQZZZZ".															
Ref	W	W	W	W	Z	W	W	W	W	W	Z	Q	Z	Z	Z	Z
1																
2																
3																
4																

Q2 Assume that for each STRING statement, StringVar2 has the value shown in the **Ref** row of the following table. Show what value StringVar2 holds after each STRING statement is executed:

```
01 Source1   PIC X(10)  VALUE "the grass".
01 Source2   PIC X(6)   VALUE "is ris".
01 StrPtr    PIC 99     VALUE 3.
```

1. STRING Source2 DELIMITED BY SPACES
          SPACE DELIMITED BY SIZE
          Source1 DELIMITED BY SIZE
          INTO StringVar2

2. STRING SPACE, "See" DELIMITED BY SIZE
        Source1 DELIMITED BY SPACES
        INTO StringVar2 WITH POINTER StrPtr

	01 StringVar2 PIC X(16) VALUE "Spring is sprung".															
Ref	S	p	r	i	n	g		i	s		s	p	r	u	n	g
1																
2																

Q3   A four-line poem is accepted into StringVar3 as a single line of text. Each line of the poem is separated from the others by a comma. Using the declarations that follow, write an UNSTRING statement to unpack the poem into individual poem lines and then display each poem line as well the number of characters in the line. For instance, given the poem

"I eat my peas with honey,I've done it all my life,It makes the peas taste funny,But it keeps them on the knife,"

Display

```
24 - I eat my peas with honey
24 - I've done it all my life
29 - It makes the peas taste funny
30 - But it keeps them on the knife
01 StringVar3       PIC X(120).
01 PoemLine OCCURS 4 TIMES.
   02 PLine         PIC X(40)
   02 CCount        PIC 99.
```

Q4   Given these strings, write what will be displayed by the following DISPLAY statement:

```
01  Str1   PIC X(25)   VALUE "I never saw a purple cow".
01  Str2   PIC X(25)   VALUE "I never hope to see one".

DISPLAY Str3((36 - 12) + 1:)
DISPLAY Str1(1:2) Str2(9:5) Str2(1:7) Str2(16:4) Str1(12:)
```

Q5   Given the following string description, write what will be displayed by the following DISPLAY statement:

```
01 Str3       PIC X(36) VALUE "abcdefghijklmnopqrstuvwxyz0123456789".

DISPLAY Str3((36 - 12) + 1:)
```

Q6 Given the following ACCEPT statement, using INSPECT, reference modification, and intrinsic functions, write a set of statements to discover the actual size of the string entered and store it in StrSize. Hint: The actual string is followed by trailing spaces:

```
01 Str4    PIC X(60).
01 StrSize PIC 99.

ACCEPT Str4.
```

Q7 Given Str4 and the ACCEPT statement in Q6, write statements to trim any leading spaces from the string entered and then store the trimmed string back in Str4.

LANGUAGE KNOWLEDGE EXERCISES: ANSWERS

Q1 Assume that for each INSPECT statement, StringVar1 has the value shown in the **Ref** row of the following table. Show what value StringVar1 holds after each INSPECT statement is executed:

1. INSPECT StringVar1 REPLACING LEADING "W" BY "6"

2. INSPECT StringVar1 REPLACING ALL "W" BY "7"
        AFTER INITIAL "Z" BEFORE INITIAL "Q"

3. INSPECT StringVar1 REPLACING ALL "WW" BY "me" BEFORE INITIAL "ZZ"

4. INSPECT StringVar1 CONVERTING "WZQ" TO "abc"

01 StringVar1 PIC X(16) VALUE "WWWWZWWWWWZQZZZZ".															
Ref	W	W	W	W	Z	W	W	W	W	W	Z	Q	Z	Z	Z	Z
1	6	6	6	6	Z	W	W	W	W	W	Z	Q	Z	Z	Z	Z
2	W	W	W	W	Z	7	7	7	7	7	Z	Q	Z	Z	Z	Z
3	m	e	m	e	Z	m	e	m	e	W	Z	Q	Z	Z	Z	Z
4	a	a	a	a	b	a	a	a	a	a	b	c	b	b	b	b

Q2 Assume that for each STRING statement, StringVar2 has the value shown in the **Ref** row of the following table. Show what value StringVar2 holds after each STRING statement is executed:

```
01 Source1   PIC X(10) VALUE "the grass".
01 Source2   PIC X(6)  VALUE "is ris".
01 StrPtr    PIC 99    VALUE 3.
```

```
1.   STRING Source2 DELIMITED BY SPACES
            SPACE DELIMITED BY SIZE
            Source1 DELIMITED BY SIZE
            INTO StringVar2

     STRING SPACE, "See" DELIMITED BY SIZE
            Source1 DELIMITED BY SPACES
            INTO StringVar2 WITH POINTER StrPtr
```

01 StringVar2 PIC X(16) VALUE "Spring is sprung".															
Ref	S	p	r	i	n	g		I	s		s	p	r	u	n	g
1	i	s		t	h	e		g	r	a	s	s		u	n	g
2	S	p		S	e	e	t	h	e		s	p	r	u	n	g

Q3 A four-line poem is accepted into StringVar3 as a single line of text. Each line of the poem is separated from the others by a comma. Using the declarations that follow, write an UNSTRING statement to unpack the poem into individual poem lines and then display each poem line as well the number of characters in the line. For instance, given the poem

"I eat my peas with honey,I've done it all my life,It makes the peas taste funny,But it keeps them on the knife,"

Display

```
24 - I eat my peas with honey
24 - I've done it all my life
29 - It makes the peas taste funny
30 - But it keeps them on the knife
```

```
01 StringVar3        PIC X(120).
01 PoemLine OCCURS 4 TIMES.
   02 PLine          PIC X(40)
   02 CCount         PIC 99.
```

UNSTRING StringVar3 DELIMITED BY "," INTO
PLine(1) COUNT IN CCount(1)
PLine(2) COUNT IN CCount(2)
PLine(3) COUNT IN CCount(3)
PLine(4) COUNT IN CCount(4)
END-UNSTRING

Q4   Given these strings, write what will be displayed by the following DISPLAY statement:

```
01  Str1   PIC X(25)   VALUE "I never saw a purple cow".
01  Str2   PIC X(25)   VALUE "I never hope to see one".
```

```
DISPLAY Str3((36 - 12) + 1:)
DISPLAY Str1(1:2) Str2(9:5) Str2(1:7) Str2(16:4) Str1(12:)
```

I hope I never see a purple cow

Q5   Given the following string description, write what will be displayed by the following DISPLAY statement:

```
01 Str3      PIC X(36) VALUE "abcdefghijklmnopqrstuvwxyz0123456789".
```

```
DISPLAY Str3((36 - 12) + 1:)
```

yz0123456789

Q6   Given the following ACCEPT statement, using INSPECT, reference modification, and intrinsic functions, write a set of statements to discover the actual size of the string entered and store it in StrSize. Hint: The actual string is followed by trailing spaces:

```
01 Str4          PIC X(60).
01 StrSize       PIC 99.
01 NumOfChars    PIC 99.
```

```
ACCEPT Str4.
```

ACCEPT Str4.
INSPECT FUNCTION REVERSE(Str4) TALLYING NumOfChars
FOR LEADING SPACES
COMPUTE StrSize = (60 - NumOfChars)
DISPLAY Str4(1:StrSize) ": is " StrSize " characters in size."

Q7   Given Str4 and the ACCEPT statement in Q6, write statements to trim any leading spaces from the string entered and then store the trimmed string back in Str4.

DISPLAY "Old string is - " Str4
MOVE 1 TO NumOfChars
INSPECT Str4 TALLYING NumOfChars FOR LEADING SPACES
MOVE Str4(NumOfChars :) TO Str4
DISPLAY "New string is - " Str4

■ ■ ■

CHAPTER 16

Creating Large Systems

All the programs you have seen so far in this book have been small stand-alone programs. But a large software system is not usually written as a single monolithic program. Instead, it consists of a main program and many independently compiled subprograms, linked together to form one executable run-unit. In COBOL, a program that is invoked from another program is called a *subprogram*. In other languages, these might be called procedures or methods.

This chapter shows you how to create a software system that consists of a number of programs linked together into one executable run-unit. You see how to create contained (internal) and external subprograms and how to use the CALL verb to pass control to them. You discover how to pass data to a subprogram through its parameter list, and you learn about state memory and how to create subprograms that exhibit state memory and subprograms that do not. Because COBOL subprograms introduce a number of data-declaration issues, this chapter also examines the COPY verb and the IS GLOBAL and IS EXTERNAL clauses.

Subprograms and the COPY Verb

Prior to the ANS 74 version, a large software system written in COBOL consisted of a series of large monolithic programs that ran under the control of a Job Control Language. Each program in the series did a piece of work and then passed the resulting data to the next program through the medium of files. The Job Control Language controlled the order of execution of the programs and provided access to the required files. For instance, a validation program might validate the data in a file to create a validated file that was then passed to the next program for processing.

The ANS 74 version of COBOL introduced external subprograms and the CALL and COPY verbs. These changes allowed you to create software systems that consisted of the following:

- A main program

- Record, file, and table descriptions imported from a central source text library

- A number of independently compiled external subprograms

These elements were linked together to form one executable run-unit.

The ANS 85 version of COBOL improved on this by introducing the concept of *contained subprograms*. These subprograms are called *contained* because their source code is contained within the source code of the main program. Contained subprograms are closed subroutines. They are very similar to the procedures or methods found in other languages. As you will discover, OO-COBOL methods are so similar to contained subprograms that once you have learned how to create one, the other requires little additional instruction.

It is easy to see how a system that consists of a main program and its contained subprograms can be compiled to create one executable image. It is perhaps not so obvious how a system that consists of a number of external subprograms, all independently compiled at different times, can be made into a single executable.

To create a single executable from a number of independently compiled programs, the object code (binary compiled code) of the main program and the subprograms must be bound together by a special program called a *linker*. One purpose of the linker is to resolve the subprogram names (given in the PROGRAM-ID clause) into actual physical addresses so that the computer can find a particular subprogram when it is invoked. Nowadays many software development environments hide the linker step in this traditional sequence:

source code (.cbl) -> **compiler** -> object code (.obj) -> **linker** -> executable code (.exe)

A system that consists of a main program and linked subprograms requires a mechanism that allows one program to invoke another and to pass data to it. In many programming languages, the procedure or function call serves this purpose. In COBOL, the CALL verb is used to invoke one program from another.

The CALL Verb

The CALL verb is used to transfer control (program execution) to an external, independently compiled subprogram or a contained subprogram. When the subprogram terminates, control reverts to the statement after CALL. The metalanguage for the CALL verb is given in Figure 16-1.

$$
\underline{\text{CALL}} \quad \begin{Bmatrix} \text{ProgNameIdentifier} \\ \text{ProgNameLiteral} \end{Bmatrix}
$$

$$
\left[\underline{\text{USING}} \begin{Bmatrix} \begin{bmatrix} \text{BY } \underline{\text{REFERENCE}} \end{bmatrix} \\ \text{BY } \underline{\text{CONTENT}} \end{Bmatrix} \text{ParamIdentifier} \dots \end{Bmatrix} \dots \right]
$$

$$
\begin{Bmatrix} \begin{bmatrix} \text{ON EXCEPTION StatementBlock} \end{bmatrix} \\ \begin{bmatrix} \underline{\text{NOT}} \text{ ON } \underline{\text{EXCEPTION}} \text{ StatementBlock} \end{bmatrix} \\ \begin{bmatrix} \text{ON } \underline{\text{OVERFLOW}} \text{ StatementBlock} \end{bmatrix} \end{Bmatrix}
$$

$$
\begin{bmatrix} \underline{\text{END - CALL}} \end{bmatrix}
$$

Figure 16-1. *Metalanguage for the CALL verb*

Some notes relating to the metalanguage follow:

- BY REFERENCE and BY CONTENT are parameter-passing mechanisms. BY REFERENCE is the default and so is sometimes omitted (hence the square brackets).

- If the called program has not been linked (does not exist in the executable image), the statements following ON EXCEPTION execute. Otherwise, the program terminates abnormally.

- If the CALL passes parameters, then the called subprogram must have a USING phrase after the PROCEDURE DIVISION header and a LINKAGE SECTION to describe the parameters that are passed.

- The CALL statement may only have a USING phrase if the PROCEDURE DIVISION header of the called subprogram also has a USING phrase.

- Both USING phrases must have the same number of parameters.

- Unlike some languages, COBOL does not check the type of the parameters passed to a called subprogram. It is your responsibility to make sure that only parameters of the correct type and size are passed.

- As shown in Figure 16-2, the parameters passed from the calling program to the called subprogram correspond by position, not by name. That is, the first parameter in the USING phrase of the CALL corresponds to the first parameter in the USING phase of the called program, and so on.

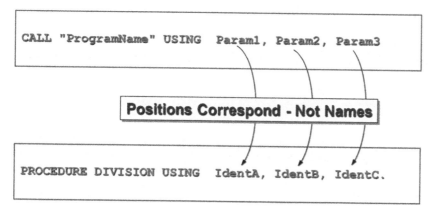

Figure 16-2. *CALL parameters correspond by position not name*

- Implementers often extend CALL by introducing BY VALUE parameter passing and by including a GIVING phrase. These are nonstandard extensions.

Parameter-Passing Mechanisms

As you can see from the metalanguage in Figure 16-1, the CALL verb has two parameter-passing mechanisms: BY REFERENCE and BY CONTENT. You should use BY REFERENCE only when the called subprogram needs to pass data back to the caller. You should always use BY CONTENT when data needs to be passed to, but not received from, the called program.

It is a principle of good program design that you should not expose a subprogram to more data than it needs in order to work. If you pass your data BY REFERENCE, the possibility exists that it may be corrupted by the called subprogram. When you pass data BY CONTENT, there is no possibility of that happening.

Figure 16-3 and Figure 16-4 show how each of these mechanisms works.

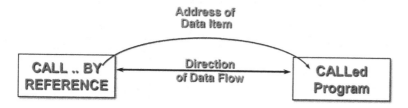

Figure 16-3. *The CALL..BY REFERENCE parameter-passing mechanism*

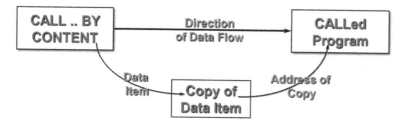

Figure 16-4. *The CALL..BY CONTENT parameter-passing mechanism*

CALL..BY REFERENCE

When data is passed BY REFERENCE, the address of the data item is supplied to the called subprogram (see Figure 16-3). Therefore, any changes made to the data item in the subprogram are also made to the data item in the main program, because both items refer to the same memory location.

CALL..BY CONTENT

When a parameter is passed BY CONTENT, a copy of the data item is made, and the address of the copy is supplied to subprogram (see Figure 16-4). Any changes made to the data item in the subprogram affect only the copy.

Subprograms

I have said that a subprogram is just a program that is invoked by another program rather than by the user/operator. In most ways, this is true. A subprogram may have all the divisions, sections, and paragraphs that a program has, but subprograms may also have additional sections and phrases. In addition, because it is contained within the source text of a containing program, a contained subprogram is not quite the same as an external subprogram (one whose source code is in a document separate from the main program source).

Example 16-1 is a template for a subprogram that shows the additional sections and clauses in bold. The subprogram in Example 16-1 might be invoked with a CALL statement such as this:

```
CALL "ValidateCheckDigit" USING BY CONTENT StudentId
                                BY REFERENCE CKD-Result
```

Note that the CALL uses a literal value to identify the subprogram being invoked and that therefore the name is enclosed in quotes. This is the usual way a subprogram is invoked, because when you write a program, you usually know which subprogram you want to call. If you wanted to choose dynamically which program to call, you would use a data item to hold the program name. For instance:

```
DISPLAY "Enter the subprogram name - " WITH NO ADVANCING
ACCEPT SubprogramName
CALL SubprogramName
```

Example 16-1. Subprogram Template

```
IDENTIFICATION DIVISION.
PROGRAM-ID. ValidateCheckDigit IS INITIAL.
DATA DIVISION.
WORKING-STORAGE SECTION.
   :    :    :    :    :    :    :
   :    :    :    :    :    :    :
LINKAGE SECTION.
01 NumToValidate        PIC 9(7).
01 Result               PIC 99.


PROCEDURE DIVISION USING NumToValidate, Result.
Begin.
   :    :    :    :    :    :    :
   :    :    :    :    :    :    :
    EXIT PROGRAM.
```

Note that the name given in the CALL statement (ValidateCheckDigit) corresponds to the name given in the PROGRAM-ID of the called program. The main purpose of the PROGRAM-ID clause is to identify programs in a run-unit (the group of programs that have been compiled and linked into one executable image). The CALL transfers control from one program in the run-unit to another.

In this template, the IS INITIAL clause is attached to the PROGRAM-ID. I discuss the IS INITIAL clause and the problem of state memory, which it solves, in the next section.

This template uses a LINKAGE SECTION. A LINKAGE SECTION (which comes after the WORKING-STORAGE SECTION) is always required if parameters are passed to a subprogram. The LINKAGE SECTION is used to define the parameters and reserve storage for them. If a LINKAGE SECTION is required, then the subprogram's PROCEDURE DIVISION header requires a USING phrase. The USING phrase matches the *actual parameters* of the CALL (by position in the parameter list) to the *formal parameters* in the subprogram.

■ **Note**   You probably know what I mean by *actual parameters* and *formal parameters*; but in case you don't, here is an explanation. Any useful subprogram is likely to be called from a number of different places and for different purposes. For instance, the check-digit validation subprogram might be called by various programs to validate NewStudentId, OldStudentId, GraduatedStudentId, TransferStudentId, or even (because it validates any seven-digit number) StockId. These data-item names are the names of the *actual parameters* that are passed to the subprogram. When you write the subprogram, you don't always know the names of the data items that will be passed as parameters (a maintenance programmer, for instance, might write a new routine and call your subprogram); and in any case, there are multiple names—which do you choose? So, the name that you use in the subprogram is a placeholder (or *formal parameter*) for the *actual parameter* that is passed to the subprogram.

The EXIT PROGRAM statement in Example 16-1 stops the execution of the subprogram and transfers control back to the caller. You place the EXIT PROGRAM statement where you would normally place STOP RUN. The difference between STOP RUN and an EXIT PROGRAM statement is that STOP RUN causes the entire run-unit to stop (even if STOP RUN is encountered in a subprogram) instead of just the subprogram.

Contained Subprograms

As I explained earlier, a contained subprogram is a program contained within the source code of another program. When you use contained subprograms, the END PROGRAM header is required to delimit the scope of each subprogram and to wrap your subprograms within the scope of the main (container) program. The END PROGRAM header has this format: END PROGRAM ProgramIdName.

Example 16-2 shows the ValidateCheckDigit subprogram implemented as a contained subprogram. In this instance, it is contained within a main program called CheckDigitDrv.

Example 16-2. Outline of a Main Program and Its Contained Subprogram

```
IDENTIFICATION DIVISION.
PROGRAM-ID. CheckDigitDrv.
 :    :    :    :    :    :    :
 :    :    :    :    :    :    :
    CALL "ValidateCheckDigit" USING BY CONTENT StockId
                                    BY REFERENCE CKD-Result
 :    :    :    :    :    :    :
 :    :    :    :    :    :    :
```

```
IDENTIFICATION DIVISION.
PROGRAM-ID. ValidateCheckDigit IS INITIAL.
 :    :    :    :    :    :    :
 :    :    :    :    :    :    :
PROCEDURE DIVISION USING NumToValidate, Result.
 :    :    :    :    :    :
 :    :    :    :    :    :    :
END PROGRAM ValidateCheckDigit.
END PROGRAM CheckDigitDrv.
```

Contained Subprograms vs. External Subprograms

I mentioned that contained subprograms are not quite the same as external subprograms. You have already seen one difference: the END PROGRAM header. Another difference is the visibility of data. In an external subprogram, it is obvious that it can't see data declared in the main program or other subprograms (although this is not entirely true, as you will see when you examine the IS EXTERNAL clause), because it is a separate, independent program. But because the text of a contained subprogram is contained within the text of the main (container) program, you may wonder whether the subprogram can see the data declared in the main program and whether the main program can see the data declared in the subprogram. In COBOL, data declared in a subprogram cannot be seen outside it, and data declared in the main (containing) program cannot be seen in the subprogram, unless ... unless what? For the answer, you have to wait for the explanation of the IS GLOBAL clause later in this chapter.

An issue that does not arise in relation to external subprograms but is a burning issue for contained subprograms is invokability. Contained subprograms can be nested: that is, a contained subprogram may itself contain a subprogram. So the question arises, can a nested subprogram be called from anywhere? Or are there restrictions? Sadly, there are restrictions. A contained subprogram can only be called by its immediate parent (container) program or by a subprogram at the same level. Even this isn't entirely true; a subprogram can only be called by a subprogram (sibling) at the same level if the called program uses the IS COMMON PROGRAM clause (see the next section) in its PROGRAM-ID.

State Memory and the IS INITIAL Phrase

The first time a subprogram is called, it is in its initial state: all files are closed, and the data items are initialized to their VALUE clauses. The next time the subprogram is called, it remembers its state from the previous call. Any files that were opened are still open, and any data items that were assigned values still contain those values.

Although it can be useful for a subprogram to remember its state from call to call, systems that contain subprograms with *state memory* are often less reliable and more difficult to debug than those that do not. A subprogram that does not have state memory is predictable, because for the same input value, it produces the same result. Subprograms that have state memory are more difficult to debug because they may produce different results for the same input values.

You can force a subprogram into its initial state each time it is called by including the IS INITIAL clause in the PROGRAM-ID. The metalanguage for the IS INITIAL clause is given in Figure 16-5. Note that INITIAL is only one of the clauses that can be attached to the PROGRAM-ID. IS COMMON PROGRAM may also be applied to a subprogram. I examine the IS COMMON PROGRAM clause in more detail later in the chapter.

IS[COMMON][INITIAL]PROGRAM.

Figure 16-5. Metalanguage for the IS COMMON and IS INITIAL clauses

Listing 16-1 has a dual purpose. It shows how contained subprograms are created and used, and it demonstrates the difference between a subprogram that has state memory and one that does not. The listing consists of a main program and two subprograms named Steady and Dynamic. Steady is so named because every time you call it with the same parameter values, it produces the same results. But Dynamic, because it remembers its state from the previous call, produces different results when it is called with the same input values.

Listing 16-1. State Memory Demonstration with Steady and Dynamic

```
IDENTIFICATION DIVISION.
PROGRAM-ID. Listing16-1.
DATA DIVISION.
WORKING-STORAGE SECTION.
01 Increment      PIC 99 VALUE ZERO.
   88 EndOfData   VALUE ZERO.

PROCEDURE DIVISION.
Begin.
*> Demonstrates the difference between Steady
*> and Dynamic.  Entering a zero ends the iteration
   DISPLAY "Enter an increment value (0-99) - " WITH NO ADVANCING
   ACCEPT Increment
   PERFORM UNTIL EndOfData
      CALL "Steady"  USING BY CONTENT Increment
      CALL "Dynamic" USING BY CONTENT Increment
      DISPLAY SPACES
      DISPLAY "Enter an increment value (0-99) - " WITH NO ADVANCING
      ACCEPT Increment
   END-PERFORM
   STOP RUN.


IDENTIFICATION DIVISION.
PROGRAM-ID. Dynamic.
DATA DIVISION.
WORKING-STORAGE SECTION.
01 RunningTotal   PIC 9(5) VALUE ZERO.
01 PrnTotal       PIC ZZ,ZZ9.

LINKAGE SECTION.
01 ValueToAdd     PIC 99.
PROCEDURE DIVISION USING ValueToAdd.
Begin.
   ADD ValueToAdd TO RunningTotal
   MOVE RunningTotal TO PrnTotal
   DISPLAY "Dynamic total = " PrnTotal
   EXIT PROGRAM.
END PROGRAM Dynamic.


IDENTIFICATION DIVISION.
PROGRAM-ID. Steady IS INITIAL.
DATA DIVISION.
```

```
                  Listing 16-1 Output

Enter an increment value (0-99) - 66
Steady   total =       66
Dynamic total =        66

Enter an increment value (0-99) - 66
Steady   total =       66
Dynamic total =       132

Enter an increment value (0-99) - 66
Steady   total =       66
Dynamic total =       198

Enter an increment value (0-99) - 22
Steady   total =       22
Dynamic total =       220

Enter an increment value (0-99) - 22
Steady   total =       22
Dynamic total =       242

Enter an increment value (0-99) -
```

```
WORKING-STORAGE SECTION.
01 RunningTotal   PIC 9(5) VALUE ZERO.
01 PrnTotal       PIC ZZ,ZZ9.

LINKAGE SECTION.
01 ValueToAdd   PIC 99.
PROCEDURE DIVISION USING ValueToAdd .
Begin.
    ADD ValueToAdd  TO RunningTotal
    MOVE RunningTotal TO PrnTotal
    DISPLAY "Steady total  = " PrnTotal
    EXIT PROGRAM.
END PROGRAM Steady.
END PROGRAM Listing16-1.
```

Notice that each time Steady is passed the same value, it produces the same result; but each time Dynamic is passed the same value, it produces a different result, because it remembers the state of the data items from the previous invocation. Sometimes, such as when you need to keep a running total, you want the subprogram to have state memory. But as a rule, unless you explicitly want a subprogram to remember its state, you should use the IS INITIAL phrase to set the program to its initial state each time it is called.

The CANCEL Verb

A program may need state memory only part of the time. That is, it needs to be reset to its initial state periodically. In COBOL, you can do this using the CANCEL verb. The metalanguage for the CANCEL verb is given in Figure 16-6.

$$\text{CANCEL} \quad \begin{Bmatrix} \text{ProgNameIdentifier} \\ \text{ProgNameLiteral} \end{Bmatrix} \dots$$

Figure 16-6. *Metalanguage for the CANCEL verb*

When the CANCEL command is executed, the memory space occupied by the subprogram is freed. If the subprogram is called again, it is in its initial state (all files declared in the subprogram are closed, and all data items are initialized to their VALUE clauses). As shown in Example 16-3, you can use the CANCEL verb to force Dynamic to act like Steady.

Example 16-3. Using the CANCEL Verb to Force Dynamic to Act Like Steady

```
DISPLAY "First  Call"
CALL "Dynamic" USING BY CONTENT 77.
CANCEL "Dynamic"
DISPLAY SPACES
DISPLAY "Second Call"
CALL " Dynamic" USING BY CONTENT 77.
```

Example 16-3 Output
First Call
Dynamic total =   77
Second Call
Dynamic total =   77

The IS GLOBAL Clause

I noted earlier that data declared in a contained subprogram cannot be seen in the main (containing) program, and data declared in the main program cannot be seen inside a contained subprogram. In general, this is true; but sometimes you may want to share a data item with a number of contained subprograms. For instance, consider the program fragments in Example 16-4. This program produces a report showing the purchases of new automobiles in the United States. The data is accumulated in a table and then printed.

The program is partitioned into a main program and two subprograms. One subprogram adds the value of each new car purchase to the appropriate state in the table. The other subprogram prints the report when the new car purchases have been processed. Both subprograms need access to the table. The table cannot be declared local to the subprogram because any local declarations cannot be seen outside the subprogram. So the table must be declared in the outer scope: the main (container) program. The problem then is how to allow the table to be seen by the subprograms.

One approach might be to pass the table through the parameter list. The problem with this approach is that there is a lot of data in the table, and every time AddToStateTotal is called, the table must be passed. A better solution is to make the table visible inside the subprograms. You can do this using the IS GLOBAL clause. Any data item to which the IS GLOBAL clause is attached is visible within the subordinate subprograms.

Example 16-4. Program Outline Showing the Use of the IS GLOBAL Clause

```
IDENTIFICATION DIVISION.
PROGRAM-ID. CarPurchasesReport.
  :    :    :    :    :    :    :
01 StateTable IS GLOBAL.
   02 State OCCURS 50 TIMES.
      03 TotalCarPurchases    PIC 9(9)V99.
  :    :    :    :    :    :
PROCEDURE DIVISION.
      :    :    :    :    :    :
    CALL AddToStateTotal USING BY CONTENT StateNo, ValueOfCarPurchase
      :    :    :    :    :
    CALL PrintTotalCarPurchases
    STOP RUN.

IDENTIFICATION DIVISION.
PROGRAM-ID. AddToStateTotal.
  :    :    :    :    :    :    :
END-PROGRAM AddToStateTotal.

IDENTIFICATION DIVISION.
PROGRAM-ID. PrintTotalCarPurchases.
  :    :    :    :    :    :    :
END PROGRAM PrintTotalCarPurchases.
END PROGRAM CarPurchasesReport.
```

The IS COMMON PROGRAM Clause

I mentioned earlier that a contained subprogram can only be called by its immediate parent (container) program or by a subprogram at the same level. I noted that even then, a contained subprogram can call a subprogram at the same level only if the subprogram to be called uses the IS COMMON PROGRAM clause in its PROGRAM-ID. You already saw the metalanguage for the IS COMMON PROGRAM clause in Figure 16-5, but it is repeated here for convenience:

IS[COMMON] [INITIAL] PROGRAM.

When IS COMMON PROGRAM is attached to the PROGRAM-ID clause of a contained subprogram, that subprogram may be invoked by any subprograms at the same level (siblings) but only by them. As you can see from the metalanguage, both the COMMON and INITIAL clauses may be used in combination. The words IS and PROGRAM are noise words that may be omitted. The IS COMMON PROGRAM clause can be used only in nested programs.

Example Programs and Their Subprograms

Listing 16-2, Listing 16-3, and Listing 16-4 are programs that consist of simple examples to demonstrate some of the issues discussed so far. Listing 16-5 is a more practical example that implements a game to test your knowledge of the American states. Listing 16-6 is a demonstrator for the external subprogram used by Listing 16-5.

External Subprogram

Listing 16-2 is an example program that calls an external subprogram to validate Student IDs. It is followed by the external subprogram Listing 16-2sub, which applies check-digit validation to any seven-digit number supplied to it.

Listing 16-2. Creating and Calling an External Subprogram

```
IDENTIFICATION DIVISION.
PROGRAM-ID. Listing16-2.
AUTHOR.  Michael Coughlan.
DATA DIVISION.
WORKING-STORAGE SECTION.
01 StudentId              PIC 9(7).

01 ValidationResult       PIC 9.
   88 ValidStudentId      VALUE ZERO.
   88 InvalidStudentId    VALUE 1.


PROCEDURE DIVISION.
Begin.
    PERFORM 3 TIMES
        DISPLAY "Enter a Student Id : " WITH NO ADVANCING
        ACCEPT StudentId
        CALL "ValidateCheckDigit" USING BY CONTENT StudentID
                                  BY REFERENCE ValidationResult
        IF ValidStudentId
          DISPLAY "The Student id - " StudentId " - is valid"
         ELSE
          DISPLAY "The Student id - " StudentId " - is not valid"
        END-IF
        DISPLAY SPACES
    END-PERFORM
    STOP RUN.
```

```
Listing 16-2 Output

Enter a Student Id : 1234567
The Student id - 1234567 - is not valid

Enter a Student Id : 7654321
The Student id - 7654321 - is not valid

Enter a Student Id : 9320288
The Student id - 9320288 - is valid
```

Listing 16-2sub. The ValidateCheckDigit External Subprogram

```
IDENTIFICATION DIVISION.
PROGRAM-ID. ValidateCheckDigit IS INITIAL.
DATA DIVISION.
WORKING-STORAGE SECTION.
```

```
01 SumOfNums            PIC 9(5).
01 Quotient             PIC 9(5).
01 CalcResult           PIC 99.


LINKAGE SECTION.
01 NumToValidate.
    02  D1              PIC 9.
    02  D2              PIC 9.
    02  D3              PIC 9.
    02  D4              PIC 9.
    02  D5              PIC 9.
    02  D6              PIC 9.
    02  D7              PIC 9.


01 Result               PIC 9.
    88 InvalidCheckDigit VALUE 1.
    88 ValidCheckDigit   VALUE 0.


PROCEDURE DIVISION USING NumToValidate, Result.
*> Returns a Result of 1 (invalid check digit) or 0 (valid check digit)
Begin.
    COMPUTE SumOfNums = (D1 * 7) + (D2 * 6) + (D3 * 5) + (D4 * 4) +
                        (D5 * 3) + (D6 * 2) + (D7).
    DIVIDE SumOfNums BY 11 GIVING Quotient REMAINDER CalcResult
    IF CalcResult EQUAL TO ZERO
       SET ValidCheckDigit TO TRUE
     ELSE
       SET InvalidCheckDigit TO TRUE
    END-IF
    EXIT PROGRAM.
```

Parameter Passing and Data Visibility

Listing 16-3 is an abstract example that demonstrates how to create contained subprograms. It shows the various kinds of parameters and parameter-passing mechanisms you can use and demonstrates the visibility of any data item declared with the IS GLOBAL clause.

Listing 16-3. Contained Subprograms and Parameter Passing and Data Visibility

```
IDENTIFICATION DIVISION.
PROGRAM-ID. Listing16-3.
AUTHOR.  Michael Coughlan.
DATA DIVISION.
WORKING-STORAGE SECTION.
01 DaysOfTheWeek  VALUE "MonTueWedThuFriSatSun" IS GLOBAL.
    02 DayName      PIC XXX OCCURS 7 TIMES.

01 Parameters.
    02 Number1             PIC 9(3)  VALUE 456.
    02 Number2             PIC 9(3)  VALUE 321.
    02 FirstString         PIC X(20) VALUE "First parameter  = ".
```

```
    02 SecondString        PIC X(20) VALUE "Second parameter = ".
    02 Result              PIC 9(6)  USAGE IS COMP.
    02 DiscountTable VALUE "12430713862362".
       03 Discount         PIC 99 OCCURS 7 TIMES.

01 PrnResult               PIC ZZZ,ZZ9.

PROCEDURE DIVISION.
DemoParameterPassing.
    DISPLAY "FirstString  value is - " FirstString
    DISPLAY "SecondString value is - " SecondString

    CALL "MultiplyNums"
        USING BY CONTENT Number1, Number2, FirstString,
              BY REFERENCE SecondString, Result
              BY CONTENT DiscountTable

    DISPLAY SPACES
    DISPLAY "FirstString  value is - " FirstString
    DISPLAY "SecondString value is - " SecondString
    MOVE Result TO PrnResult
    DISPLAY "COMP value is " PrnResult
    STOP RUN.


IDENTIFICATION DIVISION.
PROGRAM-ID. MultiplyNums.
AUTHOR. Michael Coughlan.
DATA DIVISION.
WORKING-STORAGE SECTION.
01 idx           PIC 9.

LINKAGE SECTION.
01 Param1        PIC 9(3).
01 Param2        PIC 9(3).
01 Answer        PIC 9(6) USAGE IS COMP.
01 StrA          PIC X(20).
01 StrB          PIC X(20).
01 TableIn.
   02 TNum   PIC 99 OCCURS 7 TIMES.


PROCEDURE DIVISION USING Param1, Param2, StrA,
StrB, Answer, TableIn.
Begin.
    DISPLAY SPACES
    DISPLAY ">>> In the MultiplyNums subprogram"
    DISPLAY StrA Param1
    DISPLAY StrB Param2
    MULTIPLY Param1 BY Param2 GIVING Answer.
```

```
              Listing 16-3 Output

FirstString  value is - First parameter  =
SecondString value is - Second parameter =

>>> In the MultiplyNums subprogram
First parameter  =  456
Second parameter =  321

Mon discount is   12%
Tue discount is   43%
Wed discount is   07%
Thu discount is   13%
Fri discount is   86%
Sat discount is   23%
Sun discount is   62%

>>>> In InnerSubProg
Days of the week = MonTueWedThuFriSatSun
<<<< Leaving InnerSubProg

<<<< Leaving MultiplyNums

FirstString  value is - First parameter  =
SecondString value is - VALUE OVERWRITTEN
COMP value is 146,376
```

```
*>  Displays table values. One passed as a parameter and the other global
    DISPLAY SPACES
    PERFORM VARYING idx FROM 1 BY 1 UNTIL idx > 7
       DISPLAY DayName(idx) " discount is  " Tnum(idx) "%"
    END-PERFORM

*>  Transfer control to a subprogram contained within MultiplyNums
    CALL "InnerSubProg"

*>  Demonstrates the difference between BY CONTENT and BY REFERENCE.
    MOVE "VALUE OVERWRITTEN" TO StrA
    MOVE "VALUE OVERWRITTEN" TO StrB
    DISPLAY SPACES
    DISPLAY "<<<< Leaving MultiplyNums"
    EXIT PROGRAM.

IDENTIFICATION DIVISION.
PROGRAM-ID. InnerSubProg.
AUTHOR. Michael Coughlan.
PROCEDURE DIVISION.
Begin.
*>  Demonstrates that the GLOBAL data item is even visible here
    DISPLAY SPACES
    DISPLAY ">>>> In InnerSubProg"
    DISPLAY "Days of the week = " DaysOfTheWeek
    DISPLAY "<<<< Leaving InnerSubProg"
    EXIT PROGRAM.

END PROGRAM InnerSubProg.
END PROGRAM MultiplyNums.
END PROGRAM LISTING16-3.
```

The first displayed items show the current value of the two strings in the main program. There is a purpose to this. One string is passed BY REFERENCE and the other BY CONTENT. When these strings are displayed after the CALL has executed, the one passed BY REFERENCE has been corrupted. The lesson should be obvious.

In addition to normal numeric items, one of the parameters is a USAGE IS COMP data item. It holds the result of multiplying the two numbers Param1 and Param2. One thing I must stress here is that the description of numeric items in the main program must be the same as the description in the LINKAGE SECTION. If you describe an item as signed in the subprogram, it must be signed in the main program. If it is a USAGE IS COMP item in the subprogram, it must be the same in the main program. Be aware that the complier provides you with absolutely no protection in this regard. It is up to you to make sure the data types and sizes correspond. Working with COBOL subprograms is akin to driving down a twisty mountain road with no protection barrier—one mistake, and you plunge into the abyss.

The percentage displays are used to show that an array can be passed as a parameter. But in this example I also take the opportunity to show that the DaysOfTheWeek table, which is declared as GLOBAL in the outer scope (main program), is also visible inside the contained subprogram.

Just to emphasize the visibility of GLOBAL data items, the subprogram InnerSubProg is nested within the subprogram MultiplyNums. Even in InnerSubProg, the DaysOfTheWeek table is visible.

Using IS COMMON PROGRAM

Listing 16-4 shows that the program to be called can be assigned at runtime. In this example, instead of using a literal value as the target of the CALL, a data item containing the name of the subprogram to be called is used. The name of the subprogram is supplied by the user. Because the user is supplying the name of the program, there is a possibility that they will get the name wrong; the ON EXCEPTION clause is used to make sure the named program exists.

Listing 16-4. Creating and Using a COMMON Subprogram

```
IDENTIFICATION DIVISION.
PROGRAM-ID. Listing16-4.
AUTHOR. Michael Coughlan.
DATA DIVISION.
WORKING-STORAGE SECTION.
01 Operation            PIC XXX.
01 NumericValue         PIC 999.
   88 EndOfData         VALUE ZEROS.


01 FILLER               PIC 9.
   88 ValidSubprogName  VALUE ZERO.
   88 InvalidSubprogName VALUE 1.


PROCEDURE DIVISION.
Begin.
    PERFORM 3 TIMES
        SET ValidSubprogName TO TRUE
        DISPLAY SPACES
        DISPLAY "Enter the required operation (Dec or Inc) : " WITH NO ADVANCING
        ACCEPT Operation
        DISPLAY "Enter a three digit value : " WITH NO ADVANCING
        ACCEPT NumericValue
        PERFORM UNTIL EndofData OR InvalidSubprogName
           CALL Operation USING BY CONTENT NumericValue
                ON EXCEPTION    DISPLAY Operation " is not a valid operation"
                                SET InvalidSubprogName TO TRUE
                NOT ON EXCEPTION SET ValidSubprogName   TO TRUE
                                DISPLAY "Enter a three digit value : "
                                        WITH NO ADVANCING
                                ACCEPT NumericValue

           END-CALL
        END-PERFORM
        CANCEL Operation
    END-PERFORM
    STOP RUN.


IDENTIFICATION DIVISION.
PROGRAM-ID. Inc.
AUTHOR. Michael Coughlan.
```

```
                    Listing 16-4 Output

Enter the required operation (Dec or Inc) : Dec
Enter a three digit value : 234
The current value is    -234
Enter a three digit value : 111
The current value is    -345
Enter a three digit value : 222
The current value is    -567
Enter a three digit value :

Enter the required operation (Dec or Inc) : Div
Enter a three digit value : 111
Div is not a valid operation

Enter the required operation (Dec or Inc) : Inc
Enter a three digit value : 111
The current value is    +111
Enter a three digit value : 222
The current value is    +333
Enter a three digit value : 999
The current value is  +1,332
Enter a three digit value :
```

```
DATA DIVISION.
WORKING-STORAGE SECTION.
01 RunningTotal     PIC S9(5) VALUE ZEROS.

LINKAGE SECTION.
01 ValueIn          PIC 9(3).

PROCEDURE DIVISION USING ValueIn.
Begin.
    ADD ValueIn TO RunningTotal
    CALL "DisplayTotal" USING BY CONTENT RunningTotal
    EXIT PROGRAM.
END PROGRAM Inc.

IDENTIFICATION DIVISION.
PROGRAM-ID. Dec.
AUTHOR. Michael Coughlan.
DATA DIVISION.
WORKING-STORAGE SECTION.
01 RunningTotal     PIC S9(5) VALUE ZEROS.

LINKAGE SECTION.
01 ValueIn          PIC 9(3).

PROCEDURE DIVISION USING ValueIn.
Begin.
    SUBTRACT ValueIn FROM RunningTotal
    CALL "DisplayTotal" USING BY CONTENT RunningTotal
    EXIT PROGRAM.
END PROGRAM Dec.

IDENTIFICATION DIVISION.
PROGRAM-ID. DisplayTotal IS COMMON INITIAL PROGRAM.
AUTHOR. Michael Coughlan.
DATA DIVISION.
WORKING-STORAGE SECTION.
01 PrnValue     PIC +++,++9.

LINKAGE SECTION.
01 ValueIn          PIC S9(5).

PROCEDURE DIVISION USING ValueIn.
Begin.
    MOVE ValueIn TO PrnValue
    DISPLAY "The current value is " PrnValue
    EXIT PROGRAM.
END PROGRAM DisplayTotal.
END PROGRAM LISTING16-4.
```

In this example, both Inc and Dec display RunningTotal via a CALL to their sibling program DisplayTotal, which has the IS COMMON PROGRAM clause.

A Practical Example

In Chapter 13, I introduced a table that held the codes, names, and capitals of all the states in America. You might have thought at the time that that information could prove useful in a number of programs. In the next example I take that table, expand it to include the population of each state and from it create an external subprogram called GetStateInfo. Listing 16-5 and Listing 16-6 both use GetStateInfo, but in different ways. Listing 16-5 is a game that uses GetStateInfo to test your knowledge of the American states. Listing 16-6 simply returns the other information about a state when you give it one piece of information, such as the state name.

GetStateInfo External Subprogram

Before examining Listing 16-5 and Listing 16-6, let's look at the external subprogram that both of these programs call (see Listing 16-5sub).

Listing 16-5sub. External Subprogram to Supply Information About the States

```
IDENTIFICATION DIVISION.
PROGRAM-ID.  GetStateInfo IS INITIAL.
AUTHOR.  Michael Coughlan.
DATA DIVISION.
WORKING-STORAGE SECTION.
01 StatesTable.
   02 StateValues.
      03 FILLER PIC X(38)   VALUE "ALAlabama        Montgomery    04822023".
      03 FILLER PIC X(38)   VALUE "AKAlaska         Juneau        00731449".
      03 FILLER PIC X(38)   VALUE "AZArizona        Phoenix       06553255".
      03 FILLER PIC X(38)   VALUE "ARArkansas       Little Rock   02949131".
      03 FILLER PIC X(38)   VALUE "CACalifornia     Sacramento    38041430".
      03 FILLER PIC X(38)   VALUE "COColorado       Denver        05187582".
      03 FILLER PIC X(38)   VALUE "CTConnecticut    Hartford      03590347".
      03 FILLER PIC X(38)   VALUE "DEDelaware       Dover         00917092".
      03 FILLER PIC X(38)   VALUE "FLFlorida        Tallahassee   19317568".
      03 FILLER PIC X(38)   VALUE "GAGeorgia        Atlanta       09919945".
      03 FILLER PIC X(38)   VALUE "HIHawaii         Honolulu      01392313".
      03 FILLER PIC X(38)   VALUE "IDIdaho          Boise         01595728".
      03 FILLER PIC X(38)   VALUE "ILIllinois       Springfield   12875255".
      03 FILLER PIC X(38)   VALUE "INIndiana        Indianapolis  06537334".
      03 FILLER PIC X(38)   VALUE "IAIowa           Des Moines    03074186".
      03 FILLER PIC X(38)   VALUE "KSKansas         Topeka        02885905".
      03 FILLER PIC X(38)   VALUE "KYKentucky       Frankfort     04380415".
      03 FILLER PIC X(38)   VALUE "LALouisiana      Baton Rouge   04601893".
      03 FILLER PIC X(38)   VALUE "MEMaine          Augusta       01329192".
      03 FILLER PIC X(38)   VALUE "MDMaryland       Annapolis     05884563".
      03 FILLER PIC X(38)   VALUE "MAMassachusetts Boston         06646144".
      03 FILLER PIC X(38)   VALUE "MIMichigan       Lansing       09883360".
      03 FILLER PIC X(38)   VALUE "MNMinnesota      Saint Paul    05379139".
      03 FILLER PIC X(38)   VALUE "MSMississippi    Jackson       02984926".
      03 FILLER PIC X(38)   VALUE "MOMissouri       Jefferson City06021988".
```

```
    03 FILLER PIC X(38)  VALUE "MTMontana        Helena        01005141".
    03 FILLER PIC X(38)  VALUE "NENebraska       Lincoln       01855525".
    03 FILLER PIC X(38)  VALUE "NVNevada         Carson City   02758931".
    03 FILLER PIC X(38)  VALUE "NHNew Hampshire  Concord       01320718".
    03 FILLER PIC X(38)  VALUE "NJNew Jersey     Trenton       08864590".
    03 FILLER PIC X(38)  VALUE "NMNew Mexico     Santa Fe      02085538".
    03 FILLER PIC X(38)  VALUE "NYNew York       Albany        19570261".
    03 FILLER PIC X(38)  VALUE "NCNorth CarolinaRaleigh       09752073".
    03 FILLER PIC X(38)  VALUE "NDNorth Dakota   Bismarck      00699628".
    03 FILLER PIC X(38)  VALUE "OHOhio           Columbus      11544225".
    03 FILLER PIC X(38)  VALUE "OKOklahoma       Oklahoma City 03814820".
    03 FILLER PIC X(38)  VALUE "OROregon         Salem         03899353".
    03 FILLER PIC X(38)  VALUE "PAPennsylvania   Harrisburg    12763536".
    03 FILLER PIC X(38)  VALUE "RIRhode Island   Providence    01050292".
    03 FILLER PIC X(38)  VALUE "SCSouth CarolinaColumbia      04723723".
    03 FILLER PIC X(38)  VALUE "SDSouth Dakota   Pierre        00833354".
    03 FILLER PIC X(38)  VALUE "TNTennessee      Nashville     06456243".
    03 FILLER PIC X(38)  VALUE "TXTexas          Austin        26059203".
    03 FILLER PIC X(38)  VALUE "UTUtah           Salt Lake City02855287".
    03 FILLER PIC X(38)  VALUE "VTVermont        Montpelier    00626011".
    03 FILLER PIC X(38)  VALUE "VAVirginia       Richmond      08185867".
    03 FILLER PIC X(38)  VALUE "WAWashington     Olympia       06897012".
    03 FILLER PIC X(38)  VALUE "WVWest Virginia Charleston    01855413".
    03 FILLER PIC X(38)  VALUE "WIWisconsin      Madison       05726398".
    03 FILLER PIC X(38)  VALUE "WYWyoming        Cheyenne      00576412".
  02 FILLER REDEFINES StateValues.
    03 State OCCURS 50 TIMES
          INDEXED BY StateIdx.
      04 StateCode    PIC XX.
      04 StateName    PIC X(14).
      04 StateCapital PIC X(14).
      04 StatePop     PIC 9(8).


LINKAGE SECTION.
01 StateNum-IO       PIC 99.
   88 ValidStateNum  VALUE 1 THRU 50.
01 StateCode-IO      PIC XX.
01 StateName-IO      PIC X(14).
01 StateCapital-IO   PIC X(14).
01 StatePop-IO       PIC 9(8).
01 ErrorFlag         PIC 9.
   88 NoErrorFound    VALUE ZERO.
   88 InvalidStateNum VALUE 1.
   88 NoSearchItems   VALUE 2.
   88 NoSuchStateCode VALUE 3.
   88 NoSuchStateName VALUE 4.
   88 NoSuchCapital   VALUE 5.


PROCEDURE DIVISION USING StateNum-IO, StateCode-IO, StateName-IO,
                   StateCapital-IO, StatePop-IO, ErrorFlag.
```

```
Begin.
    SET NoErrorFound TO TRUE
    SET StateIdx TO 1
    EVALUATE                TRUE
        WHEN StateNum-IO      NOT EQUAL ZEROS  PERFORM SearchUsingStateNum
        WHEN StateCode-IO     NOT EQUAL SPACES PERFORM SearchUsingStateCode
        WHEN StateName-IO     NOT EQUAL SPACES PERFORM SearchUsingStateName
        WHEN StateCapital-IO  NOT EQUAL SPACES PERFORM SearchUsingStateCapital
        WHEN OTHER SET NoSearchItems TO TRUE
    END-EVALUATE
    EXIT PROGRAM.

SearchUsingStateNum.
    IF NOT ValidStateNum SET InvalidStateNum TO TRUE
        ELSE
            MOVE StateCode(StateNum-IO)    TO StateCode-IO
            MOVE StateName(StateNum-IO)    TO StateName-IO
            MOVE StateCapital(StateNum-IO) TO StateCapital-IO
            MOVE StatePop(StateNum-IO)     TO StatePop-IO
    END-IF.

SearchUsingStateCode.
    SEARCH State
        AT END SET NoSuchStateCode TO TRUE
        WHEN FUNCTION UPPER-CASE(StateCode(StateIdx)) EQUAL TO
             FUNCTION UPPER-CASE(StateCode-IO)
            SET StateNum-IO  TO StateIdx
            MOVE StateCode(StateIdx)     TO StateCode-IO
            MOVE StateName(StateIdx)     TO StateName-IO
            MOVE StateCapital(StateIdx)  TO StateCapital-IO
            MOVE StatePop(StateIdx)      TO StatePop-IO
    END-SEARCH.

SearchUsingStateName.
    SEARCH State
        AT END SET NoSuchStateName TO TRUE
        WHEN FUNCTION UPPER-CASE(StateName(StateIdx)) EQUAL TO
             FUNCTION UPPER-CASE(StateName-IO)
            SET StateNum-IO  TO StateIdx
            MOVE StateCode(StateIdx)     TO StateCode-IO
            MOVE StateName(StateIdx)     TO StateName-IO
            MOVE StateCapital(StateIdx)  TO StateCapital-IO
            MOVE StatePop(StateIdx)      TO StatePop-IO
    END-SEARCH.

SearchUsingStateCapital.
    SEARCH State
        AT END SET NoSuchCapital TO TRUE
        WHEN FUNCTION UPPER-CASE(StateCapital(StateIdx)) EQUAL TO
             FUNCTION UPPER-CASE(StateCapital-IO)
            SET StateNum-IO  TO StateIdx
```

```
        MOVE StateCode(StateIdx)    TO StateCode-IO
        MOVE StateName(StateIdx)    TO StateName-IO
        MOVE StateCapital(StateIdx) TO StateCapital-IO
        MOVE StatePop(StateIdx)     TO StatePop-IO
    END-SEARCH.
```

This program takes as parameters StateNum-IO, StateCode-IO, StateName-IO, StateCapital-IO, StatePop-IO, and ErrorFlag. Whichever of the first four parameters has a value is used as the search term to find the other information about the state. For instance, if StateName-IO has a value, then that is used as the search term to find the state number, state code, state capital, and state population.

If an error condition is detected, such as none of the fields having a value, then the appropriate error condition is set; this results in an error code being returned in the ErrorFlag parameter. If ErrorFlag contains zero, then no error was detected. The errors detected are given by the following condition names:

```
88  NoErrorFound     VALUE ZERO.
88  InvalidStateNum  VALUE 1.
88  NoSearchItems    VALUE 2.
88  NoSuchStateCode  VALUE 3.
88  NoSuchStateName  VALUE 4.
88  NoSuchCapital    VALUE 5.
```

The State Knowledge Game

Listing 16-5 is a game to test your knowledge of the names, codes, capitals, and populations of American states. It uses the GetStateInfo external subprogram.

Listing 16-5. A Game to Test Your Knowledge of American States

```
IDENTIFICATION DIVISION.
PROGRAM-ID.  Listing16-5.
AUTHOR.  Michael Coughlan.
DATA DIVISION.
WORKING-STORAGE SECTION.
01 Parameters.
    02 StateNum       PIC 99.
    02 StateCode      PIC XX.
    02 StateName      PIC X(14).
    02 StateCapital   PIC X(14).
    02 StatePop       PIC 9(8).
    02 ErrorFlag      PIC 9.

01 idx  PIC 99.

01 CurrentTime.
    02 FILLER         PIC 9(4).
    02 Seed           PIC 9(4).
01 RandState          PIC 99.
01 RandChoice         PIC 9.
```

```
                    Listing 16-5 Output
Of what state is Santa Fe the capital? New mexico
That is correct

What is the population of Georgia? 6500300
That is incorrect.  The population of Georgia is  9,919,945

What is the population of New Jersey? 8900500
That answer is close enough.  The actual population is  8,864,590

Of what state is Madison the capital? texas
That is incorrect.  The state for Madison is Wisconsin

What is the capital of Pennsylvania? harrisburg
That is correct

What is the capital of Illinois? dublin
That is incorrect.  The capital of Illinois is Springfield

What is the state code for Tennessee? tn
That is correct

What is the population of Illinois? 12500500
That answer is close enough.  The actual population is 12,875,255
```

```
01 Answer           PIC X(14).
01 PopAnswer        PIC 9(8).
01 MinPop           PIC 9(8).
01 MaxPop           PIC 9(8).
01 PrnStatePop      PIC ZZ,ZZZ,ZZ9.
01 StrLength        PIC 99.


PROCEDURE DIVISION.
Begin.
   ACCEPT CurrentTime FROM TIME
   COMPUTE RandState = FUNCTION RANDOM(Seed)
   PERFORM 8 TIMES
      COMPUTE RandState  = (FUNCTION RANDOM * 50) + 1
      COMPUTE RandChoice = (FUNCTION RANDOM * 4) + 1
      CALL "GetStateInfo"
           USING BY REFERENCE  RandState, StateCode, StateName,
                               StateCapital, StatePop, ErrorFlag
      EVALUATE RandChoice
         WHEN       1    PERFORM TestCapitalFromState
         WHEN       2    PERFORM TestCodeFromState
         WHEN       3    PERFORM TestPopFromState
         WHEN       4    PERFORM TestStateFromCapital
      END-EVALUATE
      DISPLAY SPACES
   END-PERFORM
   STOP RUN.


TestCapitalFromState.
   CALL "GetStringLength" USING BY CONTENT StateName
                                BY REFERENCE StrLength
   DISPLAY "What is the capital of " StateName(1:StrLength) "? "
           WITH NO ADVANCING
   ACCEPT Answer
   IF FUNCTION UPPER-CASE(Answer) = FUNCTION UPPER-CASE(StateCapital)
      DISPLAY "That is correct"
    ELSE
      DISPLAY "That is incorrect.  The capital of " StateName(1:StrLength)
              " is " StateCapital
   END-IF.


TestCodeFromState.
   CALL "GetStringLength" USING BY CONTENT StateName
                                BY REFERENCE StrLength
   DISPLAY "What is the state code for " StateName(1:StrLength) "? "
           WITH NO ADVANCING
   ACCEPT Answer
   IF FUNCTION UPPER-CASE(Answer) = FUNCTION UPPER-CASE(StateCode)
      DISPLAY "That is correct"
    ELSE
      DISPLAY "That is incorrect.  The code for " StateName(1:StrLength)
              " is " StateCode
   END-IF.
```

```
TestPopFromState.
    CALL "GetStringLength" USING BY CONTENT StateName
                                 BY REFERENCE StrLength
    DISPLAY "What is the population of " StateName(1:StrLength) "? "
            WITH NO ADVANCING
    ACCEPT PopAnswer
    COMPUTE MinPop = PopAnswer - (PopAnswer * 0.25)
    COMPUTE MaxPop = PopAnswer + (PopAnswer * 0.25)
    MOVE StatePop TO PrnStatePop
    IF StatePop > MinPop AND < MaxPop
      DISPLAY "That answer is close enough.  The actual population is "  PrnStatePop
    ELSE
      DISPLAY "That is incorrect.  The population of " StateName(1:StrLength)
              " is " PrnStatePop
    END-IF.

TestStateFromCapital.
    CALL "GetStringLength" USING BY CONTENT StateCapital
                                 BY REFERENCE StrLength
    DISPLAY "Of what state is " StateCapital(1:StrLength) " the capital? "
            WITH NO ADVANCING
    ACCEPT Answer
    IF FUNCTION UPPER-CASE(Answer) = FUNCTION UPPER-CASE(StateName)
      DISPLAY "That is correct"
    ELSE
      DISPLAY "That is incorrect.  The state for " StateCapital(1:StrLength)
              " is " StateName
    END-IF.


IDENTIFICATION DIVISION.
PROGRAM-ID.  GetStringLength IS INITIAL.
AUTHOR.  Michael Coughlan.
DATA DIVISION.
WORKING-STORAGE SECTION.
01 CharCount       PIC 99 VALUE ZEROS.

LINKAGE SECTION.
01 StringParam     PIC X(14).
01 StringLength    PIC 99.

PROCEDURE DIVISION USING StringParam, StringLength.
Begin.
    INSPECT FUNCTION REVERSE(StringParam) TALLYING CharCount
          FOR LEADING SPACES
    COMPUTE StringLength = 14 - CharCount
    EXIT PROGRAM.
END PROGRAM GetStringLength.
END PROGRAM Listing16-5.
```

This program contains a number of interesting features. First, it uses the RANDOM intrinsic function. The first time RANDOM is invoked, it generates a sequence of pseudo-random numbers using the current time as a seed. Subsequent uses of RANDOM return instances of those numbers.

The program gets two random numbers: one to choose which state to ask about and the other to choose what kind of question to ask. Once the program has chosen the number of the state to ask about, it uses the CALL verb to get all the other information about the state. Depending on what question is asked, the program gets an answer from the user and then compares it with state information returned by the CALL.

Although most answers must be exact, conversion to uppercase is done so the letter case of the answer is not an issue. And because you can't expect users to know the exact population of a state, any answer within 25 percent (higher or lower) of the actual value is accepted as correct.

An interesting problem is caused by displaying state names and capitals when the text does not fill the data item. In that case, the data item is space filled, which causes unsightly output when the text is be displayed. For instance, a question about the capital of Delaware might display as follows:

```
: Of what state is Dover        the capital?
```

To solve this issue, reference modification is used to slice out the actual text. To enable this slicing, the program calculates the length of the text. Because this operation is performed a number of times, it is removed to the contained subprogram GetStringLength.

Getting State Information

Listing 16-6 also uses the subprogram GetStateInfo, but in a more straightforward way. When the user provides a piece of information, such as a state name, the program displays all the other information about the state. The state number and the state code are two of the items displayed and you might think that having both of these items in the table is redundant. However, the importance of the state code is obvious and when I wrote the game in Listing 16-5 the state number proved useful because it made it easy to select the state at random. One other advantage of the state number is that you can use it to dump out all the values in the table (see Example 16-5).

Example 16-5. Fragment Showing How to Display the State Table Values

```
PERFORM VARYING idx FROM 1 BY 1 UNTIL idx > 50
    MOVE idx TO StateNum
    CALL "GetStateInfo"
        USING BY REFERENCE  StateNum, StateCode, StateName,
                            StateCapital, StatePop, ErrorFlag
    DISPLAY StateNum ". " StateCode SPACE StateName
            SPACE StateCapital SPACE StatePop
END-PERFORM
```

Listing 16-6. Using the GetStateInfo Subprogram as Intended

```
IDENTIFICATION DIVISION.
PROGRAM-ID.  Listing16-6.
AUTHOR.  Michael Coughlan.
DATA DIVISION.
WORKING-STORAGE SECTION.
01 Parameters.
    02 StateNum     PIC 99.
    02 StateCode    PIC XX.
    02 StateName    PIC X(14).
```

```
    02 StateCapital   PIC X(14).
    02 StatePop       PIC 9(8).
    02 ErrorFlag      PIC 9.
       88 NoError     VALUE ZERO.

01 CurrentTime.
    02 FILLER         PIC 9(4).
    02 Seed           PIC 9(4).
01 RandChoice         PIC 9.
01 PrnStatePop        PIC ZZ,ZZZ,ZZ9.

PROCEDURE DIVISION.
Begin.
    ACCEPT CurrentTime FROM TIME
    COMPUTE RandChoice = FUNCTION RANDOM(Seed)
    PERFORM 8 TIMES
        DISPLAY SPACES
        INITIALIZE Parameters
        COMPUTE RandChoice = (FUNCTION RANDOM * 4) + 1
        EVALUATE RandChoice
          WHEN       1    DISPLAY "Enter a state number - " WITH NO ADVANCING
                          ACCEPT StateNum
          WHEN       2    DISPLAY "Enter a two letter code - " WITH NO ADVANCING
                          ACCEPT StateCode
          WHEN       3    DISPLAY "Enter a state name - " WITH NO ADVANCING
                          ACCEPT StateName
          WHEN       4    DISPLAY "Enter a state capital - " WITH NO ADVANCING
                          ACCEPT StateCapital
        END-EVALUATE
        CALL "GetStateInfo"
            USING BY REFERENCE   StateNum, StateCode, StateName,
                                 StateCapital, StatePop, ErrorFlag
        IF NoError
          MOVE StatePop TO PrnStatePop
          DISPLAY StateNum ". " StateCode SPACE StateName
                  SPACE StateCapital SPACE PrnStatePop
        ELSE
          DISPLAY "There was an error.  Error Code = " ErrorFlag
        END-IF
    END-PERFORM
    STOP RUN.
```

Listing 16-6 Output

```
Enter a state name - maryland
20. MD Maryland          Annapolis      5,884,563

Enter a state number - 23
23. MN Minnesota         Saint Paul     5,379,139

Enter a state number - 12
12. ID Idaho             Boise          1,595,728

Enter a state capital - topeka
16. KS Kansas            Topeka         2,885,905

Enter a state name - arkansas
04. AR Arkansas          Little Rock    2,949,131

Enter a state name - Mane
There was an error.  Error Code = 4

Enter a two letter code - me
19. ME Maine             Augusta        1,329,192

Enter a state number - 50
50. WY Wyoming           Cheyenne         576,412
```

In this program the search term type is chosen at random, the user is asked to supply a value for it, and then GetStateInfo is called to return the appropriate values for that search term.

The IS EXTERNAL Clause

The IS GLOBAL clause allows a program and its contained subprograms to share access to a data item. The IS EXTERNAL clause does the same for any subprogram in a run-unit (that is, any linked subprogram), but it has restrictions that make it much more cumbersome to use than the IS GLOBAL phrase. Whereas a data item that uses the IS GLOBAL phrase only has to be declared in one place, each of the subprograms that wish to access an EXTERNAL shared item must declare the item—and it must be declared *exactly the same way* in each subprogram. Figure 16-7 illustrates the IS EXTERNAL data-sharing mechanism.

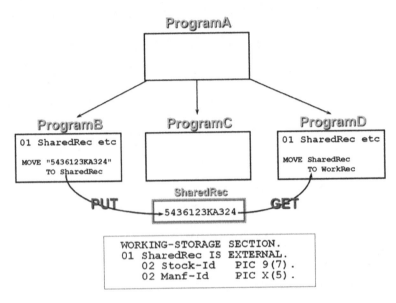

Figure 16-7. *The IS EXTERNAL data-sharing mechanism*

Figure 16-7 shows the calling structure of a run-unit that consists of four linked programs: a main program (ProgramA) and three subprograms. In the illustration, ProgramB and ProgramD share data using the IS EXTERNAL mechanism. In order to share the data, both subprograms must declare the data, and the declarations have to be exactly the same. That is, they must each have the following declaration:

```
01 SharedRec IS EXTERNAL.
   02 Stock-Id   PIC 9(7).
   02 Manf-Id    PIC X(5).
```

In this system, ProgramB communicates with ProgramD by passing it data through the shared data item SharedRec. This might work as follows: ProgramA does some work and then calls ProgramB, which moves a value into SharedRec as part of its work. When control returns to ProgramA, it does some more work, calls ProgramC to do some work, and then calls ProgramD. ProgramD then uses the data from the shared area SharedRec to perform its task.

IS EXTERNAL Problems

The problem with using the IS EXTERNAL phrase is that the transfer of data between ProgramB and ProgramD is detectable only by inspecting B and D. Even though ProgramA invokes B and D, a programmer inspecting A will not realize that B and D are secretly communicating. Even worse, at some point in the future, a maintenance programmer may decide that ProgramC needs to communicate with ProgramD using the shared area and may overwrite the data placed there by ProgramB.

The kind of hidden data communication between subprograms that you see when you use the IS EXTERNAL clause is generally regarded as very poor practice. According to the measures of module goodness discussed by Myers[1] *common coupling* is almost the worst kind of data connection you can have between modules. Subprograms that use the IS EXTERNAL clause to create shared data items are common coupled. Common-coupled modules exhibit a number of problems, such as naming dependencies, creation of dummy structures, and exposure to unnecessary data. Most of these issues are caused by the requirement that each subprogram that wants to use the shared area must describe it exactly the same way.

To illustrate the problem, consider the following scenario. A programmer creates a module to do check digit validation for the Stock-Id. Instead of using the parameter list to get the number to be validated, the programmer takes advantage of the fact that the Stock-Id is an EXTERNAL shared data item and gets access to the Stock-Id using this shared area. The first problem the programmer has is to make sure that their module is not overwriting the data moved into the shared area by some other subprogram. The second problem the programmer has is that their module has to describe the shared area as follows:

```
01 SharedRec IS EXTERNAL.
   02 Stock-Id   PIC 9(7).
   02 Manf-Id    PIC X(5).
```

Even though the module only requires access to the Stock-Id, the programmer has to create a dummy Manf-Id data item also. A maintenance programmer who was trying to understand how this subprogram worked might spend quite a bit of time trying to figure out the role of the dummy Manf-Id. A naming dependency problem might occur later.

Suppose a programmer writing a subprogram for the system to validate customer records discovers that the seven-digit Customer-Id uses a check digit for validation; so, the programmer decides to use the check-digit validation subprogram that has already been written. To use the subprogram, the programmer must pass the number to be validated through the shared data item. This requires the use of the following declaration:

```
01 SharedRec IS EXTERNAL.
   02 Stock-Id   PIC 9(7).
   02 Manf-Id    PIC X(5).
```

Again, a maintenance programmer examining the ValidateCustomerRecord subprogram might wonder why the program includes references to Stock-Id and Manf-Id when it is about validating customer records. The maintenance programmer might also wonder why the subprogram has the statement MOVE Customer-Id TO Stock-Id when these are clearly two very different items.

Using IS EXTERNAL Data Items

Even though using the IS EXTERNAL phrase to create a shared data item has many drawbacks, it may still be preferable to alternative solutions. For instance, sometimes a data item may need to be accessed by many of the subprograms in a system. In that case, your alternatives are to use the IS EXTERNAL phrase to allow the data item to be seen by

---

[1]Myers G. Composite/structured design. New York: Van Nostrand Reinhold; 1978.

any subprogram that requires it or to pass the data item as a parameter. The problem with passing the data item as a parameter is that many of the subprograms that do not require access to the data item then only serve as conduits through which the data item is passed to a subordinate subprogram. This kind of data is called *tramp data*.

Tramp data has a number of drawbacks. It widens the parameter list for subprograms that don't directly use the data; it exposes those subprograms to unnecessary data, which increases the risk that the data will be compromised; and it unnecessarily complicates the code of those subprograms. Figure 16-8 illustrates the problem. In this system, the data item used by ProgG, ProgI, and ProgK is created in ProgJ. Because none of the subprograms that use the data item are directly called by ProgJ, the data item has to be passed up and down the calling chain as tramp data.

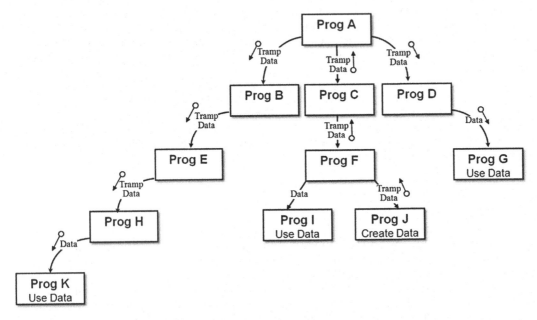

Figure 16-8. *The problem of tramp data. Connecting arrows show the direction of calls. Circle arrows show the direction of data flow*

If you have to use the IS EXTERNAL phrase, there are some things you can do to ameliorate the problems. First, to eliminate the need to create dummy structures, and to reduce exposure to unnecessary data, you should use IS EXTERNAL only with elementary data items. Second, only one subprogram should be permitted to assign a value to an IS EXTERNAL data item. All other subprograms should only be allowed to read that value.

The COPY Verb

The COPY verb is a library statement that includes prewritten library source code in a COBOL program or a subprogram. It is generally used when creating large software systems. These systems are subject to a number of problems that the COPY verb helps to alleviate. For instance, many of the files in a large software system are processed by more than one program. One issue with this is that if each programmer who creates a program or subprogram is allowed to define the files and records used, then there is a strong possibility that in some cases they will get the definitions wrong. They may make errors in defining the key fields (Indexed files); the file organization; the type of access allowed; or the number, type, and size of the fields in a record. At the very least, these kinds of errors will likely result in the failure of the program that contains the erroneous descriptions; but if the program writes to a file, bugs may result that are much harder to find. For instance, if one program writes to a file using an incorrect record description while other programs read from the file using the correct description, a crash may occur in one of the correct subprograms rather than in the one that actually has the problem.

In a large software system, when file, record, or other data descriptions are common to a number of programs, it is very important that those descriptions be described in a central source text library under the control of a copy librarian. In such a system, only the copy librarian has permission to change the data definitions, but any programmer who needs to use the data resource can copy its description into their program using the COPY verb. Using copy libraries makes it more difficult for programmers to make ad hoc changes to file and record formats and makes implementation simpler by reducing the amount of coding required and by eliminating transcription errors. For instance, when a number of programs need to access the same file, the relevant file and record descriptions can be copied from a copy library instead of each programmer having to type their own (and possibly get them wrong).

The COPY verb can also make some maintenance tasks easier and safer. For instance, if a record description in a copy library is changed, then all that is required for that change to take effect is for each affected program to be recompiled.

The COPY Metalanguage

The metalanguage for the COPY verb is given in Figure 16-9. Text can be copied from the copy file or copy library and inserted into the program source code as is, or *text words* in the copied text can be replaced by the text specified in the REPLACING phrase. If REPLACING is used, then the items before the word BY are the text-matching arguments used to identify the text words in the copied text that should be replaced by the text specified.

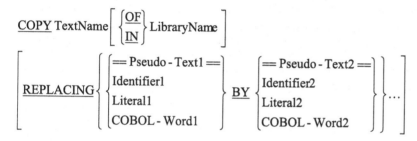

Figure 16-9. *COPY verb metalanguage*

How COPY Works

The COPY verb operates in an unusual way. Whereas other COBOL statements are executed at runtime, a COPY statement is executed at compile time. A COPY statement allows programmers to include in their programs the text of frequently used file, record, or other data descriptions. The included text is copied from a copy file or a copy library. The COPY statement is similar to the #include used in C or C++.

When a COPY statement is used in a COBOL program, the source-code text is copied into the program from a copy file or from a copy library before the program is compiled. A *copy file* is a file containing a segment of COBOL code. A *copy library* is a collection of code segments, each of which can be referenced using a name. Each client program that wants to use the items described in the copy library uses the COPY verb to include the descriptions it requires. When COPY statements copy source code into a program, the code can be included without change or the text can be changed as it is copied into the program. The ability to change the code as it is being included greatly adds to the versatility of the COPY verb.

How the REPLACING Phrase Works

When the REPLACING phrase is used, as the text is copied from the copy file, each properly matched occurrence of Pseudo-Text1, Identifier1, Literal1, and COBOL-Word1 in the library text is replaced by the corresponding Pseudo-Text2, Identifier2, Literal2, or COBOL-Word2 in the REPLACING phrase:

- Pseudo-Text is any COBOL text enclosed in double equal signs (for example, ==ADD 1==). It allows you to replace a series of words or characters as opposed to individual items.

- COBOL-Word is any single COBOL reserved word.

For the purposes of matching, the REPLACING phrase operates on text words. A text word may be defined as follows:

- Any literal, including opening and closing quotes

- Any separator except a space, a pseudo-text delimiter (==), a comma, or a semicolon

- Any other sequence of contiguous characters bounded by separators, except comment lines

COPY Examples

It can be very difficult to get a feel for how REPLACING works by reading textual descriptions alone, so this section presents a number of examples that I hope help your understanding. Listing 16-7 is a simple example that shows how you can use the COPY statement to copy a record description from a copy file. It also shows how to copy a table description from a copy file in a copy library. The REPLACING phrase is used with the second COPY statement to change the size of the table when the text is copied. Don't look for any significant meaning in this program—it simply shows how you can the COPY statement to include text in your program source code.

Listing 16-7. Using the COPY Statement to Include Text

```
IDENTIFICATION DIVISION.
PROGRAM-ID. Listing16-7.
AUTHOR.  Michael Coughlan.

ENVIRONMENT DIVISION.
FILE-CONTROL.
    SELECT StudentFile ASSIGN TO "STUDENTS.DAT"
    ORGANIZATION IS LINE SEQUENTIAL.

DATA DIVISION.
FILE SECTION.
FD StudentFile.
COPY StudentRec.

WORKING-STORAGE SECTION.
01 Idx      PIC 9(3).

01 NameTable.
COPY StudentNameTable IN EG-Lib
    REPLACING XYZ BY 120.
```

```
            StudentRec Copy File

01  StudentRec.
    88  EndOfSF VALUE HIGH-VALUES.
    02  StudentNumber        PIC 9(7).
    02  StudentName.
        03 Surname           PIC X(12).
        03 Initials          PIC XX.
    02  CourseCode           PIC X(5).

    02  Gender               PIC X.
```

```
       StudentNameTable Copy File in EG-Lib

StudSurname PIC X(12)  OCCURS XYZ TIMES.
```

```
PROCEDURE DIVISION.
BeginProg.
   OPEN INPUT StudentFile
   READ StudentFile
      AT END SET EndOfSF TO TRUE
   END-READ
   PERFORM VARYING Idx FROM 1 BY 1 UNTIL EndOfSF
      MOVE Surname TO StudSurname(Idx)
      DISPLAY StudentNumber SPACE StudentName SPACE CourseCode
      READ StudentFile
         AT END SET EndOfSF TO TRUE
      END-READ
   END-PERFORM
   CLOSE StudentFile
   STOP RUN.
```

Listing 16-8 is a program used as a container for a number of COPY..REPLACING examples. I inserted comments into the program to indicate the purpose of the particular example, and the output shows that the replacements have been made.

Listing 16-8. COPY Statements with REPLACEMENT Text

```
IDENTIFICATION DIVISION.
PROGRAM-ID. Listing16-8
AUTHOR.  Michael Coughlan.

DATA DIVISION.
WORKING-STORAGE SECTION.
01 CopyData.

COPY Copybook1
      REPLACING S BY 15.
* Changes the size of a data item

COPY Copybook2 REPLACING ==V99== BY ====.
* Changes the type of a data item to an integer

COPY Copybook3 REPLACING "CustKey" BY "MyValue".
COPY Copybook3 REPLACING CustKey BY NewKey.
* demonstrates the difference between a literal and a COBOL-Word

COPY Copybook3 REPLACING CustKey BY
==CustAddress.
      03 Adr1        PIC X(10).
      03 Adr2        PIC X(10).
      03 Adr3        PIC X(10).
   02 CustId==.
```

```
                 Copybook1

02 CustomerName     PIC X(S).
* S is a textword because it is
* bounded by the ( and ) delimiters
```

```
                 Copybook2

02 CustomerOrder           PIC 9(6)V99.
* V99 is a textword because it is
* bounded by ) and . delimiters
```

```
*Changes the CustKey declaration to add some new data items.
*After REPLACEMENT the included text will be -
*    02 CustAddress.
*      03 Adr1         PIC X(10).
*      03 Adr2         PIC X(10).
*      03 Adr3         PIC X(10).
*    02 CustId         PIC X(7) VALUE "CustKey".
```

```
                                        Copybook3
                        02 CustKey            PIC X(7) VALUE "CustKey".
                        * "CustKey" including the quotes is a text word
                        * CustKey is a different text word
```

```
PROCEDURE DIVISION.
BeginProg.
  MOVE "12345678901234567890901234567890" TO CustomerName
  DISPLAY "CustomerName - " CustomerName

  MOVE 1234.56 TO CustomerOrder
  DISPLAY "CustomerOrder - " CustomerOrder

  DISPLAY "CustKey value changed to - " CustKey

  DISPLAY "NewKey value - " NewKey

  MOVE "Dublin"  TO Adr3

  DISPLAY "CustId value - "CustId

STOP RUN.
```

```
                    Listing 16-8 Output

        CustomerName  -  123456789012345
        CustomerOrder  -  001234
        CustKey value changed to - MyValue
        NewKey value - CustKey
        CustId value - CustKey
```

Summary

This chapter introduced you to the COBOL elements required when you create a large software system. You learned about subprograms and how to create both contained and external subprograms. The chapter discussed the COBOL parameter-passing mechanisms and introduced the LINKAGE SECTION. You learned about state memory and saw how to use the IS INITIAL phrase or the CANCEL verb to create a subprogram that does not have state memory. The chapter covered the need for some shared data items in a system partitioned into subprograms and introduced the IS GLOBAL and IS EXTERNAL clauses.

The final section explored the benefits of holding file, record, and other data descriptions in a centralized library. You also learned about the COPY verb, which allows you to include such descriptions in your program's source code. You saw how to use the COPY verb to include the text from a copy file or copy library in your program.

The next chapter returns to the subject of file handling. You learn about COBOL's direct-access file organizations: relative files and indexed files. These direct-access file organizations are more versatile than sequential files, and to take advantage of that versatility, COBOL introduces a number of new verbs and makes changes to some of the file-handling verbs with which you are already familiar. Chapter 17 introduces the DELETE, REWRITE, and START verbs and the concepts of the *key of reference* and the *next record pointer*. The chapter concludes with a discussion of the advantages and disadvantages of all the COBOL file organizations and when to use one rather than another.

PROGRAMMING EXERCISE

Ah! Exercise time again. If only I had shares in a 2B pencil company.

Introduction

It has long been suspected that compatibility of Zodiac signs (also called star signs or birth signs) is a strong indicator of sexual and emotional compatibility. By processing the information in the Married Persons Date of Birth file, the program you write will test this hypothesis empirically. For each record in the file, the program will use the couple's dates of birth to identify their signs and discover whether those signs are compatible.

The program should display the following items:

- The count of the total number of records in the file

- The count of the total number of valid records (that is, records where neither is a cusp birth)

- The count of the number of compatible pairs, and the percentage of the total valid records that this represents

- The count of the number of incompatible pairs, and the percentage of the total valid records that this represents

Every Zodiac sign is compatible with itself and five other signs. A chance selection of life partner should therefore result in 50% of the pairings having compatible Zodiac signs. A significant deviation either way would be of interest, but if significantly more than 50% of the pairings have compatible signs, you would have to conclude that Zodiac signs are a good indicator of compatibility.

The File

The Census Office has made available to you the Married Persons Date of Birth file (Listing16-9MPDOB.Dat). This file consists of information extracted from the most recent census. The file is an unordered sequential file; each record contains the dates of birth of a married couple. The records have the following description:

Field	Type	Length	Value
MaleDOB	9	8	Date in mmddyyyy format
FemaleDOB	9	8	Date in mmddyyyy format

The Problem of the Cusp

In astrology, people whose birth dates fall near the changeover from one sign to the next are said to be "born on the cusp." The problem is that these persons may exhibit characteristics from both signs. If this is true, then being born on the cusp may distort the compatibility results. To prevent this, the program should treat as invalid all records where one or both of the dates of birth fall on the cusp.

The Zodiac Table

The Zodiac Table is given next. It contains the SignName, SignType, StartDate, and EndDate of each sign. The cusp is defined as a two-day gap between the EndDate of one sign and the StartDate of the next and is built into the dates shown in the table.

SignType indicates sign compatibility where

- Air and Fire signs are compatible with themselves and with each other.
- Earth and Water signs are compatible with themselves and with each other.

The Zodiac Table

SignCode	Sign	SignType	StartDate	EndDate
1	Aquarius	Air	01-22	02-18
2	Pisces	Water	02-21	03-19
3	Aries	Fire	03-22	04-19
4	Taurus	Earth	04-22	05-20
5	Gemini	Air	05-23	06-20
6	Cancer	Water	06-23	07-22
7	Leo	Fire	07-25	08-22
8	Virgo	Earth	08-25	09-22
9	Libra	Air	09-25	10-22
10	Scorpio	Water	10-25	11-21
11	Sagittarius	Fire	11-24	12-20
12	Capricorn	Earth	12-23	01-19
13	Cusp	Cusp	Cusp	Cusp

Processing

Write a contained subprogram called IdentifySign to identify the Zodiac sign for a given birth date. The IdentifySign subprogram should take DateOfBirth as an input parameter and should return SignCode (shown in the previous table) as its return/output parameter. A code of 13 should be returned for cusp births.

For each record in the file, do the following:

- Increment the TotalRecords count.
- Call IdentifySign to get ZodiacSign for MaleDOB.
- Call IdentifySign to get ZodiacSign for FemaleDOB.

If either spouse had a cusp birth, then ignore the record. Otherwise, if the signs are compatible, increment the CompatiblePairs count; and if they are incompatible, increment the IncompatiblePairs count.

PROGRAMMING EXERCISE: ANSWER

Listing 16-9. Zodiac Sign Compatibility Tester

```
IDENTIFICATION DIVISION.
PROGRAM-ID. Listing16-9.
AUTHOR. Michael Coughlan.

ENVIRONMENT DIVISION.
INPUT-OUTPUT SECTION.
FILE-CONTROL.
    SELECT BirthsFile ASSIGN TO "Listing16-9MPDOB.DAT"
        ORGANIZATION IS LINE SEQUENTIAL.

DATA DIVISION.
FILE SECTION.
FD BirthsFile.
01 BirthsRec.
   88 EndOfFile   VALUE HIGH-VALUES.
   02 MaleDOB          PIC X(8).
   02 FemaleDOB        PIC X(8).

WORKING-STORAGE SECTION.
01 Counts.
   02 CompatiblePairs     PIC 9(7)  VALUE ZEROS.
   02 CompatiblePrn       PIC ZZZZ,ZZ9.
   02 CompatiblePercent   PIC ZZ9.
   02 IncompatiblePairs   PIC 9(7)  VALUE ZEROS.
   02 IncompatiblePrn     PIC ZZZZ,ZZ9.
   02 IncompatiblePercent PIC ZZ9.
   02 ValidRecs           PIC 9(8) VALUE ZEROS.
   02 ValidRecsPrn        PIC ZZ,ZZZ,ZZ9.
   02 TotalRecs           PIC 9(9) VALUE ZEROS.
   02 TotalRecsPrn        PIC ZZ,ZZZ,ZZ9.

01 MaleSignType         PIC 99.
   88 ValidMale         VALUE 1 THRU 12.

01 FemaleSignType       PIC 99.
   88 ValidFemale       VALUE 1 THRU 12.

01 SumOfSigns           PIC 99.

PROCEDURE DIVISION.
Begin.
   OPEN INPUT BirthsFile.
   READ BirthsFile
      AT END SET  EndOfFile TO TRUE
   END-READ
   PERFORM ProcessBirthRecs UNTIL EndOfFile
```

431

```
        COMPUTE ValidRecs = CompatiblePairs + IncompatiblePairs
        COMPUTE CompatiblePercent ROUNDED   = CompatiblePairs / ValidRecs * 100
        COMPUTE InCompatiblePercent ROUNDED = InCompatiblePairs / ValidRecs * 100


        PERFORM DisplayResults

        CLOSE BirthsFile.
        STOP RUN.

    DisplayResults.
        MOVE CompatiblePairs   TO CompatiblePrn
        MOVE IncompatiblePairs TO IncompatiblePrn
        MOVE TotalRecs TO TotalRecsPrn
        MOVE ValidRecs TO ValidRecsPrn

        DISPLAY "Total records = " TotalRecsPrn
        DISPLAY "Valid records = " ValidRecsPrn
        DISPLAY "Compatible pairs   = " CompatiblePrn
                " which is " CompatiblePercent "% of total".
        DISPLAY "Incompatible pairs = " IncompatiblePrn
                " which is " InCompatiblePercent "% of total".

    ProcessBirthRecs.
    *  Get the two sign types and add them together
    *  If the result is even then they are compatible
        ADD 1 TO TotalRecs
        CALL "IdentifySign" USING BY CONTENT   MaleDOB
                                  BY REFERENCE MaleSignType


        CALL "IdentifySign" USING BY CONTENT   FemaleDOB
                                  BY REFERENCE FemaleSignType
        IF ValidMale AND ValidFemale
           COMPUTE SumOfSigns = MaleSignType + FemaleSignType
           IF FUNCTION REM(SumOfSigns 2)  = ZERO
              ADD 1 TO CompatiblePairs
            ELSE
              ADD 1 TO IncompatiblePairs
           END-IF
        END-IF
        READ BirthsFile
           AT END SET  EndOfFile TO TRUE
        END-READ.

    IDENTIFICATION DIVISION.
    PROGRAM-ID. IdentifySign IS INITIAL.
    DATA DIVISION.
    WORKING-STORAGE SECTION.
    01 WorkDate.
        88 Aquarius     VALUE "0122" THRU "0218".
        88 Pisces       VALUE "0221" THRU "0319".
        88 Aries        VALUE "0322" THRU "0419".
```

```
     88 Taurus       VALUE "0422" THRU "0520".
     88 Gemini       VALUE "0523" THRU "0620".
     88 Cancer       VALUE "0623" THRU "0722".
     88 Leo          VALUE "0725" THRU "0822".
     88 Virgo        VALUE "0825" THRU "0922".
     88 Libra        VALUE "0925" THRU "1022".
     88 Scorpio      VALUE "1025" THRU "1121".
     88 Sagittarius  VALUE "1124" THRU "1220".
     88 Capricorn    VALUE "1223" THRU "1231", "0101" THRU "0119".
     02 WorkMonth    PIC XX.
     02 WorkDay      PIC XX.

 LINKAGE SECTION.
 01 DateOfBirth.
     02 BirthMonth   PIC XX.
     02 BirthDay     PIC XX.
     02 FILLER       PIC 9(4).

 01 SignType        PIC 99.

 PROCEDURE DIVISION USING DateOfBirth, SignType.
 Begin.
     MOVE BirthDay   TO WorkDay.
     MOVE BirthMonth TO WorkMonth.
     EVALUATE TRUE
       WHEN Aquarius    MOVE  1 TO SignType
       WHEN Pisces      MOVE  2 TO SignType
       WHEN Aries       MOVE  3 TO SignType
       WHEN Taurus      MOVE  4 TO SignType
       WHEN Gemini      MOVE  5 TO SignType
       WHEN Cancer      MOVE  6 TO SignType
       WHEN Leo         MOVE  7 TO SignType
       WHEN Virgo       MOVE  8 TO SignType
       WHEN Libra       MOVE  9 TO SignType
       WHEN Scorpio     MOVE 10 TO SignType
       WHEN Sagittarius MOVE 11 TO SignType
       WHEN Capricorn   MOVE 12 TO SignType
       WHEN OTHER       MOVE 13 TO SignType
     END-EVALUATE.
     EXIT PROGRAM.
 END PROGRAM IdentifySign.
 END PROGRAM Listing16-9.
```

CHAPTER 17

Direct Access Files

When I learned COBOL many years ago, direct access files, and particularly indexed files, were the jewel in COBOL's crown. No other mainstream programming language provided native support for file organizations of such versatility. Nowadays, the predominance of databases means that the importance of direct access files in modern COBOL programming is greatly reduced. Nevertheless, the huge inventory of legacy programs that still use direct access files makes these file organizations a worthwhile topic of discussion.

This chapter introduces you to COBOL's direct access file organizations: indexed and relative files. These organizations are called *direct access organizations* because they allow you to access data records directly based on a key field. Direct access files are more versatile than sequential files. They let you update or delete records in situ and access records sequentially or directly using a key field. Needless to say, direct access files only work on direct access media such as hard disks. You can't use indexed or relative files with serial media such as magnetic tapes. To take advantage of the versatility of direct access files, you use a number of new COBOL verbs and concepts. This chapter introduces the DELETE, REWRITE, and START verbs and the concepts of *file status,* the *key of reference, and the next-record pointer.*

Sequential, indexed, and relative file organizations all have strengths and weaknesses. No one organization is best for all situations. This chapter concludes with a discussion of the advantages and disadvantages of all the COBOL file organizations and when you should use one rather than another.

Direct Access vs.Sequential Files

As you learned in Chapter 10, access to records in a sequential file is serial. To reach a particular record, you must read all the preceding records. You also learned that if the sequential file is unordered, the only practical operations are to read records from the file or add records to the end of the file. It is impractical to update records or delete records in an unordered sequential file. In addition, even if the file is ordered, inserting, updating, or deleting records is a problem because when you apply these operations, you must preserve the ordering of the file—and the only way to do that is to create a copy of the file to which these operations have been applied.

Although sequential files have a number of advantages over other types of file organization (as discussed in the final section of this chapter), the fact that you must create a new file when you delete, update, or insert records is problematic.

These problems are addressed by direct access files. Direct access files allow you to read, update, delete, and insert individual records in situ on the basis of a key value. For instance, to delete a customer record in a direct access file, you supply the customer ID of the record to be deleted and then execute a DELETE statement.

In COBOL, there are two direct access file organizations: relative files and indexed files.

Organization of Relative Files

Before you see how relative files are declared and used, let's look at how they are organized. As you can see from the schematic representation in Figure 17-1, the records in a relative file are organized on ascending *relative record number*. You can visualize a relative file as a one-dimensional table stored on disk, and you can think of the relative record number as the index into that table.

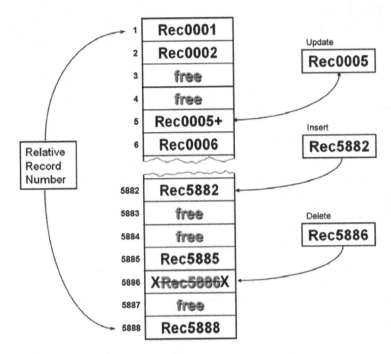

Figure 17-1. *Schematic representation of a relative file*

Some restrictions should be obvious from Figure 17-1. First, only one relative key is supported, and that key must be numeric and take a value between 1 and the number of the highest relative record written to the file. Another restriction is that, even when the file is only sparsely populated, enough disk space has to be allocated to hold all the records between 1 and the record with the highest relative record number. For instance, if a record with a relative record number of 150,000 is written to the file, then room sufficient for 150,000 records is allocated to the file—even though that may be the only record actually written to the file. You can see this illustrated in Figure 17-1. In the example file, the record with the highest relative record number is 5,888, so disk space sufficient to store 5,888 records has been allocated. However, not all the record locations contain records. The record areas labelled "free" have been allocated but have not yet had record values written to them.

Being restricted to a single numeric key in a defined range is onerous, but there are ways to loosen the shackles. For instance, you might add a base value to the relative record number to change the range. For instance, in Figure 17-1 you could use a base of 10,000 so that the first record key value would be 10,001 and the last would be 15,888. Obviously, before you used the key, you would subtract 10,000 to convert it into the relative record number.

Using a base value is a very simple key transformation, and in COBOL this is probably about as much manipulation as you want to do. In other languages, you might write a sophisticated hashing algorithm to map even alphanumeric keys onto range of relative record numbers; but in COBOL, when you need keys with this level of sophistication, you use indexed files.

In addition to showing how records are organized in a relative file, Figure 17-1 also shows how updates, insertions and, deletions are applied:

- To update a record, you use the relative record number to READ the record from the file into the record buffer. Then you make the changes to the record data and REWRITE the record to the file.

- To insert a record, you use the relative record number to tell the system where to WRITE the record. Obviously, the allocated space must be free, or an error condition will occur.

- To delete a record, you use the relative record number to tell the system which record to DELETE. Obviously, the record must exist. For instance, in Figure 17-1, an error condition would occur if you tried to delete the record with the relative record number 5,887 because there is no record in that position. In a relative file, when you delete a record, all the file system does is to mark it as deleted. It does not really delete the record.

Processing Relative Files

As mentioned at the beginning of this chapter, direct access files are declared and processed using a number of new declaration clauses and verbs. Instead of boring you with a dry, formal introduction, this section shows you some simple examples. Once you have a feel for how it all works, I introduce the required clauses and verbs more formally.

Let's start with a simple program that reads a relative file both sequentially and directly. Then you learn how to create a relative file from a sequential file. Most programming environments have tools that allow you to do this, but it is interesting to see how to do it by hand. The final example shows you how to apply a file of transactions to the relative file.

Reading a Relative File

The program in Listing 17-1 reads a relative file either sequentially or directly, depending on the choice made by the user.

Listing 17-1. Reading a Relative File Sequentially or Directly Using a Key

```
IDENTIFICATION DIVISION.
PROGRAM-ID. Listing17-1.
AUTHOR.   MICHAEL COUGHLAN.
* Reads a Relative file directly or in sequence

ENVIRONMENT DIVISION.
INPUT-OUTPUT SECTION.
FILE-CONTROL.
    SELECT VehicleFile ASSIGN TO "Listing17-1.DAT"
        ORGANIZATION IS RELATIVE
        ACCESS MODE IS DYNAMIC
        RELATIVE KEY IS VehicleKey
        FILE STATUS  IS VehicleStatus.

DATA DIVISION.
FILE SECTION.
FD  VehicleFile.
01  VehicleRec.
    88  EndOfVehiclefile        VALUE HIGH-VALUES.
    02  VehicleNum              PIC 9(4).
    02  VehicleDesc             PIC X(25).
    02  ManfName                PIC X(20).
```

```
WORKING-STORAGE SECTION.
01  VehicleStatus              PIC X(2).
    88  RecordFound            VALUE "00".

01  VehicleKey                 PIC 9(4).

01  ReadType                   PIC 9.
    88  DirectRead             VALUE 1.
    88  SequentialRead         VALUE 2.

01  PrnVehicleRecord.
    02    PrnVehicleNum        PIC 9(4).
    02    PrnVehicleDesc       PIC BBX(25).
    02    PrnManfName          PIC BBX(20).

PROCEDURE DIVISION.
BEGIN.
    OPEN INPUT VehicleFile
    DISPLAY "Read type : Direct read = 1, Sequential read = 2 --> "
                 WITH NO ADVANCING.
    ACCEPT ReadType
    IF DirectRead
       DISPLAY "Enter vehicle key (4 digits) --> " WITH NO ADVANCING
       ACCEPT VehicleKey
       READ VehicleFile
         INVALID KEY DISPLAY "Vehicle file status = " VehicleStatus
       END-READ
       PERFORM DisplayRecord
    END-IF

    IF SequentialRead
       READ VehicleFile NEXT RECORD
          AT END SET EndOfVehiclefile TO TRUE
       END-READ
       PERFORM UNTIL EndOfVehiclefile
          PERFORM DisplayRecord
          READ VehicleFile NEXT RECORD
             AT END SET EndOfVehiclefile TO TRUE
          END-READ
       END-PERFORM
    END-IF
    CLOSE VehicleFile
    STOP RUN.

DisplayRecord.
    IF RecordFound
       MOVE VehicleNum  TO PrnVehicleNum
       MOVE VehicleDesc TO PrnVehicleDesc
       MOVE ManfName    TO PrnManfName
       DISPLAY PrnVehicleRecord
    END-IF.
```

```
                    Listing 17-1 Output
                          Run 1
Read type : Direct read = 1, Sequential read = 2 --> 2
0001  Roadster                   Tesla Motors
0002  Volt                       Chevrolet
0005  ZOE                        Renault
0007  Focus Electric             Ford
0011  Fit EV                     Honda
0016  Model S                    Tesla Motors
0017  Prius                      Toyota
0018  Spark EV                   Chevrolet
0113  i-MiEV                     Mitsubishi
0124  Twizzy                     Renault
0126  BMW i3                     BMW
0133  Fluence Z.E                Renault
0135  C-Zero                     Citroen
0136  Model X                    Tesla Motors
0200  Leaf                       Nissan
0210  e-Golf                     Volkswagen
230 iON                          Peugeot

                          Run 2
Read type : Direct read = 1, Sequential read = 2 --> 1
Enter vehicle key (4 digits) --> 0016
0016  Model S                    Tesla Motors
```

The first thing to note is that the SELECT and ASSIGN clause has a number of new entries. First, ORGANIZATION is now RELATIVE. Second, because a relative file allows you to access the records in the file directly or sequentially, you must have an ACCESS MODE phrase to say what kind of access you desire on the file. Three types of access are available: RANDOM (key-based access only), SEQUENTIAL (sequential only), and DYNAMIC (a mixture of keyed and sequential access). Third, to allow key-based access, you must specify a RELATIVE KEY phrase to tell the system where it can find the key value used for direct access. Note that the key mentioned here *cannot* be part of the record description.

The final entry is the FILE STATUS clause. The FILE STATUS clause allows you to identify a two-character area of storage to hold the result of every I/O operation for the file. The FILE STATUS data item is declared as PIC X(2) in the WORKING-STORAGE SECTION. Whenever an I/O operation is performed on the file, some value is returned to FILE STATUS indicating whether the operation was successful. I introduce these FILE STATUS values as and when they occur; for this program, you only need to know that a value of "00" indicates that the operation (READ, in this case) was successful.

The FILE STATUS clause is not restricted to direct access files. You can use it with sequential files, but that isn't necessary because with those files there are not many states that you need to detect. However, with direct access files, a number of file states need to be detected. For instance, you need to detect when an attempt is made to READ, DELETE, or REWRITE a record when a record with that key value does not exist in the file. Similarly, you need to be able to detect when an attempt to WRITE a record finds that there is *already* a record with that key value in the file.

The next item of note is the change to the READ verb. The direct READ now takes the INVALID KEY clause. This clause allows you to execute some code when an error condition is detected. The sequential read may now use the NEXT RECORD phrase. This phrase is required when ACCESS MODE is DYNAMIC, to indicate that this is a sequential read. If ACCESS MODE is SEQUENTIAL, then you use the standard READ statement.

Creating a Relative File from a Sequential File

Listing 17-2 shows how to create a relative file from a sequential file. A relative file is a binary file. It can't be edited in a standard text editor. This makes it a bit awkward to create test data, but most COBOL programming environments have tools that allow you to generate a relative file from a sequential one. Of course, you don't have to use the tools; you can write a program to do it, as in this example.

Listing 17-2. Creating a Relative File from a Sequential File

```
IDENTIFICATION DIVISION.
PROGRAM-ID. Listing17-2.
AUTHOR.  MICHAEL COUGHLAN.
* Reads a Relative file directly or in sequence

ENVIRONMENT DIVISION.
INPUT-OUTPUT SECTION.
FILE-CONTROL.
    SELECT VehicleFile ASSIGN TO "Listing17-2.DAT"
        ORGANIZATION IS RELATIVE
        ACCESS MODE IS RANDOM
        RELATIVE KEY IS VehicleKey
        FILE STATUS  IS VehicleStatus.

    SELECT Seqfile ASSIGN TO "Listing17-2.SEQ"
            ORGANIZATION IS LINE SEQUENTIAL.
```

```
DATA DIVISION.
FILE SECTION.
FD  VehicleFile.
01  VehicleRec.
    02  VehicleNum              PIC 9(4).
    02  VehicleDesc             PIC X(25).
    02  ManfName                PIC X(20).

FD  SeqFile.
01  VehicleRec-SF.
    88  EndOfSeqfile            VALUE HIGH-VALUES.
    02  VehicleNum-SF           PIC 9(4).
    02  VehicleDesc-SF          PIC X(25).
    02  ManfName-SF             PIC X(20).

WORKING-STORAGE SECTION.
01  VehicleStatus              PIC X(2).
    88  RecordFound            VALUE "00".

01  VehicleKey                 PIC 9(4).

PROCEDURE DIVISION.
BEGIN.
    OPEN INPUT SeqFile
    OPEN OUTPUT VehicleFile
    READ SeqFile
       AT END SET EndOfSeqFile TO TRUE
    END-READ
    PERFORM UNTIL EndOfSeqFile
       MOVE VehicleNum-SF TO VehicleKey
       WRITE VehicleRec FROM VehicleRec-SF
            INVALID KEY DISPLAY "Vehicle file status = " VehicleStatus
       END-WRITE
       READ SeqFile
          AT END SET EndOfSeqFile TO TRUE
       END-READ
    END-PERFORM

    CLOSE SeqFile, VehicleFile
    STOP RUN.
```

In this program, the first thing to note is that because the relative file only uses direct access, the ACCESS MODE specified is RANDOM.

The relative file is created as follows. For each record in the sequential file, the program reads the record, moves the contents of the VehicleNum field to the relative key VehicleKey, and then writes the relative record from the sequential record. The record is written into the position indicated by the relative record number in VehicleKey.

Applying Transactions to a Relative File

In this final example program (see Listing 17-3), you see how to apply a sequential file of transactions to the relative vehicle master file. The transaction file contains only enough transactions to demonstrate valid and invalid insertions, valid and invalid updates (VehicleDesc is updated), and valid and invalid deletions. To keep the program short, it uses displays to report transaction errors. To make the updates clear, the contents of the vehicle master file are displayed before and after the transactions are applied. The contents of the transaction file are shown in Example 17-1.

Example 17-1. Contents of the Transaction File

```
I0001 *** invalid insert ***   Tesla Motors
D0006 *** invalid delete ***
U0017FCV  +valid update
U0117 *** invalid update ***
D0135 +valid delete
I0205Model C +valid insert    Tesla Motors
I0230 *** invalid insert ***  Peugeot
```

Listing 17-3. Applying a Sequential File of Transactions to a Relative File

```
IDENTIFICATION DIVISION.
PROGRAM-ID.  Listing17-3.
AUTHOR.  MICHAEL COUGHLAN.

ENVIRONMENT DIVISION.
INPUT-OUTPUT SECTION.
FILE-CONTROL.
    SELECT VehicleMasterFile ASSIGN TO "Listing17-3.DAT"
        ORGANIZATION IS RELATIVE
        ACCESS MODE IS DYNAMIC
        RELATIVE KEY IS VehicleKey
        FILE STATUS  IS VehicleFileStatus.

    SELECT TransFile ASSIGN TO "Listing17-3Trans.DAT"
            ORGANIZATION IS LINE SEQUENTIAL.

DATA DIVISION.
FILE SECTION.
FD  VehicleMasterFile.
01  VehicleRec-VMF.
    88  EndOfVehiclefile  VALUE HIGH-VALUES.
    02  VehicleNum-VMF       PIC 9(4).
    02  VehicleDesc-VMF      PIC X(25).
    02  ManfName-VMF         PIC X(20).
```

```
FD  TransFile.
01    InsertionRec.
        88   EndOfTransFile          VALUE HIGH-VALUES.
        02   TransType               PIC X.
             88   InsertRecord       VALUE "I".
             88   DeleteRecord       VALUE "D".
             88   UpdateRecord       VALUE "U".
        02   VehicleNum-IR           PIC 9(4).
        02   VehicleDesc-IR          PIC X(25).
        02   ManfName-IR             PIC X(20).

01    DeletionRec                    PIC X(5).

01    UpdateRec.
        02   FILLER                  PIC X(5).
        02   VehicleDesc-UR          PIC X(25).

WORKING-STORAGE SECTION.
01    VehicleFileStatus              PIC X(2).
        88   OperationSuccessful     VALUE "00".
        88   VehicleRecExists        VALUE "22".
        88   NoVehicleRec            VALUE "23".

01    VehicleKey                     PIC 9(4).

01    ReadType                       PIC 9.


PROCEDURE DIVISION.
Begin.
    OPEN INPUT TransFile
    OPEN I-O   VehicleMasterFile
    DISPLAY "Vehicle Master File records before transactions"
    PERFORM DisplayVehicleRecords
    DISPLAY SPACES

    READ TransFile
        AT END SET EndOfTransFile TO TRUE
    END-READ
    PERFORM UNTIL EndOfTransFile
        MOVE VehicleNum-IR TO VehicleKey
        EVALUATE   TRUE
            WHEN InsertRecord   PERFORM InsertVehicleRec
            WHEN DeleteRecord   PERFORM DeleteVehicleRec
            WHEN UpdateRecord   PERFORM UpdateVehicleRec
            WHEN OTHER          DISPLAY "Error - Invalid Transaction Code"
        END-EVALUATE
        READ TransFile
            AT END SET EndOfTransFile TO TRUE
        END-READ
    END-PERFORM
```

```
                        Listing 17-3 Output
Vehicle Master File records before transactions
0001 Roadster                       Tesla Motors
0002 Volt                           Chevrolet
0005 ZOE                            Renault
0007 Focus Electric                 Ford
0011 Fit EV                         Honda
0016 Model S                        Tesla Motors
0017 Prius                          Toyota
0018 Spark EV                       Chevrolet
0113 i-MiEV                         Mitsubishi
0124 Twizzy                         Renault
0126 BMW i3                         BMW
0133 Fluence Z.E                    Renault
0135 C-Zero                         Citroen
0136 Model X                        Tesla Motors
0200 Leaf                           Nissan
0210 e-Golf                         Volkswagen
0230 iON                            Peugeot

InsertError - Record at - 0001 - already exists
DeleteError - No record at - 0006
UpdateError - No record at - 0117
InsertError - Record at - 0230 - already exists

Vehicle Master File records after transactions
0001 Roadster                       Tesla Motors
0002 Volt                           Chevrolet
0005 ZOE                            Renault
0007 Focus Electric                 Ford
0011 Fit EV                         Honda
0016 Model S                        Tesla Motors
0017 FCV  +valid update             Toyota
0018 Spark EV                       Chevrolet
0113 i-MiEV                         Mitsubishi
0124 Twizzy                         Renault
0126 BMW i3                         BMW
0133 Fluence Z.E                    Renault
0136 Model X                        Tesla Motors
0200 Leaf                           Nissan
0205 Model C +valid insert          Tesla Motors
0210 e-Golf                         Volkswagen
0230 iON                            Peugeot
```

```
            DISPLAY SPACES
            DISPLAY "Vehicle Master File records after transactions"
            PERFORM DisplayVehicleRecords

            CLOSE TransFile, VehicleMasterFile
            STOP RUN.

    InsertVehicleRec.
        MOVE ManfName-IR     TO ManfName-VMF
        MOVE VehicleDesc-IR TO VehicleDesc-VMF
        MOVE VehicleNum-IR   TO VehicleNum-VMF
        WRITE VehicleRec-VMF
            INVALID KEY
              IF VehicleRecExists
                 DISPLAY "InsertError - Record at - " VehicleNum-IR " - already exists"
               ELSE
                  DISPLAY "Unexpected error. File Status is - " VehicleFileStatus
              END-IF
        END-WRITE.


    DeleteVehicleRec.
        DELETE VehicleMasterFile RECORD
            INVALID KEY
              IF NoVehicleRec
                 DISPLAY "DeleteError - No record at - " VehicleNum-IR
              ELSE
                 DISPLAY "Unexpected error1. File Status is - " VehicleFileStatus
              END-IF
        END-DELETE.

    UpdateVehicleRec.
        READ VehicleMasterFile
            INVALID KEY
              IF NoVehicleRec
                 DISPLAY "UpdateError - No record at - " VehicleNum-IR
              ELSE
                 DISPLAY "Unexpected error2. File Status is - " VehicleFileStatus
              END-IF
        END-READ
        IF OperationSuccessful
          MOVE VehicleDesc-UR TO VehicleDesc-VMF
          REWRITE VehicleRec-VMF
              INVALID KEY DISPLAY "Unexpected error3. File Status is - " VehicleFileStatus
          END-REWRITE
        END-IF.

DisplayVehicleRecords.
*  Position the Next Record Pointer to the start of the file
    MOVE ZEROS TO VehicleKey
    START VehicleMasterFile KEY IS GREATER THAN VehicleKey
```

```
        INVALID KEY DISPLAY "Unexpected error on START"
END-START
READ VehicleMasterFile NEXT RECORD
        AT END SET EndOfVehiclefile TO TRUE
END-READ

PERFORM UNTIL EndOfVehiclefile
    DISPLAY VehicleNum-VMF SPACE VehicleDesc-VMF  SPACE ManfName-VMF
    READ VehicleMasterFile NEXT RECORD
        AT END SET EndOfVehiclefile TO TRUE
    END-READ
END-PERFORM.
```

The most interesting thing about this program is that it uses all five of the direct access file processing verbs: READ, WRITE, REWRITE, DELETE, and START. The program begins by displaying the current contents of the vehicle master file. You may wonder what the purpose of the START verb is at the beginning of DisplayVehicleRecords. For relative files, the START verb is used to position the next-record pointer. When a file is accessed sequentially, the next-record pointer points to the position in the file where the next record will be read from or written to.

This first time through DisplayVehicleRecords, the START verb is not strictly necessary, because when you open the file, the next-record pointer points to the first record in the file by default. But the second time through the file, the START verb is required in order to position the next-record pointer at the beginning of the file—when you read through the file the first time, the next-record pointer was left pointing to the last record in the file. Closing the file and opening it again also positions the next-record pointer at the first record in the file, but doing so carries a significant processing penalty.

Note how you use the START verb. You move zeros into the relative-key data item; then, when START executes, its meaning is this: position the next-record pointer such that the relative record number of the record pointed to is greater than the current value of the relative-key data item. Because the current value of the relative-key data item is zero, the first valid record in the file satisfies the condition.

The first statement in the PERFORM UNTIL EndOfTransFile iteration is MOVE VehicleNum-IR TO VehicleKey. This takes the key value in the transaction record and places it in the relative-key data item. Now any direct access operation such as WRITE, REWRITE, or DELETE will use that key value.

If the transaction is an insertion, then a direct WRITE is used to write the transaction record to the vehicle master file at the relative record number indicated by the value in VehicleKey. If the WRITE fails, then INVALID KEY activates, and the file status is checked to see if it has failed because there is already a record in that relative record number position or because of an unexpected error. If the anticipated error condition occurs, an error message is displayed, indicating the offending record's key value; otherwise, an error message and the current value of the file status are displayed. The second part of the IF statement is there as an alert regarding a possible programming or test data error; you don't expect this branch of IF to be triggered.

If the transaction is a deletion, then the direct DELETE is used to delete the record at the relative record number position pointed to by the value in VehicleKey. If there is no record at that position, INVALID KEY activates.

If the transaction is an update, then a direct READ is used to fetch the record from the file and place it in the record buffer. If the record exists, the VehicleDesc-VMF field is updated, and REWRITE is used to write the record back to the file. REWRITE has to be used because WRITE would return an error if it found a record already in place.

Relative Files: Syntax and Semantics

This section provides a formal introduction to the file-processing verbs and declarations specific to relative files.

Relative Files: SELECT and ASSIGN Clause

The metalanguage for the SELECT and ASSIGN clause for relative files is shown in Figure 17-2.

SELECT [OPTIONAL] FileName

    ASSIGN TO FileSpec

    [ORGANIZATION IS] RELATIVE

$$\left[\; \underline{\text{ACCESS}}\text{ MODE IS}\; \begin{cases} \underline{\text{SEQUENTIAL}}\; [\underline{\text{RELATIVE}}\text{ KEY IS RelKey}] \\ \left.\begin{cases}\underline{\text{RANDOM}}\\\underline{\text{DYNAMIC}}\end{cases}\right\} \underline{\text{RELATIVE}}\text{ KEY IS RelKey} \end{cases} \right]$$

    [FILE STATUS IS FileStatus]

Figure 17-2. *Metalanguage for the specific relative SELECT and ASSIGN clause*

Normally, when a file is opened for INPUT, I-O, or EXTEND, the file must exist or an error condition occurs. The OPTIONAL phrase allows you to specify that the file does not have to exist (presumably because you are going to write records to and read records from it) when OPEN INPUT, OPEN I-O, or OPEN EXTEND executes.

ACCESS MODE refers to the way in which the file is to be used. If you specify that ACCESS MODE is SEQUENTIAL, then it is only possible to process the records in the file sequentially. If RANDOM is specified, it is only possible to access the file directly. If DYNAMIC is specified, the file may be accessed both directly and sequentially.

The RECORD KEY phrase is used to define the relative key. There can be only one key in a relative file. RelKey must be a numeric data item and *must not be* part of the file's record description, although it may be part of another file's record description. It is normally described in the WORKING-STORAGE SECTION.

The FILE STATUS clause identifies a two-character area of storage that holds the result of every I/O operation for the file. The FILE STATUS data item is declared as PIC X(2) in the WORKING-STORAGE SECTION. Whenever an I/O operation is performed, some value is returned to FILE STATUS, indicating whether the operation was successful.

There are a large number of FILE STATUS values, but three of major interest for relative files are as follows:

- "00" means the operation was successful.

- "22" indicates a duplicate key. That is, you are trying to write a record, but a record already exists in that position.

- "23" means the record was not found. That is, you are trying to access a record, but there is no record in that position.

Relative File Verbs

Direct access files are more versatile than sequential files and support a greater range of operations. In addition to the new file-processing verbs DELETE, REWRITE, and START, many of the verbs you already know—such as OPEN, CLOSE, READ, and WRITE—operate differently when processing direct access files.

INVALID KEY Clause

If you examine the metalanguage of any of the direct access verbs, you see that the INVALID KEY clause is in square brackets, indicating that this clause is optional. In reality, the INVALID KEY clause is mandatory *unless* declaratives have been specified. Declaratives allow you to create specialized exception-handling code. You explore declaratives in the next chapter.

When the INVALID KEY clause is specified, any I/O error, such as attempting to read or delete a record that does not exist or write a record that already exists, activates the clause and causes the statement block following it to be executed.

OPEN/CLOSE

The CLOSE syntax is the same for all file organizations.

The syntax for OPEN changes when used with direct access files: an I-O (input/output) entry is added. I-O is used with direct access files when you intend to update or both read from and write to the file. The full metalanguage for the OPEN verb is given in Figure 17-3.

$$\text{OPEN} \left\{ \begin{array}{l} \text{INPUT} \\ \text{OUTPUT} \\ \text{I-O} \\ \text{EXTEND} \end{array} \right\} \text{FileName} \ldots$$

Figure 17-3. *Full metalanguage for the OPEN verb*

Consider the following:

- If the file is opened for INPUT, then only READ and START are allowed.

- If the file is opened for OUTPUT, then only WRITE is allowed.

- If the file is opened for I-O, then READ, WRITE, START, REWRITE, and DELETE are allowed.

- If OPEN INPUT is used, and the file does not possess the OPTIONAL clause, the file must exist or the OPEN will fail.

- If OPEN OUTPUT or I-O is used, the file will be created if it does not already exist, as long as the file possesses the OPTIONAL clause.

READ Verb

There are two new formats for the READ verb. One format is used for a direct READ on a relative file, and the other is used when you want to read the file sequentially but an ACCESS MODE of DYNAMIC has been specified for the file. When an ACCESS MODE of SEQUENTIAL is specified, all file organizations use the standard READ format.

The metalanguage in Figure 17-4 shows the READ format used to read a relative file sequentially when an ACCESS MODE of DYNAMIC has been specified. The only difference between this format and the format of the ordinary sequential READ is the NEXT RECORD phrase. This format of READ reads the record pointed to by the next-record pointer (the current record if positioned by START, or the next record if positioned by a direct READ).

READ FileName <u>NEXT</u> RECORD [<u>INTO</u> DestItem$i]
      [AT <u>END</u> StatementBlock]
[END – READ]

Figure 17-4. *Metalanguage for the sequential READ when the ACCESS MODE is DYNAMIC*

The format of READ used for a direct read on a relative file is shown in Figure 17-5. To read a relative file using a key, the relative record number of the required record is placed in the RELATIVE KEY data item (specified in the RELATIVE KEY phrase of the file's SELECT and ASSIGN clause), and then READ is executed. When READ executes, the record with the relative record number equal to the present value of the relative key is read into the file's record buffer (defined in the FD entry). If READ fails to retrieve the record, the INVALID KEY activates, and the statement block following the clause is executed. If READ is successful, NOT INVALID KEY (if present) activates, and the next-record pointer is left pointing to the next valid record in the file.

READ FileName RECORD [INTO DestItem$i]
    [INVALID KEY StatementBlock]
    [NOT INVALID KEY StatementBlock]
[END – READ]

Figure 17-5. *Metalanguage for the direct* READ

WRITE Verb

The format for writing sequentially to a direct access file is the same as that used for writing to a sequential file. But when you want to write directly to a relative file, a key must be used, and this requires the WRITE format shown in Figure 17-6.

WRITE RecName [FROM SourceItem$i]
    [INVALID KEY StatementBlock]
    [NOT INVALID KEY StatementBlock]
[END – WRITE]

Figure 17-6. *Metalanguage for writing to a relative file using a key*

Writing a record to a relative file using a key requires you to place the record in the record buffer, place the key value in the RELATIVE KEY data item, and then execute the WRITE statement. When WRITE executes, the data in the record buffer is written to the record position with a relative record number equal to the present value of the key.

If WRITE fails, perhaps because a record already exists at that relative record number position, the INVALID KEY clause activates, and the statements following the clause are executed.

REWRITE Verb

The REWRITE verb is used to update a record in situ by overwriting it. The format of REWRITE is given in Figure 17-7. The REWRITE verb is generally used with READ because you can only update a record by bringing it into the record buffer first. Once the record is in the buffer, you can make the changes to the required fields; when the changes have been made, you REWRITE the record to the file.

REWRITE RecName [FROM SourceItem$i]
    [INVALID KEY StatementBlock]
    [NOT INVALID KEY StatementBlock]
[END – REWRITE]

Figure 17-7. *Metalanguage for the* REWRITE *verb*

To use REWRITE to update fields in a record, you first place the key value in the RELATIVE KEY data item and do a direct READ. This brings the required record into the record buffer. Next you make the required changes to the data in the record. Then you execute a REWRITE to write the record in the buffer back to the file.

Keep the following in mind:

- If the file has an ACCESS MODE of SEQUENTIAL, then the INVALID KEY clause cannot be specified, and the record to be replaced must have been the subject of a READ or START before the REWRITE is executed.

- For all access modes, the file must be opened for I-0.

DELETE Verb

The syntax for the DELETE verb is given in Figure 17-8. To delete a record, you place the key value in the RELATIVE KEY data item and then execute DELETE. The record in the relative record number position indicated by the RELATIVE KEY data item is marked as deleted (it is not actually deleted). If the DELETE attempt fails, perhaps because there is no record at that position, INVALID KEY activates.

DELETE FileName RECORD
    [INVALID KEY StatementBlock]
    [NOT INVALID KEY StatementBlock]
[END – DELETE]

Figure 17-8. *Metalanguage for the DELETE verb*

Note the following:

- To use DELETE, the file must have been opened for I-0.

- When ACCESS MODE is SEQUENTIAL, a READ statement must have accessed the record to be deleted (that's how the system knows which record to delete).

START Verb

For relative files, the START verb is only used to control the position of the next-record pointer. Where the START verb appears in a program, it is usually followed by a sequential READ or WRITE because START does not get data from or put data into the file. It merely positions the next-record pointer.

To use the START verb to position the next-record pointer at a particular record (so that subsequent sequential accesses will use that record position), you place the key value of the record at the desired position into the RELATIVE KEY data item and then execute a START..KEY IS EQUAL TO statement.

To use the START verb to position the next-record pointer at the first active record in the file, you move zeros to the RELATIVE KEY data item and then execute a START..KEY IS GREATER THAN statement. You can't move the number 1 to the RELATIVE KEY data item, because there may be no active record in the first record position.

The metalanguage for the START verb is given in Figure 17-9. When START executes, it has the following interpretation: position the next-record pointer such that the relative record number of the record pointed to is EQUAL TO or GREATER THAN or NOT LESS THAN or GREATER THAN OR EQUAL TO the current value of the RELATIVE KEY data item.

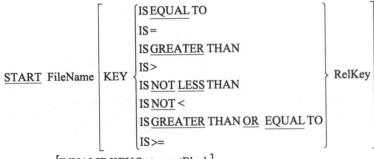

Figure 17-9. *Metalanguage for the START verb*

Organization of Indexed Files

Unlike relative files, which only allow a single, numeric key, an indexed file may have up to 255 alphanumeric keys. The key on which the data records are actually ordered is called the *primary key*. The other keys are called *alternate keys*. Although a relative file allows you to access records sequentially or directly by key, an indexed file lets you access the records directly or sequentially using any of its keys. For instance, suppose an indexed file supporting a video rental system has VideoId as its primary key and VideoTitle and SupplierId as its alternate keys. You can read a record from the file using any of the keys, and you can also read through the file in VideoId sequence, VideoTitle sequence, or SupplierId sequence. This versatility is what makes indexed files so useful.

How is this flexibility achieved? How can it be possible to read through the file sequentially in different sequences?

The data records in an indexed file are sequenced in ascending primary-key order. Over the data records, the file system builds an index. This arrangement is shown schematically in Figure 17-10.

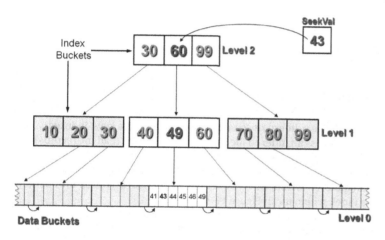

Figure 17-10. *Primary-key index: seeking a record with a key value of 43*

A number of terms relating to Figure 17-10 need clarification. A *bucket* is the smallest number of characters of disk storage that can be read or written in one I/O operation. It is the equivalent of a block on a PC disk—the smallest segment of disk space that can be addressed. *Index depth* is the number of levels of index above level 0, which is the data bucket (or base bucket) level (in Figure 17-10, the index depth is 2).

When direct access is required, the file system uses the index to find, read, insert, update, or delete the required record. Figure 17-11 shows how the index is used to locate the record with a key value of 43. The file system starts at the first level of index (one I/O operation is required to bring the records in this bucket into memory). In the index buckets, each index record contains a pointer to the highest key value in the next-level buckets. Using the condition IF SeekVal <= IndexKeyVal, a bucket is retrieved from the next level of index (another I/O operation is required to bring the records in this bucket into memory). Again the condition is applied, and the bucket at level 0 (the data buckets) is retrieved (another final I/O is required to bring the records in this bucket into memory). Once the actual data records are in memory, the file system searches them sequentially until the required record is found.

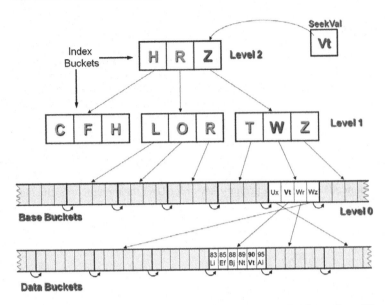

Figure 17-11. *Alternate-key index: seeking a record with a key value of Vt*

In addition to allowing direct access to records on the primary key or any of the 254 alternate keys, indexed files may also be processed sequentially. When you process an indexed file sequentially, you can read the records in ascending order on the primary key or on any of the alternate keys.

Because the data records are held in ascending primary-key sequence, it is easy to see how the file may be accessed sequentially on the primary key. It is not quite so obvious how you achieve sequential access on the alternate keys. For this, you need to examine the alternate index schematic in Figure 17-11.

For each of the alternate keys specified in an indexed file, an alternate index is built. However, unlike the primary-key index, which contains the data buckets at the lowest level of the index, the lowest level of an alternate index is made up of base records that contain only the alternate-key value and a pointer to where the actual record is. These base records are organized in ascending alternate-key order; by reading though these base records in sequence, you achieve sequential access using the alternate key. This arrangement is shown schematically in Figure 17-11.

Figure 17-11 shows how the index is used to locate the record with a key value of Vt. As with the primary key, each level of index points to the next level until level 0 is reached. Each of the base buckets at level 0 contains records that consist of the alternate-key value and a pointer to the data bucket where the record with that key value is to be found. In Figure 17-11, for example, the Vt record in the base buckets points to a bucket that actually contains the record. Note that the records in this bucket are in ascending primary key order.

Processing Indexed Files

Just as with relative files, this section introduces indexed files by showing you some simple examples. When you have a feel for how it all works, you learn about the required clauses, verbs, and concepts more formally.

Let's start with a simple program that reads an indexed file both sequentially and directly on a number of keys. Then you see how to create an indexed file from a sequential file. In the third example, you learn how to use indexed files in combination: you use an indexed file of film directors and an indexed file containing film details together to display all the films directed by a particular director. In the final example, you apply a set of transactions to the film file and cover the issue of *referential integrity* that crops up when a new film record is inserted.

Reading an Indexed File

Listing 17-4 displays the contents of an indexed file in the key sequence chosen by the user and then displays one record directly using the key chosen by the user.

Listing 17-4. Reading an indexed file sequentially and then directly using any key

```
IDENTIFICATION DIVISION.
PROGRAM-ID.  Listing17-4.
AUTHOR.  Michael Coughlan.
*Reads the file sequentially and then directly on any key

ENVIRONMENT DIVISION.
INPUT-OUTPUT SECTION.
    SELECT FilmFile ASSIGN TO "Listing17-4Film.DAT"
        ORGANIZATION IS INDEXED
        ACCESS MODE IS DYNAMIC
        RECORD KEY IS FilmId
        ALTERNATE RECORD KEY IS FilmTitle
                    WITH DUPLICATES
        ALTERNATE RECORD KEY IS DirectorId
                    WITH DUPLICATES
        FILE STATUS IS FilmStatus.

DATA DIVISION.
FILE SECTION.
FD FilmFile.
01 FilmRec.
    88 EndOfFilms          VALUE HIGH-VALUES.
    02 FilmId              PIC 9(7).
    02 FilmTitle           PIC X(40).
    02 DirectorId          PIC 999.

WORKING-STORAGE SECTION.
01 FilmStatus              PIC XX.
    88 FilmOK VALUE ZEROS.

01 RequiredSequence        PIC 9.
    88 FilmIdSequence       VALUE 1.
    88 FilmTitleSequence    VALUE 2.
    88 DirectorIdSequence   VALUE 3.

PROCEDURE DIVISION.
Begin.
    OPEN INPUT FilmFile
    DISPLAY "*** Get Records Sequentially ***"
    DISPLAY "Enter key : 1 = FilmId, 2 = FilmTitle, 3 = DirectorId - "
            WITH NO ADVANCING.
    ACCEPT RequiredSequence.

    EVALUATE TRUE
       WHEN FilmIdSequence         PERFORM DisplayFilmData
```

```
        WHEN FilmTitleSequence        MOVE SPACES TO FilmTitle
                                      START FilmFile KEY IS GREATER THAN FilmTitle
                                          INVALID KEY DISPLAY "FilmStatus = " FilmStatus
                                      END-START
                                      PERFORM DisplayFilmData
        WHEN DirectorIdSequence       MOVE ZEROS TO DirectorId
                                      START FilmFile KEY IS GREATER THAN DirectorId
                                          INVALID KEY DISPLAY "FilmStatus = " FilmStatus
                                      END-START
                                      PERFORM DisplayFilmData
    END-EVALUATE

    DISPLAY SPACES
    DISPLAY "*** Get Records Directly ***"
    DISPLAY "Enter key : 1 = FilmId, 2 = FilmTitle, 3 = DirectorId - "
            WITH NO ADVANCING.
    ACCEPT RequiredSequence.
    EVALUATE TRUE
        WHEN FilmIdSequence        PERFORM GetFilmByFilmId
        WHEN FilmTitleSequence     PERFORM GetFilmByFilmTitle
        WHEN DirectorIdSequence    PERFORM GetFilmByDirectorId
    END-EVALUATE

    CLOSE FilmFile
    STOP RUN.

DisplayFilmData.
    READ FilmFile NEXT RECORD
        AT END SET EndOfFilms TO TRUE
    END-READ
    PERFORM UNTIL EndOfFilms
        DISPLAY FilmId SPACE FilmTitle SPACE DirectorId
        READ FilmFile NEXT RECORD
            AT END SET EndOfFilms TO TRUE
        END-READ
    END-PERFORM.

GetFilmByFilmId.
    DISPLAY "Enter the FilmId - " WITH NO ADVANCING
    ACCEPT FilmId
    READ FilmFile
        KEY IS FilmId
        INVALID KEY DISPLAY "Film not found - " FilmStatus
        NOT INVALID KEY DISPLAY FilmId SPACE FilmTitle SPACE DirectorId
    END-READ.

GetFilmByFilmTitle.
    DISPLAY "Enter the FilmTitle - " WITH NO ADVANCING
    ACCEPT FilmTitle
```

```
  READ FilmFile
    KEY IS FilmTitle
    INVALID KEY DISPLAY "Film not found - " FilmStatus
    NOT INVALID KEY DISPLAY FilmId SPACE FilmTitle SPACE DirectorId
  END-READ.


GetFilmByDirectorId.
  DISPLAY "Enter the Director Id - " WITH NO ADVANCING
  ACCEPT DirectorId
  READ FilmFile
    KEY IS DirectorId
    INVALID KEY DISPLAY "Film not found - " FilmStatus
    NOT INVALID KEY DISPLAY FilmId SPACE FilmTitle SPACE DirectorId
  END-READ.
```

```
                        Listing 17-4 Output
*** Get Records Sequentially ***
Enter key : 1 = FilmId, 2 = FilmTitle, 3 = DirectorId - 2
8713669 Alien                                       023
8805288 Cape Fear                                   005
8805806 Carlito's Way                               015
8805156 Carrie                                      015
8805245 Catch Me If You Can                         005
8805334 Desperado                                   002
8805385 First Knight                                003
8805474 Ghost                                       003
8805253 Heavenly Creatures                          009
8805504 Jackie Brown                                002
8805121 Jaws                                        005
8805091 Lord of the Rings:Fellowship of the Ring 009
8805075 Lord of the Rings:Return of the King        009
8805164 Lord of the Rings:The Two Towers            009
8805261 Master and Commander                        012
8805105 Mission Impossible                          015
8805296 Overboard                                   004
8805415 Pulp Fiction                                002
8805229 Saving Private Ryan                         005
8805326 The Color Purple                            005
8812438 The Untouchables                            015

*** Get Records Directly ***
Enter key : 1 = FilmId, 2 = FilmTitle, 3 = DirectorId - 1
Enter the FilmId - 8805415
8805415 Pulp Fiction                                002
```

There is quite a bit to talk about in this program. The first thing to note is the new entries in the SELECT and ASSIGN clause. Because an indexed file has a primary key and, perhaps, some alternate keys, you must have entries in SELECT and ASSIGN for each key, and you must distinguish the primary key from the alternate keys. One very important thing to remember is that whereas the key defined in the RELATIVE KEY entry of a relative file *cannot be* a field in the relative file's record description, the keys defined for an indexed file *must be* fields in the record defined for the file.

Another item of interest is the WITH DUPLICATES phrase, which is specified with the ALTERNATE KEY clause in the SELECT and ASSIGN clause. In a relative file, the key must be unique; and in an indexed file, the primary key defined in the RECORD KEY clause must be unique, but the alternate keys may have duplicates if they use the WITH DUPLICATES phrase. For instance, in this program, the same DirectorId appears for many films. If the WITH DUPLICATES phrase is omitted, the alternate key has to be unique.

The program starts by asking the user what key to use when displaying the contents of the file sequentially. This raises an interesting question. If you examine the code in the paragraph `DisplayFilmData,` you see that the READ format used is the one for reading a file sequentially. So the question is, how does the system know to read through the file in FilmId order on one occasion, in FilmTitle order on another occasion, and in DirectorId order on yet another occasion? The answer is that the system relies on a concept called the *key of reference*. The key of reference refers to the key that is used to process an indexed file sequentially. A particular key is established as the key of reference by using that key with START or a direct READ. You can see this in the program. If FilmTitleSequence is selected, START is used with the FilmTitle key to both establish FilmTitle as the key of reference and position the next-record pointer at the first record. Similarly, if DirectorIdSequence is selected, START is used to establish DirectorId as the key of reference and to position the next-record pointer at the first record in the file. What about FilmIdSequence, though? Why doesn't that WHEN branch have a START verb? I could have used START with that branch, too, but I wanted to make the point that when the file is opened, the primary key is the default key of reference and the next-record pointer is pointing at the first record in the file.

When the program has displayed the contents of the file in the required sequence, the user is asked which key they wish to use for a direct READ. Then that key is used to read the required record from the file. If you examine the READ operation in any of the paragraphs that read the record from the file, you see that this format of READ is different from that used for relative files. For relative files, READ does not require a KEY IS phrase because there is only one key; but because indexed files use many keys, you have to say which key you are using to read the record.

One final issue needs to be discussed. The paragraph GetFilmByDirectorId returns only one record, but the same director occurs many times in the file. How can you show the other films made by this director? The answer lies once more in the key of reference. When a direct READ is made, the key used is established as the key of reference, and the next-record pointer is pointing at the next record in the file. You can display all the films made by a particular director by doing a direct READ followed by sequential READs. You stop reading the records when the Director Id changes. This procedure is shown in the revised version of GetFilmByDirectorId in Example 17-2.

Example 17-2. Revision of GetFilmByDirectorId to Show All of a Director's Films

```
GetFilmByDirectorId.
    DISPLAY "Enter the Director Id - " WITH NO ADVANCING
    ACCEPT DirectorId
    READ FilmFile
        KEY IS DirectorId
        INVALID KEY DISPLAY "Film not found - " FilmStatus
        NOT INVALID KEY  DISPLAY FilmId SPACE FilmTitle SPACE DirectorId
                         PERFORM GetOtherFilmsByThisDirector
    END-READ.


GetOtherFilmsByThisDirector.
    MOVE DirectorId TO PrevDirectorId
    READ FilmFile NEXT RECORD
        AT END SET EndOfFilms TO TRUE
    END-READ
    PERFORM UNTIL DirectorId NOT EQUAL TO PrevDirectorId
                OR EndOfFilms
        DISPLAY FilmId SPACE FilmTitle SPACE DirectorId
        READ FilmFile NEXT RECORD
            AT END SET EndOfFilms TO TRUE
        END-READ
    END-PERFORM.
```

Creating an Indexed File from a Sequential File

In Listing 17-5, an indexed file is created from a sequential file. Sequential files are useful because you can create them with an ordinary editor. There are tools available that can convert a sequential file into an indexed file, but this program does the job itself.

Listing 17-5. Creating an Indexed File from a Sequential File

```
IDENTIFICATION DIVISION.
PROGRAM-ID.  Listing17-5.
AUTHOR.  Michael Coughlan.
*Creating an Indexed File from a Sequential File

ENVIRONMENT DIVISION.
INPUT-OUTPUT SECTION.
    SELECT FilmFile ASSIGN TO "Listing17-5Film.DAT"
        ORGANIZATION IS INDEXED
        ACCESS MODE IS DYNAMIC
        RECORD KEY IS FilmId
        ALTERNATE RECORD KEY IS FilmTitle
                    WITH DUPLICATES
        ALTERNATE RECORD KEY IS DirectorId
                    WITH DUPLICATES
        FILE STATUS IS FilmStatus.

    SELECT SeqFilmFile ASSIGN TO "Listing17-5Film.SEQ"
        ORGANIZATION IS LINE SEQUENTIAL.

DATA DIVISION.
FILE SECTION.
FD FilmFile.
01 FilmRec.
    02 FilmId           PIC 9(7).
    02 FilmTitle        PIC X(40).
    02 DirectorId       PIC 999.

FD SeqFilmFile.
01 SeqFilmRec           PIC X(50).
    88 EndOfFilmFile    VALUE HIGH-VALUES.

WORKING-STORAGE SECTION.
01 FilmStatus           PIC XX.
    88 FilmOK VALUE ZEROS.

PROCEDURE DIVISION.
Begin.
    OPEN INPUT  SeqFilmFile
    OPEN OUTPUT FilmFile

    READ SeqFilmFile
       AT END SET EndOfFilmFile TO TRUE
    END-READ
```

```
PERFORM UNTIL EndOfFilmFile
   WRITE FilmRec FROM SeqFilmRec
        INVALID KEY DISPLAY "Error writing to film file"
   END-WRITE
   READ SeqFilmFile
       AT END SET EndOfFilmFile TO TRUE
   END-READ
END-PERFORM
CLOSE SeqFilmFile, FilmFile
STOP RUN.
```

The first issue to bring to your attention is the statement WRITE FilmRec FROM SeqFilmRec. When you consider this statement, you may wonder why there is no KEY IS phrase as there is with the direct READ. The reason is that records are always written to an indexed file based on the value in the primary key, so no KEY IS phrase is required.

You may also wonder why I don't put the key value into the primary-key data item before the WRITE is executed. The answer is that I do put the key value into the primary-key data item—but I do it in a different way. WRITE FilmRec FROM SeqFilmRec has the same effect as

```
MOVE SeqFilmRec TO FilmRec
WRITE FilmRec
   INVALID KEY DISPLAY "Error writing to film file"
END-WRITE
```

Using Indexed Files in Combination

Listing 17-6 uses an indexed file of film directors and an indexed file containing film details in combination to display all the films directed by a particular director. The program accepts the name of a director from the user and then displays all the films made by that director. For each film, the director ID, the surname of the director, the film ID, and the title of the film are displayed.

Listing 17-6. Using Indexed Files in Combination

```
IDENTIFICATION DIVISION.
PROGRAM-ID.  Listing17-6.
AUTHOR. Michael Coughlan.
ENVIRONMENT DIVISION.
INPUT-OUTPUT SECTION.
   SELECT FilmFile ASSIGN TO "Listing17-6Film.DAT"
        ORGANIZATION IS INDEXED
        ACCESS MODE IS DYNAMIC
        RECORD KEY IS FilmId-FF
        ALTERNATE RECORD KEY IS FilmTitle-FF
                    WITH DUPLICATES
        ALTERNATE RECORD KEY IS DirectorId-FF
                    WITH DUPLICATES
        FILE STATUS IS FilmStatus.

   SELECT DirectorFile ASSIGN TO "Listing17-6Dir.DAT"
        ORGANIZATION IS INDEXED
        ACCESS MODE IS DYNAMIC
```

```
               RECORD KEY IS DirectorId-DF
               ALTERNATE RECORD KEY IS DirectorSurname-DF
               FILE STATUS IS DirectorStatus.

    DATA DIVISION.
    FILE SECTION.
    FD FilmFile.
    01 FilmRec-FF.
        88 EndOfFilms      VALUE HIGH-VALUES.
        02 FilmId-FF            PIC 9(7).
        02 FilmTitle-FF         PIC X(40).
        02 DirectorId-FF        PIC 999.

    FD DirectorFile.
    01 DirectorRec-DF.
        88 EndOfDirectors  VALUE HIGH-VALUES.
        02 DirectorId-DF        PIC 999.
        02 DirectorSurname-DF   PIC X(20).


    WORKING-STORAGE SECTION.
    01 AllStatusFlags  VALUE ZEROS.
        02 FilmStatus          PIC XX.
           88 FilmOk    VALUE "02", "00".

        02 DirectorStatus      PIC XX.

    01 DirectorName            PIC X(20).


    PROCEDURE DIVISION.
    Begin.
        OPEN INPUT FilmFile
        OPEN INPUT DirectorFile
        DISPLAY "Please enter the director surname :- "
                WITH NO ADVANCING
        ACCEPT DirectorSurname-DF
        READ DirectorFile
            KEY IS DirectorSurname-DF
            INVALID KEY DISPLAY "-DF ERROR Status = " DirectorStatus
            NOT INVALID KEY PERFORM GetFilmsForDirector
        END-READ

        CLOSE FilmFile
        CLOSE DirectorFile
        STOP RUN.

    GetFilmsForDirector.
        MOVE DirectorId-DF TO DirectorId-FF
        READ FilmFile
            KEY IS DirectorId-FF
```

```
        INVALID KEY DISPLAY "-FF ERROR Status = " FilmStatus
    END-READ
    IF FilmOk
        PERFORM UNTIL DirectorId-DF NOT Equal TO DirectorId-FF OR EndOfFilms
            DISPLAY DirectorId-DF SPACE DirectorSurname-DF SPACE
                    FilmId-FF      SPACE FilmTitle-FF
            READ FilmFile NEXT RECORD
                AT END SET EndOfFilms TO TRUE
            END-READ
        END-PERFORM
    END-IF.
```

Listing 17-6 Output

```
Please enter the director surname :- Spielberg
005 Spielberg            8805121 Jaws
005 Spielberg            8805229 Saving Private Ryan
005 Spielberg            8805245 Catch Me If You Can
005 Spielberg            8805326 The Color Purple
```

This program uses two indexed files in combination. Used this way, indexed files are similar to a database where each file is a table, the records in the file are the table rows, and the fields in the records are the table columns.

The program starts by getting the name of the director from the user. This name is used as the key value for a direct READ on the director file. When the record is retrieved, DirectorId-DF is used to get all the director's film titles.

One item of interest in the program is the file status for FilmFile. Note that one of two codes is specified to indicate the operation was successful. Normally, "00" indicates that the operation was successful; but in this case, the code "02" indicates success and also carries extra information. A code of "02" may be returned for indexed files only and is returned in these cases:

- When after a READ operation, the next record has the same key value as the key used for the READ

- When a WRITE or a REWRITE creates a duplicate key value for an alternate key that has the WITH DUPLICATES phrase

If you want to detect when you have processed all the films directed by a particular director without having to compare keys, you can use the returned "02" code as shown in Example 17-3.

Example 17-3. Using the "02" File Status to Create a More Succinct Loop

```
01 AllStatusFlags  VALUE ZEROS.
    02 FilmStatus              PIC XX.
        88 AnotherFilmForThisDirector     VALUE "02".



:   :   :   :   :   :   :   :   :   :   :   :   :   :   :   :

GetFilmsForDirector.
    MOVE DirectorId-DF TO DirectorId-FF
    READ FilmFile
        KEY IS DirectorId-FF
        INVALID KEY DISPLAY "-FF ERROR Status = " FilmStatus
```

```
      NOT INVALID KEY DISPLAY DirectorId-DF SPACE DirectorSurname-DF SPACE
                             FilmId-FF    SPACE FilmTitle-FF
   END-READ
   PERFORM UNTIL NOT AnotherFilmForThisDirector
        READ FilmFile NEXT RECORD
           AT END SET EndOfFilms TO TRUE
        END-READ
        DISPLAY DirectorId-DF SPACE DirectorSurname-DF SPACE
                FilmId-FF    SPACE FilmTitle-FF
   END-PERFORM.
```

Applying Transactions to an Indexed File

Listing 17-7 applies a set of transactions (deletions, insertions, and updates) to the film file. The result of applying the transactions is shown in Figure 17-12. Applying the insertions to the film file is complicated by the issue of referential integrity. It should not be valid to insert a new film record when there is no record in the directors file for the director of the film. In a relational database system, referential integrity is automatically enforced by the database; but in COBOL, you have to do it yourself. The failure of programs to enforce referential integrity in COBOL legacy systems is one of the problems of legacy data. If you try to load such legacy data into a relational database that does enforce referential integrity, uniqueness, and other standards, the database system will probably crash.

Listing 17-7. Applying Transactions to an Indexed File

```
IDENTIFICATION DIVISION.
PROGRAM-ID.  Listing17-7.
AUTHOR.  Michael Coughlan.
*Applies transactions to the Indexed FilmFile and enforces referential integrity
*with the Indexed Directors File

ENVIRONMENT DIVISION.
INPUT-OUTPUT SECTION.
   SELECT FilmFile ASSIGN TO "Listing17-7Films.DAT"
        ORGANIZATION IS INDEXED
        ACCESS MODE IS DYNAMIC
        RECORD KEY IS FilmId-FF
        ALTERNATE RECORD KEY IS FilmTitle-FF
                   WITH DUPLICATES
        ALTERNATE RECORD KEY IS DirectorId-FF
                   WITH DUPLICATES
        FILE STATUS IS FilmStatus.

   SELECT DirectorsFile ASSIGN TO "Listing17-7Dir.DAT"
        ORGANIZATION IS INDEXED
        ACCESS MODE IS DYNAMIC
        RECORD KEY IS DirectorId-DF
        ALTERNATE RECORD KEY IS DirectorSurname-DF
        FILE STATUS IS DirectorStatus.

   SELECT TransFile ASSIGN TO "Listing17-7Trans.dat"
        ORGANIZATION IS LINE SEQUENTIAL.
```

```
DATA DIVISION.
FILE SECTION.
FD FilmFile.
01 FilmRec-FF.
   88 EndOfFilms     VALUE HIGH-VALUES.
   02 FilmId-FF            PIC 9(7).
   02 FilmTitle-FF         PIC X(40).
   02 DirectorId-FF        PIC 9(3).

FD DirectorsFile.
01 DirectorsRec-DF.
   88 EndOfDirectors  VALUE HIGH-VALUES.
   02 DirectorId-DF        PIC 9(3).
   02 DirectorSurname-DF   PIC X(20).

FD TransFile.
01 DeletionRec-TF.
   88 EndOfTrans     VALUE HIGH-VALUES.
   02 TypeId-TF            PIC X.
      88 DoDeletion        VALUE "D".
      88 DoInsertion       VALUE "I".
      88 DoUpdate          VALUE "U".
   02 FilmId-TF            PIC 9(7).

01 InsertionRec-TF.
   02 FILLER               PIC 9.
   02 InsertionBody-TF.
      03 FILLER            PIC X(47).
      03 DirectorId-TF     PIC 9(3).

01 UpdateRec-TF.
   02 FILLER               PIC X(8).
   02 FilmTitle-TF         PIC X(40).

WORKING-STORAGE SECTION.
01 AllStatusFlags  VALUE ZEROS.
   02 FilmStatus           PIC XX.
      88 FilmOK VALUE ZEROS.
   02 DirectorStatus       PIC XX.
      88 MatchingDirectorFound  VALUE ZEROS.

PROCEDURE DIVISION.
Begin.
    OPEN I-O FilmFile
    OPEN INPUT DirectorsFile
    OPEN INPUT TransFile
    DISPLAY "*** Film file before updates ***"
    PERFORM DisplayFilmFileContents
    DISPLAY SPACES
    READ TransFile
      AT END SET EndOfTrans TO TRUE
    END-READ
```

```
        PERFORM UpdateFilmFile UNTIL EndofTrans
        DISPLAY SPACES
        DISPLAY "*** Film file after updates ***"
        PERFORM DisplayFilmFileContents
        CLOSE FilmFile, DirectorsFile, TransFile
        STOP RUN.

    DisplayFilmFileContents.
        MOVE ZEROS TO FilmId-FF
        START FilmFile KEY IS GREATER THAN FilmId-FF
            INVALID KEY DISPLAY "Error1 - FilmStatus = " FilmStatus
        END-START
        READ FilmFile NEXT RECORD
           AT END SET EndOfFilms TO TRUE
        END-READ
        PERFORM UNTIL EndOfFilms
           DISPLAY FilmId-FF SPACE DirectorId-FF SPACE FilmTitle-FF
           READ FilmFile NEXT RECORD
              AT END SET EndOfFilms TO TRUE
           END-READ
        END-PERFORM.

    UpdateFilmFile.
        EVALUATE TRUE
            WHEN DoDeletion  PERFORM DeleteFilmRec
            WHEN DoInsertion PERFORM InsertFilmRec
            WHEN DoUpdate    PERFORM UpdateFilmRec
        END-EVALUATE
        READ TransFile
            AT END SET EndOfTrans TO TRUE
        END-READ.

    DeleteFilmRec.
        MOVE FilmId-TF TO FilmId-FF
        DELETE FilmFile RECORD
            INVALID KEY DISPLAY FilmId-FF " - Delete Error. No such record"
        END-DELETE.

    InsertFilmRec.
    *To preserve Referential Integrity check director exists for this Film
        MOVE DirectorId-TF   TO DirectorId-DF
        START DirectorsFile
            KEY IS EQUAL TO DirectorId-DF
            INVALID KEY DISPLAY FilmId-FF " - Insert Error. No matching entry for director - "
    DirectorId-TF
        END-START

        IF MatchingDirectorFound
           MOVE InsertionBody-TF TO FilmRec-FF
           WRITE FilmRec-FF
               INVALID KEY DISPLAY FilmId-FF " - Insert Error. That FilmId already exists."
           END-WRITE
        END-IF.
```

```
UpdateFilmRec.
    MOVE FilmId-TF TO FilmId-FF
    READ FilmFile RECORD
        KEY IS FilmId-FF
        INVALID KEY DISPLAY FilmId-FF " - Update error. No such record exists"
    END-READ
    IF FilmOk
        MOVE FilmTitle-TF TO FilmTitle-FF
        REWRITE FilmRec-FF
            INVALID KEY DISPLAY "Unexpected Error1. FilmStatus - " FilmStatus
        END-REWRITE
    END-IF.
```

```
                                Listing 17-7 Output
*** Film file before updates ***
8713669 023 Alien
8805075 009 Lord of the Rings:Return of the King
8805091 009 Lord of the Rings:Fellowship of the Ring
8805105 015 Mission Impossible
8805121 005 Jaws
8805156 015 Carrie
8805164 009 Lord of the Rings:The Two Towers
8805229 005 Saving Private Ryan
8805245 005 Catch Me If You Can                        Transactions
8805253 009 Heavenly Creatures
8805261 012 Master and Commander
8805288 033 Cape Fear          D8805334    +++valid delete
8805296 004 Overboard          D8844444    ---invalid delete
8805326 005 The Color Purple   I8833333Raiders of the Lost Ark - valid insert   005
8805334 002 Desperado          I8805111    invalid Insert no matching dir code   008
8805385 003 First Knight       I8805245    invalid Insert rec already exists     005
8805415 002 Pulp Fiction       U8805326Color Purple, The +++ valid update
8805474 003 Ghost              U8811111    --- invalid update
8805504 002 Jackie Brown       U8812438Untouchables, The +++ valid update
8805806 015 Carlito's Way
8812438 015 The Untouchables
8822334 023 Blade Runner

8844444 - Delete Error. No such record
8833333 - Insert Error. No matching entry for director - 008
8805245 - Insert Error. That FilmId already exists.
8811111 - Update error. No such record exists

*** Film file after updates ***
8713669 023 Alien
8805075 009 Lord of the Rings:Return of the King
8805091 009 Lord of the Rings:Fellowship of the Ring
8805105 015 Mission Impossible
8805121 005 Jaws
8805156 015 Carrie
8805164 009 Lord of the Rings:The Two Towers          Directors File
8805229 005 Saving Private Ryan
8805245 005 Catch Me If You Can          002Tarantino
8805253 009 Heavenly Creatures          003Zucker
8805261 012 Master and Commander        004Marshall
8805288 033 Cape Fear                   005Spielberg
8805296 004 Overboard                   009Jackson
8805326 005 Color Purple, The +++ valid update  012Weir
8805385 003 First Knight                015De Palma
8805415 002 Pulp Fiction                023Scott
8805474 003 Ghost                       033Scorsese
8805504 002 Jackie Brown
8805806 015 Carlito's Way
8812438 015 Untouchables, The +++ valid update
8822334 023 Blade Runner
8833333 005 Raiders of the Lost Ark - valid insert
```

Figure 17-12. *Output from Listing 17-7*

There is not much to talk about here that I have not already discussed in relation to relative files, but let's touch once more on the issue of referential integrity. When an insertion record has to be applied to FilmFile, you must make sure the director of that film has an entry in DirectorsFile. You do this in InsertFilmRec by using START with DirectorsFile and the director ID from TransFile to make sure there is a director with that ID in DirectorsFile. If there is a director with that ID, you try to apply the insertion.

Indexed Files: Syntax and Semantics

This section formally introduces the specific verb formats, clauses, and concepts required for indexed files.

Indexed Files: SELECT and ASSIGN Clause

The metalanguage for the SELECT and ASSIGN clause for indexed files is shown in Figure 17-13.

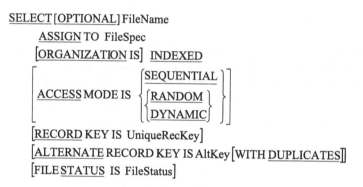

Figure 17-13. *Metalanguage for SELECT and ASSIGN specific to indexed files*

Consider the following:

- The key defined for a relative file by the RELATIVE KEY phrase in the SELECT and ASSIGN clause *cannot be* a field in the record of the relative file. In total contrast to this, every key (primary and alternates) defined for an indexed file *must be* a field in record of the indexed file.

- Every indexed file must have a primary key and may have up to 254 alternate keys.

- The primary key must be unique for each record and must be a numeric or alphanumeric data item. The primary key is identified by the RECORD KEY IS phrase in the SELECT and ASSIGN clause.

- Each alternate key must be numeric or alphanumeric and may be unique or may have duplicate values. The alternate keys are identified by the ALTERNATE RECORD KEY IS phrase in the SELECT and ASSIGN clause.

- If an alternate key can have duplicate values, then the WITH DUPLICATES phrase must be used. If WITH DUPLICATES is not used and you attempt to write a record that contains an alternate-key value that is already present in another record in the file, WRITE will fail, and a file status "22" (record already exists) will be returned.

The Key of Reference

When you define an indexed file with ACCESS MODE IS SEQUENTIAL, the file is always processed in ascending primary-key order. But if the file is defined with ACCESS MODE IS DYNAMIC and is processed sequentially, the file system must be able to tell which of the keys to use as the basis for processing the file. Because the format of the sequential READ does not have a key phrase, the file system refers to a special item called the *key of reference* to discover which key to use for processing the file. Before reading a file defined as ACCESS MODE IS DYNAMIC sequentially, you must establish one of the file's keys as the key of reference. You do so by using the key in a START or a direct READ. When the file is opened, the primary key is by default the key of reference, and the next-record pointer is pointing at the first record.

Indexed File Verbs

Indexed files use the same verbs for file manipulation as relative files, but in some cases there are syntactic or semantic differences. This section examines only those verbs that differ in syntax or semantics from those used with relative files.

The READ Verb

When an indexed file is defined with ACCESS MODE IS SEQUENTIAL, the READ format is the same as for sequential files. But when the file is defined with ACCESS MODE IS DYNAMIC, sequential processing of the file is complicated by the presence of a number of indexes. The order in which the data records are read depends on which index is being processed sequentially, and the index used is established by the key of reference.

For indexed files, the format of the READ used to read sequentially is the same as for relative files. But in the case of the direct READ, the format requires a KEY IS phrase to specify the key on which the file is to be read. The metalanguage for this format of READ is given in Figure 17-14.

<u>READ</u> FileName RECORD [<u>INTO</u> DestItem]
      [<u>KEY</u> IS KeyName]
      [<u>INVALID</u> KEY StatementBlock]
      [<u>NOT</u> <u>INVALID</u> KEY StatementBlock]
[<u>END – READ</u>]

Figure 17-14. READ format used to read an indexed file directly

To read a record directly from an indexed file, a key value must be placed in the KeyName data item (the KeyName data item is the area of storage identified as the primary key or one of the alternate keys in the SELECT and ASSIGN clause). When READ executes, the record with a key value equal to the present value of KeyName is read into the file buffer.

After the record has been read, the next-record pointer points to the next logical record in the file. If the key of reference is the primary key, then this record is an actual data record; but if the key of reference is one of the alternate keys, the pointer points to the next alternate index base record.

If duplicates are allowed, only the first record in a group with duplicates can be read directly. The rest of the duplicates must be read sequentially using the READ NEXT RECORD format.

Here are some things to remember:

- If the record does not exist, the INVALID KEY clause activates, and the statement block following the clause is executed.

- If the KEY IS clause is omitted, the key used is the primary key.

- When READ is executed, the key mentioned in the KEY IS phrase is established as the key of reference.

- If there is no KEY IS phrase, the primary key is established as the key of reference.

- The file must have an ACCESS MODE of DYNAMIC or RANDOM and must be opened for I-O or INPUT.

The WRITE, REWRITE and DELETE Verbs

The syntax and semantics of the WRITE, REWRITE, and DELETE verbs is the same as for relative files, except that

- Direct access for all these verbs is based on the primary key only.

- Although REWRITE may not change the value of the primary key, it may change the value of any of the alternate keys.

The START Verb

The syntax for the START verb is the same as for relative files, except that instead of the format START FileName KEY Condition RelKey, the format is as is shown in Figure 17-15. The key of comparison is any of the keys specified in the indexed file's SELECT and ASSIGN clause.

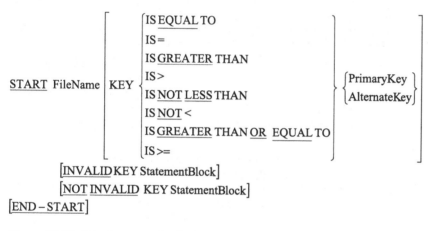

Figure 17-15. *Metalanguage for the START verb*

Just as with relative files, the START verb may be used to control the position of the next-record pointer. In addition, with indexed files, the START verb may be used to establish a particular key as the key of reference.

The primary key or one of the alternate keys is the key of comparison. To establish a particular key as the key of reference and position the next-record pointer at a particular record, you first move the key value to the key-of-comparison data item. Then you execute the statement START..KEY IS EQUAL TO .. if you want to position the next-record pointer at the record with a key equal to the value in the key of comparison, or START..KEY IS GREATER THAN .. if you want to position the next-record pointer at the succeeding record.

Remember these things:

- The file must be opened for **INPUT** or **I-O** when START is executed.

- Execution of the START statement does not change the contents of the record area (that is, START does not read the record—it merely positions the next-record pointer and establishes the key of reference).

- When START is executed, the next-record pointer is set to the first logical record in the file whose key satisfies the condition. If no record satisfies the condition, the INVALID KEY clause is activated.

Comparison of COBOL File Organizations

Now that you have examined all the COBOL file organizations, you may wonder which is the best one to use. The answer is that it depends. This section examines the advantages and disadvantages of each organization; from this information, you should be able to figure out which organization to use in a given situation.

First some terminology. The *hit rate* refers to the number of records in the file that are impacted when you process a file. For instance, if only 100 records are affected by an insert, a delete, or an update operation in a file of 100,000 records, the hit rate is low. But if 90,000 records are affected, the hit rate is high.

Sequential File Organization

The records in a sequential file are held serially, one after another, on disk, tape, or other media. This organization has both advantages and disadvantages.

Disadvantages of Sequential File Organization

Sequential files have the following disadvantages:

- *They are slow when the hit rate is low.* To read a particular record, you have to read all the preceding records. To update records, you have to read all the records in the file and write them to a new file. This is a lot of work if all you are doing is changing a few of the records in the file.

- *They are complicated to change.* Changes to sequential files are batched together in a transaction file to minimize the low-hit-rate problem, but this makes updating sequential files much more complicated than updating direct access files. The complications arise from having to match the records in the transaction file with those in the master file (that is, the file to be updated).

- *They take up double the storage when they are updated.* The records in sequential files cannot be updated in situ; instead, a new file must be created that consists of all the records in the old file plus the insertions and minus the deletions. Of course, this storage problem may be transient, because once the new file has been created, you can delete the old file.

Advantages of Sequential File Organization

Sequential file organization also has a number of advantages:

- *When the hit rate is high, it is the fastest file organization* because the record position does not have to be calculated and no indexes have to be traversed. Because the records are stored contiguously, this organization takes advantage of the fact that the file system doesn't access records on a per-record basis but instead scoops up a block or bucket at a time. When a block contains a number of records, the number of disk accesses required to process the file is greatly reduced.

- *It is the most storage efficient of all the file organizations.* No indexes are required, the space from deleted records is recovered, and only the storage actually required to hold the records is allocated to the file.

- *It is the simplest file organization.* Records are held serially, so you read them one after another.

- *It allows the space from deleted records to be recovered.* To delete records from a sequential file, you create a new file that does not contain the deleted records. Once you delete the old file, all the storage previously used by the deleted records is recovered and can be used for storing something else.

- *Sequential files may be stored and processed on serial media such as magnetic tape.* These media are cheap, removable, and voluminous.

Relative File Organization

You can think of the records in a relative file as a one-dimensional table stored on disk. The file system can calculate where each record is on the disk because it knows the start location for the file, and it knows the amount of storage required to store each record. The record location is calculated as `RecordLocation = BaseLocation + (SizePerRecord * (RelativeRecordNumber - 1))`.

Disadvantages of Relative File Organization

Relative file organization has a number of disadvantages:

- *It wastes storage if the file is only partially populated with records.* The file is allocated enough disk storage to hold records from 1 to the highest relative record number used, even if only a few records have been written to the file. For instance, if the first record written to the file has a relative record number of 100,000, room for that many records is allocated to the file.

- *It cannot recover the space from deleted records.* When a record is deleted in a relative file, it is marked as deleted, but the space that was occupied by the record is still allocated to the file. This means if a relative file takes up 1.5MB of disk space when full, it still occupies 1.5MB when 99% of the records have been deleted.

- *It allows only a single, numeric key.* The single key is limiting because often you need to access a file on more than one key. For instance, in a file of student records, you might want to access the records on student ID, student name, course code, or module code. The mention of using student name, course code, or module code highlights another drawback with relative files: you frequently need to access a file using an alphanumeric key.

- *The relative file key must map on to the range of the relative record numbers for the file.* The facts that the key must be in the range between 1 and the highest key value and that the file system allocates space for all the records between 1 and the highest relative record number used impose severe constraints on the key. For instance, even though `StudentId` is numeric, you can't use it as a key because the file system allocates space for records between 1 and the highest `StudentId` written to the file. If the highest `StudentId` written to the file is 9976683, the file system will allocate space for 9,976,683 records. Universities rarely have this many students, so most of the file will be wasted space.

   Sometimes you can get around the limitations of the relative key by using a transformation function to map the actual key onto the range of relative record numbers. There are a number of possible transformation or *hashing* functions. These transformations include *truncation* (using only some of the digits in the key as the relative record number), *folding* (breaking the key into two or more parts and summing the parts), *digit manipulation* (manipulating some of the digits in the key to produce a relative record number), and *modulus division* (using the remainder of a division operation as the relative record number). Some sophisticated transformation functions may even allow alphanumeric keys.

- *Relative files must be stored and processed on direct access media.* Because relative files are direct access files, they must be processed on direct access media such as a hard disk. They cannot be processed on magnetic tape or other cheap serial media; and if stored on tape, they must be loaded onto a hard disk before they can be used.

Advantages of Relative File Organization

Although relative file organization has many disadvantages, it also has the following advantages:

- *It is the fastest direct access organization.* Only a few simple calculations have to be done to locate a particular record.

- *Records in a relative file have very little storage overhead.* Unlike indexed files, which must store the indexes as well as the data, relative files have only a small storage overhead for each record (such as the record-deletion indicator).

- *Records in a relative file can be read sequentially.* In addition to allowing direct access, relative files allow sequential access to the records in the file.

Indexed File Organization

As shown in the Figure 17-10 earlier, the records in an indexed file are arranged in ascending primary-key order in a series of chained buckets/blocks. In addition to the actual data records, the primary key has a number of index records. For each alternate key specified for the file, there is a similar arrangement; but instead of data records at the final level, there are records arranged in ascending alternate-key order that consist only of the key and a pointer to where the actual record may be found. As shown earlier in Figure 17-11, in addition to the records at the base level, there are a number of alternate-key index records.

Disadvantages of Indexed File Organization

Indexed file organization has many disadvantages:

- *It is the slowest direct access organization,* because indexed files achieve direct access by traversing a number of levels of index. Indexed files must have a primary-key index and an index for each alternate key. Each level of index implies an I/O operation on the hard disk. For instance, three I/O operations are required to read the record shown earlier in Figure 17-10: two for the index records and one for data record).

- *It especially slow when writing or deleting records* because then the primary-key index and the alternate-key indexes may need to be rebuilt.

- *It is not very storage efficient,* because indexed files must store the index records, the alternate index records, the data records, and the alternate data records.

- *Space from deleted records is only partially recovered* until the indexes are rebuilt (which has to be done periodically).

- *Indexed files may only be processed on direct access media,* because they are direct access files. They cannot be processed on magnetic tape.

Advantages of Indexed File Organization

As you have seen, indexed files have many disadvantages, but these are far outweighed by their advantages:

- They can use multiple, alphanumeric keys.

- They can have duplicate alternate keys.

- They can be read sequentially on any of their keys.

- They can partially recover space from deleted records.

- They can have multiple alphanumeric keys, and only the primary key must be unique.

Although indexed files have their disadvantages, the versatility afforded by having multiple, alphanumeric keys and being able to process the file both directly and sequentially on any of its keys overrides all their disadvantages. As a result, indexed files are the most widely used direct access file organization.

Summary

This chapter introduced COBOL's direct access file organizations: indexed and relative files. You learned about the arrangement of records in each of these file organizations, along with new concepts such as file status, the next-record pointer, and key of reference. You explored the syntactic and semantic changes that allow the existing file-processing verbs to process direct access files, and you were introduced to new COBOL file-processing verbs such as DELETE, REWRITE, and START. In the final section of the chapter, you saw the advantages and disadvantages of each of the COBOL file organizations.

The next chapter discusses the COBOL Report Writer. The Report Writer allows you to write programs that produce reports using declarative rather than procedural/imperative techniques. In imperative programming, you tell the computer how to do what you want done. In declarative programming, you tell the computer what you would like done, and the computer works out how to do it.

The Report Writer also uses a kind of specialized exception handling called *declaratives*. You can also use declaratives with files. When you specify the declaratives for a file, an exception that would normally activate the AT END or INVALID KEY clause instead executes the code you have written in the DECLARATIVE SECTION to deal with the problem.

By way of introduction, the answer to the exercise at the end of this chapter uses the Report Writer to print a small report. Because you don't know how to use the Report Writer yet, you have to do the exercise the hard way. There is nothing like the pain of coding a report program to make you appreciate the benefits of the Report Writer!

PROGRAMMING EXERCISE

Time for a little exercise. Whip out your 2B pencil and see if you can come up with a solution to this problem.

Introduction

Acme Automobile Parts Limited sells motorcycle and automobile spare parts. Recently, the company purchased a computer and retained your firm to write the programs required. Your supervisor has asked you to write the program detailed next.

General Description

The program is required to perform file maintenance on the vehicle master file using a transaction file of validated amendment records. The transaction file has been sorted on ascending date (YYYYMMDD). If an error is encountered when attempting to apply transactions to the vehicle master file, then the transaction record must be written to an error file (Listing17-8-Err.DAT). When a vehicle record is deleted, the spare parts stocked for that vehicle are no longer required and so must be printed to a redundant stock report (Listing17-8-Stk.RPT).

There are two types of records in the transaction file, and they are distinguished from one another by the codes "I" (insert vehicle record) and "D" (delete vehicle record) in the first character position of the record.

Vehicle Master File

The vehicle master file (Listing17-8-VMF.DAT) is a relative file. VehicleNumber is used for the relative record number. Each record has following description:

Field	Type	Length	Value
VehicleNumber	9	4	1-9999
VehicleDescription	X	25	–
ManufacturerName	X	20	–

Stock Master File

The stock master file (Listing17-8-SMF.DAT) is an indexed file. It is required so that you can report all the stock records that are affected when a vehicle is deleted from the vehicle master file. Each record in the stock master file has the following record description:

Field	Key Type	Type	Length	Value
PartNumber	Primary	9	7	1-9999999
VehicleNumber	Alt with duplicates	9	4	1-9999
PartDescription	–	X	25	–

Transaction File

The transaction file (AcmeTrans.DAT) is validated file, sequenced on ascending DateOfEntry. Records in the file have the following description:

Record Type	Field	Type	Length	Value
InsertVehicleRecord	TypeCode	X	1	I
	DateOfEntry	9	8	YYYYMMDD
	VehicleNumber	9	4	1-9999
	VehicleDescription	X	25	–
DeleteVehicleRecord	TypeCode	X	1	D
	DateOfEntry	9	8	YYYYMMDD
	VehicleNumber	9	4	1-9999

Maintenance Procedure

Type Code	Action
I	If a record with this VehicleNumber already exists in either the stock or vehicle master file, then write the transaction record to the error file. Otherwise, insert the record.
D	If the record does not exist in the vehicle master file, then write the transaction record to the error file.
	If there is no error, then read all the stock records with the same VehicleNumber as the record to be deleted and write the details to the redundant stock report.
	Rewrite the VehicleNumber field in each of these stock records with zeros. Delete the vehicle master file record.

The Redundant Stock Report

Headings should be printed at the top of each page. See the print specification in Figure 17-16 for further details.

```
       1234567890123456789012345678901234567890123456789012345678901234567890:
01
02                          REDUNDANT  STOCK  REPORT
03                          ---------------------------
04
05
06     PART NUMBER      PART DESCRIPTION         VEHICLE NO.    MANUFACTURER  NAME
07
08     XXXXXXX     XXXXXXXXXXXXXXXXXXXXXXXXX      XXXX      XXXXXXXXXXXXXXXXXXXX
09
10     XXXXXXX     XXXXXXXXXXXXXXXXXXXXXXXXX      XXXX      XXXXXXXXXXXXXXXXXXXX
11
12     XXXXXXX     XXXXXXXXXXXXXXXXXXXXXXXXX      XXXX      XXXXXXXXXXXXXXXXXXXX
13
14     XXXXXXX     XXXXXXXXXXXXXXXXXXXXXXXXX      XXXX      XXXXXXXXXXXXXXXXXXXX
15
16     XXXXXXX     XXXXXXXXXXXXXXXXXXXXXXXXX      XXXX      XXXXXXXXXXXXXXXXXXXX
17
18     XXXXXXX     XXXXXXXXXXXXXXXXXXXXXXXXX      XXXX      XXXXXXXXXXXXXXXXXXXX
19
20     XXXXXXX     XXXXXXXXXXXXXXXXXXXXXXXXX      XXXX      XXXXXXXXXXXXXXXXXXXX
21
22     XXXXXXX     XXXXXXXXXXXXXXXXXXXXXXXXX      XXXX      XXXXXXXXXXXXXXXXXXXX
23
24     XXXXXXX     XXXXXXXXXXXXXXXXXXXXXXXXX      XXXX      XXXXXXXXXXXXXXXXXXXX
25
26
```

Figure 17-16. *Print specification. Line numbers and column numbers added*

PROGRAMMING EXERCISE: ANSWER

```
IDENTIFICATION DIVISION.
PROGRAM-ID.  Listing17-8.
AUTHOR.  MICHAEL COUGHLAN.
*Applies Insertions and Deletions in TransFile to the VehicleFile.
*For Insertions - If a vehicle already exists in either the Stock or
*Vehicle file, the transaction record is written to the Error File otherwise inserted
*For Deletions - If the vehicle does not exist in the Vehicle File the transaction
*record is written to the Error File otherwise the Vehicle record is deleted
*If the vehicle record is deleted all the Stock records with the same VehicleNumber
*as the deleted record are written to the Redundant Stock Report and the VehicleNumber
*field in each of these Stock records is overwritten with zeros.

ENVIRONMENT DIVISION.
INPUT-OUTPUT SECTION.
FILE-CONTROL.
    SELECT StockFile ASSIGN TO "Listing17-8-SMF.DAT"
        ORGANIZATION IS INDEXED
        ACCESS MODE IS DYNAMIC
        RECORD KEY IS PartNumSF
        ALTERNATE RECORD KEY IS VehicleNumSF
                    WITH DUPLICATES
        FILE STATUS IS StockErrStatus.

    SELECT VehicleFile ASSIGN TO "Listing17-8-VMF.DAT"
        ORGANIZATION IS RELATIVE
        ACCESS MODE IS DYNAMIC
        RELATIVE KEY IS VehicleNumKey
        FILE STATUS IS VehicleErrStatus.

    SELECT TransFile ASSIGN TO "Listing17-8-TRANS.DAT"
        ORGANIZATION IS LINE SEQUENTIAL.

    SELECT ErrorFile ASSIGN TO "Listing17-8-ERR.DAT"
        ORGANIZATION IS LINE SEQUENTIAL.

    SELECT RedundantStockRpt ASSIGN TO "Listing17-8-STK.RPT".

DATA DIVISION.
FILE SECTION.
FD  StockFile.
01  StockRecSF.
    02  PartNumSF           PIC 9(7).
    02  VehicleNumSF        PIC 9(4).
    02  PartDescSF          PIC X(25).
```

```
FD  VehicleFile.
01  VehicleRecVF.
      02  VehicleNumVF         PIC 9(4).
      02  VehicleDescVF        PIC X(25).
      02  ManfNameVF           PIC X(20).


FD  TransFile.
01  TransRecTF.
      02  TransTypeTF          PIC X.
          88  InsertionRec     VALUE "I".
          88  DeletionRec      VALUE "D".
      02  DateTF               PIC X(8).
      02  VehicleNumTF         PIC 9(4).
      02  VehicleDescTF        PIC X(25).
      02  ManfNameTF           PIC X(20).


FD  RedundantStockRpt REPORT IS StockReport.


FD  ErrorFile.
01  ErrorRec                   PIC X(56).


WORKING-STORAGE SECTION.
01  ErrorStatusCodes.
      02  StockErrStatus       PIC X(2).
          88  StockFileOpOK    VALUE "00", "02".
          88  StockRecExistis  VALUE "22".
          88  NoStockRec       VALUE "23".
      02  VehicleErrStatus     PIC X(2).
          88  VehicleFileOpOK  VALUE "00".
          88  VehicleRecExists VALUE "22".
          88  NoVehicleRec     VALUE "23".

01  FileVariables.
      02  VehicleNumKey        PIC 9(4).
      02  PrevVehicleNum       PIC 9(4).

01  ConditionNames.
      02  FILLER               PIC X.
          88  EndOfStockFile      VALUE HIGH-VALUES.
          88  NotEndOfStockFile   VALUE LOW-VALUES.
      02  FILLER               PIC X.
          88  EndOfTransFile      VALUE HIGH-VALUES.

REPORT SECTION.
RD  StockReport
    PAGE LIMIT IS 66
    HEADING 1
    FIRST DETAIL 6
    LAST DETAIL 50
    FOOTING 55.
```

```
01  TYPE IS PAGE HEADING.
    02  LINE 2.
        03  COLUMN 31          PIC X(24) VALUE
                "REDUNDANT  STOCK  REPORT".
    02  LINE 3.
        03  COLUMN 30          PIC X(26) VALUE ALL "-".

    02  LINE 6.
        03  COLUMN 2           PIC X(36) VALUE
            "PART NUMBER        PART DESCRIPTION".
        03  COLUMN 45          PIC X(35) VALUE
            "VEHICLE NO.    MANUFACTURER  NAME".

01  DetailLine TYPE IS DETAIL.
    02  LINE IS PLUS 2.
        03  COLUMN 3           PIC 9(7) SOURCE PartNumSF .
        03  COLUMN 17          PIC X(25) SOURCE PartDescSF.
        03  COLUMN 48          PIC 9(4) SOURCE VehicleNumSF.
        03  COLUMN 60          PIC X(20) SOURCE ManfNameVF.

PROCEDURE DIVISION.
Begin.
    OPEN INPUT  TransFile.
    OPEN I-O    StockFile
                VehicleFile.
    OPEN OUTPUT ErrorFile
                RedundantStockRpt.

    INITIATE StockReport

    READ TransFile
        AT END SET EndOfTransFile TO TRUE
    END-READ
    PERFORM UNTIL EndOfTransFile
        MOVE VehicleNumTF TO VehicleNumKey
                            VehicleNumSF

        EVALUATE   TRUE
            WHEN InsertionRec  PERFORM CheckStockFile
            WHEN DeletionRec   PERFORM DeleteVehicleRec
            WHEN OTHER         DISPLAY "NOT INSERT OR DELETE"
        END-EVALUATE
        READ TransFile
            AT END SET EndOfTransFile TO TRUE
        END-READ
    END-PERFORM

    TERMINATE StockReport
```

```
        CLOSE   ErrorFile
                RedundantStockRpt
                TransFile
                StockFile
                VehicleFile

        STOP RUN.

CheckStockFile.
    READ StockFile KEY IS VehicleNumSF
        INVALID KEY CONTINUE
    END-READ
    IF StockFileOpOK
        PERFORM WriteErrorLine
     ELSE IF NoStockRec
            PERFORM InsertVehicleRec
          ELSE
            DISPLAY "Unexpected Read Error on Stockfile"
            DISPLAY "Stockfile status = " StockErrStatus
          END-IF
    END-IF.

InsertVehicleRec.
    MOVE ManfNameTF TO ManfNameVF
    MOVE VehicleDescTF TO VehicleDescVF
    MOVE VehicleNumTF TO VehicleNumVF
    WRITE VehicleRecVF
        INVALID KEY CONTINUE
    END-WRITE
    IF VehicleRecExists PERFORM WriteErrorLine
    ELSE IF NOT VehicleFileOpOK
            DISPLAY "Unexpected Write Error on VehicleFile."
            DISPLAY "Vehicle file status = " VehicleErrStatus
          END-IF
    END-IF.

DeleteVehicleRec.
    READ VehicleFile
        INVALID KEY CONTINUE
    END-READ
    IF NoVehicleRec PERFORM WriteErrorLine
    ELSE IF VehicleFileOpOK
            DELETE VehicleFile RECORD
                INVALID KEY
                DISPLAY "Unexpected Delete Error on VehicleFile"
                DISPLAY "Vehicle file status = " VehicleErrStatus
            END-DELETE
            PERFORM UpdateStockFile
          ELSE
            DISPLAY "DeleteProblem = " VehicleErrStatus
          END-IF
    END-IF.
```

```
WriteErrorLine.
    MOVE TransRecTF TO ErrorRec
    WRITE ErrorRec.

UpdateStockFile.
    MOVE VehicleNumSF TO PrevVehicleNum
    READ StockFile KEY IS VehicleNumSF
        INVALID KEY CONTINUE
    END-READ
    IF StockFileOpOK
        SET NotEndOfStockFile TO TRUE
        PERFORM PrintStockRpt
            UNTIL VehicleNumSF NOT EQUAL TO PrevVehicleNum
                OR EndOfStockFile
    END-IF.

PrintStockRpt.
    GENERATE DetailLine
    MOVE ZEROS TO VehicleNumSF
    REWRITE StockRecSF
        INVALID KEY DISPLAY "ERROR ON REWRITE"
    END-REWRITE
    READ StockFile NEXT RECORD
        AT END SET EndOfStockFile TO TRUE
    END-READ.
```

■ ■ ■

CHAPTER 18

The COBOL Report Writer

This chapter introduces the COBOL Report Writer. In a series of increasingly complex programs, you learn how to use the Report Writer to create control-break-based report programs. By examining these programs, you are gradually introduced to the new verbs, clauses, sections and concepts of the Report Writer. You see how to use the RD entry in the REPORT SECTION to specify control-break items and define the basic layout of the page. The chapter explores report groups and how to create report groups linked to the control-break items specified in the report's RD entry. You learn how to use the SUM clause for subtotaling and rolling forward. The final program introduces declaratives and how to use them to extend the capabilities of the Report Writer. Once you've seen the capabilities of the Report Writer through the example programs, the chapter explores the verbs, clauses, and concepts of the Report Writer more formally.

Declaratives can be used to extend the capabilities of the Report Writer, but you can also use them to define exception-handling procedures for files. The final section explains how to create declaratives for file error handling.

Report Writer

Producing reports is an important aspect of business programming. Nowadays, reports may consist of rows and columns of figures and be supported by summary information in the form of a variety of charts and graphs. In the past, reports consisted solely of printed figures. You've probably seen such reports in old films, where a management person is poring over page after page of green-lined, fan-fold computer printout.

Although producing reports is important, unfortunately the report programs produced using standard COBOL print files (see Chapter 8) are often tedious to code. Report programs are long, achieving correct placement of horizontal and vertical print items is laborious, and the programs frequently consist of repetitions of the tasks and techniques (such as control-break processing) used in other report programs. In recognition of the importance of reports in the business domain, and to simplify the task of writing report programs, COBOL provides the Report Writer.

Like indexed files, the COBOL Report Writer used to be one of the jewels in COBOL's crown. But today, just as relational databases have eroded the importance of indexed files, so off-the-shelf packages such as Crystal Reports with its array of charts and graphs have put COBOL's Report Writer in the shade. Nevertheless, although summary information in the form of charts and graphs is very useful, there is still a need for printed reports; and you can learn a lot from a close acquaintance with the Report Writer.

I start by showing you an example of a report produced by the Report Writer. Then, through a series of increasingly complex report programs, you learn how to create the program that produced that report. The final example program takes the complexity one stage further.

Example Report: Solace Solar Solutions

This report shows the sales made by agents selling solar power products in each of the 50 American states. You see the program specification and the report, and then I follow up with a discussion that highlights the report's features. After discussing the report, I show you the PROCEDURE DIVISION code that produced the report.

Problem Specification

Solace Solar Solutions is a company that sells solar power products through its sales agents all over the United States. Sales agents are paid a base salary (which is different from state to state) and a commission of 8% on the value of the products they sell.

The monthly report shows the value of the individual sales and the total sales made by each Solace sales agent. The total sales made for the state and the base salary for the state are also shown. The report is printed on ascending sales agent number within ascending state name.

The report is based on a sequential sales file, which contains details of each sale made in the country. The sales file is ordered on ascending sales agent number within ascending state number. Each record of the sales file has the following description:

Field	Type	Length	Value
StateNum	9	2	1–50
SalesAgentNum	9	3	1–999
ValueOfSale	9	7	0.50–99999.99

Example Report

The first page of the example report is shown in Example 18-1. For ease of reference, I have attached line numbers to the report.

Example 18-1. Solace Solar Solutions Example Report: First Page

```
01                    Solace Solar Solutions
02          Sales Agent - Sales and Salary Report Monthly Report
03
04       State         Agent         Value
05       Name          Number        Of Sales
06       Alabama         38            $9,325.14
07                                    $11,839.19
08                                    $19,102.61
09                    Sales for sales agent  38   =   $40,266.94
10
11
12       Alabama         73            $4,503.71
13                                    $11,659.87
14                                    $19,540.19
15                    Sales for sales agent  73   =   $35,703.77
16
17                    Total sales for Alabama      $75,970.71
18                    Base salary for Alabama       $1,149.00
19       -------------------------------------------------------------
20
21
```

```
22    Alaska              55          $18,981.84
23                                     $3,065.97
24                                    $10,686.92
25                        Sales for sales agent  55   =   $32,734.73
26
27
28    Alaska              89          $11,187.72
29                                    $14,145.82
30                        Sales for sales agent  89   =   $25,333.54
31
32
33    Alaska              104         $18,005.42
34                                    $17,614.20
35                        Sales for sales agent 104   =   $35,619.62
36
37                        Total sales for Alaska       $93,687.89
38                        Base salary for Alaska        $1,536.00
39    ---------------------------------------------------------------
40
41
42    Arizona             23           $4,237.72
43
44
45
46
47
48
49    Programmer - Michael Coughlan                    Page :    1
```

Report Writer Tasks

To get a feel for what the Report Writer can do, let's examine in some detail what it has to do to produce this report:

- Print the report heading lines (lines 01–02). These are printed, once only, at the beginning of the report.

- Print the subject heading lines (page headings). These are printed at the top of each page—on lines 04–05 on the first page and lines 01–02 on subsequent pages.

- Print a footer at the bottom of each page (showing the name of the programmer and a page number: line 49). To print the page number, the Report Writer must keep a page count.

- Keep a line count, and change the page when the count is greater than 42 (unless the next thing to print is a sales agent total line, a state total line, a base salary line, or the final total line).

- Print the details of a sales agent's sales (for example, as shown for sales agent 38 on lines 06–08). Because the sales file only contains a state number, the Report Writer must get the state name from a lookup table.

- Suppress the sales agent number and state name after their first occurrence (but restore them if there is a change of page, sales agent, or state name: see lines 06, 12, 22, 28, 33, 42).

- When the sales agent number changes, print the total sales accumulated for the sales agent (lines 15, 25, 35)

- When the state number changes, print the total sales accumulated for the state (lines 17, 37).

- When the state number changes, get the base salary for the state from a lookup table, and print it (lines 18, 38).

- When the state number changes, print a line of hyphens to separate this state from the next (lines 19, 39).

Accumulate all the sales values, and print them as a final total at the end of the report (not shown on the example page).

Report Writer PROCEDURE DIVISION

If you had to create the Solace Solar Solutions sales report using the approach shown in Chapter 8 (that is, using a control-break program and the WRITE verb), you would probably write a program that had a PROCEDURE DIVISION with more than 100 lines of code. It is interesting to discover that the Report Writer can do all this work in just the 10 COBOL statements shown in Example 18-2.

Example 18-2. PROCEDURE DIVISION That Produces the Sales Report

```
PROCEDURE DIVISION.
Begin.
    OPEN INPUT SalesFile.
    OPEN OUTPUT PrintFile.
    READ SalesFile
        AT END SET EndOfFile TO TRUE
    END-READ.
    INITIATE SolaceSalesReport.
    PERFORM PrintSalaryReport
            UNTIL EndOfFile.
    TERMINATE SolaceSalesReport.
    CLOSE SalesFile, PrintFile.
    STOP RUN.

PrintSalaryReport.
    GENERATE DetailLine.
    READ SalesFile
            AT END SET EndOfFile TO TRUE
    END-READ.
```

So Much Work, So Little Code

How can so much work be done in so little PROCEDURE DIVISION code? How does the Report Writer know that page headings or page footers are required? If you wrote a program to print this report using WRITE statements, you would need a control-break program with a PERFORM UNTIL StateNum NOT EQUAL TO PrevStateNum loop to process each state and an inner loop PERFORM UNTIL SalesAgentNum NOT EQUAL TO PrevSalesAgentNum to process the sales for each sales agent. Without those loops, how does the Report Writer know it is time to print the sales agent totals or the state totals, and how does it accumulate those totals in the first place?

To achieve so much in so little PROCEDURE DIVISION code, the Report Writer uses a declarative approach to programming rather than the imperative (procedural) approach familiar to most programmers. In imperative programming, you tell the computer how to do what you want done. In declarative programming, you tell the computer what you would like done, and the computer works out how to do it. When you use the Report Writer, you declare *what* to print when a page heading, page footer, sales agent total, state total, or final total is required, and the Report Writer works out *when* to print these items. In keeping with the adage that "there is no such thing as a free lunch," the PROCEDURE DIVISION of a Report Writer program is short because most of the work is done in the (greatly expanded) DATA DIVISION.

How the Report Writer Works

The Report Writer works by recognizing that many reports take (more or less) the same shape. There may be headings at the beginning of the report and footers at the end. There may be headings at the top of each page and footers at the bottom. Headings or footers may need to be printed whenever there is a control break (that is, when the value in a specified field changes, such as when the sales agent number or state number changes in Example 18-1). In addition, the detail lines that display the information summarized in control-break totals also need to be printed.

The Report Writer calls these different report items *report groups*. Reports are organized around report groups. The Report Writer recognizes the seven types of report group shown in Example 18-3; the indentation shows their relative importance/order of execution.

Example 18-3. Report Group Types

```
REPORT HEADING or RH group
- printed once at the beginning of the report
     PAGE HEADING or PH group
     - printed at the top of each page
          CONTROL HEADING or CH group
          - printed at the beginning of each control break
               DETAIL or DE group
               - printed each time the GENERATE statement is executed
          CONTROL FOOTING or CF group
          - printed at the end of each control break
     PAGE FOOTING or PF group
     - printed at the bottom of each page
REPORT FOOTING or RF group
- printed once at the end of the report.
```

For each report, there must be a Report Description (RD) entry in the REPORT SECTION of the DATA DIVISION that fully describes the report. The report groups that describe the report are defined as records in the RD entries. Most groups are defined once for each report, but control groups are defined for each control-break item. For instance, in the example program, control footings are defined on SalesAgentNum, StateNum, and FINAL. FINAL is a special control group that is invoked before or after the normal control groups (before if CONTROL HEADING FINAL is used, and after if CONTROL FOOTING FINAL is used).

Ordinary control groups are defined on a control-break data item. The Report Writer monitors the contents of the designated data item, and when the value changes, a control break is automatically initiated. When the control break is initiated, the CONTROL FOOTING group of the breaking item (if there is one) and the CONTROL HEADING group of the next item are printed.

Writing a report program consists of a number of tedious tasks such as keeping track of the line count to ensure that page headings or footers are printed when required, or simply moving data values into their corresponding items in the print line. In addition, when you write a report according to a program specification, you often have to adhere to the report layout specified in a print layout form such as that shown in Figure 18-1. When you have to adhere to such a form, it can be tricky to get the vertical and horizontal placement of printed items correct. Counting characters to figure out what size to make each of the fields that define a print line is tedious and time consuming.

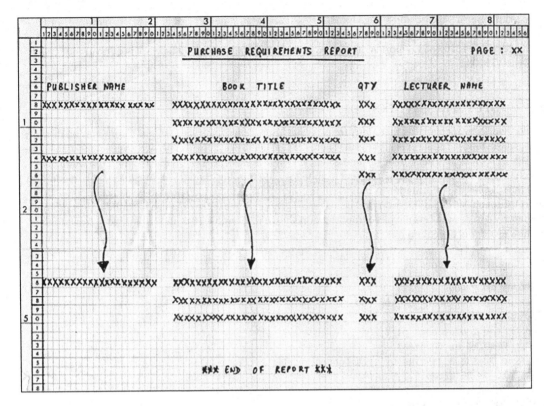

Figure 18-1. *Print layout form showing the layout required for a report*

The Report Writer makes it easier to write report programs by

- Allowing simple vertical and horizontal placement of printed items using the LINE IS and COLUMN IS phrases in the data declaration

- Automatically moving data values to output items using the SOURCE phrase

- Keeping a line count, and automatically generating report and page headers and footers at the appropriate times

- Keeping a page count that can be referenced in the report declaration

- Recognizing control breaks, and automatically generating the appropriate control headings and footers

- Automatically accumulating totals, subtotals, and final totals

Writing a Report Program

Let's see how to write a report program using the Report Writer. I start with a simplified version of the program that produced the report in Example 18-1. Succeeding examples add to it to demonstrate additional Report Writer facilities. The final example demonstrates even more than the report in Example 18-1.

Modifying the Specification

This first example program creates a report program that does the following:

- Prints a report heading

- Prints a heading and a footer on each page

- For each sale record, prints the state name (obtained from a table), the sales agent number, and the value of the sale

- Prints the total value of the sales made by each sales agent

- Prints a line of hyphens at the end of each state to separate the states from one another

The first page of the report produced by this program is shown in Example 18-4 (line numbers have been added). The program that produces the report is shown in Listing 18-1.

Example 18-4. Simplified Version of the Report Showing Only Sales Agent Totals

```
01                    Solace Solar Solutions
02           Sales Agent - Sales and Salary Report Monthly Report
03
04       State           Agent            Value
05       Name            Number          Of Sales
06       Alabama           38            $9,325.14
07       Alabama           38           $11,839.19
08       Alabama           38           $19,102.61
09                       Sales for sales agent  38   =   $40,266.94
10
11
12       Alabama           73            $4,503.71
13       Alabama           73           $11,659.87
14       Alabama           73           $19,540.19
15                       Sales for sales agent  73   =   $35,703.77
16       ---------------------------------------------------------
17
18
19       Alaska            55           $18,981.84
20       Alaska            55            $3,065.97
21       Alaska            55           $10,686.92
22                       Sales for sales agent  55   =   $32,734.73
23
24
25       Alaska            89           $11,187.72
26       Alaska            89           $14,145.82
27                       Sales for sales agent  89   =   $25,333.54
28
29
30       Alaska           104           $18,005.42
31       Alaska           104           $17,614.20
32                       Sales for sales agent 104   =   $35,619.62
33       ---------------------------------------------------------
34
35
```

```
36     Arizona          23           $4,237.72
37     Arizona          23          $13,315.00
38                      Sales for sales agent  23   =   $17,552.72
39
40
41     Arizona          90           $2,078.93
42     Arizona          90          $17,228.88
43     Arizona          90           $8,929.96
44                      Sales for sales agent  90   =   $28,237.77
45     --------------------------------------------------------
46
47
48
49     Programmer - Michael Coughlan                  Page :    1
```

Listing 18-1. Simplified Report Program

```
IDENTIFICATION DIVISION.
PROGRAM-ID.  Listing18-1.
AUTHOR.  Michael Coughlan.

ENVIRONMENT DIVISION.
INPUT-OUTPUT SECTION.
FILE-CONTROL.
    SELECT SalesFile ASSIGN TO "Listing18-1-Sales.DAT"
           ORGANIZATION IS LINE SEQUENTIAL.

    SELECT PrintFile ASSIGN TO "Listing18-1.Rpt".

DATA DIVISION.
FILE SECTION.
FD  SalesFile.
01  SalesRecord.
    88 EndOfFile   VALUE HIGH-VALUES.
    02 StateNum         PIC 99.
    02 SalesAgentNum    PIC 999.
    02 ValueOfSale      PIC 9(5)V99.

FD  PrintFile
    REPORT IS SolaceSalesReport.

WORKING-STORAGE SECTION.
01  StateNameTable.
    02 StateNameValues.
       03 FILLER  PIC X(14) VALUE "Alabama".
       03 FILLER  PIC X(14) VALUE "Alaska".
       03 FILLER  PIC X(14) VALUE "Arizona".
       03 FILLER  PIC X(14) VALUE "Arkansas".
       03 FILLER  PIC X(14) VALUE "California".
       03 FILLER  PIC X(14) VALUE "Colorado".
       03 FILLER  PIC X(14) VALUE "Connecticut".
       03 FILLER  PIC X(14) VALUE "Delaware".
       03 FILLER  PIC X(14) VALUE "Florida".
       03 FILLER  PIC X(14) VALUE "Georgia".
```

```
        03 FILLER  PIC X(14) VALUE "Hawaii".
        03 FILLER  PIC X(14) VALUE "Idaho".
        03 FILLER  PIC X(14) VALUE "Illinois".
        03 FILLER  PIC X(14) VALUE "Indiana".
        03 FILLER  PIC X(14) VALUE "Iowa".
        03 FILLER  PIC X(14) VALUE "Kansas".
        03 FILLER  PIC X(14) VALUE "Kentucky".
        03 FILLER  PIC X(14) VALUE "Louisiana".
        03 FILLER  PIC X(14) VALUE "Maine".
        03 FILLER  PIC X(14) VALUE "Maryland".
        03 FILLER  PIC X(14) VALUE "Massachusetts".
        03 FILLER  PIC X(14) VALUE "Michigan".
        03 FILLER  PIC X(14) VALUE "Minnesota".
        03 FILLER  PIC X(14) VALUE "Mississippi".
        03 FILLER  PIC X(14) VALUE "Missouri".
        03 FILLER  PIC X(14) VALUE "Montana".
        03 FILLER  PIC X(14) VALUE "Nebraska".
        03 FILLER  PIC X(14) VALUE "Nevada".
        03 FILLER  PIC X(14) VALUE "New Hampshire".
        03 FILLER  PIC X(14) VALUE "New Jersey".
        03 FILLER  PIC X(14) VALUE "New Mexico".
        03 FILLER  PIC X(14) VALUE "New York".
        03 FILLER  PIC X(14) VALUE "North Carolina".
        03 FILLER  PIC X(14) VALUE "North Dakota".
        03 FILLER  PIC X(14) VALUE "Ohio".
        03 FILLER  PIC X(14) VALUE "Oklahoma".
        03 FILLER  PIC X(14) VALUE "Oregon".
        03 FILLER  PIC X(14) VALUE "Pennsylvania".
        03 FILLER  PIC X(14) VALUE "Rhode Island".
        03 FILLER  PIC X(14) VALUE "South Carolina".
        03 FILLER  PIC X(14) VALUE "South Dakota".
        03 FILLER  PIC X(14) VALUE "Tennessee".
        03 FILLER  PIC X(14) VALUE "Texas".
        03 FILLER  PIC X(14) VALUE "Utah".
        03 FILLER  PIC X(14) VALUE "Vermont".
        03 FILLER  PIC X(14) VALUE "Virginia".
        03 FILLER  PIC X(14) VALUE "Washington".
        03 FILLER  PIC X(14) VALUE "West Virginia".
        03 FILLER  PIC X(14) VALUE "Wisconsin".
        03 FILLER  PIC X(14) VALUE "Wyoming".
    02 FILLER REDEFINES StateNameValues.
        03 State OCCURS 50 TIMES.
            04 StateName  PIC X(14).

REPORT SECTION.
RD  SolaceSalesReport
    CONTROLS ARE StateNum
                 SalesAgentNum
    PAGE LIMIT IS 54
    FIRST DETAIL 3
    LAST DETAIL 46
    FOOTING 48.
```

```
01   TYPE IS REPORT HEADING NEXT GROUP PlUS 1.
        02 LINE 1.
            03 COLUMN 20     PIC X(32)
                             VALUE "Solace Solar Solutions".

        02 LINE 2.
            03 COLUMN 6      PIC X(51)
                 VALUE "Sales Agent - Sales and Salary Report Monthly Report".

01   TYPE IS PAGE HEADING.
        02 LINE IS PLUS 1.
            03 COLUMN 2      PIC X(5)  VALUE "State".
            03 COLUMN 16     PIC X(5)  VALUE "Agent".
            03 COLUMN 32     PIC X(8)  VALUE "Value".

        02 LINE IS PLUS 1.
            03 COLUMN 2      PIC X(4)  VALUE "Name".
            03 COLUMN 16     PIC X(6)  VALUE "Number".
            03 COLUMN 31     PIC X(8)  VALUE "Of Sales".

01   DetailLine TYPE IS DETAIL.
        02 LINE IS PLUS 1.
            03 COLUMN 1      PIC X(14)
                             SOURCE StateName(StateNum).
            03 COLUMN 17     PIC ZZ9
                             SOURCE SalesAgentNum.
            03 COLUMN 30     PIC $$$,$$$.99 SOURCE ValueOfSale.

01   SalesAgentGrp
        TYPE IS CONTROL FOOTING SalesAgentNum  NEXT GROUP PLUS 2.
        02 LINE IS PLUS 1.
            03 COLUMN 15     PIC X(21) VALUE "Sales for sales agent".
            03 COLUMN 37     PIC ZZ9 SOURCE SalesAgentNum.
            03 COLUMN 43     PIC X VALUE "=".
            03 TotalAgentSales COLUMN 45 PIC $$$$$,$$$.99 SUM ValueOfSale.

01   StateGrp TYPE IS CONTROL FOOTING StateNum NEXT GROUP PLUS 2.
        02 LINE IS PLUS 1.
            03 COLUMN 1      PIC X(58) VALUE ALL "-".

01   TYPE IS PAGE FOOTING.
        02 LINE IS 49.
            03 COLUMN 1      PIC X(29) VALUE "Programmer - Michael Coughlan".
            03 COLUMN 55     PIC X(6) VALUE "Page :".
            03 COLUMN 62     PIC ZZ9 SOURCE PAGE-COUNTER.

PROCEDURE DIVISION.
Begin.
     OPEN INPUT SalesFile.
     OPEN OUTPUT PrintFile.
     READ SalesFile
         AT END SET EndOfFile TO TRUE
     END-READ.
```

```
      INITIATE SolaceSalesReport.
      PERFORM PrintSalaryReport
            UNTIL EndOfFile.
      TERMINATE SolaceSalesReport.
      CLOSE SalesFile, PrintFile.
      STOP RUN.

  PrintSalaryReport.
      GENERATE DetailLine.
      READ SalesFile
            AT END SET EndOfFile TO TRUE
      END-READ.
```

The first thing to note is that the PROCEDURE DIVISION for this program is the same as for the program that produced the report in Example 18-1. This is your first indication that most of the work is being done in the DATA DIVISION. As I add complexity to the program in the succeeding examples, eventually I have to make some changes to the PROCEDURE DIVISION code.

The second thing to note is that just like an ordinary print file, a Report Writer file must have a SELECT and ASSIGN clause in the ENVIRONMENT DIVISION and an FD entry in the DATA DIVISION. But look at the FD entry. Instead of a record description, you have a REPORT IS SolaceSalesReport entry. This entry tells you that the Report Writer is being used and that this particular report is called SolaceSalesReport. This entry links the PrintFile with the report described in the REPORT SECTION. That is the next thing to note; when you use the Report Writer, you describe the report in the REPORT SECTION.

The first entry in the REPORT SECTION is the RD entry, which is followed by the name of the report. This is the same name you use in the REPORT IS entry in the FD entry of the PrintFile. The RD entry has a number of clauses. The first is the CONTROLS ARE clause, which allows you to identify the control-break item(s) that the Report Writer must monitor in order to detect a control break. These entries usually identify fields in an input file, but they don't have to. The remaining RD clauses specify information about the page, such as the size of the page, the first line where a detail line may be printed, and the line after which the footer may be printed.

The remaining entries identify the required report groups. Each report group is a record and must start with a 01 level number. As noted in Example 18-3, there are seven possible types of report groups, and the first entry in the report group must specify the type of the group. Listing 18-1 has the following report groups:

- A REPORT HEADING group that specifies what is to be printed at the start of the report.

- A PAGE HEADING group that specifies what is to be printed at the top of each page.

- A DETAIL group that specifies what is to be printed for each sales record.

- CONTROL FOOTING groups for the SalesAgentNum control-break item and the StateNum control-break item. These groups specify what is printed when a control break occurs on SalesAgentNum or StateNum.

- A PAGE FOOTING group that specifies what is to be printed at the bottom of each page.

Report Groups

Let's look at some of the entries in these report groups in more detail. The REPORT HEADING group is of interest because it demonstrates absolute position using the LINE clause. It also demonstrates the COLUMN clause, which you use to specify the horizontal placement of the material to be printed. The final item of interest in this group is the NEXT GROUP PLUS clause, which specifies that the next group will start one line down from this group. Although, as you see with the PAGE HEADING group, you can specify vertical placement using a relative reference rather than an absolute line number, that is not always sufficient for all your positioning needs. Sometimes you require a combination of the NEXT GROUP PLUS and the LINE IS PLUS clauses.

You might think that the PAGE HEADING group would also use absolute positioning, but in this example, the page headings are not printed on the same line on every page. On the first page, they are printed after the report heading lines; but on the other pages, they are printed on the first line. For this reason, LINE IS PLUS relative positioning is used for this group. Because the other groups, except the PAGE FOOTING group, are also printed on different lines on the page, they also use LINE IS PLUS relative positioning.

The main clause of interest in the DETAIL report group is the SOURCE clause. This clause specifies that the data for this print item is to come from some source data item. This is how the Report Writer gets values for the state name (from the table), the sales agent number, and the value of the sale.

SalesAgentGrp is a CONTROL FOOTING group. It is printed whenever there is a control break on SalesAgentNum. When you create a CONTROL group, you have to associate the group with a control item mentioned in the RD..CONTROLS ARE phrase. This is how the Report Write associates a particular control-break item with a CONTROL HEADING or FOOTING group. At the moment, this group only prints a line of hyphens; but the next program uses it to accumulate and print the total sales agent sales.

The final group to consider is the PAGE FOOTING group. The item of interest in this group is PAGE-COUNTER, which is identified as the source of the page number printed in this footer. PAGE-COUNTER is a special Report Writer register that automatically keeps a count of the pages printed.

PROCEDURE DIVISION Notes

Now that you have seen the role played by the DATA DIVISION entries in producing the report, you need to know how the report is driven from the PROCEDURE DIVISION. The Report Writer introduces three new verbs: INITIATE, GENERATE, and TERMINATE.

When the INITIATE verb is executed, all the heading groups, such as REPORT HEADING and the first PAGE HEADING, are produced. All the system registers, such as PAGE-COUNTER, are set to their starting values.

When the TERMINATE verb is executed, all the relevant FOOTING groups, such as REPORT FOOTING and the last PAGE FOOTING, are produced.

The report is driven by the GENERATE verb. GENERATE is normally associated either with the DETAIL group (as it is in this example) or with the report name. When GENERATE is associated with a DETAIL group, each time the GENERATE statement is executed, the DETAIL group is printed. Obviously this makes sense only if each time GENERATE executes, the DETAIL group is fed new data. In this program, the new data is provided by reading the sales file.

Adding Features to the Report Program

Let's add some features to the Solace Sales Report program. Let's change the program so that the report now shows the total sales for the sales agent, total sales for the state, and a final total for the country. The report should also show the base salary paid to sales agents in each state. To do this, the state table has to be modified to include the salary information. One final thing needs to change. If you look at the report in Example 18-4, you see that each line that prints a sales value also prints the state name and the sales agent number. This looks unsightly. The state name and the sales agent number should be suppressed after their first occurrence. Instead of this

```
04      State       Agent        Value
05      Name        Number       Of Sales
06      Alabama       38         $9,325.14
07      Alabama       38         $11,839.19
08      Alabama       38         $19,102.61
09                 Sales for sales agent  38   =   $40,266.94
```

the report should print this:

```
04      State       Agent           Value
05      Name        Number          Of Sales
06      Alabama       38            $9,325.14
07                                 $11,839.19
08                                 $19,102.61
09                  Sales for sales agent  38   =   $40,266.94
```

You probably have realized by now that these specification changes are satisfied by the report shown in Example 18-1. Listing 18-2 is the program that produced that report.

Listing 18-2. Program to Create a Report with Sales Totals

```cobol
IDENTIFICATION DIVISION.
PROGRAM-ID.  Listing18-2.
AUTHOR.  Michael Coughlan.


ENVIRONMENT DIVISION.
INPUT-OUTPUT SECTION.
FILE-CONTROL.
    SELECT SalesFile ASSIGN TO "Listing18-2-Sales.DAT"
           ORGANIZATION IS LINE SEQUENTIAL.

    SELECT PrintFile ASSIGN TO "Listing18-2.Rpt".

DATA DIVISION.
FILE SECTION.
FD  SalesFile.
01  SalesRecord.
    88 EndOfFile   VALUE HIGH-VALUES.
    02 StateNum        PIC 99.
    02 SalesAgentNum   PIC 999.
    02 ValueOfSale     PIC 9(5)V99.

FD  PrintFile
    REPORT IS SolaceSalesReport.

WORKING-STORAGE SECTION.
01  StateNameTable.
    02 StateNameValues.
       03 FILLER  PIC X(18) VALUE "1149Alabama".
       03 FILLER  PIC X(18) VALUE "1536Alaska".
       03 FILLER  PIC X(18) VALUE "1284Arizona".
       03 FILLER  PIC X(18) VALUE "1064Arkansas".
       03 FILLER  PIC X(18) VALUE "1459California".
       03 FILLER  PIC X(18) VALUE "1508Colorado".
       03 FILLER  PIC X(18) VALUE "1742Connecticut".
       03 FILLER  PIC X(18) VALUE "1450Delaware".
       03 FILLER  PIC X(18) VALUE "1328Florida".
       03 FILLER  PIC X(18) VALUE "1257Georgia".
```

```
         03 FILLER  PIC X(18) VALUE "1444Hawaii".
         03 FILLER  PIC X(18) VALUE "1126Idaho".
         03 FILLER  PIC X(18) VALUE "1439Illinois".
         03 FILLER  PIC X(18) VALUE "1203Indiana".
         03 FILLER  PIC X(18) VALUE "1267Iowa".
         03 FILLER  PIC X(18) VALUE "1295Kansas".
         03 FILLER  PIC X(18) VALUE "1126Kentucky".
         03 FILLER  PIC X(18) VALUE "1155Louisiana".
         03 FILLER  PIC X(18) VALUE "1269Maine".
         03 FILLER  PIC X(18) VALUE "1839Maryland".
         03 FILLER  PIC X(18) VALUE "1698Massachusetts".
         03 FILLER  PIC X(18) VALUE "1257Michigan".
         03 FILLER  PIC X(18) VALUE "1479Minnesota".
         03 FILLER  PIC X(18) VALUE "0999Mississippi".
         03 FILLER  PIC X(18) VALUE "1236Missouri".
         03 FILLER  PIC X(18) VALUE "1192Montana".
         03 FILLER  PIC X(18) VALUE "1261Nebraska".
         03 FILLER  PIC X(18) VALUE "1379Nevada".
         03 FILLER  PIC X(18) VALUE "1571New Hampshire".
         03 FILLER  PIC X(18) VALUE "1743New Jersey".
         03 FILLER  PIC X(18) VALUE "1148New Mexico".
         03 FILLER  PIC X(18) VALUE "1547New York".
         03 FILLER  PIC X(18) VALUE "1237North Carolina".
         03 FILLER  PIC X(18) VALUE "1290North Dakota".
         03 FILLER  PIC X(18) VALUE "1256Ohio".
         03 FILLER  PIC X(18) VALUE "1155Oklahoma".
         03 FILLER  PIC X(18) VALUE "1309Oregon".
         03 FILLER  PIC X(18) VALUE "1352Pennsylvania".
         03 FILLER  PIC X(18) VALUE "1435Rhode Island".
         03 FILLER  PIC X(18) VALUE "1172South Carolina".
         03 FILLER  PIC X(18) VALUE "1206South Dakota".
         03 FILLER  PIC X(18) VALUE "1186Tennessee".
         03 FILLER  PIC X(18) VALUE "1244Texas".
         03 FILLER  PIC X(18) VALUE "1157Utah".
         03 FILLER  PIC X(18) VALUE "1374Vermont".
         03 FILLER  PIC X(18) VALUE "1607Virginia".
         03 FILLER  PIC X(18) VALUE "1487Washington".
         03 FILLER  PIC X(18) VALUE "1062West Virginia".
         03 FILLER  PIC X(18) VALUE "1393Wisconsin".
         03 FILLER  PIC X(18) VALUE "1393Wyoming".
 02 FILLER REDEFINES StateNameValues.
         03 State OCCURS 50 TIMES.
             04 BaseSalary  PIC 9(4).
             04 StateName   PIC X(14).


 REPORT SECTION..
 RD  SolaceSalesReport
     CONTROLS ARE FINAL
                   StateNum
                   SalesAgentNum
```

```
        PAGE LIMIT IS 54
        FIRST DETAIL 3
        LAST DETAIL 42
        FOOTING 48.


01   TYPE IS REPORT HEADING NEXT GROUP PlUS 1.
        02 LINE 1.
           03 COLUMN 20      PIC X(32)
                             VALUE "Solace Solar Solutions".


        02 LINE 2.
           03 COLUMN 6      PIC X(51)
              VALUE "Sales Agent - Sales and Salary Report Monthly Report".


01   TYPE IS PAGE HEADING.
        02 LINE IS PLUS 1.
           03 COLUMN 2      PIC X(5)  VALUE "State".
           03 COLUMN 16     PIC X(5)  VALUE "Agent".
           03 COLUMN 32     PIC X(8)  VALUE "Value".


        02 LINE IS PLUS 1.
           03 COLUMN 2      PIC X(4)  VALUE "Name".
           03 COLUMN 16     PIC X(6)  VALUE "Number".
           03 COLUMN 31     PIC X(8)  VALUE "Of Sales".


01   DetailLine TYPE IS DETAIL.
        02 LINE IS PLUS 1.
           03 COLUMN 1      PIC X(14)
                            SOURCE StateName(StateNum) GROUP INDICATE.
           03 COLUMN 17     PIC ZZ9
                            SOURCE SalesAgentNum   GROUP INDICATE.
           03 COLUMN 30     PIC $$$,$$$.99 SOURCE ValueOfSale.


01   SalesAgentGrp
        TYPE IS CONTROL FOOTING SalesAgentNum  NEXT GROUP PLUS 2.
        02 LINE IS PLUS 1.
           03 COLUMN 15     PIC X(21) VALUE "Sales for sales agent".
           03 COLUMN 37     PIC ZZ9 SOURCE SalesAgentNum.
           03 COLUMN 43     PIC X VALUE "=".
           03 TotalAgentSales COLUMN 45 PIC $$$$,$$$.99 SUM ValueOfSale.


01   StateGrp TYPE IS CONTROL FOOTING StateNum NEXT GROUP PLUS 2.
        02 LINE IS PLUS 2.
           03 COLUMN 15      PIC X(15) VALUE "Total sales for".
           03 COLUMN 31      PIC X(14) SOURCE StateName(StateNum).
           03 TotalStateSales COLUMN 45  PIC $$$$,$$$.99 SUM TotalAgentSales.


        02 LINE IS PLUS 1.
           03 COLUMN 15      PIC X(15) VALUE "Base salary for".
           03 COLUMN 31      PIC X(14) SOURCE StateName(StateNum).
           03 COLUMN 48      PIC $$,$$$.99 SOURCE BaseSalary(StateNum).
```

```
        02 LINE IS PLUS 1.
           03 COLUMN 1      PIC X(58) VALUE ALL "-".

01  TotalSalesGrp TYPE IS CONTROL FOOTING FINAL.
        02 LINE IS PLUS 2.
           03 COLUMN 15     PIC X(11)
                            VALUE "Total sales".
           03 COLUMN 46     PIC X VALUE "=".
           03 COLUMN 48     PIC $$,$$$,$$$.99 SUM TotalStateSales.

01  TYPE IS PAGE FOOTING.
        02 LINE IS 49.
           03 COLUMN 1      PIC X(29) VALUE "Programmer - Michael Coughlan".
           03 COLUMN 55     PIC X(6) VALUE "Page :".
           03 COLUMN 62     PIC ZZ9 SOURCE PAGE-COUNTER.


PROCEDURE DIVISION.
Begin.
    OPEN INPUT SalesFile.
    OPEN OUTPUT PrintFile.
    READ SalesFile
        AT END SET EndOfFile TO TRUE
    END-READ.
    INITIATE SolaceSalesReport.
    PERFORM PrintSalaryReport
            UNTIL EndOfFile.
    TERMINATE SolaceSalesReport.
    CLOSE SalesFile, PrintFile.
    STOP RUN.


PrintSalaryReport.
    GENERATE DetailLine.
    READ SalesFile
        AT END SET EndOfFile TO TRUE
    END-READ.
```

Let's look at the changes. The major differences between Listing 18-1 and Listing 18-2 are shown in bold. The PROCEDURE DIVISION has not changed. But there is a new control group: in order to print the final total for the country, a CONTROL FOOTING group is required. This control group is controlled by a special control item called FINAL. Note that now the CONTROLS ARE phrase in the report's RD contains the word FINAL. The FINAL control-break item activates when the report is terminated. You should also take note of the *order* of the control-break items in the CONTROLS ARE phrase. FINAL is the major control break, StateNum is next in importance, and SalesAgentNum is the least important. A break on a major control item causes a break on all the subordinate control items.

If you examine the report in Example 18-5, you'll see that now StateName and SalesAgentNum are suppressed after their first occurrence. This is done by specifying the GROUP INDICATE clause for the data item.

Another change to the program was required to accumulate and print the total sales for the sales agent. The Report Writer has three ways of incrementing totals: subtotaling, rolling forward, and crossfooting. All these methods use the SUM clause but target different types of data item. *Subtotaling* targets data items in the FILE SECTION or the WORKING-STORAGE SECTION. *Rolling forward* targets data items in a subordinate CONTROL FOOTING group. *Crossfooting* targets data items in the same group. This example uses subtotaling and rolling forward.

Subtotaling is used in SalesAgentGrp to sum the sales made by the agent. A SUM clause is used that targets the ValueOfSale data item so that every time a GENERATE statement is executed, the current value of ValueOfSale is added to a sum counter. When the control break occurs, the CONTROL FOOTING group activates, and the value accumulated in the sum counter is printed.

There is something else here that you note. As you have no doubt noticed, in the REPORT SECTION you don't have to follow a level number with a data-item name or even the word FILLER. This saves a lot of unnecessary work. But you can include a name if you want to. In the SalesAgentGrp, I have included the name TotalAgentSales. The reason for naming this item is shown in the StateGrp CONTROL FOOTING group, where it is used as the target of the SUM clause. Every time there is a control break on SalesAgentNum, the current value of TotalAgentSales is added to the sum counter in StateGrp. When there is a control break on StateNum, the accumulated value of the sum counter is printed. This is an example of rolling forward.

Rolling forward is also used with TotalStateSales in StateGrp. TotalStateSales is used as the target of the SUM clause in TotalSalesGrp to sum each state total into a final total. When the TERMINATE statement is executed, the final total is printed.

Adding More Features to the Report Program

In the specification at the start of this section, I mentioned that Solace sales agents are paid a base salary and a commission of 8% on the value of the products they sell. In Listing 18-3, each time the total sales for an agent are printed, the commission they have earned and their total salary (base salary + commission) should also be printed. The first page of the report produced by Listing 18-3 is shown in Example 18-5.

Listing 18-3. Adding the Sales Agent Commission and Salary to the Report

```
IDENTIFICATION DIVISION.
PROGRAM-ID.  Listing18-3.
AUTHOR.  Michael Coughlan.


ENVIRONMENT DIVISION.
INPUT-OUTPUT SECTION.
FILE-CONTROL.
    SELECT SalesFile ASSIGN TO "Listing18-3-Sales.DAT"
           ORGANIZATION IS LINE SEQUENTIAL.

    SELECT PrintFile ASSIGN TO "Listing18-3.Rpt".

DATA DIVISION.
FILE SECTION.
FD  SalesFile.
01  SalesRecord.
    88 EndOfFile  VALUE HIGH-VALUES.
    02 StateNum        PIC 99.
    02 SalesAgentNum   PIC 999.
    02 ValueOfSale     PIC 9(5)V99.

FD  PrintFile
    REPORT IS SolaceSalesReport.
```

```
WORKING-STORAGE SECTION.
01  StateNameTable.
O   02 StateNameValues.
        03 FILLER  PIC X(18) VALUE "1149Alabama".
        03 FILLER  PIC X(18) VALUE "1536Alaska".
        03 FILLER  PIC X(18) VALUE "1284Arizona".
        03 FILLER  PIC X(18) VALUE "1064Arkansas".
        03 FILLER  PIC X(18) VALUE "1459California".
        03 FILLER  PIC X(18) VALUE "1508Colorado".
        03 FILLER  PIC X(18) VALUE "1742Connecticut".
        03 FILLER  PIC X(18) VALUE "1450Delaware".
        03 FILLER  PIC X(18) VALUE "1328Florida".
        03 FILLER  PIC X(18) VALUE "1257Georgia".
        03 FILLER  PIC X(18) VALUE "1444Hawaii".
        03 FILLER  PIC X(18) VALUE "1126Idaho".
        03 FILLER  PIC X(18) VALUE "1439Illinois".
        03 FILLER  PIC X(18) VALUE "1203Indiana".
        03 FILLER  PIC X(18) VALUE "1267Iowa".
        03 FILLER  PIC X(18) VALUE "1295Kansas".
        03 FILLER  PIC X(18) VALUE "1126Kentucky".
        03 FILLER  PIC X(18) VALUE "1155Louisiana".
        03 FILLER  PIC X(18) VALUE "1269Maine".
        03 FILLER  PIC X(18) VALUE "1839Maryland".
        03 FILLER  PIC X(18) VALUE "1698Massachusetts".
        03 FILLER  PIC X(18) VALUE "1257Michigan".
        03 FILLER  PIC X(18) VALUE "1479Minnesota".
        03 FILLER  PIC X(18) VALUE "0999Mississippi".
        03 FILLER  PIC X(18) VALUE "1236Missouri".
        03 FILLER  PIC X(18) VALUE "1192Montana".
        03 FILLER  PIC X(18) VALUE "1261Nebraska".
        03 FILLER  PIC X(18) VALUE "1379Nevada".
        03 FILLER  PIC X(18) VALUE "1571New Hampshire".
        03 FILLER  PIC X(18) VALUE "1743New Jersey".
        03 FILLER  PIC X(18) VALUE "1148New Mexico".
        03 FILLER  PIC X(18) VALUE "1547New York".
        03 FILLER  PIC X(18) VALUE "1237North Carolina".
        03 FILLER  PIC X(18) VALUE "1290North Dakota".
        03 FILLER  PIC X(18) VALUE "1256Ohio".
        03 FILLER  PIC X(18) VALUE "1155Oklahoma".
        03 FILLER  PIC X(18) VALUE "1309Oregon".
        03 FILLER  PIC X(18) VALUE "1352Pennsylvania".
        03 FILLER  PIC X(18) VALUE "1435Rhode Island".
        03 FILLER  PIC X(18) VALUE "1172South Carolina".
        03 FILLER  PIC X(18) VALUE "1206South Dakota".
        03 FILLER  PIC X(18) VALUE "1186Tennessee".
        03 FILLER  PIC X(18) VALUE "1244Texas".
        03 FILLER  PIC X(18) VALUE "1157Utah".
        03 FILLER  PIC X(18) VALUE "1374Vermont".
        03 FILLER  PIC X(18) VALUE "1607Virginia".
        03 FILLER  PIC X(18) VALUE "1487Washington".
        03 FILLER  PIC X(18) VALUE "1062West Virginia".
```

```
        03 FILLER  PIC X(18) VALUE "1393Wisconsin".
        03 FILLER  PIC X(18) VALUE "1393Wyoming".
    02 FILLER REDEFINES StateNameValues.
        03 State OCCURS 50 TIMES.
            04 BaseSalary  PIC 9(4).
            04 StateName   PIC X(14).

01  MiscVariables.
    02 SalesCommission  PIC 9(5)V99.
    02 Percentage       PIC V99 VALUE .08.
    02 FullSalary       PIC 9(6)V99.
    02 ActualStateNum   PIC 99.

REPORT SECTION.
RD  SolaceSalesReport
    CONTROLS ARE FINAL
                StateNum
                SalesAgentNum
    PAGE LIMIT IS 66
    HEADING 1
    FIRST DETAIL 6
    LAST DETAIL 54
    FOOTING 56.

01  TYPE IS PAGE HEADING.
    02 LINE 1.
        03 COLUMN 20    PIC X(32)
                        VALUE "Solace Solar Solutions".

    02 LINE 2.
        03 COLUMN 6     PIC X(51)
            VALUE "Sales Agent - Sales and Salary Report Monthly Report".

    02 LINE 4.
        03 COLUMN 2     PIC X(5)  VALUE "State".
        03 COLUMN 16    PIC X(5)  VALUE "Agent".
        03 COLUMN 32    PIC X(8)  VALUE "Value".

    02 LINE 5.
        03 COLUMN 2     PIC X(4)  VALUE "Name".
        03 COLUMN 16    PIC X(6)  VALUE "Number".
        03 COLUMN 31    PIC X(8)  VALUE "Of Sales".

01  DetailLine TYPE IS DETAIL.
    02 LINE IS PLUS 1.
        03 COLUMN 1     PIC X(14)
                        SOURCE StateName(StateNum) GROUP INDICATE.
        03 COLUMN 17    PIC 999
                        SOURCE SalesAgentNum  GROUP INDICATE.
        03 COLUMN 30    PIC $$$,$$$.99 SOURCE ValueOfSale.
```

```
01  SalesAgentGrp
    TYPE IS CONTROL FOOTING SalesAgentNum  NEXT GROUP PLUS 2.
    02 LINE IS PLUS 1.
       03 COLUMN 15     PIC X(21) VALUE "Sales for sales agent".
       03 COLUMN 37     PIC 999 SOURCE SalesAgentNum.
       03 COLUMN 43     PIC X VALUE "=".
       03 TotalAgentSales COLUMN 45 PIC $$$$$,$$$.99 SUM ValueOfSale.

    02 LINE IS PLUS 1.
       03 COLUMN 15     PIC X(19) VALUE "Sales commission is".
       03 COLUMN 43     PIC X VALUE "=".
       03 COLUMN 45     PIC $$$$$,$$$.99 SOURCE SalesCommission.

    02 LINE IS PLUS 1.
       03 COLUMN 15     PIC X(22) VALUE "Sales agent salary is".
       03 COLUMN 43     PIC X VALUE "=".
       03 COLUMN 45     PIC $$$$$,$$$.99 SOURCE FullSalary.

01  StateGrp TYPE IS CONTROL FOOTING StateNum NEXT GROUP PLUS 2.
    02 LINE IS PLUS 2.
       03 COLUMN 15     PIC X(15) VALUE "Total sales for".
       03 COLUMN 31     PIC X(14) SOURCE StateName(StateNum).
       03 TotalStateSales COLUMN 45  PIC $$$$$,$$$.99 SUM TotalAgentSales.

    02 LINE IS PLUS 1.
       03 COLUMN 15     PIC X(15) VALUE "Base salary for".
       03 COLUMN 31     PIC X(14) SOURCE StateName(StateNum).
       03 COLUMN 48     PIC $$,$$$.99 SOURCE BaseSalary(StateNum).

    02 LINE IS PLUS 1.
       03 COLUMN 15     PIC X(26)
                        VALUE "Actual state number is    -".
       03 COLUMN 42     PIC Z9 SOURCE ActualStateNum.

    02 LINE IS PLUS 1.
       03 COLUMN 15     PIC X(26)
                        VALUE "Supplied state number is -".
       03 COLUMN 42     PIC Z9 SOURCE StateNum.

    02 LINE IS PLUS 1.
       03 COLUMN 1      PIC X(58) VALUE ALL "-".

01  TotalSalesGrp TYPE IS CONTROL FOOTING FINAL.
    02 LINE IS PLUS 4.
       03 COLUMN 15     PIC X(11)
                        VALUE "Total sales".
       03 COLUMN 46     PIC X VALUE "=".
       03 COLUMN 48     PIC $$,$$$,$$$.99 SUM TotalStateSales.
```

```
01  TYPE IS PAGE FOOTING.
    02 LINE IS 58.
        03 COLUMN 1      PIC X(29) VALUE "Programmer - Michael Coughlan".
        03 COLUMN 55     PIC X(6) VALUE "Page :".
        03 COLUMN 62     PIC ZZ9 SOURCE PAGE-COUNTER.


PROCEDURE DIVISION.
DECLARATIVES.
Calc SECTION.
    USE BEFORE REPORTING SalesAgentGrp.
Calculate-Salary.
    MULTIPLY TotalAgentSales BY Percentage
        GIVING SalesCommission ROUNDED
    ADD SalesCommission, BaseSalary(StateNum)
        GIVING FullSalary.
END DECLARATIVES.

Main SECTION.
Begin.
    OPEN INPUT SalesFile
    OPEN OUTPUT PrintFile
    READ SalesFile
        AT END SET EndOfFile TO TRUE
    END-READ
    INITIATE SolaceSalesReport
    PERFORM PrintSalaryReport
        UNTIL EndOfFile
    TERMINATE SolaceSalesReport
    CLOSE SalesFile, PrintFile
    STOP RUN.


PrintSalaryReport.
    GENERATE DetailLine
    READ SalesFile
        AT END SET EndOfFile TO TRUE
    END-READ
    MOVE StateNum  TO ActualStateNum.
```

Example 18-5. Report Showing Commission Earned and Total Salary

```
                Solace Solar Solutions
    Sales Agent - Sales and Salary Report Monthly Report


State           Agent           Value
Name            Number          Of Sales
Alabama         038               $9,325.14
                                 $11,839.19
                                 $19,102.61
                Sales for sales agent 038  =   $40,266.94
                Sales commission is        =    $3,221.36
                Sales agent salary is      =    $4,370.36
```

```
Alabama          073            $4,503.71
                               $11,659.87
                               $19,540.19
                 Sales for sales agent 073   =   $35,703.77
                 Sales commission is          =    $2,856.30
                 Sales agent salary is        =    $4,005.30

                 Total sales for Alabama          $75,970.71
                 Base salary for Alabama           $1,149.00
                 Actual state number is    -  2
                 Supplied state number is -  1
-------------------------------------------------------------

Alaska           055           $18,981.84
                                $3,065.97
                               $10,686.92
                 Sales for sales agent 055   =   $32,734.73
                 Sales commission is          =    $2,618.78
                 Sales agent salary is        =    $4,154.78

Alaska           089           $11,187.72
                               $14,145.82
                 Sales for sales agent 089   =   $25,333.54
                 Sales commission is          =    $2,026.68
                 Sales agent salary is        =    $3,562.68

Alaska           104           $18,005.42
                               $17,614.20
                 Sales for sales agent 104   =   $35,619.62
                 Sales commission is          =    $2,849.57
                 Sales agent salary is        =    $4,385.57

                 Total sales for Alaska           $93,687.89
                 Base salary for Alaska            $1,536.00
                 Actual state number is    -  3
                 Supplied state number is -  2
-------------------------------------------------------------

Programmer - Michael Coughlan                 Page :    1
```

The major differences between Listing 18-2 and Listing 18-3 are shown in bold. To print the agent commission and total salary, I have added a number of entries to SalesAgentGrp. Note, though, that the sources of these items are data items declared outside the REPORT SECTION. The reason is that these items require calculations beyond what the Report Writer can handle automatically. To calculate these items, you must use declaratives. I discuss declaratives presently; but for now, I want to discuss another issue.

Look at the StateGrp CONTROL FOOTING and in particular at these lines:

```
03 COLUMN 31    PIC X(14) SOURCE StateName(StateNum).
03 COLUMN 48    PIC $$,$$$.99 SOURCE BaseSalary(StateNum).
```

Notice anything strange? This footer is printed when there is a control break on StateNum—in other words, when the value of StateNum changes. This means StateNum in the previous lines should refer to the next state and not the one for which the totals have just been accumulated. And yet, if you examine the report, you see that the correct state name and base salary are printed. How can this be? Remember this:

> In a CONTROL FOOTING or in the DECLARATIVES SECTION, when a control data item is referenced, the value supplied is the previous value and not the value that has just caused the control break.

To emphasize this point, I have printed the actual state number value (the one in the record buffer) and the state number supplied by the Report Writer. To get the actual state number, each time a record is read, the StateNum in the record is moved to the ActualStateNum in the WORKING-STORAGE SECTION. This data item is used as a SOURCE when the CONTROL FOOTING is printed.

Report Writer Declaratives

The Report Writer is a wonderful tool if the structure of the required report fits the way the Report Writer does things. But sometimes the structure or requirements of a report are such that the standard Report Writer alone is not sufficient. In these cases, you can use declaratives to extend the functionality of the Report Writer.

The USE BEFORE REPORTING phrase allows code specified in the declaratives to be executed just before the report group mentioned in the USE BEFORE REPORTING phrase is printed. The code in the declaratives extends the functionality of the Report Writer by performing tasks or calculations that the Report Writer cannot do automatically or by selectively stopping a report group from being printed (using the SUPPRESS PRINTING command).

In Listing 18-3, declaratives are used to calculate SalesCommission and FullSalary before SalesAgentGrp is printed.

Report Writer Syntax and Semantics

I have shown you a number of example programs that use the Report Writer. That informal introduction should have given you a good idea of the new verbs and declarations required when you write a Report Writer program. This section deals with the syntax and semantics of Report Writer elements.

ENVIRONMENT DIVISION Entries

Just like ordinary reports, the reports generated by the Report Writer are written to an external device—usually a report file. The ENVIRONMENT DIVISION entries for a report file are the same as those for an ordinary file. The same SELECT and ASSIGN clauses apply. You can either omit the ORGANIZATION phrase as in the example programs, in which case the default of ORGANIZATION IS SEQUENTIAL applies, or you can specify ORGANIZATION IS SEQUENTIAL explicitly, as in the following example:

```
FILE-CONTROL.
    SELECT SalesFile ASSIGN TO "Listing18-4-Sales.DAT"
           ORGANIZATION IS LINE SEQUENTIAL.

    SELECT PrintFile ASSIGN TO "Listing18-4.Rpt"
           ORGANIZATION IS SEQUENTIAL.
```

FILE SECTION Entries

The entries in the ENVIRONMENT DIVISION are the same as those for ordinary print files. But in the FILE SECTION, the normal file description is replaced by the REPORT IS phrase, which points to the RD in the REPORT SECTION. The metalanguage for the phrase is

$$\begin{Bmatrix} \underline{\text{REPORT}} \text{ IS} \\ \underline{\text{REPORTS}} \text{ ARE} \end{Bmatrix} \{ \textit{ReportName} \} \ldots$$

where ReportName must be the same as the ReportName used in the RD entry. You can see this in Listing 18-3, where the REPORT IS SolaceSalesReport phrase links the PrintFile with the RD in the REPORT SECTION.

Note that before the report can be used, it must be opened for output. For instance, in Listing 18-3, the PrintFile is opened for output before the SolaceSalesReport is generated.

Report Description (RD) Entries

The RD entry in the REPORT SECTION defines the report. There must be a separate RD entry for each report you want to print. The RD entry names the report, specifies the format of the printed page, and identifies the control-break items.

Each RD entry is followed by one or more 01 level-number entries. Each 01 level-number entry identifies a report group and consists of a hierarchical structure similar to a COBOL record. Each report group is a unit consisting of one or more print lines and cannot be split across pages. The metalanguage for the RD is given in Figure 18-2.

RD *ReportName*

$$[\text{IS} \underline{\text{GLOBAL}}]$$

$$\left[\begin{Bmatrix} \underline{\text{CONTROL}} \text{ IS} \\ \underline{\text{CONTROLS}} \text{ ARE} \end{Bmatrix} \begin{Bmatrix} \{ \text{ControlName\$\#i} \} \ldots \\ \underline{\text{FINAL}} [\text{ControlName\$\#i}] \ldots \end{Bmatrix} \right]$$

$$\left[\underline{\text{PAGE}} \begin{bmatrix} \underline{\text{LIMIT}} \text{ IS} \\ \underline{\text{LIMITS}} \text{ ARE} \end{bmatrix} \textit{PageSize\#l} \begin{bmatrix} \underline{\text{LINE}} \\ \underline{\text{LINES}} \end{bmatrix} \right]$$

$$\left[\begin{bmatrix} \underline{\text{HEADING}} \textit{HeadingLine\#l} \end{bmatrix} \\ \begin{bmatrix} \underline{\text{FIRST}} \underline{\text{DETAIL}} \textit{FirstDetailLine\#l} \end{bmatrix} \\ \begin{bmatrix} \underline{\text{LAST}} \underline{\text{DETAIL}} \textit{LastDetailLine\#l} \end{bmatrix} \\ \begin{bmatrix} \underline{\text{FOOTING}} \textit{HeadingLine\#l} \end{bmatrix} \right]$$

***Figure 18-2.** Metalanguage for the Report Description (RD) entry*

Keep the following points in mind:

- ReportName can appear in only one RD entry.

- When more than one report is declared in the REPORT SECTION, ReportName may be used to qualify the LINE-COUNTER and PAGE-COUNTER report registers.

- ControlName$#i must not be a data item defined in the REPORT SECTION.

- Each occurrence of ControlName$#i must identify a different data item.

- ControlName$#i must not have a variable-length table subordinate to it.

- ControlName$#i and FINAL specify the levels of the control-break hierarchy, where FINAL (if specified) is the highest, the first ControlName$#i is the next highest, and so on.

- When the value in any ControlName$#i changes, a control break occurs. The level of the control break depends on the position of the ControlName$#i in the control-break hierarchy.

- HeadingLine#1 must be greater than or equal to 1.

- The following must hold: HeadingLine#1 <= FirstDetailLine#1 <= LastDetailLine#1 <= FootingLine#1 <= PageSize#1

- The line numbers used in a REPORT HEADING or PAGE HEADING group must be greater than or equal to HeadingLine#1 and less than FirstDetailLine#1. But when a REPORT HEADING appears on a page by itself, any line number between HeadingLine#1 and PageSize#1 may be used.

- The line numbers used in a DETAIL or CONTROL HEADING group must be in the range FirstDetailLine#1 to LastDetailLine#1, inclusive.

- The line numbers used in CONTROL FOOTING groups must be in the range FirstDetailLine#1 to FootingLine#1, inclusive.

- The line numbers used in a REPORT FOOTING or PAGE FOOTING group must be greater than FootingLine#1 and less than or equal to PageSize#1. But when a REPORT FOOTING appears on a page by itself, any line number between HeadingLine#1 and PageSize#1 may be used.

- All the report groups must be defined so that they can be presented on one page. The Report Writer never splits a multiline group across page boundaries.

Report Group Entries

The RD entry specifies the name of the report, identifies the control items, and lays down the basics of how the page is to be formatted. After the RD entry, you specify the report groups to be used in the report. Each report group is represented by a report-group record. As with all record descriptions in COBOL, a report-group record starts with level number 01. The subordinate items in the record describe the report lines and columns in the report group.

Each report group starts with a level 01 report group definition. The metalanguage for the report group definition is given in Figure 18-3.

01 *ReportGroupName*

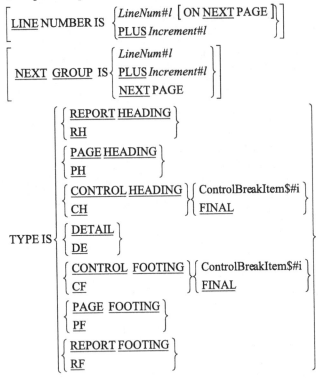

Figure 18-3. *Metalanguage for the report group definition*

RD Entry

When you create an RD entry, keep in mind that ReportGroupName is required only when the group

- Is a DETAIL group referenced by a GENERATE statement or the UPON phrase of a SUM clause

- Is referenced in a USE BEFORE REPORTING sentence in the declaratives

- Is required to qualify the reference to a SUM counter

LINE NUMBER Clause

When you use the LINE NUMBER clause, keep the following in mind:

- The LINE NUMBER clause is used to specify the vertical positioning of print lines. Lines can be printed on

    - A specified line (absolute)

    - A specified line on the next page (absolute)

    - The current line number plus some increment (relative)

- The LINE NUMBER clause specifies where each line is to be printed, so no item that contains a LINE NUMBER clause may contain a subordinate item that also contains a LINE NUMBER clause (subordinate items specify the column items).

- Where absolute LINE NUMBER clauses are specified, all absolute clauses must precede all relative clauses, and the line numbers specified in the successive absolute clauses must be in ascending order.

- The first LINE NUMBER clause specified in a PAGE FOOTING group must be absolute.

- The NEXT PAGE clause can appear only once in a given report group description, and it must be in the first LINE NUMBER clause in the report group.

- The NEXT PAGE clause cannot appear in any HEADING group.

NEXT GROUP Clause

When you use the NEXT GROUP clause, keep the following things in mind:

- The NEXT GROUP clause is used to specify the vertical positioning of the start of the next group. This clause can be used to specify that the next report group should be printed on

  - A specified line (absolute)

  - The current line number plus some increment (relative)

  - The next page

- The NEXT PAGE option in the NEXT GROUP clause must not be specified in a page footer.

- The NEXT GROUP clause must not be specified in a REPORT FOOTING or PAGE HEADING group.

- When used in a DETAIL group, the NEXT GROUP clause refers to the next DETAIL group to be printed.

The TYPE Clause

The TYPE clause specifies the type of the report group. The type of the report group governs when and where it is printed in the report (for instance, a REPORT HEADING group is printed only once: at the beginning of the report).
When you use the TYPE clause, keep the following things in mind:

- Most groups are defined once for each report, but control groups (other than CONTROL ..FINAL groups) are defined for each control-break item.

- In REPORT FOOTING, and CONTROL FOOTING groups, SOURCE and USE clauses must not reference any data item that contains a control-break item or is subordinate to a control-break item.

- PAGE HEADING and FOOTING groups must not reference a control-break item or any item subordinate to a control-break item.

- DETAIL report groups are processed when they are referenced in a GENERATE statement. All other groups are processed automatically by the Report Writer. There can be more than one DETAIL group.

- The REPORT HEADING, PAGE HEADING, CONTROL HEADING FINAL, CONTROL FOOTING FINAL, PAGE FOOTING, and REPORT FOOTING report groups can each appear only once in the description of a report.

Report Group Lines

The subordinate items in a report-group record describe the report lines and columns in the report group. There are two formats for defining items subordinate to the report-group record. The first is usually used to define the lines of the report group, and the second defines and positions the elementary print items.

Defining the Print Lines

Print lines in a report group are usually defined using the metalanguage given in Figure 18-4. This format is used to specify the vertical placement of a print line, and it is always followed by subordinate items that specify the columns where the data items are to be printed.

$$02 - 48 \; [\; ReportLineName \;]$$

$$\left[\; \underline{\text{LINE}} \text{ NUMBER IS } \left\{ \begin{array}{l} LineNum\#l \; [\; \text{ON } \underline{\text{NEXT}} \text{ PAGE }] \\ \underline{\text{PLUS}} \; Increment\#l \end{array} \right\} \right]$$

Figure 18-4. *Metalanguage for vertical print line positioning*

As shown in the metalanguage, the level number is from 2 to 48, inclusive. If ReportLineName is used, its only purpose is to qualify a SUM counter reference.

Defining the Elementary Print Items

The elementary print items in the print line of a report group are described using the metalanguage shown in Figure 18-5. As you can see, the normal data-description clauses such as PIC, USAGE, SIGN, JUSTIFIED, BLANK WHEN ZERO, and VALUE may be applied when describing an elementary print item. The Report Writer provides a number of additional clauses that may also be used with these items.

$$02 - 49 \; SumCounterName$$

$$\left\{ \begin{array}{l} \underline{\text{PICTURE}} \\ \underline{\text{PIC}} \end{array} \right\} \text{ IS } PictureString$$

$$[\; [\; \underline{\text{USAGE}} \text{ IS }] \; \underline{\text{DISPLAY}} \;]$$

$$\left[\; \underline{\text{SIGN}} \text{ IS} \left\{ \begin{array}{l} \text{LEADING} \\ \text{TRAILING} \end{array} \right\} \; \underline{\text{SEPARATE}} \text{ CHARACTER} \right]$$

$$\left[\; \left\{ \begin{array}{l} \underline{\text{JUSTIFIED}} \\ \underline{\text{JUST}} \end{array} \right\} \text{ RIGHT} \right]$$

$$[\; \underline{\text{BLANK}} \text{ WHEN } \{\; \text{ZERO} \;\} \;]$$

$$[\; \underline{\text{COLUMN}} \text{ NUMBER IS } ColNum\#l \;]$$

$$[\; \underline{\text{GROUP}} \text{ INDICATE}]$$

$$\left[\; \underline{\text{LINE}} \text{ NUMBER IS } \left\{ \begin{array}{l} LineNum\#l \; [\; \text{ON } \underline{\text{NEXT}} \text{ PAGE }] \\ \underline{\text{PLUS}} \; Increment\#l \end{array} \right\} \right]$$

$$\left\{ \begin{array}{l} \text{SOURCE IS } SourceName\$\#i \\ \text{VALUE IS } Value\$\#l \\ \{\; \underline{\text{SUM}} \; \{\; SumName\#i \;\} \; [\; \underline{\text{UPON}} \; \{\; DetailReportGroupName\$i \;\} \ldots\;] \;\} \ldots \\ \left[\; \underline{\text{RESET}} \text{ ON} \left\{ \begin{array}{l} ControlBreakItem\#\$i \\ \underline{\text{FINAL}} \end{array} \right\} \right] \end{array} \right\}$$

Figure 18-5. *Metalanguage to define elementary report items*

SumCounterName can only be referenced if the entry uses the SUM clause to define a sum counter.

The COLUMN NUMBER Clause

When you use the COLUMN NUMBER clause, keep the following things in mind:

- COLUMN NUMBER specifies the position of a print item on the print line. When this clause is used, it must be subordinate to an item that contains a LINE NUMBER clause.

- In a given print line, the ColNum#1s should be in ascending sequence.

- ColNum#1 specifies the column number of the leftmost character position of the print item.

The GROUP INDICATE Clause

The GROUP INDICATE clause can only appear in a DETAIL report group. It is used to specify that a print item should be printed only on the first occurrence of its report group after a control break or page advance. For instance, in Listing 18-3, the state name and sales agent number are suppressed after their first occurrence. As a reminder, I have repeated the DETAIL group declaration here:

```
01  DetailLine TYPE IS DETAIL.
    02 LINE IS PLUS 1.
        03 COLUMN 1      PIC X(14)
                         SOURCE StateName(StateNum) GROUP INDICATE.
        03 COLUMN 17     PIC 999
                         SOURCE SalesAgentNum  GROUP INDICATE.
        03 COLUMN 30     PIC $$$,$$$.99 SOURCE ValueOfSale.
```

The SOURCE Clause

The SOURCE clause is used to identify a data item that contains the value to be used when the print item is printed. For instance, the SOURCE ValueOfSale clause in the previous example specifies that the value of the item to be printed in column 30 is to be found in the data item ValueOfSale.

The SUM Clause

The SUM clause is used both to establish a sum counter and to name the data items to be summed. A SUM clause can appear only in the description of a CONTROL FOOTING report group. Statements in the PROCEDURE DIVISION can be used to alter the contents of the sum counters.

You can do three forms of summing in the Report Writer:

- Subtotaling

- Rolling forward

- Crossfooting

Subtotaling

When the SUM clause is used with a data item declared in the FILE or WORKING-STORAGE SECTION, then each time a GENERATE is executed, the value to be summed is added to the sum counter. If there is more than one DETAIL group in the report, the SUM..UPON option allows you to select which sum counter to total. For instance, if the report contains two DETAIL groups—one called DetailLine and the other called AlternateDetailLine—you can use SUM..UPON to specify that subtotaling is to be done only each time a GENERATE AlternateDetailLine is executed.

Rolling Forward

When the SUM clause is used with a data item representing the sum counter of another CONTROL FOOTING group, then each time the other group is executed, the value of its sum counter is added to the value of the sum counter of the current group.

Listing 18-3 contains good examples of both subtotaling and rolling forward. Example 18-6 provides a reminder of the relevant code. Each time a DETAIL line is GENERATED, the ValueOf Sale is added to the TotalAgentSales sum counter. When a control break occurs on SalesAgentNum, the accumulated sum is printed and is added to the TotalStateSales sum counter. When a control break occurs on StateNum, the sum accumulated in the TotalStateSales sum counter is added to the final total sum counter.

Example 18-6. Subtotaling and Rolling Forward from Listing 18-3

```
01  SalesAgentGrp
        TYPE IS CONTROL FOOTING SalesAgentNum  NEXT GROUP PLUS 2.
        :  :  :  :  :  :  :  :  :  :  :  :  :  :
            03 TotalAgentSales COLUMN 45 PIC $$$$$,$$$.99 SUM ValueOfSale.


01  StateGrp TYPE IS CONTROL FOOTING StateNum NEXT GROUP PLUS 2.
        02 LINE IS PLUS 2.
        :  :  :  :  :  :  :  :  :  :  :  :  :  :
            03 TotalStateSales COLUMN 45  PIC $$$$$,$$$.99 SUM TotalAgentSales.


01  TotalSalesGrp TYPE IS CONTROL FOOTING FINAL.
        :  :  :  :  :  :  :  :  :  :  :  :  :
            03 COLUMN 48      PIC $$,$$$,$$$.99 SUM TotalStateSales.
```

Crossfooting

In crossfooting, the sum counters in the same CONTROL FOOTING group can be added together to create another sum counter. In Example 18-7, each time a GENERATE statement is executed, the value of NetWeightOfGoods (in the file record) is added to the NWG sum counter, and the value of WeightOfPackingMaterials (in the file record) is added to WPM (subtotaling). When a control break occurs on OrderNumber, the values of the NWG and WPM sum counters are added together to give the combined total identified as GrossWeight and printed in column 40 (crossfooting).

Example 18-7. Crossfooting to Create the GrossWeight Sum Counter

```
01  ShippingGrp
        TYPE IS CONTROL FOOTING  OrderNumber  NEXT GROUP PLUS 3.
                        : other entries :
                        : other entries :
        03 NWG            COLUMN 20  PIC Z,ZZ9    SUM NetWeightOfGoods.
        03 WPM            COLUMN 30  PIC ZZ9      SUM WeightOfPackingMaterials.
        03 GrossWeight    COLUMN 40  PIC ZZ,ZZ9   SUM GNW, PMW.
```

The RESET ON Clause

Sum counters are normally reset to zero after a control break on the control-break item associated with the report group. For instance, in Example 18-6, if you wanted SalesAgentGrp to show a rolling total of the sales in the state, you could change SalesAgentGrp as shown in Example 18-8. In this example, TotalAgentSales prints the sales of a particular agent and is reset to zero when the footer group is printed, whereas StateSalesToDate prints a rolling total of sales for the state and is reset to zero only when there is a control break on StateNum.

Example 18-8. Using the RESET ON Clause

```
01   SalesAgentGrp
     TYPE IS CONTROL FOOTING SalesAgentNum  NEXT GROUP PLUS 2.
     :   :   :   :   :   :   :   :   :   :   :   :
        03 TotalAgentSales   COLUMN 45 PIC $$$$$,$$$.99 SUM ValueOfSale.
        03 StateSalesToDate  COLUMN 60 PIC $$$$$,$$$.99 SUM ValueOfSale
                                                  RESET ON StateNum.
```

Special Report Writer Registers

The Report Writer maintains two special registers for each report declared in the REPORT SECTION.: LINE-COUNTER and PAGE-COUNTER.

LINE-COUNTER

LINE-COUNTER is a reserved word that can be used to access a special register that the Report Writer maintains for each report in the REPORT SECTION. The Report Writer uses the LINE-COUNTER register to keep track of where the lines are being printed on the report. It uses this information and the information specified in the PAGE LIMIT clause in the RD entry to decide when a new page is required.

Although the LINE-COUNTER register can be used as a SOURCE item in the report, no statements in the PROCEDURE DIVISION can alter the value in the register.

References to the LINE-COUNTER register can be qualified by referring to the name of the report given in the RD entry.

PAGE-COUNTER

The reserved word PAGE-COUNTER is used to access a special register that the Report Writer maintains for each report in the REPORT SECTION. It keeps track of the number of pages printed in the report. The PAGE-COUNTER register can be used as a SOURCE item in the report, but the value of the PAGE-COUNTER may also be changed by statements in the PROCEDURE DIVISION.

PROCEDURE DIVISION Report Writer Verbs

The Report Writer introduces four new verbs for processing reports:

- INITIATE
- GENERATE
- TERMINATE
- SUPPRESS PRINTING

The first three are normal PROCEDURE DIVISION verbs, but the last one can only be used in the declaratives. I will postpone discussion of that verb until I deal with declaratives.

The INITIATE Verb

An INITIATE statement starts the processing of the ReportName report or reports. The metalanguage for the INITIATE verb is given in Figure 18-6.

INITIATE{ *ReportName*}...

Figure 18-6. *Metalanguage for the INITIATE verb*

Before INITIATE is executed, the file associated with the ReportName must have been opened for OUTPUT or EXTEND. This is illustrated in Listing 18-3 by these statements:

```
SELECT PrintFile ASSIGN TO "Listing18-3.Rpt".
   :    :    :    :    :    :    :    :    :
FD  PrintFile
    REPORT IS SolaceSalesReport.
   :    :    :    :    :    :    :    :
RD  SolaceSalesReport
   :    :    :    :    :    :    :    :
OPEN OUTPUT PrintFile
   :    :    :    :    :    :    :    :
INITIATE SolaceSalesReport
```

The GENERATE Verb

The GENERATE statement drives the production of the report. The metalanguage for GENERATE is given in Figure 18-7.

GENERATE{ *ReportName*}...

Figure 18-7. *Metalanguage for the GENERATE verb*

The target of a GENERATE statement is either a DETAIL report group or a ReportName. When the target is a ReportName, the report description must contain the following:

- A CONTROL clause
- Not more than one DETAIL group
- At least one group that is not a PAGE or REPORT group

When all the GENERATE statements for a particular report target the ReportName, the report performs summary processing only, and the report produced is called a *summary report*. For instance, to make a summary report using Listing 18-3, all you have to do is change

```
GENERATE DetailLine
```

to

```
GENERATE SolaceSalesReport.
```

If you specify GENERATE SolaceSalesReport, then the DETAIL group is never printed, but the other groups *are* printed.

The TERMINATE Verb

You use a TERMINATE statement to instruct the Report Writer to finish the processing of the specified report. The metalanguage for TERMINATE is given in Figure 18-8.

<u>TERMINATE</u>{ *ReportName*}...

Figure 18-8. *Metalanguage for the TERMINATE verb*

When TERMINATE is executed, the Report Writer prints the PAGE and REPORT FOOTING groups, and all the CONTROL FOOTING groups are printed as if there had been a control break on the most senior control group.

After the report has been terminated, the file associated with the report must be closed. For instance, in Listing 18-3, the TERMINATE SolaceSalesReport statement is followed by the CLOSE PrintFile statement.

Declaratives

The main structural elements of a COBOL program are divisions, sections, and paragraphs. This section introduces a new structural element: *declaratives*. When declaratives are used, they are the first element in the PROCEDURE DIVISION and start with the word DECLARATIVES and end with END DECLARATIVES. Declaratives specify USE procedures that are executed when certain conditions occur. You write the USE procedures in the declaratives in consecutive sections.

When declaratives are used, the remainder of the PROCEDURE DIVISION must consist of at least one section. Example 18-9 is a template the shows the structure of declaratives.

Example 18-9. Structure of Declaratives

```
PROCEDURE DIVISION.
DECLARATIVES
SectionName SECTION.
    USE statement
ParagraphName.
    COBOL Statements
END DECLARATIVES.
Main SECTION.
```

Declaratives are used for two main purposes:

- To extend the functionality of the Report Writer
- To handle file operation errors

Using Declaratives with the Report Writer

Declaratives are used to extend the functionality of the Report Writer by performing tasks or calculations that the Report Writer cannot do automatically or by selectively stopping a report group from being printed (using the SUPPRESS PRINTING command). When you use declaratives with the Report Writer, the USE BEFORE REPORTING phrase lets you specify that a particular section of code is to be executed before the identified report group is printed. The metalanguage for the USE statement used with the Report Writer is given in Figure 18-9.

<u>USE</u> [<u>GLOBAL</u>]<u>BEFORE</u> <u>REPORTING</u> *ReportGroupName*

Figure 18-9. *Metalanguage for the Report Writer version of USE*

Note the following:

- ReportGroupName must not appear in more than one USE statement.

- The GENERATE, INITIATE, and TERMINATE statements must not appear in the declaratives.

- The value of any control data items must not be altered in the declaratives.

- Statements in the declaratives must not reference procedures outside the declaratives.

Listing 18-3 has a good example of how declaratives may be used to extend the functionality of the Report Writer. They are used to calculate the sales agent SalesCommission and FullSalary before SalesAgentGrp is printed. For convenience, the code is repeated in Example 18-10.

Example 18-10. Declaratives from Listing 18-3

```
PROCEDURE DIVISION.
DECLARATIVES.
Calc SECTION.
    USE BEFORE REPORTING SalesAgentGrp.
Calculate-Salary.
    MULTIPLY TotalAgentSales BY Percentage
        GIVING SalesCommission ROUNDED
    ADD SalesCommission, BaseSalary(StateNum)
        GIVING FullSalary.
END DECLARATIVES.
Main SECTION.
Begin.
    OPEN INPUT SalesFile
    OPEN OUTPUT PrintFile
```

The SUPPRESS PRINTING Statement

The SUPPRESS PRINTING statement is used in a DECLARATIVES section to stop a particular report group from being printed. The report group suppressed is the one mentioned in the USE statement associated with the section containing the SUPPRESS PRINTING statement. The SUPPRESS PRINTING statement must be executed each time you want to stop the report group from being printed.

In Example 18-11, the CONTROL FOOTING data for StateGrp is printed only if the state sales total is above a certain threshold.

Example 18-11. Suppressing the Printing of a Report Group

```
PROCEDURE DIVISION.
DECLARATIVES.
CheckStateSales SECTION.
    USE BEFORE REPORTING StateGrp.
PrintImportantStatesOnly.
    IF TotalStateSales < 100000
        SUPPRESS PRINTING
    END-IF.
END DECLARATIVES.
```

Control-Break Registers

The Report Writer maintains a special control-break register for each control-break item mentioned in the CONTROLS ARE phrase in the RD entry. When a control-break item is referred to in a control footer or in the declaratives, the Report Writer supplies the value held in the control-break register and not the value in the item itself. If a control break has just occurred, the value in the control-break register is the previous value of the control-break item.

This point is demonstrated in the report produced by Listing 18-3 by printing the actual state number (the one in the record buffer) and the supplied state number (the one in the control-break register) each time StateGrp group is printed.

Using Declaratives with Files

You can also use declaratives to handle file operation errors. The metalanguage for the version of USE used with files is given in Figure 18-10.

$$
\underline{\text{USE}} \, [\, \underline{\text{GLOBAL}} \,] \underline{\text{AFTER}} \; \text{STANDARD} \left\{ \begin{array}{l} \underline{\text{EXCEPTION}} \\ \underline{\text{ERROR}} \end{array} \right\} \underline{\text{PROCEDURE}} \; \underline{\text{ON}}
$$

$$
\left\{ \begin{array}{l} [\, \text{FileName} \,] \ldots \\ \underline{\text{INPUT}} \\ \underline{\text{OUTPUT}} \\ \underline{\text{I-O}} \\ \underline{\text{EXTEND}} \end{array} \right\}
$$

Figure 18-10. *Metalanguage for the files version of USE*

When you use this version of the declaratives, you can create code that deals with any I-O error on a particular file or more generalized code that deals with INPUT, OUTPUT, I-O, or EXTEND errors on any file. When declaratives exist for a file, the INVALID KEY clause and the AT END clause are optional.

The program fragment in Example 18-12 shows how you can use declaratives to handle errors on a particular file.

Example 18-12. Declarative Procedures to Handle Unexpected File Errors

```
PROCEDURE DIVISION.
DECLARATIVES.
SupFile SECTION.
   USE AFTER ERROR PROCEDURE ON SupplierFile.
DisplaySupplierFileStatus.
   DISPLAY "Unexpected error on Supplier file. Status = " SupplierStatus
   DISPLAY "The file name used was :- " SupplierFileName
   STOP RUN.

VidFile SECTION.
   USE AFTER ERROR PROCEDURE ON VideoFile.
DisplayVideoFileStatus.
   DISPLAY "Unexpected error on Video file. Status = " VideoStatus
   DISPLAY "The file name used was :- " VidFileName
   STOP RUN.
```

```
END DECLARATIVES.
Main SECTION.
Begin.
    OPEN INPUT SupplierFile
    OPEN INPUT VideoFile
                etc
```

Summary

This chapter introduced you to the COBOL Report Writer. In a series of increasingly complex programs, you learned how to use the Report Writer to create control-break-based reports. You were introduced to a number of new verbs, clauses, sections, and concepts. You saw how to use the RD entry in the REPORT SECTION to specify control-break items and define the basic layout of the report page. You were introduced to the idea of a report group and shown how to create report groups linked to control-break items. You learned how to use the SUM clause for totaling and rolling forward. The final program demonstrated how to extend the capabilities of the Report Writer by using declaratives. You then covered the verbs, clauses, and concepts of the Report Writer. And in the final section, you saw how to use declaratives for error handling in files.

The final chapter introduces OO-COBOL. This book adheres to the ANS 85 COBOL standard, so the ISO 2002 OO-COBOL is somewhat outside its remit. Nevertheless, some of the drawbacks of contained subprograms are remedied by OO-COBOL, and it is from this perspective that I examine the topic. Do not expect a course in object-oriented programming.

PROGRAMMING EXERCISE

And now for a programming exercise that tests your understanding of the last two chapters. For this, you need a really sharp 2B pencil.

Introduction

Two months before the beginning of each semester, Campus Bookshop produces a Purchase Requirements Report. This report details the books that have to be purchased for the coming semester. In the past, this was done manually; but now management has decided to computerize the operation. Accordingly, lecturers' requirements have been captured and the results used to update a purchase requirements file. This is a permanent file that contains details of the lecturers' book requirements for both semesters.

You are required to write a program to produce a Purchase Requirements Report from the publisher, book, and purchase requirements files. The report should be sequenced on ascending publisher name and should only detail the purchase requirements for the semester under scrutiny.

The semester number (1 or 2) should be accepted from the user at the start of the program using a simple ACCEPT and DISPLAY.

File Descriptions
Purchase Requirements File (Indexed)

There is a record for each book title required by a lecturer. Note that a book may be required by more than one lecturer.

Field	KeyType	Type	Length	Value
PR-Number	Primary	9	4	1–9999
Lecturer-Name	Alt with duplicates	X	20	--
Book-Number	Alt with duplicates	9	4	1–9999
Module-Code	--	X	5	--
Copies-Required	--	9	3	1–999
Semester	--	9	1	1/2

Book File (Indexed)

Field	KeyType	Type	Length	Value
Book-Number	Primary	9	4	1–9999
Publisher-Number	Alt with duplicates	9	4	1–9999
Book-Title	--	X	30	--

Publisher File (Indexed)

Field	KeyType	Type	Length	Value
Publisher-Number	Primary	9	4	1–9999
Publisher-Name	Alt with duplicates	X	20	--
Publisher-Address	--	X	40	--

Print Specification

The report must be printed according to the print specification given in Figure 18-11.

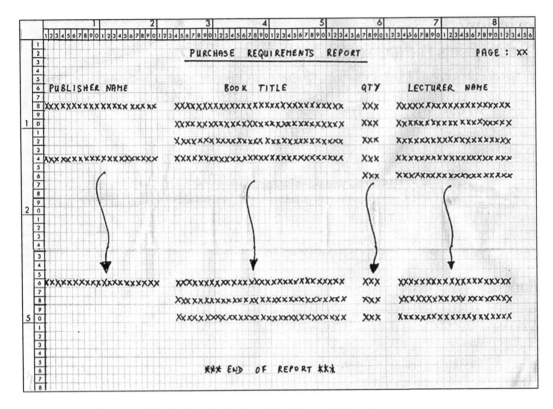

Figure 18-11. *Print specification for the Purchase Requirements Report*

The publisher name must be suppressed after its first occurrence. The headings should be printed at the top of each page, and *** *END OF REPORT* *** should be printed on line 56 on the last page of the report.

Ordinarily, a new page is required after line 50.

The Qty field, which is a synonym for Copies-Required, should be zero suppressed up to but not including the last digit.

The page number field should also be zero suppressed.

PROGRAMMING EXERCISE: SOLUTION

```
IDENTIFICATION DIVISION.
PROGRAM-ID. Listing18-4.
AUTHOR.  MICHAEL COUGHLAN.
*The Campus Bookshop Purchase Requirements Report (DP291-91-EXAM)
*Originally written for VAX COBOL 1991
*Converted to Microfocus COBOL 2002
*Modified for COBOL book 2014

ENVIRONMENT DIVISION.
INPUT-OUTPUT SECTION.
FILE-CONTROL.
    SELECT PurchaseReqFile  ASSIGN TO "Listing18-4-PRF.DAT"
```

```
            ORGANIZATION IS INDEXED
            FILE STATUS IS FileStatus-PRF
            ACCESS MODE IS DYNAMIC
            RECORD KEY IS PRNumber-PRF
            ALTERNATE RECORD KEY IS LecturerName-PRF
                    WITH DUPLICATES
            ALTERNATE RECORD KEY IS BookNum-PRF
                    WITH DUPLICATES.

    SELECT BookFile ASSIGN TO "Listing18-4-BF.DAT"
            ORGANIZATION IS INDEXED
            FILE STATUS IS FileStatus-BF
            ACCESS MODE IS DYNAMIC
            RECORD KEY IS BookNum-BF
            ALTERNATE RECORD KEY IS PublisherNum-BF
                    WITH DUPLICATES.

    SELECT PublisherFile ASSIGN TO "Listing18-4-PF.DAT"
            ORGANIZATION IS INDEXED
            FILE STATUS IS FileStatus-PF
            ACCESS MODE IS DYNAMIC
            RECORD KEY IS PublisherNum-PF
            ALTERNATE RECORD KEY IS PublisherName-PF.

    SELECT ReportFile ASSIGN TO "Listing18-4.RPT".

DATA DIVISION.
FILE SECTION.
FD  PurchaseReqFile.
01  PurchaseRec-PRF.
    88 EndOfPRequirements      VALUE HIGH-VALUES.
    88 NotEndOfPRequirements   VALUE LOW-VALUES.
    02  PRNumber-PRF           PIC 9(4).
    02  LecturerName-PRF       PIC X(20).
    02  BookNum-PRF            PIC 9(4).
    02  ModuleCode-PRF         PIC X(5).
    02  CopiesRequired-PRF     PIC 9(3).
    02  Semester-PRF           PIC 9.

FD  BookFile.
01  BookRec-BF.
    88 EndOfBooks             VALUE HIGH-VALUES.
    88 NotEndOfBooks          VALUE LOW-VALUES.
    02  BookNum-BF            PIC 9(4).
    02  PublisherNum-BF       PIC 9(4).
    02  BookTitle-BF          PIC X(30).

FD  PublisherFile.
01  PublisherRec-PF.
    88  EndOfPublishers       VALUE HIGH-VALUES.
    02  PublisherNum-PF       PIC 9(4).
```

```
      02  PublisherName-PF       PIC X(20).
      02  PublisherAddress-PF    PIC X(40).

  FD  ReportFile
      REPORT IS PurchaseRequirementsReport.

  WORKING-STORAGE SECTION.
  01  File-Stati.
      02  FileStatus-PRF         PIC X(2).
          88 PurchaseRec-PRF-Not-Found   VALUE "23".
      02  FileStatus-BF          PIC X(2).
          88 BookRec-Not-Found   VALUE "23".
      02  FileStatus-PF          PIC X(2).


  01  Current-Semester           PIC 9.


  REPORT SECTION.
  RD  PurchaseRequirementsReport
      CONTROLS ARE      FINAL
                        PublisherName-PF
      PAGE LIMIT IS 66
      HEADING 2
      FIRST DETAIL 8
      LAST DETAIL 50
      FOOTING 55.

  01  TYPE IS REPORT FOOTING.
      02  LINE 56.
          03  COLUMN 29       PIC X(23)
                      VALUE "*** END  OF  REPORT ***".


  01  TYPE IS PAGE HEADING.
      02  LINE 2.
          03  COLUMN 27       PIC X(30)
                      VALUE "PURCHASE  REQUIREMENTS  REPORT".
          03  COLUMN 77       PIC X(6)
                      VALUE "PAGE :".
          03  COLUMN 84       PIC Z9 SOURCE PAGE-COUNTER.

      02  LINE 3.
          03  COLUMN 26       PIC X(32) VALUE ALL "-".

      02  LINE 6.
          03  COLUMN 2        PIC X(24) VALUE "PUBLISHER NAME".
          03  COLUMN 33       PIC X(11) VALUE "BOOK  TITLE".
          03  COLUMN 57       PIC X(3)  VALUE "QTY".
          03  COLUMN 65       PIC X(14) VALUE "LECTURER  NAME".
```

```
01  PReq-PrintLine TYPE IS DETAIL.
    02  LINE IS PLUS 2.
        03  COLUMN 1        PIC X(20) SOURCE PublisherName-PF
                            GROUP INDICATE.
        03  COLUMN 24       PIC X(30)  SOURCE BookTitle-BF.
        03  COLUMN 57       PIC ZZ9    SOURCE CopiesRequired-PRF.
        03  COLUMN 63       PIC X(20)  SOURCE LecturerName-PRF.

PROCEDURE DIVISION.
BEGIN.
    DISPLAY "Enter the semester number (1 or 2) - " WITH NO ADVANCING
    ACCEPT Current-Semester
    OPEN INPUT PurchaseReqFile
    OPEN INPUT BookFile
    OPEN INPUT PublisherFile
    OPEN OUTPUT ReportFile
    INITIATE PurchaseRequirementsReport

    MOVE SPACES TO PublisherName-PF
    START PublisherFile
          KEY IS GREATER THAN PublisherName-PF
          INVALID KEY DISPLAY "START Pub file status" FileStatus-PF
    END-START
    READ PublisherFile NEXT RECORD
          AT END SET EndOfPublishers TO TRUE
    END-READ
    PERFORM PrintRequirementsReport UNTIL EndOfPublishers

    TERMINATE PurchaseRequirementsReport
    CLOSE   PurchaseReqFile, BookFile,
            PublisherFile, ReportFile
    STOP RUN.

PrintRequirementsReport.
    SET NotEndOfBooks TO TRUE
    MOVE PublisherNum-PF TO PublisherNum-BF
    READ BookFile
        KEY IS PublisherNum-BF
        INVALID KEY
            DISPLAY SPACES
            DISPLAY "Book File Error.  FileStatus = " FileStatus-BF
            DISPLAY "Publisher Number - " PublisherNum-BF
            DISPLAY "Publisher Rec = " PublisherRec-PF
            MOVE ZEROS TO PublisherNum-BF
    END-READ

    PERFORM ProcessPublisher
        UNTIL PublisherNum-PF NOT EQUAL TO PublisherNum-BF
                OR EndOfBooks
```

```
        READ PublisherFile NEXT RECORD
            AT END SET EndOfPublishers TO TRUE
        END-READ.


    ProcessPublisher.
        SET NotEndOfPRequirements TO TRUE
        MOVE BookNum-BF TO BookNum-PRF
        READ PurchaseReqFile
            KEY IS BookNum-PRF
            INVALID KEY
                DISPLAY SPACES
                DISPLAY "PurchReqFile Error. FileStatus = " FileStatus-PRF
                DISPLAY "Book Num PRF = " BookNum-PRF
                DISPLAY "Book Rec = " BookRec-BF
                MOVE ZEROS TO BookNum-PRF
        END-READ

        PERFORM UNTIL BookNum-BF NOT EQUAL TO BookNum-PRF
                OR EndOfPRequirements
                    IF Current-Semester = Semester-PRF THEN
                Generate PReq-PrintLine
            END-IF
            READ PurchaseReqFile NEXT RECORD
                AT END SET EndOfPRequirements TO TRUE
            END-READ
        END-PERFORM

        READ BookFile NEXT RECORD
            AT END SET EndOfBooks TO TRUE
        END-READ.
```

CHAPTER 19

OO-COBOL

This chapter introduces you to OO-COBOL. This book adheres to the ANS 85 COBOL standard, so ISO 2002 OO-COBOL is somewhat outside its remit. The ANS 85 version of COBOL was designed to bring structured programming to COBOL, but failings in the way contained subprograms were implemented meant this version did not fully live up to its promise. However, the structured programming weaknesses of ANS 85 COBOL are remedied by OO-COBOL, and the chapter examines OO-COBOL from this perspective. In this chapter, you see how OO-COBOL can be used to create informational strength modules that fully realize Parnas's[1] idea of information hiding. I show you some OO-COBOL programs and introduce you to classes and methods, but the chapter does not delve deeply into topics such as inheritance, polymorphism, properties, and interfaces. In other words, do not expect a course in object-oriented programming.

Module Strength and Module Coupling

Prior to the introduction of the ANS 74 version of COBOL, many COBOL systems consisted of huge, monolithic programs containing as many as 100,000 lines of code. It soon became clear that it was difficult, if not impossible, to maintain programs of this size. As a result, the ANS 74 version of COBOL introduced external subprograms that allowed programmers to create modular systems consisting of a number of independently compiled programs bound together into one run-unit. Unfortunately, this did not entirely solve the maintenance crisis. It turned out that some kinds of partitioned programs were as bad, or worse, than the monolithic programs they replaced. Using empirical research done at IBM as the basis for their ideas, Stevens, Myers, and Constantine[2] addressed this issue by introducing structured programming and the criteria for decomposing a system into modules. In structured programming, a module is defined as any collection of executable program statements that meets all the following criteria:

- It is a closed subroutine.

- It can be called from any other module in the system.

- It has the potential of being independently compiled.

Although structured programming introduced a number of criteria for decomposing a system into modules, the main criteria for judging the quality of a module were module strength and module coupling (see Table 19-1).

---

[1] On the Criteria to Be Used in Decomposing Systems into Modules. *Commun. ACM* 15, no. 12 (December 1972).
[2] Wayne P. Stevens, Glenford J. Myers, and Larry L. Constantine. "Structured Design," in *Classics in Software Engineering*, ed. Edward N. Yourdon (Upper Saddle River, NJ: Yourdon Press, 1979), 205–232.

Table 19-1. *Module Strength and Module Coupling*[3]

		Module Coupling	Module Strength/Cohesion
Best	1	No direct coupling	Functional strength
⇧	2	Data coupling	and informational strength
Better	3	Stamp coupling	Communicational strength
	4	Control coupling	Procedural strength
Worse	5	External coupling	Classical strength
⇩	6	Common coupling	Logical strength
Worst	7	Content coupling	Coincidental strength

Module strength (sometimes called *module cohesion*) is a measure of the association between the elements of a module. Modules whose elements are strongly related to each other are regarded as more desirable than modules whose elements only have a weak or nonexistent connection. For instance, a *functional-strength* module is one in which all the elements combine to perform a single specific function or is one that coordinates subordinate modules such that they perform a single function. Modules such as ValidateCheckDigit, ValidateDate, GetStateCode, and GetCustomerRecord are functional-strength modules: they perform one specific task. On the other end of the scale, a *coincidental-strength* module is one in which the elements are only weakly related to one another and are more strongly related to the elements of other modules. Coincidental-strength modules are likely to be created when, for example, management mandates that a monolithic program be partitioned into subprograms, each 100 lines long.

Module coupling is a measure of the degree to which one module is connected to another. Modules that have low coupling are regarded as being more desirable than those that are highly coupled. A module with no direct coupling (the best) does not rely on data from other modules and provides no data to other modules. This data independence means this module is unlikely to be affected by bugs in other modules, and a bug in this module is unlikely to affect other modules.

In terms of module strength, a functional-strength module is often considered to be the best. However, this is not always the case. An informational-strength module has characteristics that may make it even more desirable than a functional-strength module. An informational-strength module has the following characteristics:

- It contains multiple entry points.

- Each entry point performs a single function.

- All the functions are related by a concept, data structure, or resource that is hidden in the module

For instance, in the dictionary module shown in Figure 19-1, the dictionary is held in a table. The DictionaryModule has four separate entry points: one that allows words to be added to the dictionary, one that allows the dictionary to be searched for a particular word, one that prints the contents of the dictionary, and a final entry point that allows the definition of a dictionary word to be retrieved. Each entry point has functional strength but shares access to the table.

The advantage of this arrangement is that because knowledge of *how* the dictionary is represented is hidden in the module, you can change it without causing knock-on effects for the modules that use it. In Figure 19-1, the dictionary is held in a table; but if you decide to hold it as a dynamic structure or even an indexed file, the modules that use the dictionary will not be affected. This is the benefit of *information hiding*:[4] the knowledge of the data structure, concept, or resource is isolated in a single module. It is the idea on which information-strength modules are based.[5]

---

[3]Glenford J. Myers, *Composite/Structured Design* (New York: Van Nostrand Reinhold, 1978).
[4]David Parnas, "On the Criteria to Be Used in Decomposing Systems into Modules. *Commun. ACM* 15, no. 12 (December 1972).
[5]Glenford J. Myers, *Reliable Software through Composite Design* (New York: Van Nostrand Reinhold, 1975).

DictionaryModule

DictionaryTable			
Add word to dictionary	Search dictionary for word	Print dictionary contents	Get word definition

Figure 19-1. *Dictionary module with four entry points*

Informational-Strength Modules in COBOL

The desirability of being able to create informational-strength modules is self evident. In COBOL, the combination of the IS GLOBAL phrase and contained subprograms seems to allow you create modules of this type. For instance, you could imagine that the dictionary module is an external subprogram that contains the AddWordToDictionary, SearchDictionaryForWord, PrintDictionaryContents, and GetWordDefinition subprograms and in which the dictionary is held in a table made available to all the contained subprograms. Example 19-1 shows the outline of an attempt to create such an external subprogram. This arrangement reflects the structure of the informational-strength module shown in Figure 19-1. Unfortunately, the attempt to create an informational-strength module in this way is prevented by the rule that says a subprogram may only be called by its parent. In other words, the only program that can call AddWordToDictionary, SearchDictionaryForWord, PrintDictionaryContents, and GetWordDefinition is the containing program DictionaryModule. They can't be called by any other program in the run-unit that wants to use the dictionary. This situation is illustrated in Figure 19-2, where the program UseDictionary is not permitted to call the subprograms contained in DictionaryModule. You might think the IS COMMON PROGRAM clause provides a solution to the problem, but unfortunately that clause only allows the sibling subprograms to call one another.

Example 19-1. Attempting to Create an Informational-Strength Module

```
IDENTIFICATION DIVISION.
PROGRAM-ID. DictionaryModule.
WORKING-STORAGE SECTION.
01 DictionaryTable IS GLOBAL.
   02 DictionaryEntry  OCCURS 1000 TIMES.
      03 DictionaryWord   PIC X(20).
      03 WordDefinition   PIC X(1000)

IDENTIFICATION DIVISION.
PROGRAM-ID.  AddWordToDictionary IS INITIAL.
PROCEDURE DIVISION USING WordToAdd, WordDefinition.
END PROGRAM AddWordToDictionary.

IDENTIFICATION DIVISION.
PROGRAM-ID.  SearchDictionaryForWord IS INITIAL.
PROCEDURE DIVISION USING WordToFind, WordFoundFlag.
END PROGRAM SearchDictionaryForWord.

IDENTIFICATION DIVISION.
PROGRAM-ID.  PrintDictionaryContents IS INITIAL.
PROCEDURE DIVISION.
END PROGRAM PrintDictionaryContents.

IDENTIFICATION DIVISION.
PROGRAM-ID.  GetWordDefinition IS INITIAL.
PROCEDURE DIVISION USING WordToFind, WordDefinition.
END PROGRAM GetWordDefinition.
END PROGRAM DictionaryModule.
```

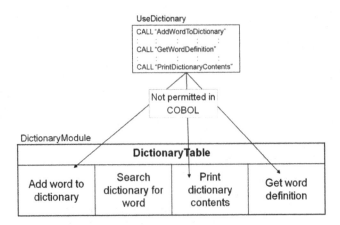

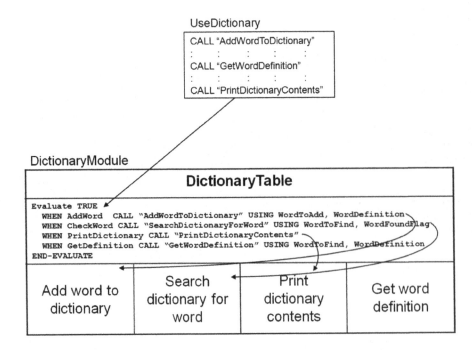

Figure 19-2. COBOL only allows a subprogram to be called by its parent

The only way any kind of informational-strength module can be achieved is for UseDictionary to call the external subprogram DictionaryModule and for DictionaryModule to call the appropriate subprogram, as shown in Figure 19-3. To do this, UseDictionary has to pass a code to DictionaryModule to tell it which of the subprograms to use; and the parameter list passed to DictionaryModule has to be wide enough to accommodate the needs of the contained subprograms. This means even when PrintDictionaryContents is called, you must pass WordToAdd, WordToFind, WordFoundFlag, and WordDefinition as parameters. The problem with this solution is that although you may have created a kind of informational-strength module, the programs UseDictionary and DictionaryModule are now control coupled. The exposure to unnecessary data is not particularly egregious in this example, but it might prove a serious drawback if the contained programs had more significant data needs.

Figure 19-3. Workaround to create an informational-strength module in COBOL

The workaround to the problem of creating an informational-strength module in COBOL is not very satisfactory. Module coupling has been traded for module strength. A kind of informational-strength module has been created, but at the expense of control coupling the `DictionaryModule` and `UseDictionary` programs.

When you come to use `DictionaryModule`, you may discover another limitation: there is only one instance of the dictionary. This means you cannot use the `DictionaryModule` to create specialized dictionaries for acronyms, networking terms, or slang words without running the program multiple times.

OO-COBOL

OO-COBOL provides a solution to many of the problems outlined so far. In OO-COBOL, you can create a *class* in which to hide the implementation details of the dictionary, and you can create *methods* to put words into the dictionary and retrieve word definitions from the dictionary. In addition, a class-based solution goes one step beyond the informational-strength module because it allows you to create instances of the dictionary. This means you can create a dictionary to hold acronyms, a dictionary to hold networking terms, or even a dictionary to hold slang words.

The UseDictionary Program

Listing 19-1 uses OO-COBOL to create a `Dictionary` class and shows how it can be used to create and use multiple instances of dictionaries. Once you have seen an example program and have a feel for how OO is implemented in COBOL, I introduce the topic more formally. I have kept the `Dictionary` class short by only implementing the `AddWordToDictionary` and `PrintDictionaryContents` methods as well as the internal method `SetDictionaryName`.

Listing 19-1. COBOL Program that Uses the Dictionary Class

```
IDENTIFICATION DIVISION.
PROGRAM-ID. Listing19-1.
AUTHOR.  Michael Coughlan.
*UseDictionary program

REPOSITORY.
    CLASS DictionaryCls AS "dictionary".

DATA DIVISION.
WORKING-STORAGE SECTION.
01 AcronymDictionary  USAGE OBJECT REFERENCE DictionaryCls.
01 NetworkDictionary  USAGE OBJECT REFERENCE DictionaryCls.
01 SlangDictionary    USAGE OBJECT REFERENCE DictionaryCls.
01 CurrentDictionary  USAGE OBJECT REFERENCE.

01 WordToAdd          PIC X(20).
   88 EndOfInput      VALUE SPACES.

01 WordDefinition     PIC X(1000).

PROCEDURE DIVISION.
Begin.
    INVOKE DictionaryCls "new" USING BY CONTENT "Acronym Dictionary"
                                    RETURNING AcronymDictionary
    INVOKE DictionaryCls "new" USING BY CONTENT "Network Dictionary"
                                    RETURNING NetworkDictionary
```

```
INVOKE DictionaryCls "new" USING BY CONTENT "Slang Dictionary"
                                RETURNING SlangDictionary

    SET CurrentDictionary TO AcronymDictionary
    DISPLAY "Fill the Acronym dictionary"
    PERFORM FillTheDictionary WITH TEST AFTER UNTIL EndOfInput

    SET CurrentDictionary TO NetworkDictionary
    DISPLAY "Fill the Network dictionary"
    PERFORM FillTheDictionary WITH TEST AFTER UNTIL EndOfInput

    SET CurrentDictionary TO SlangDictionary
    DISPLAY "Fill the Slang dictionary"
    PERFORM FillTheDictionary WITH TEST AFTER UNTIL EndOfInput

    DISPLAY SPACES
    INVOKE AcronymDictionary "PrintDictionaryContents"

    DISPLAY SPACES
    INVOKE NetworkDictionary "PrintDictionaryContents"

    DISPLAY SPACES
    INVOKE SlangDictionary "PrintDictionaryContents"

    INVOKE SlangDictionary    "finalize" RETURNING SlangDictionary
    INVOKE NetworkDictionary  "finalize" RETURNING NetworkDictionary
    INVOKE AcronymDictionary  "finalize" RETURNING AcronymDictionary
    STOP RUN.

FillTheDictionary.
    DISPLAY "Enter a word to add (press return to end) - " WITH NO ADVANCING
    ACCEPT WordToAdd

    DISPLAY "Enter the word definition - " WITH NO ADVANCING
    ACCEPT WordDefinition

    INVOKE CurrentDictionary "AddWordToDictionary"
        USING BY CONTENT WordToAdd, WordDefinition.
```

Listing 19-1 uses the dictionary class to create three instances of the dictionary: one to hold acronyms, one for network terms, and the third to hold slang words. The program demonstrates that three instances of the dictionary have been created by filling each with relevant words and then displaying the words in each dictionary.

It is interesting to note how little the language has been changed to accommodate the syntax required to write OO-COBOL programs. In Listing 19-1, the first difference between this and an ordinary COBOL program is the REPOSITORY paragraph. This paragraph lists the classes used in the program. The AS clause specifies the external name for the class.

The second difference is the USAGE OBJECT REFERENCE clause, which is an extension of the USAGE clause that allows you to specify that a data item is capable of holding a reference (handle) to an object. In the program, three data items capable of holding references to dictionary objects are created, and a fourth is created that can hold a reference to any object. I could have made this last a dictionary reference also, but I wanted to show that you can create object-reference data items that are not bound to a particular type of object.

The first thing done in the PROCEDURE DIVISION is to create three instances of the dictionary and assign their references (handles) to the appropriate object-reference data item. This is done by using the INVOKE verb to execute the new method in the dictionary class (or, to describe it in OO-COBOL terms, the INVOKE verb is used to send the new message to the dictionary class.) Because there are three instances of the dictionary, you need to tell each instance its name, so the name of the dictionary is passed to new as a parameter. The new method creates an object instance and places a reference to the instance (the object handle) in the object-reference data item.

At this point, three instances of the dictionary object have been created, and the next step is to fill each dictionary with the appropriate words. I could have done this by repeating the code in the paragraph FillTheDictionary three times and each time targeting a different dictionary (this is what I do to display the contents of each dictionary). But I wanted to create one piece of code to handle all three dictionaries. To do this, instead of referring to a specific dictionary in the FillTheDictionary paragraph, I refer to the CurrentDictionary object reference and then, just before the FillTheDictionary paragraph is performed, move the appropriate dictionary object reference to CurrentDictionary.

When the dictionaries have been filled with words, the contents of the dictionaries are displayed. This is done by sending the PrintDictionaryContents message to the appropriate dictionary object.

Finally, the storage used by the dictionaries is released by sending a finalize message to the appropriate dictionary object. This is often a vital step because if the program ends without destroying the object, the memory allocated to the object is still allocated but the object references that allow you to access the object in memory are lost.

The Dictionary Class

Listing 19-1 showed how to use the dictionary class to create and use dictionary object instances. Listing 19-1-cls (identified as Listing 19-1-cls.cbl in the online sources) shows how to define the dictionary class.

Listing 19-1-cls. The Dictionary Class

```
CLASS-ID.  DictionaryCls AS "dictionary"
           INHERITS FROM Base.
AUTHOR. Michael Coughlan.

REPOSITORY.
   CLASS Base AS "base"
   CLASS DictionaryCls AS "dictionary".

FACTORY.
METHOD-ID. New.
LINKAGE SECTION.
01 TestObject-lnk  OBJECT REFERENCE.
01 DictionaryName  PIC X(20).

PROCEDURE DIVISION USING DictionaryName RETURNING TestObject-lnk.
Begin.
*Create a new dictionary object by invoke "new" in the base class
     INVOKE SUPER "new" RETURNING TestObject-lnk.

*Set the dictionary name in the dictionary object
     INVOKE TestObject-lnk "SetDictionaryName"
            USING BY CONTENT DictionaryName
     EXIT METHOD.
END METHOD New.
END FACTORY.
```

```
OBJECT.
WORKING-STORAGE SECTION.
*Items declared here are visible only to methods of this
*instance.  They have state memory.
01 DictionaryTable.
   02 DictionaryEntry  OCCURS 0 TO 1000 TIMES
      DEPENDING ON NumberOfWords
      INDEXED BY WordIdx.
      03 DictionaryWord   PIC X(20).
      03 WordDefinition   PIC X(1000).

01 NumberOfWords          PIC 9(4) VALUE ZERO.


01 DictionaryName         PIC X(20).

METHOD-ID. SetDictionaryName.
LINKAGE SECTION.
01 DictionaryNameIn       PIC X(20).
PROCEDURE DIVISION USING DictionaryNameIn.
Begin.
    MOVE DictionaryNameIn TO DictionaryName
END METHOD SetDictionaryName.


METHOD-ID. AddWordToDictionary.
LINKAGE SECTION.
01 WordIn                 PIC X(20).
01 DefinitionIn           PIC X(1000).
PROCEDURE DIVISION USING WordIn, DefinitionIn.
Begin.
    MOVE FUNCTION UPPER-CASE(WordIn) TO WordIn
    SET WordIdx TO 1
    SEARCH DictionaryEntry
       AT END ADD 1 TO NumberOfWords
           MOVE WordIn TO DictionaryWord(NumberOfWords)
           MOVE DefinitionIn TO WordDefinition(NumberOfWords)
       WHEN WordIn = DictionaryWord(WordIdx)
           DISPLAY WordIn " is already in the dictionary"
    END-SEARCH
    EXIT METHOD.
END METHOD AddWordToDictionary.

METHOD-ID.  PrintDictionaryContents.
LOCAL-STORAGE SECTION.
PROCEDURE DIVISION.
Begin.
    DISPLAY "Words in  - " DictionaryName
    PERFORM VARYING WordIdx FROM 1 BY 1 UNTIL WordIdx = NumberOfWords
       DISPLAY "Word = " DictionaryWord(WordIdx)
```

```
        END-PERFORM
        DISPLAY "------ End of dictionary words  --------"
        EXIT METHOD.
    END METHOD PrintDictionaryContents.
    END OBJECT.
    END CLASS DictionaryCls.
```

The first difference between this class program and a normal COBOL program is that there is no IDENTIFICATION DIVISION. Actually, the IDENTIFICATION DIVISION is now optional. If you are nostalgic, you can still use it. The second difference is that instead of the PROGRAM-ID, you have a CLASS-ID. The CLASS-ID names the class and specifies from what classes it inherits. In this program, the DictionaryCls class inherits from the Base class. The Base class is a system class from which all classes inherit. It corresponds to the class Object in many other OO languages.

The REPOSITORY paragraph allows you to associate internal names with the name of the external file that contains the code for the class. Internally the dictionary class is known as DictionaryCls, but the system knows it as dictionary.

The next item to consider is the FACTORY. The entries from FACTORY to END FACTORY specify the factory object. The main function of the factory object is to create new object instances where initialization is required. If initialization is not required, the new method inherited from the Base class may be used. For instance, if no initialization was required, you could create new acronym dictionary using the statement

```
INVOKE DictionaryCls "new" RETURNING AcronymDictionary
```

In this example, initialization *is* required, so FACTORY contains a new method that overrides the new method inherited from the Base class. What this new method does is to create a new dictionary object. It does this by using the predefined object identifier SUPER to invoke the new method in the Base class. Once a new dictionary object has been created, it is sent the SetDictionaryName message, and this sets the dictionary name into the dictionary instance object by storing it in a data item declared in the instance object. The factory object could not be used for this purpose because there is only one instance of the factory object (created by including the CLASS entries in the REPOSITORY), and the next time you tried to create a new dictionary, the previous name would be overwritten.

You have probably noticed by now that methods in COBOL bear a very strong resemblance to contained subprograms (with some minor differences). Instead of a PROGRAM-ID, you use a METHOD-ID; instead of delimiting the scope with END PROGRAM, you use END METHOD; instead of terminating the method using an EXIT PROGRAM statement, you use EXIT METHOD; and instead of WORKING-STORAGE SECTION, you use LOCAL-STORAGE SECTION.

In Listing 19-1-cls, the next item of interest is the entries that define the instance object. These entries start at OBJECT and end at END OBJECT and specify the data and methods of each dictionary instance. This is where the table that holds the dictionary entries is defined; each dictionary instance has a separate table. Defining the table in the WORKING-STORAGE SECTION of the OBJECT keeps it alive for the life of the instance and makes it available to the methods of the object. It is also where DictionaryName is defined.

SetDictionaryName is an internal method. It is only invoked by the new method in the factory. Its only purpose is to take the dictionary name passed as a parameter and move it to less transient storage. It can't be stored in the method because method storage only persists as long as the method is alive. When the method ends, any data stored in the method is lost.

AddWordToDictionary adds the word and definition passed as parameters to the appropriate place in the table. PrintDictionaryContents displays the words in the dictionary. The list of words is preceded by the name of the dictionary. The name of the dictionary is obtained from DictionaryName in the WORKING-STORAGE SECTION of the OBJECT.

To keep the class short, so that you are not overwhelmed by detail, I did not include the methods SearchDictionaryForWord and GetWordDefinition. These are left as an exercise for you.

A Formal Introduction to OO-COBOL

Now that you have seen an OO-COBOL program and have an idea about how to create such programs, this section introduces some of the elements of OO-COBOL more formally. But keep in mind that this book is not about OO-COBOL or object-oriented programming, so I skim over many of the constructs and only stop to deal more thoroughly with those I consider particularly salient.

When you remember all the new syntax that was required for the Report Writer, you may find it amazing that object orientation has been brought to COBOL with so few additions to the language. There is only one new verb (INVOKE), one new data type (OBJECT REFERENCE), and a few new entries such as these:

- CLASS-ID and END CLASS

- REPOSITORY

- FACTORY and END FACTORY

- METHOD-ID and END METHOD

- OBJECT and END OBJECT

- EXIT METHOD

Objects, Classes, and Methods

Before I begin a discussion about creating objects, classes, and methods in COBOL, I should define some of these terms. An *object* is an encapsulation of data and procedures that operate on that data. In object orientation, the data is known as the object's attributes, and the procedures are known as its methods. For instance, a Stock object might need attributes such a StockId, QtyInStock, ReorderLevel and ReorderQty and might support such methods as GetStockId, AddToStockQty, SubtractFromStockQty, GetStockQty, GetReorderQty, ChangeReorderQty, GetReorderLevel, and ChangeReorderLevel. *Encapsulation* means the structure and implementation of the attributes (data) is completely hidden in the object and the only access to the attributes of an object is through the object's methods. For instance, the only way to change the ReorderLevel of a particular stock item is to invoke that item's ChangeReorderLevel method.

The user of an object can only discover the value of an attribute or change the value of an attribute by making requests to the object. These requests are known as *messages*. Each message invokes a method supported by the object. The messages to which an object responds is known as the *object interface*. Each class actually defines two interfaces: an interface defining the methods supported by the class object (such as the new method) and the interface defining the methods supported by each instance of the class (such as ChangeReorderQty).

A *class* is a template for creating objects. A class contains all the information you need to create objects of a particular type. In OO-COBOL, a class is called an *object factory* because it "manufactures" the object instances. This idea is reinforced by identifying the area of the program where the factory object is defined using the keywords FACTORY and END FACTORY. The factory object may contain its own factory methods and its own factory data. For instance, the Stock class would allow you to create instances of Stock items by sending the new message to the factory object of the Stock class.

In OO-COBOL, a *class definition* is a program that starts with a CLASS-ID and ends with an END CLASS statement. The class program may contain its own ENVIRONMENT, DATA, and PROCEDURE DIVISIONS. When you write a class program, you need to distinguish between three different but related entities:

- The *class* is the source code program defining the class.

- The *factory object* is the class at runtime.

- *Instance objects* are created by the factory object at runtime.

Programming with Objects

OO-COBOL is not a fully object-oriented language. This means objects can be used inside a COBOL program that is not itself object oriented. However, whether the program you want to write is an OO-COBOL class or an ordinary procedural COBOL program that uses OO-COBOL objects, the same rules for using the objects apply.

Your program must have a REPOSITORY paragraph. The REPOSITORY lists all the class that the program is going to use. If the program itself is an OO-COBOL class, the REPOSITORY paragraph also lists its superclass (the class from which it is derived).

Your program must declare one or more data items of type OBJECT REFERENCE. An OBJECT REFERENCE data item holds an object handle. An object handle enables you to send messages to the object. Object references can be moved from one OBJECT REFERENCE data item to another or can be passed as parameters when you INVOKE a method or CALL a subprogram.

Your program must use the INVOKE verb to send messages to the object. Sending a message to an object invokes the named method in the object. A *method* is a piece of code that performs one of the functions of the object. Some methods receive or return parameters, so when you invoke a method you may have to include the parameters as part of the message in the INVOKE statement.

Registering a Class

Before you can use an OO-COBOL class, you must register it by declaring it in the REPOSITORY paragraph. Entries in this paragraph link the internal class name with the name of the external file that contains the code for the class. Registering the class in the REPOSITORY using the CLASS clause creates a data item for each class named, and at runtime this data item holds an object handle to the factory object.

Declaring Object References

When you have declared the class in the REPOSITORY (an action that creates a factory object for the class), you have to declare the data items that will hold the handles of any instance object you may create. To do this, you declare the data items as USAGE OBJECT REFERENCE. For instance, the following data items are declared in Listing 19-1:

```
01 AcronymDictionary  USAGE OBJECT REFERENCE DictionaryCls.
01 NetworkDictionary  USAGE OBJECT REFERENCE DictionaryCls.
01 SlangDictionary    USAGE OBJECT REFERENCE DictionaryCls.
01 CurrentDictionary  USAGE OBJECT REFERENCE.
```

An object reference can be used

- As the target of an INVOKE statement

- As a parameter to a program or method

- With the SET verb to set one object reference to the value of another or to NULL

- In a comparison comparing one object reference for equality with another or to NULL

The object reference for the factory objects is automatically created when you register a class.

An object reference may be typed or untyped. As demonstrated in Listing 19-1, an untyped object reference data item (called a *universal object reference*) can hold an object reference for any object. A typed object reference data item can only hold an object reference of the type specified. For instance, the AcronymDictionary data item can only hold a handle (object reference) to a DictionaryCls object instance.

Sending Messages to Instance Objects

You interrogate, or change, the values of an object's attributes by sending messages to the object instance. You send messages to an object instance using the INVOKE verb. When you send a message to an object instance, it causes the method named in the message text to execute. If the method is not found in the object, it is passed up the method inheritance chain until it is recognized and executed. This is how the new and finalize methods that create and destroy object instances are executed. These methods are part of the system provided Base class inherited by every COBOL class.

As you can see from Figure 19.4, the INVOKE verb has a strong similarity to the CALL verb and so requires little in the way of explanation. The ObjectIdentifier is the data item that holds the object reference. MessageLiteral is the name of the method to be invoked. Parameters are passed using the same syntax as the CALL verb except that an additional mechanism (BY VALUE) has been added. The RETURNING phrase allows the invoked method to return a value.

$$\underline{\text{INVOKE}} \ \{ \text{ObjectIdentifier} \} \left\{ \begin{array}{l} \text{MessageLiteral} \\ \text{MessageIdentifier} \end{array} \right\}$$

$$\left[\underline{\text{USING}} \left\{ \begin{array}{l} [\text{BY} \ \underline{\text{REFERENCE}}] \left\{ \begin{array}{l} \text{Identifier} \\ \underline{\text{ADDRESS}} \ \underline{\text{OF}} \ \text{Identifier} \end{array} \right\} \dots \\ \text{BY} \ \underline{\text{CONTENT}} \left\{ \begin{array}{l} \text{Identifier} \\ \text{Literal} \\ \text{Arithmetic Expression} \end{array} \right\} \dots \\ \text{BY} \ \underline{\text{VALUE}} \left\{ \begin{array}{l} \text{Identifier} \\ \text{Arithmetic Expression} \end{array} \right\} \dots \end{array} \right\} \dots \right]$$

$$[\{ \underline{\text{RETURNING}} \} \{ \text{Identifier} \}]$$

Figure 19-4. *Metalanguage for the INVOKE verb*

Creating a New Object Instance

Once you have created a data item capable of holding an object reference, you need to create an object instance and store its reference in the data item. You create an object instance by sending a creation message to its factory object (the factory object itself is created when you register it in the REPOSITORY). For objects that do not have any initialization parameters, the creation message is new (see Example 19-2 and Example 19-3). When the new method executes, it allocates the storage required for the object and returns the object handle.

Example 19-2. Registering a Class, Declaring an Object Reference Data Item, and Creating an Object Instance

```
REPOSITORY.
    CLASS StockCls AS "stockclassprogram"
    :    :    :    :    :    :    :
WORKING-STORAGE SECTION.
    01  StockItem USAGE OBJECT REFERENCE StockCls.
    :    :    :    :    :    :    :    :
PROCEDURE DIVISION.
    :    :    :    :    :    :    :    :
    INVOKE StockCls "new" RETURNING StockItem
```

Example 19-3. Registering a Class, Declaring an Object Reference Data Item, and Invoking new with an Initialization Parameter to Create a Dictionary Instance

```
REPOSITORY.
    CLASS DictionaryCls AS "dictionary".
    :    :    :    :    :    :    :    :
WORKING-STORAGE SECTION.
01 AcronymDictionary  USAGE OBJECT REFERENCE DictionaryCls.
    :    :    :    :    :    :    :    :
PROCEDURE DIVISION.
    :    :    :    :    :    :    :    :
    INVOKE DictionaryCls "new" USING BY CONTENT "Acronym Dictionary"
                                RETURNING AcronymDictionary
```

Destroying Objects

When you have finished using an object, you must destroy it. This frees the memory it uses. There is no automatic garbage collection in OO-COBOL, so the memory for objects that have been allocated but whose object handles have been lost cannot be recovered. Once an object has been created, it remains in existence until it is destroyed explicitly, even if the data item that holds its object handle is destroyed or the object handle is overwritten.

You destroy an object by sending it the finalize message. Like the new method, finalize is a method provided by the Base class and inherited by all classes. When you finalize an object, the method returns a NULL object reference. Example 19-4 shows how to use INVOKE with the finalize message to destroy an object.

Example 19-4. Using finalize to Destroy an Object

```
INVOKE AcronymDictionary "finalize" RETURNING  AcronymDictionary
```

Predefined Object Identifiers

I mentioned the NULL object reference in the previous section. NULL is one of three predefined object identifiers. The identifiers and their significance are given in Table 19-2.

Table 19-2. *Predefined Object Identifiers*

Predefined Object Identifier	Meaning
| NULL | The predefined object reference NULL contains the null object-reference value that is a unique value guaranteed by the implementer never to reference an object. It represents a value used to indicate that data items defined as USAGE OBJECT REFERENCE do not contain a valid address. NULL must not be specified as a receiving operand, but it can be used in a comparison such as<br><br>```
IF AcronymDictionary = NULL
    DISPLAY "The acronym dictionary object does not exist"
END-IF
``` |
| SELF | SELF is a predefined object identifier used in the PROCEDURE DIVISION of a method. SELF refers to the object instance used to invoke the currently executing method. By using SELF you can cause an object to send a message to itself. This is useful if you want a method to invoke one of its siblings. For instance, in Listing 19-1-cls you could use SELF to invoke the SetDictionaryName method from one of the other methods using a statement such as<br><br>```
INVOKE SELF "SetDictionaryName"
    USING BY CONTENT NewDictionaryName
```<br><br>You might want to use SELF because you have placed a piece of code that is used by several different methods in a method on its own and want to use this method like a subroutine. |
| SUPER | SUPER allows an object to send a message to itself, but the method invoked is a not a method in the class itself but rather a method in one of the superclasses of the class. If SUPER is used from an instance method, the system searches its way up through the instance methods of all the superclasses until it finds a method matching the message.<br><br>If SUPER is used from a factory method, the system searches for a factory method beginning with the factory object code of the superclass immediately above the class and searches its way up through the factory methods of all the superclasses until it finds a method matching the message.<br><br>For instance, in Listing 19-1-cls, the new method in the FACTORY needs to invoke the new method in the base class. This is achieved using the statement<br><br>```
INVOKE SUPER "new" RETURNING TestObject-lnk.
``` |

Writing Your Own Classes

When you write an OO application, you need to create your own classes. A class program has the structure shown in Figure 19-5, and the entries required are outlined in the class template in Example 19-5.
```

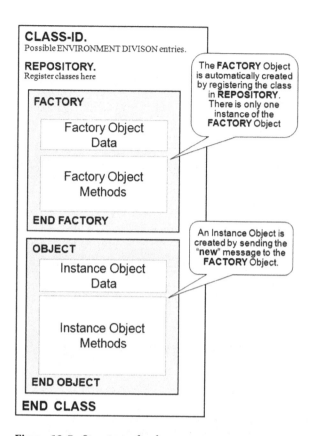

Figure 19-5. *Structure of a class program*

Example 19-5. A Class Program Template

```
CLASS-ID.  Template-cls AS "template"
           inherits from Base.
* Class identification.
ENVIRONMENT DIVISION.
* Optional but when used all normal ENVIRONMENT DIVISION entries are valid
   :    :    :    :    :    :    :    :    :

CONFIGURATION SECTION.
* Optional entry but the REPOSITORY is part of the CONFIGURATION SECTION
   :    :    :    :    :    :    :    :    :
REPOSITORY.
* The Repository paragraph names the files containing the executables
* for each class.
* The executable for Template-cls is in the file template.
   CLASS BASE AS "base"
   CLASS Template-cls AS "tester".

FACTORY
* Defines the start of the factory object.
ENVIRONMENT DIVISON.
DATA DIVISION.
```

```
* Defines factory object data
WORKING-STORAGE SECTION.
* Defines factory object data
    :     :     :     :     :     :     :     :     :
METHOD-ID. new.
* If initialization is required there may be a "new" of factory method.
* This overrides "new" coming from Base.
    :     :     :     :     :     :     :     :     :
END METHOD new.
END FACTORY.


OBJECT.
* Start of the code that defines the behaviour of class instances.
WORKING-STORAGE SECTION.
* Defines instance data visible to all methods of the instance.
    :     :     :     :     :     :     :     :     :
METHOD-ID. ExampleTemplateMethod.
* Start of instance method "ExampleTemplateMethod "
    ...
END METHOD ExampleTemplateMethod.
END OBJECT.
* End of code for instance objects.
END CLASS Example.
```

The Issue of Scope

Whenever you write a class program, you have to be aware of the consequences of declaring data items in various parts of the program. When I refer to the *scope* of a data item, I am referring to its lifetime: how long it persists. The scoping issues of data items declared in the class program are summarized in Table 19-3, and Listing 19-2 demonstrates these issues in an example program.

Table 19-3. *Class Program Scoping Issues*

Where Declared	Scope
WORKING-STORAGE SECTION **of the** FACTORY	A data item declared in the WORKING-STORAGE SECTION of the FACTORY is visible only to factory methods; and because there is only one factory object, there is only one instance of the data item. The item persists as long as the class program is alive.
WORKING-STORAGE SECTION **of the** OBJECT	A data item declared in the WORKING-STORAGE SECTION of the OBJECT is visible only to object instance methods. There is an instance of the data item for each object, and the data item will persist as long as the instance is alive (has not been finalized).
LOCAL-STORAGE SECTION **of any method**	A data item declared in the LOCAL-STORAGE SECTION of any method (factory of instance object) visible only to the method, and it persists only as long has the method is alive.

Listing 19-2. Example Program to Demonstrate Scoping Issues

```
IDENTIFICATION DIVISION.
PROGRAM-ID. Listing19-2.
* AUTHOR.  Michael Coughlan.
* Demonstrates the difference between Factory methods & data
* and instance methods & data.
* It is also used to demonstrate the scope of
* data items declared in different parts of the program.

REPOSITORY.
    CLASS Tester-cls AS "tester".

DATA DIVISION.
WORKING-STORAGE SECTION.
01 Test1-obj  OBJECT REFERENCE Tester-cls.
01 Test2-obj  OBJECT REFERENCE Tester-cls.
01 Test3-obj  OBJECT REFERENCE Tester-cls.

PROCEDURE DIVISION.
Begin.
    INVOKE Tester-cls "new" RETURNING Test1-obj
    INVOKE Tester-cls "new" RETURNING Test2-obj
    INVOKE Tester-cls "new" RETURNING Test3-obj

    DISPLAY SPACES
    DISPLAY "--------- Test3-obj ViewData -----------"
    INVOKE Test3-obj "ViewData"

    DISPLAY SPACES
    DISPLAY "--------- Test1-obj ViewData -----------"
    INVOKE Test1-obj "ViewData"

    DISPLAY SPACES
    DISPLAY "--------- Test3-obj ViewData again -----"
    INVOKE Test3-obj "ViewData"

    DISPLAY SPACES
    DISPLAY "--------- Test2-obj ViewData -----------"
    INVOKE Test2-obj "ViewData" USING BY CONTENT 5

    INVOKE Test1-obj "finalize" RETURNING Test1-obj
    INVOKE Test2-obj "finalize" RETURNING Test2-obj
    INVOKE Test3-obj "finalize" RETURNING Test3-obj
    STOP RUN.
```

Listing 19-2 Output

```
Factory Working-Storage data has state memory   - 2
but Factory Method Local-Storage data does not - 2

Factory Working-Storage data has state memory   - 4
but Factory Method Local-Storage data does not - 2

Factory Working-Storage data has state memory   - 6
but Factory Method Local-Storage data does not - 2


--------- Test3-obj ViewData -----------
This is instance 3 of 3
Instance Object Data = 30
Instance Method Data = 30

--------- Test1-obj ViewData -----------
This is instance 1 of 3
Instance Object Data = 10
Instance Method Data = 10

--------- Test3-obj ViewData again -----
This is instance 3 of 3
Instance Object Data = 60
Instance Method Data = 30

--------- Test2-obj ViewData -----------
This is instance 2 of 3
Instance Object Data = 20
Instance Method Data = 20
```

The program starts by creating three instances of the tester class object. It does this by sending the new message to the class. There is a new method in the class factory, so that method is executed. The purpose of the new method is to demonstrate the difference between data items declared in the WORKING-STORAGE SECTION of the factory and items declared in the LOCAL-STORAGE SECTION of a factory method. The output from the program shows that while the WORKING-STORAGE data items remember their values from invocation to invocation, which allows them to be incremented each time new is invoked, the LOCAL-STORAGE items always show the same value.

There is one other thing going on here under the surface. If you look at the ViewData displays in the Listing 19-2 output, note that the first line displayed shows which instance it is and how many instances there are. In order to display this information, you must note the instance when new is invoked. But although the number of instances can be stored in the factory, the particular instance number cannot. It has to be stored with the particular instance. When you examine the class program, you can see how this is done.

The ViewData displays are also used to show that there are separate data items for each instance. The increment value used to show the difference between data items declared in the WORKING-STORAGE of the OBJECT and those declared in LOCAL-STORAGE of the ViewData method is computed as 10 multiplied by the instance number. That is 10 for instance one, 20 for instance two, and 30 for instance three.

The purpose of the ViewData displays is to show that separate instances have been created and that when you invoke an object for the second time, you can see that it has remembered the contents of one variable but not the other. The class program used by Listing 19-2 is given in Listing 19-2-cls.

Listing 19-2-cls. Class Program Used by Listing 19-2

```
CLASS-ID. Tester-cls AS "tester"
         INHERITS FROM Base.
* AUTHOR. Michael Coughlan.
* Demonstrates the difference between Factory methods and data and Instance methods
* and data.  Also demonstrates persistence of data items declared in different areas.

REPOSITORY.
    CLASS BASE AS "base"
    CLASS Tester-cls AS "tester".


FACTORY.
WORKING-STORAGE SECTION.
*Items declared here are visible only to factory methods and have state memory
01 InstCounter-fws   PIC 9 VALUE ZEROS.
01 FactoryData-fws   PIC 9 VALUE ZEROS.


METHOD-ID. New.
LOCAL-STORAGE SECTION.
*Items declared here are visible only to this method but do not have state memory.
01 LocalData-mls   PIC 9 VALUE ZEROS.

LINKAGE SECTION.
01 TestObject-lnk   OBJECT REFERENCE.

PROCEDURE DIVISION RETURNING TestObject-lnk.
Begin.
    ADD 2 TO FactoryData-fws LocalData-mls
    DISPLAY "Factory Working-Storage data has state memory  - "
            FactoryData-fws
    DISPLAY "but Factory Method Local-Storage data does not - "
            LocalData-mls
    DISPLAY SPACES
    INVOKE SUPER "new" RETURNING TestObject-lnk
    ADD 1 TO InstCounter-fws
    INVOKE TestObject-lnk "InitialiseData"
          USING BY CONTENT InstCounter-fws
    EXIT METHOD.
END METHOD New.


METHOD-ID. GetTotalInstCount.
LINKAGE SECTION.
01  TotalInstCount-lnk    PIC 9.
PROCEDURE DIVISION RETURNING TotalInstCount-lnk.
Begin.
```

```
    MOVE InstCounter-fws TO TotalInstCount-lnk.
END METHOD GetTotalInstCount.
END FACTORY.

OBJECT.
WORKING-STORAGE SECTION.
*Items declared here are visible only to methods of this
*instance.  They are persist for the life of the object instance.
01  ThisInstanceNum-ows        PIC 9 VALUE ZEROS.
01  InstObjectData-ows         PIC 99 VALUE ZEROS.

METHOD-ID. InitialiseData.
LINKAGE SECTION.
01 InstNumIn-lnk               PIC 9.
PROCEDURE DIVISION USING InstNumIn-lnk.
Begin.
    MOVE InstNumIn-lnk TO ThisInstanceNum-ows
    EXIT METHOD.
END METHOD InitialiseData.

METHOD-ID. ViewData.
LOCAL-STORAGE SECTION.
*Items declared here only exist for the life of the method.
*They do not retain their values between invocations.
01  InstMethodData-mls         PIC 99 VALUE ZEROS.
01  TotalInstCount-mls         PIC 9  VALUE ZEROS.
01  Increment-mls            PIC 99 VALUE ZEROS.

PROCEDURE DIVISION.
Begin.
    COMPUTE Increment-mls = 10 * ThisInstanceNum-ows
    ADD Increment-mls TO InstObjectData-ows, InstMethodData-mls
    INVOKE Tester-cls "GetTotalInstCount"
                       RETURNING TotalInstCount-mls
    DISPLAY "This is instance " ThisInstanceNum-ows
            " of " TotalInstCount-mls
    DISPLAY "Instance Object Data = " InstObjectData-ows
    DISPLAY "Instance Method Data = " InstMethodData-mls
    EXIT METHOD.
END METHOD ViewData.
END OBJECT.
END CLASS Tester-cls.
```

The first thing to note about Listing 19-2-cls is that I have attached a suffix to each data item to assist your understanding. The suffix meanings are as follows:

```
-ows indicates a data item in the OBJECT WORKING-STORAGE
-mls indicates a data item in the method LOCAL-STORAGE
-lnk indicates a data item in the LINKAGE-SECTION
-fws indicates a data item in the FACTORY WORKING-STORAGE
```

The factory contains a new method. This method overrides the new method in the Base class and its purpose is to note the number of the particular object instance created and to keep a count of how many instances have been created. There are two data items in the WORKING-STORAGE SECTION of the FACTORY: FactoryData-fws and InstCounter-fws. FactoryData-fws is used for the purpose of contrast with the LocalData-mls data item declared in the new method. As you can see from the output, FactoryData-fws remembers its value from invocation to invocation, whereas LocalData-mls starts with a value of ZEROS each time the new method is called. InstCounter-fws holds the count of the number of instances that have been created. Each time new is invoked, this count is incremented. InstCounter-fws, however, can't be used to hold the instance number (as soon as the next instance is created, the number is overwritten). Instead, as soon as an instance has been created by the statement

```
INVOKE SUPER "new" RETURNING TestObject-lnk
```

the method InitialiseData in the instance just created is invoked and is passed the current value of InstCounter-fws. InitialiseData then records the number in the instance variable ThisInstanceNum-ows.

Two data items have been declared in the WORKING-STORAGE SECTION of the OBJECT: ThisInstanceNum-ows and InstObjectData-ows. As I have already mentioned, ThisInstanceNum-ows is used to hold the instance number. InstObjectData-ows is used to show the contrast between items declared in the WORKING-STORAGE of the OBJECT and items declared in the LOCAL-STORAGE of the method.

One last issue needs some explanation. ViewData can display the instance number because it is stored in the instance data item ThisInstanceNum-ows, but ViewData does not know how many instances have been created. That information is stored in the factory in InstCounter-fws. The problem is that an instance method cannot see a data item declared in the factory. In order to get access to that information the statement

```
INVOKE Tester-cls "GetTotalInstCount"
                  RETURNING TotalInstCount-mls
```

invokes the factory method GetTotalInstCount. This method returns the number of instances as a parameter. Pay particular attention to the target of the INVOKE statement. Instead of targeting the instance object, or SELF, or SUPER, the class name is used (registering the class in the REPOSITORY created the factory object.)

Summary

This chapter introduced OO-COBOL from a particular perspective. The ANS 85 version of COBOL was supposed to bring structured programming to COBOL, but although it had many fine features, it was not entirely successful in this respect. This chapter discussed the shortcomings of the ANS 85 version when attempting to create informational-strength modules and showed how OO-COBOL can be used to fulfill the structured programming promise of ANS 85 COBOL. You then saw an OO program that implemented the information hiding techniques of an informational-strength module. Having demonstrated how to create an OO program through an example, I introduced the topic more formally, and you saw the entries required to use a class, invoke a method, and create a class program. The final section discussed the issue of data-item scope and demonstrated the effect of declaring data items in various parts of the class program.

This has been a long journey. I hope that you have enjoyed the trip and have learned something along the way. Although COBOL has its flaws, its many strengths in the area of its chosen domain account for its dominance in the world of enterprise computing.

PROGRAMMING EXERCISE

Well, it's time for the final exercise. If you can locate the stub of your 2B pencil, why not have a go at writing an OO-COBOL program?

The Zodiac Signs Compatibility exercise in Chapter 16 required you to write a program that used a contained subprogram called `IdentifySign` to identify the Zodiac sign for a given birth date. Using the program that you wrote for that exercise as a starting point, write a `Zodiac` class that supplies the following methods, and then rewrite the Zodiac Sign Compatibility Experiment program so that it uses that `Zodiac` class:

```
METHOD-ID. "getSignHouse".
LINKAGE SECTION.
01 InDate.
    02 InDay          PIC XX.
    02 InMonth        PIC XX.
01 OutZodiacHouse     PIC 99.
01 OpStatus           PIC 9.
* value of 0 indicates operation was successful
* value of 1 indicates sign is a Cusp Sign
* value of 2 indicates date supplied was invalid
PROCEDURE DIVISION USING InDate, OutZodiacHouse RETURNING OpStatus.
*Accepts a date in form DDMM and returns the Zodiac House value (01-12)
*The twelve houses are Aries, Taurus,Gemini, Cancer, Leo, Virgo,
*Libra, Scorpio, Sagittarius Capricorn, Aquarius, Pisces
*Method should note if the sign is a cusp sign
END METHOD "getSignHouse".

METHOD-ID. "getSignName".
LINKAGE SECTION.
01 INZodiacHouse    PIC 99.
01 OutSignName          PIC X(11).
01 OpStatus             PIC 9.
* value of 0 indicates operation was successful
* value of 1 indicates InZodiacHouse value not in range 01-12
PROCEDURE DIVISION USING InZodiacHouse, OutSignName RETURNING OpStatus.
*Accepts a Zodiac House value and returns the Zodiac Sign name
*For instance house 3 = Gemini
END METHOD "getSignName".

METHOD-ID. "getSignElement".
LINKAGE SECTION.
01 InZodiacHouse      PIC 99.
    88 ValidSignHouse  VALUE 01 THRU 12.
01 OutSignElement     PIC X(5).

01 OpStatus    PIC 9.
    88 InvalidSignHouse    VALUE 1.
    88 OperationOk         VALUE 0.
```

```
PROCEDURE DIVISION USING InZodiacHouse, OutSignElement RETURNING OpStatus.
*Accepts a Zodiac House value and returns the element of the sign
*Viz - Fire Earth Air  Water.
*Houses 1,5,9 = Fire; 2,6,10 = Earth; 3,7,11 = Air; 4,8,12 = Water
END METHOD "getSignElement".
```

Before you rewrite the Zodiac Sign Compatibility Experiment program, you can test the Zodiac class you have written using the following test program:

```
IDENTIFICATION DIVISION.
PROGRAM-ID. UseZodiac.
AUTHOR.  Michael Coughlan.
REPOSITORY.
    CLASS ZodiacFactory AS "zodiac".

DATA DIVISION.
WORKING-STORAGE SECTION.
01 MyZodiac    USAGE OBJECT REFERENCE ZodiacFactory.

01 Date-DDMM   PIC X(4).
   88  EndOfData  VALUE SPACES.

01 SignCode    PIC 99.

01 OpStatus1    PIC 9.
   88 CuspSign   VALUE 1.

01 OpStatus2    PIC 9.
   88 OperationOK VALUE ZEROS.

01 SignName     PIC X(11).

01 SignElement   PIC X(5).

PROCEDURE DIVISION.
Begin.
   INVOKE ZodiacFactory "new" RETURNING MyZodiac
   DISPLAY "Enter the Date DDMM :- " WITH NO ADVANCING
   ACCEPT Date-DDMM

   PERFORM GetAndDisplay UNTIL EndOfdata
   INVOKE MyZodiac "finalize" RETURNING MyZodiac
   DISPLAY "End of Program"
   STOP RUN.

GetAndDisplay.
   INVOKE MyZodiac "getSignHouse" USING BY CONTENT Date-DDMM
                                  BY REFERENCE SignCode
                                  RETURNING OpStatus1

   INVOKE MyZodiac "getSignName"    USING BY CONTENT SignCode
                                  BY REFERENCE SignName
                                  RETURNING OpStatus2
```

```
        INVOKE MyZodiac "getSignElement"      USING BY CONTENT SignCode
                                              BY REFERENCE SignElement
                                              RETURNING OpStatus2

    DISPLAY "SignCode = " SignCode
    DISPLAY "Sign name is " SignName
    DISPLAY "Sign Element is " SignElement
    IF CuspSign
        DISPLAY "The sign is a cusp"
    END-IF
    DISPLAY "Enter the Date DDMM :- " WITH NO ADVANCING

    ACCEPT Date-DDMM.
```

PROGRAMMING EXERCISE: ANSWER

Listing 19-3. Zodiac Compatibility Program Using the Zodiac Class

```
IDENTIFICATION DIVISION.
PROGRAM-ID. Listing19-3.
* Zodiac Compatibility program
ENVIRONMENT DIVISION.
INPUT-OUTPUT SECTION.
FILE-CONTROL.
    SELECT BirthsFile ASSIGN TO "Listing19-3-MPDOB.DAT"
        ORGANIZATION IS LINE SEQUENTIAL.

CLASS-CONTROL.
    ZodiacFactory IS CLASS "zodiac".

DATA DIVISION.
FILE SECTION.
FD BirthsFile.
01 BirthsRec.
    88 EndOfFile   VALUE HIGH-VALUES.
    02 MaleDOB.
        03 MaleDate        PIC X(4).
        03 FILLER          PIC X(4).
    02 FemaleDOB.
        03 FemaleDate      PIC X(4).
        03 FILLER          PIC X(4).

WORKING-STORAGE SECTION.
01 MyZodiac   USAGE OBJECT REFERENCE.

01 Counts.
    02 CompatiblePairs    PIC 9(7)  VALUE ZEROS.
    02 CompatiblePrn      PIC ZZZZ,ZZ9.
    02 CompatiblePercent  PIC ZZ9.
```

```
      02 IncompatiblePairs    PIC 9(7)  VALUE ZEROS.
      02 IncompatiblePrn      PIC ZZZZ,ZZ9.
      02 IncompatiblePercent  PIC ZZ9.
      02 ValidRecs            PIC 9(8) VALUE ZEROS.
      02 ValidRecsPrn         PIC ZZ,ZZZ,ZZ9.
      02 TotalRecs            PIC 9(9) VALUE ZEROS.
      02 TotalRecsPrn         PIC ZZ,ZZZ,ZZ9.

   01 MaleSign         PIC 99.
   01 FemaleSign       PIC 99.
   01 SumOfSigns       PIC 99.

   01 OpStatusM        PIC 9.
      88 ValidMale     VALUE ZEROS.

   01 OpStatusF        PIC 9.
      88 ValidFemale   VALUE ZEROS.

PROCEDURE DIVISION.
Begin.
   INVOKE ZodiacFactory "new" RETURNING MyZodiac
   OPEN INPUT BirthsFile.
   READ BirthsFile
      AT END SET  EndOfFile TO TRUE
   END-READ
   PERFORM ProcessBirthRecs UNTIL EndOfFile

   COMPUTE ValidRecs = CompatiblePairs + IncompatiblePairs
   COMPUTE CompatiblePercent ROUNDED   = CompatiblePairs / ValidRecs * 100
   COMPUTE InCompatiblePercent ROUNDED = InCompatiblePairs / ValidRecs * 100

   PERFORM DisplayResults

   CLOSE BirthsFile.
   STOP RUN.

DisplayResults.
   MOVE CompatiblePairs   TO CompatiblePrn
   MOVE IncompatiblePairs TO IncompatiblePrn
   MOVE TotalRecs TO TotalRecsPrn
   MOVE ValidRecs TO ValidRecsPrn

   DISPLAY "Total records = " TotalRecsPrn
   DISPLAY "Valid records = " ValidRecsPrn
   DISPLAY "Compatible pairs  = " CompatiblePrn
         " which is " CompatiblePercent "% of total".
   DISPLAY "Incompatible pairs = " IncompatiblePrn
         " which is " InCompatiblePercent "% of total".
```

```
ProcessBirthRecs.
*  Get the two sign types and add them together
*  If the result is even then they are compatible
   ADD 1 TO TotalRecs
   INVOKE MyZodiac "getSignHouse" USING BY CONTENT MaleDate
                                        BY REFERENCE MaleSign
                                        RETURNING OpStatusM

   INVOKE MyZodiac "getSignHouse" USING BY CONTENT FemaleDate
                                        BY REFERENCE FemaleSign
                                        RETURNING OpStatusF

   IF ValidMale AND ValidFemale
      COMPUTE SumOfSigns = MaleSign + FemaleSign
      IF FUNCTION REM(SumOfSigns 2)  = ZERO
         ADD 1 TO CompatiblePairs
       ELSE
         ADD 1 TO IncompatiblePairs
      END-IF
   END-IF
   READ BirthsFile
      AT END SET  EndOfFile TO TRUE
   END-READ.
```

Listing 19-3-cls. The Zocodiac Class Program

```
CLASS-ID. Zodiac AS "zodiac" INHERITS FROM Base.
* AUTHOR. Michael Coughlan.


REPOSITORY.
    CLASS BASE AS "base"
    CLASS Zodiac AS "zodiac".


* No FACTORY in this program

OBJECT.
WORKING-STORAGE SECTION.
01 ZodiacTable.
   02 ZodiacTableData.
      03 FILLER    PIC X(20) VALUE "Aries      103210419".
      03 FILLER    PIC X(20) VALUE "Taurus     204200520".
      03 FILLER    PIC X(20) VALUE "Gemini     305210620".
      03 FILLER    PIC X(20) VALUE "Cancer     406210722".
      03 FILLER    PIC X(20) VALUE "Leo        107230822".
      03 FILLER    PIC X(20) VALUE "Virgo      208230922".
      03 FILLER    PIC X(20) VALUE "Libra      309231022".
      03 FILLER    PIC X(20) VALUE "Scorpio    410231121".
      03 FILLER    PIC X(20) VALUE "Sagittarius111221221".
      03 FILLER    PIC X(20) VALUE "Capricorn  212221231".
      03 FILLER    PIC X(20) VALUE "Aquarius   301200218".
      03 FILLER    PIC X(20) VALUE "Pisces     402190320".
```

```
    02 ZodiacSign REDEFINES ZodiacTableData
                  OCCURS 12 TIMES
                  INDEXED BY Zidx.
       03 SignName        PIC X(11).
       03 SignElement     PIC 9.
       03 StartDate       PIC X(4).
       03 EndDate         PIC X(4).

01 ElementTable VALUE "Fire EarthAir  Water".
   02 Element OCCURS 4 TIMES PIC X(5).


METHOD-ID. getSignHouse.
LOCAL-STORAGE SECTION.
01 WorkDate.
   88 SignIsCusp  VALUE "0120", "0121", "0219", "0220",
                        "0320", "0321", "0420", "0421",
                        "0521", "0522", "0621", "0622",
                        "0723", "0724", "0823", "0824",
                        "0923", "0924", "1023", "1024",
                        "1122", "1123", "1221", "1222".
   02 WorkMonth        PIC XX.
   02 WorkDay          PIC XX.

LINKAGE SECTION.
01 InDate.
   02 InDay            PIC XX.
   02 InMonth          PIC XX.

01 House               PIC 99.
01 OpStatus            PIC 9.
   88 CuspSign         VALUE 1.
   88 InvalidDate      VALUE 2.

PROCEDURE DIVISION USING InDate, House RETURNING OpStatus.
  MOVE InDay   TO WorkDay
  MOVE InMonth TO WorkMonth
  MOVE 0 TO OpStatus
  SET Zidx TO 1
  SEARCH ZodiacSign
     AT END IF WorkDate >= "0101" AND <= "0119"
                        MOVE 11 TO House
             END-IF
     WHEN WorkDate >= StartDate(Zidx) AND <= EndDate(Zidx)
         SET House TO Zidx
  END-SEARCH
  IF SignIsCusp SET CuspSign TO TRUE
  END-IF

  EXIT METHOD.
END METHOD getSignHouse.
```

```
METHOD-ID. getSignName.
LINKAGE SECTION.
01 House                 PIC 99.
   88 ValidSignHouse     VALUE 01 THRU 12.
01 OutSignName           PIC X(11).

01 OpStatus              PIC 9.
   88 InvalidSignHouse   VALUE 1.
   88 OperationOk        VALUE 0.

PROCEDURE DIVISION USING House, OutSignName RETURNING OpStatus.
   IF NOT ValidSignHouse
     SET InvalidSignHouse TO TRUE
   ELSE
     MOVE SignName(House) TO OutSignName
     SET OperationOk TO TRUE
   END-IF
   EXIT METHOD.
END METHOD getSignName.

METHOD-ID. getSignElement.
LINKAGE SECTION.
01 House     PIC 99.
   88 ValidSignHouse     VALUE 01 THRU 12.
01 OutSignElement        PIC X(5).

01 OpStatus              PIC 9.
   88 InvalidSignHouse   VALUE 1.
   88 OperationOk        VALUE 0.

PROCEDURE DIVISION USING House, OutSignElement RETURNING OpStatus.
   IF NOT ValidSignHouse
     SET InvalidSignHouse TO TRUE
   ELSE
     MOVE Element(SignElement(House)) TO OutSignElement
     SET OperationOk TO TRUE
   END-IF
   EXIT METHOD.
END METHOD getSignElement.
END OBJECT.

END CLASS Zodiac.
```

Index

▓ D

S

Get the eBook for only $10!

Now you can take the weightless companion with you anywhere, anytime. Your purchase of this book entitles you to 3 electronic versions for only $10.

This Apress title will prove so indispensible that you'll want to carry it with you everywhere, which is why we are offering the eBook in 3 formats for only $10 if you have already purchased the print book.

Convenient and fully searchable, the PDF version enables you to easily find and copy code—or perform examples by quickly toggling between instructions and applications. The MOBI format is ideal for your Kindle, while the ePUB can be utilized on a variety of mobile devices.

Go to www.apress.com/promo/tendollars to purchase your companion eBook.